ALSO BY MARK MOLESKY

Our Oldest Enemy:
A History of America's Disastrous Relationship with France

This Gulf of Fire

THIS GULF OF FIRE

The Destruction of Lisbon,
or
Apocalypse in the Age of Science and Reason

Mark Molesky

ALFRED A. KNOPF   NEW YORK   2015

THIS IS A BORZOI BOOK
PUBLISHED BY ALFRED A. KNOPF

Library of Congress Cataloging-in-Publication Data
Molesky, Mark.
This gulf of fire : the destruction of Lisbon, or apocalypse in the age of science and
reason / Mark Molesky.—First edition.
pages cm
"A Borzoi book"—Title page verso.
Includes bibliographical references and index.
ISBN 978-0-307-26762-7 (hardcover) ISBN 978-1-101-87582-7 (eBook)
1. Lisbon Earthquake, Portugal, 1755. 2. Earthquakes—Portugal—Lisbon—
History—18th century. 3. Tsunamis—Portugal—Lisbon—History—18th
century. 4. Fires—Portugal—Lisbon—History—18th century. 5. Earthquake
relief—Portugal—Lisbon—History—18th century. 6. Lisbon (Portugal)—Social
conditions—18th century. 7. Disasters—Social aspects—Europe—History—18th
century. 8. Enlightenment—Europe. I. Title.
DP762.M65 2015
946.9'42033—dc23   2015007131

Jacket image: Rua Augusta Arch, Lisbon, Portugal © UrbanTexture/Alamy
Jacket design by Chip Kidd
Cartography by Mapping Specialists

Manufactured in the United States of America
First Edition

Contents

This Gulf of Fire

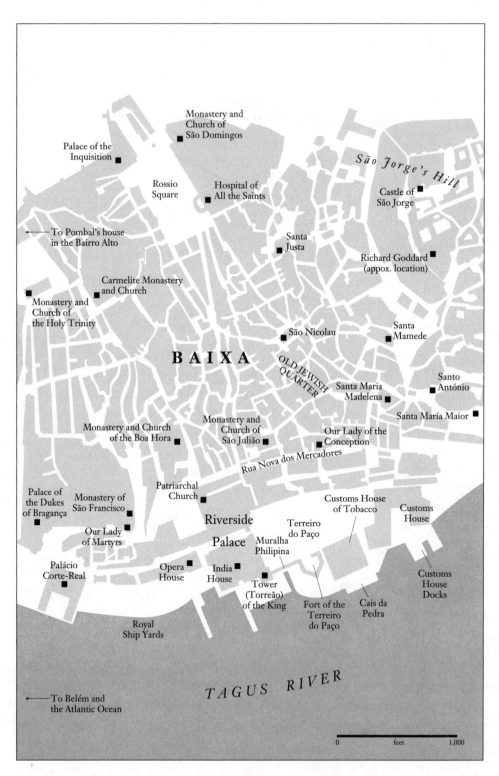

Monastery and
Church of
São Domingos

Palace of the
Inquisition

Rossio
Square

Hospital of
All the Saints

São Jorge's Hill

Castle of
São Jorge

To Pombal's house
in the Bairro Alto

Santa
Justa

Richard Goddard
(appox. location)

Carmelite Monastery
and Church

Monastery and
Church of
the Holy Trinity

São Nicolau

Santa
Mamede

BAIXA

OLD JEWISH
QUARTER

Santa Maria
Madelena

Santo
António

Santa María Maior

Monastery and Church
of the Boa Hora

Monastery and
Church of
São Julião

Our Lady of the
Conception

Rua Nova dos Mercadores

Patriarchal
Church

Palace of
the Dukes
of Bragança

Monastery of
São Francisco

Customs House
of Tobacco

Customs
House

Riverside

Terreiro
do Paço

Our Lady
of Martyrs

Palace

Muralha
Philipina

Palácio
Corte-Real

Opera
House

India
House

Tower
(Torreão)
of the King

Fort of the
Terreiro
do Paço

Cais da
Pedra

Customs
House
Docks

Royal
Ship Yards

To Belém and
the Atlantic Ocean

TAGUS RIVER

0   feet   1,000

Lisbon's city center before the earthquake

The Last Victim

Earth gapes, hell burns, fiends roar, and saints pray.

—*RICHARD III*, ACT IV, SCENE 4

On a late Sunday evening in September 1761, an old Italian priest made his way up the steps of a large, newly erected wooden platform in Lisbon's Rossio Square, where an executioner's garrote was ceremoniously looped around his neck. For Father Gabriel Malagrida, the seventy-two-year-old Jesuit missionary and former favorite of the king, it was the climactic—if unhappy—end to what had been an unusually long day. The festivities had begun at seven that morning, when Malagrida, clad in the black woolen cassock of his order, was plucked from his dungeon cell and delivered to what was left of the cloisters of the nearby Monastery of São Domingos.[1] There—in the presence of the king, his ministers, and the entire Portuguese court—he was denounced as a heretic and a traitor, stripped of his priestly functions, and, in the macabre tradition of the *Inquisição*, forced to don a pointed cardboard miter and a long gray linen sack adorned with demons and bright red flames. His hands bound behind him, a *mordaça* (or gag) placed in his mouth, he began his final journey through the streets of the capital accompanied by a pair of Benedictine monks, two attendants, and over fifty fellow prisoners of the regime.[2]

It was not the first time that Malagrida had faced execution. Years before, in the sweltering jungles of Maranhão, near the river Itapecuru in northeastern Brazil, he and a group of Indian catechumens were ambushed by members of the fearsome Guaraní tribe, and he, the lone survivor, captured and sentenced to death. Tied to a tree, he could do little but pray as his naked, shrieking executioner bore down upon him with an enormous battle club. Yet just before the fatal blow could be administered, a Guaraní matron had interceded, staying the warrior's hand. "Do not dare kill the envoy of the Great Spirit," she reputedly exclaimed. "His death will be your funeral. I knew the warrior who, many years ago, killed the first 'black-robed one' to appear among us. I saw him die a most horrible death. Eaten by animals, [he suffered] the greatest torments."[3] And so, Malagrida was denied his first chance at martyrdom. Hustled through the thick undergrowth to the banks of the Itapecuru, he was thrown into the bottom of a canoe and set adrift upon the muddy, treacherous current. Only a fortuitous encounter with an Indian boy (who had also survived the massacre) enabled him, after three arduous days, to reach the village of his Indian allies.[4]

Unfortunately, no such reprieve seemed possible now, for Portugal had become more dangerous to Malagrida than all the dark-canopied forests of Maranhão had ever been. The Old World, as he once knew it, had been transformed. Only eleven years before, he—a modest bare-footed priest from the Brazilian outback—had entered Lisbon in triumph. Hailed as a "living saint" for his legendary missions among the *selvagens* (as well as his many reputed miracles), he was received at the great Riverside Palace by His Most Faithful Majesty, the aging, half-paralyzed João V, on his knees. "Do not call me king," the starstruck monarch implored his famous visitor. "Call me sinner."[5]

Soon Malagrida was basking in the brilliant glow of his spiritual celebrity. Wherever he wandered, vast crowds followed, all jostling for the chance to kiss his hand or witness one of his impassioned extempore orations. At court, he became a fixture, leading the queen and her ladies-in-waiting in their daily Spiritual Exercises—while the dying king saw an opportunity to redeem a life marred by the gravest sexual transgressions. "Tell me, *padre*," he begged, "what must I do to quiet my conscience?"[6] To this end, he would grant all of Malagrida's requests for the construction of schools, seminaries, convents, and houses of retreat in far-off Brazil.[7] He even ordered an elaborate, custom-made dress encrusted with precious gems and decorated with gold for the much venerated statue of the Virgin Mary, *Our Lady of the Missions*, which Malagrida had carried with him on his travels and which, ultimately, would find pride of place among the relics in the king's bedside *oratório*. Yet, neither priest nor Virgin could, in the end, postpone the ravages of time and disease. "How fortunate was [the king]," remarked Pope Benedict XIV upon learning of the old sinner's demise, "that he had Malagrida as his spiritual guide, and that he expired in his arms."[8]

Less than a year after João V's death in July 1750, Malagrida returned to Brazil, but not before promising the queen mother, Maria Ana of Austria, that he would sail back immediately if her health began to fail. Three years later, he did just that—although jealous courtiers conspired to deny him access to her bedchamber. But Malagrida's bonds with the Braganças were deep. During morning prayers at the Church of Santa Maria in Setúbal on August 14, 1754, he announced to an astonished congregation, through fits of sobbing, that the queen mother had "just given up her spirit to God!"[9] When some claimed (and many more believed) that his words had been spoken at the exact moment that Her Highness had passed away that day in the capital, his already lofty reputation soared. No longer just a wildly popular priest from the colonies, he had become a kind of supra-national religious hero, the living embodiment of that centuries-old mixture of mysticism and theatrical religiosity which had taken on a new career during the recent struggles of the Counter-Reformation. Embraced, as he was, by the new monarchs, José I and Mariana Vitória, the bulk of the old aristocracy, and the great mass of the common people—as well as many admirers across Europe and the New World—Father Malagrida appeared, in late 1754, at the apex of his power and prestige.

Then—quite suddenly—on a crisp, clear All Saints' Day (November 1) morning in 1755, something occurred that would alter not only the course and trajectory of Malagrida's life, but that of the Portuguese Empire. It began as a slight tremor, followed by a dull and persistent roar, which many *lisboetas* initially mistook for a giant clattering coach—or string of coaches—bounding recklessly through the city's cobbled streets. But as the seconds wore on and the sound and intensity of the shaking increased, it became evident that this was no man-made phenomenon, but a terrible earthquake which, over the course of the next few minutes—and the arrival of two additional tremors—would bring one of the greatest cities of Europe to its knees.

Its origin (or hypocenter) lay not under the city, but several hundred kilometers off the southwest coast of the kingdom along one of the many faults that radiate out from the boundary separating the African and Eurasian continental plates.* The result of a 150–600-kilometer-long segment of that fault thrusting upward as much as 10 meters from the seafloor, the energy released was staggering: the equivalent of 475 megatons of TNT or 32,000 Hiroshima bombs. It was at least three times more powerful than the volcanic eruption of Krakatoa and a thousand times more potent than the devastating Haitian earthquake of 2010. Estimated by seismologists to have measured at least 8.5—and possibly above 9.1—on the moment magnitude scale (Mw), it was one of the most powerful earthquakes in human history, the largest ever recorded in the Atlantic Ocean—and the most powerful to strike the continent of Europe in recorded human history.[10]

It was also one of the most deadly. Arriving at 9:45 a.m. during morning mass, it turned Lisbon's churches into death traps, their arched ceilings toppling down upon thousands of terrified worshippers. Those who were not immediately buried in their homes or pinned beneath the rubble of collapsing buildings scrambled desperately to escape the chaos and confusion. "I could hardly take a step without treading on the dead or dying," recalled one survivor. "In some places lay coaches with their masters, horses and riders almost crushed in pieces . . . mothers with infants in their arms . . . ladies richly dressed. . . . Some had their backs or thighs broken; others vast stones on their breasts."[11] Perhaps as many as ten thousand souls perished in that first fatal hour.

But the terrors of the day were not over. Of those who fled to the riverbank for shelter, many were swept away by an enormous, earthquake-induced tsunami, whose giant ten- to fifteen-meter waves would ravage the western and southern coasts of the kingdom before entering the Tagus River and slamming into Lisbon's largely unpro-tected shoreline. "The water rose to such a height," reported one ship captain, "that it overcame and overflow'd the lower part of the city" and so terrified "the miserable and already dismayed inhabitants" that they believed "the dissolution of the world was at hand."[12] A rare occur-rence in the Atlantic, the Great Tsunami would pummel beaches and sink ships, and demolish piers, seawalls, and coastal buildings, and drag one newly constructed marble quay into the Tagus River. It would also

---

* The hypocenter (or *focus*) refers to the point where an earthquake occurs, while the *epicen-ter* refers to the point on the surface of the earth or sea directly above the *hypocenter.*

drown thousands, pulling many unfortunate victims miles out to sea.[13] By day's end, it would claim fatalities on four continents.

No element of the disaster, however, proved crueler than its third and final act: a terrible, seemingly unquenchable fire, which began almost immediately after the first tremor in hundreds of locations throughout the city and burned out of control for weeks. One of the most destructive conflagrations in European history, it gutted the principal institutions of Lisbon's political, religious, and economic life, laying waste to its opulent churches, palaces, monasteries, convents, theaters, public markets, and private libraries. When it was finally extinguished, the entire densely populated city center, the low-lying Baixa, where much of the business of the empire took place, was rendered little more than a charred smoking ruin.[14] "I believe," wrote one dazed survivor, that "so compleat a Destruction has hardly befallen any Place on Earth since the Overthrow of Sodom and Gomorrah."[15]

Nearly six years later, the city still lay in ruins. The Crown's ambitious rebuilding project, which promised to transform the capital into a glowing Neoclassical showplace, had only recently begun, and was,

The ruins of Lisbon's cathedral, Santa Maria Maior de Lisboa

to the regret of the majority of Lisbon's wretched inhabitants, pro-
ceeding at a snail's pace.[16] According to one visitor from France, the
city presented an appalling spectacle, "a frightful pile of fallen palaces,
burned-out churches, and rubble that resembled a fortress blown to
bits."[17] Whole neighborhoods that had once pulsed with activity had
become little more than "vast heaps of rubbish" and debris, while a
few lonely structures stood sentinel, "strange and terribly beautiful,
like the remains of the ancient Romans and Greeks."[18] Each night the
unhappy city descended into anarchy, as gangs of thieves, hooligans,
and indigent soldiers, as well as tens of thousands of stray dogs, which
ate the refuse dumped into the streets and kept the inhabitants awake
with their nocturnal howling, came into their dominion.[19] "The people
are more wretched than can be imagined," wrote one resident. "Poverty seems to preside universally among all ranks . . . [and] murders
are here so common that there is little notice taken of them."[20] Until
now, the only significant attempts at reconstruction had been those of
private citizens, who, in their desire to shelter their families and get
on with their lives, had built thousands of cramped, makeshift *barracas*
(huts) amid the ruins and in the fields outside the city. Those of lesser
means dwelt in squalid holes scraped into the foundations of collapsed
buildings.[21]

It was these humble survivors who now surged into Lisbon's squares
and *avenidas* to catch a glimpse of Malagrida as he walked at the head of
the great procession that was snaking its way silently toward the Rossio
and the waiting scaffold.[22] It had been more than two years since most
lisboetas had laid eyes on the venerable priest. Incarcerated in the bowels
of the infamous Junqueira prison until his recent move to the Palace of
the Inquisition, Malagrida had suffered greatly during his confinement,
engaging in the most excruciatingly painful contortions of self-imposed
penance, often pressing his head violently against the cold floor for
hours as he chanted his prayers.[23] While self-mortification had been
part of his daily routine since childhood (in Brazil, he had worn a hair
shirt and regularly beat himself with a horrible homemade chain tipped
with metal spurs), years of such behavior had taken their toll.[24] Alone
and ailing, clothed only in rags, he began to hear voices in the darkness.
"Who is calling me? . . . Who speaks?" he cried out in his cell.[25] At
some point, he came to believe that the voice of St. Anne, the mother
of Mary, had come to comfort him in his suffering, dictating to him an
account of her life, which he dutifully transcribed in a weak, faltering

A procession of prisoners during an auto-da-fé

hand. In a second work, a *Treatise on the Life and Empire of the Antichrist*—
a commission, he claimed, from the Blessed Virgin herself—he would
prophesy that the last of the three future Antichrists would be born in
Milan of a monk father and a nun mother in the Year of Our Lord One
Thousand Nine Hundred and Twenty and would, upon reaching adult-
hood, wed the Greco-Roman goddess Proserpine.[26]

Unfortunately, the Inquisition (and the Portuguese state that now
controlled it) was in no mood for flights of imagination, nor was it
willing to acknowledge or excuse the obvious signs of madness.[27] In its
dogged determination to prove Malagrida a heretic, the Holy Office
would pedantically assert that the "fanatical Jesuit" had "presented God
and his glorious saints speaking Portuguese, mixing Italian and Latin
words, and making more than a few grammatical errors."[28] If his fellow
Jesuits are so convinced of Malagrida's doctrinal orthodoxy, wrote the
censor (in a rare, if not unprecedented, case of inquisitorial humor),
"perhaps he should be honored with the name BONagrida."[29]

Yet now, out in the open air, among the teeming crowds, Malagrida
regained not only a rush of lucidity, but that noble bearing and "saintli-
ness" for which he had long been known.[30] Despite the absurdity of his

costume, he was instantly recognizable. Fair-complexioned and ruddy-cheeked, with piercing blue eyes and a beard that had turned from blond to chalk white when he was still a young man, he had, most likely, once appeared as an angel or apparition to the dark-skinned *mestiços*, *morenos*, *índios*, and African *escravos* (slaves) of equatorial Brazil. Later, Portuguese authorities would attempt to subvert this seraphic image, portraying Malagrida in a widely circulated broadsheet as beardless, with a gaping mouth and an expression of malignancy, his brow and neck deeply lined.[31]

Also concerned with imagery, the planners of Malagrida's execution had waited until sundown to begin the final procession so that the torches carried by each prisoner would emit a more sinister glow.[32] In one corner of the Rossio, a richly adorned wooden amphitheater had been erected so that government ministers, judges, bishops, and

Profile of Gabriel Malagrida (on the left) in an example of anti-Jesuit propaganda

priests, members of the high nobility, and dignitaries of various ranks and national origins could view the horrible event above and apart from the rabble, which was restrained from violence or any rash attempts to save the old *padre* by the presence of hundreds of strategically positioned soldiers and dragoons—each carrying eight cartridges as a precaution. Conspicuously absent was the royal family—but more than filling their shoes was the man truly in charge of the day's proceedings, the master of ceremonies and principal architect of it all, Sebastião José de Carvalho e Melo, Portugal's first minister and Count of Oeiras (later the Marquês de Pombal as he would be known to history and will hereafter be identified).[33]

Born in 1699 in the same townhouse in Lisbon's Bairro Alto (Upper District) that he now occupied with his wife and family, this ferociously ambitious son of the lower gentry had been the earthquake's greatest beneficiary. Tall and sinewy, with a long, knowing face, Pombal was both conspicuously handsome and physically imposing, his broad shoulders and six-foot frame towering over the legions of diminutive priests and stunted courtiers who flitted about the hallways of the Riverside Palace.[34] In his youth, the blond *cavalheiro* cut a dashing figure in the salons and streets of the Portuguese capital, where, it was said, he and a friend would regularly don white hats, cloaks, and shoes and challenge gangs of young, marauding noblemen.[35] Yet, for all his good manners and youthful bravura, Pombal's rise had not been without struggle. His father, Manuel de Carvalho e Ataíde, although a respected and long-serving officer in the court cavalry, had provided little in the way of financial support or useful social connections to any of his twelve children, of which the future first minister was the eldest.[36]

Seeking wisdom, young Pombal entered the Jesuit University at Coimbra, where he studied law and encountered a curriculum firmly and unapologetically rooted in the late Middle Ages—as well as a student body that spent much of its considerable spare time whittling toothpicks.[37] Upon graduation, he moved to his uncle's house in Lisbon and, following the path of his father, enlisted in the army, though the attainment of an important military post would remain elusive. He was, after all, a commoner, and Lisbon (he would soon learn) was a closed world where a tiny aristocratic minority jealously guarded entrée into its ranks and all the privileges that came with it. An audacious (and hopelessly naive) attempt to woo the daughter of one of Portugal's most illustrious families, the Távoras, would end in humiliation when the lovesick striver was unceremoniously hurled out of the wrought-iron gates of Távora palace. It was a slight that would one day be avenged. Further disappointment arrived when a coveted position was denied him as war with Spain seemed imminent. In despair, he resigned his commission and retreated to his family's small country estate at Soure, near Coimbra.[38]

There he remained in self-imposed exile for several years, seething at his rejection by both the government and Lisbon's elite for their inability to recognize his obvious talents. "You will remember," he wrote his cousin many years later, "how at a time when I was little more than twenty . . . I retired of my own accord to the Coimbra country, preferring, for more than seven years, a crust at Soure to my uncle's table [in Lisbon]."[39] Although João V would eventually appoint him to the newly created Academy of History, a sinecure that would have allowed him to spend the rest of his days in quiet study, it was his elopement with Dona Teresa, the well-to-do widow of a prominent nobleman, that catapulted Pombal's fortunes and forced all of Lisbon to take notice of this vigorous and versatile young upstart.[40] Stints as ambassador to Great Britain (1738–1748) and special envoy to Austria (1745–1749) would introduce him both to the amoral subtleties of European diplomacy and the intellectual life of a continent in full thrall to Enlightenment ideas.[41]

When the earthquake struck, Pombal was Portugal's secretary of state for foreign affairs and war and a trusted member of the inner circle of the new king, Dom José. Seizing the initiative in the chaos of the first days, he dashed off orders and proclamations with great gusto, riding amid the toppled, burning buildings on his horse with only a bowl of broth prepared by his wife (his second) to keep him going.[42] With many of his fellow ministers either wintering on their country estates or, like the king, initially paralyzed by fear and shock, Pombal became Portugal's indispensable man—and before long, its dictator. One might say that he was the earthquake's fourth tremor, so swift and violent was his rise in the weeks after the disaster.

Malagrida, too, had been in Lisbon on the first of November; and like Pombal, he had confronted the terrors of the day with undeniable courage. When the first tremor began, he looked toward the Heavens shouting, "My heart is ready, Father! . . . My heart is ready!" before bounding out of his church, crucifix in hand, to succor the injured and deliver the last rites to the dying.[43] Soon afterward, however, he was recognized by the terrified crowds and carried aloft to the Rossio, where, inspired by the momentousness of the occasion, he began to preach. A sermon published many months after the disaster conveys a sense of that first earthquake oration—as well as the hundreds that he would deliver over the course of the next three years.[44] "Know, oh Lisbon," he thundered, "that the destroyers of so many houses and palaces, the devastators of so many churches and monasteries, the killer of so many people . . . are not comets, stars, vapors, exhalations, phenomena, accidents, or natural causes—but only our intolerable sins."[45] Lisbon, he proclaimed, had become a "Babylon of inconsolable confusion," which the Good Lord, in His righteous outrage, had chosen to smash to the ground. The only option for the Portuguese was to repent, admit their transgressions, and, if possible, spend six days on retreat seeking spiritual guidance from the one terrestrial organization best able to provide these indispensable and holy services: Malagrida's order, the Society of Jesus.[46]

This was not at all what Pombal wanted to hear. Brutal, efficient, and (for his time) thoroughly modern, he was one of his country's new men, a reformer who wished to bring enlightened ideas and practices to a kingdom he considered backward and superstitious. The man who would mandate the study of Newton and Descartes in Portuguese universities wanted the *terremoto* (earthquake) to be seen not as a divine punishment or warning from God, but as a random, natural occurrence, however horrific.[47] As first minister, he believed it his first duty to see that his king's subjects occupy themselves with rebuilding the capital, not fret about the impending overthrow of the world by a vengeful God. In Malagrida, Pombal saw a fanatic and a fraud, a most dangerous and power-hungry priest, who along with his conniving Jesuit colleagues sought to incite the impressionable masses, turning them away from their national responsibilities, and driving them ever further into what he viewed as the pernicious embrace of the Companhia de Jesus. In a letter posted two days after the earthquake, Pombal implored the cardinal patriarch to forbid priests from delivering sermons that "increased the anxiety of the people" and caused them to cease working and "flee to deserted places."[48] But Malagrida refused to be silenced. He continued to preach, and when his sermon was published in late 1756, he sent the thirty-one-page pamphlet to the most prominent figures in the kingdom—including, most fatefully, the first minister himself.[49]

With this innocent yet decidedly ill-considered act, Malagrida became the special object of Pombal's wrath. As the first minister became more powerful, Malagrida's star began to fade. Exiled to Setúbal, Malagrida was, in 1758, implicated (and almost certainly framed) in an unsuccessful (and probably manufactured) attempt by the Duke of Aveiro and members of the Távora family to assassinate José I. Personally denounced by Pombal, Malagrida was thrown into the Junqueira.[50]

There, he would languish for two years until his trial and sentence of death. To ensure the outcome would be in no doubt, Pombal appointed his brother, Paulo de Carvalho e Mendonça, Portugal's inquisitor general.[51] Although the first minister had outlawed autos-da-fé as barbaric vestiges of an unenlightened past, he saw fit to make an exception for his personal enemy.[52] And while Malagrida's execution would resemble previous "acts of faith" in every respect, this time it was Pombal—and not the Church—pulling the strings. For in the wake of the earthquake, he targeted the two institutions that stood squarely in his path to power: the Church and the nobility. With so many palaces and houses of worship destroyed in the disaster (his home, by contrast, had largely been spared), he would move against their owners with a ruthlessness that foreshadowed the social and cultural upheavals of the French Revolution.[53]

The Jesuits, in particular, would fall within Pombal's crosshairs. Historically close to the royal family, they exerted enormous influence over both court politics and official state policy. And their control of vast income-generating territories in the New World, which resisted state control and harbored tens of thousands of rebellious Indians (who might otherwise have joined the regular workforce), put them increasingly in conflict with the first minister's imperial economic goals. For this, they would pay dearly.[54] For in Pombal's newly conceived absolutist state, the twin demons of modernity—political violence and an abiding contempt for tradition—would be fully realized. And there could hardly be a more eloquent rebuke to the last two and a half centuries of Portuguese history than the fact that Lisbon's last auto-da-fé would have as its victim not a Jew, but a Jesuit.[55]

For Malagrida, the irony could not have been more evident, as he, the once beloved holy man, entered the Rossio and mounted the wooden steps of the makeshift scaffold. For two full hours, he stood silently as the official charges—a long catalogue of sins, scandalous abuses, and heretical acts—were read aloud. He was called a "monster of the greatest iniquity," who had acted as if he were a "saint" and a "true prophet." An inspirer of regicide, he had faked "miracles, revelations, visions, locutions, and other *favores celestiaes*" (heavenly favors) and freely admitted to having conversed regularly with St. Ignatius, St. Bonaventure, St. Philip Neri, St. Teresa, and St. Francis de Borgia, the sixteenth-century Spanish Jesuit who had recently been appointed national protector of Portugal against earthquakes and other disasters.[56] He had even claimed, in the words of his accusers, to have heard the "clear and distinct" voices of the "Eternal Father, his Eternal Son, and the Holy Spirit."[57]

At one time, Malagrida had been revered for his ability to commune with the saints. Now, he could only marvel at the physical and spiritual collapse of that world in which he had thrived. Born in 1689 on the banks of Lake Como, in the small Italian village of Menoggio in Lombardy, he revealed early on a remarkable capacity for both piety and religious fervor—as well as a morbid fascination with death. As a schoolboy at his desk, young Gabriele was frequently observed gnawing on his hand until it bled—preparation, he explained to his classmates, for the future sufferings of martyrdom.[58] Once, he witnessed a particularly virtuous priest in the painful throes of death display a smile of such serenity and contentment that it seemed as if he had already entered the kingdom of Heaven. "Oh what a beautiful death!" he was often heard to remark afterward. "How sweet and consoling is dying at the end of a life completely devoted to the service of God."[59]

It was this strength of spirit that had animated his decision to forgo the secure and comfortable life of the religious scholar and join the Jesuit order, created in the sixteenth century to crush heresy, counter the advances of Protestantism, and spread the Word of God to the most distant and dangerous corners of the globe. Toward the end of 1721, the intrepid young priest landed in São Luís, the provincial capital of the state of Maranhão, located on an island set in the dark turbid waters of São Marcos Bay. Surrounded by mangrove swamps and vast, desolate mud flats at low tide, the small city built on bluffs was the last civilized outpost for hundreds of miles. To the north lay the equator and the Central Atlantic, to the south, scorching, barely penetrable forests filled with jungle buffalo, spotted panthers, and gargantuan snakes, which, it was believed, swallowed horses and cattle whole.[60]

It was here, against this tropical backdrop, that Malagrida developed his gift for dramatic gestures and stirring oratory. In the long silences of the jungle and the Brazilian *sertão* (scrub desert), both saints and demons cried out to him. The great biblical struggle between good and evil, between the righteous and the damned, between the prophets of salvation and those of perdition, was all around him. As he criss-crossed northeastern Brazil in his bare feet, baptizing Indians, founding churches and schools, curing the sick, and, many claimed, raising the dead, Malagrida's resemblance to the Prophets grew more and more pronounced. When, in 1749, he arrived in Portugal, it was as if John the Baptist himself, clothed in skins and a loincloth, had suddenly emerged from the wilderness to indict a corrupt and sinful age.[61]

But all of that now seemed to belong to the distant past. From his position on the scaffold, he could see along the eastern slope of the Chagas Hill the ruins of the Igreja do Carmo (Carmelite Church), whose vaulted stone ceiling had buckled with the first tremor and collapsed onto the heads of hundreds of parishioners. To the south-east, atop the imposing São Jorge's Hill, sat the crumpled ruins of the Castle of São Jorge, which for centuries had served as a fortress to both Moorish and Christian kings, and had been the site, in 1499, of King Manuel I's historic meeting with Vasco da Gama after his discovery of the sea route to India. (It would not be repaired until the 1940s.)[62] And to the south, out of sight, along the western edge of the Palace Square, lay the remains of the Riverside Palace, the fabled former abode of the Portuguese monarchy, where Malagrida had been received on his first visit to Lisbon by the affable and God-fearing Dom João.[63]

Like the old city itself, Malagrida's end had finally come, but not in circumstances that he had expected. When asked to confess his crimes, he said simply, "Since I first put my foot on Portuguese soil, I have always served my Most Faithful Majesty as a good and loyal subject. However, if, through ignorance I have offended him or anyone in the least, I ask humbly and sincerely for forgiveness."[64] It was precisely at this moment, according to one eyewitness, that the night sky cleaved apart and a radiant light illuminated the square for several minutes as if it were day, causing many of the astonished spectators to cry out *"Milagro! . . . Milagro!"* (Miracle! . . . Miracle!). Others claimed that the heavenly rays had only illuminated the prisoner's pale face.[65] Despite the determined efforts of Pombal to demonize the old man, many in the crowd still considered him a saint. Although a frequent guest in the grand *palácios* of the aristocracy, Malagrida enjoyed a special rapport with the common folk, especially those on society's lowest rungs. Per-haps his most enduring act as a missionary had been his founding of the Schools of the Sacred Heart of Mary, which housed and educated former prostitutes, the "Remorseful Magdalenes," as he called them.[66]

When the executioner moved to secure the garrote, Malagrida remained still, his hands crossed gently against his chest. "Father, have mercy on me!" he cried. "Help me in this hour! . . . Into your hands, *Senhor*, I deliver my spirit . . . Jesus! . . . Maria!"[67] Then the garrote was tightened and he was strangled without a struggle. A directive in his sentence had called for death "without the effusion of blood," a lone gesture of respect accorded him, presumably on account of his advanced age.[68] Few similar instances of compassion would be extended by the new regime. Indeed, two years before, as Pombal's assault on the aristocracy intensified, several male and female members of the Távora family, his old nemeses, had been ritually torn apart in a publicly staged bloodbath of such concentrated cruelty that the future French revolutionary executioner, Charles-Henri Sanson, might have recoiled in horror.[69]

To complete the ceremony, Malagrida's lifeless body was laid out on the scaffold, his face, recalled an eyewitness, "white as marble."[70] After this, firewood was piled on top of the corpse and set ablaze. According to a priest, the body initially refused to burn, remaining miraculously intact beneath the rising flames, the head erect "as if looking in the direction of heaven."[71] But after soldiers tossed more wood on the fire, the sanctified remains finally yielded to material realities. By four in the morning, it was all over. In accordance with the dictates of his sentence, Malagrida's ashes were carefully collected and cast into the Tagus so that they would not be gathered up by admirers and so that "there . . . [would] be no memory of him or his remains."[72] However, one oft-repeated story tells of a pious old matron who found the Jesuit's heart completely unharmed beneath the cinders and carried it home to worship as a relic.[73]

As word of Malagrida's death spread across Europe and the Atlantic, reactions varied widely. In Spain, Jesuit churches rang their bells in mourning and remembrance for days, while in Paris, anti-Jesuit rejoicing—undoubtedly inspired by Pombal's recent propaganda campaign—broke out. In northeastern Brazil, thousands mourned the white-bearded saint who, for so many years, had carried the Word of God to the deepest recesses of that largely untamed land, while in Protestant Britain, the response was more muted (in time, the name

Malagrida would become synonymous there with those who practiced disloyalty, religious fanaticism, or treason against the state).[74] In Switzerland, the aging philosophe and literary bane of the Church, Voltaire, whose career had been reinvigorated by the recent continent-wide debate on the meaning and causes of the earthquake, was personally outraged by Malagrida's death. "Thus," he wrote, "was the excess of the ridiculous and the absurd joined to the excess of horror."[75] But closer to the centers of power, at Versailles, a genuinely saddened Louis XV—perhaps sensing that a new, more pitiless age was dawning—could offer up but a simple lament: "It is as if I burned the old lunatic in the Petites [Maisons] asylum who says he is God the Father."[76]

Six years after the Great Lisbon Earthquake, the world had indeed changed. In Portugal, a violent new regime had emerged from the rubble. Its aggressive reformist agenda, which some would later dub "earthquake politics," was transforming the broad landscape of Portuguese national life and challenging the notion of what it meant to be modern in the eighteenth century. At the helm was Pombal—a force of nature all his own—who well understood that his power and authority were attributable to much more than talent, ambition, and a special rapport with the king. "Terrible physical phenomena," wrote one contemporary, "frequently change the face of empires."[77]

But the destructive reach of the earthquake was by no means limited to Portugal or the Iberian Peninsula. Tremors were reported as far away as Sweden, Norway, Ireland, Italy, Cape Verde, and the Azores—while across the wide arc of Northern and Central Europe, strange agitations of the water were observed in ponds, inland lakes, streams, springs, fjords, and canals.[78] In Derbyshire, England, lead miners deep underground were jolted by as many as five tremors over a span of twenty minutes—while in Venice, over twelve hundred miles from the epicenter, a twenty-nine-year-old Casanova, imprisoned for impiety in the depths of the Doge's Palace, lost his balance during a tremor and saw the ceiling beam in his jail cell suddenly turn on its axis, though not collapse, as he had hoped.[79] When the shaking returned, he would cheer it on with mounting excitement. "Another, another, great God, but stronger [!]," he cried.[80] Although delighted when, many weeks later, he realized that he had experienced the "shock" that had "flattened Lisbon," he was, at the same time, despondent that it had not deposited him "safe, sound, and free" on the Piazza San Marco. "It was thus," he wrote, "that I began to go mad."[81]

Unfortunately for Casanova, most of the significant earthquake damage outside of Iberia occurred in northwest Africa.[82] At Fez, Rabat, Algiers, and Marrakesh, and hundreds of tiny villages across Algeria and Morocco, the quake caused considerable destruction and many deaths—while the resultant tsunami battered the coasts of Portugal, Spain, and Morocco, and propelled waves of unusual size as far as the West Indies and the shores of northeastern Brazil, over four thousand miles to the southwest.[83] In all, the total area physically impacted by the earthquake encompassed more than 5.8 million square miles (3 percent of the earth's surface), more than any other known disaster of its kind.[84]

It was the Lisbon Earthquake's impact on human history, however, that distinguishes it from all other natural catastrophes, before or since. Striking in the middle of the eighteenth century, when many believed that the natural world had been effectively tamed, if not mastered, by modern science, the great quake had, in the view of one historian, "shocked western civilization more than any event since the fall of Rome in the fifth century."[85] With three violent shivers (and the destruction of a major capital city), Europeans were suddenly confronted with a phenomenon of nature that could, without warning, throw one back into the chaos of blind and destructive forces. Once again in its history, the West found its conceptions of God, Nature, and Providence under a barrage of scrutiny. And many, as a result, began to ask the all-important yet profoundly disturbing question of theodicy: How could a Creator, both beneficent and all-powerful, have permitted such a catastrophe?

The size and scope of the reaction were unprecedented—and deeply revealing. Over the next five years, theologians, philosophers, preachers, journalists, poets, and scientists from across Europe and the New World—including the three most celebrated minds of the century: Voltaire, Kant, and Rousseau—would weigh in on the disaster. The sum of their reflections—the Great Lisbon Earthquake Debate—would prove one of the defining events of the European Enlightenment.

For scientists, the disaster offered an unprecedented opportunity to once and for all unlock the mysteries of one of the last great terrestrial phenomena to have hitherto eluded scientific understanding. To this end, geological data on earthquakes and tsunamis were collected and analyzed; academic papers were published and distributed; and universities and scholarly institutes offered prizes to anyone who could explain the cataclysm.

While some interpreted the disaster as part of God's overarching plan for the universe, others saw it as a reminder of His ongoing intervention in the world, if not a sign of the impending chaos of the Last Days. For it was still widely believed by Christians in the eighteenth century that when the sixth seal was opened on Judgment Day a catastrophe of terrifying seismic and cosmological dimensions would ensue.

And, lo, there was a great earthquake, and the sun became as black as sackcloth of hair, and the moon became as blood.

— REVELATION 6:12[86]

By the early 1760s, however, the Lisbon disaster had been largely forgotten. Over time, it would slip into a state of near-permanent historical oblivion. "Have you heard of the Lisbon Earthquake?" Lodovico Settembrini asks fellow patient Hans Castorp in Thomas Mann's early twentieth-century novel *The Magic Mountain*. "No—an earthquake?" Castorp replies. "I haven't been reading newspapers here."[87] Today, few would be capable of answering differently.

Occasionally, however, the memory of All Saints' Day 1755 did break through the cultural fog. During the final days of that most tumultuous year in European history, 1848, Londoners of all social classes would stream into the Colosseum near Regent's Park to witness a spectacular new Cyclorama exhibition on the Lisbon disaster. "As an effort of scenic illusion," wrote the *Spectator*, "it surpasses anything before attempted of this kind in boldness of design and the artistic skill and ingenuity with which it is attempted."[88]

As the audience sat in the darkness, surrounded by faux marble columns, gilded sculptures, and "hangings of crimson silk velvet," a procession of large painted panels was presented to them—the first showing the Tagus filled with ships, another the great city as viewed from the river. When the earthquake arrived, "rumbling and rushing" could be heard offstage—followed by "the tolling of bells," "the crash of falling buildings," and, finally, the shrieks and cries of victims.

To heighten the mood, various musical works were performed on an Apollonicon organ by a Mr. Pittman—including Beethoven's *Pastoral Symphony*, an aria from the *Marriage of Figaro*, Mendelssohn's "Wedding March," a Brazilian melody, and a Portuguese dance called "The

Earthquake." A final scene showed Lisbon in ruins. In the words of the *Spectator*, the exhibition offered "as good an idea of the horrors of an earthquake (the tremulous shock excepted) as mechanical means may produce." A box office sensation, it would continue to entertain audiences until 1851.[89]

Like London's celebrated Cyclorama, this book seeks to provide an accurate and absorbing re-creation of the terrible events of All Saints' Day 1755 as possible. To this end, documents and printed materials from four continents have been gathered and employed; and the latest historical and scientific scholarship have been consulted. While the international nature of the disaster is a major theme, a special effort has been made to preserve Portugal's place at the center of the narrative. To accomplish this, the eyewitness testimonies of two Oratorian priests (the first, almost entirely unknown to scholars, the second known only through an incomplete transcription) undergird the text.[90]

This book, like all works of history, is at its heart concerned with memory—with how individuals and nations choose to recall, commemorate, and, in some cases, forget or suppress an event of lasting importance. One place where the earthquake was never forgotten but lingered on in the collective memory of its inhabitants was Lisbon. No municipality suffered as much in the disaster; and none was more deeply or meaningfully transformed. Indeed, the forces that brought down Portugal's capital on the morning of November 1, 1755, did more than just demolish buildings and extinguish lives, they put an effective end to one of the most vibrant, singular, and (to later generations) largely unfamiliar urban cultures in European history. "Of that global emporium," wrote the poet Francisco de Pina e de Mello in 1756,

> *Where Neptune raised his trident,*
> *And all the Orient, America, and the most distant provinces*
> *Bestowed their treasures in continuous fleets,*
> *There is nothing more, except a pitiable memory.*[91]

Today, proud but clear-eyed *lisboetas* still refer to their beloved capital as the earthquake city (*"a cidade do terramoto"*), so decisive was that event in the shaping of its history, a dividing line between the greatness of its past and the obscurity of the last two and a half centuries.

CHAPTER ONE

Babylonia Portugueza

Lisbon might be said to be at once the most visibly rich, and the most
abandonly wicked and superstitious city in the world.

— *The London Magazine*, JANUARY 1756

QUEEN OF THE SEAS

If there was one thing that Prince José may have enjoyed more than
hunting—both wild game and the daughters of the nobility—it was
opera. All of the Braganças were music lovers, and during the first
four decades of the eighteenth century the Portuguese royal family had spared little expense in luring Europe's finest singers, dancers,
and musicians to the banks of the Tagus.[1] But in April of 1740, José's
father—the legendary João V—suffered the first of several debilitating
strokes and the music halls fell silent. "The King has forbidden all theatrical performances and balls," complained a composer from Bologna.
"[He] wants to force people into becoming saints."[2]

Now, after ten long years of religious processions and somber
masses, the old king was dead; and his pleasure-loving son conceived of
a plan that would bring glory to his new reign and, he fervently hoped,
revive the jaunty, permissive spirit of his youth. He would build a glit-
tering opera house near his Riverside Palace that would rival any on the
continent. A gift to his people, his court, and, of course, himself, the
new theater would celebrate the dramatic resurgence of Portugal's fortunes over the last half century as well as provide him with a cushioned,
royal perch from which to inspect his comeliest subjects.[3]

Completed in the spring of 1755, Lisbon's Casa da Ópera was nothing short of a sensation, "[surpassing] in magnitude and decorations all that modern times can boast," wrote one visitor from England.[4] Its immense stage, 180 feet long and 60 feet wide, easily accommodated the lavish and inventive sets designed by renowned Italian architect Giovanni Carlo Galli-Bibiena—although one writer complained that "the spectators were unwittingly distracted . . . by the richness of the house and all the gilded decorations."[5] With its 350 seats and 38 boxes, it was not quite the largest theater in Europe, but it could easily accommodate everyone who counted in eighteenth-century Lisbon: generals and judges, bishops and merchants, government officials and their female servants. Even the court bloodletter and the king's three illegitimate half brothers, the so-called Boys of Palhavã, had their assigned places in this most exclusive of institutions.[6]

For decades, foreign visitors had complained that despite the extraordinary wealth and extravagance of the Portuguese Crown, Lisbon lacked the ceremonial diversions of Versailles and Vienna.[7] "There is no court in Portugal," sniffed the Chevalier des Courtils in 1755. "One never sees the King or the Queen eat. Nobody attends the King's *lever* and *coucher* [the public waking and putting-to-bed rituals]. The Queen does not [even] have her *toilette* in public."[8] But now the Portuguese had a true royal theater where both king and queen could be entertained (and observed) in the presence of their opera-starved subjects.

And so, on March 31, 1755, when the curtain went up for the first time in honor of Queen Mariana Vitória's thirty-eighth birthday, it appeared that her husband's dream of a city transformed through spectacle had finally been realized.[9] He had, after all, assembled "the greatest singers then existing": Domenico Luciani, Anton Raaff, Giuseppi Morelli, Carlo Reina, and the incomparable "Caffarelli" (Gaetano Majorano), who had been paid the princely sum of 40,000 cruzados for a year of service in the Portuguese capital. Although the swoon-inducing Italian castrato Farinelli (arguably the most famous singer of the eighteenth century) was not present, one audience member affirmed that the Lisbon production exceeded "all that Farinelli had attempted" during his previous year in Spain.[10] The protagonist of the evening's opera—*Allessandro nell' Indie* (*Alexander in India*) by David Perez—was, like Dom José, a European monarch known for his extensive global empire. But whereas the immortal Macedonian had once claimed conquests on three continents, Portugal's king—it was commonly known—had possessions on four.[11]

At the center of the empire was Lisbon, Queen of the Seas. For two and a half centuries, her storehouses along the Tagus River had overflowed with riches from the four corners of the globe: pepper from India, sugar from Pernambuco and São Tomé, cloves, mace, and nutmeg from the Spice Islands of Indonesia, fine porcelains and silks from China and Japan, rugs from Persia, and, most recently and momentously for the empire, vast quantities of gold and precious gems from the mines of central Brazil.[12] By 1755, Lisbon had become perhaps the most ostentatiously wealthy city in the world, an opulent, Baroque metropolis that, in its way, rivaled Rome, Paris, Vienna, and London. Now, with the construction of the Casa da Ópera, its aspiration to become one of Europe's foremost cultural centers had been greatly bolstered—though some, like Malagrida, saw the darker side of such hubris, envisioning the capital instead as a "new Babylon," whose "theaters, songs, immodest dances, obscene comedies, amusements, [and] bullfights" made it guilty in the eyes of God.[13]

Yet one suspects that few, on that glorious March evening in 1755, raised any such objections. As the spectacle rose to a delirious, showstopping climax, several hundred armor-clad warriors were joined on stage by a troop of twenty-five horsemen led by the king's own riding master atop Bucephalus, Alexander's fabled steed. According to one observer, the clomping of the horses' hooves was integrated into the rhythm of Perez's grand march.[14]

Unfortunately, the only image that has survived of Dom José's Casa da Ópera (besides a few architectural sketches found in the National Museum of Art in the 1930s) is a romanticized depiction of its ruins by the French engraver Jacques-Philippe Le Bas.[15] Rendered in 1757, two years after the disaster, the composition reveals not a theater, but an immense crumbling shell of mortar and brick exposed to a sun-drenched day. Along shattered walls once covered in bronze, disparate clumps of vegetation have taken root—while inside the hollowed-out foundation, a few sightseers clad in coats of brilliant red and blue stroll about like pilgrims to the Roman Forum, contemplating the overthrow of a once fabled if decadent city.[16]

. . .

The ruins of Dom José's Casa da Ópera

Like Rome, Lisbon was built on seven hills, and like the Eternal City, ancient Olisipo could trace its origins to the aftermath of the Trojan War. According to legends championed by Renaissance scholars, the Greek warrior Odysseus founded the city on one of his westward voyages in search of the garden of the Hesperides nymphs, said to lie at the very edge of the known world.[17] Over time, it was claimed, the name of its founder, Ulysses, evolved into the present-day Lisboa through a number of intermediary forms (Olisipo-Olispona-Lisipona-Lisibona-Lixbona) in a tantalizing, though almost certainly apocryphal, etymological link to a now forgotten heroic past.[18] What *is* certain is that for most of its history the future capital of Portugal existed in obscurity, an insignificant backwater on the periphery of several large ancient empires.

Archaeological evidence indicates that a variety of Paleolithic peoples once lived in the hills and verdant valleys at the mouth of the Tagus, hunting the abundant herds of deer, bison, goat, wild cattle (*aurochs*), and elephant (as well as the occasional rhinoceros) that once populated the area. Sharing their territory and competing for food were

small bands of Neanderthals, the thick-browed, barrel-chested cousins
of modern humans who made the Iberian Peninsula one of their last
redoubts before their mysterious extinction some forty thousand years
ago.[19]

Like their kinsmen at Altamira and Lascaux, these Paleolithic fore-
bears left hauntingly beautiful images of their quarry on cave walls,
buried their dead in graves streaked with ocher powder, and thus began
to experience the first stirrings of religious sentiment (a dominant
theme in Portuguese history).[20] They also started to exploit the great
bounty of marine life along the Atlantic coastline. One early tool was a
kind of pick or chisel used to separate mussels and other shellfish from
the rocks.[21]

Although humans first cultivated crops and formed settlements in
the lands of the Fertile Crescent around 10,000 BC, it took over seven
thousand years for these developments to find their way to eastern
Iberia. By this time, the civilizations of Egypt and Mesopotamia were
already highly advanced and Portugal was home to a mysterious culture
that littered the landscape with hundreds of giant stone monuments or
megaliths, used primarily as tombs.[22] These pioneers of the Neolithic
Era were the first to plant wheat and barley in the Portuguese soil, coax
animals into domestication, consume cow's milk, and use copper and
bronze to fashion their weapons. As their culture became more complex, they employed a still undecipherable form of writing (possibly
derived from a Phoenician script) to mark their burial sites.[23]

Around 1000 BC, however, their world was violently upended,
when a rapacious, fair-haired invader from Central Europe—the
Celts—swept across the Pyrenees into Spain and northwest Portugal,
raiding villages and towns and seizing everything in their path. These
tall, mustachioed horsemen of Indo-European origin quickly subju-
gated the indigenous populations of Iberia, imposing their language,
their religion, and their distinct and elevated culture, which included a
facility with metalwork and a corollary interest in mining. They were
not, however, the only outside influence on the peninsula.[24]

Two centuries before, Phoenician sailors from the Levant first
ventured out of the Mediterranean into the Atlantic and built trading
settlements along the Portuguese coast where they exchanged salt, silver, tin, copper, and horses with the rustic natives of the interior. At
some point, they constructed an outpost along the southern slope of
what would one day be known as São Jorge's Hill in Lisbon (the rem-

nants of which are believed to lie beneath the present-day cathedral of Santa Maria Maior). In their wake came the Greeks, who managed a flourishing commercial market along the coastal region of southern Iberia, shipping their wares in amphorae-laden ships to the far ends of the Mediterranean and beyond. One local product, *garos* (or *garum* in Latin), a type of fish sauce made from the entrails of tuna, mackerel, or eel, was greatly prized in Classical Athens and would later become the principal condiment (a kind of ancient catsup) consumed by both rich and poor throughout the Roman Empire.[25] As Greece's power waned, the Carthaginians—a seafaring, Semitic people from North Africa—closed off the Strait of Gibraltar to rival shipping and penetrated deep into Iberia looking for able-bodied men and the much coveted Spanish swords to aid them in their wars against the Romans.

But the renowned Carthaginian general Hannibal failed in his attempt to capture his enemy's capital city in the Second Punic War; and, thus weakened, the lands of Iberia fell to the brutal armies of Rome. As a consequence, Lisbon, now called Olisipo, became a far-flung western outpost in the newly created Roman province of Lusitania.[26] Although local resistance by the native Lusitani was fierce (one legendary guerrilla leader named Viriatus won a series of improbable, yet ultimately Pyrrhic, victories against the Italian invaders between 146 and 139 BC), by the end of the first century Lisbon had accepted its fate and begun to transform itself into a proper Roman city.[27] In recognition of its loyalty in the struggle against the Lusitani, it would receive the title *Felitias Julia* from an ambitious and self-regarding young magistrate posted to Spain named Julius Caesar.[28]

Over time, temples to Jupiter, Cybele, Tethys, and Diana were constructed in addition to a sizable forum, a theater, public baths, a necropolis, sophisticated drainage systems, conduits to deliver fresh water, scores of multistoried apartment buildings (or *insulae*), as well as a number of peristyle villas and an immense city wall to protect the populace against the ever rebellious inhabitants of the surrounding plains. Roads now connected the principal cities of Iberia; and wealthy locals who had proven their worth to the state were rewarded for their service with Roman citizenship, while the fractious peasantry was enslaved and forced to work on large farms *(latifundia)* in the great fertile expanses along the Tagus River. In the fourth century, a new religion, Christianity (which had originated in the eastern province of Judea), began to win adherents from the traditional pagan religions and popular oriental cults of the day, and Olisipo, like many large cities of the period, played an important role in its dissemination.[29]

As Roman culture became more entrenched, the use of Latin spread widely, crowding out and ultimately extinguishing the indigenous languages of the province. In time, this spoken Latin (as distinct from its ecclesiastical form) would develop into a new vernacular: Galician-Portuguese. Originally spoken in the northwest corner of Iberia during the Middle Ages, it would expand southward, and becoming not only the national language of Portugal but the official tongue of the lands of its future empire: Brazil, Angola, Mozambique, Cape Verde, Guinea-Bissau, East Timor, Macau (China), Goa (India), São Tomé, and Príncipe.[30]

In the fifth century AD, the Roman dam burst. Armed barbarians from Central and Eastern Europe and Asia overwhelmed the legions along the Rhine and poured into Italy, Gaul, and Hispania. In 411, the Suevi tribe overran Lusitania, and Roman Olisipo was sacked. For a time, all was peaceful as the pagan interlopers traded their swords for plows and settled their women and children on their newly conquered lands.

Then, in 416, another tribe hungry for conquest—the Visigoths (or "Western Goths")—crossed into Iberia from neighboring Gaul. By 476, when the last Roman emperor in the West was deposed, they controlled the entire peninsula, despite comprising just 2 percent of the population. Unlike the pagan Suevi, the Visigoths were Arians (Christians who denied the Trinity as well as the divinity of Jesus)—though in 589 their king, Reccared I, was converted to Catholicism, and over the course of the seventh century the Roman creed would take permanent hold over the remaining pagan inhabitants of Portugal and Spain.[31]

But the Visigothic peace did not last. For on Monday, June 8, 632, in the faraway Arabian city of Mecca, a sixty-two-year-old former merchant named Muhammad took his final breath. The Prophet, as he was known by his followers, was not only the founder of a revolutionary new faith, he was a skilled military leader who, during his eventful life, united the formerly divided tribes of the Arabian Peninsula into a seemingly unstoppable military force. Within a decade of Muhammad's demise, Muslim armies were racing across the Arabian Peninsula, conquering Persia, Mesopotamia, Syria, and Egypt, before marching westward along the northern coast of Africa. On April 30, 711, a force of ten thousand Arabs and Berbers landed in Gibraltar and slashed its way northward toward the Spanish cities of Toledo and Córdoba, killing Roderic, the last Visigothic king. By 713, the Moors (as Christians collectively referred to North African Muslims of Arab, Berber, and African descent) held most of the territory of modern-day Portugal and Spain.[32]

Over the next four centuries, a small Moorish minority would reign peaceably, though firmly, over a substantially larger Christian population and a tiny Jewish presence in the cities. After years of neglect, the city of al-'Isbunah (as Lisbon was now called) would be largely rebuilt, her new rulers residing in the great castle fortress called the Alcaçova, constructed upon the hill that would later be named for São Jorge (St. George). Unlike their barbarian predecessors, the Moors possessed a highly advanced culture, which boasted a variety of innovations in science and medicine (of which many were inspired by Arabic translations of ancient Greek and Roman texts long lost to the West). Most fateful for Portugal's future was the introduction during this period of cutting-edge nautical equipment, like the astrolabe and the compass, which Muslim sailors had perfected during open-sea voyages on the Indian Ocean. Other advances included roofed chimneys, improved irrigation techniques, brick paving, and glazed wall tiles called *azulejos*, which, in time, would become a hallmark of Portuguese, Spanish, and Latin American architecture.[33]

Although Christians were free to practice their religion during the Muslim occupation, most became thoroughly Arabized. Many spoke both Arabic and Lusitano, a Latin-based dialect with a significant Arabic influence.[34] As a result, hundreds of Arabic words made their way into Portuguese, including *guitarra* (guitar), *álgebra* (algebra), *café* (coffee), *damasco* (apricot), *azul* (blue), *alfageme* (swordsmith), *algodão* (cotton), *alface* (lettuce), *arroz* (rice), *azeite* (oil), *alfândega* (customs house), *chafariz* (fountain), *alfaiate* (tailor), *almofada* (cushion), and *alfinete* (pin).[35] Also of possible Moorish origin (at least in the opinion of some) is the mournful folk music called *fado* (fate), which is still performed in the dimly lit bars of Coimbra and in Lisbon's Alfama and Mouraria districts.[36]

Yet, despite their many successes, the *mouros* failed in their attempt to conquer the whole of Iberia—for still surviving in the mountainous regions of the north were several small Christian kingdoms, which in time would embark on a centuries-long movement—the Reconquista—to reclaim the peninsula from the Infidel and restore

Christianity to its rightful dominion.[37] In 1096, Henry of Burgundy, a French-born nobleman called to Iberia to help fight the Muslims, secured the territory around the northern coastal city of Oporto called Portucale or Portugal ("the land of the port").[38] Two years later, Henry would seize all the lands between the River Minho and the River Mondego, a third of the way down the Portuguese coast.

It was Henry's son, however, who, in the wake of his famous victory over the Muslims in the Battle of Ourique on July 25, 1139, would proclaim himself Portugal's first king and secure his nation's independence from the Spanish kingdom of León. According to legend, on the eve of the battle Christ appeared to young Afonso Henriques and assured him that, though outnumbered, he would vanquish his foes. "It is my wish," said the Son of God, "to create through you and your descendants an illustrious state that shall carry my name all over the world, even to the most distant nations.[39] These words would not only inspire and sustain the Portuguese during their rise as a great power but comfort them in the aftermath of the great earthquake seven hundred years later.[40]

In 1147, Afonso I (as the victor of the Battle of Ourique was now known) enlisted the aid of thirteen thousand crusaders from England, Germany, France, and Flanders, who were sailing southward along the Portuguese coast to the Holy Lands, to recapture al-'Isbunah.[41] After a brutal four-month siege (during which the defenders may have resorted to cannibalism) and several days of pillaging and massacres, Lisbon once again became a Christian city.[42] Upon the site of the great mosque, a cathedral, Santa Maria Maior, was constructed; and those Muslims and Jews who had survived the bloody transition of power were henceforth confined by law to special urban quarters, called *mourarias* and *judiarias*, where commercial business could be conducted during the day, but whose gates were locked at night.[43]

Although banned from holding most military and civilian posts and forced to wear identifying marks on their clothing, Lisbon's Jews (who had lived in Portugal for over a thousand years) would continue to play a significant role in the life of the city, serving as merchants, physicians, bankers, and artisans in a society that for most of its history lacked a sizable middle class.[44] By the close of the fifteenth century, the Jews of Portugal may have possessed 20 percent of all movable property in the kingdom and were in firm control of its successful financial services industry.[45] "I visited the Jewish synagogue," recalled the German humanist Hieronymus Münzer while traveling in Lisbon in the late fifteenth century, "and I must confess that I have never seen its equal. . . . There is a patio covered by an enormous vine whose circumference measures four palmas . . . and there is a cathedra to preach from, just like in the mosques! Inside there are ten lighted candelabra, with fifty or sixty lamps each. Women have a separate synagogue, which also has many lamps. Lisbon Jews are extremely wealthy, as they collect the royal duties."[46] Some historians have drawn a causal link between Portugal's rise as a European power and its thriving Jewish population, which, according to one scholar, "played a more important role in Portugal than in any other European country."[47]

Although less affluent than their Jewish neighbors, Lisbon's Muslims lived in their own densely populated district along the northwestern slope of São Jorge's Hill; there they had their own mayor (*alcaide*), their own mosques, schools, hospitals, butcher shops, prisons, bathhouses, and brothels, as well as their own religious leaders, the muezzins and imams. Forced to wear the half crescent on their turbans and unable to participate in trade, they worked primarily as artisans and craftsmen.[48] In 1249, Afonso III captured Silves, the final Moorish stronghold in the southern kingdom of the Algarve, and Portugal acquired the basic geographical shape and size that it retains to this day, making it one of the oldest states in Europe.[49] Its new capital, Lisboa, was strategically located halfway down the Atlantic coast and boasted an excellent deepwater port a few leagues upriver from the mouth of the Tagus.

Yet Portugal remained isolated and was still relatively weak. For this reason, it chose to enter into a comprehensive treaty with England, another small maritime power, on May 17, 1386, in the Star Chamber at Westminster. "There shall be between the subjects of both kingdoms," read the pact, "an inviolable, eternal, solid, perpetual, and true league of friendship, alliance, and union not only between each other, their heirs and successors, but also between . . . their kingdoms, lands, dominions and subjects . . . wherever they may be."[50] This "perpetual alliance"—the longest-standing such agreement in the world—was one of the decisive factors that enabled Portugal to retain its independence from its larger and more powerful neighbor, Spain. It was also the beginning of a unique political and cultural bond between two seafaring peoples who would soon take full advantage of their strategic positions on the western edge of the Atlantic Ocean.[51]

The Anglo-Portuguese Treaty could not have come at a better time for Portugal, which less than forty years before may have lost half its population during the Black Death of 1348–1349.[52] As a whole, the fourteenth century proved unusually grim for the Portuguese. From 1309 to 1404, no fewer than twenty-two famines and eleven earth-quakes visited the country.[53] Because of its proximity to the geologi-cal boundary between the ever shifting African and Eurasian tectonic plates, Portugal has always been vulnerable to earthquakes, experienc-ing large seismic events at fairly regular two-hundred-year intervals throughout its recorded history.[54] In 60 BC, a particularly devastating temblor shook Roman Lusitania, laying waste to numerous towns and triggering a tsunami surge along the coast—although the most power-ful quake to strike Lisbon before 1755 occurred a little after 4 a.m. on Thursday, January 26, 1531.[55] Registering between 6.5 and 7.0 (Mw), it destroyed over fifteen hundred houses (including many churches and palaces), killed hundreds if not thousands of people, and unleashed a tsunami that laid bare the Tagus riverbed, before crashing against the shoreline and sinking many ships.[56]

It was the fifteenth century, however, that would prove the most momentous to Portugal's future, for it was during these years that the small maritime nation led Europe almost single-handedly out of its medieval isolation into the great oceanic expanses of the globe. Unlike most European states at the time, Portugal found itself united and polit-ically cohesive—and was thus able to escape absorption by Spain upon the marriage of Fernando of Aragon and Isabel of Castile in 1469. With many of its potential European rivals embroiled in periods of strife—the War of the Roses, the Hundred Years War, the Turkish incursions into the Levant and the Balkans—the Portuguese were able to push ahead with their plan for Atlantic exploration largely unchallenged.[57] Inspired by both Christian zeal and the promise of economic gain, the third son of João I, Prince Henrique ("Henry the Navigator") founded a nautical school at Sagres along the southern Portuguese coast.[58] Although the singular importance of Sagres has been exaggerated, the Portuguese did, in these years, make heroic strides under Henrique's direction in the fields of mapmaking, course plotting, and open ocean sailing, build-ing on the solid foundation in the seafaring arts bequeathed them by the Moors.[59]

Thus equipped, Portugal's new generation of *marinheiros* was dispatched out into the treacherous Atlantic in their newly designed oceangoing *caravelas* (caravels). Soon, the islands of Madeira, the Canaries, and the Azores were seized. These relatively small, elegantly bowed ships were manned by only twenty sailors, but they were fast and maneuverable, and able to cover great distances and weather the most hazardous seas. When, on August 22, 1415, twenty thousand Portu- · guese troops captured the seaport of Ceuta on the Moroccan coast, the era of European global expansion had begun. Previously thwarted in their attempts to enlarge the boundaries of Western civilization by setting up permanent Christian kingdoms in the Middle East during the Crusades, Europeans (and all the pent-up energies of the Renaissance) were suddenly unleashed upon the globe.[60]

Beyond an impulse to destroy the Infidel and find the elusive (and entirely mythic) Christian ruler Prester John, the primary objective of the Portuguese was gold. Throughout the High Middle Ages, the economy of Europe had suffered from a growth-stifling lack of coinage due to a perennial shortage of precious metals. Most of Europe's small quantity of gold was purchased on the northern coast of Africa from Muslim traders, who had acquired it from the great camel caravans that had carried it across the Sahara from Timbuktu and the jungles of West Africa. With so many middlemen and a limited supply, prices remained high. If the Portuguese could circumvent these traders and purchase the gold at its source, the world, they believed, would be at their feet. When, in the second half of the fifteenth century, Portuguese sailors finally arrived at what became known as the Gold Coast in Ghana, they built a heavily fortified trading post christened St. George of the Mines and exchanged horses and grain for ivory, coral, and gold dust. Before long, the coveted metal was streaming into Lisbon in staggering quantities, over half a ton per year.[61]

One age-old industry that was reinvigorated during this period was the slave trade. In antiquity, European and Middle Eastern slaves had played a significant role in the Portuguese economy. Used for both field labor and domestic service, they enjoyed a variety of legal rights and privileges, such as the protection that was afforded female slaves against the sexual advances of their masters.[62] By contrast, African slaves—who were now being purchased in large quantities from African traders for work in the sugarcane fields of São Tomé and the fruit plantations of southern Portugal—had few such rights. Over time, the original 35,000 African slaves imported to Portugal would be blended, through miscegenation, into the general Portuguese population.[63]

Yet neither African gold nor the slave trade proved sufficient to transform Portugal into a leading European power.[64] The decisive event occurred late in the fifteenth century when Admiral Vasco da Gama and his four *caravelas* rounded the Cape of Good Hope and sailed out into the Indian Ocean.[65] Aided by a pilot supplied by the East African Sultan of Malindi, da Gama landed in Calicut, India, on May 28, 1498—thus discovering the long-dreamed-of sea route to the Indies. When, in the summer of 1499, his two surviving ships returned to Lisbon laden with pepper, cloves, nutmeg, cinnamon, silks, and porcelain, a new era in world history had begun.[66] To celebrate da Gama's accomplishment, the new king, Manuel I, ordered the striking of a ten-cruzado coin, the português, whose 98.96 percent gold content made it wildly popular throughout Europe, further elevating him into the top ranks of European monarchs.[67] If, in 1500, the kingdoms of Europe and Asia found themselves in relative parity in the economic and technological spheres, the voyages of discovery initiated by da Gama decisively shifted the balance, ushering in four centuries of Western European dominance.[68] "Forget all the Muse sang in ancient days," wrote Luís de Camões at the beginning of his epic poem *As Lusíadas*. "For nobler valor yet is now to praise."[69]

Although Portugal's João II had turned down the chance to finance Christopher Columbus's expedition to the West Indies in 1492—thus losing out on an opportunity, subsequently seized by the Spanish, to claim an even greater portion of the Western Hemisphere—it is difficult to see the achievements of the Portuguese in the fifteenth century as anything short of miraculous.[70] For the second time in a century, they had managed to break a powerful merchant monopoly, this time of traders from the Middle East and Venice who controlled the spice trade of the Levant and the eastern Mediterranean. By 1514, even the Venetians were buying their pepper in Lisbon.[71]

Over the next seventy-five years, Portugal would become the most important and possibly the most powerful nation in the world. With a population of barely one million (Spain's, by contrast, was seven million) and a fleet that numbered just three hundred ships at its peak, the little European kingdom would—through superb organization, the skilled use of diplomacy and force, and a chain of well-fortified trading posts and military garrisons—maintain and jealously defend a trading monopoly over the entire Indian Ocean, which, for all intents and purposes, had been transformed into a vast Portuguese lake.[72] One significant reason for Portugal's success was that all of its potential rivals in Asia—the Ming Dynasty of China, the principalities of India, and Shogun Japan—were either politically divided or in a state of precipitous decline. And the Muslim merchants who then plied the waters of the Indian Ocean were mostly unarmed.[73] Into this vacuum, tiny Portugal threw itself with great purpose and ferocity.

In short order, the Portuguese captured the cities of Malacca, Ormuz (Hormuz), and Goa and set up a string of trading posts across the region, ruthlessly imposing their will at every turn. (During the struggle for Goa as many as nine thousand Muslim defenders were either slain or drowned.)[74] Soon, all trade coming out of Portugal's Asian ports was subject to a duty payable directly to the Portuguese Crown; and any ship that resisted ran the risk of being sunk by heavily armed Portuguese warships. On the whole, the Portuguese showed little interest in penetrating into the interiors of these Asian states as future colonial powers would do. With limited manpower and resources, they were content to control the sea lanes and trading routes of an empire that soon stretched from Morocco to Macau.[75] At the center of it all was "Golden Goa." With a population of more than forty thousand and as many as three hundred churches within its limits, it would become the largest and richest city in Asia.

By the early sixteenth century, it had become clear to Manuel I that Portugal's future lay with her oceangoing fleets, and in an act replete with symbolism, the king left his apartments atop São Jorge's Hill to reside permanently in the newly constructed Riverside Palace.[76] There, in his royal tower at water's edge, this newly anointed "Lord of the conquest, navigation, and commerce of Ethiopia, India, Arabia, and Persia" could monitor his fleets' comings and goings from across the globe, the lifeblood of a mighty Empire.[77]

It was during this era—Portugal's first Golden Age—that Lisbon was transformed into a true city of the world. Almost overnight, foreign merchants from England, Germany, France, Holland, and Scandinavia streamed into the Portuguese capital, their imaginations stirred by the sight of seemingly endless cargoes of merchandise from Asia, Africa, and South America. Pepper was the chief commodity of the imperial economy, perhaps as high as 90 percent of the total (in an era before refrigeration, when even the wealthiest European's diet was decidedly bland, it was worth its weight in gold)—although a vast array of other goods were either purchased or traded for, including cinnamon, nutmeg, camphor, saffron, cardamom, cloves, ginger, mace, sugar, rhubarb, coconut oil, assorted gums and resins, indigo, sandal and aloe wood, cotton, tobacco, molasses, rubies, diamonds, honey, beeswax and baleen, cages filled with monkeys and parrots, elephant tusks (as well as the occasional live pachyderm from India), musk from the glands of the civet cat, shark, deer, and seal skins, *pau de china*, or sarsaparilla (an alleged aphrodisiac and cure for venereal disease), various manufactured products like perfume and porcelain, wine, calico cloths, medicines, silks, lacquers, and fine inlaid furniture, as well as a steady supply of African slaves, Brazilian Indians, and young boys from China and India to be employed as servants.[78] Those goods that did not stay in Lisbon were traded for products coveted by the Portuguese (like wheat, textiles, timber, and silver) and shipped on to markets in London, Hamburg, Antwerp, Amsterdam, and Genoa.[79]

To aid in the running of the empire, a new class of civil servants was created.[80] Whereas most Portuguese explorers had been noblemen, these newly commissioned bureaucrats hailed from the middle classes and would soon be manning posts from Bahia to Nagasaki—all the while maintaining their personal and economic contacts with the burgeoning metropole. Many came from the formerly Jewish or New Christian communities of the Baixa. In 1497, Dom Manuel, under pressure from his future in-laws, Fernando and Isabel of Spain, had ordered all Jews and Muslims expelled from the kingdom if they refused to convert to Christianity.[81] Although most chose conversion over exile, they remained, in the words of one historian, "a thoroughly traumatized community."[82] In 1506, a violent mob stirred up by the Dominicans murdered several thousand of Lisbon's New Christians, whose bodies were hurled into an enormous bonfire in the Rossio.[83]

To adorn the capital (which by the middle of the sixteenth century had become Iberia's most populous city with 100,000 inhabitants), Portuguese architects developed a sumptuous new architectural style, the Manueline (in recognition of Manuel I), which incorporated ornamental motifs and images from the field of navigation and the aquatic realm: anchors, crosses, pearls, and mermaids, twisted ropes and cables, exotic animals and plants, shells and strings of seaweed, all celebrating in intricately carved stone Portugal's momentous achievements across the watery globe.[84] Adding to Lisbon's unusual visual aspect was the fact that many of its buildings were constructed of a local variety of pink marble, which, despite a tendency to crack, is strikingly beautiful.[85]

City life, for the most part, revolved around two squares: the centrally located Rossio and the Terreiro do Paço (or Palace Square), which was situated along the Tagus next to the Riverside Palace. This royal expanse of land—200 paces wide and 620 paces long—was both the physical and symbolic center of the empire. Unlike Versailles, where the approach to the monarch and the seat of power was made by land, Lisbon's great stage was meant to be viewed from the sea. In his *Journal of a Voyage to Lisbon*, Henry Fielding, the author of *Tom Jones*, would compare the city's physical layout to an amphitheater, with its central low-lying valley of tightly clustered red-roofed houses—the Baixa— surrounded by hills on either side. In the words of a visting Scotsman: "It is almost impossible to conceive anything more magnificent than the appearance this stately city made at a distance; owing, [as much] . . . to its situation on the declivity of several hills, as to the many grand edifices with which it abounded."[86] On the city's largest hill lay the now forgotten remains of São Jorge's Castle.[87]

Over the course of his reign, Dom Manuel "the Fortunate" would finance over sixty building projects, of which the most notable were the imposing Hospital of All the Saints, which served the poor of the city; the Jeronimos Monastery, the magnificent and fantastically decorated Manueline masterpiece in white marble that holds the graves of both Vasco da Gama and Luís Camões; the Belém Tower, another Manueline tour de force, which guarded Lisbon from attack from its posi-

A view of pre-earthquake Lisbon, from the opposite bank of the Tagus. The Terreiro do Paço can be seen at the center.

tion in the middle of the Tagus; and the fabled Riverside Palace (Paço da Ribeira). Completed in 1505, the new palace was surrounded by a complex of buildings essential to the workings of the empire, including the India House, which Damião de Góis in his *Urbis Olisiponis Descriptio* (1554) called "the most opulent emporium of aromas, pearls, rubies, emeralds, and other types of precious gems," where trade with Asia was administered and where the precious objects of that trade were stored; the Flanders House, which directed exports to Portugal's merchant community in Antwerp; the War Amory, where 43,000 suits of armor were stored; the Naval Yard; the Money Exchange; and various high court and administration buildings.[88]

But the true center of power in Lisbon was the Riverside Palace. It was here that the king, his queen, and their children spent most of their time, where foreign diplomats, military officers, and heads of state were received, where courtiers and court officials jostled with one another for influence and authority, and where newly appointed poets and court musicians sang the praises of the new imperial order. Throughout, an exotic and dazzling hybrid aesthetic reigned, as much Asian as European, African as Iberian, a veritable Renaissance *cabinets de curiosités* multiplied a thousandfold: exquisite Chinese ceramics (a favorite

The Rossio in the years before the disaster. The Church of São Domingos is at center left. The Hospital of All the Saints is at center right (with stairs leading up to its entrance). The Castle of São Jorge sits atop São Jorge's Hill (on the top right).

of Dom Manuel), Indian rarities of every imaginable type, damasks, precious objects made of amber and chalcedony, intricately carved furniture inlaid with ivory and silver, textiles from Florence and Genoa, brocade curtains from Gujarat lined in gold and blue silk, Indian silver, Flemish paintings, silk carpets (a gift from the monarch of Mombassa), an ebony casket inlaid in silver and seed pearls, and a small natural history museum—perhaps the first of its kind in the world—containing stuffed animal specimens from Africa, South America, and Asia, including an ostrich egg and a coconut on silver stands.[89] There was also a royal menagerie, which boasted five Indian elephants, a pet rhinoceros, a Persian horse, and a hunting lynx, which Dom Manuel took with him on royal processions throughout the capital.[90] But the highlight of the royal collections was twenty-six oversized tapestries manufactured in Tournai, France, each depicting an episode from da Gama's expedition to the subcontinent. Special care had been taken so that each panel would record as accurately as possible the customs, clothing, rituals and even the skin color of the people of India.[91]

In imitation of the royal move to the river's edge, Portuguese *fidalgos* (noblemen) and wealthy European merchants began to relocate their families and business concerns to the city center, which had previously been occupied by Jews and artisans. Many of Lisbon's leading com-

The heart of the Portuguese Empire: A view of the Riverside Palace and the Terreiro do Paço

mercial families—the Alegretes, the Teles de Melos, the Marialvas, and the Távoras—built luxurious new urban palaces to flaunt their good fortune. In 1554, Damião de Góis recalled houses "constructed with such elegance and sumptuousness that it was difficult to believe. . . . The interior walls and arches are completely covered in wood from Sarmatia, carved objects, gold, and multicolored paintings."[92] Within the Casa dos Bicos (House of the Beaks), so named after the whimsically pointed decorations covering its facade, Brás de Albuquerque, son of a former viceroy to India, lived in pashalike opulence and was said to store the jewelry collection of an African queen.[93] In 1589, in his treatise *The Reason of State*, the Italian Jesuit Giovanni Botero ranked Lisbon second only to Paris in a list of the greatest cities of Christendom. The capital of Portugal, he wrote, is "somewhat larger" than London, Naples, Prague, Milan, and Ghent "by means of the commerce and traffic of Ethiopia, India and Brazil. . . . [and] in Spain there is not a city of any such greatness."[94]

But the years of good fortune did not last. In 1578, Portugal's impetuous young king, Sebastian I, perished in an ill-conceived attempt to capture Morocco in the Battle of Alcácer-Quibir; and, as His Majesty left no heir, the Portuguese throne passed to the Habsburgs of Spain.[95] Suddenly, proud, fiercely independent Portugal and all her colonial possessions were subsumed within the sprawling Spanish Empire, where

The Portuguese Empire at its peak

they would remain for the next sixty years. Over the preceding century, Portugal and Spain had rarely locked horns, the result of Pope Alexander VI's farsighted Treaty of Tordesillas (1494), which had divided the known world between the two potential rivals—Spain receiving everything west of the line and much of the Western Hemisphere and Portugal retaining its African possessions and claiming Brazil, the easternmost region of South America, which was discovered in 1500 by Pedro Álvares Cabral during the India-bound voyage that directly followed da Gama's.[96]

Now, both kingdoms were united in an enormous conglomeration of interests that one scholar has called "the first world-empire on which the sun never set."[97] Although the Portuguese experienced an understandable loss of national pride, there were benefits. Portuguese merchants could now freely sell their wares in the lands of the Spanish Empire; and cultural contacts between the upper classes of both Iberian nations increased. Most important, Spanish silver could now be used to buy products in Portuguese-controlled Asia, where it was more prized than gold.

Unfortunately, the new arrangement put Portugal's empire at risk. Former allies, England and the Netherlands, were now foes due to their enmity with Spain. The upstart Dutch, who had emerged as a rising power in the late sixteenth and early seventeenth centuries after throwing off the yoke of Spanish dominance, were of particular concern. Employing superior firepower and even shrewder strategy, the small, dike-covered republic would, within just a few decades, carve out a global merchant empire that would finance one of the world's first true consumer cultures—and cultivate the flowering of Dutch genius in the persons of Huygens, Leeuwenhoek, Rembrandt, Vermeer, and Hals. The Dutch plan of action was simple: first, isolate and attack Portuguese forts and fortified cities throughout the world (which the overstretched Iberians had difficulty reinforcing) and then sink all Portuguese ships in the Indian and Atlantic Oceans—or at least sink them at a faster rate than they could be replaced. In both of these endeavors, the Dutch proved highly successful.[98]

When, in 1640, the Portuguese—now led by a new king, João IV, and a new royal family, the Braganças—finally managed to free themselves from an increasingly weakened Spain, their once mighty empire lay in shambles. In the New World much of Brazil's northeastern coast was now in the hands of the rapacious *holandeses*, while in Asia, Portugal's trading monopoly had long ceased to exist, as the Dutch had taken the Spice Islands (1605), Pulicat (1609), Malacca (1641), Ceylon (1658), Nagappattinam (1660), Cochin, and Cranganore (1662). In 1622, an Anglo-Persian force had captured Ormuz (Hormuz), and in 1632, the Mughals of India took Hooghly. In 1639, the Dutch expelled the last Portuguese traders from Japan; and in 1665, Bombay and Tangier were handed over to the British as dowry for Catherine of Bragança's marriage to Charles II. With British and Dutch assistance, the Ya'arubi imams of Oman took Muscat (1650) and Mombassa (1698) and then seized the East African states of Malindi, Zanzibar, Pate, and Pemba.

Although the Portuguese did retain control of Goa, Macau, Mozambique, Angola, Príncipe, São Tomé, and—after repeated assaults by British, French, and Dutch forces—the Azores, the situation remained precarious.[99] According to an assessment by the Portuguese treasury in 1657: "India finds itself miserably reduced to six principal squares; Mozambique, defenseless; Goa, with little security; Diu at risk; Cochin, relying on the friendship of the King; Columbo, invaded by the Dutch; Macau, lacking in commerce and desperate; Angola, the power behind Brazil, needs help against the desires of the Castilians, English, and the Dutch . . . Brazil, the principal possession of the Crown, asking for help, and it is necessary."[100] Although Portugal prevailed over Spain in the War of Restoration (1640–1668) that followed its independence, the economy of Lisbon suffered an understandable decline during these years and with it the fortunes of thousands of its citizens. To many, it appeared as if Portugal's days of imperial glory were a thing of the past.

Then—quite unexpectedly—in the final decade of the seventeenth century, a series of discoveries in the central Brazilian highlands resuscitated the fortunes of the empire and laid the foundation for what would (quite literally) become Portugal's second Golden Age. Although claimed for the Crown in 1500, Portugal's New World colossus had, for two centuries, taken a backseat to the more lucrative spice trade of the East. Unlike Mexico and Peru, where gold and silver had been found almost immediately after the Conquest (making Spain the most powerful country in the world by the end of the sixteenth century), Brazil had been something of a disappointment for the Portuguese.

Named for a plant (*pau-brasil*) used in the production of red dye, Brazil was a reliable—if not spectacularly profitable—producer of agricultural goods. Unlike Portugal's other colonial holdings, Brazil had, from the start, been divided into large strips of land or *captanias* (captaincies) which were doled out to select individuals who penetrated deep into the interior in search of arable land.[101] Soon, tens of thousands of Africans were being shipped westward to the sugarcane fields of Pernambuco and Bahia, replacing the indigenous workers who were less able to endure the backbreaking work, and, as the years went by, fell increasingly under the protection of the Jesuits. By 1580, Brazil had become the leading producer of sugar in the world. But in 1654, when the Dutch were driven from their footholds along Brazil's northeastern coast, they took their sugar-producing know-how with them to the Caribbean, and Portugal's monopoly was definitively broken.[102]

In the late 1690s, however, everything changed when roving bands of barefooted prospectors from São Paulo—*os Bandeirantes*—uncovered the elusive yellow metal in Brazil's central inland plain and turned hitherto obscure mining settlements like Vila Rica do Ouro Preto, Cataguases, Arraial do Tejuco, and Mariana into seemingly limitless founts of wealth. Soon, tens of thousands of prospectors from Bahia, Rio de Janeiro, and Portugal surged into the region. The technology they employed was primitive; and the competition between different groups frequently led to violence, but within a few years the amount of gold arriving in Brazil's ports was staggering. "So much gold is [being] sent to the city of Bahia," reported one observer, "that the amount cannot be counted in pounds but in hundredweights."[103]

To meet the demands of the burgeoning frontier camps, the colonial economy expanded exponentially. Thousands of new slaves were brought from Africa by French slavers (who had been awarded the coveted supply contract in 1701) and the traditional industries of cattle ranching, whaling, and tobacco cultivation all grew in tandem with the explosion of transatlantic commerce. When, in the late 1720s, diamonds, emeralds, and other precious gems were discovered in Rio das Velhas (later Minas Gerais or "General Mines"), Brazil became the singular obsession of the money-mad Portuguese regime.[104] One advisor even suggested moving Portugal's capital permanently to Brazil and appointing a Viceroy to oversee Portugal.[105]

Much of the wealth flowed directly to Lisbon, where merchant barons built stately new villas along the Tagus and in the fashionable districts upriver.[106] The most shameless beneficiaries, however, were the royal family, who entitled themselves to an astonishing 20 percent of the output of all colonial mines (although in practice they received less than 5 percent, thanks in part to rampant smuggling by monks who hid the gold dust in the folds of their robes).[107] Considered wealthier than the Bourbons of France, the pious Braganças flaunted their newfound riches in rivalry with Lisbon's mercantile elite, building churches, convents, and monasteries, and financing an array of public building projects that further transformed the capital's topography.[108]

THE NEW SOLOMON

Although the first gold strikes were made during the last years of Pedro III's reign, it was his son and heir—Dom João V—who is most closely associated with its second Golden Age. "My grandfather owed and feared. My father owed. I neither fear nor owe," the young king would reputedly boast.[109] In 1706, he ascended the throne at the tender age of seventeen, and after a five-year period in which power temporarily resided in the hands of the Royal Council, he snatched the levers of state and ruled with energy and panache for thirty years of a forty-four-year reign.[110]

Of average height, with the slightly rotund torso that was common among the Braganças, he was nevertheless considered handsome, if not strikingly so. His almond-shaped eyes were large and dark and his lips full and well formed, revealing two missing teeth when he smiled. In his youth, he wore monstrous beehive-shaped wigs of curly gray hair and his taste in clothing was, like his taste for most things, decidedly extravagant.[111] The most highly educated of all Portuguese monarchs, he was taught Spanish, French, English, Italian, and mathematics by his Jesuit tutors—as well as an unflinching belief in the divine right of kings. It was a conviction from which he never wavered. Buoyed by the vast wealth pouring out of the Brazilian mines (which allowed him to rule as an absolute monarchy without the *Cortes* or Parliament), and largely insulated from overseas entanglements, the young sovereign, who modeled himself on France's "Sun King," Louis XIV, found himself completely at leisure to pursue all the protean pleasures of mind, soul, and flesh.[112] A portrait miniature of 1720 shows the gregarious and self-possessed monarch surrounded by courtiers as a cup of hot chocolate (a considerable delicacy at the time) is served to him by his uncle, the Duke of Lafões, in an apron.[113] When a youthful plan to travel incognito across Europe to Jerusalem with a hundred attendants and bodyguards was deemed impractical, a disappointed Dom João decided instead to embark on a series of domestic projects that would bring the best of European culture directly to him.[114]

His most celebrated cultural indulgence was his library, which contained more than seventy thousand volumes and which rivaled, if not surpassed, the collections of the Vatican, the Sorbonne, and Louis XV.[115]

João V when he was thirty-two (1721)

Although Portugal's kings had been actively acquiring books since the fifteenth century, for Dom João it would become a priority of state.[116] Early in his reign, the Portuguese diplomatic corps was informed that one of its principal duties was to purchase large quantities of books, maps, atlases, musical scores, coins, medallions, and rare manuscripts and send them directly to the Riverside Palace, where three great marble rooms had been set aside for their display.[117] There, on shelves of ebony and carved Brazilian jacaranda wood, books on history, politics, philosophy, canon law, commerce, theology, literature, medicine, navigation, and the sciences resided alongside six thousand titles from the Bragança family's private collection. In 1743, Pombal sent the king an assortment of Hebrew Bibles and books on the Jewish religion he had acquired in England while ambassador there.[118]

During João V's reign, entire manuscript collections were purchased in France and England, and many works were sent by the authors themselves. In addition to priceless documents pertaining to the history of Portugal and illuminated manuscripts from the Middle Ages (such as French King Francis I's *Book of Hours* and a history of the Jewish Wars by Flavius Josephus), there was an early Bible printed in Mainz in 1462, all 120 volumes of the *Atlas Boendermaker*, the first printed edition of Giovanni Balbi de Genoa's *Catholicon* (a Latin dictionary), in addition to etchings by Rembrandt and Rubens, and prints after Michelangelo, Titian, and Rafael. One two-volume book contained 1,439 etchings by the fearless chronicler of the Thirty Years War, Jacques Callot.[119] In order to provide the king with a comprehensive overview of European art, prints and engravings were acquired by the thousands.[120] Bound in volumes of red morocco and stamped in gold with Dom João's coat of arms, the print collection became one of the central focuses of the library and was considered one of the foremost treasures of Europe.[121]

Similar attention was given to decoration.[122] The walls were covered with oil paintings by Van Dyck, Rembrandt, Jan Breughel de Velours, Paul Bril, Rubens, Luca Giordano, Filippo Lauri, David Teniers the Elder, and Francesco Albani.[123] To provide illumination, gargantuan candelabras with yellow candles were stationed throughout. There were giant terrestrial and celestial globes, rare clocks, an armillary sphere, pendulums to determine longitude, as well as an assortment of telescopes and other state-of-the-art astronomical and mathematical devices. In charge of science and experimentation, a leading Jesuit mathematician and theologian, Padre Giovanni Battista

Carbone, organized the library so that researchers could consult the scientific literature alongside the appropriate instruments.[124] At the center of each room, long wooden tables were placed for the comfort of visiting scientists, lay scholars, and members of the clergy. It was said that the king spent many contented hours here, finding special satisfaction when a long-sought-after volume was successfully acquired.[125] For Dom João, the Royal Library was an extension of the monarchy itself, a cultural repository that reflected not only the pride he felt in his country's achievements but his belief that pathfinder Portugal was one of the centers of world civilization.

This modern-day Solomon (as he was known) also spent liberally to enlarge, restore, and decorate the Riverside Palace.[126] Royal agents stationed in major European capitals acquired thousands of works of art to augment the already legendary collections that had existed from the time of Manuel I. Dom João expanded the extensive portrait collection he had inherited, commissioning oil likenesses of dozens of European monarchs and popes. "Here for all your delight," exclaims a character from Resende's *Mirror on the Court* describing the fabled palace, "is Rome in Painting, Persia in carpets, Venice in crystal, the Orient in precious stones, Osir in gold and Mexico in silver."[127] Ceilings were painted in illusionistic perspectival style by the Florentine artist Vincenzo Baccherelli; and fabulous sums were spent on tapestries (many by Gobelins) to cover the ever expanding number of marble walls.[128]

One noteworthy addition was the art and furniture collection of Catherine of Bragança, who had returned to Portugal after the death of her husband, Charles II of England.[129] Among the many paintings, textiles, carpets, porcelains, gilt mirrors, and masterpieces of English Restoration furniture were Hans Holbein the Younger's *Virgin and Child with Saints*, Cornelis van Cleve's *The Virgin of the Annunciation* (given to her by Pope Innocent XI for aiding the cause of English Catholics), as well as a gold toilet service that had been a gift of her husband.[130]

One room—the Casa dos Relogios—was devoted entirely to clocks. (Like the future Louis XVI of France, Dom João loved all things mechanical.) One extraordinary timepiece, fashioned by one of the founders of the Rococo style, Sébastien-Antoine Slodtz, measured eleven feet in height, was made of bronze and lapis lazuli, and stood on a base of Scottish marble. The central allegorical figures of marriage, which featured Prince José and his future wife, the Spanish infanta Mariana Vitória, were rendered in ormolu.[131] Of the contents of the king's private quarters, little is known, although they were rumored to contain chests brimming with relics and other objects of inestimable value. Reputedly, the hand of St. Teresa of Ávila lay on a table next to the royal bed.[132]

For the king was not only a connoisseur; he was deeply religious. In this, he resembled the typical *lisboeta*, for Catholicism (to the great horror of visiting Protestants) had penetrated profoundly into the life and rhythms of the city.[133] Lisbon's seven hills were covered with the spires of churches, chapels, monasteries, and convents whose opulent interiors rivaled those found in Rome. Visitors were struck dumb by the sheer quantity of gold, silver, and precious gems that appeared to drip from the altars and side chapels of these sacred spaces. One such chapel dedicated to St. John the Baptist inside the Jesuit church of São Roque had been specially constructed in Rome at the request of the king. Produced by Italy's foremost architects, artisans, craftsmen, and painters, who had worked feverishly on it for over a decade, it was reputedly the most expensive chapel in Europe. Assembled from a shimmering array of precious materials—alabaster, porphyry, amethyst, several kinds of marble, lapis lazuli, coral, jasper, ivory, silver, bronze, and granite— its installation during the final months of Dom João's life in 1750 was cause for national rejoicing.[134]

Indeed, a preoccupation with the lives and special powers of the saints was something of an obsession in eighteenth-century Lisbon. Along every street, religious figures and crucifixes could be found affixed to walls or placed inside specially constructed niches. When pedestrians passed by, they would routinely bow, recite a prayer, or sing religious songs.[135] Within Lisbon's churches, there were at least twenty images of Jesus believed to have special abilities and healing powers. One statue of the Holy Infant, whose growing nails were regularly and dutifully clipped by parish priests, was said to descend regularly from the Virgin's embrace to play with urchins on the steps of the church.[136]

Although everyone in Lisbon had a patron saint (or *padroeiro*) on whose feast day they were born, most *lisboetas* invoked the aid of an assortment of other saints because of the special powers they were believed to possess. Santa Ines, for example, protected virgins; São Marcos, cattle. São Marçal warded off fires, while Santa Bárbara provided defense against thunderstorms. Santa Rita granted courage to unhappy wives, while São Gonçalo possessed the unique ability to arrange the marriages of old men and spinsters. The patron saint of Lisbon, São Vicente, protected vintners and makers of vinegar, although by far the most popular saint was Santo António, the *padroeiro* of Portugal. Born in the twelfth century in a modest house in the shadow of Santo Maria Maior on São Jorge's Hill, he was believed to be attuned to the painful little problems of daily life and was said to possess the ability to repair broken pitchers and find lost objects.[137]

Within almost every Portuguese home there was an *oratorio*, a small, usually wooden shrine that contained precious religious objects passed down through the generations: locks of Christ's hair, pieces of the true cross, reliquaries filled with the bones, eyelashes, hair, teeth, and clothing of long-dead martyrs, as well as small polychrome or wooden statuettes of favorite saints. Sometimes these beloved little figurines were adorned in tiny dresses or covered in flowers. When one had a special request, votive candles were lit in their presence. And if, for some reason, one's prayers were not satisfactorily answered, the ineffectual *santo* might be relegated to a drawer or a box under a bed— only to be returned when the request was fulfilled.[138] The Chevalier de Oliveira recalled how he once placed his Santo António and São Gonçales de Amarante statuettes in a water tank when a certain young lady did not return his affections—while a friend of his would regularly twist the head of Santo António when his favors were not granted so that António could no longer see the infant Jesus in his arms (something the saint, apparently, could not endure).[139]

On practically every other day in Lisbon, there was a religious procession commemorating one of the hundreds of church festivals and saints' days that governed the city's calendar. On such occasions, shops and businesses were closed and the entire capital was decorated with colorful banners, and bedspreads were hung from windows. At the head of the procession, a venerated relic or the statue of an honored saint was carried aloft, while thousands of the faithful followed behind on streets strewn with red sand. As the multitudes passed by, women threw flower petals and fireworks were sent aloft; and every spectator, including soldiers employed to keep the peace, bowed their heads and knelt to the ground.

The largest procession of the year was that of Corpus Christi, where tradition called for the king himself to carry one of the rods supporting the canopy above the cardinal patriarch, who, as he walked, clutched the Holy Sacrament.[140] During Lent, processions were held every Friday, although the mood was considerably less festive. According to the Anglican preacher and initiator of the Great Awakening George Whitefield:

> The penitents themselves were clothed and covered all in white linen vestments, only holes being made for their eyes to peep out of. All were barefooted, and all had heavy chains fastened to their ankles, which when dragged along the street, made a dismal rattling. . . . Some carried great stones on their backs, and others dead mens' bones and skulls in their hands. . . . Most of them whipped and lashed themselves, some with cords, and others with flat pieces of iron.[141]

Such fervor had its rewards. Those who walked in the Procession of the Stations of the Cross for seven straight years received the comforting assurance that they would not die in a state of mortal sin.[142]

Even on days without a procession, Lisbon's streets were normally choked with monks, nuns, and priests. According to one scholar, Portugal was "more priest-ridden than any other country in the world, with the possible exception of Tibet." In a country of two million souls, roughly 200,000 (or one tenth of the population) had taken holy orders. In Lisbon, the percentage was even higher. One out of every six people was a member of the clergy.[143] Some were *seculares*, the simple and often impoverished parish priests, while others were members of the wealthy and powerful religious orders such as the Augustinians, the brown-hooded Capuchins, the Dominicans, the Oratorians, the Celestines, the Bernardines, and the Carthusians.[144]

Over the previous 250 years, the Portuguese had taken their proselytizing to the four corners of the globe. In the fifteenth and early sixteenth centuries, the Franciscans and Dominicans led the charge. But after the formation of the Society of Jesus in 1540, much of the responsibility had fallen to the Jesuits. Between 1541 and 1724, these black-robed pioneers—Malagrida among them—would convert over a million people to the Holy Roman Catholic Church. Thousands more—from humble Chinese peasants and illiterate Brazilians to such *éminences* as Descartes, Voltaire, and Diderot—would be educated in Jesuit schools, seminaries, and colleges. Known for their political savvy and keen interest in the exercise of power, the Jesuits would insinuate themselves into the highest circles of Portuguese society, eventually becoming the principal confessors to the royal family, as they had throughout much of Catholic Europe.[145]

As the principal supporter of religion in Lisbon, Dom João spent vast sums to make his capital the religious equal of the Eternal City, a veritable *Nova Roma* on the Tagus.[146] In 1721, he ordered that precise architectural models of every major Roman monument, church, palace, and altarpiece be constructed in Rome and shipped to the Riverside Palace. The results were astonishing. A scale replica of St. Peter's Basilica arrived in twenty-three crates and occupied an entire room in the palace, while the model of the Vatican Palace was so finely detailed that over eight thousand separate rooms could be discerned. The most famous replica, Bernini's fountain of the *Four Rivers* in the Piazza Navona, was crafted completely of silver.[147]

With the riches of the New World at Dom João's personal disposal (he was known to give cups filled with diamonds to his friends), the pious king would establish the equivalent of a Portuguese national church. A steady stream of payments to Rome ensured that the Vatican looked the other way as the Portuguese beatified legions of local religious figures, sanctified marriages between aristocratic cousins, and excused the amorous transgressions of its clergy (as well as its monarch). In 1716, in a move that electrified the continent, Pope Clement XI elevated Lisbon's archbishop to the status of cardinal patriarch, who joined the ranks of only three other patriarchs of the Latin rite, those of Venice, Jerusalem, and the East Indies. Thirty-two years later, Pope Benedict XIV granted Dom João the singular privilege of being addressed as "Most Faithful," just as Spain's king was known as "Most Catholic" and France's sovereign "Most Christian."[148]

For his patriarch, Dom João built a magnificent church out of the former chapel of the Riverside Palace. Meant to replicate—and indeed challenge—the pomp and ceremony of St. Peter's, the Patriarchal, as it was known, became an obsession of the king's. "One of the most magnificent churches in Europe," was the assessment of an Italian visitor. "The dazzling quantity of gold, silver, and precious stones rivaled that in the famous Temple of Solomon," remarked one Portuguese gentleman of the black and yellow marble building, which contained a main altar fashioned out of lapis lazuli, a tabernacle of rare agate, silver candelabras inlaid with diamonds designed by Antonis Arrighi, walls covered with *azulejos*, a shimmering mosaic floor, and an interior that was, in the view of another observer, "bent by the weight of the gold, silver, and rare stones."[149] One painting that hung there, Albrecht Dürer's *Lamentation over the Dead Christ*, was believed to grant miracles, while a large rock crystal crucifix made in Rome would, according to a decree by Benedict XIII, grant indulgences to all who prayed in its presence.[150]

Assigned to watch over the Patriarchal and its many treasures were 160 priests. Posted to the Sacred College next door were several bishops, twenty-four prelates dressed in scarlet, seventy-two monsignors who wore purple vestments hemmed in scarlet in imitation of the pope's chamberlain, twenty canons with the right to wear a miter, and over ninety singers and musicians. The patriarch himself—whose status in Lisbon was second only to the king's—wore a cardinal's habit of crimson velvet, shoes bordered with a gold cross, and purple gloves. When traveling through the city, he was carried in a litter pulled by six mules behind a cross bearer *(crucifer)* and was trailed by four or five priests, all hoisted aloft in sedan chairs. As two assistants held a parasol above him, His Holiness dispensed blessings to the pious crowds who dropped to their knees as he passed.[151]

Those who refused to genuflect ran the risk of being set upon by agents of the Inquisition, the infamous institution created in the sixteenth century to combat heresy and root out heretics and Jews. Although the majority of Portugal's *judeus* had chosen conversion, many New Christians were routinely accused of continuing to practice their former religion in secret. Fully 80 percent of the cases that came before the Portuguese Inquisition involved such accusations. Some scholars have seen an underlying economic component to these charges, as many former Jews were successful merchants and tradesmen who found themselves in competition with the landowning nobility.[152]

By far the most spectacular and inventive punishment devised by the Inquisition was the auto-da-fé, which in Lisbon was treated by the populace as a religious festival—which, in a sense, it was. The city was bedecked in flowers and banners. Soldiers and priests lined the streets and women donned their finest clothing and jewelry and watched the proceedings from window perches. After a morning mass, the condemned prisoners, holding candles and dressed in long robes and miters, were led through the streets to the Rossio or the Terreiro do Paço. There, they either stood or knelt before the king and other dignitaries, as their sentences were read aloud by the presiding bishop. If their crimes were severe, they were turned over to the "civilian authority" (because the Church was morally forbidden to commit executions) and were either strangled, like Malagrida, or burned alive on a vertical stake.

As the condemned writhed in agony in the midst of the flames, they were frequently taunted by their executioners, as well as the crowd, and poked with long poles. If the prevailing winds kept them from dying of smoke inhalation, their fate was even more horrific. When it was all over, the inquisitor general (as was custom) invited guests to his home for a late-night meal. Although public executions remained a common sight throughout Europe well into the nineteenth century, autos-da-fé were much rarer than many assume (as an example, between 1682 and 1691 only eighteen people were executed in this manner in all of Portugal). Yet no aspect of Portuguese civilization was more roundly condemned by European public opinion—both Catholic and Protestant—than this vestige of the Wars of Religion.[153]

Lisbon's inquisitor general was also in charge of censorship, a phenomenon that existed to varying degrees in every European country during the eighteenth century. Before any book could be published in Portugal it first had to be read and approved by officials of the Holy Office. By the middle of the eighteenth century, the list of prohibited

Victims of the Inquisition burning at the stake in the Terreiro do Paço. The Riverside Palace is in the background.

authors included not only those on Rome's Index like Machiavelli and Erasmus, but Aristotle, Dante, Cervantes, Kepler, Montaigne, Galileo, Spinoza, and even Thomas More, one of the Church's most celebrated martyrs and a future saint.[154]

Yet intellectual life in Portugal was far from stagnant. Enlightenment ideas and the latest scientific theories (as we shall see in the Portuguese debates about the causes of the earthquakes and tsunamis) were well known among the cognoscenti.[155] In 1720, the Royal Academy of History was instituted. And through Dom João's patronage a number of groundbreaking works of cultural significance were produced, like Rafael Bluteau's *Vocabulário* and the *História genealógica da Casa Real* (Genealogical History of the Royal Family), which served to strengthen the claims to nobility of Portugal's leading families.[156] Yet, on the whole, Portugal found itself in the cultural wake of countries like France, Britain, and Italy—though there was considerable hope that eventually Brazilian gold would succeed in financing a second renaissance in Portuguese civilization.[157]

Undoubtedly the most imposing architectural feat and religious gesture of João V's reign was the massive thousand-room palace-convent-church at Mafra, just north of the capital. Built to rival France's Versailles and Spain's Escorial, this monstrosity in bright pink marble ("the only monument that could in its magnificence emulate the Temple of Solomon," remarked a Brazilian priest) reflected the excesses of the monarchy in both the ostentation of its design and its veiled carnal function.[158] Begun in 1717, in gratitude for the birth of Dom João's son and heir José, it would take fifty thousand stonemasons and carpenters over thirty-two years to complete. Within its windows and towers were placed 114 bells to mark the hours of meals and religious ceremonies.[159] When the foundry at Liège questioned the high price of the original order, the profligate Dom João doubled his payment and disbursed all the funds before completion.[160] Of Mafra's landlord, Voltaire would write: "When he wanted a festival, he ordered a religious parade. When he wanted a new building, he built a convent, when he wanted a mistress, he took a nun."[161]

Voltaire did not exaggerate. The amorous king took several nuns as lovers during his long reign, fathering dozens of children by them, including two of the three Boys of Palhavã, the future inquisitor general, Dom José, and the future Archbishop of Braga, Dom Gaspar. In the 1780s, an aging Italian priest recalled Dom João passing "hours of luxurious retirement, in an apartment bedecked with mirrors and carpets, in a sort of fairy palace communicating with the nunnery of Odivelas."[162] There, he met Sister Dona Magdalena de Miranda, with whom he is believed to have sired Dom Gaspar. His most famous mistress, however, was Sister Paula Teresa de Silva, the little nun-concubine of Odivelas, who was lavished with royal attention for over twenty years and who gave birth to several of the king's bastards, including the Palhavã prince Dom José (mentioned above).[163]

In his predilection for nuns, the king was not alone. By the eighteenth century, the distinction between Lisbon's convents and its brothels was practically nonexistent. "Throwing aside their . . . habits, covered with rouge, with patches, and diamonds," the city's nuns were, to one French observer, "little more than cloistered prostitutes," who "excited . . . the most refined gallantry, and passed for the most attractive favorites of the Portuguese nobility."[164] So many noblemen frequented Lisbon's convents in pursuit of pleasure that midwives referred to newborn babies as "little canons of the Patriarchal Church" or "little capuchin nuns." To this day, certain bulbous pastries sold in the capital bear the names "nun's belly," "sighs of a nun," and "stomach of an angel."[165]

The inhabitants of Lisbon, who numbered about 200,000 at the time of the earthquake (making it the fifth-most populous city in Europe after London, Paris, Naples, and Amsterdam), were well aware of their city's amorous reputation.[166] "The sin which the Portuguese acknowledge to be the most heinous," wrote one French traveler, "is that of the flesh; and it is precisely the one into which they rush with the greatest impetuosity."[167] After sailors and day laborers, prostitutes constituted Lisbon's most popular profession. "Here we find plenty of whores whose Company ought by all means be avoided," reported one observer, "for besides the danger of losing one's health, a Man runs the risque of being knock'd on the Head if he frequents their Company."[168] Not everyone followed his advice.

Venereal disease was rampant among all classes (the strain infecting prostitutes was rumored to be so virulent that it could kill clients within a few minutes); and extramarital affairs were common.[169] So fearful were Lisbon's husbands of their wives' potential infidelity that many upper-class women, in a tradition dating back to Moorish times, were confined to their homes during their entire lifetime, only having cause to leave on three occasions: their baptism, their wedding day, and their

burial.[170] Many a grand house had its own private chapel with a corridor linking it directly to the female quarters so that the ladies of the
house could receive communion far from the leering eyes of men.[171]

Within their inner sanctum, Portuguese women spent their days in
studied indolence, relaxing on silk pillows and blankets strewn across
the floor as they had done in Moorish times.[172] There, they played cards,
gossiped with servants, strummed their Jewish guitars, and confessed
their sins to the family priest. A favorite and decidedly melancholy pas-
time was to peer through the slats of the always shuttered windows at
a world they were rarely, if ever, allowed to enter. Even their maidser-
vants were kept in seraglio-like sequestration until the age of thirty-five
(although other female domestics like cooks and washerwomen were
permitted to venture outside the home to purchase goods or carry away
trash).[173] If social visits did occur, the sexes were strictly segregated.
"The ladies dance with each other in their room, and the men do the
same in theirs," reported a foreigner. "If one is lucky enough to be
admitted to the ladies' room, one will find them sitting on a straw mat
on the floor, and the men talking to them on the border of the mat,
some fifteen feet away."[174]

For this reason, the convent proved an especially attractive option

A view of domestic life before the earthquake

to young unmarried women. For behind its supposedly cloistered walls, musical performances, dances, plays (sometimes with shockingly vulgar themes), and frequent visits from men were the norm rather than the exception—although inveterate socializing was frowned upon by Lisbon's priests, who counseled the sisters against the use of "gloves, fans, [and] make-up."[175] Of course, many *senhorinhas* saw the convent as a temporary domicile—a comfortable, entertaining haven far from the strict etiquette and parental tyranny of their childhood homes—where, if they had not taken their final vows, they might freely search for a husband of their own choosing. Arranged marriages were still common in the eighteenth century, especially among the elite.[176] For all social classes, virginity was (at least in theory) expected of a bride. One custom called for the "bedspread of the newlyweds" to be hung—complete with bloodstain— outside the bedroom window on the morning after a wedding to prove both the bride's purity and the marriage's successful consummation.[177]

Perhaps there was a reason the Portuguese were so covetous of their women. According to a French nobleman, "No females in Europe have so fine a color. . . . They have very white teeth, beautiful and abundant heads of hair . . . [that] reach down to their heels . . . [and that] they . . . turn it up into enormous cartogans, often larger than their heads; these they adorn with flowers and diamonds, which they place with great coquetry and art."[178] They have "large black eyes," wrote an admiring Englishman, and "pouting lips . . . the color and size of full-blown roses."[179]

Most upper-class women dressed seductively in eighteenth-century Lisbon, favoring velvet corsets and silk neckerchiefs that exposed their cleavage. Following the Turkish style, they wore long billowing pants of taffeta or translucent gauze as well as sandals that exposed their feet. Atop their perfumed curls, many placed a turban; and around their necks they wore a ribbon or choker with a gold cross that dangled suggestively between their breasts.[180] Because Portuguese women believe "a prominent bosom" to be "one of the principal charms of a woman," observed one foreigner, "they avail themselves of all the contrivances of art to increase its dimensions, when Nature has been parsimonious to them in that particular."[181] In their small alabaster hands, they wielded fans of ivory, tortoiseshell, or mother-of-pearl with the skill of a swordsman—though, in general, their sedentary circumstances ensured that they received little in the way of exercise—which may explain one foreigner's observation that, despite their beauty, Portuguese women had "very bad legs and large feet" and a walk that was "slow and ungraceful."[182]

If a lady did venture out into the city, she would most likely have been carried by her servants or mules in a small one-person *liteira* (litter) or *cadeirinha* (sedan chair) with curtained windows. Slightly larger two-person chaises were also common, while full-size coaches pulled by horses were generally only employed by the royal family or foreign diplomats, as they proved impractical for everyday use in the city's narrow streets.[183] Laws actually existed to determine who had the right-of-way when two coaches approached each other on a constricted lane.[184] As in most early modern European cities, Lisbon's streets were filthy. And while all were obliged by law to carry their refuse to the Tagus, many simply dumped it in the streets near their homes.[185]

Unlike their wives, Portuguese gentlemen were entirely free to escape the suffocating confines of their homes—and many could be observed parading through the streets with a long train of servants and children following behind them in single file. Properly dressed, a *cavaleiro* of the mid-eighteenth century wore a suit with lace cuffs, white

A woman riding in a *liteira* held aloft by two mules

silk stockings, a three-cornered hat of felt or taffeta, and a wig that varied with the occasion.[186] According to one contemporary: "There were wigs for the house, for taking a walk, to wear at court, to wear if one is a soldier, and I am waiting for the time when wigs can be bought to lie down in or wear in the hour of one's death." Eyeglasses were also popular (even if the wearer had no visual impairment), for it was believed they offered an air of sophistication or, at the very least, indicated literacy. Outside the home, some Portuguese men carried a fine Indian cane and most wore a sword of considerable length, which they were known to brandish at the smallest perceived insult. In general, dueling was common in Portugal, as it was in much of the continent.[187]

In keeping with the androgynous style of the eighteenth century, both Portuguese men and women wore brightly covered ribbons in the French manner as well as rouge, which gave the appearance of health, or, alternatively, facial powder to bestow the pallid look, which helped to distinguish its wearers from the sunburnt peasantry. On the street, both sexes sported a long dark cloak that covered the body from the shoulders to the ankles. The goal was to conceal one's social status (and one's weapons) from potential thieves and, if possible, blend in with the thousands of robed clerics who crowded Lisbon's streets. (It was a particularly egregious sin to assault a priest.)[188]

In imitation of the Riverside Palace, the homes of Lisbon's aristocracy were exotic spaces overflowing with the spoils of Old and New World trade: Indian silks, Japanese porcelains, jades, ivories, Persian rugs, silver candelabras, and squawking parrots—on the walls, colorful draperies and *azulejos* painted with scenes of the hunt or the lives of the saints, and beneath the floor of the family chapel, the moldering bodies of their ancestors.[189] The wealthiest families had dozens of servants (of whom most were African slaves, as the majority of native Portuguese believed domestic service to be degrading); and every family of status had at least one cook, one groom, two table servants, two governesses, two maids, and two valets.[190] Some also employed a butler (*mordomo*) who was frequently recruited from the army and, in such cases, continued to wear his old uniform. Pombal had three such ex-soldiers who served him tea and sweets every Friday at his country estate. Typically, servants spent their entire lives attached to one household, sleeping eight or ten to a room and eating all their meals in the kitchen, where a table was also set aside to feed the poor of the neighborhood.[191]

On the whole, *lisboetas* ate well. Bread, the standard staple of the eighteenth-century diet, was expensive in Portugal due to frequent shortages of wheat and rye, and was thus less popular.[192] But Lisbon's markets offered an abundance of fruits year-round, including pears, figs, limes, melons, pomegranates, pears, peaches, sweet oranges (originally from China), carobs, apples, plums, grapes, and apricots. Chestnuts were roasted and sold in the streets; and although vegetables like sweet potatoes, peas, and beans were grown in private gardens throughout the city, *lisboetas* were by nature a carnivorous lot.[193]

In the city's *azulejo*-lined meat market, the well-to-do could purchase beef, lamb, goat, rabbit, pigeon, duck, turkey, chicken, and pork.[194] But it was seafood, then as now, that dominated the city's cuisine. In a society that forbade meat on Fridays and fast days (when a single meal of fish and vegetables was permitted), seafood served both a religious and a biological need.[195] In Lisbon's riverside fish market—which many considered the finest in the world—one could find weakfish, mackerel, sole, eel, shad, hake, lamprey, sea bass, scabbard, fearsome-looking cutlass fish, as well as oysters, barnacles, periwinkles, scallops, clams, crabs, octopus, cuttlefish, and squid—though the humble sardine was by far the most ubiquitous and probably the most beloved of all Lisbon's aquatic staples.[196] Roasted on street corners by women in colorful shawls, they were cheap and nutritious, the daily repast of soldiers, sailors, beggars, and tradesmen, as well as most of the city's poor (10 percent of *lisboetas* were homeless).[197] "It is well," wrote one poet of the indispensable little fish, "that we celebrate that which sustains us most."[198]

Salted codfish (*bacalhau*) was also consumed. Caught by Portuguese fishermen in the cold waters of the Atlantic (after the European rediscovery of Newfoundland in 1497), the much coveted fish was dried and generously coated with salt to preserve it during the long ocean transport (Portugal had been a center of salt production since the Middle Ages). Prepared this way, cod has remained a favored food, especially on holidays, not only in Portugal, where it is said to have inspired a recipe for every day of the year, but also in the lands of its former empire.[199]

As in most European countries, banquets were elaborate affairs, involving dozens of different dishes and multiple courses, although most meals were eaten with the fingers while sitting on the floor in the Moorish style (forks were not commonly used until the late eighteenth century).[200] In his *Art of Cooking*, Dom João's personal chef describes an elaborate seven-course meal for every day of the week.[201] On Sundays, he suggests beginning with bowls of chicken soup topped with egg yolk and cinnamon followed by beef soup, then roasted partridges and sausages. For the third and fourth courses, rabbit "João Pires style" and veal confit, followed by round pastries stuffed with various meats and small lamb pasties made with sugar and cinnamon. Then, a saffron-spiced Castilian stew with beef, lamb, pigs' feet, ham, bread stuffing, turnips, and peppers, followed by a white pudding (blanc-mange), fried sweets, and seasonal fruits for dessert.[202] Like his modern descendant, the typical lisboeta of the eighteenth century harbored an abiding passion for sweets—the more intensely sugared the better. Jellies, custards, vanilla puddings, crèmes, pastries, and egg-yolk-based concoctions of almost infinite variety sprang from the imagination of chefs and cozinheiras throughout the city (Voltaire, like many, knew Portugal as "the land of marmalade"). "We ate liquid sweets with a spoon," recalled one satisfied French traveler, "and in the time it takes to open and shut one's eyes we consumed a pound. Then, we drank some water and afterwards returned to eat more varieties of dessert."[203]

For much of Lisbon's history, fresh water was difficult to obtain. There were few wells and fountains and transporting potable water over the hilly terrain proved difficult—although partially melted ice was occasionally brought down from the mountains of central Portugal, flavored with lemon, and eaten on hot days.[204] In 1731, work began on one of Dom João's most ambitious building projects: the Aqueduct of the Free Waters. Financed through a tax on wine, olive oil, and other goods, this graceful Gothic marvel spanned twelve miles across the nearby Alcântara valley and first began to bring water to the city in 1748.[205] Perhaps because of its scarcity, water was, quite possibly, the favorite beverage of lisboetas. To cleanse their palates during banquets, both men and women preferred a glass of agua to any other liquid. Although beer and wine were both readily available, the Portuguese generally abstained from heavy drinking. In fact, many upper-class women had never tasted wine (and this in an age when imbibing to excess was more the norm than the exception).[206]

Some Portuguese gentlemen had, according to a contemporary, "taken on the habit of the British" and "drank tea all day"—though, interestingly, that practice first became popular in the British Isles after Charles II's 1662 marriage to Portugal's Catherine of Bragança, who drank tea imported from Macau. Others developed a fondness for port, a mixture of wine made from grapes grown along Portugal's Douro

River and *aguardente* (a variety of brandy), which fortified the wine and prevented it from spoiling during long ocean voyages.[207] When the Methuen Treaty of 1703 gave Portuguese wine growers special entrée into British markets in exchange for eliminating the duty on British textiles entering Portugal, the Portuguese wine industry blossomed.[208]

By the middle of the eighteenth century, port and Madeira, another fortified wine produced exclusively on the Portuguese archipelago of that name, had become the most popular alcoholic beverages in both Britain and its North American colonies.[209] A young Virginia lawyer named Thomas Jefferson was particularly fond of Madeira, as, for that matter, were George Washington, Benjamin Franklin, John Adams, Alexander Hamilton, and the future chief justice John Marshall. In 1776, it was used to toast the signing of Jefferson's handiwork, the Declaration of Independence.[210]

Like many European cities of the mid-eighteenth century, Lisbon was dangerous after dark. At the conclusion of evening prayers, which ended around nine o'clock, the narrow, winding streets fell under the control of thieves, hooligans, and, if the authorities are to be believed, Gypsies (*ciganos*).[211] In addition to money and jewelry, men were commonly targeted for their hats, which, according to one contemporary, "the Portuguese steal during the night and then wear ostentatiously the next day as if honorably acquired."[212] Foreigners regularly complained about poor policing in the city. Indeed, many of the soldiers entrusted with keeping public order (there was no professional police force in Lisbon until 1760) were infrequently paid and, as a consequence, had become thieves themselves. Even Dom João felt moved to protest "the scandalous liberty with which . . . robberies, murders, woundings, and other crimes" were committed in the capital. "Security," lamented the king, "is completely lacking for my subjects and for those of other nations who reside here."[213]

Murders were especially common in Lisbon, particularly those instigated by sexual misconduct. Husbands regularly killed their adulterous wives along with their lovers; and wives murdered their cheating husbands. In 1733, the wife of a tavern keeper killed her husband and served his salted remains to her guests. Only when soldiers discovered the unfortunate man's head in a well did she confess.[214] Many homicides were contract killings planned and paid for by aristocrats who had no shortage of servants, slaves, and henchmen to do their nefarious bidding. "Rare is the punishment for gentlemen who do evil," complained one contemporary.[215] Laws and punishments for noble transgressors were so lenient that throughout the first half of the eighteenth century gangs of young aristocrats roamed the streets with apparent impunity, robbing, stabbing, and, frequently, killing innocent people. In the mid-seventeenth century, one of Lisbon's most infamous gangs was headed by the king himself, Afonso VI.[216]

One factor that aided criminals (whether hoodlums or Portuguese monarchs) was Lisbon's warrenlike topography. Despite the building booms of the sixteenth and early eighteenth centuries, much of pre-earthquake Lisbon remained decidedly medieval in its layout. Narrow, serpentine streets—which appeared to have no apparent direction or end—had changed very little since Moorish times and were frequently clogged with beggars and refuse. Some foreigners dismissed Lisboa as an "African city."[217] According to one Scotsman: "The interior part [of the city] . . . did by no means correspond to its external magnificence. . . . The narrowness, declivity, and irregularity of some of its streets, and the dirtiness of others, made it a very disagreeable place of Abode to strangers [i.e., foreigners]."[218] Others noticed the discrepancy between the enormous wealth of the capital and the crushing poverty that existed outside it. One Englishman compared the Portuguese Empire "to one of that sort of spider which has a large body (the capital) with extremely long, thin, feeble legs, reaching to a great distance, but are of no sort of use to it, and which it is hardly able to move."[219]

The problem, as many contemporaries saw it, was that Portugal was entirely too dependent on other nations to provide it with life-sustaining grain, fish, timber, and manufactured goods like textiles. "Portugal," wrote Pombal, "was powerless and without vigor, and all her movements were regulated by the desires of England."[220] Although Portugal had numerous trading partners, its treaties with Britain in 1654, 1661, and 1703 formed the cornerstone of its economic system, providing its longtime ally with the right to sell textiles in the country without a tariff. In return, Britain allowed Portuguese wine to be sold at reduced tariffs in England and provided protection to Portugal and her merchant fleets from pirates and rival European powers, like Spain.[221]

On the whole, the British found the system highly advantageous. As the former British envoy to Portugal Lord Tyrawley wrote in 1752, "The great body of his Majesty's subjects reside in Lisbon, rich, opulent, and everyday increasing their fortunes and enlarging their dealings."[222] Over half of the ships in the Tagus were said to be British and over the course of the century the "British Factory," as the community of British merchants was known, became an integral and highly visible part of Lisbon's economic and social landscape.[223] "It is a common observation of the natives," wrote one Englishman, "that excepting of the lowest condition of life, you shall not meet anyone on foot some hours of the day, but dogs and Englishmen."[224] Much of the profit earned by the "jolly, free Factory," as former British ambassador to Portugal Benjamin Keene referred to it, found its way back to the mother country.[225] Portuguese coins were in fact legal tender in Britain; and some have asserted that by the middle of the eighteenth century they were more plentiful than British ones in British pockets. Indeed, some have argued that this large influx of Portuguese capital played a crucial role in financing the early stages of the Industrial Revolution in Britain.[226]

But one must not lose sight of the fact that the Portuguese also benefited from the arrangement. In his treatise, *On the Principles of Political Economy and Taxation* (1817), the British economist David Ricardo (whose family was of Portuguese Jewish origins) used the example of English and Portuguese economic cooperation to explain the concept of comparative advantage. By choosing to produce a good where it has a competitive advantage (in the case of England, textiles, in the case of Portugal, wine) and then trading that good for the other, both countries end up maximizing the benefits to each other. Although contemporaries like Pombal never tired of pointing out that Portugal lacked vibrant agricultural and manufacturing sectors, it was actually in possession of the most lucrative and coveted of all early modern industries: the minting of gold. Unlike other products, gold coins could be traded for every other commodity. As a result, Portugal was free to import whatever it desired—like textiles and Italian singers—and was still able to finance the kind of extravagant court life that was considered indispensable to maintaining a strong, effective state in early modern Europe. While scholars have derided the Portuguese armed forces in the eighteenth century as small, underfunded, and corrupt, in reality, Portugal had little need for them. The vaunted British army and navy were, for all practical purposes, its paid mercenaries.[227]

Brazilian gold also funded the Church and kept a high proportion of the kingdom's citizens in holy orders, many cloistered away behind convent walls. While few modern economists would consider this an efficient or even sensible way to spend state resources, most Portuguese at the time would have disagreed. For them, it was vital that Christ find favor with their kingdom. From their perspective, the prospect of heaven was unquestionably worth the investment.

Although historians have disparaged pre-earthquake Lisbon—citing the enormous gulf that existed between rich and poor and the moral discrepancy between the overt claims of piety and the obvious cruelties of the Inquisition—one might also see a vital imperial city that blended (sometimes uneasily) elements of East and West, the medieval and the early modern, the local and the international, and the cultural traits from three great religions: Judaism, Christianity, and Islam.

It was certainly no backwater, as some have asserted.[228] In 1755, it was more populous than either Rome or Madrid, and was (with its patriarchy) an indisputable center of the Catholic faith.

It was also the third-busiest port in the world after London and Amsterdam, the principal European entryway of New World trade, and was the center of a large global empire that continued to send immense riches to its appreciative monarch. Much derided then and now, the Portuguese economy had in fact expanded continuously for seventy years with a low rate of inflation.[229] Why else would merchants from around the world (and especially the British, who were on the verge of the Industrial Revolution and the creation of the world's largest global empire) have maintained such a large and robust commercial presence there? In the words of a common proverb of the time: *"Chi non vista Lisboa, non a cosa boa"* (He who never saw Lisbon never saw a good thing).[230]

But the Portugal of João V would not last forever. In 1749, the ailing king made his thirteenth and final journey to the therapeutic hot springs of Caldas da Rainha in an ultimately unsuccessful effort to revive his health. By the late spring of 1750, it became clear that he was dying. In the hope that the Virgin would prove a more effective healer than his physicians, the king spent most days lying motionless inside the Church of Our Lady of Necessities. He was joined by the faithful figure of Malagrida, who prayed for hours with his head pressed against the marble floor. On July 11, Dom João was given extreme unction by Carmelite priests and afterward received an apostolic blessing and plenary absolution from the papal nuncio, Lucas Melchior Tempi.[231] Outside his window in the Riverside Palace, large crowds gathered. Inside, a coterie of intimates stood vigil: Queen Maria Ana, Prince José (the heir apparent), the king's two brothers (António and Pedro), Father Malagrida, the cardinal patriarch, and a gaggle of priests and monks,

who, when the king's condition worsened, held aloft a statuette of Our
Lady of Necessities for him to gaze upon. When the end seemed near,
a lighted candle was placed in his trembling hands. On the night of
July 31, 1750, the candle fell; and the old king rose one last time from his
pillow with a shudder, stared at those arrayed around him with uncom-
prehending eyes, murmured a few incomprehensible words, exhaled,
and then fell back cold and inanimate onto his bed.[232]

On the day after his father's death, Dom José appointed Pombal
secretary of state for foreign affairs and war in an act of defiance to
the old order. (The dead king had never trusted Pombal, believing he
possessed a "hairy heart," while Ambassador Keene had written that
he "would rather have any other nag put in the harness but him.")[233]
Although not as physically or intellectually commanding as his father,
Dom José would prove competent and popular during his first five years
on the throne, aided as he was by his talented and ferociously ambitious
right-hand man.[234]

Of medium height, the new king was robust of frame as well as
constitution, though a bit on the corpulent side, with a fleshy face and,
like his father, a few missing teeth. Said to be "agreeable in private, and
majestic in public," he was no dullard. Considered reasonably erudite
in conversation and skillful in the saddle, he had inherited from his
father both a love of grandeur and a wandering eye. Rumors of extramarital affairs began soon after his coronation. Driven to distraction
with jealousy, his Spanish wife, Mariana Vitória, "prohibited women
from serving at the royal table," according to a priest, and kept a close
eye on the female servants who attended to her husband. In the early
years of his reign, the king took a special fancy to the twenty-four-year-
old Marquesa of Távora, a ravishing beauty with conspicuous doll-like
features. Although already married (to her nephew, a common practice among the inbred Portuguese aristocracy), she was flattered by the
king's advances and in due course succumbed to his royal ardor.[235]

When, on June 6, 1755, Dom José celebrated his forty-first birthday, the state of the kingdom—as well as the royal libido—was strong.
At a performance of *Clemenza di Tito* that evening at the opera, the
British naval officer Augustus Hervey observed that "the Marquesa de
Tavora was very well with the King. They did nothing but eye each
other as much as they dared in the Queen's presence." Hervey had himself visited Lisbon many times over the years and had taken full advan-

José I

tage of its pleasures. This "British Casanova" (as he was then known) relished the permissive atmosphere of Dom José's capital city at mid-century, passing most of his nights in the embrace of nuns, whores, and noblewomen (of which he did not express any particular preference).[236]

Despite the rumblings of war, Portugal's borders were secure; the Tagus was clogged with ships; and the royal coffers continued to over-flow with gold and precious gems. In short, there was every hope and expectation that His Most Faithful Majesty's reign would replicate, if not ultimately surpass, the Alexandrine greatness of his illustrious father.[237]

On October 7, 1755, Dom José attended a rehearsal for *Antigono*. It would open the new fall season at the Opera House on October 16, the Feast of São Carlos.[238] On October 15, at Mafra, thousands of the faithful descended upon the gigantic pink *palácio* for the climax of the fourteen-day-long religious Jubilee that had been awarded to the kingdom by Pope Clement XII. A week later, on October 23, Portugal's only newspaper, the *Gazeta de Lisboa*, reported the shocking news that British General Edward Braddock and over a thousand of his troops had been routed by a force of "one thousand five hundred French regulars supported by six hundred Indians" in the North American colony of Pennsylvania (the actual numbers were closer to three hundred Indians and thirty Frenchmen).[239]

The Battle of the Monongahela, or more commonly "Braddock's Defeat," had taken place three months earlier on a sweltering July day; but only now was the news reaching Europe.[240] Curiously, no mention was made of the lanky young colonel from Virginia named George Washington, who had helped pull his mortally wounded commander from the field and lead the surviving troops to safety (Braddock would succumb to his wounds four days later). A partial list of the sixty or so British officers who had been either killed or wounded was no doubt of great interest to Lisbon's expatriate community who had many friends and relations serving in North America.[241] It was only a matter of time, many surely thought, before Portugal and its capital were dragged into the center of world events.

CHAPTER TWO

November 1, 1755

The day dawned serenely; the sun was bright;
and there was not a cloud in the sky.

—JOACHIM JOSEPH MOREIRA DE MENDONÇA,
HISTORIA UNIVERSAL DOS TERREMOTOS (1758)

TERREMOTO!

The first to realize that something was amiss were sailors and ship captains in the northeastern Atlantic. At 9:30 a.m. on November 1, 1755, 325 miles west of Cape St. Vincent, Portugal, a Captain Eleazer Johnson of Boston "felt his Ship shake very much two different Times," though "the Sky was very clear and the Sea very smooth," reported *The Boston Gazette*. "The first Shock lasted 2 or 3 Minutes," then "about three Minutes" later "came on the second . . . which lasted about 2 minutes and shook [Johnson's] Ship to such a Degree that it un-hung the Card of his Compass then in the Binnacle."[1] At about the same time, 120 miles west of the Cape, the crew of the *Jean* was "thrown eighteen inches from the deck" by a sudden jolt—while 750 miles southwest of Iberia, a tremor shook the *Mary* "in such a manner" that it "overturned the Compass . . . and broke most of [the] Earthen-ware, China, and Bottles" on board. "It strained the Ship as if she had been striking on the Ground," recalled the captain, "and cracked the Seams on the Deck, which afterwards leaked, though [they had been] quite tight before."[2]

One ship, sailing 310 miles west of Lisbon, "had her Cabin Windows shattered to Pieces" by a "Shock," and another vessel experienced "such a violent motion" that "every part . . . seemed to become detached" and "pieces of artillery leapt over their carriages."[3] Off San-lúcar, Spain, the *Nancy* was given such a violent and unexpected "shake" that the captain initially believed that she had run aground, but after "heaving the lead" he saw that "the water [had risen] upwards of 30 feet in two minutes," and that a second anchor "fairly swam on the water"— while less than five miles from the Portuguese coast (and about twenty-five miles south of Lisbon), the Dutch captain of the *Hollandois* "felt a violent tremor" at around 9:45 a.m. and "saw several large rocks separate themselves from Mount Sesimbra . . . and roll into the sea with a vast and horrid noise."[4]

It all began at 9:30 in the morning Lisbon time (meaning Captain Johnson and his crew were probably the first to experience a quake), when a long-dormant fault line several hundred miles off the coast of Cape St. Vincent suddenly exploded across a 150-to-600-kilometer gash in the ocean floor.[5] Driving upward like a coiled spring, the vast shelf of rock and sediment produced a tremor nine times more powerful in terms of energy released than Tsar Bomba, the largest thermonuclear device ever detonated.[6] Over the next eight to ten minutes, the fault's hanging wall would surge two more times from the seabed, each tremor radiating outward from the quake's hypocenter (or focus) at 3 to 5 kilometers per second.

Although the exact dimensions of the Lisbon Earthquake will never be known (seismographs were not introduced until the late nineteenth century), all available evidence indicates that it was one of the most powerful in recorded human history, measuring between 8.5 and 9.1 on the moment magnitude scale Mw—though it may have even been larger.* Like most giant temblors, it was a "mega-thrust" earthquake, which occurs when two tectonic plates collide and one (A in the diagram on p. 72) is pushed upward while the other (B) is forced or subducted underneath.

---

* For earthquakes above a 5.0, the local magnitude scale ML (commonly referred to as the Richter scale) has been replaced by the moment magnitude scale Mw, which measures the total energy released from an earthquake rather than the size of its seismic waves. Unlike the local magnitude scale ML, which reaches a saturation point at the upper end of the scale and assigns a magnitude of around 7.0 to all large earthquakes, the moment magnitude scale Mw has no upper limit and so is useful for gauging the dimensions of medium- and large-size temblors. Each increase of 1.0 on the moment magnitude scale (6.0 to 7.0 Mw, for example) corresponds to an increase of 32 times the energy released, while an increase of 2 equals an escalation of 1,000 times.

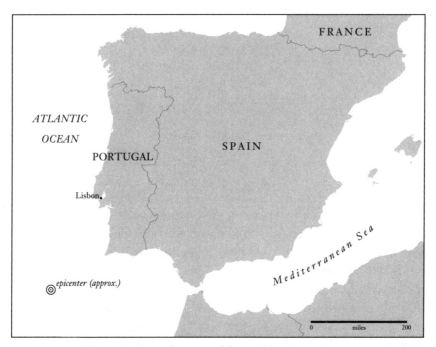

The approximate location of the earthquake's epicenter

At sea, tsunamis are frequently the result when the rising plate, acting like a giant piston, drives millions of gallons of seawater toward the surface of the ocean. In the case of Lisbon, three massive underwater tremors (which raised the ocean floor approximately 10 meters) produced three separate tsunami waves.[7]

While tsunamis are relatively rare in the Atlantic, earthquakes are not. Iberia has long been the site of seismic activity, lying as it does just north of the geologically contentious boundary between the African and Eurasian continental plates that runs horizontally east to west along the entire length of the southern Mediterranean through the Strait of Gibraltar all the way to the Mid-Atlantic Ridge. In the 1950s and '60s, the science of plate tectonics revolutionized the study of geology by revealing that the earth's crust is comprised of several large rigid plates that glide atop the earth's viscous upper mantle at a rate of a few centimeters per year.[8] Faults develop when plates collide, separate, or move laterally next to one another. Generally, the movement along fault lines is continuous and relatively stress-free. In these cases, energy is released gradually and, for the most part, without incident. However,

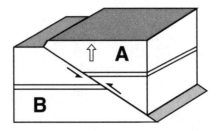

Cross section of a mega-thrust earthquake

there are times when two plates lock together for an extended period, storing up enormous quantities of energy that are released when one or both plates suddenly slip, producing an earthquake.

The two fault types that correspond to this phenomenon are reverse and strike-slip faults. The first occurs when two plates collide and one is thrust upward, while the second arises when two plates moving in opposite directions collide horizontally along points of contact known as asperities. A third fault type, the normal fault, ensues when one plate drops downward, usually as the result of two plates separating from each other.[9]

The distant cause of the Great Lisbon Earthquake—a mega-thrust temblor resulting from a reverse fault—was the slow-motion collision of the African and Eurasian continental plates. Although both plates are moving eastward at a rate of one centimeter per year, the African plate is also turning counterclockwise around a fixed rotation point several hundred miles west of the African continent. Thus, both plates are approaching each other at a speed of 5 millimeters per year.[10] The result is enormous friction (and occasional earthquakes) where the two plates find themselves in greatest conflict, most notably off the coasts of Portugal and Spain.[11]

Yet, after years of research, the precise location of the Lisbon Earthquake's hypocenter remains elusive and the subject of vigorous debate among seismologists.[12] Until recently, many believed that an area several hundred miles west of Cape St. Vincent called the Gorringe Ridge was the most likely candidate.[13] Scarred with faults, it gave birth to a string of earthquakes between 1930 and 1980, including the Mw 8.0 quake of February 18, 1969, which was felt in both Portugal and Morocco and which caused several deaths, though it did not produce a tsunami. Over the past two decades, however, new research has uncovered several other possible locations, including a fault south of Iberia in the Gulf of Cádiz, another northwest of the Gorringe Ridge, aptly christened the "Marquis de Pombal Thrust" (MPF in the diagram on p. 74), one in the Horseshoe Plain, south of the Gorringe Ridge, one in the Guadalquivir Bank, below Portugal's Algarve coast, one in the lower Tagus valley, near Lisbon, and one running from Lisbon to a point just north of the Moroccan coast. There is also growing speculation that the Lisbon disaster resulted from two or more earthquakes, whereby an initial temblor triggered a series of quakes, some possibly hundreds of miles from the original hypocenter.[14]

Whatever its size and provenance, the great quake of 1755 did not arrive without warning, both real and imagined. Eight days earlier, according to an account printed in Germany, a hitherto unknown species of cricket emerged in great numbers in the vicinity of a harbor on the Algerian coast. The mysterious black bug with "rounded horns" was thought to have hatched in a "fiery underground vapor" (then believed to be one of the principal physical causes of earthquakes) and was strikingly similar, the authors noted, to a creature that had appeared in Peru just after the Great Lima-Callao Earthquake of 1746.[15]

One week before the disaster, a whale was spotted off the shores of Lisbon. If only *lisboetas* had recalled the book of Jonah, wrote the German theologian Johann Rudolph Anton Pidorit, they might have

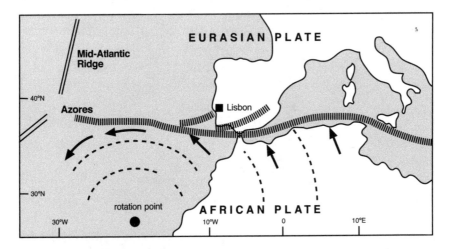

The seismically contentious boundary between the Eurasian and African continental plates

repented like the inhabitants of Nineveh after Jonah's sermon and saved themselves and their city.[16]

In the last week of October (1755), "the sea became [so] enraged" off Ericeira, Portugal, reported the *Gazeta de Lisboa*, that "fishermen, fearing a large storm, moved their boats to higher ground"—though the anticipated tempest never came. And on the day before the disaster (October 31), sailors in Lisbon noticed the tide arrive two hours late, while peasants in the tiny village of Linhares in northern Portugal witnessed "a phenomenon or a very bright comet" appear around noon and persist until two hours after midnight, when it "ended in flames."[17]

One Lisbon merchant recalled that "during the last days of October the air seemed heavy with a reddish and unhealthy fog at sunrise and sunset."[18] And on the last day of the month, October 31, Hamburg's consul, Christian Stocqueler, espied a large and ominous fog on the

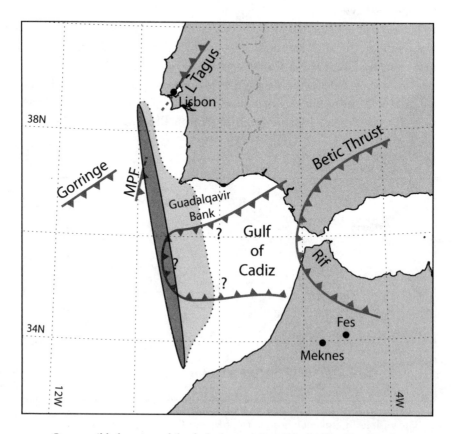

One possible location of the fault that produced the Lisbon Earthquake

surface of the ocean. "[It] came from the sea," he wrote, "and covered the vallies." Then "the wind [shifted] to the east, [and it] returned to the sea, collecting itself" and became "the thickest I ever saw."[19] During the eighteenth century, many believed there was a causal relationship between earthquakes and the weather. The still influential Aristotelian view, derived from the *Meteorologica*, posited that earthquakes were produced by the exhalation of wind from underground caverns—though the most plausible explanation for the appearance of these "dry fogs" or "tropospheric sulphate aerosols," as they are known today, was the eruption of Iceland's Katla volcano two weeks earlier.[20]

More worrying from a seismological perspective were the "two small earthquakes" and the "light movements [of the earth]" that several priests from Lisbon's Oratory of St. Philip Neri and one *lisboeta*, respectively, felt on the evening of October 31.[21] Similarly, "some ecclesiastics and some lay people" also felt a slight shaking of the earth around midnight in Madrid—while in Cork, Ireland, "betwixt Twelve and One o'clock" (on November 1), a handful of people reported "a small Shock of an Earthquake"—but because it was "so early and felt by so few, [it] passed without much Notice."[22]

At eight in the morning on All Saints' Day, according to a newspaper report, the air became so dense along the coast near Naples, Italy, that "people could not see one another"—after which "the sea became disturbed and the water rose." At approximately 9 a.m., Mount Vesuvius began to emit smoke—"leading many residents of Naples to fear an earthquake." But, by ten o'clock "the smoke [had] stopped and the people rushed to the churches to thank God for saving them."[23]

Throughout the morning of November 1, 1755, wells ran dry across Portugal and Spain; and some rivers inexplicably lost their current and stopped moving altogether.[24] According to two unsubstantiated reports, the Tagus began to swell ominously in the hour before the first tremor; and "all of the animals" in Lisbon—no doubt sensing the onset of seismic activity caused, perhaps, by a change in the electromagnetic field—"appeared alarmed and filled with fear."[25] All of this suggests that several small tremors shook the North Atlantic in the days and hours leading up to the great cataclysm (a not uncommon occurrence before the largest earthquakes).

It was even alleged that Malagrida himself had predicted the quake, when, in the last week of October, he was heard to exclaim while staring at one of Lisbon's busiest squares: "Oh! How much toil and soon it will all be extinguished!"[26] He was not Portugal's only Cassandra. For many years, a nun from Louriçal claimed that Christ had conveyed to her his profound disappointment with Portugal and how one day the country would pay for its sins. Moreover, three years before the disaster, a monk had announced that an extraordinary event on All Saints' Day that year would herald the return of the lost king Sebastian I on the Feast of São João (June 24). But when November 1, 1752, arrived and nothing remarkable happened, the date was pushed ahead to 1753—and then 1754.[27] By All Saints' Day 1755, the monk's prophecy—along with all the others—had been largely forgotten.

FESTUM OMNIUM SANCTORUM (FEAST OF ALL SAINTS)

It was, by all accounts, an uncommonly beautiful Saturday morning. "The finest I had ever seen," wrote one survivor. "The sun shone out in its full lustre," recalled another, and "the whole face of the sky was perfectly serene and clear." The temperature, a continuation of the unseasonably warm month of October, was 63.5°F; the barometer registered above 900 millibars; and the ocean and river were quiet. From the northeast, a gentle wind blew across the undulating cityscape, which, according to one eyewitness, "was bathed in a blanket of golden light."[28]

Over the previous day, thousands of the faithful—many on foot, others in rickety wooden carts pulled by mules or burros—had streamed into the capital from villages and farms in the surrounding districts. In a country where the veneration of saints was a part of the fabric of everyday life, the Feast of All Saints (or All Saints' Day) was a national holiday and one of the most cherished dates on the crowded liturgical calendar. A holy day of obligation, requiring Catholics of good health to attend mass, it honors and commemorates all those (known and unknown) who have achieved the "beatific vision," that is, those who enjoy an immediate visual knowledge of God in Heaven, like the angels and the souls of the just.

The holiday officially began before dawn with the ringing of the bells of São Jorge and São Roque, as swarms of beggars took their places outside churches and taverns in the hope that the festivities would bring an abundance of copper coins.[29] At 6:02 a.m., cannons were fired from Belém Tower to proclaim the arrival or "birth of the sun" (*nascer do sol*).[30]

By 9 a.m., Lisbon's churches were brimming with believers. Amid the pomp and festal splendor, the laity heard sermons on the communion and sacred testimony of the saints, asked God for His forgiveness, and, in keeping with long-standing tradition, bestowed *oferendas* (offerings) upon their favorite *santos* and *santas*. "Among the people [that day]," recalled one priest, "there was an extraordinary, deep-seated joy which . . . accentuated their pleasures and forecast in everything happiness and good luck."[31]

In the congested streets, great crowds were on the move. Many were destined for the popular High Mass at ten o'clock, with its full choir, somber procession of religious officials, and annual presentation of relics believed to possess miraculous powers, while others, still at home, made harried, last-minute adjustments to coats, shawls, powdered wigs, and buckled shoes. More than a few remained safe and secure in their beds.[32]

In stoves and hearths throughout the city, fires had been set in preparation for the feast day meal; and in every church, chapel, domestic altar, and convent wax candles burned. For Lisbon's religious community, the morning of All Saints' Day was an unusually busy time. "A large number of the clergy was engaged in the choirs," recollected a priest, "[while] many were on the altars celebrating the sacred sacrifice of the mass or handing out the Eucharist."[33] In the streets, legions of monks from the city's two mendicant orders—the Dominicans and the Franciscan Capuchins—moved purposefully between churches, petitioning passersby for handouts and donations. Clothed in shabby and more often than not malodorous robes, they wore tattered sandals or walked *descalços* (barefoot) on the grimy cobblestones. In their hands they clutched Bibles, crosses, portable *oratórios*, and religious statuettes, which they repeatedly and reverently kissed.[34]

Fortuitously absent from the capital that day was Portugal's royal family who, in the early hours, had traveled to their beloved palace in the suburb of Belém (Bethlehem). Unlike their main residence along the river, Belém provided the *família real* with genuine privacy, a chance to escape the stifling protocol of the court (as well as the oppressive odors of the Baixa). There, the queen and the princesses could engage in their favorite equestrian pursuits and the king could hunt (and still be only a carriage ride away from his many mistresses in the city).[35] Also absent was a sizable portion of the Portuguese nobility, who customarily spent the rain-soaked winters in their palatial villas in Belém or the neighboring provinces of Estremadura, Beira, and Alentejo.[36] Joining them were scores of foreign merchants who fled each year from the boisterous (and frequently anti-Protestant) revels of the holiday for the seclusion of their country homes (or *quintas*), where they would remain in bucolic obscurity, observed *The London Magazine*, "till the second of November, when everything is quiet."[37]

Accounts differ as to when the first tremor reached Lisbon. Pocket watches were uncommon at the time; clocks were rare; and the majority of firsthand accounts offer a wide range of starting times.[38] A careful examination of the most reliable sources, however—including one from a watch-carrying eyewitness—suggests that at 9:45 a.m. (give or take a minute or two) the capital was startled by what one survivor described as a "horrible subterranean noise"—likened variously to "the rattling of several carriages in the main street," "a chest sliding on the deck of a ship," "drums being played in the distance," or "the hollow, distant rumbling of thunder."[39] Within several seconds, the noise became as deafening as "the loudest cannon."[40]

Initially, few had any idea what was occurring. The majority of *lisboetas* had never experienced a large earthquake before and were thus "so ignorant" that they "could neither give a name to what was occurring nor decide how to flee from it," recalled a priest.[41] Apart from the relatively minor (albeit much discussed) tremor that followed the death of João V on July 31, 1750, the preceding decades had been, on the whole, geologically tranquil—though one contemporary claims that Lisbon had experienced a series of smallish earthquakes in the years leading up to All Saints' Day 1755.[42] What is certain is that the last seismic event of any significance in Portugal—the earthquake and tsunami of December 27, 1722 (est. Mw 6.5–Mw 7.8)—had taken place more than three decades before; and, while it caused widespread devastation across the kingdom's southern coast, it left little mark on the capital.[43]

For one English merchant living on the eastern edge of São Jorge's Hill, it was the flapping of picture frames against the walls of his bedchamber that indicated something out of the ordinary. At first, he had barely taken notice when his house started "gently to shake." But then the movements "gradually increased," along "with a rushing noise like the Sound of heavy Carriages driving hard at some Distance." After this, he recalled, the room began to roll and "every part of the House cracked ... the Tiles rattled ... the Walls rent on every side; [and] the Doors of a pretty large Bookcase ... burst open and the Books fell from the Shelves."[44] Terrified, he grabbed his hat and wig and rushed toward the interior of the building where he could hear the sounds of houses crashing down and "the Screams and Cries of People from every Quarter."[45]

The merchant was lucky. His decision to remain indoors and ride out the tremors in a "winding stone staircase" probably saved his life. For those "in the upper stories of houses," wrote a surgeon, "were in general more fortunate than those that attempted to escape by the doors . . . for they were buried under the ruins with the greatest part of the foot-passengers."[46] When the second tremor came, "all the inhabitants endeavored to fly," recalled one eyewitness, "tho' many thousands perished in that attempt, having their brains knocked out."[47]

The most prominent victim of the earthquake, Spain's ambassador to Portugal and the Count of Perelada, Bernardo de Rocaberti, died in his nightgown when the coat of arms above his front door fell on top of him as he attempted to escape into the street.[48] Another notable fatality, the Reverend J. Manley, the principal of the English College of Lisbon, was buried under the rubble of his school's bell tower as he tried to outrun the falling debris. "Tis thought," wrote a nun, that Manley had "lived about four and twenty hours in that Misery [and thus probably suffocated], for when they found him [under a bench], he was nowhere bruised."[49]

The first tremor caught the city's inhabitants completely by surprise. Ringing church bells and wrenching down buildings in a shower of bricks, mortar, and broken beams, it lasted all of two minutes and was, by most accounts, the strongest and most deadly of the three. Especially vulnerable were street-facing walls, which, in many instances after their collapse, left the floors and interior walls of structures largely intact.[50] According to a newspaper report, John Williamson, the chaplain of Lisbon's British Factory, "escaped most wonderfully" from the quake, "for though the Walls of the House [which he was occupying] were thrown down," they "providentially . . . fell outward, and his Life [as well as that of his family] was preserved."[51]

Then after a pause of approximately one minute (during which many mistakenly believed the danger to be over), a second tremor shook the capital for at least two and a half minutes with a terrible and sustained intensity.[52] It was this tremor that brought down two palace walls on top of the Marquesa de Louriçal as she knelt to thank God for sparing her young daughter and herself during the first shock. One of

Portugal's most prominent aristocrats, the mortally injured marquesa would expire a few days later "in the prime of her life" in the nearby village of Cascais.[53] For one (more fortunate) individual, the second tremor dislodged a beam that had pinned him almost to the point of suffocation beneath the rubble of his multistoried house—thus enabling him to escape.[54]

Following another sixty-second pause, a third and final tremor, which lasted three to four minutes, pulled down those buildings that had been structurally compromised by the previous two tremors. From beginning to end, the earthquake spanned approximately ten minutes (with eight solid minutes of shaking)—though a few witnesses claimed it persisted for as long as a quarter of an hour, and others much less.[55] By comparison, the much smaller quake that destroyed much of Port-au-Prince, Haiti, in 2010, killing 160,000 people, lasted just thirty-five seconds.[56]

Almost certainly, the first physical sensation felt by the inhabitants of Lisbon was the arrival of what geologists call P waves: seismic disturbances that ripple through the earth at 5 kilometers per second and announce themselves as a kind of sonic boom, rattling windows and causing objects on tables and walls (like picture frames) to tremble and vibrate.[57] Typically, these are followed by S waves, which shake and shear the earth and every structure upon it. In all likelihood, the ear-splitting subterranean noises heard during the length of the earthquake were the result of P and S waves (or body waves) converting their energy into acoustic waves as they reached the atmosphere.[58]

As the P and S waves arrive at the earth's surface, their energy, according to a seismologist, is "reflected back into the underlying rocks so that the surface is affected simultaneously by upward and downward moving waves."[59] One eyewitness recalled that "the earth moved vertically at times and at other times it moved side to side . . . the movements were so contrary and opposed to each other that the thickest and strongest walls easily separated and fell." Another reported that the "earthquake shook by quick vibrations the foundations of the superstructure, loosening the stones from their cement, and then with scarce a perceptible pause, the motion changed and every building was tossed like a waggon driven violently over rough stones."[60]

After this, Love and Rayleigh waves (named after their discoverers A. E. H. Love and Lord Rayleigh) arrived.[61] Known as surface waves, they amplify the structural pressures on buildings and, in the case of

Rayleigh waves, undulate across the surface of the earth like waves on the ocean or, as two *lisboetas* put it, like "waves . . . in a cornfield" or a "feverish human body when exposed to a sudden draft."[62] Another recalled "the whole city waving backwards and forwards like the sea when the wind first begins to rise."[63]

One eyewitness who had an exceptionally clear view of the disaster was a ship captain anchored in the Tagus just east of the Riverside Palace. Rising at five that morning, he had maneuvered his vessel from the Customs House to a position in front of the Royal Ship Yards (Ribeira dos Naus), when, at about 9:50 a.m., he experienced an "uncommon motion." Fearing that he had run aground, though at the same time confident that he was still in deep water, he glanced toward the city, where to his "amazement" he "beheld the tall and stately buildings . . . tumbling down with great Cracks and Noise." From São Paulo northward to the Bairro Alto, the Rossio, and the parish of São José, and "Eastward, as far as the gallows," he saw the great capital laid low by "three . . . shocks which were so violent" that people "could [only] with great Difficulty stand on their Legs." Within this area, "almost all the palaces and large churches were rent down or part fallen," he wrote, "and scarce one house . . . [was] left habitable."[64]

Another who observed Lisbon's destruction from a similarly advantageous perch was Richard Goddard, the young vicar of Lacock in Wiltshire (whose medieval abbey has served as a backdrop for numerous films, including several in the Harry Potter series).[65] Recently arrived from England in a packet boat (which ferried mail, merchandise, and people between Britain's embassies and colonial possessions), the New College, Oxford, graduate was in poor health and was hoping to spend a quiet, uneventful winter away from the cares of his vicarage. He would lodge with his younger brother, Ambrose, a merchant in the British Factory. A scion of the prominent Goddard family of Swindon, he was received with the utmost courtesy by the "most considerable" people of Lisbon's British community, including Abraham Castres and Edward Hay, Britain's ambassador and consul to Portugal.[66]

On the morning of All Saints' Day, Goddard had risen early in order to take a therapeutic stroll along the viewing platform that overlooks the city from atop São Jorge's Hill. Originally intending to return after half an hour to assist the Factory chaplain, John Williamson, with morning services, he was instead "tempted by the Delightfulness of the Morning . . . the Softness of the Air, and the Beauty of the Prospect" to

The combined assaults of the earthquake, the tsunami, and the fire

prolong his walk for a few more minutes. "To this happy . . . providential Change of Mind," he would later write, "I owe my preservation."[67] For as soon as Goddard returned to the platform, he heard what he thought was the "noise of several Coaches" and felt "a trembling of earth not greatly unlike what is felt in such an Occasion." The rocking increased so much that until he grabbed a nearby flagstaff he had great difficulty staying on his feet.

He then saw the Castle of São Jorge collapse "and the Houses round [it] share the same fate." Luckily, he was in no danger, as the platform he inhabited was situated on open ground. All around him, terrified people cried out to God "for Mercy" (Misericordia). The "Shrieks of [one] Person who ran by me," he wrote, "left me no Room to doubt of my real Situation."[68]

Yet just as Goddard began to think that the worst was over, "the shock returned with such an increase in Violence [that it] seemed to threaten everything with inevitable destruction." "No words," he wrote, "can convey an Idea of that Scene of Horror and Confusion to which I was now Witness . . . Houses, Churches, Convents, Palaces composed one undistinguished Heap of Ruins; unless . . . the more magnificent Buildings seemed distinguished by the severity of their Fate. . . . [I] expected every Moment to be swallowed up."[69]

In the midst of all the horror and confusion was Guillaume de

Rochemont, the preacher of the Dutch legation and the religious leader of Lisbon's Dutch and German Protestant communities. On the morning of All Saints' Day, he was sitting down to tea with his wife and family—and having just taken a cup in his hand—when the house began to shake. "As we raced down the steps in an attempt to save the children," he recalled, "the ceiling fell down on our heads and the stairs collapsed beneath our feet, so that we barely reached the safety of the garden." Behind him, he saw his newly built house collapse with such thundering finality that "there was not one stone which stood upon another."[70]

Like the Reverends Goddard, Williamson, and Rochemont, Manoel Portal was a man of the cloth. A Catholic priest and a resident of the Monastery of the Congregation of the Oratory of St. Philip Neri, he would become one of the principal chroniclers of the Lisbon disaster, penning a massive 389-page account entitled *The History of the Destruction of the City of Lisbon*.[71] On the evening before the earthquake, Portal experienced what he later believed was a premonition of an impending disaster, when, in a dream, Jesus warned him that he would never again see his beloved crucifix, which hung on the wall of his cell.[72]

When the earthquake began, Father Portal knew immediately what was happening, but as he dashed through the monastery corridor in an attempt to escape, the ceiling collapsed on top of him and he was buried in the rubble. "Asking God for mercy and awaiting death at any moment," he was discovered by several fellow priests and pulled from the debris. Though his eyes were covered in "crusts of blood" and his leg crushed by a large boulder, he feared being caught inside during any future tremors; and so, after confessing his sins and hearing confessions from a few other priests (some covered with blood), he ventured out into the chaos of the streets.[73]

Fortunately, most of Portal's congregation had survived—though some were severely injured. Father José Clemente had ridden out the quake by leaping into the window opening of his cell and holding on to the beam. Many, however, who had stayed in their beds, ran out into the corridor (like Portal), or found themselves in large rooms had been wounded or killed. Father Clemente's brother, Father Joaquim Ferraz, had slipped on the monastery stairs while attempting to escape the church where he had been celebrating mass and was injured in the fall of the building. He never regained consciousness and lingered for three days before succumbing to his wounds. Portal's pious and learned mentor, Father Philip Neri, was so thoroughly crushed in the collapse of the dining hall ceiling that "only a few fragments of his bones" were ever recovered, while the virtuous and erudite Father Vicente Collasso (who was, in Portal's words, "a very good friend of books") was found dead in the hallway alongside Father José da Encarnação, a young nurse monk, who was bringing medicine to his ailing friend when the earthquake struck.[74]

Farther from the center of the destruction, Catherine "Kitty" Witham, a twenty-six-year-old English nun, had already attended choir, consumed a meager breakfast, and taken communion in Syon Covent (where she lived with a community of Bridgettine nuns) when the earthquake or "the dreadful Affair," as she called it, began. She had been in the process of "washing up the tea things" (as she told her "Dearest Mama" in a letter) when she heard a sound like the "rattling of coaches" and saw everything on the table begin to "danse up and down."[75]

> I look about me and see the Walls a shakeing and a falling down then I up and took to my heells, with Jesus in my mouth, and to the quire I run, thinking to be safe there, but there was no Entranc but all falling rownd us, and the lime and dust so thick there was no seeing.

Encountering several terrified sisters, Kitty suggested they escape as a group to the garden, which—"Blessed be his holy name"—they all reached without injury.[76]

When the first tremor struck, the papal nuncio, Monsignor Filippo Acciaiuoli, was on his knees in his bedchamber, praying and preparing for the High Mass at 10 a.m. Born in Rome of a distinguished Florentine family, Acciaiuoli was fifty-five years old and had represented the Holy See in Lisbon for a year. As the vibrations coursed through his palace and the upper floor fell, he was just able to raise himself from the floor, reach for the door handle, and, though "blinded by dust and injured by the falling plaster," escape into the garden—where, half naked and covered in blood, he watched what was left of his house and stable fall on top of his private secretary, a male servant, and seven mules.[77]

In the nearby Patriarchal Palace, at the southern end of the Baixa, the cardinal patriarch, José Manuel da Câmara de Atalaia, was sitting in his bedroom, stricken with dysentery and unable to move, when the ceiling suddenly collapsed. Fortunately still "intact inside the ruins" after the first tremor, he was saved by the courage and quick thinking of two servants, who dragged the sixty-nine-year-old out of the building moments before it fell.[78]

Sir Charles Henry Frankland had also escaped death. On holiday in Lisbon on what was supposed to be the first leg of a Grand Tour of Europe, "Harry" was a baronet and a dandy as well as a direct lineal descendant of Oliver Cromwell. Born in Bengal on May 10, 1716, to an ancient and affluent family from the north of England, he was (according to a nineteenth-century biographer) possessed of a "refined and noble cast of features with a peculiarly passive and melancholy expression" as well as "a delicacy of taste." He was also a friend of such worthies of the age as Henry Fielding, Horace Walpole, and Lord Chesterfield. In 1738, he inherited a substantial fortune upon the death of his father. Three years later, when offered the choice of the governorship of Massachusetts or the lucrative collectorship of the port of Boston, he chose the latter and settled in the New World.[79]

Since 1752, Frankland had lived scandalously on a sprawling country estate in Hopkinton, Massachusetts with Miss Agnes Surriage, a comely and bewitching young woman whom he had met at a local inn when she was a barefoot servant girl of fourteen and he a dashing twenty-six-year-old on the make.[80] "Her ringlets," wrote a biographer of young Agnes, "were as black and glossy as the raven; her dark eyes beamed with light and loveliness; [and] her voice was musical, birdlike."[81] In the years that followed, Frankland saw that the fisherman's daughter was educated in Boston's finest schools—though the nature of their union elicited a "storm of just indignation" across the commonwealth.[82] In 1754, the unmarried couple had traveled to England on Frankland family business (where Agnes had received an icy reception from Sir Henry's relatives) and then on to Lisbon and their continental journey.[83]

When the first tremor began, Frankland was on his way to High Mass in his carriage in full court dress with a lady who was decidedly not Miss Surriage. As buildings collapsed into the street, the coach was buried; and Frankland was trapped under the rubble for more than an hour, his horses and riders dead. In the dark, he was set upon by his terrified female companion, who, "in the Agonies of Death," tore through the sleeve of his red broadcloth coat with her teeth, removing a chunk of flesh from his elbow.[84] Begging for mercy and asking God to forgive his sins (which, according to his biographer, were "not a few"), Frankland promised God that if he was delivered from this predicament, he would henceforth lead a noble and praiseworthy life and marry the neglected and long-suffering Agnes.[85]

In Belém, the royal family escaped from their palace largely unscathed.[86] His Most Faithful Majesty had fled from his private rooms wearing only his nightshirt, while the queen had scurried down the Moorish staircase as masonry fell all around her—one stone slightly grazing her neck, according to a report.[87] Also making it out alive were Portugal's four *princesas*—Maria, Mariana Francisca, Doroteia, and Benedita—who had been praying in the palace oratory when the tremors commenced.[88] (One German account of dubious provenance claims that after escaping from the palace the terrified king had leapt into the Tagus, where a "despicable man" had refused to take him aboard his ship.[89])

Unfortunately, the Riverside Palace in the Baixa had suffered notable, though not complete, destruction. The German Room (Sala dos Tudescos) had collapsed on top of several guards, though precise information about the extent of the damage to the palace was difficult to obtain.[90] In a letter to her mother (the queen consort of Spain), written three days after the disaster, an emotional Mariana Vitória recounted the tragic events:

November 4, 1755

Ma très chère Mère,

. . . We are all alive and in good health, a thousand thanks are offered up to God. I have now the honor of relating to you the disastrous event that has occurred. Saturday at 9 and three quarters in the morning we felt the most horrible earthquake. I ran outside only with the greatest difficulty, I left via the Arab staircase where, surely, without God's help I would have cracked my head or broken my legs for I was not able to support myself and filled with fear, as you can imagine, I believed that the last hour had arrived.

The King came to me later as he had escaped from the other side [of the building]. My daughters were in the oratory, but later came to be with us, even though their rooms were a little ruined, they were, thanks be to God, uninjured. . . .

Lisbon is practically completely flattened and there are many people crushed, among others poor Peralada [*sic*, the Spanish ambassador]. . . . If God takes pity on us, we will be saved [and] he will be praised a thousand times. There is terrible misfortune here and the desolation is universal.

I ask you very humbly to pray to God for us that we will continue to receive his mercy and be delivered to safety if that is his will.[91]

Considerably more fortunate than poor Perelada was Britain's ambassador, Abraham Castres, whose house, though damaged, had "stood out the shock." "It has been a most particular Blessing of Providence," Castres observed from a tent in his garden, "that I should have escaped with whole Bones, after having been obliged to jump out of a window from a second Storey."[92]

By contrast, the Dutch ambassador's palace was completely destroyed. According to family legend, the household was alerted to the impending disaster by the screeching of the governess's pet monkey.[93] Fortunately, the ambassador, Charles François de la Calmette, had "kept his *sang froid*" (according to a young man residing in the home) and ordered everyone to stay within its walls. "If we had gone outside we would have been crushed to death."[94] When the house began to burn, the governess, Mademoiselle Joneur, distinguished herself by scooping up the ambassador's two sons, five-year-old Charles and three-year-old Antoine, and carrying them from the building. (The young Antoine would survive the disaster and become one of the most celebrated landscape architects of the eighteenth century.)[95]

Another survivor was Count François de Baschi, the fifty-four-year-old French ambassador and former musketeer. In bed when the earthquake struck, Baschi had escaped his palace in housecoat and slippers, while his much younger wife, Charlotte-Victoire, had just enough time to throw on her skirt, round up the children, and flee before the building fell on top of her. "I am pleased to have survived," Baschi informed Versailles, "along with my wife, my children, and all my servants, who have given me the greatest signs of their affection." Sadly, twenty-seven of Baschi's fifty horses perished in their stable.[96]

Also spared were Christian Stocqueler, the consul from Hamburg; Ferdinando Aniceto Vigánego, the Genoese consul; Carlo de Guevara, the Neapolitan ambassador; Giuseppe Moreschi, the Neapolitan consul; Arvid Arfwedson, the Swedish consul; and Jan Gildemeester, the Dutch consul—though a letter written by several Hamburg merchants in the post-earthquake confusion erroneously reported that both Arfwedson and Gildemeester had died, leading to much confusion in the European press.[97] France's consul Nicolas Grenier and his family had been at their villa in the country when the earthquake occurred. All had survived.[98]

One of the first things that the Prussian ambassador, Hermann Josef Braamcamp, did after securing the safety of his family was to write to his sovereign, Frederick the Great. "I am obliged to inform his Majesty," he wrote, "how the Lord of the Universe has allowed His arm of Justice to fall upon the inhabitants of Lisbon . . . [but] through his grace, [He] has protected my life and that of my entire family."[99]

British Consul Edward Hay and his family, like many foreign diplomats, lived in a house on the outskirts of the city and had also survived. "May God Almighty ever preserve His Majesty's Dominions from the like Calamity," Hay wrote Whitehall.[100]

Twenty-nine-year-old Charles Douglas, Earl of Drumlanrig, had just sat down to write his father, the Duke of Queensberry, when the room around him began to shake. Initially unperturbed, the Scottish nobleman decided to flee when the house started "sawing from side to side." With the help of a servant, he grabbed on to a stone staircase, which he believed "might [better] resist the Shock of an Earthquake," just as the room he had left collapsed behind him.[101]

Upon sensing the first signs of an earthquake, Thomas Jacomb, a British wool merchant and the son of a Member of Parliament, escaped to the yard of his house near the Rossio. There, he witnessed the collapse of the Senate House, the palace of the Duke of Cadaval, the Palace of the Inquisição, as well as his own home. "The Earth," he wrote, "[was] shaking so much [I] could hardly stand and making so great a noise that [I] imagined [it] must be the day of Judgmt."[102]

Down in the Baixa, a German *Kaufmann* (merchant) was reading a sermon in his bedroom when the *"erschreckliche Erdbeben"* (terrible earthquake) began. Sprinting down the stairs of his five-story house, he found his servants and employees "lying on their faces and calling on God for mercy." Fearing the worst, he ran back up the stairs to his sick wife's bedroom; but no sooner had he entered than the tremors became so strong that he had to grab ahold of a pillar for support. As "stones, beams, and the ceiling itself began to fall all around" him, he managed to force his way into the room, where he found his wife praying in her bed and the children arrayed about her crying wretchedly: "*Ach Mama! Help us!*"[103]

Another survivor, twenty-year-old French-born Portuguese merchant Jácome Ratton, did not wish to become "buried in the rubble of his own house or those of his neighbors," so he wisely chose "not to descend the stairs and escape into the streets," but instead climb to the roof in order "to keep above the ruins."[104]

Similarly, the British merchant Thomas Chase ran to the uppermost floor of his house where the roof was secured by stone pillars. But the shaking became increasingly worse. "Every stone in the walls," he observed, "separating each from the other and grinding, as did all the walls of the other houses, one against another, with a variety of different motions, made the most dreadful jumbling noise ears ever heard."[105] Believing "the whole city was sinking into the earth," Chase witnessed "the tops of two of the pillars meet" and then lost consciousness, falling several stories into the collapsing ruins.[106]

"ONE CONFUS'D HEAP OF RUBBISH"

Death in every shape soon grew familiar to the eye!

—THOMAS CHASE, IN A LETTER TO HIS MOTHER (DECEMBER 31, 1755)

As the third and final tremor ended, a great cloud of dust enveloped the city. Thrown into the air by the impact and concussion of collapsing structures, the dust plunged Lisbon into what one eyewitness described as an "Egyptian Darkness," turning day into night and obscuring what Richard Goddard remembered as "the brightest sun I ever saw."[107] For several agonizing minutes, survivors choked on a noxious haze of powdered mortar, sand, dirt, and lime. "A great number of people suffocated," recalled a Swiss survivor.[108] And many, blinded, disoriented, and completely alone, were left to wonder if the world had finally come to an end.[109]

After several minutes, the dust began to settle and the sun to penetrate the grayish haze. "We went near two miles through the streets," wrote one eyewitness of this new Lisbon, "climbing over ruins of churches, houses & stepping over hundreds of dead and dying people killed by the falling of buildings; carriages, chaises and mules, lying all crushed to pieces."[110] Many survivors became lost in the tangled maze of bodies and debris. "The streets were covered with so many dead and dying people," wrote a German merchant, "that one was forced to walk over their corpses. One saw carriages with 6, 4, and 2 horses harnessed to them, in which both the people and the animals were dead."[111] On his way to the Rossio, Thomas Jacomb saw "coaches, chaises, carts, Horses, Mules, Oxen . . . some entirely some half buried under Ground, many People under the Ruins begging for assistance and none able to get [near] them, many groaning under ground, many old and hardly able to walk, now without shoes and stockings . . . hurrying to save life, but now no distinction of Sexes, Ages, Birth or Fortune are regarded."[112]

One merchant "saw shops . . . with the shopkeepers buried with them, some alive crying out from under the ruins, others half buried, others with broken limbs, in vain begging for help . . . [all] passed by crowds without the least notice or sense of humanity."[113] Another survivor witnessed "half-naked women, children covered with blood, old men and women caked with dust running to and fro, corpses disfigured by death spread across every street . . . and numerous victims trapped under the ruins with no hope of rescue."[114] A Portuguese priest recalled "creatures of both sexes, groaning and crying on the ground, some with their legs and arms broken, others with their heads split open or their entire bodies crushed."[115] Some, who had escaped death under the rubble but remained trapped, offered "great sums of money to whomever would liberate them,"[116] wrote another priest. From his rooftop perch, Jácome Ratton was able to see inside several homes whose facades had collapsed. "Their occupants, some still in their bed shirts, running terrified from place to place, pleaded for help from both the minions of Heaven and their fellow men."[117]

The principal reason that Lisbon experienced so much destruction in the earthquake was that much of the Baixa stood on a medieval landfill. Two thousand years before, this low-lying district had been an estuary fed by two small streams that ran southward (along what is now Lisbon's central thoroughfare, the Avenida da Liberdade into the Tagus).[118] As the city expanded from its original precincts along the slopes of São Jorge's Hill, the estuary and the two streams, which had been used as sewers during the Middle Ages, were covered up and the foundation stakes of new buildings were driven into the soft sands and alluvial soils of the former riverbed. On All Saints' Day 1755, this proved disastrous because seismic waves vibrate at higher amplitudes and lower frequencies in unconsolidated materials like sand than they do in either rock or clay.

As a consequence, the destructive power of Europe's most powerful earthquake was significantly magnified in the Baixa and along the banks of the Tagus, where the buildings sat on sandy stretches of earth.[119] "Those in the Rossio were astonished and amazed by the movement of the earth," wrote Father Portal, "which fluctuated like waves [during which] they were hardly able to keep on their feet). Glancing in the direction of São Domingos, they saw that famous church reduced in an instant to a pile of stones" and "the Palace of the Inquisição falling to the ground and with it the President of that institution caught in the ironwork of a window, where he died a miserable death."[120]

In this and other geologically vulnerable areas of the city—like the summit of São Jorge's Hill, the region around Santa Ana's Hill, and significant swaths of the Bairro Alto and the Alfama district (despite a modern-day misconception that it was spared)—the earthquake registered X degrees or higher on the Modified Mercalli Intensity scale, indicating a seismic event in which the majority of masonry structures are destroyed along with their foundations.* Particularly vulnerable were large structures, which typically shake more intensely at lower frequencies.[121]

For this reason, Lisbon's churches and convents suffered disproportionately, as their wide-spanning ceilings and roofs proved unable to withstand the seismic onslaught. According to one earthquake chronicle, the churches that were "completely destroyed" included

São Mamede, São Jorge, São Martinho, São Tiago, S. Thomé, Santo Andre, Santo Estevão, Salvador, São Miguel, São Pedro, São João da Praça, e Santa Marinha, Santa Cruz do Castello, São Barthulumeo, São Paulo, Our Lady of Martyrs, Sacramento, Santa Catharina, and the Church of Our Lady of Nazareth of the Bernadines, the Church of the Esperança [or Hope], Tri-

---

* The Modified Mercalli Intensity scale (MMI) is used by seismologists to calculate the effects of an earthquake on surface objects such as buildings and people.

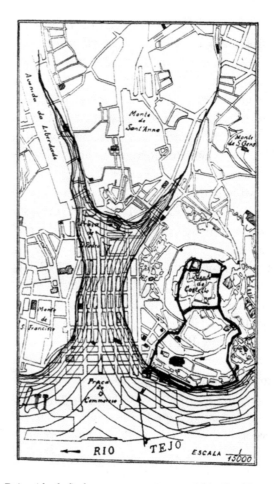

Area of the Baixa (shaded) that was once a cove within the Tagus fed by two streams

nas do Mocambo, São Pedro de Alcantar, the Holy Trinity, the Carmelite Church or Carmo, São Francisco of the City, Espirito Santo [Holy Spirit], the Boa Hora of the Discalced Augustinians, Corpus Christi of the Discalced Carmelites, São Domingos [in whose ruins Malagrida would be defrocked], Santa Ana, the Church of the Sandal-Wearing Augustinians, also called Our Lady of Grace, the Church of Santa Monica of the Augustinian Nuns, the Seminary of São Patricio, the Church of the Followers of Santa Clara, Our Lady of the Rock of France.[122]

Also reduced to rubble were scores of monasteries, convents, religious schools, and chapels, including the School of São Pedro e Paulo dos Ingleses (the "English School" headed by Father Manley), the Convent of Santo Antonio of the Capuchins, the Church of Our Lady of the Immaculate Conception of the Cardaes, the Church of the Crucifix, the Church of the Saints of the Military Order of São Tiago, and the Church of Our Lady of the Incarnation of the Order of São Bento de Aviz.[123]

One of the most conspicuous casualties was the cavernous Igreja do Carmo (Carmelite Church), which for centuries enjoyed an unobstructed view across the Baixa and the eastern flank of São Jorge's Hill. During the first tremor, its massive Gothic ceiling buckled and collapsed on the heads of hundreds of parishioners and at least seventeen sandal-shod Carmelite priests.[124] While attempting to escape, many were buried when the cloisters and church tower subsequently fell. One of the few survivors was the sacred statue, the *Holy Lady of the Carmo*, which was rescued by a Father Francisco Augusto in an act of singular courage and devotion. According to Father Portal, Augusto located the blessed *Senhora* after "climbing up mountains of stones, passing over corpses, [and] encountering danger with every step." He then hoisted her upon his saintly shoulders and carried her out of the burning church.[125]

Down by the Tagus, sixty persons, including two priests, lay dead or dying under the rubble of São Paulo's Church. Fortunately, the *Santissimo Sacramento* (Sacred Host) had survived and had been quickly transferred to the Church of São João Nepomuceno for safekeeping.[126] "The Church of the Monastery of the Trinidad fell so quickly," reported Father Portal, "that sixteen priests who had been in the confessionals or in the main chapel . . . were buried [beneath it]."[127] Likewise, the ceiling and facade of the Church of the Wounds of Jesus collapsed on top of the congregation and entombed many—although one parishioner, the Count of Vimieiro, managed to dig himself out, despite a broken leg. "He alone of his family suffered the effects of the earthquake," wrote Portal, for though "his palace collapsed, all were able to escape."[128]

Lisbon's Romanesque cathedral, Santa Maria Maior, had survived many earthquakes during the six centuries it had stood on the southern slope of São Jorge's Hill.[129] Now its roof had "fallen in" and its great stone "arches [were] broken through," wrote Richard Goddard.[130] Its clock tower had also collapsed, smashing "into pieces" as it hit the ground along with its massive bells. Most shockingly, the statue of *Nossa*

Senhora (Our Lady) which had hung above the main altar tumbled to the floor, her "head separating from her body" (and later discovered in the home of a woman on the outskirts of the city.)[131] Although the cathedral's massive, ten-foot-thick outer walls "remained standing," they formed, in the opinion of the Reverend Goddard, "the most horrid Ruin imaginable."[132]

Perhaps no work of art captures the shocking scene like João Glama Ströberle's massive oil painting, *Allegory of the Earthquake of 1755*, whose subject is the destruction of the Church of Santa Catarina. Located atop a hill overlooking the city's western district, Santa Catarina rises like a battered galleon in the top center of the canvas, its roof and tower fallen in, its facade scarred with cracks and fissures.[133] In the foreground, victims lie scattered across the crowded church square, while others wander aimlessly, gesturing to the heavens or grasping their heads in confusion and disbelief. As people tend to the injured, priests deliver sermons and offer absolution to the gathering throngs. At the lower right, a gentleman discovers a young woman in the ruins, her arms reaching out to him in desperation. At left center, two men embrace a large wooden cross, while angels slice through the smoke-filled sky, their swords drawn. Much more than a visual encapsulation of the day, Ströberle's *Allegory* is a study of order at war with chaos. Yet, for all its pathos and power, one can safely assume that it fails to capture the full extent of the horror and confusion that reigned in those desperate hours.

"It is impossible to describe the affrighted looks of the inhabitants, flying various ways to avoid destruction," recalled one survivor.[134] "Many believed themselves in the Bowels of the Earth," wrote another.[135] Some wailed and screamed or looked skyward, imploring God for His protection and forgiveness; others sat on the ground, stunned and speechless, a look of frozen horror upon their faces. A few attempted to speak, but precious little came out. For those capable of communication, *"Misericordia"* (Mercy) or *"Misericordia de Deus"* (God have mercy) became a kind of plaintive chorus of the disaster.

"The horror of the earthquake," stated one eyewitness, along with "the rumble of falling buildings, the fear of death, the shouts of men, the laments of women, and the cries of children . . . led to a general panic."[136] Indeed, "everybody [who was] not crushed to death, ran out into the large places," wrote a ship captain, "and those near the river ran down to save themselves by boats, or any other floating conveniency, running, crying, and calling to the ships for assistance."[137] Others attempted to reach the city's largest squares.

After escaping his collapsing house, Charles Douglas found the neighborhood "so totally in ruins that it was not possible for Strangers [foreigners] to know where one street had been from another." Fortunately, he encountered a *lisboeta* who was able to pick "out the way over the most terrible Ruins" to "one of the broad squares of the town" (probably the Rossio), where the earl and his company would be "out of the reach of the [falling] Stones."[138]

Soon after the German *Kaufmann* had ushered his sick wife and children out of the house, he noticed that the home of his good friend, Herr Vetter, had fallen and the occupants (he believed) crushed. Judging it best to flee to the Rossio rather than die among the ruins, he put his wife under one arm and his smallest child under the other and walked "fearlessly over hundreds—if not a thousand—dead people and falling buildings." To the family's amazement, upon finally reaching the Rossio, they encountered Herr Vetter and his wife. "I was . . . speechless with joy," recalled the merchant, who, just a few moments before thought that he would never see his *"Herzens-Freund"* (dear friend) again.[139]

Also arriving at the Rossio at about this time was Thomas Jacomb, who noted that it was now "almost full of people."

> Old, Young, Male and Female seeking their Parents, Children, Relations and Friends many sick, many maimed and wounded from the fall of the Houses, some dead and most part especially women half naked so dismal a sight was never seen, neither can thought imagine or fancy describe the various scenes of misery.[140]

And everywhere "Fryars and Priests"—and eventually Malagrida himself— "giving Absolution, Confessing and Praying with everyone."[141]

Another merchant in the Rossio recalled "many Thousands of People in the utmost Confusion and Distress, making the most hideous Noise I ever heard." He saw large "Numbers of them smiting their breasts and beating their Faces in the most cruel Manner, which were swollen to a monstrous Size, and so discoloured as to render them quite ghastly."[142] Amid the chaos, one woman's "lovely auburn hair became quite grey . . . through terror," according to her husband, while many survivors, "especially women and children and ancient people, died of the fright," reported one eyewitness.[143]

In the frenzy, familial bonds were broken. "Only the love of self dominated," wrote a survivor. "Parents deserted their children . . . spouses forgot their partners. Ties between friends dissolved. . . . No acts of virtue were performed; only the need to preserve one's life and preserve one's soul."[144] According to another, "there was no piety, nor compassion, nor humanity, nor friendship."[145] Indeed, "the fear and consternation were so great," recalled an eyewitness, "that the most resolute person . . . [did] not stay a moment to remove a few stones off the friend he loved most, though many might have been saved by so doing . . . nothing was thought of but self-preservation; getting into open places, and into the middle of streets."[146] One survivor considered the actions of the people "more Shocking . . . than even the very Operations of the Earthquake."[147]

Firmly convinced that they were the target of God's special wrath, thousands of *lisboetas* began to gather "about Priests and Friars, all falling on their Knees, kissing the Earth, beating their Breasts, slapping their Cheeks, and crying out for Absolution which was granted in general terms to Hundreds of them all at once."[148] In their frantic state, they "invoked all the celestial and angelic orations of the Our Father and the Hail Mary," stated a priest, "[while] others asked for grace from God the Father and the Virgin Mary . . . crying out their sins and asking God repeatedly for mercy, breaking the air with sighs, with what seemed to be real contrition, and the pain of sin." Some even embraced their "worst enemies" and "asked for forgiveness . . . swearing from this day forward to be faithful friends."[149]

In the midst of such terrifying assaults on the senses—imploding buildings, heart-stopping noises, spreading fires, clouds of dust and smoke, and the pitiful wails of men and beasts—a "Wreck of Worlds," as one described it—many believed that Judgment Day had finally arrived—for, as described in the book of Revelation by St. John the Divine, at the end of time the earth will be thrown into a period of great tribulation when fire and hail will fall from the skies, darkness will envelop the land, oceans will be destroyed, rivers and springs will be poisoned, the sun will scorch the surface of the earth, seas and lakes will turn to blood, armies will attack the living, and then—after the seventh angel empties his bowl into the air—a terrible earthquake will rend the world.[150]

> *And there were voices, and thunders, and lightnings; and there was*
>   *a great earthquake, such as was not since men were upon the*
>   *earth, so mighty an earthquake, and so great.*
> *And the cities of the nations fell. . . .*
> *And every island fled away, and the mountains were not found.*
> *And there fell upon men a great hail out of heaven, every stone*
>   *about the weight of a talent.*
>
>   REVELATION 16:18–21

"It is impossible in Nature to behold a Picture that bears a stronger Resemblance to the last great solemn Day," wrote one Portuguese officer. Lisbon has "become a frightful Abyss, a tremendous Gulph; in short, one of the wide Gates of the vast Empire of Death."[151]

In their frightened state, "the Portuguese . . . were fully employed in a sort of religious madness," recalled Thomas Chase, "lugging about saints without heads or arms; telling one another, in a most piteous manner, how they met with such misfortunes; and their Clergy all saying it was a judgment upon them for their wickedness."[152] They "loaded themselves with crucifixes and saints," reported another survivor, "[and] during the intervals between the shocks," they either sang "Litanies, or . . . stood harassing the dying with religious ceremonies. And whenever the earth trembled, everyone fell on their knees and ejaculated—*Misericordia!*—in the most doleful accents imaginable."[153]

In the garden of Syon Convent, Kitty Witham and her fellow nuns huddled together in feverish prayer as each new tremor appeared to threaten their successful deliverance from death. For all they (or anyone) in Lisbon knew, they were about to experience the trials of the Last Judgment (which follows the Last Day) when all nations will be judged by Christ; and the Righteous will go on to live for all eternity with God, while the Wicked—joined by Satan, Death, Hades, the Beast, and the False Prophet—will be cast into "the lake of fire and brimstone" and be "tormented day and night for ever and ever."[154]

There were a few, however, who preached hope amidst the darkness. One "old venerable priest in a stole and surplice" who had escaped from the ruins of the Church of São Paulo "was continually moving to and fro among the people exhorting them to repentance and endeavoring to comfort them."

> With a flood of tears, [he told them] that God was grievously provoked at their sins, but if they could call on the Blessed Virgin she would intercede for them. Everyone now flocked around [him], earnestly begging his benediction, and happy did that man think himself, who could get near enough to touch but the hem of his garment.[155]

Although heartened by the sight of the clergy, lisboetas were, at the same time, shocked that hundreds of previously cloistered monks and nuns now walked freely through the ruins. Unable to find domicile, these pious men and women of God had no choice but to join the great mass of Lisbon's survivors as they attempted to escape from a city which had been transformed, in the words of a priest, into a "laberinto" (labyrinth) of obstacles.[156]

For the small children, the elderly, and the severely injured, traversing the rubble proved especially difficult. Many survivors were unshod or barely clothed, "some with their beards partially-combed; some in their shirts; and others ... without a shirt or any covering whatsoever."[157] Many were suffering from a multitude of injuries, some rather severe. Moreira de Mendonça estimated that five thousand people died of their wounds in the month following the earthquake. It was a very conservative estimate.[158]

In general, the animals of Lisbon suffered more than their masters. Many were "buried inside stables, [and] in the streets; and those that did not perish immediately and were only partly covered with debris, bellowed and screamed; [while] those that were free of the rubble but still tied to carriages stuck in the ruins, stamped their hooves in frustration with such force that they could no longer rise." In the days and weeks that followed, thousands of horses, donkeys, mules, and dogs would die of their wounds or of dehydration and neglect. Although some managed to escape to the outlying fields (where they would find little food or water), most continued to wander "day and night" in search of their masters, with whom they were rarely reunited.[159]

After the final tremor, Agnes Surriage thought of only one thing: reuniting with her beloved Harry. Though the city was now largely impenetrable, she somehow followed the path of his carriage to the pile of ruins under which it lay; and recognizing his voice beneath the debris, enlisted the help of passersby (with the promise of money) to extricate the baronet from his "living tomb." Wounded and disheveled, though still very much alive, a contrite Sir Harry was conveyed to the house of a Portuguese gentleman, where his wounds were attended to, and then transported, with Agnes at his side, to Belém. (What became of his mysterious female companion is unknown.)[160]

Although unharmed, Richard Goddard suddenly found himself alone in a city where he knew neither the language, nor the customs, nor the layout of the streets. Moreover, he feared for the safety of his brother Ambrose and his friends, though "I had scarce any Room to flatter [myself] that they could escape the General Destruction." Looking around him, he found "every countenance . . . a most perfect Representation of Horror and Distraction. Everyone seemed in the greatest Hurray to leave their present Situation, though without knowing where to fly for greater Security. Not to mention the Numbers that were maimed . . . and covered with Blood."[161]

Luckily, he came upon a fellow Englishman and factory merchant who had made an "almost miraculous escape" during the earthquake. Unfortunately, their joy was short-lived, for the situation soon deteriorated. All around them, crowds of *lisboetas* "were engaged in deprecating the Vengeance of Heaven"—throwing themselves "prostrate on the Ground, beating their Breasts, tearing their Hair, lamenting their Losses in the Extasie of Grief," and bemoaning "the divine Vengeance in the most enthusiastic Transports of Devotion."[162]

Although touched by their suffering, the Protestant Goddard was "greatly scandalized by the large Mixture of Idolatry and Superstition which prevailed in them." They carried "Crucifixes" as well as the "Images and Pictures of their Saints," which they "kissed with great Eagerness and Reverence."[163] Goddard's companion advised that they steer clear of the faithful, lest they attempt to force the pair "to pay respect to their Images." But following an aftershock at 11 a.m., the crowd (which numbered about two hundred) seized the two Britons "in the most violent Manner," and began to ask questions of which Goddard understood not a "Syllable." While his Portuguese-speaking companion was able to extricate himself, Goddard was trapped by the surging mass of Catholics. "I imagined I had everything to fear from their excessive Bigotry and Enthusiasm and that they would throw us from the Platform of the Castle, a Terrace of great Height, as Hereticks who had brought this Judgement upon them."[164]

It was at this moment that a Portuguese gentleman took pity on Goddard and delivered "a long and violent Harangue . . . with the most enthusiastic Action and Emphasis." Though the people "returned to their Devotions," a priest began to pester Goddard with questions, including one in "very intelligible" Latin: *"Vis baptizari?"* (Will you be baptized?). Afraid to refuse and unable to explain that he was in fact a Christian (and thus had already been baptized), Goddard kept quiet, though the "Mob" provided him with what, for them, was the appropriate answer: *"Volo. Volo. Volo"* (I do. I do. I do.). Although Goddard later claimed he never uttered a word, the priest continued with the ceremony and baptized him anyway, sending the crowd into paroxysms of joy. He was nearly crushed with vigorous embraces; and while several priests fell down in front of him, grabbing his knees "and kissing the Feet of their new Convert."

The reason for their happiness was their belief that the conversion of an Infidel (Goddard) would provide each of them with a "Fund of Credit" in Heaven that might compensate for even the most sinful life. Though relieved at his escape, Goddard pitied the "Ignorance and Superstition" of his baptizers and sincerely hoped "that their mistaken Piety might be accepted [by God]." A few days later, the papal nuncio, Filippo Acciaiuoli, expressed outrage when he learned of the incident from Goddard and threatened to reprimand the unknown priest for his "Ignorance as well as his Presumption and Impertinence." Although religious divisions were stark in eighteenth-century Lisbon, collegiality between gentlemen and ecclesiastics of the same social stratum (though different religion) was evidently robust.[165]

Below in the Baixa, Thomas Chase had regained consciousness after his fall and found himself enclosed within "four high walls, nearly fifty feet above." Fearing he might starve to death—"immured in so hopeless a manner"—he retreated to a small archway as a shower of "tiles and rubbish" rained down upon him.[166] Finding a small hole and through it a passageway, he arrived in a tiny room where he startled a Portuguese man covered in dust. "Jesus, Maria, and José!" the man exclaimed as he beheld the severely wounded Chase, whose fractured right arm hung "motionless" in front of him. In addition, Chase's shoulder was "out and the bone broken," his legs were "covered with wounds," his right ankle was spurting a "fountain of blood," there were gashes above and below each eye; and the left side of his face, in which much of the skin had been torn off, was swollen and bleeding profusely.

Just then, another tremor—"more threatening than the former"—ripped through the city. As the Portuguese man bolted from the room, Chase felt the "violence of the concussion and the falling of houses," and heard "the screams of the people." Then, when it was all over, he stepped out into the street.[167]

"The people," he recalled, "were all at prayers, covered over with dust, and the light appeared just as if it had been a very dark day." And the street was "filled with fallen houses, as high as the tops of the remaining ones." But unable to walk due to his broken leg and his many wounds, and probably in shock, he collapsed in the middle of the wreckage-filled street. Although several people known to him (including Richard Goddard's brother Ambrose and Ambrose's business partner, Benjamin Branfil) walked close by, he was unable to rouse himself and get their attention.[168]

About to give up, Chase placed his back against the side of a house and, in doing so, drew the attention of its owner, John Ernest Forg, a merchant from Hamburg. "What miserable wretch is this?" exclaimed Forg as he cast his eyes upon the battered and bloodied form. Then, a flash of recognition. "Dear Mr. Chase, what a shocking sight is this! Let me carry you up stairs, and try what we can do for you." "Many thanks," replied the despondent Englishman, "but it is now too late." "Never think so," said Mr. Forg, "I hope the worst is over, and you shall have the very first assistance that can be procured." Before long, Forg and his uncle were dressing Chase's wounds with plaster and carrying him to a room near the top of the house.[169]

Incredibly, some structures in Lisbon—like Mr. Forg's home, Dom José's beloved Casa da Ópera, the Patriarchal Church, and the headquarters of the Jesuits, the Igreja de São Roque—remained standing, though, in the case of São Roque, its tower and part of its front entryway had collapsed.[170] In a few neighborhoods, entire streets had escaped with little or no damage, including Lisbon's most economically vital thoroughfare, the New Street of the Merchants (Rua Nova dos Mercadores), and Big Chapel Street (Rua do Capelão), notorious for its whorehouses and formerly known as Dirty Street (Rua Suja).[171]

In the suburb of Belém, the Jeronimos Monastery survived intact, as did the Aqueduct of the Free Waters (which still spans eighteen kilometers across the valley of Alcântara). In the outlying parish of Ajuda, the earthquake's intensity reached a respectable VIII degrees on the Mercalli scale, enough to bring down chimneys and poorly constructed buildings though not enough to destroy large structures (it had reached X degrees in the Baixa).[172] One priest who had been inside a confessional in the Church of Our Lady of Ajuda reported that the first tremor (which he dubbed "*o Palpitante*," or "the throbbing") moved in a vertical direction and put considerable pressure on the soles of his shoes—though it had done little harm.[173] Likewise, an eleven-year-old boy (and future Portuguese general) who had been on a farm outside the city never noticed the earthquake at all, mistaking the swaying of the fig tree that he was climbing for a sudden and sustained wind.[174] Thus Lisbon escaped complete obliteration and the vast majority of its 200,000 inhabitants were, at least at the moment, still alive.

But Lisbon was not the only Portuguese city affected. Tremors had been felt throughout the kingdom. At Mafra, several kilometers to the north, the great pink palace-convent-chapel of João V was seen "falling, rising, and swaying, from one part to another, like a ship upon the waves," although miraculously it would suffer little damage and no casualties.[175] Near the mouth of the Tagus, the village of Casais was "razed to the ground," according to a priest. "There is not a house," he wrote, "that did not fall to the earth or was shaken into a ruin. The churches, the bridge, the city and its neighborhoods are totally destroyed and turned into dust. . . . The village is without a clock because the great tower built by the Moors was reduced to ashes. . . . The streets are mountains of stones and debris, without any sign that there were streets, it is not Cascais."[176] Also destroyed was the picturesque mountain village of Sintra, where the king's palace was in ruins and the Church of São Marinho had collapsed on top of its pastor and twenty-four parishioners.[177]

"All the villages of Ribatejo suffered a great deal," reported Moreira de Mendonça, from the region south of the Tagus River.[178] In the Monastery of São Francisco in Castanheira, "several priests died along with fourteen other people," while "two priests, three novices, and thirty people perished" in the ruins of the Church of São Francisco in Alenquer.[179] In Santarém, numerous churches were lost; and cracks and fissures (which gave off the fetid smell of sulfur) were reported throughout the city.[180]

One port felt the impact of the earthquake almost as grievously as Lisbon. "Setúbal is no more," wrote Dutch ship captain Jan Pinapels.

"Two thirds of the city, with its churches, monasteries, and houses, have been transformed into a *Steinhauff* [a pile of stones]," he wrote.[181]

On the whole, regions south of Lisbon (particularly those on or near the coastline) suffered the most, while the damage was much less severe farther inland. There were reports that several of Portugal's principal mountain ranges—Estrela, Montejunto, Sintra, Marvão, Arrábida—shed chunks of rock and earth—while across the Algarve, Portugal's southern shore, tremors of greater intensity than those felt at Lisbon caused considerable devastation.[182] According to the *Gazeta de Lisboa*, "there was not a city, farm, fortification, place, or village [in the Algarve] that did not experience more or less ruin."[183]

In the provincial capital of Faro, "there was not one church or house left standing," reported the *Gazeta*. All the important buildings—"the cathedral, the archbishop's palace, the Church of São Pedro, the Capuchin Convent, the Jesuit School"—had collapsed. In Sagres, near the tip of Cape St. Vincent, the earthquake brought down every house, including the fortresses of Zavial and Baleeira, while in Portimão, all but one of the city's churches, the Corpo Santo, fell. In Silves (the former Muslim capital of the region), "the cathedral, tower, castle, senate house, jail, and a monastery were lost; and "entire streets [that had been filled with people] were destroyed." In Vila do Bispo, only a single structure survived—while in the city of Lagos, the only building of significance that remained standing was the governor's palace (though one of the governor's grandchildren had perished in the ruins of another building).[184]

In general, the northern half of the kingdom—particularly the provinces of Trás-os-Montes, Minho, and Beira—escaped significant damage.[185] At Coimbra (Pombal's alma mater), some buildings were damaged, although no one died.[186] In the city of Alcobaça, in Estremadura, the horrible earthquake caused "notable damage to some of its superb buildings," according to the *Gazeta*, including the historic and imposing Cistercian Monastery. Founded by Afonso Henriques in 1153, it was the first Gothic structure built in the kingdom.[187]

By far the greatest blow to Alcobaça, however, was the sudden stoppage of the flow of water from a place called Chaqueda, a half league away (about 1.75 miles). While the *Gazeta* had its own theory on what had happened ("The earth with its tremor absorbed the watershed"), there were other possible explanations. On November 5, the whole community of Cistercian monks, accompanied by an "infinite number of people," processed to Chaqueda, where everyone prayed "for mercy from Heaven." Father Luís de São Bento "delivered a short oration on Psalm 114, *In exitu Israel de Aegypto,*" in which the last two stanzas read:

> *Tremble, thou earth, at the presence of the Lord,*
> *   at the presence of the God of Jacob,*
> *Which turned the rock into a standing water,*
> *   the flint into a fountain of waters.*

Suddenly, the water began to flow; and everyone, reported the *Gazeta,* experienced "the relief of seeing the waters restored to their natural course and previous copious flow." When the procession returned in triumph to Alcobaça, Father São Bento "delivered a sermon that bore much fruit among the congregation; and in the days that followed, missionaries were sent out to pray in the villages of the region."[188]

At the northern city of Porto, the tremors lasted from six to ten minutes. "I saw all the world running out of their houses, and crying out, An Earthquake," recalled Theodore Jacobson, Esq.[189] Though the terrified population expected "every minute [that] the earth would open," the material damage to Portugal's second-most populous city (with around thirty thousand inhabitants) was mercifully light— confined to "the overturning [of] some pedestals from the tops of some churches and [the] cleaving of the walls of some old houses"—though a few people apparently died of fright.[190]

COMPARISONS

Fortunately, temblors as powerful as the Lisbon Earthquake are exceedingly rare, occurring once every 500 to 10,000 years.[191] Although several million earthquakes take place annually across the globe (90 percent of them along the 40,000-kilometer Circum-Pacific Belt, known as the Pacific Ring of Fire), only around 500,000 are detectable by seismometers; and of these, only 100,000 (or one fifth) are felt by human beings, the vast majority of those doing little or no damage.* In general, the larger the earthquake, the less common it is. According to the Gutenberg-Richter Law (devised by Beno Gutenberg and Charles

---

* The instrument used today to measure earthquakes, nuclear explosions, volcanic eruptions, and meteor impacts is called a seismometer (rather than the earlier seismograph).

Francis Richter, who gave his name to the famous magnitude scale), the relationship between an earthquake's size and its frequency is, by and large, exponential. Thus, for every temblor above Mw 7.0, there are roughly 10 quakes between Mw 6.0 and Mw 6.9, and 100 between Mw 5.0 and Mw 5.9, and so on. Although the total number of reported earthquakes—both large and small—has increased over the past few decades (mainly due to improvements in technology and the growing number of seismic stations), their actual frequency across the globe has remained constant.[192]

Since 1900 (when accurate seismographic readings first became available), the world has averaged one earthquake above Mw 8.0 and 18 between Mw 7.0 and Mw 7.9 per year. Over the last 115 years, only 17 earthquakes have achieved Mw 8.5 or higher—among them, the Great Chilean or Valdivia Earthquake of 1960 (Mw 9.5), the Great Alaskan Earthquake of 1964 (Mw 9.2), and the infamous 2004 Indian Ocean or Sumatra-Andaman Earthquake (Mw 9.1), whose giant tsunami ravaged the coasts of Indonesia, Sri Lanka, Thailand, and southeast India and caused the deaths of more than 230,000 people. The Great Tōhoku or Sendai Earthquake and Tsunami of 2011, which paralyzed much of northern Japan, wiping several small villages off the map and precipitating an international crisis when its 30-foot waves critically damaged several nuclear reactors, registered Mw 9.0. Considerably smaller twentieth-century temblors include the Great San Francisco Earthquake and Fire of 1906 (Mw 7.9), the Haiyuan (China) Earthquake of 1920 (Mw 7.9+), which was responsible for 200,000 deaths, the Great Tangshan (China) Earthquake of 1976 (Mw 7.8), which claimed over 240,000 lives, and the 2010 Haitian Earthquake (Mw 7.0), in which 160,000 people perished.[193]

Before 1900—and indeed throughout human history—earthquakes of extraordinary size have made dramatic, if infrequent, appearances. "The Lord *is* the true God," declares Jeremiah (10:10). "At his wrath the earth shall tremble, and the nations shall not be able to abide his indignation." In the past 2,500 years, perhaps 40 earthquakes between Mw 6.3 and Mw 8.3 have shaken the foundations of the Holy Land.[194] One such disaster around 2100 BC most likely caused the "overthrow" of Sodom and Gomorrah, while the ancient walls of Jericho show clear signs of earthquake damage inflicted over the course of the millennia.[195] In 464 BC, a powerful temblor flattened the Greek city state of Sparta, depleting its famed warrior population, and, as some scholars have speculated, laying the foundation for its decline over the next century.[196]

Eight hundred years later, on July 21, AD 365, a gargantuan quake near Crete (*Mw* 8.5 est.) "shuddered and trembled" the "solid frame of the earth," according to the Roman historian Ammianus Marcellinus. A disaster of epic proportions, surpassing everything "in legend or authentic history," it unleashed a devastating tsunami that overwhelmed the coasts of Greece, Dalmatia, Sicily, and Egypt (particularly in the low-lying Nile Delta) and drowned untold thousands.[197] For centuries afterwards, it was commemorated in Egypt by a festival known as the "Day of Horror."[198] The Antioch Earthquake (*Mw* 7.0 est.) of AD 526 would prove even more lethal, destroying the city of Antioch (in tandem with an ensuing fire) as well as a large region of northern Syria and causing the deaths of as many as 250,000 people.[199]

The deadliest temblor of all time, however, occurred more than a thousand years later on January 23, 1556. Measuring an estimated *Mw* 8.0, the Shaanxi Earthquake laid waste to a 530-mile swath of land covering ten provinces in central China during the Ming Dynasty, killing upward of 830,000 people and stripping some regions of 60 percent of their population. Most of the victims lived in man-made caves or *yaodongs*, which collapsed under the intense seismic onslaught.[200] Note: it is generally accepted by scientists that no earthquake, ancient or modern, has ever measured—or could ever measure—*Mw* 10.0 or higher, although the most devastating seismic event in the history of the Earth, the Yucatán Meteor Impact of 65 million years ago—to which some have attributed the extinction of the dinosaurs—may have achieved *Mw* 12.55, making it 32,000 times more powerful than the largest temblor ever recorded: the Great Chilean Earthquake of 1960 (*Mw* 9.5).

THE WIDER WORLD

The streets, squares, and fields [of North Africa] became
a Theater of Clamor, a Babylon of Shouting,
a Coliseum of Tragedy, and a Pantheon of Misfortune.

—ANONYMOUS[201]

Over the course of All Saints' Day 1755, the great earthquake shook the coast of northwest Africa, sped across the Iberian Peninsula at 750 miles per hour (almost the speed of sound), surged through the Pyrenees, and then penetrated into the heart of Western and Central Europe.[202] Along Spain's southern Costa de la Lu, the destruction was particularly severe.[203] At Ayamonte, just across the Spanish-Portuguese border, "almost all the buildings" were destroyed, according to one account, and "the monastery of the nuns of Our Lady of Santa Clara was reduced to fragments." At Huelva the earthquake lasted "between nine and ten minutes . . . [and] although the violent movements of the earth were continuous over that entire time," recalled the mayor, "one noted their diversity, some vibrating, others pulsing, the latter causing the greatest ruin and bringing down even the most robust structures."[204]

At Sanlúcar de Barrameda (where, in 1498, Columbus set sail on his Third Voyage and where, in 1519, Ferdinand Magellan began his expedition to circumnavigate the globe), the ground started to shake at precisely 9:58 a.m. "There were no warning signs," reported the provincial governor, "except that at 7 or 8 a.m., several wells emitted muddy water and a strange malodorous vapor. . . . For five minutes, every building in the city shook with great force, causing fear and confusion, forcing people to flee the churches and the priests to suspend the Holy Sacrifice of the mass."[205]

Farther down the Spanish coast, at Cádiz, an English gentleman complained of "Sea Sickness, a Swimming in the Head, and Qualmishness" immediately before the first tremor.[206] Then, "water in the [underground] cisterns" began to slosh "backwards and forwards so as to make a great froth upon it" before a few "tiles fell" and "several old houses were badly damaged." Yet no buildings collapsed, according to the provincial governor, and "no grave damage was done."[207]

Perhaps the most famous resident of Cádiz (and one of the most reliable earthquake eyewitnesses) was the French astronomer and mathematician Louis Godin. Educated at Paris's elite Collège Louis-le-Grand (like Molière and Voltaire before him), Godin was a member of the French Royal Academy and one of the leaders of the much celebrated Franco-Spanish expedition to Peru in 1735, which proved that the earth flattened at the poles (as Isaac Newton had postulated) and not at the equator, as most scientists in France then believed. During the 1746 Lima Earthquake and Tsunami, Godin made pioneering seismological observations, after which he oversaw the rebuilding of the Peruvian capital before returning to France in 1751 and later accepting the presidency of the Royal Naval Academy at Cádiz.[208]

On the morning of All Saints' Day 1755, Godin began to perceive "a faint movement of the earth . . . at 9 o'clock and 52 minutes."

> Others became aware of it later [but] I felt it earlier as I am used to this kind of phenomenon, having experienced more than five hundred [tremors] during the years that I lived in Peru. . . . The earthquake continued gently for two minutes, until 9:54 a.m., when the oscillations increased significantly and lasted with all its violence another three minutes. During this period there were no more than two very short pauses. . . . Then at 9:57 a.m., there was a pause which only lasted a few seconds, after which, the earthquake became almost as violent as before. Then it declined, until 10:01 a.m., when it ended.[209]

"I have developed a way to determine when an earthquake is over," boasted the fifty-one-year-old savant. "I grab an iron rod embedded in a wall by one of its two ends. [And] by this method, even the slightest movement or oscillation can be perceived. . . . I used it to determine the different phases of the great earthquake in Lima and Callao in 1746. . . . [It was in this way that] I ascertained that the earthquake in Cádiz lasted a full nine minutes. . . . As for the direction of the earthquake, I determined it as best I could by noting the oscillation of several nearby objects, then comparing them with a compass reading. I found a movement almost exactly from east to west, or perhaps more accurately, a course more to the Northeast-Southwest."[210]

At Tarifa (Europe's southernmost point), the earthquake was also felt, "but by the mercy of God," wrote one Spanish official, "it caused no damage to churches, houses, plumbing, persons, or animals."[211] At the British outpost of Gibraltar, the quake began "with a Trembling," according to an eyewitness, "then a violent Shock, after that a Trembling for five or six Seconds and then another Shock. . . . Most people were seized with a Giddiness and Sickness. . . . Some fell down, others were stupefied, and in general all were affected as if electrified."[212]

Farther inland, at Córdoba (the former capital of the Islamic caliphate in Iberia), the tower of the cathedral broke and "250 structures had to be immediately demolished," reported one royal official, while Seville, the shimmering capital of Andalusia, suffered even more destruction, more in fact than any city in Spain.[213] "It appeared," according to one *poeta sevillano*, "as if the earth had pulled the very hinges off churches, houses, and numerous buildings."²¹⁴ "Not a single Church or Convent has escaped some Damage or other," reported a Trinitarian friar, and "those which are [now] ordered to be pulled down are without Number."²¹⁵

When the temblor began, *sevillanos* had run screaming from their homes and churches, each "asking Heaven for pity and the forgiveness of their sins," though the earthquake would, in the end, claim only eight victims.²¹⁶ Still, "many families and among them, some of distinction, are left without houses to live in and have taken refuge in the gardens and ovens and wherever else they could creep."²¹⁷ Fearing that the vibrations from road traffic might cause buildings to fall, "a Proclamation [was] issued [in the city] . . . that no Coach, Chaise, or Cart should stir about the Streets upon Pain of . . . paying 500 Ducats and being imprisoned six Months."²¹⁸ Though most of the largest structures in Seville had been damaged, only about 6 percent of the city's buildings were destroyed.²¹⁹

At 10:10 a.m., the earthquake shook Madrid and lasted approximately eight minutes, causing the church bells to ring throughout the city.²²⁰ At first, *madrileños* had been "seized with a swimming in their heads," according to one account. And people inside buildings felt the tremors more distinctly than those riding in coaches or on foot.²²¹ Many believed it was the most powerful earthquake to have ever shaken the city, though little material damage was reported and the only known victims were two boys who were crushed to death when a stone cross from the front portico of a church fell on them.²²² "Divine Providence," the *Gaceta de Madrid* wrote reassuringly, "has deigned to preserve the city's inhabitants from the terrible destruction that was threatened."²²³

It was widely believed that God had also intervened to save the Spanish royal family. When the earthquake began, Fernando VI, and his Portuguese wife, Maria Bárbara (the sister of Dom José), were at their private residence within the massive palace-monastery of El Escorial in San Lorenzo, twenty-eight miles from the capital. Like the Braganças, they managed to escape into the surrounding fields without injury, though Don Fernando ordered an immediate return to Madrid. If "we had stayed in the Escorial and the tremors had continued," wrote the forty-two-year-old monarch in a letter to his stepmother, Isabel de Farnesio, "we would have had to walk a considerable distance to get outside . . . while here [in Madrid's Buen Retiro Palace]" our rooms "are very close to the exit and are without stairs." For Fernando, the quake had been a horrifying experience—a "natural fright" and "a danger so great that only the considerable mercy of God had limited its destruction."[224] (He had yet to receive word of the damage it had caused across southern Spain.) So thankful was he for the salvation of his family and his kingdom that on November 4 he personally sang the *Te Deum Laudamus* in the Church of San Jerónimo el Real.[225]

Although dutifully religious, Don Fernando was, at the same time, deeply committed to the Scientific Revolution and its national manifestation in the eighteenth century: the Spanish Enlightenment. Nicknamed "the Learned," he sent Spanish youths abroad to study the natural sciences, created professorships in experimental physics, ordered topographical maps of Spain's coast, opened the first natural history museum and metallurgy laboratory in the kingdom, instituted an array of reforms that modernized the navy and the Treasury, and streamlined trade with the New World. A patron of high culture, he founded the San Fernando Royal Academy of Fine Arts and supported the careers of famed Neapolitan composer Domenico Scarlatti as well as the incomparable Farinelli. In the realm of foreign policy, he maintained a neutrality with former foes Great Britain and France and even signed an agreement with Portugal (with his Portuguese wife's encouragement) over the disputed Colony of Sacramento in Uruguay.[226]

When he began to receive the first reports of the devastation across Iberia, Don Fernando was shaken. "While I am thankful to God that I am well, I am very grieved at the damage that has befallen almost my entire kingdom as well as Portugal."[227] On November 8, at the suggestion of his prime minister, Ricardo Wall, he ordered an *encuesta* (survey) to assess the earthquake's impact on Spain. Notable for its unambiguous embrace of the scientific method, it was sent to government officials across the kingdom and consisted of the following eight questions.

1. Did you feel the earthquake?
2. What time did it begin?
3. How long did it last?
4. What movements were observed in floors, walls, buildings, fountains, and rivers?
5. What damage did it cause to buildings?
6. Were there any deaths or injuries of people and animals?
7. Are there any other notable things to report?
8. Was the earthquake preceded by any signs?

The responses, which were received from almost every major city in Spain, provide a treasure trove of information about the disaster.[228]

Although large earthquakes were not entirely unknown in eighteenth-century Spain, they were decidedly rare. The last Spanish earthquake of any significant size had shaken the Valencian towns of Montesa, Corbera, l'Olleria, Vallada, and Xativa with moderate force on March 23, 1748.[229] There were no casualties. By contrast, on November 1, 1755, 61 people died in Spain (according to official records) as a direct result of the quake (although many more would later die in the tsunami). The majority of those 61 (84 percent) were killed by falling debris or buried under collapsed structures, while the rest died in the ensuing panic, as a result of heart attacks, et cetera.[230] Although the total value of property destroyed in Spain paled in comparision with Portuguese losses, it was still high, roughly equal to one fifth of the annual expenditure of the Spanish Crown.[231]

In France, tremors were felt in the south and west, in La Rochelle, Toulouse, Anduze-en-Languedoc, Angoulème, Cuers, Saint-Auban, Vaucluse, Gémenox, Cognac-en-Saintonge—as well as Poitou and Provence. According to a newspaper report, "the Shock was felt very smartly in Bordeaux, [and] the Waters of the Garonne were in terrible Agitation, but through the Providence of God, no great Mischief was done."[232] In the northwest, the earthquake shook Brittany and Normandy, where the market town of Caen experienced tremors of striking violence.[233] In Paris, the earthquake was not perceived at all, although the Marquis d'Argenson reported in his journal that the famed astronomer and cartographer Cassini de Thury did see fit to inform the king, Louis XV, that on November 1 "there must have taken place some great movement of the earth, judging from the motion of the pendulum at the Observatory."[234]

In Switzerland, the quake was perceived at Neuchâtel and Basel, though it apparently did no damage—while in Italy the shaking was noticeable across the north and in the Alpine regions.[235] In Turin, light tremors were felt during morning church services, while across Lombardy, in Milan, Lodi, and Pizzighettone, many houses and churches were destroyed.[236] Near Rome, the citizens of Acquapendente and Allegrotte experienced "eighteen earthquake tremors," according to one account; and a few houses apparently collapsed.[237] In Venice, the earthquake was also felt, most famously by Casanova—while in the Low Countries light tremors were reported at Leyden, Harlem, The Hague,

Gouda, Amsterdam, Rotterdam, Utrecht, and 's-Hertogenbosch (Bois-le-Duc).[238]

In northern Germany, churchgoers gaped as lamps and architectural decorations swayed for as long as fifteen minutes, while in Glückstadt, near Hamburg, chandeliers in the city's churches swung back and forth for several minutes, as did church decorations in Elmshorn, Wilster, Kellinghusen, and Meldorf.[239]

Tremors from the great quake (or possibly secondary earthquakes triggered by the initial event) were felt as far away as Sweden and Norway and many locations throughout the northeastern Atlantic, including Cape Verde, Madeira, and the Canary Islands.[240] According to one report the entire island of Sardinia "was shaken by the earthquake of the first," while an account from Copenhagen asserts that "the inhabitants [of Greenland]" were put "in a state of the greatest alarm" due to "a large earthquake"—though the details are unclear. On the island of Terceira in the Azores, violent and sustained tremors prompted clerk Mathias Pires to believe that "the day of the last Judgment" was approaching.[241] And at the southern tip of Ireland, at Cork, a "sensible" shock "was felt between Nine and Ten o'clock," according to one newspaper account. The "Motion was tremulous, like that of a Ship under easy Way." It frightened "those that were in upper Chambers," who imagined that "the Houses were falling."[242] In Great Britain, tremors were perceived in Kent, Reading, and Derbyshire.[243]

There is no evidence that the earthquake was felt in North America. No record of seismic activity has been found in any newspaper of the day or in any other contemporary source (diaries, memoirs, etc.).[244]

Outside Portugal, no region suffered more than northwest Africa. Although evidence is scant and, in some cases, imprecise or exaggerated, the region clearly met with widespread devastation and considerable loss of life.[245] In Marrakesh, "not even the sturdiest building escaped total ruin!" reported a pamphlet, and the city walls, which were "made of a mortar so solid that a pickaxe could only succeed in dislodging sparks, collapsed like ashes; the majority of its mosques [were] destroyed, swallowing up a large number of Moors who still lie buried beneath the ruins."[246] In the cities of Fez and Meknes, "many Moors and Jews [were] buried along with an infinite number of injured people in the wreckage of . . . houses [and] synagogues."[247] And according to a report in *The Scots Magazine*, "that part of the city [Meknes] where the Jews resided was entirely swallowed up and all the people of that sect (about 4000 in number) perished, except [for] seven or eight."[248] Likewise, a mosque in Fez was reported to have collapsed on top of eight hundred Muslim worshippers.[249]

Along Morocco's Atlantic coast—at Safi, Tangier, Salé, Agadir, Asilah, and Larache—the earthquake brought down an unknown number of buildings and claimed hundreds, if not thousands, of victims—while in the city of Tétouan on the Barbary Coast only a few walls were damaged.[250] Across the region, there were rock slides and reports of colored sand pouring forth from the ground. According to an account in *The Gentleman's Magazine*, "some distance from [Fez], a prodigious large mountain opened in the middle, out of which issued a river as red as blood."[251] One widely communicated (and almost certainly apocryphal) report describes the earth opening up and devouring no fewer than five thousand people along with their "camels, horses, cows, [and] herds of animals" as well as an encampment of six thousand cavalrymen, who "were sucked towards the precipice with their horses." Afterward, the earth closed up so neatly "that the next day it was difficult to recognize the place where there had been so many villages, habitations, people, and beasts."[252]

Across North Africa and Western Europe, reports of troubled waters were widespread. In Morocco, fountains, springs, and wells mysteriously dried up or flowed forth more vigorously, as they had in Spain and Portugal—while throughout Europe, seiches, or standing waves, appeared in canals, ponds, rivers, and lakes as the earthquake rippled across the surface of the earth, and animated waters that were normally placid (a hallmark of the largest temblors).[253] According to one study, the Lisbon Earthquake produced "the most widespread and varied examples of earthquake seiching" of "any [other known] earthquake."[254]

In the small village of Cranbrook in Kent, England, several ponds "were observed to have a very extraordinary motion, flowing like the sea after a storm," while in nearby Tenterden, the water in "several ponds . . . [was] forced up the banks with great violence, foaming, fretting, and roaring like the coming in of the tide." At Bocking, a flock of geese let out a scream in the moments just before the waters of a pond "ran up the hill into a ditch," according to an account in *The Gentleman's Magazine*.[255]

In London, near Old-Street, "large waves rolled slowly to and from the bank" of a fish pond next to Peerless Pool, leaving "the bed of the pond dry for several feet, and in their reflux" overflowing "the bank ten or twelve feet."[256] On the Thames at Rotherhithe, south London, a merchant, Henry Mills, was unloading timber when he and his servants "were surprised by a sudden heaving up of the barges from a swell of the water, not unlike what happens when a ship is launched." According to Mills, "the barge . . . alternatively rose and sunk three or four times with a motion gradually decreasing, [before] the water became quiet again."[257] In Scotland, Loch Lomond rose unexpectedly from its banks several times over the course of a few hours, while at Loch Ness, "a very extraordinary agitation of the water" was reported.[258]

In France, the waters were greatly disturbed at Garonne, while near Agoule, a "torrent" of red sand was observed pouring from the ground.[259] In Switzerland, a number of the republic's largest lakes— including Lucerne, Geneva, Zurich, Thun, and Brienz—rose unexpectedly, tearing boats from their moorings and depositing them on shore.[260] At Travemünde, near the German port city of Lübeck, "the water of the Trave [River] began suddenly to bubble up with great violence" and continued "with such impetuosity that . . . [those] on board . . . imagined that this strange motion proceeded from some whale or other monstrous fish."[261]

At Hamburg, the Alster rose "more or less impetuously," forming "several gentle whirlpools" before throwing mud upward from the bot-

An eighteenth-century depiction of the destruction of Meknes, Morocco

tom and then subsiding "with a copious white froth," while the Elbe in some places grew "still more violently."[262] At Eibsee in Bavaria, and in the Brandenburger towns of Templin and Röddelin, an "agitation of the water" was noticed "between eleven and twelve o'clock" in the morning. In Schleswig-Holstein, Rendsburg, the waters of the Eider took on "a very unusual motion," while at Netzow, fishermen reported "an insupportable stench."[263]

Strange movements were also perceived off the German coast at Hockensbüll and Schobüll, in the Stör River at Itzehoe, in Husum harbor in Frisia, in the Great Plön Lake at Plön, and in lakes and various bodies of water across Mecklenburg, Thuringia, Brandenburg, Hannover, and Hesse.[264]

At Töplitz (now Toplice) in Bohemia, the famous thermal springs suddenly experienced "a wonderful increase in the flow of water," although their "volume or quality had not changed in a thousand years." At noon on November 1, the *Bade-Meister* (caretaker of the spa) noticed that the waters had turned cloudy, after which they slowed to a trickle and then ran "thick and blood-red." Fifteen minutes later, however, they flowed so "bright and clear" that they filled up the various springs in half the time that it normally took. Although many from the town saw the phenomenon through a scientific lens—hypothesizing that a new spring had opened up and broken into a patch of red earth "through an act of underground violence"—the chief magistrate and city council took no chances and ordered a *Te Deum Laudamus* to be sung in the parish church.[265]

In the Netherlands—at Woubrugge, Alphen, Boshoop, and Rotterdam—the water became so agitated that "buoys were broken from their chains, large vessels snapped their cables, and smaller ones were thrown out of the water onto the land," while in 's-Hertogenbosch (Bois-le-Duc), the "wrecks of vessels, long since sunk" rose to the surface and floated "for several minutes."[266] In Norway, the water level in Farris Lake increased so suddenly and violently that one boat sank and several others had difficulty reaching the shore.[267] In Sweden, the Dal "rose so quickly," according to one report, that it broke the chains of several boats, while in Värmland and Vänersborg waves crashed against the shores of several lakes, rivers, and lochs.[268] Near the town of Smögen, not far from the Norwegian border, a terrible noise was heard just before the cold waters of the North Sea drove violently into the coast.[269]

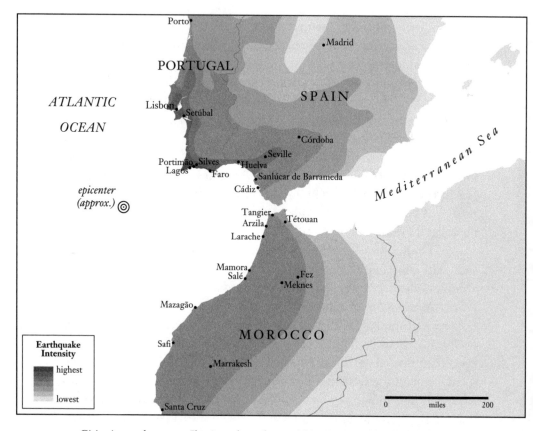

Cities in southwestern Iberia and northwest Africa impacted by the earthquake

The farthest known report of a seiche came from Turku, Finland, more than two thousand miles away from the earthquake's epicenter.[270] But because news traveled slowly in the mid-eighteenth century, it would take months before anyone began to connect these widespread and disparate phenomena with the Lisbon disaster—which for most of that city's inhabitants on the morning of November 1, 1755, was, unfortunately, just beginning.

CHAPTER THREE

An Unexpected Horror

*The sea seemed jealous that people thought they had less to fear from
her than the earth and the fire.*

—A FRENCH EYEWITNESS

INUNDAÇÃO

At approximately 10:25 a.m. (thirty minutes after the last tremor
ended), an ominous and entirely unforeseen event occurred at Lisbon.
The waters of the Tagus river basin began to recede with unusual swiftness, exposing, in a few short minutes, vast stretches of grimy river
bottom, which even during the lowest of tides "had never been seen
before."[1] Large frigate ships, sloops, and tiny skiffs that just moments
before had floated placidly in deep water were suddenly left stranded
and helpless on shoals of mud, sand, and silt. One merchant vessel got
stuck on the sandbar at the Tagus's mouth and "several large ships,"
according to one captain, "lay very high and dry at Boa Vista," near
the parish of São Paulo.[2] "In many places" the riverbed "was raised . . .
to the Surface," recalled an eyewitness, and "Ships drove from their
Anchors, and jostled together with great Violence"—their "Masters"
not knowing "if they were on Ground, or [still] afloat."[3]

What no one in Lisbon could have known was that they were witnessing the drawback phase of a gigantic tsunami, whose peak (or bore)
was bearing down on the Portuguese capital at speeds approaching fifty
miles per hour. Produced at the same time as the earthquake, when
the fault's hanging wall thrust upward three times a total of ten meters

across hundreds of miles of ocean floor, the great wave chain was just now reaching Lisbon.[4] A tele-tsunami or oceanwide tsunami, it was one of the largest, most destructive, and far-ranging of its kind in history. Comprised of three separate waves (each corresponding to a single earthquake tremor), it stretched from the center of its peak to the bottom of its trough at least a hundred and fifty miles across the surface of the sea. (By comparison, a typical wind wave spans one hundred to three hundred feet, peak to peak.)[5]

On the open ocean, the Great Tsunami almost certainly achieved speeds of 500 to 600 miles per hour (similar to a jet airplane)—but because each wave was no more than three feet high, it would have appeared as little more than a modest wave crest streaking along the ocean's surface. Ships crossing its path would have felt nothing as the largest part of each wave passed silently beneath their keels. Those sailors who did report disturbances were most likely experiencing the impact of P waves from the earthquake itself.[6] Meanwhile, on the ocean floor, an avalanche triggered by the quake created such a thick cloud of mud and silt that the majority of marine life was extinguished for hundreds of miles in several directions. The radiocarbon dating of microfossils found in core samples collected at depths of 4.5 kilometers off the Portuguese coast have allowed researchers to identify sediment from this event.[7]

As the tsunami neared shore, it was forced upward by the narrowing angle of the coastline. Consequently, its height grew, its length shortened, and its speed diminished. For this reason, it arrived in Lisbon, as it did in other locations, after the earthquake. Reaching land first was the wave trough, which pulled the water in front of it back in the direction of the incoming peak, much as a wind wave draws the water at its base back from the shore just before breaking. This is known as the drawback effect. For several minutes, this curious spectacle—occurring, as it did, without a strong breeze or any other apparent natural cause—both frightened and astonished those assembling along the Tagus—and perhaps even coaxed a few hungry survivors out onto the riverbed to collect oysters and stranded fish.[8]

As each tsunami wave entered shallow water, it became increasingly compressed and, as a result, began to drive the water in front of it in the direction of the shore. (For this reason, most tsunamis appear less like a conventional wind wave than a rapidly rising tide or flood.) But the Great Tsunami of 1755 contained so much water and energy that its three wave peaks bore some resemblance to normal waves as they approached and subsequently broke on shore. But unlike most waves they did not immediately dissipate upon landfall, but were driven forward violently and relentlessly by the force of the enormous mass of churning surf that stretched back hundreds of meters behind them.[9]

Perhaps the first to experience the tsunami was Johann Jakob Moritz, a managing clerk in a Hamburg merchant house, who on the morning of November 1 had boarded a Porto-bound ship in order to evade questioning about his possible involvement in illegal activities. As his vessel crossed the Tagus bar and sailed out into the open ocean, Moritz felt, for a brief moment, that his troubles were now behind him. "But suddenly," the wind "became still" and an eerie calm descended upon the coastline. There were, he wrote, "no sounds, no birds, not even a single ubiquitous sea gull."[10] Then—just as abruptly—"the sea rose up" with a mighty fury; and Moritz's ship was assaulted by a series of "long, roaring, foaming, white waves" which crashed against it with "thunderous Noises."[11]

The turbulent waters, however, subsided as quickly as they had come. The ship righted itself and sailed out into the Atlantic. From the direction of the shore, Moritz heard a kind of "muffled rumble," which he thought to be "distant thunder," and in the sky, he saw several "heavy, black-gray clouds." Odder still, the tide had failed to come in; and the flags that normally fluttered over the distant towers of Belém had vanished. "Was everyone dead?" he asked. "Are we alone in the world? Has everything disappeared?"[12]

In Lisbon, the first sign of trouble was the sudden appearance of a great wall of churning water moving eastward up the Tagus in the direction of the city. Breaking "feather white" over the sandbar, the tsunami's peak rolled into the river basin like a rapidly moving fog and then plowed into the northern shore.[13] From Alcântara to Belém, the water reached "up to the walls of farms and palaces"—a distance of "more than sixty yards (fifty *varas*)" . . . "leaving behind boats, frigates, and skiffs that had once been on the water," wrote a priest.[14] Along the road between Lisbon and Belém, "the waves rushed in with so much rapidity," recalled the English merchant Braddock, that several persons on horseback "were obliged to gallop as fast as possible to the upper grounds, for fear of being carried off."[15]

Moments before, the tsunami had smashed into the coastal fishing villages of Carcavelos, Oeiras, São Paço de Acros, and Cascais (all

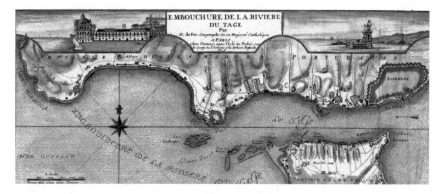

The mouth of the Tagus River where the tsunami entered. Lisbon is on the
top right.

located just outside the sandbar, and thus fully exposed to the fury of the
sea). While the first three villages somehow weathered the assault, Cascais was hit head-on.[16] "The ocean quickly entered the town," recalled
a priest, "knocking over its sturdy bridge, swallowing the houses closest
to the shore and killing many inhabitants."[17] So violent and unexpected
was the tsunami's arrival that soldiers at the Fort of São Lourenço of
the Dry Head, at the river's mouth, "fired several Guns as" a "signal for
Help," according to an eyewitness, and then fled "to the upper Part of
the Tower" for safety.[18] Likewise, Belém Tower and the riverside forts
of São Sebatião de Caparica and São Julião da Barra were assaulted by
the waves.[19] Outside the sandbar, the water may have risen as far as
forty feet above the usual high-tide mark (a difference known as the
run-up). The most severe damage and the greatest loss of life would
occur along Lisbon's populous riverbank.[20]

Even "the oldest sailors" were "astonished," recalled one survivor,
as the sea broke in "in mountainous waves over the Bar." The towering wall of water "seem'd to threaten the City with inevitable Destruction."[21] Crashing through the mouth of the Tagus, the tsunami quickly
overwhelmed the British merchant ship that was stranded on the bar,
though it did not destroy it (when the waters retreated, the vessel had
"floated out to sea").[22] Several sailors who had been "tossed on Land by
the sudden rise of the Water," wrote a ship captain, "jumped ashore to
save themselves, and immediately their Boats were carried away by the
retiring Sea, which ebb'd and flow'd, and ebb'd and flow'd" over the
course of "four or five minutes."[23] Indeed, "the water rose in less than
five Minutes more than twenty Feet," reported several ship captains.

"Many Ships drew their Anchors . . . and all were under the greatest Apprehensions of running foul of each of other and being dashed to Pieces."[24]

"Ships at anchor [however] ran a great danger," recalled Fernando Vigánego, the Genoese consul at Lisbon. "Some of them broke away and were carried off at the discretion of the sea, with considerable mortality of those who had once thought themselves saved."[25] William Clies, captain of the British packet ship *Expedition*, "actually deserted the packet" for a time, "thinking she might be lost."[26] Though Clies and his crew weathered the onslaught, others were less fortunate. "Many frigates and some crew members disappeared," wrote an eyewitness. "To this day no trace of them has reappeared, not even a hat."[27] According to another survivor: "The furious waters smashed anchors, broke cables, and then entered into the streets and squares near the riverbank"—the "sea" carrying "with it everything that it encountered, and" then bringing "back everything . . . with full force." Some sailors "who had jumped from their boats were drowned and the Tagus soon became a confusing mass of entangled ships' masts . . . a horrible cemetery of cadavers."[28]

"The whole river," recalled another eyewitness, "was overspread with boats, vessels, timber, masts, household goods, casks, etc. Not any one thing remains in the king's yard or arsenal and what timber was not washed away is [strewn] across the streets in such a manner as makes them impassable."[29] Likewise, the bay in front of the city "was transformed into a confused forest of intertwined masts, without arrangement or order," wrote a Frenchman, "cables and broken anchors, the carcasses of old ships, displaced despite their enormous weight and left almost dry on the margins of the river."[30] As the tsunami crossed and recrossed the river basin, ships were thrown about like pieces of driftwood. A few floated helplessly to the other side of the river, while others found themselves locked in a furious struggle to stay afloat.

From the middle of the Tagus, a young Swedish sailor, Fredric Christian Sternleuw, believed he was experiencing "the most tragic event ever contemplated by human eyes"—equaling if not surpassing "the cruel description of what will come to pass on the Day of Judgment."[31] Orphaned at five and raised by a distant uncle, Sternleuw was, on November 1, 1755, a veteran crewman of the *Sverige* (Sweden), which was then hauling salt from Stockholm to Sétubal, when he saw the Tagus "rise with incredible speed." "The agitation of the waters was

Lisbon assailed by the elements

such that the sloops could not reach the ships" and "many ships were dragged onto the land," he recalled, "of which the oddest example was one that came to rest in the old city square," presumably the Terreiro do Paço.[32]

Nearby, the British ship captain, who had witnessed the earthquake from his merchant ship a half hour before, saw a new tragedy unfold. "Everybody" on land, he wrote, who had not been "crushed to death" by the earthquake had run "out into the large spaces . . . and those near the river ran down to save themselves by Boats or any other floating Convenience, running, crying, and calling to the Ships for Assistance." Just then, "the Water rose to such a Height that it overcame and overflow'd the lower Part of the City, which so terrified the miserable and already dismay'd Inhabitants, that with dreadful Cries, which were heard plainly on board [the ship], it made them believe the Dissolution of the World was at Hand."[33]

In the vicinity of St. Paul's Church, Mr. Braddock "heard a general outcry, 'The sea is coming in, we shall be all lost.'" Turning toward the river, he saw it "heaving and swelling in a most unaccountable manner" although "no wind was stirring." In the distance "a large body of water" rose "like a mountain" and "came on foaming and roaring, and rushed toward the shore with such impetuosity that" although everyone "immediately ran for [their] lives, as fast as possible; many were . . .

swept away."[34] Although some found themselves "above their waist in water at a good distance from the banks," he wrote, "I had the narrowest escape, and should certainly have been lost, had I not grasped a large beam that lay on the ground" and hung on "till the water returned to its channel, which it did almost at the same instant, with equal rapidity."[35]

Three miles from Lisbon, a British merchant about to enter his boat saw the Tagus rise "so high" and so suddenly that it "obliged us to take to our heels, and run for our lives, into the fields and high ground," where he saw "the water flowing across the road which. . . . was above a quarter mile" from the low-tide mark. On the surface of the turbulent river, he could see ships whirling about, "and several people taken into the water, others driven ashore, and dashed to pieces. From the high grounds," he wrote, "we could see the sea at about a mile's distance come rushing in like a torrent, tho' against wind and tide."[36]

North of the Terreiro do Paço, another merchant making his way toward the river saw "a Crowd" of people "running from the Waterside, all crying out" that "the Sea was pouring in and would certainly overwhelm the City." "This new Alarm created such Horrors in the agitated Minds of the Populace," he wrote, "that vast Numbers of them ran screaming into the ruinated City again, where a fresh Shock of the Earthquake immediately" buried a great many "in the Ruins of falling Houses."[37] Thousands of others, recalled a priest, managed to escape "back through the hills and valleys" of the city, climbing on "top of mountains of rubble and ruined walls" to reach safety.[38]

The Reverend Goddard had just returned to the top of São Jorge's Hill, after a failed attempt to reach his brother Ambrose's house in the Baixa, when he received "a Report that the Sea was breaking in." Large crowds, among them a "Family of the Factory consisting of several Gentlemen and Ladies," began to run up the hill toward the Castle, "as the highest Ground and a Place of Safety." "We were so alarm'd with the News of the Inundation," recalled the vicar, "that we were scarce at Leisure to bestow a Thought on ourselves or our Friends."[39]

"Like a wolf with its mouth open," wrote a Spanish eyewitness, "the Tagus seemed to want to swallow the city whole."[40] According to a Portuguese priest, the "movement" of the water "appeared supernatural, flowing without restraint with great speed and arrogance." With apparent premeditation, "it targeted the shore, entering those houses closest to the river"—and seemed "to want to swallow all that it found" in its path.[41] "The sea appeared to empty its bowels," reported another survivor, "turning the waters dark green and infused with nitrous [oxide]," a chemical that is known to give off a slightly sweet odor.[42]

"Three times the sea rose up and exceeded its limits," wrote Miguel Pedegache, "and three times it receded back into river with equal speed."[43] Most agree that Lisbon's shores were beset by three separate inundations, with run-up heights of between 15 and a little more than 20 feet (4.5–6 meters). The first wave receded, wrote a survivor, "with the same impetuosity as it had risen, falling three feet lower than the lowest tides." This was immediately followed by a second wave that was "much more turbid and irritated than the first but whose impact was less."[44]

All along the northern bank of the Tagus, the violent waves surged ashore. From the Fort of Our Lady of Conceição, the Tower of Belém, and the Fort of St. John of the Junqueira, in the west, to the Docks of the Saints (Docas dos Santos), St. Paul's Church, the Riverside Palace, the Riverside Market (Mercado da Ribeira), and the Public Square (Terreiro Público), in the east, the tsunami left its mark.[45] According to the secretary of state for the navy and the overseas empire, Diogo de Mendonça, "the sea entered by way of the bar like a mountain and so rapidly left its normal limits that it covered the Junqueira bridge," which was a considerable distance from the beach.[46] At Alcântara, recalled a priest, the waters "overcame and broke apart" a bridge that spanned a small river that flowed into the Tagus.[47]

Fortunately, the royal family was never threatened. Belém Palace stood on a hilltop overlooking the river. But the king's uncle, Prince Dom António (the eldest of the boys of Palhavã), found himself in "grave danger" in the Palace of the Royal Court (Palácio Corte-Real). Falling to his knees in a palace window as the tsunami approached, the fifty-one-year-old doctor of theology at first "offered his life to God," before escaping to a small yawl (escaler) and then onto a British ship. When the waters subsided, he was returned to land, "barefoot and almost naked," in the vicinity of the Junqueira. He would live another forty-five years.[48]

At the Royal Ship Yards (Ribeira das Naus) next to the Riverside Palace, the tsunami tore into the partially constructed ships that lay about the enclosure and scattered immense quantities of boards into the already devastated Baixa. One eyewitness estimated that the losses in wood alone amounted to "five or six million" cruzados.[49]

One husk of a ship floating off the Ship Yards caught fire and was left to burn—while the western *bairro* of São Paulo was flooded along the river.[50] In the *bairro* of Boavista, "the water entered the houses, smashing apart huts and piles of boards, beams, and rafters and carrying with it everything that it found," wrote a priest.[51] At the Terreiro do Paço, the tsunami breached the Muralha Philipina, the seawall built by Philip II in the seventeenth century, and smashed into the small fortification called the Fort of the Terreiro do Paço (Forte da Vedoria), tearing down the river-facing walls of the Customs House (Alfândega) and the Customs House of Tobacco (Alfândega do Tabaco), and destroying "all the Goods brought over in the two last Fleets from Brazil," including "some twelve thousand cases of sugar," recalled Father Portal. Also wiped out were dozens of merchant warehouses filled with tobacco, timber, grain, and textiles on or near the river's edge.[52]

Perhaps the most famous architectural victim was the much admired marble quay, the Cais da Pedra, which disappeared into the Tagus along with a substantial crowd of people on top of it.[53] Recently constructed, the formidable structure of rough-hewn white stone was—at least for four months—one of Lisbon's busiest and most visited sites. During the day, precious cargo was loaded and unloaded onto and from it, while in the evenings, *lisboetas* took relaxing, river-cooled strolls upon its gleaming surface.[54]

"Upon the first shock" of the quake, reported *The Gentleman's Magazine*, people had run down to the quay for protection; and in the half hour afterward they were offering "from 10 to 50 pieces" to board "ships in the harbor."[55] Then the tsunami struck. Estimates vary as to how many were swept away. One survivor claimed that the quay sank "with about 600 persons on it," while two others reported 900 and 150 victims, respectively.[56] One *lisboeta* later wrote that he was awaiting the arrival of a pearl diver from Angola whom he had hired to confirm the precise number of victims, which he estimated to be around "three or four hundred."[57] The actual number will never be known.

Richard Goddard learned from several eyewitnesses that the quay "was entirely swallow'd up, for it was observ'd that none of the Bodies floated, nor did any of the Boats that were moor'd there appear afterwards."[58] One ship captain reported that "he saw the quay with the concourse of people on it, sink down, and at the same time every one of the boats and vessels near it were drawn into the cavity, which," he supposed, "instantly closed upon them . . . as not the least sign of a wreck was ever seen afterwards."[59]

For over two centuries, the story of the Cais da Pedra disappearing into a cavity in the earth was repeated as fact and became one of the defining images of the disaster. Yet it is wholly inaccurate. Not long after the disaster, the quay's remains were found in deep water along the riverbed by the military engineers Carlos Mardel and Eugénio dos Santos.[60] More recently, remnants were discovered during excavations for a new subway line.[61]

What then explains the quay's strange demise? One factor may have been liquefaction, a phenomenon known to occur during the most powerful earthquakes when the ground shakes so intensely that uncon-solidated water-saturated soils like sandy soils near the shore become temporarily liquefied, causing objects to sink into the ground, lique-faction is believed to have occurred numerous times in both Portugal and Spain as a result of the Lisbon quake.[62] In Spain, it was observed in Seville as well as the cities and villages in the province of Huelva.[63]

Ultimately, the quay probably succumbed to the combined assault of several fatal phenomena. After suffering severe structural damage in the earthquake and a partial submerging due to the effects of lique-faction, it was likely pounded apart by the tsunami and then scattered across the riverbed as the waters receded back into the Tagus.[64]

Many recalled that after the three great waves made landfall the Tagus continued to rise and fall for several hours, albeit with dimin-ished energy and penetrative force.[65] According to one ship captain, "the current first run violently up and then down for about half an hour and then at a stand, alternately ebbing and flowing in a gentle degree, small whirlpools, and moderate thwart currents."[66]

If accurate, this may be a description of the three tsunami waves reverberating back and forth between the opposite banks of the Tagus basin, or it is evidence that there were more than three tremors, pos-sibly from two or more separate earthquakes (as some seismologists have speculated). One eyewitness claimed that the quake first began "at the castle [of São Jorge]," then "the great blow ran like lightning down to the water-side, in a line nearly from north to south, passing under the river, where it instantly swallowed up a Dutch ship, an Irish two-masted vessel, three fishing-schooners full of men, and some boats that lay in that direction nearest the shore."[67] While the assertion that ships were lost on the river owing to the first tremor is probably inaccurate (the later arrival of the tsunami being the more likely cause), if the first tremor did indeed move from north to south, then there must have been a second earthquake.

In support of this theory, several eyewitnesses purport to have seen sparks and flames in the hills near Lisbon right after the quake. "On a hill next to Colares [a town approximately fifteen miles east of Lisbon] very credible people have assured me," wrote Father Portal, "that, although there were no houses or chimneys on the hill, sparks of fire came out of the earth at the precise moment that" the earthquake struck.[68] Another eyewitness saw something "issuing from the sides of the mountains resembling that which may be observed on the kindling of charcoal."[69] These observers may have captured the moment, seen later in California and Japan, when electrons in newly disturbed rock above a fault come into contact with the air and, in the process, give off a searing light.[70]

As the waters rushed in, most lisboetas had no real sense of what was occurring, for tsunamis were even less well understood at the time than earthquakes. Over 80 percent take place within the Pacific Rim along several active underwater faults. Ninety percent are caused by undersea earthquakes, while the rest are triggered by landslides, meteor strikes, nuclear and volcanic explosions, and, in some cases glacier and iceberg calvings.[71] Although large tsunamis had struck the Portuguese coast before (most recently in the Algarve in 1722), it had been many years since one of real consequence had reached Lisbon. Some educated lisboetas were undoubtedly aware of the devastating tsunami that, nine years before, ravaged the coast of Peru in the wake of the Great Lima Earthquake.[72] Yet there is no record of anyone exhorting survivors to stay away from the riverbank in the half hour after the earthquake.

So obscure, in fact, were tsunamis at the time that no single term for them existed in any European language. Portuguese chroniclers refer to the "inundation" (inundação), the "alteration of the waters" (alteração das aguas), the "flood" (enchente), the "waves" (ondas), the "flux and reflux" (fluxo e refluxo), or simply report that the sea or, in some cases, the river had "risen beyond its limits" (saiu dos seus limites).[73] The Spanish, for their part, speak of the "very extraordinary movement" of the sea (muy extraordinario movimiento del mar), the "inundations" (inundaciones), "the flux of the waters" (el fluxo de las aguas), and the "arrogant waves" (soberbias olas).[74]

An anonymous Spanish poet refers to "el aquemoto del Mar" (water quake of the sea) to describe the tsunami's arrival in Sanlúcar, Spain, while in Boston, Massachusetts, the Congregationalist preacher Charles Chauncy refers to "Water-quakes" in his *Sermon occasioned by the late earthquakes in Spain and Portugal* (1756). Both may be examples of *hapax legomena*, words that appear only once in the history of a language. ("Water-quake" is not, for example, to be found in Dr. Johnson's *Dictionary of the English Language* of 1755.)[75]

The term most commonly used today, "tsunami"—or "harbor wave" in Japanese (*tsu* meaning "harbor" and *nami*, "wave")—first appeared in Japan in the early seventeenth century and may have been invented to describe a wave that fishermen had not noticed while they were at sea but, in their absence, would inflict damage to their harbor.[76] The word tsunami would not become commonplace in Western scientific and public discourse until the last decades of the twentieth century, replacing the terms "tidal wave" and "seismic sea wave" in English and *maremoto* or "moving tide" in modern Portuguese and Spanish. All three are misleading in their own way.[77] In the first place, tsunamis are not caused by the tides (although both tsunamis and "tidal waves" have extraordinarily long wavelengths that can stretch hundreds and, in the case of tidal waves, thousands of miles); and "seismic sea wave" is also imprecise since not all tsunamis are caused by earthquakes.[78]

While words may have been lacking, the principal cause—divine punishment—seemed clear to many if not most *lisboetas*. All knew the story of the flood in Genesis; and many were aware that one of the signs of the Apocalypse was a significant alteration of the world's oceans.

> And the second angel poured out his vial upon the sea; and it became as the blood of a dead *man:* and every living soul died in the sea. And the third angel poured out his vial upon the rivers and fountains of waters; and they became blood.
>
> REVELATION 16:3–4

And so an already emotionally battered population was driven to even more frenzied displays of despair, piety, and self-flagellation. To one Portuguese cleric, however, the fact that Lisbon had not been completely destroyed by the sea was a sign that God had not completely given up on its inhabitants. "In the same way," he wrote, "that God in ancient times had discovered one righteous man [Noah] to save the world, so we must have faith that" during the recent disaster "some servant of the Lord ... had asked for [and received] a suspension of the greatest part of the punishment that God had originally wished to deliver on Lisbon." In light of this, the duty of *lisboetas* was to do as Noah did when he saw that the waters had receded: build an altar and offer a sacrifice to God. "All those who escaped the ruins of the city," wrote the priest, "should thank God for the great mercy that he has shown us" and pray that "we will always serve him and do his divine will."[79]

DAMAGE ASSESSMENT

Despite the destruction that the tsunami caused along the riverbank, there is little evidence that the waters penetrated very deeply into the heart of the city. One contemporary estimated "five estadios" (approximately 4,280 feet or 1,305 meters).[80] But, at the same time, there were no reports that the tsunami destroyed any monument or building of note other than the Cais da Pedra and no credible evidence that it reached the Rossio (despite the widespread belief among present-day *lisboetas* today that it did).[81]

One Spanish survivor asserted that "the waters of the Tagus ... reached into the City to the New Street" (the Rua Nova dos Mercadores), located just two streets north of the Terreiro do Paço—while the most comprehensive chronicler of the disaster, Father Manoel Portal, states unequivocally in the introduction to his *History of the Ruin of the City of Lisbon* that the majority of the damage to the capital was not caused by the tsunami.[82] "God in his mercy put an end to [the sea's] fury," Portal informs us. "Because of Divine Providence," the river "did not rise as much from its limits as it could have; [and thus] did not cause the kind of damage that one might have imagined."[83]

Why was this? In the first place, a sizable proportion of the tsunami's energy was absorbed by the sandbar at the Tagus's mouth—"breaking its greatest violence," according to one contemporary history.[84] Secondly, the Tagus basin, which is almost two miles wide at Lisbon, dispersed at least some of the raging water. "Had it not been for the great Bay, to receive and spread the great Flux," wrote Mr. Farmer, "the low Part of the City [would] ... have been under Water: For as it was, it came up to the Houses, and drove the People to the Hills."[85] Finally, the Muralha Filipina, the seawall guarding the riverbank in front of the Terreiro do Paço, together with the densely packed and rubble-strewn

Baixa, proved effective in blunting the tsunami. Thus, while much of Lisbon, and particularly the Baixa, proved vulnerable to the tremors and the subsequent fire, it was spared the worst of the tsunami's power.

Still, an analysis of the phases of the moon on November 1, 1755 (by this author), as well as the testimony of a reliable eyewitness, indicate that the Tagus was approaching high tide (which occurred around noon) when the tsunami arrived and thus was perhaps as much as six feet higher than it had been at 6 a.m.[86] If so, the run-up heights of the tsunami would have been six feet higher if it had struck at low tide in the early morning or late afternoon.[87] Testimony from the kingdom's chief architect, Manoel da Maia, that parts of the Baixa regularly flooded at high tide supports the conclusion that the tsunami penetrated at least 300 to 350 meters into the city in the area of the Terreiro do Paço—and perhaps even more in areas not protected by the seawall.[88]

Such an inundation would have caused catastrophic material damage along the northern bank of the Tagus, where so much of the merchant wealth of the city was stored in warehouses and shipyards. It would have also caused many deaths. Of the thousands who flocked to the riverside after the earthquake, many—the injured, the disoriented, and the infirm—would have been unable to escape the rising waters. Some survivors "had not noticed the alteration in the waters" at all until it was too late, recalled one priest, while others were simply "unable to flee with sufficient speed."[89] Miguel Pedegache believed that "the majority of those who had gone to the margins of the river for shelter were carried off by the waves."[90] Indeed, on November 16, a Captain Willett of the *Augusta* reported seeing "great Quantities of Household Furniture, dead Bodies, Legs, Arms, & [other objects] floating" in the open ocean near Lisbon.[91]

Most of those washed out into the Atlantic were never presumably recovered and thus never incorporated into any official or unofficial death tally. (Surviving church records from Lisbon contain no specific references to those who died in the tsunami.)[92] In the aftermath of the disaster, the paramount concern of the authorities was to bury the thousands of rotting corpses as quickly as possible, not determine how each had died. And those corpses that did wash up on shore would have, after days or weeks of decomposition, have been largely indistinguishable from those that had suffered in the earthquake or fire.

One recent study, however, of 214 skeletonized remains found under the floor of the former Franciscan Monastery of Our Lady

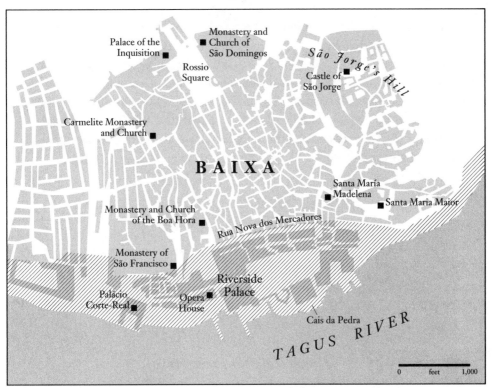

The tsunami penetrated more than 1,000 feet into the Baixa

of Jesus (now the Academy of Sciences and the Center of Geological Studies for the New University of Lisbon) has revealed that silver objects buried with the bodies bear signs of chlorine alteration from apparent immersion in saltwater, leading some researchers to conjecture that some of the dead may have been tsunami victims from the São Paulo and Conde Barão *bairros* of Lisbon.[93] As these bodies represent only a fraction of the roughly three thousand believed to be buried in this mass grave, one may assume that the number of recovered tsunami corpses (those that had not been pulled past the Tagus bar and out to sea) was not inconsiderable.

One priest observed that it would be difficult to estimate the number of people who drowned because of the large numbers of those who lived and worked by the river in "stores, tents, and huts"—not to mention all "those from outside the city who came to earn their living along the riverside or those who sought the banks of the Tagus to escape the piles of trash and puddles which covered the streets in the winter." He nevertheless estimated the number who perished "in the sea flood at more than six or eight hundred."[94] A modern study puts the tsunami death toll at 900.[95] If one assumes, however, that there were approximately 8,000 people (or about 4 percent of the population of the city, plus people visiting for the holiday) crowded along Lisbon's riverside when the tsunami arrived—and that 100 to 200 were swept away on the Cais da Pedra—then it seems reasonable to conclude that the tsunami was responsible for between 2,000 and 3,000 deaths at Lisbon.[96]

TELE-TSUNAMI

The force of the waters . . . rose up against the Heavens and . . . dissolved the eternal laws. Disturbing foreign kingdoms, it destroyed the tranquility of Nature.

—JOSÉ DE OLIVEIRA TROVÃO E SOUSA (1755)[97]

The sea swallowed the beaches.

—ABBOT PAULINO ANTONIO CABRAL[98]

However great the destruction and loss of life caused by the tsunami at Lisbon, the lion's share actually occurred along the Portuguese, Spanish, and African coasts.[99] Just as the earthquake had delivered its horrible force deep into the European continent, so would the tsunami spread its watery mayhem across great swaths of the Atlantic world. Coastal cities were battered, and villages and towns inundated or completely wiped out as the tele-tsunami barreled in unexpectedly from the ocean. At Setúbal "the sea entered the city with such fury," wrote Moreira de Mendonça, "that it toppled walls and many buildings" and "two yachts and many boats were carried five hundred feet into the city," which had already borne the full brunt of the earthquake.[100] According to Father Portal, "the sea knocked down walls and entered the city, and in the countryside it penetrated almost a quarter of a league [4,500 feet], and left boats in the streets."[101]

In the already devastated regions of the Algarve, it was the "sudden fury of the sea" that "caused the greatest unhappiness," remarked one eighteenth-century historian.[102] Dotted with fishing villages and ancient forts of white-gray stone, Portugal's southern coast was sparsely populated and largely cut off from the rest of the kingdom. Only three roads connected it to Alentejo, the region to the north.[103] In 1755 (as in 1722), its proximity to the earthquake's underwater hypocenter rendered it vulnerable to the ravages of both land and sea. While a few fortunate stretches of the coast would suffer relatively minor tsunami damage due to the protection of natural barriers (the high cliffs near São Vicente and the islands of the Sotavento region), much of the region east of Lagos was overrun by waves that, in some areas, may have risen more than 50 feet and penetrated a league (over 4,000 yards) or more inland.[104] In several places, the water carried large boulders and cobbles as far as 400 yards onto land as it choked river systems and blanketed villages with enormous quantities of sand, debris, and sediment (creating malarial conditions in some areas for decades to come).[105]

The leading wave of the tsunami reached the Algarve about a quarter of an hour before it arrived at the mouth of the Tagus, striking the western tip of Cape St. Vincent about sixteen minutes after the final tremor ended.[106] As in Lisbon, the waters receded dramatically along the entire coast before the arrival of the wave peak a few minutes later; and, as in Lisbon, the tsunami struck as the sea was approaching high tide, making run-up lengths substantially higher.[107] According to the archbishop of the Algarve, Lourenço de Santa Maria, "everything in the city of Lagos, in the settlements of Vila Nova and Albufeira, in the cities and parishes of . . . São Vicente, and many other places along the coast were completely overturned and destroyed by the sea, which knocked down earthworks, [and] walls, tearing apart hills, giant stones, dikes, stockades, trees, people and animals, and filling towns, gardens, and yards with salt, sand, and countless fish."[108]

At Albufeira, in the central Algarve, "the ocean entered the outskirts of the village," recalled Father Costa de Aragão, "and carried off the entire *bairro* of Santa Ana, which consisted of seven streets and many houses, without leaving any sign of where the houses once stood."[109] Following the earthquake, many inhabitants had run to the beach seeking safety, but then "the sea came," according to one account, "and swallowed everyone up."[110] Out of a population of about 2,500, "one hundred and ninety-seven [or 8 percent] drowned," according to a manuscript source.[111] At the village of Alvor, the sea rose perhaps 40 feet, reaching a height of 9 feet inside the Church of Mercy, whose foundation is already 33 feet above sea level.[112] There, the waves "devoured vegetable gardens and mountains of sand from neighboring beaches, carrying off the chapel of Our Lady of Ajuda" and "leaving not a trace of where it once stood," reported an eyewitness.[113]

At Cape St. Mary, the southernmost point of mainland Portugal, the fury of the incoming waters so surprised the Dutch fleet on patrol there that, according to a gentleman in Cádiz, it "fired [its] Guns . . . in Distress," while in the village of Armação de Pêra, near Silves, the ocean barreled into the center of the small settlement and "carried off the Church of Santo António by its foundation, leaving only a few stones" and killing 66 people.[114] In the parish of Boliqueime, the sea wiped out all 38 fisherman's huts along the beach, killing 28—while in Portimão, "the rapid inundation of the waters exceeded its natural limits," recalled a priest, "and entered the land in places more than eight hundred varas [over 800 yards], devastating the salt works of the city . . . razing many houses in the *bairro* of Asapal . . . ruining all of its gardens and orchards . . . [and] entering the Church of Misericordia," where it reached a "height of 12 palmos [approximately 9 feet]."[115]

In Lagos, "ninety-five people died," according to a parish priest, "some underneath the ruins, others carried out to sea."[116] There, "the ocean rose 13½ palmos in the houses" and may have penetrated more than half a mile inland, recalled another survivor. It "took with it all the furniture of great value, all the silver, gold, [and] money," as well as "twenty-eight casks of wine, wheat, corn and vegetables," and "the library of my brother, and all the farm contracts" of the surrounding houses.[117] Large sections of Lagos remained in ruins as late as the 1820s.[118] Officially, the tsunami claimed 442 people in the Algarve, although the actual numbers may be much higher due to incomplete records and the fact that many bodies in this remote region were simply carried out to sea and forgotten.[119]

In the coastal cities and villages north of Lisbon, there was considerably less tsunami damage. At Porto, the River Douro "rose and fell surprisingly every quarter of an hour, for upwards of four hours, four or five feet, and sometimes more," recalled one British eyewitness. "Four or five boats were overset by" the sea "on the bar, but no one drowned"; while "two Brazilian ships, that had just got over the bar, were . . . forced into the harbor again" and were "very nearly . . . lost."[120] Yet there were no reports of deaths or significant property damage.

Three hours after the earthquake ended, the tsunami reached Galicia (Spain) in the northwest corner of the Iberian Peninsula. At La

Coruña, "the motion of the sea was extraordinary," reported the mayor, José de Avilés. "In less than an hour it waxed and waned four times, and although expressing great anger and violence in its movements, it never overflowed or exceeded its limits."[121] At Santander, on Spain's northern coast, "the water of the estuary retreated more than normal at low tide and soon filled in again, repeating this movement three times," recalled Mayor José Pérez de Cossio—while a hundred leagues from the sea, at Toledo (in the very heart of the Spanish kingdom), "the waters of the Tagus River became cloudy and rose one vara [approximately three feet], though it caused no damage or other misfortune," reported the provincial *intendente*.[122]

It was in Andalusia, along Spain's southern Atlantic coast, that the tsunami did most of its damage.[123] At Huelva, "the first movement of the sea was to recede," wrote Mayor Don Bartolomé Ramos Dávila, "revealing more than a quarter league [.87 of a mile] of beach, after which [the water] rushed forward with great fury onto the shore, uprooting and destroying everything that resisted it."[124] According to another eyewitness, "the sea was furiously agitated [three quarters of an hour after the earthquake ended] and the waters pushed towards the coast . . . [and] the river came out of its course, sending waves into the first streets, [and] inundating the plains . . . with great damage to the boats."[125]

Salting sheds and the cabins of sardine fishermen were razed; several hundred people were drowned.[126] According to official estimates, 276 drowned at La Redondela, while at nearby Ayamonte, 400 perished.[127] "The sea . . . came in with remarkable violence," wrote an inhabitant of Ayamonte, and entered "the streets of the town. . . . Great mountains of water, black and horrible," reached "halfway up the tower at the sandbar at the mouth of the port." In the panic, survivors "from the most distinguished families to the most unfortunate (and even the sick and the disabled)" fled to the nearby hills.[128]

Farther south, at Sanlúcar de Barrameda, "the fast-moving waves rose out of the sea and . . . flooded the streets of the lower town . . . with such incredible speed and such an abundance of water that people on horseback on Exchange Street had to escape on boats," reported Mayor Juan O'Brien. "Overrunning the sand dunes," the water "penetrated a thousand paces onto shore," leaving "a twenty-paces-long boat in San Juan Street."[129] One anonymous Spanish poet, the author of a *Truthful Account of the Great Miracle Seen by Innumerable People in the City of*

Sanlúcar de Barrameda, blamed neither Nature nor the Christian God for the phenomenon, but an unlikely combination of both pagan and demonic forces. "With the sun covered in mourning clothes and murky shadows obscuring its brilliance," he wrote, "Thetis [the ancient Greek goddess of the sea] entered the campaign."[130] Joining the attack was "*el Dragon* [i.e., the Devil] who enlisted all the occupants of Hell (with permission from the great God of Battles) to destroy *in totum* every human being. Spewing venom, he ordered his soldiers to give no quarter . . . and to attack through the swift waters that were now inundating the land and flooding the cities." To this end, "he fixed his battery against Sanlúcar . . . and the salty waters flooded the City and drowned the Lower Barrio."[131]

But Santa Rita of Cascia, the patron of lost and impossible causes, heard the cries of the people. And soon afterward, "a strange, divinely inspired idea" was implanted in the mind of a cleric named Prior Burgos. Without hesitating, he remembered Rita, retrieved her statue from the church, rounded up three fellow friars, and marched off in the direction of the sea carrying the *santa* on top of a raised platform. Of the multitude of priests in Sanlúcar, only these four dared to face the watery threat. Arriving at the water's edge (with a large crowd of the faithful behind them), they demanded in the name of Santa Rita that the Devil desist. Outraged, the Evil One conjured up "a second wave so high and terrible that," according to the poet, "it would have surely submerged the city."[132]

But Burgos and his three *compañeros* stood strong. Knee deep in sea foam, they continued their prayers, now urged on by the city's chief justice *(alguacil mayor)*, who upped the ante, proposing that the city honor Santa Rita with a yearly feast day. "We vow to you Protector *(Protectriz)* and Advocate of Impossible Causes," the priests now chanted, "that if you save us from the fury of this cruel enemy . . . your glorious name will resound throughout the world and we promise you that a solemn feast in your honor will be celebrated annually at our religious house."[133]

The gambit worked, for "immediately after they had finished speaking, the approaching wave halted timidly," wrote the poet, "and the waters receded." In celebration, church bells echoed throughout the city; and all those "who had been dispersed by the disaster . . . ran into the streets and the squares and shouted with abundant joy: Viva Santa Rita! Viva! And Long Live the Virgin Queen of Charity! Long May She Reign in our Hearts!" And at ten the next morning (the approximate

time the earthquake had struck the day before), "a priest of great erudi-
tion delivered such an eloquent and persuasive homily that the congregation wept as they gave thanks to God."[134] Despite suffering a direct
hit from the tsunami and being situated in one of the most devastated
earthquake zones, Sanlúcar lost only nine people to drowning and one
to panic, according to the official Spanish records.[135]

Cádiz, however, was not so lucky. Located on a narrow strip of land
jutting out into the Atlantic, this ancient port founded by the Phoe-
nicians is the oldest inhabited city in continental Europe. It is also—
despite its high walls—exceedingly vulnerable to a direct assault from
the sea. At about 11:10 a.m., the great tsunami arrived as high tide was
approaching, some eighty minutes after the earthquake.[136] Just as "the
frightened inhabitants . . . had begun to quiet down, making their way
to the churches to give thanks, pitiful voices could be heard throughout
the city," wrote one *gaditano*, as a resident of Cádiz is called. "The sea
is swallowing the earth! We will be flooded and drowned! To the Land
Gate! . . . In the confusion, some ran without knowing where; others
injured themselves or knelt on the ground to beg for mercy, while the
majority cried out their confessions to the Almighty."[137]

"On a sudden," reported another eyewitness, "the ocean swelled . . .
upwards of eighty vars in length [approximately 200 feet] . . . from the
Caletta [or Cove Beach] to . . . the Castle and soon overflowed all the
streets thereabouts . . . carrying with it huge Pieces of the Wall . . .
[and] at the same time, the waters enter'd the Port . . . sweeping away
all before them." Everyone "ran into the streets for Confession and
Mercy." Some "ran to the Higher Grounds. [And] the Friars gave Bene-
diction to the People [who were] all in Tears, expecting instant Death,"
while "a great many ran out at the Land-Gate [in an attempt] to escape"
inland, "but, poor creatures! The two Seas met with equal Violence [on
either side of the isthmus that connects the city to the mainland] . . .
And . . . they were all drowned, Men, Women, and Children."[138]

One Englishman remembered "a prodigious large Wave of the Sea
like a Mountain pouring right down upon the Town . . . at the distance of about two Leagues."[139] It possessed "a speed that is difficult to
express," wrote a French eyewitness, "and rose to an incredible height
of more than five meters."[140] Realizing that he was situated where the
waves were likely to strike first, the Englishman and a friend ran "into
the heart of the Town as fast as [they] could . . . every Moment looking
behind [them], expecting the Water at [their] Heels." They were not

alone. "It seemed as if all the world was in the Streets," he wrote. "Such Crying, Such Confusion never was seen [before], one half did not know from whence the danger came—but we were all alike afraid and the universal cry was *Misericordia*." One could "see the best Women of the Town, fainting" and falling down "in the Streets half dressed, [and] everybody anxious for [only] himself took no Notice of his Neighbor, pushing along with the Crowd."[141]

Though the "huge Wave decreased considerably upon the Shallows and the Rocks off of the point," it divided, with "one part" sweeping "along the back of the Town, as high as the Parapet of the Wall" and the second falling "upon a fine Causeway . . . which it carried clear away with upwards of 150 Travellers upon it, all lost."[142] Officially, two hundred people drowned at Cádiz, although that is only an estimate.[143]

One of the victims on the causeway was Jean Racine, the son of the poet Louis Racine and the great-grandson of the renowned seventeenth-century French dramatist Jean Racine. Perhaps the most famous person to perish in the Lisbon disaster, the young merchant and his business partner, Joseph Juan Mason, were swept out to sea and drowned as they tried to escape along the causeway between Cádiz and Isla de León.[144] Widely reported throughout Europe, Racine's death devastated his father, who sold his library and officially retired from public life. Poets from across Europe offered up eulogies to the young man in verse. One such consoler was Jean-Jacques Lefranc, the Marquis of Pompignan and the future "enemy of Voltaire"—as he would be known after a speech delivered in the Académie Française in 1760. In his *Letter to M. L. Racine . . .* , Lefranc contended that although we must grieve the young man's death, we should not become overly distraught, for Racine is in Heaven and while the innocent may suffer in this life, we know they will receive recompense in the world beyond.[145]

The French savant Louis Godin had survived the earthquake at Cádiz, but "about an hour later" he noticed that "the sea had become very choppy far to the west of the city." Suddenly, he saw several "large towering waves," which slammed furiously into the city walls, cleaving them "in a number of places from top to bottom . . . The Caleta Gate was destroyed and the parapet that runs from there to Santa Catalina was in pieces. . . . [The waves] entered the city and flooded the Mola which was covered with barrels, pieces of wood and a thousand other objects."[146]

Along the isthmus that connected the city with the mainland (where young Racine was swept away to his death), Godin reported that a man mounted on a donkey was dragged out to sea among the cargo ships and then was returned again to the shore, where he ditched his donkey and escaped. This first "advance" of the sea, wrote Godin, "occurred at 11:10 a.m." Then, "at 11:30 a.m., the sea returned again, the same way as it did on the first occasion, and then withdrew until it appeared calm. The cycle repeated five times with almost equal force from 11:10 a.m. until 1:15 p.m." Below is a chart from Godin's written report on the disaster, giving the times the first five inundations arrived and the intervals between them.

1st Inundation: 11:10 a.m.	Intervals between:
2nd	11:30 a.m.	20 minutes
3rd	12:00 (noon)	30 minutes
4th	12:35 p.m.	35 minutes
5th	1:15 p.m.	40 minutes

From this data, Godin concluded that as the waves weakened and their speed decreased, the intervals between them became longer. "The agitation of the water lasted until midnight," he noted, though after each wave it became less and less perceptible.[147]

In an extraordinary feat of scientific thinking, Godin computed the speed of the tsunami by pointing out that a ship captain sailing from Caracas, Venezuela, on the morning of November 1 had felt a powerful movement (undoubtedly a seismic wave) at about 9:15 a.m. Since the ship was located approximately 150 leagues (520 miles) due west of Cádiz and the tsunami arrived about an hour and ten minutes after the earthquake ended, Godin postulated that before arriving in that city the "waters" had averaged "100 fathoms per second" or 410 miles per hour.[148] More than two centuries before the discovery of plate tectonics (and with it the discovery of the primary cause of most earthquakes), Godin had demonstrated the astonishing speed of a phenomenon that science had not yet even named. Today, having a better understanding of the location of the earthquake's epicenter, we must conclude that either the starting time provided by Godin's captain was about fifteen minutes too early (the most likely scenario) or else his ship was much farther west than he knew. In other words, the tsunami was, if anything, much faster than Godin had calculated.

Although the earthquake was felt throughout most of Spain, it was the tsunami that caused more deaths.[149] According to official records, 61 Spaniards died in the earthquake, and 1,214 perished in the raging waters along the coasts. As in Portugal, however, this tally was probably low owing to incomplete parish records in the small villages along the coasts and the fact that many bodies were swept permanently out to sea.[150] Still, some officials did try to be exact. A report from the village of Conil de la Frontera, near Cádiz, states that "599 heads of cattle, 120 cows, 430 sheep, [and] 3 adult and 46 juvenile mules" drowned when the sea pushed inland.[151]

Farther down the coast, at Cape Trafalgar (where half a century later Lord Nelson's fleet would vanquish the combined naval forces of the French and the Spanish), present-day evidence of the tsunami consists of almost three hundred boulders, each weighing up to ten tons, as well as hundreds of smaller stones called cobbles, strewn across the coastline.[152] Farther south, at Gibraltar—then, as now, a British territory—"the Sea rose six Feet eight Inches every fifteen Minutes and fell so low that Boats and all the Small Craft near the Shore were left a-ground, as were Numbers of small Fish," reported *The Whitehall Evening Post*.[153] Inside the Strait of Gibraltar, at Ceuta, "the sea swelled to the height of seven feet," stated the *Gazette de Cologne*, and "a quarter of an hour later, it came down so much, that great quantities of boats and fish remained dry on the sand."[154] Likewise, the Mediterranean islands of Majorca, Minorca, and Corsica felt the effects of the tsunami, while the city of Cagliari, on the southern coast of Sardinia, was hit with such an enormous wall of water that it carried off all the resident coral fishermen, along with their wives and children.[155]

Approximately thirty minutes after the earthquake, waves began to pound the shores of Algeria and Morocco. Relatively close to the epicenter and largely unprotected by islands or undersea barriers, this stretch of coastline lay tragically exposed to the sea. Although the extant European, Arab, and Hebrew sources are limited in quantity and quality and wave run-up heights and casualty figures will never be known with any precision, the legacy of the great tsunami in Africa is a grim one.[156] As along the coasts of Spain and Portugal, the sea was moving in the direction of high tide.[157] At Arzila, Mamora, Larache, Tangier, Safi, and Santa Cruz, "the never before seen rise of the sea overcame the walls and inundated the houses and fields . . . ruining many buildings, [and] killing many people," wrote an anonymous chronicler. It "sunk . . . many ships along with the people inside them, and after it receded . . . left the streets and fields filled with wreckage and abundant quantities of fish."[158]

As it had in Portugal and Spain, the incoming wave trough pulled the coastal water out to sea. "The water disappeared and the boats stood firmly on the sea bed" at Salé, Morocco, wrote the Jewish scholar Ibn Dana. Then, "the water returned suddenly with a great furor—and rising above its usual limits, it drowned all the people who were in the boats as well as those on the beach . . . among the Jewish people, no one died."[159] After this, "the sea flowed into the heart of the city and drowned several of the inhabitants, leaving a great quantity of sand and filth," while "two ferry boats overset in the river and all the people on board" perished.[160] One modern study estimates that the sea penetrated two thousand meters into the city.[161] At "Sella," according to Mohammad Adu'ayyef Al-ribati, "the sea pulled the water towards the depths and disappeared." However, when "the people left the city" to inspect the phenomenon, "the sea broke over the land and killed [them]."[162]

One account in *The Gentleman's Magazine*, mirrored in Arabic sources, reported that "a caravan with two hundred persons" traveling along the coast from Salé to Morocco "was destroyed by the sea, which rose to a prodigious height almost in an instant"—while at the same time "another caravan, with yet a greater number of persons, going from Salle to Fez, was destroyed by the sudden rise of the inland rivers."[163]

At Tangier, "the Water rose fifty Feet perpendicular," wrote *The London Evening Post*.[164] It "swallowed up . . . several boats full" of fishermen, reported another source, and "flowed into the heart of the city (a thing never seen before) leaving behind it, at its return, a vast quantity of filth and sand." Over the next eight hours, the sea "continued to rise and fall about 18 times."[165] And for some time afterward, the city's fountains stopped and then "gushed out with great Violence . . . Water the Colour of Blood."[166]

In the ports of Safi and Santa Cruz, the ocean was "so violently agitated," recalled one Frenchman, "that ships crashed into each other as they could not free themselves from the anchors." And "buildings all along the coast were destroyed by the violence of the waves; and the port was suddenly covered by wreckage, cadavers, and dead fish that floated on the surface of the waters."[167] At Safi, according to a British diplomatic dispatch, "the water penetrated to the great mosque, which was located inside the city a great distance from the sea."[168]

"At Arzila, the sea inundated more than half the city," reported a Franciscan priest, "and killed innumerable people and razed to the ground many houses and buildings and destroyed others." According to other sources, "the water rose nine feet" and "came in through one of the city walls . . . with such impetuosity that it lifted up" a ship in the bay, which "fell down with such force upon the land, that it broke into pieces." The unfortunate vessel "was found at the distance of two musket-shots [or about 400 feet] . . . from the sea."[169] Miraculously, the entire crew survived.[170]

At Mazagão, a Portuguese-controlled city on the Moroccan coast (now called El Jadida), "the sea continued in its fury until two in the afternoon," reported the *Gazeta de Lisboa*, "carrying with it cannon balls and destroying almost to the bedrock the bean and barley fields, and meadows where horses went to pasture. It ruined the fortifications [and] the fences. [And] some of his Majesty's ships were lost, others ruined. The governor *(alcaide)* of the fortress was swept away by the sea and returned . . . alive. . . . Attended to by priests, he recovered by the mercy of God," but not before "vomiting out sand, shells, and blood."[171]

There is even evidence that the tsunami put its imprint on the slave-trading coasts of West Africa. A letter addressed to the Académie Royale des Sciences de Paris states that "all the lagoons at Cape *** happened to be filled by the sea."[172] (The precise location of the lagoons was presumably omitted because it might have provided the British with valuable wartime information and, in truth, could have been anywhere from present-day Liberia to Senegal.[173])

Ninety minutes after the earthquake ceased its rumble, the tsunami arrived at Madeira, the small wine-producing Portuguese archipelago northwest of the Moroccan coast.[174] There, "the sea . . . was observed to retire suddenly," wrote an eyewitness, "and arising with a great swell" and "without the least noise . . . overflowed the shore, and entered into the city. It arose [a] full fifteen feet perpendicular above the high water mark, although the tide . . . was then at half ebb." It destroyed "several houses and cottages, forcing open doors, and breaking down the walls of several stores and magazines, and carrying away in its recess a considerable quantity of grain."[175] At the Madeiran cities of Porta da Cruz and Machico, the tsunami "did considerable damage," recalled another eyewitness, carrying "off near 200 pipes of wine and several . . . [brandy] stills."[176]

In December 1755, both *The London Evening Post* and *The White-*

hall Evening Post erroneously reported that the Azores (or the Western Islands, as they were also known), had been "totally destroyed or sunk."[177] Apparently both the Maranhão fleet (which consisted of five merchant ships and one man-of-war) and two ships carrying flour from Philadelphia reported after putting in at Lisbon that they had failed to locate the islands, while the Marquess of Carnarvon "looked for them in vain [for] two Days in the Longitude and Latitude where they should be found," according to *The London Evening Post.*[178] Although eventually corrected, this shocking information caused (as one might expect) considerable consternation in the Portuguese capital.

By the afternoon, the northern ripples of the great wave chain reached Brittany, France, where at Brest it was reported that the "waters suddenly rose to a height of three feet" in the "Basin . . . at the foot of Saint-Magdelaine's mount."[179] Around four o'clock in the afternoon, the tsunami arrived at the Irish coast. At Kinsale, the tide rose seven feet in one minute and fishing boats at another had "whirled about like so many corks . . . with a motion as quick as the fly of a jack [flag]" though "not a breath of wind was stirring." Earlier that morning, the coasts of Britain and Ireland had been hit by the seismic waves of the quake, disturbing the 40-gun *Gosford* at anchor in Portsmouth. According to a John Huxham, "the tide" at Creston near Plymouth "had a very extraordinary out (or recess) almost immediately after high water (about 4 p.m.) and left both the passage-boats, with some horses, and several persons, at once high and dry in the mud." Then, "in less than eight minutes the tide returned with the utmost rapidity, and floated both boats again, so that they" were in "near six feet [of] water." At Stone-house Lake, "the bore came in with such impetuosity, that it drove everything before it, tearing up the mud, sand, and banks, in a very shocking manner, and broke a large cable, by which the foot passage-boat is drawn from side to side of the lake."[180]

In Mount's Bay, in Cornwall, "the sea was observed at the Mount-pier to advance suddenly from the eastward," according to a Reverend Borlase. "It continued to swell and rise for the space of ten minutes" and "then began to retire . . . with a rapidity equal to that of a mill-stream descending to an undershot-wheel." At the Mount, the sea rose at least "ten feet perpendicular," which was five feet higher than at Mount-pier and two feet higher than at Penzance.[181] At Swansea (Wales), "about a mile up" the Tawe Rive "at a place called White-rock," "a great head of water rushed up with a great noise," according to one account, "floated two large vessels, the least above two hundred tons . . . broke their moorings, and hove them across the river."[182]

At Hunston, in West Sussex, it was reported that "two gentlemen and a servant went out a shooting on the sea-shore" when they suddenly found themselves "in great danger of being drowned, by the sea's sudden flowing before its usual time." They managed to save "themselves, with difficulty, by clambering up the sides of the cliffs."[183] Sedimentary deposits found on St. Agnes Island, in the Isles of Scilly off the Cornish Peninsula, strongly suggest that the tsunami struck there as well.[184] There is also a possibility that the tsunami entered the North Sea and disturbed the coast of the Netherlands (although most of the watery commotion in that region was probably caused by the earthquake's seismic waves).

Over the next several hours, the tsunami rolled westward across the Atlantic at speeds that may have topped five hundred miles per hour. By 2 p.m. (local time), it reached the Lesser Antilles in the eastern Caribbean.[185] According to an officer on board the *Warwick*, near Barbados, "the sea [which was between high and low tide] . . . rose from eight to twelve feet perpendicular," "twice in some islands, and thrice on others." In some places, where the plantations were on low ground near the sea," he wrote, "much damage was done, by drowning and washing away houses, cattle, etc."[186] At Antigua, Captain Affleck of the man-of-war *Advice* reported that "the tide rose . . . twelve feet perpendicular several times and returned almost immediately: the same at Barbadoes, at Martinique, and most of the French islands, [the sea] overflowed the low land, and returned quickly to its former boundaries." In some places, it was "dry for a mile; and in others, [it] flowed into the upper rooms of the houses and destroyed much coffee."[187]

From La Trinité Bay to the François cul-de-sac along the northeast coast of the island of Martinique, the ocean may have risen as much as thirty feet four separate times.[188] According to a French source, "all the houses in the town of Martinique were inundated with more than three feet of water" and "all the stores" which "were filled with coffee . . . were spoilt."[189] Fortunately, the sea around Martinique was almost at low tide when the tsunami arrived, so far less damage was done.[190]

At Guadeloupe, which was between high and low tide, "there was a considerable withdrawal of the sea," according to one eyewitness.[191] At Sainte-Anne, the sea first retreated and then returned again "with violence" and invaded the land.[192] In the vicinity of the Dutch Caribbean island of Saba, "a sloop that rode at anchor in fifteen feet of water was laid dry on her broadside," according to Captain Affleck. And in Carlisle Bay, Barbados, "the rising water" appeared "as black as ink, instead of the clear sea-green."[193] The ebb and flow of the ocean was observed there every fifteen minutes until ten that evening.[194]

There is an unsubstantiated but plausible nineteenth-century account that the tsunami "almost flooded the population" of Santiago de Cuba, as well as several references in the correspondence of South Carolina rice merchant and future delegate to the Second Continental Congress Henry Laurens, that the tsunami was observed at Bermuda and the Leeward Islands, where, according to Laurens, "they had a constant flux and reflux of the Sea every five or six minutes for Hours together."[195]

Strong evidence exists that the tsunami struck the cod-fishing hamlet of Bonavista, Newfoundland, in Canada. There, the sea (as elsewhere) initially retreated—draining Bonavista's harbor dry over the course of ten minutes—before returning, rising to a great height, and overflowing the surrounding meadows. No casualties were reported.[196]

Meanwhile, another branch of the tsunami hurtled across the equator and struck the sun-drenched shores of northeastern Brazil, more than three thousand miles from the epicenter. According to Luís Diogo Lobo da Silva, the governor of the *captania* of Pernambuco, writing to the secretary of the navy, Diogo de Mendonça, "there was more than one flood at Tamandaré and Itamaracá, Pernambucoon the first of November" but "because they struck on deserted beaches, they caused little more trouble than the destruction of some fishermen's huts."[197] Another Brazilian official added that, "the earthquake flood penetrated a distance of one league inland at Lucena [Paraíba] and Tamandaré and carried off some houses . . . leaving one boy and one woman missing."[198] "For several days afterwards," wrote a Portuguese priest of the Brazilian coastline, "the sea deviated from its natural movement."[199]

Intriguingly, no reports exist of the tsunami making landfall along the North American coast of the future United States, despite the considerable number of ports that might have recorded such a phenomenon.[200] One explanation for this is that the tsunami was deflected or dispersed by a range of impediments (like islands, and undersea objects) during its journey across the Atlantic.

One scenario modeled by scientists supports this theory. If the earthquake's epicenter is placed in the eastern region of the Horseshoe Plain, the tsunami disperses westward in "three main energy paths"—the first two move in the direction of the Caribbean and Newfoundland, Canada, while the third is directed toward the Brazilian coast (just like the Lisbon tsunami). Collisions with the Madeira archipelago, the Azores, and several undersea impediments (the Madeira-Tore Rise, the Great Meteor, the Cruiser Seamounts, and the Bahamas Banks) work to scatter the wave chain away from the coastline of the thirteen British American colonies.[201]

The vast scope, destructive power, and impressive run-up heights of the Great Tsunami of 1755 strongly suggest that its progenitor, the Great Lisbon Earthquake, may have been larger than previously believed.[202] Similarities to both the 2004 Indian Ocean Tsunami and the 2011 Tōhoku (or Sendai) Tsunami, whose precipitating earthquakes measured Mw 9.1 and Mw 9.0 respectively, indicate that the Lisbon quake reached or exceeded Mw 9.0.[203] For present-day scientists and government officials, such speculation is of more than mere academic interest. A future mega-quake of similar size occurring in the same general area could conceivably produce a tsunami capable of killing tens of thousands of people along the coasts of Portugal, Spain, Morocco, and possibly even claim victims in Canada, the Caribbean, and the United States.[204] One Portuguese official theorized that a Mw 8.5 quake could produce a tsunami capable of killing 3,000 people and leaving 27,000 homeless in the Algarve alone.[205] Fortunately, earthquakes of this size are exceedingly rare in the Atlantic Ocean. And geological evidence in the form of tsunami deposits called "turbidites" indicates that temblors as large as the Lisbon Earthquake (Mw 8.5–Mw 9.2) occur in this area of the Atlantic once every one to five thousand years, while slightly smaller quakes arise every two hundred years or so.[206]

Although one of the most destructive and far-ranging tsunamis in history, the Great Tsunami of 1755 was by no means the largest. That title most likely belongs to the mega-tsunami produced in the cataclysmic meteor strike in the Yucatán (Mexico) around 65 million years ago. In addition to leaving a 110-mile-wide crater, the impacting meteor created a tsunami wave that may have reached a height of 1.9 miles! In 6100 BC, several giant undersea landslides off the coast of Norway produced the epic Storegga Slides Tsunami, which devastated the North Sea coastlines of Britain and Europe and, in the process, destroyed

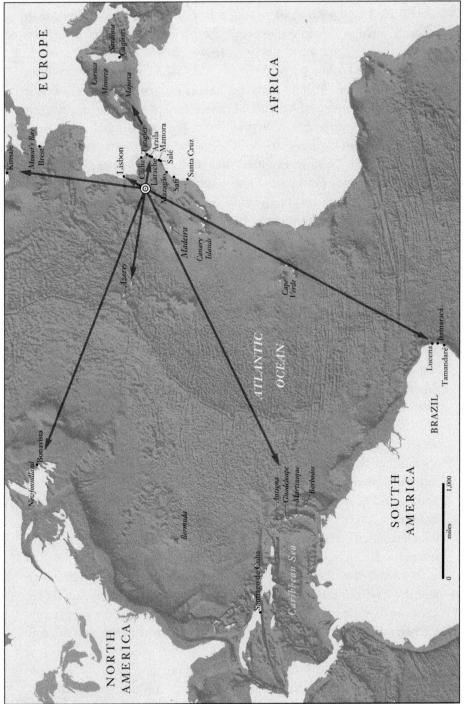

The range of the tsunami in the Atlantic Ocean

several land bridges that then linked Britain with the continent, thus severely disrupting contact between the Mesolithic people of the two regions.[207]

A hundred years later (around 6000 BC), a volcanic eruption and landslide on Mount Etna on the island of Sicily produced a 165-foot-high wave, which caused cataclysmic damage to the eastern coast of the Mediterranean, wiping out an unknown number of Neolithic settlements. About 1600 BC, another enormous tsunami was triggered by the volcanic eruption that completely devasted the Greek island of Santorini (or Thera). The resulting wall of water ravaged the island of Crete and may have led to the demise of the fabled Minoan civilization that had dominated the southern Aegean for centuries.[208] Known variously as the Santorini or Minoan Eruption, the disaster may have inspired the myth of Atlantis described by Plato in the *Critias* and the *Timaeus*.

At the height of the Roman Empire, in AD 79, Pliny the Younger was distracted just long enough from his reading of Livy to notice a small tsunami in the Bay of Naples following the eruption of Mount Vesuvius, which destroyed the cities of Pompeii and Herculaneum. Six hundred years later (AD 684), a massive (Mw 8.4 est.) earthquake in Japan triggered the Great Hakuho Tsunami, which inundated large swaths of land in Tosa province and claimed unknown numbers of victims. The first tsunami ever described in Japan, it was referred to as an *oshio* or "a high-rising tide" (the word "tsunami" would not be invented for another thousand years).

On September 20, 1498, an earthquake and tsunami killed between 26,000 and 40,000 people along the coast of Nankai, Japan, while on October 28, 1707, an earthquake (Mw 8.4) and its resultant tsunami, which reached 10 meters in height, killed 30,000. On May 21, 1772, an undersea landslide (produced by either a volcano or earthquake) caused a 100-meter-high tsunami, which killed 10,000 in the Higo province and the city of Shimbara in southwestern Japan—while on August 16, 1868, an Mw 8.5 mega-thrust earthquake originating in the Peru-Chile Trench sent waves smashing into Arica, Chile (now Peru), and the surrounding coast, killing 70,000.

On August 26–27, 1883, a mega-tsunami produced by the epic volcanic explosion of Krakatoa in Indonesia reverberated throughout the Indian and Pacific Oceans, eventually reaching the coasts of both North and South America. It would claim an untold number of victims.[209] On December 28, 1908, a tsunami triggered by an Mw 7.2 earthquake killed thousands in Messina, Sicily, and its environs; and on July 9, 1958, a mega-tsunami, caused by an earthquake-induced landslide near Lituya Bay, Alaska, reached an incredible height of 1,706 feet (520 meters). Although considerably taller than the Empire State Building, the gigantic wave resulted in only five known deaths due to the remoteness of the region.

The deadliest tsunami in history was caused by the 2004 Indian Ocean or Sumatra-Andaman Earthquake. On the day after Christmas, it plowed into the tourist-lined coasts of Indonesia, Thailand, Sri Lanka, and India and killed more than 230,000 people. Probably the costliest tsunami in material terms was that which followed the Great 2011 Tōhoku Earthquake (Mw 9.0) in northern Japan. Its waves achieved heights of more than 133 feet (40.5 meters); and it killed 15,833 people (leaving another 3,611 missing) and led to several tragic nuclear accidents, including the meltdown at the Fukushima Daiichi power plant.

THE SCIENTIFIC BACKGROUND

Where, indeed, can our fears have limit if the one thing immovably fixed, which upholds all other things in dependence on it, begins to rock, and the earth loses its chief characteristic, stability? What refuge can our weak bodies find?

—SENECA, *Natural Questions*, BOOK VI

Physical explanations for the causes of tsunamis are nothing new. More than two thousand years ago, the Greek historian Thucydides provided the earliest known eyewitness account and scientific explanation for a tsunami in his *History of the Peloponnesian War*. Arising during the summer of 426 BC off the coast of Euboea after a large earthquake, the tsunami (which would later be known as the Malian Gulf Tsunami) "caused the sea" to subside, wrote Thucydides, "from what was then the shore and afterwards swept up again in a huge wave, which covered part of the city and left some of it still underwater when the waves retreated, so that what was once land is now sea." It also forced the Spartans to abandon plans for their annual invasion of Attica. According to Thucydides, the cause of "events of this kind" are "earthquakes. . . . Where the full force of the earthquake is felt, the sea is drawn away from the shore and then suddenly sweeps back again even more violently, thus causing the inundation."[210] For Thucydides, the hardheaded materialist, neither earthquakes nor tsunamis were the work of the gods.

By contrast, his predecessor Herodotus attributed the Potidaean Tsunami (which occurred during the Persian siege of Potidaea in 479 BC) to the wrath of Poseidon. According to the Father of History, the Persians had "behaved sacrilegiously" in the presence of an image of the sea god; and, as a result, Poseidon had conjured up a tsunami (or "ebb tide" as Herodotus called it) to punish them.[211] Such explanations were more nearly the norm for much of antiquity.

The first scientific theories on the causes of earthquakes, however, can be traced back to the pre-Socratic philosophers of the sixth and fifth centuries BC. According to Thales of Miletus in the early sixth century, the earth floated on a sea of water; and earthquakes occur when that water moves, shaking the earth like a ship in a storm and then erupting through the earth's surface. Thales supported his theory by noting that it was common for new springs to burst forth in the wake of earthquakes.[212] In the second half of the sixth century BC, Anaximenes postulated that earthquakes were caused by the collapse of underground caves, while Anaxagoras, in the fifth century BC, claimed that temblors were produced when air, which had been trapped underground by rain, attempted to escape to the surface.[213]

Not surprisingly, the definitive ancient theory on the origins of earthquakes and tsunamis came from Aristotle, the fourth-century BC Greek philosopher and polymath, who formulated a systematic explanation of the physical world based on rising vapors. According to Aristotle, moist vapors, which do not ascend as high or as quickly as dry ones, produce metals, hail, snow, rain, clouds, and the "halo" in space, while dry vapors cause earthquakes, wind, thunder, lightning, comets, and the northern lights.[214] In the specific case of earthquakes, the damp earth generates subterranean winds when it is heated by underground fires and the sun. As these winds swirl around beneath the ground or, in some cases, escape into the atmosphere, they shake the ground. In Aristotle's view, there are four types of earthquakes: inclinatory earthquakes (which move the earth diagonally), shakers (which move the earth vertically), ruptures (in which trapped air escapes into the atmosphere), and howlers (in which trapped air remains underground).[215] All in all, it was an extraordinarily prescient and perceptive (though ultimately unsuccessful) attempt to explain the complex nature and variety of seismic waves.

Tsunamis, according to Aristotle, occur when one of two contrary winds pushes the sea back from the coast into a concentrated mass (an early description of the drawback effect). When, however, this initially stronger wind finally gives way, the opposing wind drives the water back toward and onto the shore. It was a theory as ingenious as it was fallacious, and it (along with his earthquake theory) would hold sway in Western science for more than two thousand years.[216]

Another idea from antiquity that would survive well into the eighteenth century was the seismological importance of subterranean caverns and fires. Both Plato and Aristotle believed in underground "fire streams" and "fire hearths." Before them, the fifth-century BC Sophist Antiphon theorized that subterranean fires produced earthquakes by causing the internal collapses of the substrata which their burning had destabilized—while another Greek hypothesized that quakes resulted from boiling water heated by subterranean fires.[217] One ancient theory (later embraced by the impressive trio of Leonardo da Vinci, Giordano Bruno, and Johannes Kepler) postulated that the earth was similar to a human body with canals running through it like arteries and veins. As the earth ages, these canals, which normally contain free-flowing air and water, become clogged (as arteries and veins invariably do in an elderly person). Unable to move without restriction through the canals, the now pressurized air and water cause powerful vibrations in the earth.[218]

From the Middle Ages (when his works were reintroduced to the West) through the sixteenth century, Aristotle's views on the origins of earthquakes and tsunamis reigned supreme. No truly original theories on the subject emerged, though most commentators now added that while Aristotle may have correctly identified the physical forces, God had been the First Cause.[219] In the seventeenth and eighteenth centuries, earthquakes began to be seen within the context of the emerging science of geology, though very little new was said. In his *Protogaea* (1690–91), the German philosopher Gottfried Wilhelm von Leibniz postulated that earthquakes and volcanoes were caused by the eruption of underground fires left over from the days when the earth resembled a fiery sun.[220]

The first half of the enlightened eighteenth century saw little or no advance in the understanding of earthquakes. Even the innovative French naturalist Buffon followed the herd, arguing that earthquakes had their origins in an explosive, fire-ravaged subterranean world.[221] But in 1749, the English antiquarian and scholar William Stukely challenged the prevailing earthquake orthodoxy by claiming that electricity, a phenomenon of growing fascination, was a more likely catalyst. "If a nonelectrical Cloud discharges its contents, upon any Part of the Earth, when in a high-electrify'd State," Stukely wrote, "an Earthquake must necessarily ensue."[222]

What Benjamin Franklin, the sage of electricity, thought of this theory is unknown. More than a decade before, in 1737, the forty-nine-year-old printer, inventor, and scientist did publish an article on the causes of earthquakes in his *Pennsylvania Gazette* in response to an earthquake that struck the Mid-Atlantic British American colonies on December 7, 1737.[223] Unfortunately, it is not his own work (as many once believed), but an edited transcription of an entry on earthquakes in Ephraim Chambers's influential *Cyclopaedia* of 1728.[224] The article in question contends (as many did at the time) that earthquakes result from underground explosions of chemicals like sulfur, pyrite, and niter, while lightning and thunder issue from similarly triggered above-ground detonations. What is perhaps most noteworthy is Chambers's concession that the issue was far from settled science. "Naturalists are here divided," he wrote. "Some ascribe [earthquakes] to Water, others to Fire, and others to Air; and all of 'em with some appearance of Reason."[225]

By the early afternoon, there were some in Lisbon who began to think that the worst might be over. "At Two [o'clock]," wrote a ship captain on the Tagus, "the Tide returned to its natural Course . . . [and] the Ships [and] Boats began to ply, and took Multitudes on board. The English Ships" loaded up "their Countrymen and Women, with which the Shore was crowded."[226] Richard Goddard reported that it was only in the evening that the tide finally returned "to its usual course," although one eyewitness recalled that it was not for another "ten to twelve days [that] the tides" returned "to their regular rhythm, sometimes arriving late, other times coming in early."[227] Nevertheless, most survivors seemed to have realized that the immediate danger from the sea was over. They had somehow managed to escape death, yet were still fully aware of the tragedy of their present situation. "It is inexpressible to behold the Fear, the Sorrow, and hear the Cries and Lamentations of the poor Inhabitants," recalled the ship captain. "Everyone begging Pardon, and embracing each other; crying, forgive me, Friend, Brother, Sister! Oh! what will become of us! neither Water nor Land will protect us."[228] It was at this point that the city was confronted with the third— and most destructive—component of the great disaster: the fire.

CHAPTER FOUR

The Great Firestorm

And after the earthquake a fire.

—I KINGS 19:12

"UM GRANDISSIMO INCÊNDIO"

It began in a hundred places throughout the city: at the Carmelite Church and the Church of São Paulo, at the Convent of the Anunciada and the Monastery of the Boa Hora (Good Hour)—as well as the imposing Church of Santo Domingos, in whose ruins Malagrida would be defrocked six years later. "The first of November" being "a high festival among the Portuguese," wrote one survivor, "every Altar in every church and chapel . . . was illuminated with a number of wax tapers and lamps." When the churches fell, an avalanche of debris collapsed on top of thousands of candles, rugs, lamps, tables, benches, tapestries, statues, crucifixes, containers of holy oil, and human bodies, setting the enormous heaps of rubble ablaze.[1] At Santo Domingos, a single candle in one of the side chapels ignited a curtain, which, according to a chronicler, rapidly communicated the flames to "pulpit, church, and monastery."[2]

Fires also broke out in private homes and residences where servants and housewives were busy preparing the feast day meal.[3] "The fire began as the houses fell," recalled an eyewitness, "and because each of them contained a fire within"—in fireplaces, stoves, kitchen chimneys—it soon "spread to the combustible matter."[4] One of the first structures to catch fire was the stately palace of the Marquês de Louriçal, which, according to one report, may have actually been burning *before* the earthquake due to an overturned taper.[5] Located in the northern reaches of the city, it was a repository of countless treasures, including a collection of over two hundred paintings by such masters as Titian, Correggio, and Rubens, and a renowned library of eighteen thousand books, which contained a history composed by the Emperor Charles V in his own hand, a collection of preserved plants (a herbarium) once owned by King Matthias Hunyadi of Hungary, and a priceless assemblage of original manuscripts, maps, and charts from the Portuguese Age of Exploration.[6]

As the morning progressed, the individual fires grew, multiplied, and, driven by an increasingly robust wind, swept swiftly across the city's fractured landscape.[7] Those fires that had begun along Lisbon's northern limits—at the Louriçal palace and the church of Santo Domingos—united and moved southward, while those on the city's eastern fringes—at the Church of São Paulo, the Carmo, and the Monastery of the Boa Hora—advanced south and east toward the Tagus.

Reaching temperatures of 1,000°C (1,832°F) or more, the fire devoured everything in its path, feasting on floorboards, beams, rafters, and building frames made of pine, cork, chestnut, and jacaranda.[8] It engulfed entire churches, palaces, private homes, and storerooms, and incinerated everything within: desks, trunks, dressers, chairs, bookcases, furniture made from slow-burning *pau brasil* (brazilwood), as well as carpets, mattresses, paintings and frescoes, painted tiles, stacks of paper, bags of flour, cotton, and grain, barrels of fish, gunpowder, butter, and olive oil, as well as slabs of meat and fowl, bottles of wine, and, of course, human bodies, both dead and alive.[9] In the intense heat, coins and all manner of metal objects melted, and sand turned to glass.[10] "It was a tremendous sight," wrote an eyewitness. "One saw merchants throwing their riches from the windows in order to save them from the [advancing] flames."[11]

With a dynamism that suggested (to some) a will of its own, the fire tore through city blocks and down long tortuous streets, leaping across narrow lanes and *avenidas* and spreading itself across the capital's congested central *bairros*. One particularly destructive blaze broke out just north of the Terreiro do Paço on the Street of the Ovens (Rua dos Fornos), so named for the concentration of bakeries and public kitchens found there.[12] By the early afternoon, the entire city center and portions of the surrounding neighborhoods were at risk of being completely overrun by an enormous conflagration, which, according to Mr. Brad-dock, "went on consuming everything the earthquake had spared."[13]

As the fire intensified, enormous quantities of hot ash were thrown hundreds of feet in the air above the city and then were scattered by the winds. Alighting on the roofs of churches, houses, and other structures, the glowing flakes kindled even more fires and, in this way, projected the conflagration across open spaces, like gardens, plazas, and squares, that might otherwise have impeded its progress. "The city was in flames in several distant parts at the same time," recalled an eyewitness, "for in the terror . . . no attempt was made to stop it, and the wind was very high, so [that the fire] . . . was communicated from one street to another by the flakes of fire driven by the winds."[14]

Unfortunately for the inhabitants of Lisbon, conditions were ideal for the creation of a truly monumental blaze. The air was cool and dry. There was a brisk, unrelenting wind and, thanks to the earthquake, an almost infinite supply of flammable material scattered about. Further-more, the location of the main fire in the Baixa served to magnify its size and intensity. Surrounded by hills to the north, east, and west—with the Tagus forming its southern border—the bowl-shaped Baixa constitutes a classic topographical setting for a firestorm, a phenome-non that thrives in confined spaces and is defined by exceptionally high temperatures, a self-sustaining wind system, the presence of radiated heat (i.e., infrared radiation), and copious amounts of hot ash.

The majority of firestorms occur when temperatures inside a large fire become so great that the surrounding air is effectively drawn into it, further increasing temperatures and combustion. As a firestorm develops, the air at its core begins to spiral upward and as a result of a powerful vacuum effect, self-generating winds pull oxygenated air and flammable material toward its center. This is known as the stack effect. As temperatures within the fire approach those found in a blast furnace, metal and glass start to melt and objects as far away as a hundred feet suddenly burst into flames. Violent wind shears drive the fire in sev-eral different directions at once, and inside a certain radius, people and animals (who might otherwise have escaped) suffocate in the oxygen-deprived conditions. In some cases, enormous columns of spinning ver-tical flame, called fire whirls or fire tornadoes, come into being—as do pyrocumulus and pyrocumulonimbus clouds, which are produced by the high levels of condensation given off during combustion (the latter have been known to generate lightning).

By late afternoon, hundreds of small and medium-sized fires began to coalesce into a single hellacious inferno, which one French chronicler described as an *embrasement universel* (an all-encompassing conflagration).[15] Father Portal thought it "one of the largest [fires] that has ever been seen," while another eyewitness called it "the cruelest fire the world has ever experienced. One does not read about its equal in the ancient histories, nor in the destruction of Carthage, nor in the burning of Troy."[16] Yet the Great Fire of Lisbon has but rarely appeared on lists of the world's most devastating conflagrations, due, one presumes, to the famous earthquake that preceded and overshadowed it, and has only recently been identified as a firestorm (by this author).[17] Nevertheless, its impact on earthquake-ravaged Lisbon was nothing short of catastrophic, and the similarities between it and other historic firestorms are as illuminating as they are undeniable.

One of the earliest and most infamous was the Great Fire of Rome (AD 64), which destroyed ten of fourteen districts of the Eternal City, during the reign of Nero. But contrary to legend, the tyrannical emperor was not the arsonist. He was far from the city when it began, and he never once fiddled during the six days and seven nights that the fire raged (fiddles were not invented until the tenth century).[18] More than a millennium and a half later, the Great Fire of London would consume the heart of another imperial capital along with eighty-seven parish churches and the homes of more than seventy thousand people.[19] Aided by a steady breeze, as in Lisbon, it would, from September 2 to September 5, 1666, completely gut a massive half-oval-shaped region north of the river Thames, destroying the old Gothic cathedral of St. Paul's and much of the fabled capital that More, Spenser, Shakespeare, and Raleigh had known so well. It was "the saddest sight of desolation that I ever saw," wrote the famed diarist Samuel Pepys.[20]

Two centuries later, someone or something other than Mrs. O'Leary's mythic cow triggered the Great Chicago Fire, which devastated more than 3.3 square miles of that Midwestern metropolis on October 8, 1871, killing upward of 350 people. (A journalist would later admit to having fabricated the fire's bovine origins.)[21] On the very same day and with no apparent connection other than severe droughtlike conditions that had prevailed for months across the upper Midwest, the deadliest fire in American history, the Great Peshtigo Fire of Peshtigo,

Wisconsin, incinerated vast expanses of alpine forest and claimed 1,500 victims.[22]

Several decades later, on the West Coast of the United States, the Great San Francisco Earthquake (7.8 Mw) of April 18, 1906, triggered a firestorm that killed more than a thousand people and, like Lisbon, caused considerably more material damage than the earthquake itself. On the other side of the globe, on the first of September, 1923, the Great Kantō Earthquake (7.9 Mw) produced a string of immense fire-storms on the Japanese island of Honshu, destroying Tokyo, Yokohama, and several other major cities.[23] Of the roughly 145,000 victims, most died in the fires, including 44,000 who were killed in the span of fifteen minutes by an enormous fire tornado that tore through Tokyo's Army Clothing Depot, where tens of thousands had sought shelter from the blaze. "The jam [in the depot] had been so congested," wrote a journal-ist, "that [the victims] had not been able to fall to the ground. . . . They stood there, packed, the dead rubbing elbows with the dead."[24]

In Lisbon, eyewitness accounts reveal all the essential elements of a firestorm. One ship captain saw the burning city ten leagues (or thirty-five miles) out at sea, while another person could see it from Santarém, forty-three miles from the capital.[25] "The flames of the fire were so numerous and so extraordinary," wrote a priest, "that . . . it eclipsed the luminous '*astro*' that God created in the sky to signal the day."[26] For more than a week, survivors were assaulted by its intense radiant heat. Many in the vicinity of the Terreiro do Paço "had their hair seared and their eyebrows and eyelashes singed off," an eyewitness reported.[27] Many others recalled the "furious" wind, which "arising at the same time [as the earthquake] and blowing on the fire, reduced," in the words of Father Portal, "the largest and the best part of unhappy Lisbon to the ultimate misfortune."[28]

ESCAPE FROM THE "CHAOTIC LABYRINTH"

> *With hurried steps those who have become nomads*
> *Seek refuge,*
> *Upon still quivering cadavers,*
> *They callously tread.*

—DOMINGO DOS REYS, *Poem on the Lamentable Earthquake* (1756)

Of the thousands now caught in the path of the fire, many were suffering from an array of crippling injuries: crushed legs, arms, backs, and chests, horrific bone fractures, broken necks, severed spines, gaping wounds, and grave internal hemorrhages. Some were unable to move, let alone walk or run.[29] Others with moderate to severe head trauma simply lay on the ground or wandered dazed and disoriented as the fire closed in upon them. Some sobbed uncontrollably or entreated passersby for help—while a few, resigned to their fate, sat stoically and alone on broken stones or piles of debris.

Thousands more remained entombed beneath the rubble, pinned under mountains of bricks, boards, stones, and shattered glass or imprisoned inside tiny caverns or pockets of air deep underground. Some held out hope that they would be rescued. Shouting toward the surface, they offered "great sums of money to whoever would free them," recalled a priest.[30] But as the hours passed, those expectations began to fade. "How can the sighs and the agonies of so many in the ruins who waited at any moment to give their last breath be portrayed?" asked one chronicler. "A spectacle so pitiful, a thing so disastrous, a horror so formidable, that it cannot be described, nor explained, nor depicted, only felt."[31]

As the fire closed in, temperatures under the rubble rose precipitously; and the first wisps of smoke began to reach those entombed underground through tiny cracks and openings in the ruins. The lucky ones died of smoke inhalation long before the flames arrived. Others choked to death when toxic gases produced by the fire caused their larynxes to constrict.[32]

The fire moved quickly—"many who could not escape or were trapped uninjured beneath the ruins were consumed alive," recalled a cleric.[33] "Entire families were burned alive," wrote another priest, while others, "sick or paralyzed in their beds," suffered a similar fate according to an eyewitness.[34] Hundreds who sought shelter inside churches and monasteries spared by the earthquake were incinerated when the fire ripped through those structures.[35] At the Church of São Paulo, the two-hundred-year-old wooden ceiling caught fire and collapsed on top of "thirty-two miserable souls," who were roasted where they fell. "Their cries," recalled Father Portal, "could be heard for a quarter of an hour."[36]

The horror, however, was not reserved only "for the wretched martyrs [of the fire], but for the despondent fathers, children, wives, and husbands, who failed to free the victims from their painful martyrdom," reported one cleric. "[I] heard of one father," he wrote, "who was helping [to rescue] his daughter. He watched as she was burned alive. He could not save her."[37] At the site of what had once been the Church of São Francisco, several priests heard the voice of a man buried deep beneath the rubble. Though they eagerly wished to rescue him, they were forbidden by the man himself, who explained that any attempt to dig him out would require the removal of a large stone, which would cause an arch to collapse and flatten his would-be saviors. Distraught, the Franciscans provided the man with absolution, which he had requested, and prayed for his generous soul, as he began, in the words of Father Portal, to "feel the fire beneath him."[38]

In another woeful case narrated by Mr. Braddock, a young Englishman known "for his modesty and affable behavior" was walking through the streets near the entrance to a parish church," when a large stone fell on top of him during the first earthquake tremor, breaking his legs. "In this miserable condition, he lay a good while," wrote Braddock, "in vain beseeching the terrified [passersby] to take some pity" on him. Fortunately, "a tender hearted Portuguese man, moved at his cries, gathered him up in his arms and carried him into the Church," believing this to be safer "than the open street." But at just "this instant, the second shock entirely blocked up the door" and the building caught fire; and "the lad was . . . burnt alive [along] with his generous assistant and many other poor wretches."[39]

High above the Baixa in the Carmelite Monastery, a young priest had been standing in the window of his cell conversing with a fellow cleric when suddenly the roof collapsed in the earthquake and an enormous stone fell on top of his friend, killing him instantly. Though he had escaped injury, the priest realized that he was no longer in his cell, but on a stone ledge suspended high above the rubble without any clear path of descent to the ground.[40]

Shouting down to the street below proved unsuccessful. "In all the commotion, voices disappeared in the wind," wrote Father Portal.[41] The streets were now almost empty, most of the inhabitants having fled in terror from the flame-engulfed church. And so, realizing that his life could not be saved, the young Carmelite instead resolved "to save his soul." Dropping to his knees and "raising his hands and eyes to heaven," reported Father Portal, he placed "his skull cap on his head" and offered himself up in sacrifice to God. He then "gazed directly at the fire," which "burned and consumed him alive. Like a phoenix, he will burn forever in the fire of divine love, exalting the supreme majesty of eternal glory."[42]

Others acted less heroically. "Infinite were the Numbers of poor broken-limbed Persons, who were forced to be deserted even by those who loved them best and left to the miserable Torture of being burnt alive," wrote one eyewitness.[43] "How can you find the proper terms to express the impious humanity," asked another, "with which parents abandoned their children, children their parents, brothers their siblings, husbands their wives to be buried alive [and subsequently burned] beneath buildings?"—and those trapped "beseeching [their family] in tender voices for help," but their family "deaf to their moans, responding with their escape, because they did not want to be delayed and suffer the same end."[44]

As the fire traversed the Baixa, thousands were forced to seek shelter in one of Lisbon's two main squares. In the Terreiro do Paço, many thought themselves fortunate to have reached an open expanse where they would be safe from falling debris. But by the late afternoon, even those who had retreated deep into its interior were under assault from the heat and the flames of a conflagration that had grown to gargantuan proportions. "A large number of people who made their way to the Terreiro do Paço," wrote one chronicler, "soon saw their relief" transformed into terror "as they found themselves surrounded by a fire" so intense that it "scorched the heads of some . . . [while] others lost their eyebrows and eyelashes, because everything was on fire and not just around the [peripheries of the] square, but in the middle . . . where the fire had been transported [by the wind]."[45]

"The fire increased and surrounded us," wrote another eyewitness, and when it "reached the houses on the north [side of the square], the wind blew upon us a large shower of fire like hail, and it became so hot and full of smoke that we were almost blind."[46] Some of this burning was blown over onto the Tagus. One French survivor reported that "a large number of boats, barges, and other vessels on the water were destroyed by the fire."[47] Many who had lugged their possessions to the square in the hope that its immense size and extensive river frontage would provide protection from the blaze were deceived. "Tongues of flames leaping from the houses [on the edges of the square] ignited some of the piles of possessions," wrote Father Portal, "and then, under the influence of a furious wind, set fire to the rest of them and reduced everything in the square to ash."[48]

Multiple eyewitnesses reported that the gentle breeze of the morning had, by the afternoon, grown substantially in strength. "About two hours after the shock," recalled Richard Wolfall, "the wind," which had been "perfectly calm, sprung up a fresh gale, which made the fire rage with such fury that at the end of three days all the city was reduced to cinders."[49] Father Morganti also remembered "the great wind, that all during the day and those immediately afterwards, blew"; one Frenchman wrote of "a serious wind" (un vent sérieux), while a British eyewitness reported "a strong northerly wind [that] blew from the shore" and "covered the water with dust" so that from "our boat we could scarce see one another."[50] Increasing in strength with the fire and continuing unabated for several days, this powerful breeze was, in all likelihood, part of the self-generating wind system of the firestorm and not, as some survivors believed, merely an intensification of the northwesterly wind of the morning of All Saints' Day.

In the Rossio, several hundred yards to the north, a petrified throng of around forty thousand survivors found temporary refuge from the chaos. But when "news was brought that the city was all in flames," recalled an eyewitness, "the confusion . . . may be conceived by a human heart, but not described by a human pen." From every direction came "the horrid and innumerable shrieks . . . of the people, expecting every moment to launch into eternity."[51] São Domingos (located just off the northeastern corner of the square) had been burning for several hours. Now, the giant Hospital of All the Saints (which occupied much of the square's eastern edge) was on fire. Although hospital personnel scrambled furiously to rescue patients from the blazing ruins and drag them into the square, upward of four hundred would die in their beds, many of them burned alive.[52]

As the fire grew, the great movement of people from the city to the fields (campos) outside it intensified. "The desertion of the population" from Lisbon "was almost universal," wrote Pombal, "leaving the city entirely empty. Almost all the inhabitants fled; terrified people without sense or destination, abandoning their houses and possessions."[53] They left, recalled Miguel Pedegache, "without remembering their father, their mother, their wife, their children, their houses, or their farms, all escaping without knowing where they were going, treading without fear on dead bodies and the injured."[54] One eyewitness saw survivors "trampling under foot some hundreds both of young and old." And in all the confusion, "great bodies of people . . . were suffocated; and numberless others, being blinded by the smoke, lost their way, and . . . ran headlong into the midst of the flames."[55]

The westward trek to Belém became so thronged with people that many were trampled; "many others, especially women and children, and ancient people died of the fright," recalled one survivor.[56] "As you passed along the streets, you saw shops . . . with the shopkeepers buried with them," wrote an eyewitness, "some alive crying out from under the ruins; others half buried; others with broken limbs, in vain begging for help. They were passed by crowds without the least notice, or sense of humanity."[57] One person claimed he saw "8 or 9,000 dead bodies, some upon the rubbish, others halfway up their bodies in the rubbish, standing like statues."[58]

Some tried to put as much distance as they could between themselves and the Portuguese capital. "It was not a few," recalled a priest, who "fled far from the city to farms a distance of two, three, four, and five leagues away and in some cases, ten or twelve."[59] Some "made their way by foot to the cities of Caldas, Alenquer, and Santarem"—seventy-six, thirty-nine, and seventy kilometers away, respectively—wrote one eyewitness.[60] "In all the disorder and confusion," reported a chronicler, the priests of the Carmo fled to Count Tarouca's farm at Cotovia, just outside Lisbon. But after a rumor spread that the fire was approaching a cache of gunpowder inside the São Jorge's castle, the Carmelites fled in panic to Campo Grande and Cotavia, taking with them "the venerated statue of *Our Lady of the Carmo* . . . and the Holy Eucharist," which they had managed to rescue from their fire-engulfed church.[61]

One of the most pressing concerns of Lisbon's clergy was indeed for the safety of the Holy Eucharist. "It is horrible even to recall," wrote Father António Pereira de Figueiredo, "that the sacred vessels which held the Holy Sacrament were burned in the flames or so profoundly buried in the rubble that even the most extraordinary efforts could not recover them."[62] As churches crumbled and burned, courageous priests and monks made desperate dashes into the ruins to rescue the body of Christ. Some, presumably, did not survive. If recovered, however, the Eucharist had to be preserved and stored in a safe location. "Priests from the Monastery of São Pedro de Alcântara," wrote a survivor, "journeyed almost the entire day with the Eucharist and the sacred vessels," in order to find "a safe place to keep" them, while clerics from eleven parish churches, according to one *padre*, "placed vessels containing the sacraments" over the course of the afternoon inside the largely unscathed and unthreatened Church of Santa Isabel.[63]

Adding to the terror and anxiety that day were several violent aftershocks. Earthquakes in their own right, they were the result of the continued slippage (and the subsequent release of energy) along the fault line of the original quake. "Almost every aftershock was preceded by a horrible noise which was like the rumble of thunder or the echo of an artillery piece fired underground," recalled Miguel Pedegache.[64] With each tremor, terrified survivors braced for a replay of the morning's devastating events.[65] The strongest aftershock occurred around 11 a.m., not long after the final tsunami wave had receded back into the river. Though much weaker than each of the three main tremors, it brought down many structurally damaged buildings and, one assumes, caused many deaths.[66] Moreira de Mendonça remembered that "in the twenty-four hours after the earthquake, the earth vibrated almost continuously, becoming stronger [or weaker] from hour to hour. Some in Lisbon felt it," he wrote—especially those inside buildings—while "others doubted it, believing it to be mere conjecture arising from the horror of the first earthquake."[67]

Lisbon in flames

One building that had survived the earthquake and the initial after-shocks was the Riverside Palace. "It was the fire that destroyed it," wrote Father Portal. Starting slowly and then gaining momentum with the rise of the wind, the flames overtook the fabled structure and over the span of several hours gutted its priceless contents. "The fire burned all of the galleries, halls, rooms, antechambers, and offices of the palace, with all of its rich decorations and furniture covered in gold, silver, and rich jewels of inestimable value," wrote Portal.[68]

Gone forever were all the singular and extraordinary objects collected by the kings of Portugal over the centuries. Gone, too, was the Royal Library, "the most excellent in Europe," added Portal. The pride of the late João V, and indeed all of Portugal, the entire library and its seventy thousand volumes, reams of priceless manuscripts, including many of the original travel logs of Vasco da Gama and other Portuguese explorers, rare tapestries, oil paintings, and engravings were incinerated (though a few objects may have been pilfered by thieves and subsequently lost).[69] In terms of cultural harm, the destruction of Portugal's Biblioteca dos Reis (Library of the Kings) ranks as one of the great tragedies in the history of the West and can be likened to the burning of the Ancient Library of Alexandria.[70]

Sadly, this was not the only library lost. The firestorm consumed several other remarkable book and manuscript collections, including those of "the Duke of Lafões, the Marquês de Louriçal [mentioned earlier], and the Count of Vimieiro," according to Father Figueiredo, as well as the famous ecclesiastical libraries of the Carmelites and the Oratorians. The Dominicans lost two libraries, the largest of which housed 15,188 volumes, was open to the public, and was staffed by two librarians.[71] The Oratorian library contained a comprehensive collection of Marian literature ("almost everything ever written on the Virgin Mary," in the opinion of Father Figueiredo) that had been assembled over many years by a Father Domingos Pereira and supported through the generosity of João V.[72] Also lost were the notable libraries of the Monasteries of São Francisco, the Holy Spirit, the Trinity, and the Boa Hora, as well as the extensive and much admired library of the inquisitor general, Simão Joseph Silveiro Lobo, and the entire inventories of twenty-five bookstores and the private collections of several prominent merchants.[73]

Another victim of the flames was Dom José's Casa da Ópera. Like the Riverside Palace, it had escaped significant damage in the quake—

but according to a "very credible" woman who was in the Terreiro do Paço at the time, the blaze took hold of the enormous building with such "vehemence," that feeding off the "oily frames" and other combustible objects within, it triggered an explosion similar to the discharge of "artillery" and burned swiftly to the ground. Of all the losses suffered in the disaster, few were more heartbreaking for the king.[74]

Also destroyed was the palace of the Dukes of Bragança, the irreplaceable depository of the royal family. Also still standing after the quake, it was "reduced to ashes" in the fire, reported Father Portal. "Its interior, with all of its rich furnishings, the family archive, and other things of great importance were consumed." Another victim of the flames was the palace of the Corte-Real (Royal Court), located just west of the Riverside Palace and the Royal Ship Yards along the Tagus. They were destroyed by fire in 1751 and subsequently rebuilt, but the Great Firestorm delivered the definitive coup de grâce.[75]

Over the course of the next few days, the fire would consume the churches of Santa Maria Madalena, Our Lady of the Conception, Our Lady of Martyrs, the Sacrament, São Paulo, Chagas (Wounds of Christ), Our Lady of Loreto of Italy, Our Lady of the Incarnation, Santa Justa, São Nicolau, Santa Mamede, São Batholomeu, São Jorge, and São João

The ruins of São Nicolau's Church in the Baixa

of the Square, along with each of "their parishes," reported Moreira de Mendonça.[76] It burned the churches of São Sebastião, São Julião, and the Church of the Chapter of the Conception of the Monks of the Order of Christ, as well as the chapels of the Assumption, Our Lady of Oliveira, Our Lady of the Palm, Our Lady of Victory (along with its hospital), the Ascension of the Lord, Our Lady of Amparo, Our Lady of Grace, Our Lady of Alecrim, and the Chapel of the College of Santa Catarina.[77] Perhaps "the greatest punishment for us," wrote one priest, was the destruction of the city's churches. "So profane had these houses of God become in God's eyes that he felt obligated to destroy them and, by doing so, purify them."[78]

Also destroyed by the blaze, according to Moreira de Mendonça, were "the monasteries of the Holy Trinity, Our Lady of the Carmo, São Francisco, Our Lady of the Irish Rosary, the Holy Spirit, Our Lady of the Boa Hora, Corpus Christi, Santo Domingos, Santo Eloyo [Saint Eligius], with its two majestic and ornate churches," as well as "the houses of retreat of the Castle [of São Jorge], the Converted, Santa Maria Madalena, and the Orphans of Our Lady of the Carmo of the Count São Lourenço."[79]

Lisbon's thick-walled cathedral, Santa Maria Maior, had suffered horrendous damage in the earthquake, but it was the fire that did it in, destroying "all of its chapels, offices, and interior houses," wrote Moreira de Mendonça.[80] Likewise, Dom João's Patriarchal Church would succumb to the flames, though "it had not fallen in the earthquake," according to Father Portal. Its fate was sealed when "a tongue of flame leapt from houses belonging to [the theologian and philosopher] Antonio Verney . . . [and] set it ablaze. . . . It was an incredible thing. Soon after the fire entered one part of the church, it burned completely to the ground . . . [and] consumed everything inside it . . . [reducing it] to powder and ashes. . . . All that was saved was a silver *banqueta* . . . and some candle holders." Unfortunately, "the Holy Sacrament . . . was buried and could not be saved." An urn that had contained the Patriarch's jewels "was found completely intact, however everything inside had turned to ashes." Neither "the venerated statue of the *Conception of the Lady*," nor the precious set of lapis lazuli candlesticks, which had "cost one hundred and twenty thousand cruzados, was ever found."[81]

As previously mentioned, a fire broke out on the roof of the Church of São Paulo and "destroyed what was left of the structure and everything inside it," wrote a chronicler. The only good news was that the Holy Sacrament had been saved and quickly transferred to the Church of São João Nepomuceno.[82] The fire also consumed much of what was left of the enormous complex of the Carmelites. Likewise, the ruins of the Monastery and Church of the Trinity were reduced to ashes; and many trapped beneath it "were burned alive," according to Father Portal. Among the victims was a priest found still clutching the vessel that contained the Holy Eucharist, while "another deceased cleric was found in the confessional with his right hand raised in the act of giving absolution to the dead penitent at his feet." One priestly corpse was discovered in the ruins surrounded by dead churchgoers, all clutching the cleric's robes.[83]

The church that suffered the most damage in the disaster was São Julião. One of Lisbon's oldest houses of worship, it was constructed in the Baixa at some point before 1200 but had been completely and luxuriously renovated in the sixteenth century by Dom Manuel.[84] On November 1, 1755, it experienced almost complete ruin. When the first "tremor began," wrote Father Portal, "the people fled to the church-yard," after which "the church fell and the surrounding houses collapsed and buried almost all of the people" there.[85] The fire then burned all those trapped beneath the rubble as well as "all the ornaments, wall decorations, silver, and sacred figures" of the church, though "the statue of *Our Lady of Cadeias* was saved . . . as was the church registry." It was "an extremely rich [*riquissima*]" parish church, whose "gilt silver was valued at 50,000 cruzados." Though "much silver was dug out of the rubble . . . it was all burnt."[86]

The contiguous Monastery of São Julião, run by the Venerable Community of Poor Clerics of São Julião, also suffered gravely in the blaze. Lost, according to Father Portal, were enormous quantities of "gilt silver, chalices and cruets, a cross, a censer, an incense boat, a holy water vase, a cross for the hands of the dead, . . . four silver candle hold-ers . . . and the crown worn by *Our Lady of the Conception* made of fine stones," as well as "ornate tapestries . . . [and] one parameter of gold cloth which was bordered in gold. . . . [and] worth almost ten thousand cruzados. . . . All were reduced to ashes."[87]

Also consumed were many of the homes of Portugal's nobility. In addition to the grand *palácio* of the Marquês de Louriçal, the confla-gration destroyed the palaces "of the Dukes of Bragança . . . Alofoens, Aveiro, and Cadaval; the Marquises of Valença, Marialva, Anjeja, Fronteira, and Cascais; the Counts of São-Thiago, Ribeira, Cuculim, Villa-Flor, Valadares, Aveiras, Atouguia, Vemieiro, and Alva; as well as the Viscount of Barbacena," according to Moreira de Mendonça.[88] It also devastated the riverside palace of Pombal's great nemeses: the Távora family.[89]

One bright spot was the Royal Mint (Casa de Moeda), which was saved, along with all the Brazilian gold inside it, by the heroic efforts of a single intrepid officer, Lieutenant Batholomeu de Sousa Mexia, assisted by a sergeant and three soldiers. While the rest of the infantry company assigned to guard the mint had fled in panic during the earthquake, Sousa Mexia and his men had stood their ground and, for several harrowing and eventful days, successfully defended the building from the encroaching fire and numerous assaults by thieves. For his act of bravery (which was widely reported in the foreign press), the young lieutenant was appointed captain of the king's first company by Dom José himself.[90]

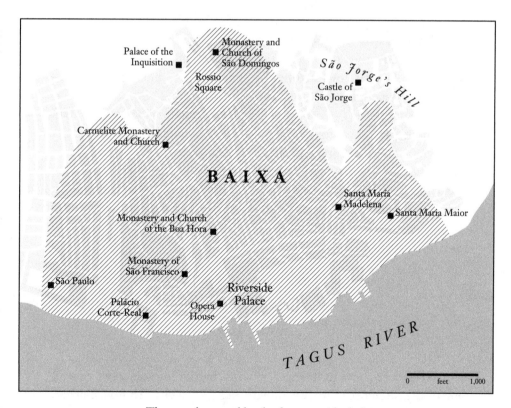

The area destroyed by the firestorm (shaded)

Also saved were much of the collection of the Royal Archive of the Tower of Tombo (Torre do Tombo) located in the tower keep of the Castle of São Jorge on São Jorge's Hill. The hero in this instance was Manoel da Maia, the indefatigable eighty-three-year-old director general of the archive and Portugal's chief military engineer. Almost immediately after the collection was buried in the collapse of the castle, Maia and his loyal staff (which included the earthquake chronicler Moreira de Mendonça) set about digging it up and carrying it to safety. Although Maia's house had been destroyed in the disaster, he focused all of his efforts on salvaging the contents of the archive and its priceless cache of agreements, contracts, royal chancellorship books, and land registry *(tombo)* records covering many centuries of Portuguese history.[91] Perhaps the most historically important set of records saved from the rubble were 82,902 documents concerning the years 1161 to 1699 from the Corpo Cronológico (Chronological Collection), which contains, among many other things, the correspondence between the viceroys of Brazil and India.[92]

Five days after the quake, Maia asked Pombal to order the construction of a wooden house with a roof in the Armaments Square of the Castle" in order to protect the salvaged collection from the elements as well as for "two sentinels" to guard it "day and night."[93] Pombal complied, congratulating Maia on his efforts and bestowing on him wide-ranging powers to carry out his plans, which included asking the inhabitants of Lisbon to bring books and documents recovered from the ruins to the new archive. Because of these actions, General Maia should not only be credited with saving the bulk of the Torre do Tombo's collection, but many precious books and documents from libraries and homes that might otherwise have been lost, stolen, or destroyed.[94]

"ONE FURNACE"

He looketh on the earth, and it trembleth:
he toucheth the hills, and they smoke.

—PSALM 104:32

Down below in the Baixa, Thomas Chase had an unobstructed view of one of the large fires that was moving across the city. And once again, he was gripped by fear. "All that afternoon, I had time to make the most melancholy reflections, whilst the flames were speeding everywhere within my view with inexpressible swiftness," he wrote. At "about five o'clock," the flames "seemed approaching close to the window where I lay." Believing escape was impossible and terrified at the prospect of being burned alive, the severely injured merchant, who, several hours before, had found shelter in the home of the Hamburg merchant Mr. Forg, crawled out of the bedroom and into the next room. "I begged with tears in my eyes," Chase wrote, "that before [Mr. Forg]" decided "to quit his house, he would either throw me over the gallery, or any other way dispatch me; and not leave me, in violent agonies, to linger out a few hours, and at last to die a most dreadful death."⁹⁵

But Forg would have none of it. "He desired me not to talk in that manner," recalled Chase, "assuring me most affectionately that he never had intended to leave me; and [that] if no other help came, he would himself carry me out upon his back, and we should take our chances together." At 11 p.m., Forg, who had been following the fire's progress from a window at the top of his house, decided that it was time to leave. Placing Chase in a chair, he covered the British merchant with a quilt, and, with the help of a servant, carried him down the stairs and out into the street, and then southward in the direction of the Terreiro do Paço, where, it was hoped, they might escape the flames.⁹⁶

With a torch-bearing servant leading the way, Chase could see all around him the devastation the earthquake had wrought, as well as the danger the firestorm now posed to the structures that remained standing. "There [from the western flank of São Jorge's Hill], I saw the middle part of the city, extending to the King's palace and . . . up the hill opposite to us, leading to the Bairro Alto, and containing a number of parishes, all in one great blaze."⁹⁷

Moving carefully down Rua das Pedras Negras (Black Rocks Street), Chase and his companions "heard some poor wretches begging for help," but continued on. "At the bottom of the alley stood a church belonging to a convent of friars." Inside the open door "there stood lighted candles upon the high altar . . . [and] the friars seemed to be very assiduously occupied, arrayed in their ecclesiastical habits, and in the porch lay some dead bodies." He could see that "the Church of St. Mary Magdalen was likewise undemolished, the doors open, and some lights and people in it." More ominously, he "observed that the fire had already taken possession of the street leading to the cathedral; [while] in the Silversmiths' Street there were no houses quite fallen, and some people seemed to be employed in throwing bundles out the windows."[98] As for the Rua Nova dos Mercadores (New Street of the Merchants), he could see plainly that "both sides of it were on fire."[99]

Upon reaching the square, Chase found a small crowd of British survivors, exhausted by the ordeal of the last few hours, sitting on small bundles of clothes and other possessions. Along the entire western side of the square lay the great Riverside Palace, which was at that time still largely intact. But like so many of the largest structures in the Baixa, it had caught fire and was now "burning slowly, the little wind driving . . . [the fire] gently onwards."[100]

Chase noted with alarm that many of the Portuguese survivors who had crowded into the massive square believed that "Judgment-Day" had arrived. "They had loaded themselves with crucifixes and saints," and then set about "harassing the dying with religious ceremonies." Whenever the earth shook, they fell to their knees and "ejaculated *Misericordia!* [Mercy!] in the most doleful accents imaginable." At this delicate moment, "when all government was at a stand" and when "it was impossible to guess what turn their furious zeal might take against that worst of criminals, a *Heretic,*" Chase feared for his personal safety and "dreaded the approach of every person."[101]

Danger seemed to be everywhere. Though the waves of the tsunami had retreated, Chase was afraid that, as he put it, "the least rising of the water would overflow us all." And no one—as he would soon learn—was safe from the flames. Though the Terreiro do Paço was immense and bounded by the Tagus along its southern border, the fire had now surrounded it on its three other sides and gave off such intense heat and blew such unrelenting showers of hot ash across it that it threatened everyone who had taken refuge there.

"Beat down the Cabanas[!]" the crowd began to yell, as the small wooden shed in which Chase had taken shelter caught fire. Somehow, he managed to drag himself out only seconds before it collapsed. After this, he was laid on some bundles belonging to a British family, of which one member suddenly pointed out in horror that "the flames were approaching the gun-powder shops" just north of the square. This "new terror" rendered Chase speechless. "We all silently awaited the event," he wrote, "which [unexpectedly] proved . . . most favorable; for though there were three explosions immediately succeeding each other with a loud report, they were not attended . . . with any mischief."[102]

Suddenly, a "poor, half-mad Irish beggar woman," who put "her trust in Saint Somebody with a strange name," recalled Chase, ran head-long into the fire on the Rua Nova dos Mercadores and then returned unscathed with a bottle of wine in her gnarled hand. Despite her dangerous labors, wrote the uncharitable Chase, "she would retrieve no gratuity at such a time as this," though he was grateful for the opportunity to partake of this "most welcome refreshment" at the end of such an extraordinary day.[103]

High above the Baixa, on São Jorge's Hill, it didn't take Reverend Goddard long to realize that the advancing fire would become "a still greater Calamity than either [the tsunami] or the Earthquake." He could see "Clouds of Smoke" beginning "to rise from several Parts" of the city. And by its size and ferocity, he immediately grasped that the "Misfortunes of the Earthquake" would be immeasurably worsened by it and that the blaze would go on to devour "the wretched Remains of Lisbon." It was, he wrote, "the only Circumstance that was wanting to complete the Destruction of that Unhappy City."[104]

Three hours after the quake had ended and the fire begun, Goddard and his small party "agreed that it was High Time to determine upon something." And so, "after much Debate and great Irresolution," they decided "to proceed to a small House about two Miles out into the Country" that was owned by an acquaintance of one of them. It would be a journey, recalled Goddard, filled with "Difficulty and no small Danger."[105]

After a short trek, they reached an olive grove, where they encountered the British consul, Edward Hay. He was, "the first Person," recalled Goddard, whom "I saw after the Earthquake that I had known before." With him was his wife, Lady Hay (née Mary Flower), who just twelve days earlier had given birth to a daughter, Margaret.[106] Her Ladyship had been in bed and had only been saved by a quick-thinking maid, who, when the earthquake began and the room began to split in two, "had scooped her up and carried her naked into the street" (along with little Margaret). There, Lady Hay had encountered her husband, who, after covering his wife with his cloak, watched their house successfully withstand the second tremor, "tho' the Walls of it were rent in a surprising Manner," he told Goddard. With Her Ladyship safe in the arms of her faithful and, apparently, muscle-bound servant, she and the consul had then traveled the half mile to their present location. "I congratulated Mr. Hay," wrote Goddard, "on his having escaped so happily with his Family, but he was still in very great Perplexity."[107]

It was here, in the company of a growing clutch of English survivors, that Goddard first learned from his brother's servants that Ambrose had survived along with his business partner Benjamin Branfil. Apparently everyone from their household had escaped from the building alive, except for the housekeeper, Mrs. Hussey, "who was so much bruised by the Fall of part of the House in the First Shock," wrote Goddard, "that she dyed within half an Hour." Although Ambrose had spent much of the morning making his business rounds in the Baixa, he had providentially returned home only five minutes before the first tremor, and in so doing had probably escaped death. After riding out the earthquake in his house, he then escaped to the British packet boat, where he remained.[108]

The greatest fear among the Britons was for Lady Hay, whose nakedness was covered by only a few cloaks that had been given to her by her husband and several acquaintances during the nearly half-mile journey to the olive grove. "It was apprehended that to remain . . . exposed to the open Air . . . might prove fatal to a Person in her condition," wrote Goddard. Because of this, the consul decided to proceed without delay to a country house belonging to Her Ladyship's uncle, "though it was [known to be] very much shattered." "Poor dear Woman!" Hay later wrote of his wife. "She is blessed with so good a Disposition, and so much Strength of mind that She has born [sic] all She has gone thro' with surprizing Spirits."[109]

Though invited to join the Hays, Goddard declined, not wishing to be "an Incumbrance." Instead, he decided to continue on with his small party, which, after much effort, traveled to a spot "some Distance from the City." Though Lisbon was obscured from sight by a hill, Goddard and his companions were "sufficiently convinced by the Clouds of Smoke which rose in great Abundance that the Fire had got to such a Height that nothing would be able to escape its Fury."[110]

Like the good Reverend Goddard and most of his fellow Oratorians, Father Portal decided it was time to flee from the city. Although his monastery (despite some damage) remained standing, the injured Portal feared that more tremors were in the offing. Most ominously, a fire had broken out on the Street of the Ovens, which was now threatening the entire *bairro*. And so, with little time to waste, Portal decided to journey to the Monastery of the Necessities (Necessidades), which was run by his order and which was located more than a mile to the west. It would not be easy. The route was strewn with rubble and corpses, and Portal was unable to walk.[111]

Yet with the help of two priests holding each of his arms, he made his way out the front door and hobbled up the steep hill toward the once stately and commanding Church of Santa Catarina. Upon his arrival there, he encountered several priests he knew, including a cousin. Wading into the terrified crowds surrounding the battered church, he gave absolution and heard confessions. But after starting off toward the Necessidades and finding every path to the west blocked, instead he decided to make for the country farm owned by his order in the outlying parish of Campolide. On the way, he encountered an old acquaintance, Father Manoel Rodriques, busily "praying," while at the Church of São Pedro d'Alcântara, he found "nothing but corpses and ruins." At the Palace of the Count of Tarouca, Portal was overcome with pain and could go no further.[112]

Taking pity on the miserable priest, several *lisboetas* hoisted him on top of a beast of burden and led him forward. Outside the Silk Factory, a violent aftershock rocked the city and people suddenly appeared from all directions, flushed out by the furious shaking of the earth. Falling on their knees before the injured Oratorian, they exhorted him to "absolve them of their sins," which he did to the best of his abilities. When he arrived at the *quinta*, he was, by his own estimation, "in a dreadful state." But he was treated with exceptional kindness and placed "with great consideration" in a chair at the base of a tree in the garden and covered with a cloak. As he rested, the Patriarch himself arrived in a *cadeirinha* (litter) after his own traumatic escape from the city, during which he had lost six or seven servants.[113] Later, Portal was carried to a makeshift shack, whose cramped conditions he found uncomfortable. After so many trials, he was anxious "to be bled."[114]

In the crowded Rossio, Charles Douglas, the Earl of Drumlanrig, had spent more than two hours, "mostly on [his] knees."[115] There, he and his faithful band of servants had survived two aftershocks. Then they saw one corner of the square catch fire. "The Crowd was so great and the Smoke so suffocating," recalled the young aristocrat, "we determined to endeavor to get over the Ruins into the Country" to the home of the British envoy, Abraham Castres, where Douglas hoped to receive "some Succor and Protection." The journey took three hours, though it was only "about a mile the common way," wrote Douglas.[116] Along the route, they were joined by the Dutch ambassador Charles de la Calmette and his large family. When they reached Castres's house, they found it had survived the earthquake (and being located on the outskirts of the city it was never menaced by the fire). But no one dared enter it (let alone sleep in it) while the tremors continued. Instead, Douglas and his party, the Dutch contingent, and several other survivors were placed in the large garden, where they "received some Refreshment and rest" and gratefully spent the remainder of the afternoon and their first evening far from the horrors of the capital.[117]

Thomas Jacomb was also in the crowded Rossio when São Domingos caught fire and began to burn. "The Smoke . . . and the Concourse of People was so great," he recalled, that many—"fearing to be suffocated"—resolved to escape. This would prove difficult, however. "The Distresses on the Road are not to be described," wrote Jacomb. "Everyone in Tears and Knowing not whether to fly or to remain and almost all the Houses on the Road having met the same fate and no one place remaining entire except the grand Aqueduct which seems to have no damage." Few *lisboetas* were seen on the road, he noted, without "an Image of our Saviour on the Cross, the Virgin Mary, St. Anthony, and . . . other wooden and brick Images which they embraced and prayed to save them." For him, the scene was reminiscent of "the burning of Troy, when the Trojans took such good care of their Household Gods."[118]

Another survivor just now arriving in the Rossio was the German merchant who had escaped death with his wife and children earlier in the Baixa. No sooner, however, had he set his half-dead spouse and the *kinder* down in the square that he felt the city jolted by "a strong shock" and witnessed the extraordinary effect it had on the thousands of survivors, each of whom, he thought, harbored the "greatest fear of death." For four hours, the Germans endured this atmosphere of angst, "until the fire broke out in every corner of the city and the Rossio was surrounded by flames; and everyone, thought they would be burned alive." After petitioning the Almighty to deliver them from this hell, they fled from the square in the direction of the open fields and, in doing so, passed over "countless dead and half-dead bodies through streets lined with fire."[119]

After witnessing the collapse of his house, the Dutch preacher Guillaume de Rochemont spent many hours in his garden pondering his next move. But as the fires grew, he decided to risk the two-mile journey with his wife, children, and maid to the home of the brother of the Dutch consul. None of the Rochements had shoes. "The whole city was a frightening spectacle," he wrote, "where one could no longer determine where the streets had been, so covered were they with rubble; and everything else was consumed by the flames."[120]

In the words of a ship captain watching the scene from the safety of the Tagus:

> The fear, the sorrow, the cries and lamentations of the poor inhabitants are inexpressible, every one begging pardon, and embracing each other; crying, forgive me, friend, brother, sister! Oh! what will become of us! neither water nor land will protect us, and the third element, fire, seems now to threaten our total destruction! as in effect it happened.[121]

At the center of the chaos was the Countess of Atouguia. "When the earthquake occurred," she wrote, "I survived by the mercy of God along with the Count, my six children, my father-in-law, my parents, and my siblings. Everything I had in my house and the house of my parents the earthquake destroyed and afterwards the fire consumed. . . . [But] I prefer the life of these people to possessions." As for "the houses, the furniture, and the silver, everything was lost, [and] we were left with only the clothes we had on our bodies. My mother did not even have that, only a shirt; and out of compassion a man covered her with his cloak at the doors of Santa Catarina, where, after escaping, she had walked by foot, for she was in her bed when the earthquake began." It was in front of Santa Catarina that the countess was reunited with her parents and her family. "It seemed," she wrote, after finding all alive, "that I had not lost anything."[122]

Ostensibly safe within his garden refuge, Filippo Acciaiuoli kept watch over the few things he was able to salvage from the ruins of his palace. Still clad in his pajamas, a borrowed cap, and some slippers, the Nuncio was unable to fashion a proper makeshift shelter for himself because all the materials he might have used were underneath the rubble. Though small tremors continued to shake the city, "a subterranean fire," he noted with alarm, had taken hold among the downed buildings in the neighborhood.[123]

This was good news for the one group who stood to benefit from the continuing disorder: thieves. After the earthquake, hundreds of criminals had escaped from Lisbon's three main prisons—the Limoeiro, the Tronco, and the Aljube—as well as most of the jails of "the court, the city, and the Castle" and the galley ships on the Tagus.[124] "All of the inmates fled," wrote a priest, "because [in the panic] their jailors . . . did the same."[125] The quake had aided their getaway by bringing down prison walls, doors, towers, and iron gates. In the Limoeiro, "it was necessary [for the jailers] to set prisoners free so that they would not be buried," recalled Father Portal.[126]

For several days, these "thieves," "ruffians," "*malvados*" (evildoers), "wicked incendiaries," and "brigands," as they were variously called, descended on Lisbon like a pack of ravening wolves, murdering, plundering, and raping their way through the burning *bairros*. They smashed into churches, palaces, monasteries, and private homes, stealing everything they could get their hands on in a frenzied (and increasingly violent) hunt for riches. In their impatience to separate people from their jewelry, they sliced off the fingers and earlobes of those they found in the ruins, regardless of whether they were living or dead.[127] They rescued nuns from the rubble, only to murder them or treat them "with great brutality," recalled one eyewitness.[128] Adding to their ranks, according to local lore, were two marginalized groups found year-round in Lisbon: Gypsies and foreign deserters.[129]

Some thieves posed as Good Samaritans—offering to help survivors move their valuables to safer locations and then brazenly carting off everything for themselves.[130] "Many families whose houses had not been ruined by the earthquake or destroyed by the fire became destitute on account of the robberies," recalled Moreira de Mendonça.[131] One band of "six or seven Catalonians proved so efficient in their looting of the contents of the Riverside Palace and the Patriarchal Church," wrote one priest, "that their ship, the *Cétya*, sank halfway into the water under the weight of their ill-gotten loot."[132] In their greed some thieves took unnecessary risks and ended up "crushed under the Ruins [of buildings] too weakened by the Earthquake to bear the least Motion," reported *The London Evening Post*.[133]

"Who could have believed," wrote Miguel Pedegache, "that there were individuals so perverted that they scorned the flames and death" to seek "a criminal fortune in the public ruin?"[134] "They were men," wrote a priest, "whose hearts more closely resembled those of beasts than rational creatures," Yet, in the end, he believed they had been guided less by their own depraved consciences than "by Providence." "God wanted us to suffer and for this purpose he made rouse against the sinners, not only the elements, but people one against the other." Not satisfied with the havoc caused by the earthquake, the tsunami, and the fire, God, in his opinion, had ordered a fourth punishment: a scourge of thieves.[135]

In order to facilitate their larceny, some "malefactors" started fires in order to flush the remaining population out of the city.[136] "I cannot conceive what could have induced them to this hellish work," wrote Mr. Braddock, "except to add to the horror and confusion, and that they might, by this means, have the better opportunity of plundering with security."[137] Although some expressed skepticism of these accounts at the time, their sheer number suggests that at least some arson did occur in the chaotic and lawless days that followed the earthquake.[138] Father Portal, for his part, believed the rumors.[139]

In a few striking cases, revenge against the regime appears to have been a motivation for the arsonists. According to one eyewitness, "a Moor" who had escaped "with the rest from the [galleys] . . . confessed, before he was hung up, that he set fire to the city in seven places," while another Moor, reported Mr. Braddock, "confessed at the gallows that he set fire to the King's Palace with his own hand; at the same time glorifying in the action, and declaring with his last breath that he hoped to have burnt all the Royal Family."[140] According to an account in *The Gentleman's Magazine*, a "French deserter confessed" that he set fire to the city "in three places" including "the India House adjoining the palace," while a Spaniard alleged that "Jews who had been in the custody of the Inquisition" along with "other incarcerated criminals set fire to the Riverside Palace, which, despite being a strong structure, was reduced to ashes and earth."[141] Admittedly, the veracity of these accounts must be weighed with caution because of the real and palpable prejudice that existed against Muslims and Jews in Iberia at the time. On the other hand, it was precisely this kind of intolerance that may have motivated individuals to commit such crimes.

CAUSES: UNNATURAL AND NATURAL

The earth, the air, and the water had been conjured up
against unhappy Lisbon and her afflicted citizens.
All that was missing was the fire to complete our ruin.

—MIGUEL PEDEGACHE

Who maketh his angels spirits; his ministers a flaming fire.

—PSALM 104:4

For many survivors, the multiple stages of the disaster were proof that they were witnessing the unfolding of the events prophesied in Revelation. "This day [November 1, 1755]," wrote a Portuguese priest, "is so similar to that which St. John describes in his Apocalypse."[142] In Revelation 8:7–10,

> The fire angel sounded, and there followed hail and fire mingled with blood, and they were cast upon the earth: and the third part of trees was burnt up, and all green grass was burnt up.

> And the second angel sounded, and as it were a great mountain burning with fire was cast into the sea: and the third part of the sea became blood. . . .

> . . . the third angel sounded, and there fell a great star from heaven, burning as if it were a lamp.

In Revelation 9:1,

> . . . the fifth angel sounded, and I saw a star fall from heaven unto the earth: and to him was given the key of the bottomless pit.

> And he opened the bottomless pit; and there arose a smoke out of the pit, as the smoke of a great furnace; and the sun and the air were darkened by reason of the smoke of the pit. . . .

Later, in Revelation 9:17–18, John writes that an army of 200 million horsemen will descend upon the earth wearing

> breastplates of fire, and of jacinth, and brimstone: and the heads of the horses *were* as the heads of the lions: and out of their mouths issued fire and smoke and brimstone.

> By these three was the third part of men killed. . . .

Echoing the biblical Apocalypse and employing a historical logic that united Aristotelian physics with Christianity, one Portuguese cleric described the fire as the final blow "from the sword of Divine Justice" in which each assault corresponded to the four "elements of earth, water, air, and fire." In much the same way, another cleric argued that the "four vices of vanity, arrogance, anger, and lust" had compelled God to deliver his "pitiful punishment" using "the four elements," in which each was matched to a different vice.[143]

Satan himself may have even played a role in the disaster. According to an elderly bachelor (a very "reliable person" in the opinion of Father Portal), "a gigantic black figure launching fire from his mouth" and "jumping from one place to another without stopping" appeared beneath the rubble "at the moment of the greatest darkness." In Portal's view, it "must have been the devil" trying to tempt the living "so that they would die impenitent and condemned [by God]."[144]

But Portal did not believe that the Devil had been responsible for the fire. Like many savants (both inside and outside the Church), he believed that the true origin of the blaze was also the principal cause of most earthquakes: underground fires. Joachim Joseph Moreira de Mendonça's brother, Veríssimo António, held this view, as did the German philosopher Immanuel Kant. Father Bento Morganti, a Portuguese priest, concurred. "Knowing that the earth is full of subterranean fire," he wrote, "it is not impossible [to believe] that through openings that form [during the earthquake] strange flames are exhaled, which taking hold of the combustible material . . . created the fire."[145] This was certainly the popular view. *The London Evening Post* informed its readers that in Lisbon "the Earth opened in divers Places, and through the Apertures, Torrents of Fire gush'd out, completing the Destruction of what the Shocks of the Earthquake had left standing."[146] And according to a German poet,

> . . . *that which had been spared from the wrath [of the earthquake and tsunami],*
> *Was transformed into horror,*
> *By fire from the earth.*[147]

But some were skeptical of such claims. Thomas Chase wrote that to the best of his knowledge "no fire came out of the ground, nor were there any openings of the earth."[148] Mr. Braddock agreed. "As to the fiery eruptions then talked of, I believe they are without foundation, though it is certain," he wrote, that "I heard several complaining of strong sulphureous smells, a dizziness in their heads, a sickness in their stomachs, and difficulty of respiration, not that I felt such symptoms myself."[149] Indeed, at the time, many believed that sulfur was one of the explosive gases that caused earthquakes. Though this connection is now known to be false, it does seem plausible that as the fire burned its way through the city it produced odors vaguely sulfurous. Interestingly, Braddock's personal observations of the disaster left him skeptical of the current state of earthquake science. "It is not to be doubted," he wrote, "that the bowels of the earth must have been excessively agitated to cause these surprising effects, but whether the shocks were owing to any sudden explosions of various minerals mixing together, or to air pent up, and struggling for vent, or to a collection of subterraneous waters forcing a passage, God only knows."[150]

Finding science inadequate to explain the Lisbon fire, many mid-eighteenth-century commentators looked to ancient precedents. Miguel Pedegache thought Lisbon was "a second Troy," the legendary city set ablaze by the Mycenaean Greeks after an epic siege around 1190 BC and later immortalized by Homer.[151] Others saw in Lisbon's fiery overthrow both the destruction of Carthage, which was razed and burned by the Romans in 146 BC, and the siege of Jerusalem (AD 70), after which the legions set fire to and destroyed the Second Temple. "Oh how I fear that the sins of Lisbon are equal to those of Jerusalem!" wrote one Portuguese writer. Like Lisbon, Jerusalem was "filled with innumerable people, respected for so many things by the entire world, known to the most barbarous nations, selected as the head of an empire established by God, where in many sumptuous and magnificent temples admiringly adorned with so many riches of the East, thousands of sacrifices, offerings, and rituals are daily repeated."[152] Both fabled for their opulence and degeneracy (as well as their piety), Jerusalem and Lisbon were now united in their destruction.

Others compared the Lisbon disaster with the Great Fire of Rome of 64 BC and the eruption of Mount Vesuvius in AD 79, which buried the Roman cities of Pompeii and Herculaneum. But to one French eyewitness, the Lisbon fire was the more awe-inspiring. "It consumed everything in front of it, all was hostage to the flames. Never did Mount Vesuvius produce a more horrible sight."[153]

Discovered only a few years earlier (in 1748 and 1738, respectively), the remains of Pompeii and Herculaneum—and their ongoing excavations—had become a continent-wide sensation in keeping with a general fascination with ruins soon to loom large in Neoclassical and Romantic aesthetics. In the late 1750s, paintings and etchings of Lisbon's devastated landscape would help propel and nurture this interest alongside images of ruined antiquity by such artists as Piranesi, Charles-Louis Clérisseau, and Robert Adam.[154]

In the popular and poetic imagination of the time, Pompeii, Herculaneum, Rome, Carthage, Jerusalem, and Troy had all been victims of their sins and excesses. For many, Lisbon's reputation for wickedness was as central to its fall as the scope and scale of the disaster itself. As a moral and human tragedy of epic proportions, the Lisbon Earthquake would (many believed) join the ranks of history's greatest catastrophes—and cautionary tales.

MISÉRIA

All the vengeance of Heaven was [directed] against Lisbon.

—AN ITALIAN IN LISBON TO A NUN IN ITALY

Throughout the first day, survivors from the city arrived in the fields. Their "clothes torn," they were "covered in dirt, filthy, bloody, bruised, mistreated and disfigured by fear," recalled a priest.[155] Some "appeared as if they had [just] been exhumed," wrote another survivor.[156] "Here, we see none but People who either stare aghast, or look down desponding; whole Minds are possessed by Fear or Grief," added an eyewitness. They "entertain each other with the most frightful Tales and the most dismal predictions. One bewails his own Misfortune, another the cruel Fate of his Friends or Relations. And they all most bitterly weep over their dear Lisbon, which from one of the most opulent Cities in the World, is become the Center of Woe and Misery."[157]

For months, they would subsist in crowded, makeshift camps that originally and spontaneously appeared in the Campo de Ourique (Ourique Field) and the Largo do Rato (Rat Square), but were later constructed in a variety of different sites outside the capital: the Campo Grande (Big Field), Campo Pequeno (Little Field), Campo do Curral (Corral Field), the Alto da Cotavia (Cotavia Heights), Chelas, Penha de França (French Cliff), Graça (Grace), São Bento (St. Benedict), Senhora da Boa Morte (Lady of the Good Death), Alcântara, Boavista (Good View), the property of the Count of Tarouca, the Campos of Santa Clara (Fields of Saint Clara), Santa Ana, São Sebastião da Pedreira (St. Sebastian of the Quarry), and Santa Izabel, as well as the Terreiro do Paço.[158]

As they arrived, the survivors glanced back at the inferno that Lisbon had now become. "Everyone," wrote Mr. Braddock, "had his eyes turned toward the flames, and stood looking on with silent grief, which was only interrupted by the cries and shrieks of women and children, calling on the Saints and angels for succor whenever the earth began to tremble."[159] One priest recalled that "all during the day, the female sex passed the hours reciting the Rosary . . . and other hymns and orations."[160]

As the day wore on, the panic of the morning was transformed into despair. "The absence of loved ones started to be felt," wrote Pedegache. "One saw the father bathed in tears looking everywhere for his child . . . the distraught daughter calling loudly for her beloved mother. The anxious, frightened woman, asking everyone she encountered about a husband. . . . One heard nothing but cries, tears, and sobbing. Those who found each other embraced and drenched each other in their tears. People congratulated one another for having escaped a seemingly inevitable death, and some cried with friends over their losses."[161] In the recollection of one priest, "those who did not know with certainty whether their wives, children, brothers, relatives, and servants were dead or alive never stopped asking people that they knew or met if they had by any chance seen" them. Some poor souls wandered "without peace or rest for days without hearing the least bit of news."[162]

Yet life went on. "Women big with Child were delivered in the open Fields, amidst the Groans and the Cries of [the] Trembling Multitudes," recalled one survivor.[163] Few had sufficient clothing, and some were "almost completely nude."[164] Fortunately, the temperature would be mercifully mild for the next few days, allowing people to sleep outdoors without too much discomfort. Autumns in Portugal are frequently colder than winters, however; and conditions would soon worsen.[165]

During the first few days or so after the disaster, food and water were scarce. The fire had destroyed the contents of most family larders; and the earthquake had done damage to the piping "that brought water to many wells and fountains."[166] "There was such a want of food," remembered Father Figueiredo, "that those who were able to eat *pão seco* [dry bread] were considered rich and fortunate."[167] Almost universally, the fire was blamed for the lack of foodstuffs and supplies. "If the fire had not happened," wrote a survivor, "people would have recovered their effects out of the ruins."[168] And "even those few effects that had the luck of escaping the first flames," recalled Mr. Braddock, "found no security in the open spaces they were carried to" because they were "either burnt" by "the sparks that fell on every side or lost in the hurry and confusion [of the] people" or "stolen by those abandoned villains, who made their doubly wicked advantage of this general calamity."[169] The situation cried out for a savior.

CHAPTER FIVE

The Hour of Pombal

*A little genius who has a mind to be a great one
in a little country is a very uneasy animal.*

— SIR BENJAMIN KEENE,
BRITISH AMBASSADOR TO PORTUGAL, DESCRIBING
POMBAL TO THE BRITISH CONSUL, ABRAHAM CASTRES (1745)

A CITY TO SAVE

Pombal's house on the Rua Formosa had suffered only negligible damage in the quake and because of its location in the northeastern reaches of the Bairro Alto was never seriously threatened by the fire.[1] Consequently, Pombal was able to escape straightaway to Belém without having to spend the day like so many others searching for shelter or extricating relatives from the rubble (though he would lose his stepfather in the ruins of the Carmo). He "left his wife and children [in the] Rua Formosa," wrote a chronicler, "mounted a stallion, and rode through streets choked with collapsed walls and the bodies of the dead."[2]

In Belém, he found the situation chaotic and the king surrounded by priests. Few high-ranking government officials were in attendance. The secretary of war, Pedro de Melo Paz Ataide, was dead, as was the king's counselor, Manoel de Vasconcellos Gajo. Both the secretary of the navy, Diogo de Mendonça, and High Court judge António da Costa Freire had fled the capital in panic, the latter to his country estate in Santarém, some forty miles away. Also absent were the chief justice and Duke of Lafões, Pedro Henrique de Bragança, who was wintering at his villa north of the city, and the prime minister, Pedro da Mota, who, though he had survived the earthquake, was not urgently expected in Belém. Aged and sickly, Mota had spent much of the previous decade bedridden in Lisbon, seeing visitors and conducting most state business only after midnight.[3]

Sensing a power vacuum, Pombal took immediate command of the situation (and one might say of Portugal itself), for it was his energy, his vision, and his sheer ruthlessness in the aftermath of the disaster that would lay the groundwork for his dictatorship—and his legend. Realizing that the path to power lay through the recovery effort, he began to give orders and shove directives into the anxious hands of courtiers and aides. Over the next two years he would dictate hundreds of these *providências* (measures), many signed in his distinctive chicken scratch scrawl. Compiled with other government edicts and decrees in *An Account of the Principal Measures Taken in the Earthquake Suffered by the Court of Lisbon in the Year 1755* (1758), they collectively tell the story of the largest national relief effort in world history to date.[4]

According to an oft-repeated story, that effort began when Dom José greeted Pombal in Belém with the simple question: "What is to be done?" "We must bury the dead and feed the living, Sire," was the secretary's succinct reply. It would become the most celebrated utterance of the disaster—though it was a myth.[5] It was the Marquês de Alorna, the elderly war hero and former Portuguese governor of India, who had spoken these words, though they would become forever attached to Pombal in the popular imagination because of his no-nonsense leadership style and his central role in the kingdom's recovery.[6] They are all illustrative of the remarkable and unprecedented transfer of power that was then taking place between the king and his hard-charging minister.

It was not that Dom José disliked being monarch. It was simply that he had developed a desire for private pleasures over public responsibilities, and the earthquake disaster had provided him with the perfect pretext to hand over the day-to-day decision making to an older, wiser steward.[7] By 1755, Pombal had become the obvious choice for the position. The brightest star in Dom José's inner circle, he had earned the king's confidence through his loyalty, unceasing drive, and uncanny ability to deal swiftly and efficiently with important matters of state. Compared with most high officials in the kingdom, he was worldly and experienced, having served as Portugal's ambassador to Great Britain from 1738 to 1745, and then as special envoy to Austria from 1745 to 1749.[8] When João V died on July 31, 1750, he was appointed secretary of state for foreign affairs and war by the new king.

From the start, Pombal's abundant talents were recognized—and as a result, his power grew. Although careful to pay the requisite deference to Prime Minster Mota, he quickly assumed most of the invalid statesman's responsibilities. Pombal "may be looked upon as the principal minister," wrote the French chargé d'affaires in Lisbon. "He is indefatigable, active, and expeditious. He has won the confidence of the King, his master, and in all political matters none [retains it] more than he."[9] The Austrian envoy agreed. "To all appearances it is . . . [Pombal] who governs with full power, to the exclusion of everyone else . . . [he] possesses alone, and, without partners, the King's confidence."[10] By 1755, Dom José and his favorite secretary had developed not only an effective working relationship, but a genuine personal bond.

But this coziness with the king drew the ire of Portugal's tiny but powerful aristocracy. They were threatened by Pombal's domestic reforms, which championed the interests of merchants and the new urban bourgeoisie at the expense of the old nobility, and they were incensed that when making appointments Pombal favored men of talent over those, like themselves, who saw government service as largely a matter of birthright.[11] But when Pombal took the audacious step of bestowing upon the merchant class the privilege of wearing a sword in public (previously a prerogative of the nobility alone), he overplayed his hand. Almost immediately, plots against him were hatched and the ranks of his enemies swelled.[12] Suddenly, the upstart minister from the lower gentry found his career imperiled by a seemingly indomitable alliance of Portugal's most ancient families. But then the earthquake came and the political landscape of the capital was transformed almost as abruptly and profoundly as Lisbon's topography.

"Recognizing the great destruction and the deplorable state of the city of Lisbon and its environs," wrote an eighteenth-century chronicler, "the King directed his Secretary of State, the *excellentissimo Senhor* Sebastião José de Carvalho e Melo, to take the necessary measures for the restoration" of the capital and instructed him to "call together some gentlemen and ministers" for a discussion of the situation.[13] The torch of political power had officially been passed.

Pombal's first order of business on November 1, 1755, was to muster together all the military forces in and around the city. He instructed the Marquês de Alegrete to join with the Marquês de Marialva (the master of the horse), the Marquês de Abrantes, and the lieutenant general of artillery "to do whatever is necessary—with troops, artillery, and matériel—to alleviate Lisbon's unhappiness."[14] This was no easy task. Hundreds of soldiers had died in the disaster, and many of those who had survived were, like the civilian population, desperately trying to escape the burning capital. There was "no order whatsoever" among the troops, recalled an eyewitness. "The majority had fled on foot and subsequently scattered to various places outside the city."[15]

Initially, only a few cavalry regiments from nearby Alcântara heeded Pombal's call. They had been in their barracks when the earthquake struck and, for this reason, had survived intact.[16] But Pombal was not to be deterred. "If you need people or money," he wrote the Marquês de Alegrete, "I have been ordered [by the king] to inform you that . . . it will be provided."[17]

Pombal realized that the most effective way to get things done was to exploit the talents and resources of the most powerful and capable people in the kingdom. By positioning himself as the king's primary advisor and mouthpiece (yet always leaving the impression that it was Dom José, and not he, who was giving the orders) and by delegating jobs to men of talent, he both achieved his goals and monopolized power. Among those at the pinnacle of the regime serving Pombal's agenda were the Duke of Lafões, who served as chief justice; the Marquês de Marialva, who was master of the horse; the Marquês de Alegrete, who was the president of the Lisbon city council; and the cardinal-patriarch.

After attempting to rally the troops, Pombal ordered the master of the horse to make sure that "every necessary measure be taken to dig up" the body of the "Ambassador of the Catholic King [of Spain]" from the ruins of his palace. After the young Racine, Count Perelada was the most notable victim of the disaster and retrieving his body was both a political and humanitarian imperative for the Crown.[18]

Although Pombal would remain at the king's side throughout much of that terrible first day, at some point he jumped back on his stallion and returned to the burning city. It is still widely believed that he spent the first week after the disaster traveling about Lisbon in his coach even though the city's rubble-strewn streets would have rendered such bulky conveyance useless.[19] He probably continued to ride his stallion or walk when necessary.

Over the months to come, Pombal would become a common sight in Lisbon: rallying the populace and shouting orders. An engraving from the period shows the secretary standing amid the ruins surrounded by a clutch of white-wigged assistants. Clad in a darkish coat and breeches, with a cocked bicorne *chapeu* on his head and the cross of the Order of Christ dangling from his neck, Pombal gestures grandly toward the horizon with his right hand, while his left hand rests on a map held

Pombal giving orders amid the ruins

open by solicitous attendants.[20] "Monsieur Carvalho . . . is the leading man," wrote Edward Hay. "Nothing is done without him."[21]

Although Pombal made frequent forays into the city during these critical days, Belém remained his home base. There, he lived out of his coach in the royal garden, consulting with the king and managing the recovery efforts far from the ongoing firestorm and the threat of falling buildings—though he must have returned from time to time to his home in the Bairro Alto to see his wife and five children.[22] The survival of Pombal's palace, the king's jester later declared, was clear proof that God had been watching over the minister. "This is no doubt true, *Senhor*," replied the Count of Oviedo, "but similar heavenly protection was also enjoyed by the residents of the Rua Suja [i.e., the prostitutes of Dirty Street]."[23]

Whether the king also received divine protection cannot be known. But contrary to a widespread impression, he was not psychologically paralyzed by the disaster and did, in fact, make several critical and timely decisions concerning the care of his subjects. While Pombal worked to save the city and the kingdom, Dom José sought to alleviate the suffering of those in his immediate vicinity—testament to both his charitable nature and the declining scope of his royal responsibilities.

"The first act of " Dom José's "piety and generosity," according to a little known account of the disaster, "was to make sure that everyone who arrived in Belém on . . . [November 1] and the next [day] would be fed." This was no small undertaking, for the number and variety of survivors—"the sick and the healthy, the small and the large, nobles and laborers"—soon became so great that Belém began to resemble "a new and opulent city." To satisfy the overwhelming demand, the king gave orders to fire up the royal kitchens.[24]

He also decreed that a building near the Tagus known as the Palace of the Farm Down Below, where young colts were trained for the court, be made available to treat and house the legions of the battered and bleeding. Here, the earliest known attempts at medical triage in history took place—whereby patients, upon their arrival, were sorted by the severity of their injuries.[25] The most critical cases, according to a chronicler, "those with fractured legs, arms, and skulls," were housed inside six horse stalls (with approximately twenty-four beds each), while those with lesser wounds—the ambulatory or the convalescent—were sent for treatment in what had once been the riding circle. About four hundred could be accommodated at any one time in the facility, though the total number cared for is not known; as soon as "some were treated, others came and took their place."²⁶

The king also ordered priests from the Monastery of Our Lady of Belém to hear confessions and offer communion to the sick and the dying, who were buried in the monastery's churchyard. During the cold of winter, the Monastery of the Patriarch São Bento provided much-needed shelter, courtesy of the king.²⁷ According to a priest, Dom José supplied those who arrived in Belém with "chickens, calves, a pharmacy, doctors, and surgeons, and everything else, so that they were not in want of anything."²⁸ He opened his private coffers, recalled Father Freire, "with a liberality equal to the tenderness and greatness of his heart." In a letter to a governor in Brazil, Pombal would praise "the heroic and unalterable constancy of the King."²⁹

Belém was not the only place receiving refugees. Over 100,000 were now gathered in the fields north and west of the capital and thousands more were arriving every hour. Except for the occasional farmhouse or hut, there was nothing to be found in the way of shelter across the vast expanse of fallow fields and evergreen shrubland. Although the earthquake's destruction was less noticeable here, "the Earth [had] opened and closed in many Places," according to one account, and some eyewitnesses "perceived the Ground flung up as if it had been done with Shovels."³⁰ Finding comfort in this alien environment proved difficult. When the sun dropped below the horizon at 5:37 p.m., survivors had little option but to wrap themselves in their coats, cloaks, cassocks, and shawls and lie down on the cold earth. "Some of the boldest, whose houses were not yet burnt, ventured home for clothes," recalled a survivor. "A blanket has now become of more value than a suit of silk."³¹

FIRST NIGHT (AND THE SECOND DAY)

That Night . . . equaled . . . the Terror of the Day.

—MR. FARMER, *Two very Circumstantial Accounts of the late dreadful Earthquake at Lisbon* (1756)

Exhausted, disheveled, famished, and grieving, Lisbon's survivors spent their first full night under the stars. Their troubles, unfortunately, did not disappear with the sun. For "as soon as it grew dark, another scene presented itself," recalled Mr. Braddock. "The whole city appeared in a blaze, which was so bright that I could easily see to read by it. It may be said without exaggeration [that] it was on fire in at least a hundred different places at once."[32] "The City [was] all in Flames," reported Mr. Farmer, "and if you happened to forget yourself by Sleep, you were awoke by the Trembling of the Earth, and [the] Howlings of the People: Yet the Moon shone, and the Stars, with unusual Brightness."[33] According to Jácome Ratton, there arose that night "the most horrible spectacle of flames, which devoured and illuminated the city as if it were day. It was not the same city. One could hear only cries, lamentations, and the chanting of prayers."[34]

"All during the evening," recalled Miguel Pedegache, "the dogs howled and the horses neighed in such a way that it created a sense of horror and a new cause for fear."[35] And "because of the repeated tremors of the earth and the smoke from the city," wrote Father Figueiredo, "no one dared sleep."[36] It was truly an appalling spectacle. The once great capital was shrouded in flame and almost completely deserted except for those still trapped beneath the ruins and those "execrable villains" who spent that night—and many afterward—rifling greedily through the rubble in search of plunder.[37] Around midnight, the crew of a ship that had departed Lisbon that morning reported seeing on the horizon "a prodigious Cloud of Smoke, which covered the whole City."[38]

"Many survivors," recalled a priest, "had promised those they had left behind [in the ruins] that they would return in the morning to dig them out."[39] But the growth of the fire during the night made this increasingly unlikely. Most despaired of ever seeing their family and friends again. In their grief and suffering, survivors felt united—"reduced to one common level," as one eyewitness put it.[40] "We lay in the Fields all Night," wrote Mr. Fowke. "I was extremely cold. I had no other Clothing but my Night-gown and Slippers; my Wife and all her Company [were] in much the same Condition. But God preserved us."[41]

In Belém, the king, queen, and four princesses passed the evening in coaches tethered to their horses, steadfastly refusing to return to their palace or any other building with a stone or plaster ceiling out of fear of a future earthquake.[42] In the coming days, Princess Maria would become "dangerously ill," according to a newspaper report, though the twenty-year-old would eventually recover.[43] Decades later, as Maria I, she would lose her sanity—possibly due to porphyria, the genetic disorder that afflicted George III of Great Britain—and be forced to relinquish power to her son, the future Dom João VI.

When the "long wished for day at last appeared," recalled a survivor, "the sun rose with great splendor on the desolated city."[44] Unfortunately, the fire had grown in both size and intensity. During the night, a strong wind (probably generated by the fire itself) spread the flames steadily across the Baixa and down the western slope of São Jorge's Hill toward the northern and eastern edges of the Terreiro do Paço, where they had trapped all those who had not already escaped. There, survivors would spend most of the day fleeing from the flames and the intense heat, beating from their clothes the burning flakes of hot ash that continually rained down upon them.

At 5 a.m., Thomas Chase perceived that the wind in the Terreiro do Paço had abruptly changed direction. "Blowing fresh, it drove the flames with the utmost rapidity down the hill from the Cathedral towards our side of the Square," he wrote. In order to save himself, he ordered several black servants to carry him to its western edge. "But so quick was the progress of the flames," he recalled, "that they presently seized the Custom-House, and [burst] out all at once with a violent heat. I attempted all I could to get away; [but] being unable to do [so], I remained scorching there, till good Mr. Forg appeared, and removed me [across the square to a place near the Riverside Palace,]" whose roof "had already fallen in." There, "the fire was so much decreased, that there seemed but little left to burn"—though Chase now feared that he would be crushed to death by the collapse of the palace walls, which were "almost all . . . still standing."[45]

Noticing that the tide had returned to normal on the Tagus and that ships had once again begun to carry away survivors, Chase and several of his party trekked to the riverbank to try to secure passage. "I found the cool air from the water very refreshing," he wrote. "But it did not last long, for in a little time it grew increasingly hot, and we soon perceived that the fire, which we imagined [we had] left so far behind us, had crept along through the low buildings by the water-side close by us." But after returning to the square, they saw that the fire had flared up there as well, fueled by "a large quantity of timber that lay upon the shore" in front of the palace. "To our great surprise," Chase wrote, the fire "blazed out afresh, though before it had seemed to be quite extinguished." Before long, "we found ourselves surrounded by a prodigious

fire, attended with such a rain of ashes from the timber by the water-
side, that, to keep them off" and to avoid "the violent heat, I was forced
to close my quilt over my face."[46]

Once again, he was relocated to the northwest corner of the square,
where there were fewer bundles and where Chase believed there was
less danger. Here, he watched as a small group of men and women
tried to escape from the square "through the ruin of the [still burning]
Riverside Palace." He saw them scramble over the "rubbish" and then
disappear. When an arch that stood in their path collapsed, a "compassionate cry" arose from the crowd. "As none of the adventurers
returned," Chase wrote, "I would hope they were successful."[47]

About an hour later—with "the fire still gaining" on them—Chase's
pathetic figure "excited the pity" of a Portuguese woman, who raised a
crucifix over his head, and with a small group of the faithful, encircled
him on their knees and began to pray "in a melancholy tone." Greatly
disturbed by the unwanted attention, Chase feigned senselessness. But
no sooner had he done this than the woman "abruptly stopped and a
dismal roar of 'Misericordia!' resounded" from the crowd, as it normally
did during and following an aftershock.[48]

But as he covered his head and braced for another tremor, Chase
felt nothing. The reason for the uproar was not a new tremor, but the
realization that the fire had "become the more threatening danger."
Across the entire expanse of the Terreiro do Paço, he witnessed "everyone kneeling down, and the great Square full of flames." Almost every
bundle and pile of personal effects that had been carried here over the
past two days was now on fire.[49] "The wind blew very fresh," Chase
wrote, "and drove the flames in sheets of fire close slanting over our
heads. Expecting them at any minute to seize upon us, I again lost all
my spirits, and abandoning myself to despair, thought it still impossible,
after so many escapes, to avoid the sort of death I so much dreaded."
But just then "the wind suddenly abated" and, as a consequence, the
fire began to burn "upright" and, at least for the time being, "made no
farther progress."[50]

During this much-wished-for respite, Mr. Forg offered Chase
a piece of bread and went off in the direction of the river—never to
return. Oddly unfazed by his abandonment, Chase later confided that
he was actually "surprised that [Forg] had not done it before." He
thought himself fortunate "that, after saving my life so many times,"

Forg "had not deserted me till the most imminent dangers were almost over. . . . I . . . wished him the utmost happiness which the warmest gratitude for my preservation could dictate."[51]

On his own now, Chase asked a British gentleman if he could join his family on one of the boats, only to receive the curt reply "that his own family was sufficient to fill any boat he was likely to get [and] therefore . . . could not pretend to offer any such thing." Forced to make his own arrangements, Chase immediately employed a black servant and ordered him to the riverbank to see if he could secure a spot on one of the ships. To his surprise, the servant returned with news of an offer of passage for eighteen shillings. Chase readily accepted and, employing another black boy, he was carried by his two porters to "a large boat, almost full of people," where he was "laid upon a board in the middle of it." But the trip ended abruptly, and when Chase complained to the boatmen that he had not been taken far enough away from the city center, he was rebuffed and put "roughly" on shore—after which, the epithets *"Hertick!"* and *"Devils!"* were hurled at him and his porters.[52]

Back on terra firma, Chase was carried by his servants almost a mile along a road "full of people, going silently along, with the most dejected countenances." Arriving at the *quinta* owned by his friend Joseph Hake, he learned from those present that Hake had lost his wife (the sister of New York governor Sir Charles Hardy) and his three children in the disaster and had probably already boarded a ship.[53] "Utterly in despair [about] what to do," Chase then caught sight of Mr. Hake, who was "astonished to hear the voice of a person whom he had been informed the previous day was either dead or dying." Calling "out in the greatest surprise," Hake "came running to me immediately." To Chase's great relief and happiness, he was received "in the most affectionate manner possible." He told Hake that he "most sincerely thanked God for lengthening out [his] days" so that he could "die under his protection!"[54]

Chase was then carried to "a sort of tent made with carpets under a vine-walk" in the garden, where beds had been placed. There, he slaked his thirst with some "strong white wine" and appeased his hunger with some bread and butter that to him were "so exquisite and refreshing that they were afraid of giving me too much." To each of his black porters, he handed eighteen shillings, which they accepted with great joy before returning to their masters. Then Mr. Hake called for "the King's farrier," who, though normally engaged with the care of horses' hooves, had achieved fame as a bonesetter. Examining Chase, he and "a sort of barber-surgeon" found, besides many bruises, only a single broken bone in his arm, which they set. "If a fever could be kept off," the farrier told Chase, he would "do very well again." Unfortunately, they had overlooked his dislocated shoulder, which during the night gave him such excruciating pain "that it almost took away [my] breath," he recalled. After "a numbing coldness" overtook his arm, Chase thought that he "had only a few moments to survive." But Mr. Hake and his son—most of the family had in fact survived—awoke and nursed him safely through the long night. In the morning, Chase was bled five times, which "relieved [him] greatly."[55]

Throughout the day, rumors of various kinds abounded. One particularly vile one (alleged to have been started by thieves) was that soldiers stationed on São Jorge's Hill were about to launch an artillery barrage on several of Lisbon's neighborhoods in an attempt to halt the progress of the fire by leveling buildings in its path. Completely unfounded, the story nevertheless caused many to flee even farther out into the fields, in some cases, a "distance of three or four leagues [about one mile]," reported a priest.[56] There were, however, those braver souls who chose to venture in the opposite direction, defying the terrors of the city in order to recover a small portion of their property or attempt to rescue family members and friends. Many found their houses burned to the ground or ransacked. Others perished when the walls of their homes collapsed on top of them.[57]

When Monsignor Acciaiuoli saw that the fire was approaching the ruins of his palace, on November 2, he realized it was time to flee. The previous night he had watched anxiously from his garden as flames consumed all the houses surrounding his. And so, clad in only his pajamas, the nuncio set off through the ruins with his surviving servants. After several hours, he arrived at a rural monastery, where he was sheltered in a tent made of rugs and wooden planks. There he sat, exhausted but safe, providing absolution, communion, and indulgences to those who sought them. Others just wanted to kiss his hand.[58]

From his servants, the nuncio learned that the body of his secretary had been recovered from the rubble, along with some of the monsignor's clothes.[59] Discovering a small piece of paper (which had become an extremely rare commodity in Lisbon), he wrote a letter to one of his brothers in Rome, which he addressed "from the desolate place that last Friday was Lisbon" (Dalla desolata terra ove fu venerdì scorso Lisbona).[60]

The phrase alluded to the well-known lines in Virgil's *Aeneid* (3.8–12), in which Aeneas recounts how he left Troy after its sack at the end of the Trojan War. It received much attention at the time in the European press and bound both tragedies together—the ancient one and the modern—in the popular imagination.

> Weeping, I leave behind the shores and harbors of my country, and the fields where Troy [once] was. I am carried as an exile into the deep sea with my companions, my child, and the great household gods.

Recounting his own exodus from Lisbon, Acciaiuoli fretted that the fire was now approaching the crumbled remains of his palace. "I am filled with confusion and pain," he ended his letter. "*Addio.*"[61]

At some point during the day, Pombal ordered the now recovered body of Ambassador Perelada to be "carried with every magnificence to the Monastery of São Bento where," according to Father Figueiredo, it would be given burial.[62] At approximately 8:30 that evening, November 2, in an armchair in the Hofburg Palace in Vienna, the Empress Maria Theresa gave birth to her fifteenth child, the Princess Maria Antonia Josepha, the future monarch Marie Antoinette of France.

MEASURES TAKEN

It appeared for some days like a Place without either King or Laws.

—*The Whitehall Evening Post,* LETTER DATED NOVEMBER 18, 1755

We have profited from measures so timely and so well-proportioned to our great calamity.

—POMBAL, IN A LETTER TO GOMES FREIRE DE ANDRADE, GOVERNOR OF RIO DE JANEIRO, MINAS GERAIS, AND SÃO PAULO, APRIL 14, 1756

On November 2, Pombal ordered all available troops to the burning capital without delay. "His Majesty so commands that as soon as this notice is received that the Regiment of Dragoons at Évora [sixty-seven miles to the east] will march with haste to Lisbon, where it can assist the urgent need of the court."[63] The dragoons were specifically instructed to bring "as many wooden huts that could be carried on the backs of pack animals and porters."[64] Worsening conditions in the fields outside the city had spurred Pombal's action. He likewise ordered regiments to Lisbon from the nearby regions of Alentejo and Beira as well as the cities of Cascais, Peniche, and Setúbal.[65] "In the event that those cities have experienced the same amount of damage [as Lisbon] then only send half of each regiment," Pombal added.[66] By flooding the capital with troops, he hoped to restore order as quickly as possible and, in doing so, relieve Lisbon's priests and monks, who had been actively defending the city's churches, monasteries, and private homes for more than twenty-four hours, but were now becoming overwhelmed.

Before the regiments arrived, however, some of the king's soldiers—many of them foreign deserters—"mutinied and joined the Mob," reported an eyewitness.[67] "Instead of assisting the people," they "turned plunderers," recalled Mr. Chase. "Even adding . . . to those fires, which already were dreadfully numerous from the fallen houses."[68] Although shocking, incidents like these were far from uncommon in early modern Europe. After a fire broke out in the French city of Rennes in 1720, a regiment from the province of Auvergne ignored orders to protect the populace and went on a riotous spree of pillaging and arson.[69]

Pombal's greatest fear in these early days was that decomposing corpses would "infect the air" and trigger an outbreak of contagious disease—possibly even the plague (peste in Portuguese). It might "produce another calamity," he wrote, "equal to the one that through the mercy of God appears to have been suspended."[70] Before the development of the germ theory of disease in the nineteenth century, little was known about the cause of epidemics. It was widely believed at the time that decomposing organic matter spread disease through the air. For this reason, on November 2, Pombal directed the chief justice to appoint ministers in each of the city's twelve neighborhoods to oversee the collection and burial of dead bodies.[71] "Signs are to be posted," ordered Pombal, "inviting all people and priests in their respective neighborhoods to work together in the spirit of Christian piety or in the service of those [dead] relatives, friends, and property covered in the rubble." "No one," he added, "should be given an exemption."[72]

On the same day, Pombal ordered that "barges or large ships be made available so that they could be filled with bodies and [then], after the necessary Christian pieties, carry the bodies many leagues past the sandbar at the mouth of the Tagus, where they could be thrown into the sea with weights."[73] One large ship, according to an eyewitness, "was ordered to be filled with as many corpses as it could hold, and then sunk on the high seas."[74]

So that large numbers of corpses could be buried at one time (either at sea or in large mass graves on land) Pombal asked the patriarch (and he agreed, in a rare act of doctrinal flexibility) to waive the normal church custom of providing an individual burial for each Christian.[75] Several days later, Pombal directed the public registrar, Nicolau Luís da Silva, and a former magistrate, António Rodrigues de Leão, "to cooperate with the religious estates and the nobility in the merciful and indispensable work of burying the dead" and encouraged both men to prosecute and imprison anyone who turned their backs on their "urgent obligations." Such work, in the opinion of Father Freire, was both "Christian and heroic."[76] But much of it would have to wait until the firestorm had burned itself out.

Not every human body pulled from the ruins had experienced decomposition (or it was so reported). In the Church of the Holy Sacrament, where "seventy-two people of both sexes perished in the ruins," the body of a priest, Sebastião de Carvalho, was found, according to church records, in perfect condition eighteen months later, his body completely "without corruption, his clerical garb having suffered no damage whatsoever."[77]

Nor was every excavated body deceased. According to Father Figueiredo, several people were found alive in the rubble "after four days, others after six, and some after nine."[78] In the ruins of the Hospital of All the Saints, two mental patients—one the brother of the city's religious prosecutor, the other a former colonel and military engineer from nearby Alentejo—were heard groaning under the rubble five days after the disaster. During the forty-eight hours it took to dig them out, they were sent water and broth through a pipe that was snaked down to them—though, after being freed and given absolution, the engineer promptly died.[79]

Two days later, Dr. Manoel Madeira de Sousa (the manager of the Hospital of All the Saints) rushed to the Street of the Pipes, where he and a group of medics extricated a fourteen-year-old girl who was found completely uninjured and, it was said, clutching a statuette of Santo António. She had not eaten for nine days and had been lying, according to Father Figueiredo, "in the midst of cadavers."[80]

In Setúbal, some stories of survival were deemed so unbelievable they had to be authenticated by public notaries.[81] In the ruins of one house, a woman and the infant girl she was cradling were recovered alive "without a single injury," while another woman was found after three days under the earth locked in the arms of her dead lover. When one famished five-year-old boy was pulled from the rubble asking for bread, he was handed a chestnut instead and "ran off jumping for joy."[82]

Among those who first greeted the rescued girl with the Santo António statuette was one of the undisputed heroes of the earthquake disaster, Monsignor Sampaio. Counselor to the king and prelate of the now destroyed Patriarchal Church, this brave man not only "helped to dig out many citizens alive from the rubble, he also, according to Father Figueiredo, "buried 240 people with his bare hands."[83] Another hero was Dom João de Bragança. The cousin of Dom José and brother of the Duke of Lafões, "he crossed the city many times on foot," recalled Father Figueiredo, "one hour burying people; another hour digging out survivors from the ruins." For this and other acts of devotion, "he won for himself immortal glory."[84]

Before long, damage reports began to arrive from across the kingdom. Most areas inland and north of the capital had suffered relatively little. Though the cities of Porto and Évora had been shaken, they were still standing. Along the coasts of southern Portugal (as has been mentioned), the situation was very different. Entire villages had been leveled and, in some cases, dragged into the sea. In the Algarve, the situation was particularly grim. Closer to the epicenter than Lisbon, it had been rocked by powerful tremors before taking the full brunt of the tsunami. Only because of its sparse population was it spared the horrendous death tolls seen at Lisbon and on the Moroccan coast.[85] At once, Pombal realized the south's vulnerability and ordered the Marquês de Tancros to march five companies of cavalry to those coastal regions "which," wrote Pombal, "find themselves exposed to Moorish invasion because of the destruction of their forts and [the deaths of] . . . their inhabitants."[86]

Fortunately, the Algarve had a man as capable and determined as Lourenço de Santa Maria in charge. Born in Faro to an aristocratic family in 1704, Santa Maria was ordained a Franciscan priest in 1730 and made archbishop of Goa thirteen years later. But in the heat of the subcontinent his health declined and in 1752 he returned to Portugal. When the earthquake struck, he had been archbishop and provincial superintendent of the Algarve for almost three years. "There were so many extraordinary things taking place on that memorable day," he later wrote of November 1, 1755, "that there is only room for admiration."[87]

Like Pombal, Santa Maria seemed to draw energy and strength from the chaos swirling around him. He immediately ran to Faro's damaged hospital in an attempt to rescue as many patients as he could—relocating the survivors to a new hospital constructed of boards and financed entirely by him. As head of the provincial military and secular administration, he ordered the army to dig up bodies from the ruins and burn them on the beaches to prevent contagion. He distributed food and medicine and rebuilt mills and ovens destroyed in the quake. He expelled vagabonds and set prices and salaries across the region to their "just value." He organized religious processions and publicly begged the Mother of Mercy for her help and protection. He even attempted to embolden fishermen, who had abandoned their nets for fear of the sea—exhorting them to return to their livelihood. "I clothed the naked," he wrote in an accounting of his actions that was sent to Rome.

> I gave drink to those who were thirsty; I visited the sick; I liberated the oppressed; I offered dowries to virgins; I protected widows and wives; I received the meek and the poor. At a time of such danger, I did everything for everyone, as a communal father, never sparing work or goods, never resting my body or my senses; I helped and embraced everyone with feelings of charity.[88]

In 1773, Pombal divided the Algarve into two bishoprics and sent the independent, popular (and therefore dangerous) Santa Maria into exile.[89]

In Lisbon, as in the Algarve, fear of an attack by pirates—or perhaps even a foreign power—was widespread.[90] On November 3, the court was informed that several "Algerians" in a small boat had tried to cut the cable of a ship anchored behind the Tower of Belém. Worried that after "seeing the destruction in Cascais and . . . other places," these pirates (*corsários*) might launch a full-scale attack upon the capital, Pombal ordered a corps of cavalry and other troops to secure the riverbank from Belém to Bom Sucesso. He had sentinels posted on every beach and prohibited ships from disembarking at night.[91] According to Father Figueiredo, those in charge of the forts and towers along the river were commanded to prohibit "the entry and exit of every ship that did not have a passport signed by the hand of General Rodrigo António de Noronha." Pombal then ordered Noronha "to explore the river with [his] soldiers and carefully inspect and observe every ship and every sailor" on it.[92]

On November 3, Dom José left Belém to survey the damage to the capital on horseback. According to the Prussian ambassador, Hermann Braamcamp, the king toured the outskirts of the capital, gave orders, and comforted his subjects with His Royal Presence. What he saw would not have been very reassuring, for "the city of Lisbon," wrote Braamcamp, "will in three or four days be ruined forever by the fire. . . . One hopes that God will protect us from famine or any other plagues that the disaster has brought with it."[93]

Herr Braamcamp and his family were now living "in the open air," not far from his "substantially destroyed country house" three miles from the city. "I am at a loss," he informed Frederick the Great, "how to feed the more than hundred people who have taken refuge with me." Lacking proper clothing, he had not yet made an appearance at court—though he hoped "to pay his respects to their Majesties in two or three days."[94]

On November 3, Thomas Chase was treated by the official surgeon of the British Factory, Mr. Scafton, who over the previous two days had been, in his words, "almost pulled to pieces" by people seeking medical attention. Indeed, Chase and his hosts, the Hakes, felt increasingly imperiled by the throngs of starving people just outside the estate walls clamoring for bread and "threatening continually to break in upon us."[95] According to one survivor, "the poor go around like hungry wolves, and there is no doubt, that in a few days they will use violence to search for their food, and will kill friend or foe for a piece of bread."[96]

Throughout the day, according to Chase, there circulated "reports of robberies and murders which were committed all around." When the British community urged Mr. Hake to leave Lisbon immediately by ship for "his own protection," Chase was initially overtaken by despair at the possibility of losing another guardian. "I knew not where to form another hope!" he wrote. But then, to his great relief, he overheard Mr. Hake tell a ship captain that he would not leave Portugal without his family and Mr. Chase, "who he could not abandon in so distressful a condition."[97]

When the provincial troops finally arrived later in the week, Pombal ordered them to surround the city and then, "at the same hour" and in one coordinated movement, sweep through the *bairros* and "apprehend all the malefactors and vagrants."[98] Likewise, he posted soldiers to the city gates with instructions to search people for stolen goods. In effect, Pombal had taken control of Portugal's armed forces and was now in a position to exert his will over the entire kingdom. It was the single most important step toward the creation of a Pombaline military state.

To deal with those taken prisoner, the king, according to a chronicler, "ordered the *excellentissimo* Chief Justice [and Duke of Lafões] to return with all haste from his *quinta* in Alpriate." Upon his arrival, the duke instructed "every magistrate" within a radius of twenty-eight miles of Lisbon "that if they found someone running away from the city they should be quickly examined, and if there was some suspicion of a crime, to detain them and send them back" to the capital to be tried in one of the numerous open-air courts being set up around the city.[99]

The duke erected his headquarters in Santa Isabela's Field, "where he quickly made contact with the relevant ministers and the clerks," reported an eyewitness, and provided "them with the necessary orders for the good administration of justice." There, he worked with his assistants "all day and a part of some nights, sitting on stones that were [now being] used in church services in the newly created suburban parishes." For hours on end, "they asked questions of the accused and summarily sentenced them according to the proof that they found." The duke toiled "without peace and without domicile, only resting for a short period at night in a hut constructed of sheets."[100] In the interest of efficiency, there were no written records. And "all sentences" were carried out "on the same day that they were given" by order of the Crown.[101] Most were uncompromisingly severe.

Those condemned to death were strung up and hanged on scaffolds hastily constructed at eleven sites throughout the city, including "the Cross of Buenos Aires, Boa Vista, the residence of the Count of Tarouca, the Rossio, Corral Field, and the Cross of the Four Paths."[102] To instill the necessary "terror" in the populace and thereby suppress lawlessness, Pombal ordered that scaffolds be built "as high as possible" on elevated ground and that the bodies be left there for a sufficient time so that they would begin "to decay in the elements." Such "a just and indispensable punishment" would, he believed, serve as an example (and a warning) to the people.[103]

Within a few days, "thirty-four people were hanged," reported

Father Figueiredo, "including eleven Portuguese, ten Castilians, five Irish, three Savoyards, two Frenchmen, one Pole, a Fleming, and a Moor."[104] "Several villains have been apprehended and executed," wrote a British observer, "mostly foreigners, and to our reproach among other nations some *English* sailors for robbing and plundering the palace and king's chapel [the Patriarchal Church] . . . of a great deal of rich plate. The others were *French* and *Spanish* deserters, and some from the common prisons, which, in the general havoc . . . let forth their contents [i.e., prisoners] in common with other edifices."[105] Those who were found guilty of lesser crimes were sent to prison, "where they were put to work and later occupied themselves with cleaning the rubble from the principal streets of the city." Joining them in their work were numerous Portuguese soldiers, who, by special order of the king, earned "four *vinténs* and frequently a *tostão* in addition to their military salary," according to a priest.[106]

To apprehend criminals working from ships along the Tagus, Pombal commanded the navy to stop all vessels entering or leaving the sandbar at the mouth of the river "under penalty of death."[107] Ships were searched for stolen goods by "armed sloops" and "small sailboats" manned by government officials or even the lord high admiral *(almeirante mor)* himself.[108] If loot was found, it was ordered to be returned to its rightful owners—though, under the circumstances, this was rarely possible.[109]

None of the thieving ships was more infamous than the *Cétya*, the tiny vessel (mentioned in chapter 4) that appeared so overloaded with cargo that it became the object of wonder, astonishment, and suspicion, as it was known to have previously unloaded its cargo of wheat.[110] On inspection, it was found to be stuffed to the gills with "silver and other precious objects" taken from the Patriarchal Church and the Treasury of the Riverside Palace. The entire Catalonian crew, including the captain, was immediately arrested and—"except for one boy who escaped with a more moderate punishment" because of his age—sentenced to death by the chief justice in Santa Isabela's Field.[111]

To deter such acts, Pombal posted soldiers at every site in the city that still housed gold, silver, and precious gems.[112] He ordered that the safe at the Jesuit Church of São Roque, which held money for orphans, be retrieved and sent guards to secure Lisbon's Public Depository.[113] Much later, after the fires had burned themselves out, soldiers and prisoners dug in the ruins of the Treasury, the Patriarchal Church, the Cathedral of Santa Maria Maior, and other prominent buildings. All money and valuables recovered, though much of them disfigured beyond recognition, were to be placed in a guarded "depository," where anyone with sufficient proof of ownership could come and make their claim.[114] With so many dead, however, the total value of unclaimed property would, according to Father Portal, "exceed three million [cruzados]."[115]

FIREFIGHTING

Tears were useless because of the lack of spirit and means to stop the fire.

—FATHER FRANCISCO JOSÉ FREIRE, *An Account of the Principal Measures Taken in the Earthquake Suffered by the Court of Lisbon in the Year 1755* (1758)

Despite the full-scale mobilization of troops, only a few serious attempts at extinguishing the great fire were made. On November 3, Pombal ordered the Marquês de Marialva to remove piles of coal and firewood from the Santarém Docks and "other places along the riverbank" because they were fueling the blaze (and presumably endangering shipping), after which he instructed the chief justice to prevent the fire from overtaking the Customs House of Tobacco.[116]

Two days later, Pombal commanded that all court and government officials enter the city and begin "to rip out the woodwork, roofs, and wood from houses in order to stop the progress of the fire."[117] To this end, "the Chief Justice" and the military engineer "Colonel [Carlos] Mardel," along with "several military people and some experts from the shipyards," conferred in the burning capital.[118] But apparently little was accomplished. The government was simply too busy trying to restore order to attempt to grapple with such a massive and unpredictable force of nature. "Fires broke out in several parts of the ruins," recalled Englishman E. Turnville, "and there [was] no capability of extinguishing them, the streets being . . . impassable by the rubbish of the fallen houses and the general panick that . . . hindered the Portuguese from giving the assistance that they might."[119]

Even under normal circumstances, the city's firefighting capabilities were limited. Narrow, crooked streets and steep hills, a lack of water, poor sanitation, and an abundance of wood-framed structures rendered Lisbon unusually vulnerable.[120] Now the streets were clogged with fallen masonry, broken carriages, and rotting bodies.

Like most European cities, Lisbon had taken measures over its history to reduce the peril. In 1395, the Senate decreed that town criers be dispatched each night in every parish to remind the populace to put out their candles and chimney fires. In the fourteenth and fifteenth centuries, when a fire did occur, all of the city's carpenters were expected to rush to the scene with their axes to help contain it through demolition or the creation of firebreaks. Likewise, "all women" were mandated by local laws to bring "pitchers and pots" of water, a rare civic duty for the normally homebound other sex.[121]

In 1681, the Senate authorized the purchase of leather buckets, axes, hoes, pickaxes, and primitive hoses from Holland, where the best firefighting equipment was made, and funds were to be distributed to neighborhood crews.[122] Unfortunately, the reforms proved inadequate. Organization was lacking, the equipment was poorly maintained, and the shortage of water continued. And the cutting-edge mobile water pumps purchased from Holland in 1683 were of little use on Lisbon's narrow streets and steep inclines.[123]

In 1734, four state-of-the-art pump tanks were purchased in England to great public acclaim (the term "firefighter," *bombeiro*, which is derived from the word "pump," *bomba*, first came into use in Portugal during this period).[124] In 1750, after a large fire completely destroyed the Royal Hospital of All the Saints in the Rossio, Pombal bowed to popular demand that the water pumps be placed in the supposedly more responsible hands of local magistrates.[125] Proper fire brigades first came into being in the first half of the nineteenth century, but even had they existed in 1755, it seems highly unlikely that they would have made a significant difference, assuming they and their equipment even survived.

BREAD, BEANS, MEAT, AND *BACALHAU*

The King orders that all boats and ships bringing bread, beans, rice, butter, flour, dried fish, fresh fish, and provisions will anchor and land in the area from the bridge of the India House to the Stone Docks.

—POMBAL, NOVEMBER 4, 1755

Another pressing concern for Pombal was how to feed and care for the more than 150,000 survivors who had fled their homes with little more than the clothes on their backs. For all intents and purposes, the economy had collapsed, and Pombal saw it as his responsibility to ensure that food and supplies reached those in the fields as well as those who remained in their homes on the outskirts of the capital. So that the populace had enough fresh water, he had the rubble cleared from the city's aqueduct along the Rua dos Canos (Pipes Street).[126] And because the city's private granaries had burned in the fire, he commanded the nobility from the surrounding regions to gather as much bread and every bit of grain that they could spare for shipment to Lisbon. Several aristocrats—including his brother, Monsignor Paulo de Carvalho e Mendonça—were dispatched to the cities of Villa Nova, Alenquer, Mafra, Torres Vedras, Cascais, Cintra, and Oeiras to purchase wheat.[127]

Pombal then commanded the president of the Senate and various ministers to intercept foodstuffs at the city gates and distribute them "to the twelve *bairros* in ratios that corresponded to the size and needs of the populations of those areas."[128] To maintain order while the food was being handed out, reported Father Figueiredo, Pombal sent a company of soldiers ("armed and ready") to the Rossio.[129] He also directed that bakers be put to work in the city's still functioning ovens "with the flour that can be found."[130] "And orders were given to set all the mills at work," recalled an eyewitness."[131]

Fortunately, the public grain silos outside Lisbon had survived, and despite considerable hunger and distress during the first three days of November, the much feared famine never materialized.[132] "Great care [has been] taken about Provisions and as it has been a plentiful Year there [are] no prospects of Want in this particular," reported Edward Hay reported to Whitehall. "Besides, the number of inhabitants . . . [is] much lessened either by death or Flight."[133] Still, the British merchant community donated substantial quantities of grain, flour, and rice to the needy—evidence, according to the editors of *The Whitehall Evening Post*, not only of a "Humane Disposition," but "Proof of great Prudence . . . for amidst an unhoused and distracted People there was no Security for Property of that Kind."[134]

One commodity that was in extremely short supply was sugar. Much of the city's supply had gone up in flames in the Customs House. And according to Father Portal, there were only two thousand boxes of it left in the entire city. This caused the price of sugar to rise precipitously—one arrátel (about sixteen ounces) sold for eight vinténs, or several times the normal price.[135]

On November 3 and 4, the Crown "ordered meat carts accompanied by guards to distribute meat to everyone in the fields," recalled an eyewitness.[136] "Butcheries were ordered to be opened and bullocks and sheep [were] sent from all parts of the kingdom," wrote a ship captain.[137] And "to prevent disorder" on the beaches in front of the Terreiro do Paço, where bread and other foodstuffs were sold, Pombal instructed the master of the horse to send two patrols of troops.[138] To discourage hoarding, "ships were stopped" and "a strict search was made and captains were forced to swear "that they had received no goods but [those] which belonged to the merchant or [the] owners," according to one ship captain.[139]

In early November it had "come to attention of the King," according to Pombal, "that bakers, shopkeepers, craftsmen, and businessmen were impiously abusing the disaster . . . by charging exorbitant prices for indispensable goods and services," and in doing so were "acting against the Law of God and the King and . . . of the Providence that the Lord has imposed." On November 10, Pombal ordered the Marquês de Alegrete to post signs and placards in every *bairro* announcing price controls on all goods, including food. They would henceforth be fixed at pre-earthquake (that is, October 1755) levels.[140] On the other hand, imported goods would be admitted tax free until the end of the month—"even fish, which before paid a high duty," recalled a ship captain.[141] Price gougers were put to work clearing rubble.[142]

While eliminating duties on imports undoubtedly helped Lisbon's inhabitants by increasing the supply, price fixing on domestic goods would have had the opposite effect—as would be seen later during the French Revolution when attempts to fix prices in the face of rampant inflation led to severe shortages and economic chaos throughout France. "As soon as we fixed the price of wheat and rye," officials from the French département of the Nord reported in 1793, "we saw no more of those grains."[143] By keeping prices artificially low, Pombal was in effect discouraging vendors from assuming the substantial risks of transporting their wares into a disaster zone.[144] It was a situation that called out for market forces such as Adam Smith would discuss in *The Wealth of Nations* (1776). Put succinctly, if prices had simply been allowed to adjust naturally, *lisboetas* would have been rewarded with greater supplies.

Apparently, many in Lisbon understood this—for within weeks
of the disaster, the Senate voted to modify Pombal's decree and allow
prices to rise "on cod and butter." (Some French towns would react
in the same way to Jacobin price fixing.)[145] But Pombal was livid and
reminded the Senate in a strongly worded rebuke that they "could
not interpret or change royal decrees."[146] The prices of October 1755
would remain in effect—at least officially. Fortunately, this suppression of supply was at least partially mitigated by the bountiful harvest
of the previous year as well as the willingness of the Crown to expend
considerable national resources on food aid and other supplies. As the
higher price of sugar (noted earlier) suggests, a black market existed in
Lisbon, presumably providing many of the goods and services that the
government and other suppliers could not.

Normally, an instantaneous boost to Lisbon's economy would have
come with the arrival of one of the large trading fleets from Bahia,
Pernambuco, Rio de Janeiro, and Maranhão. Unfortunately, they had
unloaded their cargos in Lisbon just a few days before the disaster.
Consequently, it would be many weeks before they could set sail again
for South America, this time with orders to return with extra quantities
of sugar and other essentials.[147] In Brazil, rumors that Lisbon had been
completely destroyed initially made traders reluctant to risk sending
their gold and other merchandise to Portugal. One ship from Rio de
Janeiro, *Our Lady of the Conception*, arrived in May 1756 with few goods
to speak of, and another brought only 400,000 cruzados' worth of merchandise to Porto and a paltry 2.2 million cruzados for Dom José.[148]

It was not until August 18, 1756, that the first Brazilian trading
fleet since the disaster arrived at Lisbon. It came from Pernambuco and
consisted of fifteen ships and a man-of-war and was laden with 4,000
chests of sugar, 110,000 hides and half hides, and 600,000 cruzados in
gold.[149] On the same day, a ship from Bengal and India's Coromandel
Coast arrived carrying silk, ivory, beds, sheets, pepper, and rice. And
several weeks later, the first cargo from China was unloaded.[150] Only
in the winter and spring of 1756–1757, however, did the Brazil fleets
begin to land at Lisbon with some regularity.[151]

A much more immediate problem for the Crown than reviving the
economy was caring for the thousands of critically wounded survivors
who lay about the fields and the city, like the hundreds of patients from
the Hospital of All the Saints still littering the Rossio. The ratio of
doctors to patients was shockingly low, and even if one was lucky

enough to be seen by a physician, treatment options were limited. Most doctors and barber-surgeons, and some farriers, could set broken bones and apply simple compresses to wounds, but none could have performed any but the simplest of surgeries. In an age before antibiotics, the majority of open-wound injuries were difficult to treat. Even relatively minor cuts and lacerations were potentially fatal. Both gangrene and tetanus must have been widespread.

Most medical care and humanitarian aid was in fact provided not by doctors but by Lisbon's priests, monks, and nuns. Although modern historians have criticized Portuguese society for subsidizing such large numbers of clerics, it cannot be denied that they saved thousands of lives in the aftermath of the disaster and were probably more responsible for the success of the recovery efforts than agents of the Crown. As the firestorm swept across the capital, many stayed at their posts. With no children or spouses to care for, they could apply themselves without hesitation to the aid of others: tending to the sick, rescuing people and property, and hearing confessions (which now all men who had taken holy orders could do, by order of the patriarch).[152] To care for the infants and children who were being abandoned by their parents and guardians in appalling numbers, they set up an orphanage called Nossa Senhora da Lapa.[153]

One priest even presided over the hastily prepared nuptials in Belém of Agnes Surriage and Sir Henry Frankland, who had made good on his vow to marry his savior. "I hope," the baronet confided to his diary, that "my providential Escape [from the ruins] will have a lasting good Effect upon my mind," for "National Calamities . . . proceed from the hand of God and . . . are designed by divine Power as Warnings, to teach the inhabitants of the World Righteousness." (A Protestant ceremony was later performed aboard a Britain-bound ship.)[154]

One continuing problem on the minds of every *lisboeta* was the multitudes of formerly cloistered monks and nuns still without domicile and forced, for the first time, to witness life at its most desperate and degrading. "A considerable number of the Wives of Christ," wrote Father Freire, "walked around experiencing the same disgraces as the people." It was nothing short of a "public scandal."[155]

To calm the gathering furor over this, Pombal urged these pious folk to seek shelter in the homes of parents, relatives, and other "praiseworthy people" until permanent accommodations could be found.[156] Over time, many were sent to religious communities in other parts of the kingdom—while some were resettled in Lisbon, like the nuns from the convents of Santa Clara, Santa Ana, and Calvary, who were relocated to the Convent of Hope, where, according to Father Freire, they succeeded in fashioning "a truly rigorous claustral confinement."[157]

Finally, there was the problem of depopulation. By mid-November, letters from Porto confirmed that "so great a Number of Persons, English, Dutch, [and] Portuguese, were arriving . . . that the Town being . . . [unable to accommodate] them . . . had built a great many Huts for their present Reception, and were building many others."[158] Pombal feared that Lisbon might become a ghost town.

An abandoned capital would not only thwart recovery efforts, it might paralyze the kingdom. It would certainly discourage foreign trade and might even tempt pirates, brigands, if not a foreign state, to attack. To thwart the exodus, Pombal ordered the roads outside the city to be patrolled, and soldiers and naval vessels were instructed to turn back persons—"regardless of quality or condition"—caught attempting to flee. Only those in possession of an official passport would be allowed to leave the city or the kingdom or even pass from one province to another.[159] In the coming months, Pombal would need as many able-bodied men as he could find.[160]

To ensure a steady supply of workers for the future task of clearing and rebuilding the city, Pombal ordered magistrates from each of Lisbon's neighborhoods on November 4 "to promptly and carefully examine . . . the lives, habits, and professions of all the [city's] inhabitants . . . and to apprehend all those vagabonds and beggars young enough and healthy enough to work . . . and to sentence them in verbal trials" to participate in public works projects.[161] This chilling directive, written just three days after the earthquake, revealed the fundamentally despotic nature and growing power and reach of the emergent Pombaline state.

Under normal circumstances, the traditional powers within Portugal—the Church, the nobility, the military, and the merchant classes—would have resisted such a comprehensive usurpation of government duties and responsibilities by the Crown. But the disaster had been so unexpected, so sudden, and so destructive that these institutions had had little time to react. Thus would aggressive statism in the name of reform and national survival fundamentally alter the character and trajectory of the kingdom. The earthquake, in short, had brought about a revolution.

CHAPTER SIX

City of Ashes, Huts of Wood

After the tempestuous storm,
Nocturnal shadows and wheezing wind.

—FATHER RODRIGO JOSÉ DOURADO DE MARIS SARMENTO,
ABBOT OF THE CHURCH OF SÃO MARTINHO, LISBON

BARRACAS

Despite the raging fire, "great numbers" of people returned to the city on November 4 "to see what effects could be saved" from their homes, recalled one survivor. "Unfortunately, the far greater number never returned, and those that did were hardly recompensed for their trouble."[1] In the haunting words of James O'Hara, the 2nd Baron Tyrawley, who bravely entered the ruins that day with his friend Commodore Thomas Broderick,

> Never did any eye behold so awful, so tremendous, and so solemn a scene. The moon, which was then at the full, shining resplendently on the Tagus, gave us a night view of this wreck of nature. The howling of the dogs, the stench of the dead bodies, together with the gloom which now and then diffused itself around, from the moon's being sometimes obscured, gave me some idea of that general crash, when sun and moon shall be no more; and filled my mind with meditations, that only such a scene could inspire.[2]

According to another survivor, the fire "reduced [the] whole Metropolis to Ashes, rendering it such a Spectacle of Terror and Amazement, as well as of Desolation to Beholders, as perhaps has not been equaled from the Foundation of the World."[3]

"Going into the town a few days after the earthquake," wrote Mr. Braddock, "[I] saw several bodies lying in the streets, some horribly mangled, as [I] supposed, by the dogs; others half burnt, some quite roasted; and . . . in certain places, particularly near the doors of Churches, they lay in vast heaps, piled one upon another."[4] The "intolerable stench from the dead bodies" was so strong, continued Braddock, "that I was ready to faint away."[5] There may, however, have been a silver lining. "The fire," wrote one survivor, "was an act of mercy sent by the Almighty because it consumed the exposed dead bodies that could have, with time, infected the air and led to much harm."[6]

There had been many acts of mercy in Lisbon. But none was more important than that of the Virgin Mary, who, in the opinion of most *lisboetas*, had saved the city from complete annihilation through her special intercession. One should never forget "the powerful protection of Holy Mary," wrote Father Morganti, "who remembers to help mankind in its time of greatest distress." Despite the terrible carnage, the majority of Lisbon's population had survived the disaster, along with the royal family and the great majority of the nobility. As an indication of the Holy Mother's powers, Morganti presented the fact that though the fire had "reduced the stones [of his church] to ashes," it had "lost its strength" when it approached the ancient and venerated statue of the Virgin Mary known as the *Senhora a Grande* (the Great Lady). "She remained intact," he wrote, and "not even the silver embroidery on her dress showed any sign that it had come close to the fire."[7]

Overflowing with piety and fear, *lisboetas* sought out the comforting rituals of the Catholic mass. "Moved by devotion, some attended services inside churches that had suffered minimal damage," recalled a cleric. But "many times, when they were inside and the priests were celebrating mass, small tremors were felt; and the people fled once again to the fields with their priests behind them carrying the chalice in their hands, only to return when the tremor had ended to complete the mass." On such occasions, some were trampled and injured and, in a few cases, even killed. Thus, it was decided that most masses should be held out in the fields under the open sky.[8]

In the first weeks after the earthquake, "everyone . . . spent their days and nights outside in the inclement weather," recalled a priest. But because "the tremors continued" and because people did not want to spend the night in houses "for fear that they would collapse," many began to search for sticks of wood and drive them into the ground. Over these, they draped "pieces of cloth, covers, oiled handkerchiefs, rugs, tapestries, and carpets" and, in doing so, fashioned little tents that offered some shelter from the cold and the rain, which began on Monday, November 3, with a few scattered drops.[9] Some of the rope and cloth came directly from the royal storerooms—lent by the king to specific individuals, who never returned it—while some of the sailcloth was salvaged from the Naval Yard.[10] Inside their crude shelters, survivors gave thanks to God and considered themselves more privileged, in the words of one survivor, "than if they were in the finest palaces that once adorned the noble city of Lisbon."[11]

For eight days, Kitty Witham and her fellow nuns lay under a pear tree overhung with a carpet, experiencing terror every time the wind blew. For some time after that, they slept under the stars. The only true inconvenience for Kitty, which she asked "God to accept . . . as a small Pennance," was being forced to sleep in her clothes. Yet she could not help but despair, "for only God knows how long we have to live for I believe this world will not last long. Happy are those that has gon well out of itt."[12]

Survivors of the earthquake living in tents outside the city

On November 5, Abraham Castres and Charles Calmette both waited upon Dom José outside his makeshift lodgings in Belém. Although "the loss His Most Faithful Majesty has sustained on this occasion is immense," wrote Castres, "he received us with more Serenity that we expected." Queen Mariana Vitória and the princesses, however, sent their regrets. Having spent the last four days in tents, they no longer possessed dresses that they thought "fit to appear in."[13]

Others, like the Countess of Atouguia, were also discomfited by the new accommodations. "We walked on foot to my parents' farm in the Campo Pequeno (Small Field), in which there were some magnificent houses, but we found them in ruins so we stayed on the farm in small make-shift huts . . . with [all] the inconveniences shared by everyone *for a long time*."[14] Standards of basic personal hygiene, which were not exceptionally high before the earthquake, plummeted. "Some people wore the same shirt which they had worn when they had escaped from their houses for fifteen or twenty days," recalled one priest.[15]

As a result, there followed an appalling infestation of fleas, lice, and "those bad smelling little [blood-sucking] creatures called bedbugs," reported an eyewitness.[16] No one was spared. Lice became so prevalent and pernicious that one priest believed them to be "more supernatural than natural," yet another scourge sent to punish Lisbon's sinful inhabitants.[17] It was reminiscent, for many, of the third plague (of lice) that God had inflicted on Egypt in the time of Moses. "God sent the earthquake to Portugal as a punishment," wrote the priest, and "after this the waters of the ocean," and then "the fire, the thieves, and finally . . . the plague of those bugs."[18] In John's Apocalypse, too, swarms of insects were sent to torture humanity in its time of troubles.

> And there came out of the smoke locusts upon the earth: and unto them was given power, as the scorpions of the earth have power.
>
> And it was commanded them that they should not hurt the grass of the earth, neither any green thing, neither any tree; but only those men which have not the seal of God in their foreheads. . . .
>
> And in those days shall men seek death and shall not find it; and shall desire to die, and death shall flee from them.
>
> REVELATION 9:4–6.

Amid the bugs, the vermin, and the cold, *lisboetas* began to realize that their crude shelters would not preserve them through the winter. Many therefore "resolved to construct another form of habitation to accommodate their families" and better protect them from the weather, recalled a priest. They began "to search for wood and boards," even though they were "difficult to find because the fire had reduced the city to ashes," and the tsunami "had carried off the majority of the wood in the timber yards along the river."[19]

To satisfy demand, vast supplies of timber would be procured and sent from northern Europe over the next few months; and ships carrying wood from Brazil were redirected to the Portuguese capital.[20] Other building materials like bricks and tile, as well as coal and firewood, were allowed to enter the city duty-free, while the sale of contraband materials was prohibited.[21]

As many as nine thousand wooden huts (*barracas*) would be built in and around the city. Most were constructed of wooden boards and variously roofed with woven straw, bunches of green pinewood, and fibers from an herb called pita.[22] A few were "covered in tile."[23] Unfortunately, most were inadequately constructed. Although they kept their occupants drier than the tents and lean-tos they had replaced, they proved ineffective against the temperature extremes of the winter and summer. The problem was that the majority of Lisbon's skilled laborers were then engaged in building shelters for the nobility and the king's enormous and extravagant Real Barraca (Royal Hut).[24] Because of this, *lisboetas* began to purchase prefabricated huts from the Netherlands that could be unloaded and erected in about twenty-four hours with only a minimum investment of labor and plaster.[25]

These ready-made Dutch domiciles, however, paled in comparison with the homes being built by Lisbon's aristocracy. "The *barraca* of the Marquês de Louriçal is a palace," wrote Father Portal, "which they say cost upwards of thirty or forty thousand cruzados." Nearby stood "the *barraca* of the Chief Judge [the Duke of Lafões]," which was "made of wooden partitions and painted with great perfection. The *barraca* of the Inquisição is [also] beautifully made, very spacious, and much more comfortable than what they had before. . . . Towards Belém, it is incredible how many *barracas* there are, some very expensive and exquisite. That of the Secretary of State Sebastião José de Carvalho [i.e., Pombal] could serve as a *palácio*."[26] As for the king and his family, before the Real Barraca was completed, they lived in Belém in a luxurious wooden structure owned by the Duke of Aveiro, who less than five years later would be executed by order of Pombal and the king.[27]

A few members of the upper classes found their new digs less than satisfactory. "We are all in a little cubbyhole [surrounded by] children, masters, and servants, and we cannot even close off a little corner," complained a young Swiss gentleman to his mother. "I must end my letter as I began it, in the middle of a thousand noises. It is torture."[28]

When the fires subsided, the building of *barracas* inside the capital began in earnest, as many survivors wished to live as close as they could to their former homes and parishes. Before long, most of the city's open spaces were covered in wooden huts—the Rossio, the Terreiro do Paço, the Ribeira, and the Fields of Santa Ana, Santa Bárbara, and Santa Clara—as well as many streets, and the land surrounding monasteries and convents.[29] "The entire riverbank is so filled with *barracas*," reported Father Portal, "that passage through it is very tight and difficult."[30]

In addition to domiciles these simple wooden structures also served as churches, warehouses, stores, and workshops.[31] According to Father Portal, many people continued to sleep inside their *barracas* well after their homes and palaces had been rebuilt, out of fear of a future earthquake.[32] During the long winter of 1755–1756, they saved countless lives—although many, overwhelmed by stress, grief, and disease, ultimately succumbed. "Every day," wrote one German survivor, a corpse "was carried to the grave so thin, pale, and misshapen that it barely resembled a human being anymore."[33]

NOBLESSE OBLIGE

All of Dom José's residences in and around the city had been either destroyed or rendered unusable, resulting in enormous personal financial losses. His uncles Dom Manuel and Dom Pedro did go "to survey the Ruins, attended by a Guard of 100 Soldiers, in order to see if any Thing could be recovered out of . . . the [Riverside] Palace," according to a newspaper account. But, alas, their expedition came "to no Purpose."[34]

Lacking funds, the king was suddenly unable to pay the salaries of those who worked for him. In the near term, he needed money to continue to care for the thousands of survivors who continued to stream into Belém. And so, in an effort to economize, he "diminished the number of delicacies on the royal table," according to a priest, "and ordered all the ferocious beasts that resided at the Belém Palace be killed because—being lions and tigers and other dangerous animals—they might, if they escaped, cause injury." But "the most pressing reason [for the animal slaughter] was to avoid the four thousand cruzados per year [to feed them] . . . not counting the salaries of their keepers."[35]

The king was not the only member of the royal family who provided assistance to survivors. Mariana Vitória and her daughters collected cloth and made clothing for those in need, while the royal princes also did their part. Dom António, another of the king's uncles, allowed "as many who wanted to stay" at his residence on the farm of the Alcântara Palace—while Dom Manuel lodged and cared for great multitudes at his palace in the Monastery of Our Lady of Necessities, west of the capital.[36]

Likewise, the three bastard princes—Dom António, Dom Caspar, and Dom José—"showed by their actions that they were real Catholics" when they allowed survivors to stay on the grounds of their palace or even in their house "without turning anyone away." There the Boys of Palhavã provided doctors, surgeons, medicines, medical supplies, and every kind of care that the wretched masses required. Though their palace garden was one of the marvels of the city (and one of their greatest joys), they discontinued its upkeep in order to focus exclusively on aiding the sick and the dispossessed—even to the point of uprooting beloved plants to make room for more refugees. Nor did their generosity end at the palace gates. According to a chronicler, it flowed out to all those camping in the fields adjacent to their land. And their good works "lasted more than a year."[37]

Like Dom José, many nobles lost their palaces in the Baixa, along with all of the property they contained: private libraries, irreplaceable collections of family documents, priceless paintings and furniture and other precious irreplaceable objects collected over the centuries. Even more severely affected were those merchants and businessmen whose wealth was entirely concentrated in their homes, shops, and warehouses. "It was astonishing in those first months," recalled a survivor, "to encounter . . . women of means begging in the streets because they had lost everything they owned."[38]

The most fortunate possessed palaces on the outskirts of the city. These had a much better chance of surviving the earthquake, and they were not seriously threatened by the fire. With their fortunes intact, these grandees could focus their attention and munificence on relatives, friends, and others who had lost everything in the disaster. One aristocrat who deserves special mention is the Count of Redondo, who provided accommodations for many at his palace at the foot of the Convent of Santa Maria. He treated the injured and the sick at his own expense, visiting them faithfully and inquiring if they needed medicine or food, which, if they did, he would immediately send to them.[39]

On November 3, Pombal asked the patriarch to order all members of Lisbon's religious communities to begin burying all the corpses strewn about the city.[40] "This they promptly and cheerfully did," wrote Father Figueiredo.[41] Leaving their monasteries, farms, and temporary lodgings in the outlying parishes, they marched back into the heart of the capital armed with ladders, digging tools, and a "holy resolution," in the words of one cleric, to accomplish their grim mission.[42]

All day they "searched with great diligence through all the hills and mountains of rubble and fragments of buildings," recalled a priest, pulling battered, foul-smelling, ash-smeared corpses from the earth, placing them "on ladders and stretchers, and carrying them in the direction of their monasteries." Sometimes they gave a simple blessing over a corpse or body part, scratched out a shallow grave, and buried the remains "with their own holy hands." Although most corpses, after a few days, reached a level of advanced (and no doubt nauseating) putrescence, they "were always treated with gentleness."[43]

Some bodies trapped under large stones were not disturbed, only covered up with dirt, "so that they would not infect the air," a priest recalled. Then, after two years, when they had become skeletonized, they were dug up for reburial elsewhere. Because many corpses were not visible from the surface, it was common practice for priests to ask people where they thought bodies might be located or where they had once heard voices under the ruins, often enlisting the help of laymen to dig them up.[44] While many distinguished themselves with their zeal at burying the dead, none brought more honor upon themselves than "the secular priests of the habit of São Pedro" and the "illustrious Monsignors of the Patriarchal Church," who, clothed in "their prelates' robes," trudged resolutely through the streets alongside their fellow ecclesiastics, climbing ladders, digging up bodies, and dragging them across the capital for burial.[45] Despite these efforts, corpses would continue to be found in the ruins for many years. When they were, hygienic considerations dictated that the body be coated in "tar and pitch" and then set on fire.[46]

Adding to the fear and anxiety were the terrifying aftershocks that continued to rock the capital. One large tremor on the morning of November 8 was felt not only in Lisbon but aboard a British ship sixty leagues (more than two hundred miles) from the Portuguese coast. "The earth shook with a violent impulse," recalled Moreira de Mendonça, "though only for a short time."[47] Several of these tremors may have even generated tsunamis. According to an article in *Mercurio Histórico y Político*, Madrid's other principal newspaper, "the waters of the Tagus rose and fell many feet on the 1st, 10th, 15th, and 18th" of November.[48] If true, the same fault that had produced the All Saints' Day earthquake continued to slip along the seabed and, in these instances, propel water and energy the two hundred or so miles to the Portuguese coast.

For many, these recurring aftershocks were proof that God was still angry at Lisbon. Popular preachers adopted the theme, prophesying a host of future calamities: a second devastating quake, another cataclysmic inundation, and, in one sermon, the destruction of the entire planet by the heat of the sun. Some of these self-styled prophets were actually thieves who wished to flush out any remaining inhabitants from the Baixa—but most were earnest clerics, like Malagrida, intent on drawing attention to the moral failings of the people.

To counter this fear-mongering, Pombal outlawed provocative utterances of all kinds; and in a series of public notices sought to affirm the natural origins of the earthquake. Yet at the same time he partnered with the Church "to placate the Divine Justice who has not yet put down his sword," as Father Portal put it. To this same end, the cardinal-patriarch ordered public and private prayers, fasting on most Saturdays, and a decree that every mass must include "special orations against earthquakes."[49] On November 12, Pombal asked the Senate, in the name of the king, to recognize the Virgin Mary for her special and decisive intercession in preventing the complete destruction of the city.[50]

Four days later, a citywide procession of thanksgiving was held at the king's urging. Beginning at the Hermitage of São Joachim in Alcântara, located between Belém and the western boundaries of the city, it would proceed through the rubble-lined streets to the Church of Our Lady of Necessities, the headquarters of the Oratorians. Among those walking the route were Dom José and Mariana Vitória. They were joined by the entire court, various members of Portugal's high nobility, affiliates of the Patriarchal Church and the Cathedral of Santa Maria Maior, most of Lisbon's clergy and religious communities, and the entire Senate. Three days earlier, that body had proclaimed that a procession in honor of the Virgin Mary would be held in Lisbon every second Sunday of November "while the world endures."[51]

A month later, on December 13, another enormous procession was organized to solicit God's mercy and the protection of the saints. It followed the same route as the procession of November 16 and was headed by the titular Archbishop of Lacedaemonia, José Dantas Barbosa, who walked barefoot behind a single elevated cross.[52] Behind him trudged thousands of barefoot *lisboetas*, their heads bowed in prayer. Joining them were several princes of the Church, multitudes of priests, monks, and nuns, and a few aristocrats, including the brother of the Duke of Lafões and the Counts of Obidas and São Lourenço. At the Church of Our Lady of Necessities, the papal nuncio himself, Monsignor Filippo Acciaiuoli, surprised and delighted everyone by joining members of the Oratory in washing the feet of the faithful. Many were moved to tears at his faith and humility.[53] One Oratorian who was conspicuously absent that day was Manoel Portal, who was still recovering from the grisly leg injury he sustained on November 1. "God knows," he wrote in his account of the disaster, "but this sinner did not deserve to walk among so many just people."[54]

In the months that followed, a number of other processions invaded the streets of Lisbon, including one led by the Franciscan order "with great spirit and fervor." With a statue of their patron leading the way, the Franciscans surged through the ravaged city in their coarse robes, praying and performing sundry acts of mortification. Some walked barefoot with gags in their mouths, while others occupied themselves with "instruments of penance."[55]

To further placate the population, Pombal petitioned Benedict XIV to proclaim St. Francis de Borgia the official protector of Portugal and its empire against earthquakes and national calamities. Deceased since 1572, the Spanish Jesuit general was the great-grandson of Pope Alexander VI and had a proven track record of preventing disasters. He had also shown good taste earlier in his life by taking a Portuguese wife, who died before he took his vows. On May 24, 1756, the proclamation was granted. It required churches throughout the empire to celebrate

Borgia's feast day (September 30) every year with a solemn mass and a strict obligation that a choir of priests sing "in all the churches."[56] Although the Oratorians would have preferred their own patron, Philip Neri, the choice of St. Francis de Borgia did much to comfort the average *lisboeta*, who nevertheless remained panic-prone and fretful.[57]

CHAPTER SEVEN

Word Spreads

Never before has the Demon of Fright spread his Terror so quickly and powerfully over the land.

—JOHANN WOLFGANG VON GOETHE,
Truth and Poetry (1811)

"UN EXPRESSO"

On the morning of November 4, a lone courier, carrying packets stuffed with letters, bolted from the still burning capital. For several days, he rode eastward through the granite hills and gray-green valleys of Alentejo and Extremadura in Spain before turning north at the dry windswept plateau of Castile. Though difficulty in procuring a horse during one leg of the journey forced him to continue on foot for many miles, he arrived in Madrid at 4 p.m. on November 8, exhausted and caked with dust.[1]

Several days earlier, the *Gaceta de Madrid* had reported what every *madrileño* already knew, that a *"considerable Temblor de Tierra"* had shaken the Spanish capital and caused "the inhabitants . . . the most dreadful consternation." It was the strongest "earthquake in living memory," declared the editors, though happily "His Majesties," who were residing in the El Escorial palace at San Lorenzo, were unhurt and the loss of life and property had been minimal.[2]

The letters arriving from Lisbon would tell a much different story. Written by authors both high and low—Dom José, Monsignor Acciaiuoli, the ambassadors of France, Naples, and Prussia, the secretary of the late Count Perelada (who paid for the courier), as well as several merchants and private citizens—they were quickly opened and distributed to people of prominence throughout the capital.[3] Before long, copies were affixed to city walls, along with hastily produced accounts of the earthquake. In Madrid's principal squares and markets, the resonant voices of *noveleros* (newsmongers) kept the city's largely illiterate population abreast of the latest developments.[4]

Perhaps no phrase uttered in the aftermath of the disaster proved more disconcerting to eighteenth-century sensibilities than Dom José's oft-quoted words to the Spanish throne. "I am without a House, in a Tent, without Servants, without Subjects, without Money, and without Bread," he informed Fernando VI, his brother-in-law, and Maria Bárbara, his older sister. Both were understandably horrified.[5] "Their Catholic Majesties have been affected with this news as souls like [theirs] should be affected in such terrible calamities," reported a British ambassador to Spain, Benjamin Keene.[6] According to Keene, "the King immediately wrote a Letter to his Sister the Queen of Portugal in the most tender & most generous Terms: offering all in his Power to assist and relieve them; and expressing his great Concern that the Distance deprived Them from applying such immediate Remedies as He could wish."[7] "We must give a thousand thanks to God," wrote Don Fernando to his stepmother, "that the [Portuguese] royal family has successfully escaped from such a great danger."[8]

Within hours, he and Maria Bárbara dispatched their first shipment of aid to Belém and "gave orders," according to a newspaper account, "to supply [the Portuguese] court with everything else that would be wanted."[9] "They send as much ready money every day as a messenger can carry," wrote Keene. "And . . . [Don Fernando's] letter to his sister [Queen Mariana Vitória] offers all *her* King can ask and he can send."[10] To facilitate the flow of goods and royal cash, which may have totaled as much as 150,000 pieces of eight or about £37,000, Fernando abolished all tariffs along the Spanish-Portuguese border.[11]

It was the opening act of the first international relief effort in world history. In the case of Spain, it was the close familial bonds between the two royal houses that, despite the age-old antagonism between the two Iberian kingdoms, proved decisive. Undoubtedly, the pivotal factor was Maria Bárbara, Spain's Lisbon-born queen. The oldest child of João V, she was, despite her homeliness, much beloved by her husband, over whom she exercised considerable influence. After ascending the throne in 1746, she had worked tirelessly to improve relations with

Portugal, lobbying strenuously for the Treaty of Boundaries, which had eased border tensions in the New World between the two Iberian kingdoms. Later, to the delight of both Portugal and Britain, she supported Spain's neutrality during the early stages of the Seven Years War.[12]

But despite the improved relations, the Portuguese refused to embrace Spain's earthquake largesse with open arms. According to Keene, Dom José only accepted the money "conditionally" and requested that the funds "remain in the Hands of the Spanish Treasurer residing in Lisbon" until "he should have Occasion for Them."[13] Pombal must have reasoned that it was better to regard monetary gifts from former adversaries with a degree of caution than run the risk of later feeling obligated to them. The implication is that Portugal did accept some Spanish aid in the form of supplies (though, in at least one case, the Portuguese were forced to return a shipment of clothing because treaty obligations prohibited their importation from Spain).[14]

On November 11, the *Gaceta de Madrid* published the first Spanish account of the earthquake in Portugal. "A special news bulletin [*un expresso*] has been received from Lisbon, that the same earthquake that was felt [here] ... on the first of the month caused the most pitiful destruction" there. "Although specific information on the devastation was not yet available, it is said that His Excellency, Count Perelada, the Spanish Ambassador to the Portuguese Court, has perished along with several members of his family."[15] One of the few survivors was the count's only son and heir, a lad of about seven.[16] Upon hearing the news, Fernando VI appointed the boy a "Gentleman-in-Waiting" and awarded him "an annual pension of 500 gold doubloons" out of a sense of gratitude for his father's service to the Crown.[17]

Reliable information from Lisbon remained scarce, however. "We are stunned at the lack of news," wrote Don Fernando.[18] According to Mr. Keene, "Count Unhão [Portugal's ambassador to Spain] is half dead for fear of his father and his daughter. He has not heard a word about either."[19] For his part, Keene knew nothing about the condition and whereabouts of Mr. Castres and Mr. Hay—though he tried mightily to interpret this as a positive sign. "I console myself from this very silence," Keene wrote Castres on November 10, "that no harm is personally taken upon you and that your house is situated in such a manner as not to be exposed to the flames which we hear are consuming the miserable remains of what survived the earthquake. . . . Send me good news of yourself and believe the tender sentiments with which I embrace you."[20]

By the end of November, most Spaniards knew that the Portuguese capital had been destroyed. At this time, the *Mercurio Histórico y Político* began its monthly coverage of the Lisbon disaster, modestly offering its readers "a brief compendium of the innumerable and miserable ruins and pitiful destruction that the great city and court of Lisbon experienced on November 1, 1755, through the violent collusion of all four elements."[21] In November and December, the first pamphlets and books on the disaster were published in Spain. In hard-hit Seville, over fifty titles would appear before the end of the year.[22]

Back in Lisbon, the most extraordinary thing about the press coverage was that it occurred at all. The shop that printed the *Gazeta de Lisboa*, Portugal's only newspaper, was located in the heart of the Baixa on the Rua Nova dos Ferros (as the central section of the Rua Nova dos Mercedores was called) and was almost certainly destroyed.[23] Although the November 6 edition of the weekly did appear—leading many later to applaud the superhuman efforts of its staff—it was almost certainly delayed for several weeks.[24] The *Gazeta* declared on the last page of the November 6 edition,

> The first day of the month will forever be remembered in every country for the earthquakes and fires that ruined a great part of this city; fortunately, the royal coffers and the greater part of the royal property were recovered in the ruins.[25]

Such was the entire initial news coverage of the greatest natural disaster in Portuguese history.

In the edition that followed, on November 13, *lisboetas* learned that Spain had experienced the same *"formidavel tremor de Terra"* as they had and that the cities of Córdoba, Seville, and Cádiz had suffered substantial damage.[26] In the coming months, the *Gazeta* would report on the devastation in the Algarve as well as the damage sustained by several Portuguese cities—although almost nothing on Lisbon itself.

The reasons for this lie not with any lack of interest in the disaster, but with the nature of the *Gazeta* itself. Created by royal charter in 1715 and still managed by its first editor, the now eighty-five-year-old José Freire Monterroio Mascarenhas, the paper was practically as well as conceptually ill-equipped to cover such a momentous and complex

Num. 45.   353

GAZETA

DE

LISBOA

Com Privilegio   de S. Mageſtade.

Quinta feira 6. de Novembro de 1755.

FRANÇA.
Pariz 3. Outubro.

Corte ſe acha ao preſente em *Fon
tainebleau*, onde eſtá muy brilhan-
te, mas Domingo proximo ſe veſ-
tirá de luto, e o continuará poc
tempo de onze dias pela morte de
Luiz Auguſto de Bourbon Princi-
pe ſoberano de *Dombes*, Cavaleiro das Ordens do Rey, Tenente
General dos ſeus exercitos, Coro-
nel General dos Eſguiſaros, e Griſoens; e Governador
por Sua Mageſtade nas Provincias do Alto e Bayxo
Languedoc, que faleceu no primeiro do corrente em ida-
de de 55. annos, 6. mezes, e 26. dias, neto do grande
Luiz 14. filho de ſeu filho legitimado *Luiz Auguſto de*
                 Zz   *Borbon*

The first issue of the *Gazeta de Lisboa* (November 6, 1755) published after the
disaster

event. Like most European newspapers of the day, the *Gazeta*'s job was
to keep the urban elite apprised of distant events as well as the doings
of foreign courts. Except for an obligatory and brief accounting of
the public activities of the Portuguese royal family and high nobility
in the final pages of each issue, the *Gazeta* did not cover national and
local news at all.[27] It offered no political commentary and contained
no headlines or illustrations, and, as was customary at the time, the
most important and arresting stories were almost never featured on
the front page.[28] The paper was also rigidly controlled by the government—becoming, after the disaster, a tool of Pombal, who sought from
the start to downplay the impact of the earthquake on Lisbon in order

to convince business interests and foreign governments that Portugal had not been destroyed or irreparably damaged.

If literate *lisboetas* wished to learn more about the disaster, they (like their Spanish counterparts) would have consulted the growing number of handwritten accounts, letters, and official proclamations that circulated among the elite or were plastered to city walls.[29] Within weeks, published narratives, poems, sermons, and scientific treatises on the disaster began to appear in Lisbon, Porto, and Coimbra. For the illiterate majority, most news on the topic would have been obtained through word of mouth.[30]

BEYOND THE PYRENEES

On November 10, several couriers left Madrid for Paris and Versailles. Their ride across Castile, Navarre, the Pyrenees, Guyenne, Gascony, and Poitou was colder, wetter, and almost twice as long as the journey from Lisbon to Madrid.[31] In the eighteenth century, most overland mail was delivered by coach, but for urgent messages—those requiring an "express"—an individual rider was used.[32] At intervals of around twenty miles, fresh horses were provided at "posts," usually taverns or inns. If offered extra money, a rider would increase his speed, normally around five miles per hour, and limit his periods of rest. The courier who carried the news on November 4 from Lisbon to Madrid averaged about 3.8 miles per hour (factoring in periods of sleep and rest) during his 103-hour, 390-mile journey.[33] Such efforts were necessary, for the majority of ships in Lisbon's harbor had been detained for inspection or the urgent need to collect people and property.[34]

On November 18, the French ambassador's letter (of November 4) arrived at Versailles. Addressed to Louis XV from "a field near Lisbon" and composed on two small and uncharacteristically plain leaves of paper, it contains almost no punctuation, a testament, Count de Baschi explained, to the enormous strain under which it was produced.

> I have taken advantage of the departure of the courier of the secretary of the Spanish Embassy and [my] first moment of peace to share with you the horrible event which has overwhelmed Lisbon ... Most of the houses have been destroyed ... and the fire has yet to complete its consuming of this unfortunate

city that will not be rebuilt in a hundred years[.] My house has collapsed like all the others[.] But my people have courageously saved many of my effects[,] but for some chairs beds and two tapestries[,] everything is [beneath the ruins.] I am overjoyed that my life has been saved as well as that of my wife my children and all of my servants[.]

The Baschis were now living (the ambassador reported) on the grounds of French consul Nicolas Grenier's villa, sitting on pillows in the open air and sleeping in tents fashioned from towels, which somehow provided adequate protection "from a violent wind that blows every night."[35] Joining them was the surviving son of Count Perelada, whom Baschi had saved from the ruins, in addition to the servants and staff of the Spanish embassy who had followed the ambassador there after Perelada's death.[36]

In his memoirs, the Marquis d'Argenson, the former French foreign minister, recalled the moment that the "awful news" that Lisbon had "been suddenly swallowed up" arrived at Versailles. "The engulfed churches, the palaces, the residences of the Portuguese and the foreign ministers—what wealth destroyed!" he wrote. "We . . . fear bankruptcy for our merchants . . . [though] the English, too, will have heavy losses."[37]

Similarly distressed was Madame de Pompadour, the king's "official chief mistress," who feared for the safety of her sister-in-law and protégée, Charlotte-Victoire Le Normant, Count de Baschi's wife. It was Pompadour, after all, who had first brought this younger sister of her own cuckolded husband, Charles-Guillaume Le Normant d'Étiolles, to the attention of the king and court. And it was Pompadour who, two years earlier, had secured for Madame de Baschi's husband, François (a provincial aristocrat and well-known incompetent), the coveted ambassadorship to Portugal.[38] Now she found herself powerless to do anything more than inset a few "valuable presents" in the shipment of supplies the government was readying to send the Baschis.[39]

On November 15, Madame de Baschi composed a letter that would be quoted in newspapers as far away as St. Petersburg. "His Majesty has ordered six people, who have confessed to setting fire to the Royal Palace and the Patriarch's house, to be hanged," she wrote, and in addition he "has ordered gallows to be erected to terrify such godless people around the city." Not long ago, the king "toured the whole city to inspect the damage and endeavored to dig up anything that was possible from underneath the rubble. . . . My husband found his silver plate [in the ruins of our house] . . . only a few pieces have been damaged."[40]

This last fact caught the attention of the great and ever-alert Voltaire, indirectly inspiring his greatest masterpiece four years later.[41] "I see my dear Monsieur from your last letter," the philosopher wrote to a friend on December 9, 1755, "that the End of the World and the Last Judgment is not yet come, and since M. Baschi's furniture is in good condition, all is well in Lisbon."[42]

For his part, Louis XV was more impressed with Baschi's conduct during the disaster. To see him through the new year, the king sent him a remittance of 25,000 livres, and in January 1756 he conferred upon Baschi the "cordon bleu" of the Order of the Holy Spirit, France's most prestigious chivalric honor.[43] "The king has certainly given me a nice Christmas bonus," wrote the count on January 16, 1756.[44]

On November 22, France's official newspaper, the *Gazette de France*, announced to the nation that a mighty earthquake had "toppled half the city [of Lisbon], all the churches, as well as the King's palace." Fifty thousand inhabitants, it was believed, had died, and "the royal family was living in huts, [and] sleeping in their coaches," having "spent the [first] twenty-four hours without servants or anything to eat."[45] As copies of the *Gazette* made their way across the continent, this image of the Braganças as the victims of cruel fortune built sympathy for the Portuguese and may have added emotional fuel to the international relief effort.

In December 1755, the *Journal étranger* published a four-page account of the catastrophe by its correspondent in Lisbon, Miguel Pedegache. It was the first news release authorized by the Portuguese government.[46] "I have no colors vibrant enough to paint you a picture of the disaster to which almost all of Portugal and the majority of its inhabitants have fallen victim," wrote the Portuguese soldier, poet, engineer, playwright, amateur scientist, and social critic. "Imagine the four Elements conspiring and competing against each other to bring about our ruin. Some may fear this picture will never approach the truth."[47]

Pedegache's description combines the empirical—he recorded the precise barometric pressure (27.07) and temperature (63.5°F) readings at the time of the first tremor—with the poetic:

The sky darkened again and the earth seemed to want to return into chaos. The tears and cries of the living, the groans and complaints of the dying, the shaking of the earth and darkness, compounded the horror and the fright. But finally, after several minutes everything was calm. . . . Our misfortune, however, was not yet at its height.[48]

Like many in Lisbon, Pedegache's losses were both personal and financial.

As for my property—furniture, jewelry, silverware, etc.— everything is still under the stones and ashes of my house that the fire burned completely. I lost my library that contained three thousand well-chosen volumes and all of my own works which were numerous enough to have made me a reputation in the Republic of Letters. But what I regret the most are fifty very rare manuscripts. [As well as] a work . . . on morals, customs, usages, prejudices, Portuguese studies, manufacturing, the police & the government of Portugal. It is the fruit of six years of toil and reflection; plus, *Historical Researches on Portugal*, a Critical *Examination of the Articles on Portugal in [Louis] Moreri's Diction- ary*, *Dissertations on Different Subjects*, my *Astronomical Observa- tions*, a *Dissertation on the Atmosphere of the Moon*, etc. . . . But these are feeble losses in comparison to the hundred thousand crowns that this tragic event has cost me. I am writing you from the fields because there are no habitable houses. Lisbon is no more and will never be rebuilt in the place where it once was.[49]

From Paris, news of the earthquake traveled south to Avignon, where, on November 28, *Le Courrier* announced that the "beautiful, large, and flourishing city [of Lisbon] has been entirely destroyed . . . [And] at least half of its inhabitants lie buried beneath its ruins."[50] Four days later, it reported that the disaster had grabbed "the attention of the [French] public" and effectively "crossed out the joy" that had come with the birth of the latest Bourbon baby on November 17.[51] This child—Louis Stanislas Xavier, the Count of Provence and the younger brother of the Duke of Berry (the future Louis XVI)—would, fifty-nine years later, succeed Napoleon Bonaparte and rule for ten uninspiring years as Louis XVIII.

On December 8, the grandfather of the infant count, Louis XV, wrote a moving letter of condolence to Dom José. Motivated by diplomatic necessity (as well as the likely urging of Madame de Pompadour), the popular forty-five-year-old monarch, known as "Louis the Beloved," seemed genuinely distressed.

> When we first received news from Count de Baschi of the misfortune that your Majesty's capital city had suffered, the utmost feeling was excited in our hearts. From the details given in the ambassador's account of this sad event, we feel the size of the evil *[la grandeur du mal]*. . . . [And] we admire the true Christian and royal virtues that you have displayed in being much less affected by your own misfortunes than your subjects. Your Majesty must know that we keenly share your sorrow and that we offer to contribute with the greatest zeal to the comfort and relief of your nation. We ask our ambassador [in consultation with you] to instruct us more precisely of your needs.

> From His Majesty's good friend and cousin, Louis.[52]

In late December, Louis's letter was presented to Dom José by Ambassador Baschi, who offered the Portuguese 20,000 pistoles (£16,600) in aid.[53] Though grateful for the gesture, His Most Faithful Majesty refused the money.[54] No doubt, he and Pombal were, once again, wary of a gift that might come with strings attached. Furthermore, they knew that accepting such a sum would almost certainly provoke Great Britain, France's global rival and Portugal's ally. With war on the horizon, that alliance had become more important than ever.

ACROSS THE CHANNEL

Lisbon is no more.

—*The Public Advertiser* (LONDON), DECEMBER 2, 1755

Before it reached Avignon, news of the disaster traversed the English Channel and arrived in London at "about Change Time" (i.e., business hours) on November 24. There, "it struck such a general Panic," according to *The Whitehall Evening Post*, "that the Merchants immediately withdrew . . . [the Royal Exchange] shut up, and no Business was transacted"—and not a single member of the "Club of Lisbon Merchants, who [had] been accustomed to meet at the Fountain Tavern in Bartholomew-Lane" was seen in public.[55]

Over the preceding days, the British press had started to draw connections between the latest reports of an earthquake in Iberia with the waves, tremors, and strange agitations of bodies of water that occurred across southern England on November 1. In the opinion of the editors of *The Whitehall Evening Post*, "the Earthquake lately felt at Portsmouth and other Places in Europe, far distant from each other, appears (by the Accounts we have received) to be of a different Kind from any mentioned by Naturalists."[56]

On November 25, the first accounts of the disaster began to appear in the British press.[57] "Yesterday, Advice came by the Way of Paris," announced *The Public Advertiser*, "that a most dreadful Earthquake happened at Lisbon on the 1st [of November] . . . the Day on which the Water was so much agitated here [in England] and in many other Places, that the Earth opened and swallowed up great Numbers of Houses, and Flames issuing at the same time, set on Fire those that stood; [and] that two Thirds of that great City were destroyed and 100,000 lives lost."[58]

In reports published that day in a handful of evening newspapers, there was much contradictory and inaccurate information. According to *The General Evening Post*: "the Spanish Ambassador and his Family were swallowed up . . . [and] the King was obliged to run out in his Shirt and" he "sat . . . without any other Clothing for three hours in his Coach." While *The Whitehall Evening Post* reported "60,000 people perished," *The London Evening Post* said "the Shocks began at Seven in the Evening" and that there were "about 100,000" dead.[59]

One newspaper reported that the British consul had died, another that the king and queen had perished as a result of a second earthquake on November 8 (though the editors added that this second report was "groundless").[60] Things became so confused that *The Whitehall Evening Post* was forced to confess that "the Account of the dreadful earthquake at Lisbon is variously reported. Some say . . . that two thirds of the City is swallowed up, and others one half: so that we shall not pretend to give any further Account . . . till [we are] better informed, and especially as the Account came by the Way of France."[61]

Skepticism was widespread. "There is a most dreadful account of an earthquake in Lisbon," wrote Horace Walpole on November 25, "but several people will not believe it."[62] The next day a friend informed the Duke of Bedford that "the terrible report from Lisbon is not believed in the extent it is talked of, but [it is] feared much damage is done."[63] One "Man of Business," as he referred to himself, became so upset by the inaccurate reporting that he published a compilation of the worst offenses and labeled those responsible "dastardly mongrels, insects, scribbling incendiaries, starveling savages, human-shaped tygers, [and] senseless yelping curs," among many other things.[64]

Much later, when Samuel Johnson was asked whether he had given any credence to the initial reports of the Lisbon disaster, he allegedly replied: "Oh! not for six months, at least. I did think that story too dreadful to be credited, and can hardly yet persuade myself that it was true to the full extent that we all of us have heard."[65] Earlier in the year, Johnson had matter-of-factly defined the word "earthquake" in his groundbreaking *Dictionary of the English Language* as a "tremor or convulsion of the earth."

Such skepticism must also be understood in the context of the Great London Earthquake Panic of 1750, which most adults in the city could still recall. On February 8 and March 8 of that year, two small tremors caused an avalanche of fear, anxiety, and undeniable coward-ice in the British capital. Although there were no serious injuries and little physical damage to speak of, preachers across London tumbled over themselves to interpret the mini-quakes as undeniable proof that God was a real and consequential force in the world. "The clergy, who have had no windfalls of a long season," recalled Walpole, "have driven horse and foot into this opinion. There has been a shower of sermons and exhortations."[66] Before long, the preachers were joined by a chorus of quacks, seers, and madmen who began to proclaim loudly and confi-dently that the end of the world was nigh. When a trooper in the King's Royal Guards named Mitchell announced to all who would listen that London would be completely flattened by an earthquake on the night of April 4 or the morning of April 5, people began to flee from the city.[67]

In the three days before the prophesied cataclysm, a "frantic fear" prevailed in the capital, Walpole noted: "730 coaches have been counted passing Hyde Park Corner, with whole parties removing for the coun-try."[68] In towns just outside the city limits, rooms in private homes and inns were completely rented out, and thousands trekked to the city's parks to sleep in coaches and boats or under the open sky. Some women wore fashionable "earthquake gowns" produced especially for the occasion. On the angst-filled night of April 4–5, "perhaps 100,000 persons," according to one estimate, slept in Hyde Park.[69] But when the dreaded date arrived and the earth remained stubbornly silent, many of London's inhabitants faced ridicule—or worse. Trooper Mitchell was carted off to a madhouse, and *The Daily Examiner* sneered: "Low stupid panics speak a pygmy race."[70]

Now, five years later, the news from Lisbon was all too real. "The dismal fate of [the Portuguese capital has] sunk our spirits to such a degree that for my part I have not been able to raise them since," wrote Mary Delany, a prominent bluestocking. Like many of her class, she knew people who had suffered serious financial injury in the disaster. Diamond merchants Gore and Bristow experienced losses of £30,000 and £100,000, respectively, while the Bishop of Asaph (the older brother of Edward Hay) lost £7,000 of his wife's money. "Every day will make, I fear, some new unhappy discovery," wrote Delany. "What a scene . . . to awaken those who think of nothing but greatness and wealth! and to those of a better turn it will, I hope, strengthen their pursuit after immortal happiness. I am so thoroughly touched with these distresses that I can think of nothing else."[71]

She was not alone. "The earthquake, the [Tory] opposition, and the war," wrote Horace Walpole on December 4, 1755, "are the only topics" that people are discussing.[72] On December 19, representatives of the British East India Company in London described in a letter to their colleagues in Bengal the grave impact the Lisbon disaster was having on European trade.

> This Melancholy Event [has] caused so great and Immediate a Stagnation in Business, and so much affected Publick Credit in the Negotiations of Exchange with most Parts of Europe, that We [have] found ourselves under a Necessity on the pressing Instances of many of our Principal Buyers to postpone the Sale, And whether It will be possible for us to have it ended by the Time of our latter Ships for Coast and Bay sail is yet incertain.[73]

There is even some anecdotal evidence that a preoccupation with the earthquake led to an economic downturn in the British capital.[74] In a letter to the prime minister, Thomas Pelham-Holles, the Duke of

Newcastle, a London hat maker, several shopkeepers, and a city prosecutor requested a pardon for a young artisan named Daniel Brasel,
who was convicted on February 25, 1756, of stealing a silk handker-
chief in front of St. Dunstan's Church in London on January 16. Brasel
had been driven to steal, his supporters argued, because in the months
following the Lisbon Earthquake the hat trade had "totally stagnated"
and he had lost his job.[75] Though the prime minister was somewhat
sympathetic to their claim, Brasel was nevertheless sentenced to seven
years in a penal colony.[76]

That an earthquake in Iberia might harm the British economy was
not an unreasonable assumption. The two economies were, as has been
discussed, closely connected. And not only did a large percentage of
King George's subjects enjoy the jingling of Portuguese coins in their
pockets, many were acquainted with Portugal, either having done business there or having stopped there while sailing to and from India or
the Mediterranean.

A few Londoners held out hope that the worst was not true. On
November 29, the editors of *The Whitehall Evening Post* noted that no
one had yet seen or received any letters from British citizens in Lisbon. Because of this, they began to entertain "some Reason to hope"
that "the Case may not be so dreadful as the Parisian Accounts set
forth."[77]

In some instances, the exaggerated death tolls were replaced by
equally exaggerated reports of minimal damage and death. "We have
good grounds to hope," announced the *Post*, "that the Fate of Lisbon
is not so dreadful as represented. . . . In a Letter . . . by the French
Mail, the Number of Persons perished is reduced from One Hundred
Thousands to Ten Thousand; and there is not the least Doubt but the
greatest Part of the Specie [i.e., money] will be in Time recovered,
especially as the Merchants [kept] their Cash in Iron Chests."[78] In other
accounts, the number of British casualties was sharply reduced. "There
are not more than five English Persons lost in that dreadful Disaster,"
one assured readers. "Immediately upon the first Shock . . . most of the
English Families repaired on board the Ships in the Harbor."[79]

But the merchants of London could not afford to indulge such
unfounded optimism. On November 27, several sent letters via "an
Express from London's General Post Office" to their correspondents
in Portugal, and the next day, some traveled to Falmouth to catch the
Lisbon-bound packet boat so they could post letters and packages to

their colleagues, relatives, and friends.[80] "We are assured," wrote one newspaper editor, "that several Expresses have been sent to Falmouth and other . . . Ports, with Orders to send Ships with Provision and Necessities for the speedy Relief and Support of the many unhappy Sufferers in Portugal . . . an Express was also dispatched for Yarmouth with Directions . . . to send there with all possible Expedition a large Quantity of Herrings and other necessary Provisions" so it could be shipped on to Lisbon.[81] The next day, the British relief effort would take on national dimensions.

BEEF, BUTTER, AND BISCUITS

On November 28, the British prime minister read a message from George II to both Houses of Parliament.[82]

> His majesty, being moved with the greatest concern for so good and faithful an ally as the King of Portugal, and with the utmost compassion for the distresses to which that city and kingdom must be reduced . . . recommends to the House of Lords the consideration of this dreadful and extensive calamity . . . and desires the concurrence and assistance of the House of Lords, in sending such speedy and effectual relief as may be suitable to so afflicting and pressing an exigency.[83]

Both king and prime minister realized at once how perilous the situation was. In the fragile, globally interconnected economy of the mideighteenth century, an unforeseen and disruptive calamity like an earthquake had the potential to do enormous harm.[84]

On the following day, November 29, the prime minister convened a meeting at his London residence, Newcastle House, "to consider what might be the properest Relief to be immediately sent to Portugal."[85] Those present included the chancellor of the exchequer, Sir George Lyttelton; the lords of the treasury, Henry Vane and Robert Craggs-Nugent; the secretary of state for the Southern Department, Henry Fox; the lord mayor of London, Sir John Barnard; and four wealthy London merchants: Mr. Burrell, Mr. Bristow, Mr. Gore, and Mr. Cleveland.[86] It was an exercise in consensus politic—later known as "the Whig Supremacy"—so typical of this era, when king and Parliament (then dominated by the powerful landowning families of the Whig party) worked in almost complete unison.[87]

At the meeting, Newcastle ordered a man-of-war to be sent straightaway to Lisbon with £30,000 in "Portugal Gold" and £20,000 in silver "Pieces of Eight."[88] A day or two later, three more ships would follow with orders to provide protection for the inhabitants of Lisbon, who, according to Monsignor Acciaiuoli quoted in a British newspaper, "were fearful of being put to the Sword by the neighboring Barbarians" (i.e., pirates or Moors from Africa's Barbary Coast).[89]

In addition to the cash gift, Newcastle directed the merchants Burrell, Bristow, and Gore to procure and send the following provisions to the Portuguese capital. (They would later be reimbursed by the government.)

Irish beef (60,000 barrels)	£10,000
Butter (4,000 firkins)	£ 3,000
Flower (10,000 quarters)	£15,000
Wheat (10,000 quarters)	£15,000
Biscuits (1,000 bags)	£ 1,200
Rice (1,200 barrels)	£ 1,000
Pix-axes, spades, crows and screws and/or other proper utensils	£ 1,000
Shoes, if necessary	£ 1,000[90]

All in all, it was an impressive display of political skills and organization by the prime minister, who many contemporaries believed was hopelessly out of his depth. "He [Newcastle] loses half an hour every morning," quipped the earl of Wilmington, "and runs after it all the rest of the day without being able to overtake it."[91]

On December 1, George II wrote a letter of condolence to Dom José in French.

> *Monsieur mon Frère*, it is with the deepest sorrow that I received from my ambassador at the court of Madrid news of the . . . earthquake and the even more awful fire that arrived at your capital. Yet what Consolation for Europe that it has pleased the Divine Providence to preserve the Sacred Person of Your Majesty and his royal house. I cannot convey to

you how deeply I have been affected by the knowledge that so many of Your Majesty's subjects have perished in such a general ruin. I am also very aware of the deplorable state to which those who have escaped have been reduced.

And [therefore] to enable Your Majesty to bear the woes that have overwhelmed him . . . I have given orders to my Parliament that all sorts of Relief and various kinds of Provisions be dispatched to you without Delay. Your Majesty should know that I am very interested in your well-being. Would to God that I was not given such a sad Opportunity to affirm to you the sincere and perfect Friendship between us.

I am, my brother, your good brother,

George Rex.[92]

Ten days later, the House of Commons announced "that 100,000*l.* [British pounds] be granted to his majesty . . . to defray the expenses which have been, or may be incurred . . . in giving assistance to the distressed people of Portugal and our unhappy fellow subjects residing and trading there."[93] By comparison, Parliament spent £2.6 million in 1755 to maintain Britain's 50,000 sailors and 9,138 marines, £930,000 to finance all of its land forces at home as well as care for 3,759 invalids, and nearly £300,000 to defray the cost of its troops and garrisons across the globe.[94] "I was touched," wrote the British diplomat Horace Mann, "with the King's humane and compassionate message to the Parliament and their generous resolution to send such speedy relief. This resolution, worthy of both, does them great honour, and will be recorded to future ages with just applause!"[95] Benjamin Keene was equally enthusiastic when writing to his superiors at Whitehall: "I believe there have been Few Examples in the World, where Publick Generosity was ever applied to a more Noble Purpose, or ever met with a more ample Retribution, of National Honor."[96]

Because no one knew at the time whether Abraham Castres and Edward Hay were dead or alive, Henry Fox, the secretary of state for the Southern Department, ordered Charles Townsend, the secretary of the British embassy in Madrid, to Lisbon to take Castres's place in the event he had perished and to convey to the king and queen "the strongest Assurances of our great Concern at the late calamitous Events and of our entire Friendship and Esteem for him."[97]

Townsend was also instructed to inform Dom José of the coming money and provisions and to ask Hay, if he too was alive, "for an Account of the Number and Names of our Subjects that may have been lost in the late Calamity, and of the Condition of those who may have survived." Otherwise, he was ordered "to give all possible Council and Assistance to our subjects and all others whose Distress may justly entitle them to the Same."[98] When, however, George II received word the next day from Ambassador Keene in Madrid that Castres had "happily escaped the General Ruin," Fox ordered Castres to carry out the royal embassy himself.[99]

As it happened, Castres had several weeks earlier (on November 6) finally found the time to write to Whitehall of his survival and overall good fortune.[100] Somewhat annoyingly for him, the Dutch ambassador's entire household—M. Calmette, his wife, Antoinette, their three children, several servants, a few friends, and their inimitable monkey—had, along with a few British merchants and their families, taken refuge in his garden. But it was "the lower sort of His Majesty's Subjects," Castres confided, "who all fly to me for Bread, and lie scattered up and down in my Garden with their Wives and Children. I have helped them all hitherto, and shall continue to do so, as long as provisions do not fail us, which I hope will not be the case."[101]

One of Castres's first challenges was to find a way to shelter "the poorer sort" of British citizens, estimated at about three hundred, before he could send them back to Britain on either a rented "Portuguese Hulk" or an English vessel.[102] Many of the poor, however, desired to remain, if only for a little longer, in the hope that they might recover some of their "little Cash" in the ruins of their homes.[103] Although Castres had once been on difficult terms with Pombal, he liberally praised the secretary of state in the same letter for his orders "preventing Rapine & Murder." A few days earlier, he had asked Pombal for guards to protect his house from the "Ruffians" who had surrounded it the previous night.[104]

On November 15, it was Hay who wrote to his superiors back in Westminster. Though many merchants were intent on returning to England, Hay affirmed it was his "Duty not to stir from hence until I have his Majesty's Commands to do so." He had anticipated the turmoil that news of the quake would cause in London, but advised "that the Merchants be persuaded not to withhold the usual Supply of Clothing and Provisions from coming hither." In other words, he wished to normalize the flow of trade between the two countries as soon as possible, seeing no good reason for a pause in the export of textiles to Portugal. "May God Almighty," he ended his letter, "ever preserve His Majesty's Dominions from the like Calamity."[105]

It was the British Factory's hope that the disaster would prove only a hiccup in the hitherto cozy economic relationship between the two countries, and that the Methuen Treaty (and the low tariffs it afforded Britain) would be maintained. On Sunday, November 9, Hay expressed this sentiment to Dom José in his royal garden in Belém in a formal declaration prepared in Portuguese.[106]

> The Consul General and Merchant Subjects of His Britannick Majesty beg leave to offer at Your Royal Feet their sincere Condolences on the late Calamity, which the Almighty hath permitted to befall your capital City, and several other Parts of your Majesty's Dominions.
>
> Truly sensible as they are of your Majesty's gracious disposition, and grateful for the repeated instances they have received of your Royal Protection, they beg leave to assure your Majesty of their cheerful and determined resolution to prosecute under your auspicious Influence and Sovereign Justice a Commerce so particularly necessary at this time, and always so advantageous to the Kingdoms of Great Britain and Portugal.
>
> They think it, in a peculiar manner, their Duty to express the strong reliance they have on your Majesty's Princely Care for making such wise regulations for the security of Commerce and reestablishment of mercantile Credit, as may fix them on the justest and firmest Foundations: such as may, by their public Utility reflect the brightest Glory on your Royal Name and make Your Dominions prosperous and happy to latest posterity.[107]

"His Majesty received us very graciously," wrote Hay, "and made answer that he would look over the Paper at his leisure and assured the

Envoy [Castres] of the regard he knew he always had for the British nation and particularly for His Britannick Majesty."[108]

CRACKS APPEAR

In early December, the consuls of the several trading nations began meeting in Castres's home to discuss how to normalize trade.[109] (Conspicuously absent was the French consul, M. Grenier, who refused to attend because of the growing friction between Britain and France.) Pombal's recent heavy-handed decrees had left the merchant community up in arms. British ships were being harassed and searched, allegedly to intercept contraband, Hay complained; meanwhile, Pombal had given orders that all ships arriving in the Portuguese capital must unload their entire cargos even if Lisbon was not their final destination.[110] This had infuriated ship captains who hoped to sell their goods elsewhere—especially now that price controls were in effect. In one recent instance, too many shiploads of fish had arrived in Lisbon, and even though they were at risk of spoilage, Pombal forced them to remain.[111]

For his part, George II was not worried. He blamed the harassment on overzealous underlings.[112] "The King has no doubt," Fox conveyed to Castres, "that His Most Faithful Majesty and his Ministers will show all possible Facilities to the Merchants in the dispatch of their commercial Affairs—not load their Trade with any new and unnecessary Burdens or delay, which would besides, not be quite consistent with the King of Portugal's intention of Rebuilding Lisbon, and inducing the Merchants to continue there."[113] But George II was unaware that Pombal was now firmly in control.

Hay also expressed concern that members of the British Factory remained dispersed throughout the countryside because Pombal had forbidden anyone to build houses near the new Customs House. Instead, the government was encouraging people to move back into the shattered Baixa. But the area they wished people to inhabit—around the old Terraço do Paço—had been "so totally destroyed," Hay observed, that this was not feasible.[114]

Back in London, the mood remained subdued, if not downright gloomy. At White's, the notorious gentlemen's club, the betting stakes had been sharply reduced.[115] And masquerade balls had been abolished across the city for fear of provoking the Almighty's wrath—though, a reader of *The London Evening Post* remarked in early December that the "Playhouses and all Conventicles of Vanity and Wickedness are as crowded as ever."[116]

On December 18, George II called for a "General Fast" to be held on February 6 in England, Wales, Scotland, and Ireland.

> From the deepest Sense . . . of the Miseries which our People would suffer if a like Visitation should be shewed forth upon these Kingdoms, and placing our whole Truth and Confidence in the Mercy of Almighty God, [we] have resolved, that a general and public Fast be observed, that both we, and our People, may humble ourselves before Almighty God, and in a most devout and solemn Manner, send up our Prayers and Supplications to the Divine Majesty, to divert all those Judgments which we most justly have deserved, to continue his Mercies, and to perpetuate the Enjoyment of the Protestant Religion among us, and Safety and Prosperity to our Kingdoms and Dominions, and to implore his Protection and Blessing, upon our Fleets and Armies.[117]

The fast was a penitential gesture, a way to beseech the Almighty to safeguard London and the empire from both natural and man-made dangers. "When we look round the World and consider the boisterous Winds and Storms, Thunders, Lightning, Earthquakes, and other Disasters that have lately happened in Europe," wrote the editors of *The Whitehall Evening Post*, "we have the greatest Reason to be highly thankful to a kind Providence that our Fleets . . . are all safe in our Harbors, and will very soon be ready to put to Sea again, if any emergent Occasion should offer."[118]

It was an oddly pietistic attitude in a Protestant country in the midst of the Age of Enlightenment. Realizing this, some tried to convince themselves that the fast was not a repudiation of science, logic, and reason. "That Earthquakes are Effects of natural Causes is true," wrote one author in *The London Evening Post*. "But to conclude it from thence superstitious to entreat the Almighty to defend us from them, is not Argument but Folly. He is the Author and the Lord of Nature, all these Causes are in his Hands, and his Providence is over all his Works."[119]

Back in the Portuguese capital, on November 29, Mr. Hake personally carried the still crippled Thomas Chase aboard a ship bound for Britain. Only the second British-destined vessel to leave the Tagus since the disaster, it departed the next day with twenty-four passengers. "How great . . . must be my thankfulness to Divine Providence," wrote Chase, "for raising me up assistance, not only unasked, but even unhoped for, among persons almost strangers to me!" Looking back, he found himself especially obliged to the Hamburg merchant Mr. Forg, "with whom I had but a slight acquaintance; and who, like a guardian angel, appeared almost ready to assist me in the utmost extremities!"[120]

He learned later that Mr. Forg had not abandoned him in the Terreiro do Paço as he had been led to believe. After crossing the river to safety, Forg had in fact sent someone back to look for him. But when Chase could not be found, the man assumed he had been carried away and left. Until his death in 1788 at the age of fifty-nine, Chase would never forget the horrors of that November.[121] "It more than once occurred to me," he later wrote of his experiences, "that the Inquisition, with all its utmost cruelty, could not have invented half such a variety of tortures for the mind as we were then suffering."[122]

In early December, the first British survivors began to set foot on their native soil. One merchant named "Mr. Dodd," reported *The Whitehall Evening Post*, "arrived at his Father's House [on December 15] in New Palace-Yard [London] from Lisbon, where he was much wounded by the falling of the Buildings by the Earthquake."[123] A week later, a large group of survivors disembarked in the capital after a ten-day voyage. "The images [they provide] of the misery of the remaining inhabitants," recalled one witness, "are so lamentable that hardly anyone can remember it without tears."[124]

One of the first earthquake survivors to arrive in London was an inhabitant of Canton, China, referred to as "Cheequa" (possibly Qi Guo) in a solicitor's letter to the court of the East India Company dated December 8, 1755. According to his lawyer, this "Unhappy Stranger" had been "deprived of all his Effects to a considerable Value" by "the Earthquake at Lisbon," and "without the means of Supporting himself & returning home," he had decided to fall on the mercy of the illustrious company and ask that they "bear the Charges" of his trip back to China on a company ship. His petition was granted on the same day.[125]

OF DIKES AND DOLPHINS

When news of the disaster reached Holland in late November, the Dutch were still debating what had caused church chandeliers to sway and ships to break free from their moorings on the first of the month. Some blamed natural forces, while others, like the Amsterdam office clerk Jan De Boer, felt that "the all-governing hand of God" had played a role.[126] There was, in short, no clear consensus, and little definitive evidence either way. In early November, when a porpoise was fished out of the inland harbor at Oudewater, some forty miles from the sea, a few thought that the unusual occurrence was somehow connected to the quake.[127]

Then, the *Gazette d'Amsterdam* reported on November 25 that "a shock from an earthquake" had been felt in Madrid on November 1 and the *Gazette de Leyde* (Leiden) announced that "a violent earthquake" had struck both Spain and Italy.[128] The next day, Jan De Boer read the first terrifying accounts of Lisbon's destruction in the *Hague Current* (*'s-Gravenhaegse Courant*), which, he recalled, could not be purchased "for any sum of money."[129] At Amsterdam's stock exchange, traders were sent "into the most extreme bewilderment," according to a German newspaper.[130] The *Gazette de Leyde*—Europe's newspaper of record and the leading journal of the European Enlightenment—declared that "half the city was ruined" and "more than 50,000 people" had perished. And at midnight on November 2, "a thick cloud of smoke was seen above the city and the sky was red."[131]

More news arrived over the coming days via merchants' letters and conversations with ship captains returning from Iberia. Jan De Boer personally spoke with a ship captain named Booij who had experienced the earthquake at Lisbon, and recalled that on November 29 the Amsterdam merchant Louis Michel learned in a letter that his son had perished in the disaster.[132]

The first post-disaster correspondence from the Dutch ambassador in Lisbon arrived on December 5 at The Hague, a month and a day after it was written. "We are all here in a state of the utmost consternation and misery," wrote M. Calmette from a tent in Abraham Castres's garden on November 4. "I have had by God's grace the good luck to have survived with my wife and children." In his flustered state, he dated the letter "4. Oct. 1755." Throughout the remainder of the year, Calmette wrote regularly to The Hague (November 11, 18, 25, and December 16, 23, 30), keeping it apprised of his condition and the state of affairs in the Portuguese capital.[133]

On November 15, both Calmette and Jan Gildemeester, the Dutch consul, met with Dom José and offered him, in the name of their gov-

A seventeenth-century view of the Riverside Palace and the Terreiro do Paço by the Dutch painter Dirk Stoop

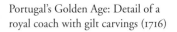

Portugal's Golden Age: Detail of a royal coach with gilt carvings (1716)

Dom João being served chocolate by his uncle, the infante Dom Miguel (1720)

Allegorical depiction of the marriage on January 19, 1729, of Dom José and Mariana Vitória, the daughter of Philip V of Spain

CONCORDIA FRATRUM

Pombal flanked by his two brothers: Paulo de Carvalho, Portugal's inquisitor general, and Francisco Mendonça Furtado, the governor of Grão-Pará and Maranhão and later secretary of state for overseas possessions

Pombal looking robust and in command at the age of seventy (1769)

João Glama Ströberle's *Allegory of the Earthquake 1755* (circa 1760) showing
the destruction of the Church of Santa Catarina

A family's tribute: The monkey that warned the Calmette family of the impending earthquake memorialized at Liselund, Antoine de Bosc de la Calmette's country estate and landscaped park on the island of Møn in Denmark.

Devotional (ex-voto) painting of a young girl being rescued from the ruins. The text on the left reads: "A votive offering made to Our Lady of the Star by Leonardo Rodrigues who invoked her Holiness's help after his three-year-old daughter was lost for seven hours after the earthquake of 1755. After discovering her in the ruins with a dangerous wound to her head, he attributed her survival to the intercession of the Lady."

Pombal's revenge: The public execution of the Távoras on January 13, 1759

Pombal gestures triumphantly toward the city he both rebuilt and terrorized

The ruins of the Carmelite Church today

The equestrian statue of José I in the Praça do Comércio. In the background is the triumphal Arch of the Rua Augusta which leads to the Rossio.

The Pombaline Baixa as seen from the river. The Praça do Comércio or Commerce Square (previously the Terreiro do Paço) is in the foreground. The western slope of São Jorge's Hill can be seen on the right.

ernment, all the assistance that he required. "My special esteem for the Republic of the United Provinces," Dom José replied, "will always force me to take care of their interests, as I am persuaded of their concerns about the fatal event that has recently afflicted my kingdom. I appreciate the offer made by the Minister in the name of his entire country; and I will happily use it to contribute to the relief of my poor subjects."[134] But Calmette and Gildemeester, it seems, did not have authorization to make such a promise for the Dutch Republic, whose merchants comprised only around 2 percent of the foreign total, ultimately sent no aid.[135]

On November 28, the Rhineland learned of the disaster from letters in the *Gazette de Cologne*. According to one, the Patriarchal Church and the Riverside Palace had been "reduced to cinders along with the treasures and archives of the court."[136] On December 9, the *Gazette*'s editors observed that "the entire western part of our continent" had been affected by the "great Phenomenon." Indeed, from the Strait of Gibraltar to the ponds and rivers of central Europe, few regions had not experienced some manifestation of the seismic event. In northern Germany, "the rising and falling of the water" in several lakes, reported the *Gazette de Cologne*, "was accompanied by a deadly stench which . . . suffocated fishermen, and was so violent that nets filled with fish were driven onto shore."[137]

On November 29, Dubliners first read about the quake in *The Dublin Gazette*, the British government's official newspaper in Ireland. Three weeks later, *The Cork Journal* conveyed the unhappy news to the kingdom's southern counties.[138] On December 20, William Cavendish, the Lord Lieutenant of Ireland and 4th Duke of Devonshire, composed a letter to Dom José from Dublin Castle in which he informed the king (in French) that he had received orders from George II to send 6,000 barrels of Irish beef and 4,000 casks of butter to Lisbon. "Permit me, Monsieur," wrote the thirty-five-year-old future nominal prime minister of Britain, "to assure Your Excellency how much I have been affected by the tragedy which has befallen your Portuguese Majesty and his realm."[139]

In late November, Count Perelada's replacement met with Fernando VI in Madrid before departing for Lisbon. "Offer [Portugal's] king, my brother-in-law, the continuation of all my help as well as that of my vassals," the monarch instructed his new ambassador to Portugal, Pedro Pablo Abarca de Bolea, the 10th Count of Aranda. "Let me know what his needs are. The hardships of his kingdom I consider my own, because I care about [the Portuguese]." On December 5, the fifty-seven-year-old Aranda arrived in Lisbon to a thunderous welcome.[140]

HAMBURG TO THE RESCUE

No country reacted to the news of the Lisbon disaster with more genuine horror than the Free and Hanseatic City of Hamburg. Situated at the confluence of the Elbe and Alster Rivers in northern Germany, the proud little trading republic had been an important commercial center since the Middle Ages and an original member of the Hanseatic League. By the middle of the eighteenth century, Hamburg was the third wealthiest trading hub in Northern Europe, after London and Amsterdam. Home to a bustling population of foreign merchants from Great Britain, Flanders, Portugal, and Holland, it specialized in trade with the British Isles, the Low Countries, and Iberia, where it purchased New World goods (primarily in Lisbon) to sell in central European markets. On All Saints Day 1755, there were more merchants from Hamburg living in the Portuguese capital than from any other nation other than Great Britain.[141]

The first report of an earthquake on November 1 to reach Hamburg appeared in the city's leading newspaper, *Hamburgischer Unparteyischer Correspondent* (Hamburg Nonpartisan Correspondent), on November 8, 1755. It came from Glückstadt, a city on the lower Elbe, and described an unexpected movement and rise of the waves in the harbor, a "strange phenomenon," which caused ships to break free of their moorings and "which the old people had never experienced." "Whether this was caused by a shaking of the earth," wrote the editors, "one cannot know for certain."[142]

In the weeks that followed, the *Correspondent* published several accounts of unusual disturbances of the water in northern Germany and Holland. On November 28 it reported that an earthquake had shaken Milan. "[It] is noteworthy," the editors remarked, "that . . . on that day, the same tremors were felt in the Netherlands."[143]

Then, in the late evening of November 28, letters arriving from France told of "a very great Earthquake at Lisbon," recalled the British ambassador to Hamburg, Emanuel Mathias.[144] The next day, the *Correspondent* published the first German account of the disaster. In just seven minutes, half of the city had been destroyed and 100,000 people, including the papal nuncio and the Spanish and English Ambassadors, had died. "With the next Post, we will have further details about this misfortune which has been equally great for merchants from many different kingdoms and cities."[145]

Three days later, the *Correspondent* ran a *Spitzmeldung* (news lead) on the front page, describing the disaster "with all its horrible details and unhappy consequences." But there was good news as well. The papal nuncio had in fact survived, and the number of fatalities had been reduced to fifty thousand.[146] In January, that number would drop to "only 5,000," as a result of letters "from a very good hand."[147] Was this none other than Pombal himself?

Over the coming year, no European paper ran more articles on the disaster than the *Hamburgischer Unparteyischer Correspondent*—more than 3,300 lines of coverage through June of 1756.[148] Demand for information about the earthquake was intense in the Hanseatic city. Inhabitants wished to know the fate of relatives, business associates, and friends, and many were terrified that the disaster might spell financial ruin not only for individual trading firms but for the tiny trading republic itself. Capitalizing on the fear that God might be planning more catastrophes, Lutheran ministers in the city called on their flocks to repent. "O Hamburg! Hamburg!" thundered one such preacher. "Like Lisbon you have no firm ground beneath you."[149]

On December 8, Hamburg's mayor, Nicolaus Schuback, proposed to the city government that a *Don Gratuit* (free gift) consisting of several merchant ships loaded with timber, building supplies, foodstuffs, and other goods be immediately sent to José I—a demonstration, he argued, of the special bond that existed between the two trading cities. The Admiralty, the seven commerce deputies, and the leading merchants of the Senate agreed. Immediately afterward the Senate set about drafting a most solicitous letter to Dom José. "We have ordered that ships be immediately loaded with stocks of beams and rafters," read the missive written in Latin. "We earnestly ask that your Majesty . . . not refuse this humble little gift."[150]

To finance the relief effort, the Senate pledged 80,000–100,000 mark bancos, the famous silver-backed currency of Hamburg (about £54,000–67,000), and the commerce deputies 150,000 mark bancos (£100,000).[151] Four ships were chosen for the mission: the *Sara* (captained by Samuel von der Smisten), the *Miss Elizabeth* (captained by Joahnn Eggers), the *Gerhardus* (captained by Bernard Johann Lange), and the *Peter* (captained by Joachim Ehlers). Each would carry approximately two hundred loads of timber in addition to other supplies.[152]

Detailed lists of each ship's cargo survive—a testament to both the generosity of Hamburg's elite and the thoroughness of the mercantile mind.[153] In addition to wooden boards and beams of varying lengths and sizes, there were great quantities of bricks and stones, and tools of every type and size: shovels and saws, hammers, clamps, mallets, planes, pliers, screwdrivers, drills and hatchets, as well as hundreds of barrels of nails and screws. To feed the survivors were casks of salted beef and pork and generous quantities of *Zuckerzweiback*, a dry sugary biscuit, as well as 199 bundles of food earmarked specifically for those from Hamburg.[154]

There were also hats, caps, socks, blankets, bolts of linen, sewing needles, and sailcloth to make tents, as well as bundles of paper and the writing quills and the quill knives *(Federmessern)* used to sharpen them. For Dom José's personal use, the thoughtful merchants included several barrels of "Rhine wine" and a single barrel containing both refined and crystalized sugar.[155] Such largesse came easily to a city that had enjoyed an impressive charitable infrastructure for more than three decades.[156]

The first relief ship set sail on December 17 (eleven days after Schuback's call to action), but slack winds initially impeded its progress. By December 29, both ships had only advanced up the Elbe as far as Neumühlen, while the third ship had still not left the harbor and the fourth had been deliberately held back until more information was received on exactly what kinds of supplies were needed. Almost a month would pass before the first two ships entered the North Sea. When Britain learned of the convoy, it offered to send warships to escort them to Lisbon. Although appreciative of the offer, Hamburg's Senate refused, believing it would only cause further delay.[157]

During the second week of January 1756, Hamburg's consul in Lisbon, Christian Stocqueler, hand-delivered the Senate's letter to Dom José. On January 20, the Portuguese monarch replied in Latin:

> Noble and Praiseworthy Consuls and Senators of the Republic of Hamburg! . . . We take special comfort from your letter. For we see that not only were you moved by this calamity of ours, but that you very diligently planned for the rebuilding [of our city] from so great a ruin. . . .
>
> For this gift . . . we thank you and we will remember it for-

ever, and with the same care in mind . . . we shall look out for
the business of your Republic . . . for only in this way are we
able to accept your help. In the meantime, we ardently pray to
the best and greatest God that he kindly avert a similar calamity
from befalling your city and all your territories. Given on the
twentieth day of January, in the year of our Lord 1756.

    Josephus[158]

Despite having declared that he would refuse all future gifts from any
country other than Great Britain, Dom José did, in the end, accept
Hamburg's *Don Gratuit*. The Hanseatic city-state was apparently too
nonthreatening for any of the major European powers to object. When,
in late April 1756, the four relief ships finally arrived in Lisbon, Dom
José announced that the supplies would be used for the construction of
his new palace in Belém.[159]

    From Hamburg, news of the disaster traveled north to Copenha-
gen, capital of the Kingdom of Denmark-Norway, and appeared in the
Copenhagen Danish Post Gazette on December 5.[160] "[T]he great European earthquake . . . has also made a great impression here, as you can
well imagine," wrote the German poet and Copenhagen resident Friedrich Gottlieb Klopstock to his parents back in Germany.[161] From the
Danish capital, the news crossed into Sweden, where three days later
its population learned of the quake in the pages of Stockholm's oldest
newspaper, the *Regular Mail Times*. After this, it was carried forty-five
miles due north to Uppsala, the ecclesiastical center of the kingdom,
"by a rider on a foaming horse."[162]

PRUSSIAN BLUES

It appears that Nature is in complete disarray.

—*The Berlin News (Berlinische Nachrichten)*, DECEMBER 23, 1755

It is likely that Frederick the Great first received word of the disaster in
early December from his envoy in London, Andrew Mitchell.[163] "You
must send me the most faithful and accurate account [of the destruc-
tion] that has been received in England," wrote the Prussian monarch
in reply on December 9. "Let me know if this calamity, which is occurring in a country with such strong business connections to England,

causes a great revolution in the economy of that country and give me your opinion on the impact."[164] Anxious for any intelligence, the forty-three-year-old Frederick then fired off letters to his ambassadors in France and the Netherlands, Baron Knyphausen and Bruno von der Hellen.[165] From the latter, he wished to know what manner of "revolution this event will bring about in Holland" and requested, as he had of Mitchell, a detailed report on the events in Lisbon.[166]

A week later, Frederick asked of Mitchell "if any of the losses suffered by English merchants have led to bankruptcies and if the circulation of money will stop and if this will result in the cessation of borrowing by the English government, making its operations more difficult."[167] The reason for this inquiry was that Frederick had just entered into discussions with Great Britain about forming a military alliance, and its economic prospects were of great concern to him. According to the agreement, Prussia promised to protect Hannover (over which the Hanoverian George II ruled) from a French invasion in exchange for money and Britain's promise to give no future aid to its former ally and Prussia's nemesis. Although Frederick initially feared that the quake had produced "a general desolation in English trade," the alliance went forward.[168]

After learning that his ambassador to Portugal, Hermann Braam-camp, had survived, Frederick instructed his minister of state, Heinrich Graf von Podewils, to draft "an obligatory and very affectionate letter of condolence from me to the King of Portugal."[169] It was signed by the Prussian king on December 18. "We have just learned of the sad fate of Your Majesty's Capital [and our] heart is pierced by the deepest sorrow," he wrote.

> We pray to God that he holds you—most High, Most Excellent, Most Powerful Prince, Our Cherished and Beloved Brother—in his holy and deserving protection.
>
> Your Good Brother
>
> Frederick[170]

Evidence exists that Frederick did offer some aid to the Portuguese, but, in the end, he failed to make good on it.[171] In the fifteen years since the publication of his celebrated treatise, *Anti-Macchiavel*, in which he espoused a moral politics that systematically refuted the views of the cynical Florentine philosopher, Frederick had ruled as a despot. He had waged war if his self-interest called for it. He had torn up agreements and treaties. And despite his continent-wide reputation as a poet, composer, and musician of considerable talent, he was widely viewed as one of the most conniving and thoroughly deceitful monarchs of his age. By such means, he had transformed Prussia into one of Europe's great powers. "I begin by taking," he allegedly said of his foreign policy. "I shall find scholars later to demonstrate my perfect right."

From the perspective of Fredrick's Prussian realpolitik, sending aid to Portugal made little sense. Unlike the Free City of Hamburg, Prussia had few economic ties with Lisbon, and although Prussia was in the process of becoming a British ally, the treaty that had cemented that relationship was simply too recent (it was signed in Westminster on January 16, 1756) and too narrow in scope for Frederick to contemplate providing anything substantial to Britain's oldest ally.[172] Besides, Frederick was a notorious skinflint—a family trait—and spent nearly every thaler and pfennig he possessed on his beloved and much-feared army.

Frederick's sangfroid notwithstanding, there seemed an almost insatiable desire among his Prussian subjects, and Germans in general, for news and information about the disaster. In 1755 and 1756, publishers in Breslau produced a series of twelve numbered pamphlets entitled *Accounts of the Frightening Lisbon Earthquake,* which extracted letters and eyewitness reports from a variety of European newspapers.[173] Also appearing (as in other countries) were hundreds of sermons, essays, and poems on the catastrophe by preachers, poets, and scholars—as well as several large and comprehensive volumes, which, in addition to a detailed description of the disaster provided an overview of the history and culture of Lisbon and the Portuguese empire.[174] They fed a growing interest among the Germans in the importance and uses of history, a trend that would culminate in the revolutionary advances in German and, ultimately, European historical scholarship in the next century.

The generosity of other heads of state is also open to question. In the city of Dresden, Augustus III—the King of Poland, Grand Duke of Lithuania, and Elector of Saxony—may or may not have put charity before national interest when he learned of the disaster. According to an article in the *Gazette de Cologne* in late January, a courier "left [Dresden] for Lisbon carrying a considerable sum of money that the King had sent to be distributed to those inhabitants who suffer in the

midst of the worst misfortunes that have happened to that great city."[175]
Whether these funds were received or even sent is unknown. Since ties
between Poland and Portugal were relatively weak, one must view this
claim with skepticism.

News of the disaster reached Vienna in early December. On
December 6, the *Wienerisches Diarium* (the Vienna Daily) ran an *Extra-
Blatt* (extra page) describing the "terrible earthquake" and the miraculous survival—"God be praised" ("*Gottlob*")—of the Braganças.[176] On
December 8, the Holy Roman Emperor, Francis I, wrote to Dom
José in his own hand in Italian. "I am deeply affected [by the news],"
confessed the forty-six-year-old husband of Maria Theresa and father
of five-week-old Antonia, the future Marie Antoinette. "Feelings of
humanity and sympathy" have welled up in "the depths of my heart,"
he wrote. I give "thanks to the Almighty that he has spared your fair
Majesty, the queen, and the entire royal family." An illness following
the birth of their daughter, he explained, had kept the Empress (and
real ruler of the empire) from offering her personal well wishes.[177]

According to an Italian newspaper report, "his Imperial Majesty
[Francis I] was touched by Lisbon's misfortunes and gave 300,000 Florins [£45,000] in relief to the poor Inhabitants" of that city.[178] A similar
story in *Hamburgischer Unparteyischer Correspondent* gives the amount as
"300,000 Guldens" (£45,000).[179] *The Boston Weekly News-Letter* stated
that the gift was sent by both the emperor and empress, while *The
Maryland Gazette* said that it was "the Empress Queen" Maria Theresa
who was responsible.[180] Whether these funds were ever sent and, if they
were, did Dom José accept them, is unknown.

On January 18, 1756, the distraught Portuguese ambassador in
Vienna wrote to Pombal seeking word of the Azores, which, according
to rumors, had fallen into the sea.[181]

ITALY LEARNS OF "THE GENERAL SLAUGHTER"

When word of the quake arrived in Rome in early December, Pope
Benedict XIV instructed Romans to pray daily in all the "convents,
monasteries, and churches . . . so that the Almighty would not extend
[to Italy] the terrible earthquake that had desolated Spain and Portugal."[182] According to a newspaper account, he "ordered three days of
prayers, with the showing of the Venerable [image] in the Church of

Santo Antonio dos Portugueses" and gave "plenary indulgences to all the faithful" who offered special thanks to God for having spared Dom José and his family.[183]

As early as December 6, Romans began to contemplate the impact of the earthquake on their own city.

> We are thunderstruck by the disaster at Lisbon, from which City large Sums were yearly remitted hither for the support of the Churches and Religious Houses founded by the Kings of Portugal, and for Pensions to a Multitude of Ecclesiastics and others.[184]

No one better understood Portugal's importance to the Holy See than Benedict, who on December 10 composed a letter of condolence to Dom José from his offices in the Basilica of Santa Maria Maggiore.

> Greetings and apostolic blessings to our dearest son in Christ. The news of the terrible earthquake and the fire that followed in the royal city of Lisbon, which caused such damage and injury to its inhabitants and such consternation in all of Europe, has been a bitter sorrow to us in light of the paternal affection with which we hold your Royal Majesty, your royal family, and your dominion, the royal Portuguese nation. With so large a desolation we cannot suggest to your Majesty any great consolation . . . except to accept that what He has done and will do has been for the benefit of our souls; among many indications of Divine Wrath, we see indications of Divine Mercy; having learned in letters [from Lisbon] that your Royal Person and all of your royal family, the Cardinal Patriarch and our Monsignor Nuncio have survived . . . I will not forget to give thanks to the Almighty for his mercy and to beg him vigorously to suspend further scourges that men, because of their sins, perhaps merit.
>
> In spite of the great distances between us, if there is anything that we can do to aid Your Majesty and relieve the suffering of your subjects, [let us know]; we are obligated to do everything we can. In the meanwhile . . . I give the Papal benediction to Your Majesty, the Queen, and the entire royal family.[185]

The next day, Silvio Valenti Gonzaga, the cardinal secretary of state of the Vatican, wrote to Monsignor Acciaiouli in Lisbon. "I do not have words or phrases to sufficiently express and explain to Your Illustrious Lordship how touched and injured was the paternal heart of our Lord [Pope Benedict] to hear such dreadful accounts of the inestimable damage caused in that city by the horrible earthquake."[186] A week later, Gonzaga expressed his anxiety at not having received a second letter from the nuncio. "We do hope," wrote Gonzaga, "that the Mercy of the Lord has preserved your life in the [midst of the] general slaughter."[187]

On December 25, the cardinal informed Acciaiouli, after finally receiving additional letters from him, that "Our Lord [Pope Benedict] thanks Your Illustrious Lordship for the attention that you have given to consoling and offering all of your energy to His Majesty [Dom José]. . . . His Blessedness will also be happy if in his pontifical name you offer His Majesty everything that can be done with the spiritual power that Jesus Christ grants to console his Majesty and comfort his afflicted people."[188] In other words, the eighty-year-old pontiff had no intention of sending anything but spiritual aid to his Most Faithful Benefactor.

Several weeks earlier, on November 18, the Genoese consul to Portugal, Ferdinando Aniceto Vigánego, wrote his government from the fields outside Lisbon.

> For my part, I can assure Your Serene Lordships that I was not even able to save a [single] shirt from my house. I have been reduced, with my three children, to the most extreme poverty. I explain this to Your Serene Lordships to implore you kindly to send me the relief that you deem appropriate to my dismal state or I will almost be forced to beg in the streets with my sons. . . .
>
> I ask Your Serene Lordships to forgive my confused style, for I have not yet recovered from my horror and fright when I found myself in the midst of so many ruins and the death of relatives and friends.[189]

Over the next few months, Vigánego dutifully sent reports to his superiors in the seaside republic. "For the last several weeks, I have not felt any more tremors of the earth," he wrote on June 22, 1756. "But people continue to remain in their huts partly out of fear and partly because of the lack of houses."[190]

The Neapolitan ambassador, Carlo de Guevara, and his entire

family had also survived—although his house and everything in it was destroyed. "I am living in the fields under a tent made of curtains, covers, and sheets," wrote the forty-year-old diplomat on November 4. "I am about to construct a *barraca*, if I can get the materials and the workers, regardless of the cost."[191]

Although Guevara and Vigánego stayed at their posts, many Italians fled the city. "Your musitians come tumbling in naked upon us every day," wrote Keene to Castres on November 20.[192] In the words of Monsignor Acciaiuoli, those leaving Lisbon included "all the musicians, ballet dancers, painters, tailors, and other artists, who in considerable numbers and with enormous annual salaries from his Majesty had come from Italy and other countries, but mostly from Italy."[193] Dom José's dream of transforming Lisbon into an international music center was definitively over.[194]

According to official documents, the Most Serene Republic of Venice first learned "the terrible news of the Lisbon Earthquake" on December 1 from a courier arriving from Paris.[195] Several days later, Venice's consul in Madrid, Girolamo Ascanio Giustinian, informed his government that "everything" in Lisbon had been "reduced to a mountain of stones and cadavers."[196] Strange, then, that the brief letter subsequently sent by Venice's doge, Francesco Loredano, to Dom José was so cheery.

"We hope," wrote the seventy-year-old on December 27, "that God compensates you for this auspicious event with prosperity and many long and happy years." A largely ineffectual leader and frequent figure of mockery during his ten-year rule, Loredano offered to send aid to Venice's old trading rival, but, like Frederick the Great, never followed through. Although not a trait of the Prussian king, passivity was Loredano's hallmark, which explained both his decision not to help Lisbon and Venice's future neutrality in the Seven Years War. The latter policy led (unexpectedly) to a temporary resurgence in the declining republic's fortunes, allowing it to access markets it had been previously denied.[197]

On January 14, 1756, Dom José replied to Pope Benedict's letter, which he had received directly from the hands of Monsignor Acciaiuoli.

> Blessed Father *[Beatissimo Padre]*. The paternal feelings
> expressed in your letter from December only reinforce the
> great confidence that I have always had in Your Holiness. But
> at the same time it has also brought me the most powerful

consolation from the legitimate emotion that the damage
from the earthquake on November 1 . . . has caused me. . . .
I recognize in such a deadly event that the Divine Mercy was
much greater than the Divine Justice. . . . And [I realize that]
to end the effects of the latter and permanently exercise the
former, to benefit the royal family and the people that God
has entrusted to me, that I must recommend to them the
devoted prayers of Your Holiness, offering myself beneath
your Apostolic Blessing.

Belém the fourteen of January seventeen fifty-five.

Very Obedient Son of Your Holiness Joseph[198]

On the final day of January 1756, Charles Emanuel III, Duke of
Savoy and King of Piedmont, sent two letters of condolence to Dom
José—one in Italian, the other in French.

Monsieur Mon Frère. I trust that Your Majesty is persuaded
that I share in the sad events that have struck your dominions
and in the dangers that you face. Although I think the present
is still filled with horror, a thousand blessings to the Lord for
protecting Your Majesty and Your Majesty's Royal Family, and,
in doing so, providing your afflicted peoples with the greatest
consolation they could have in their present misfortunes. . . .
I hope that Your Majesty can judge the tender feelings that I
have for you and with which I am very sincerely,

Monsieur Mon Frère Your Majesty's Good Brother Your
Friend

Turin, January 31, 1756[199]

As far as can be determined, the fifty-four-year-old uncle of Louis XV
sent no aid.

THE TSARITSA'S DECISION

Despite being separated from the Portuguese capital by more than
2,200 miles, the inhabitants of St. Petersburg, Russia, were apparently

captivated by the news of the disaster. The first public mention of the earthquake appeared in the *St. Petersburg News (Sankt-Peterburgskie Vedomosti)* on December 5, or December 16 in the Gregorian calendar used by most Western European countries.[200] "More than half of the Portuguese capital collapsed," the paper declared, "and within a few minutes around 100 thousand people were crushed."[201]

From its founding in April 1756, the *Moscow News (Moskovskiye Vedomosti)* also covered the topic extensively, running articles written by correspondents in Lisbon not found in any other European paper. One such article on April 30, 1756, claimed that Dom José was attempting to "restore trust between England and France." This "shows," said the author, "that he has calmed down somewhat after the misfortune that happened at Lisbon." Throughout the spring and summer of 1756, both newspapers kept Russian elites apprised of the developing situation in Portugal.[202]

It is probable that the Tsaritsa Elizaveta Petrovna first learned of the disaster from her minister plenipotentiary in Great Britain, Prince Aleksandr Mikhailovich Golitsyn, who posted a letter on the subject from London on November 25.[203] Two days later, he wrote her that "confirmation . . . of the horrible event" had arrived with the French mail. He further informed the empress that Fernando VI of Spain had sent 60,000 pistoles (£50,000) to Portugal along with clothing and other provisions and that "His Royal British Majesty" had asked Parliament for £100,000 worth of provisions for the Portuguese.[204] The result, Golitsyn noted, was "much praise for the Spanish King on account of his lofty sentiments and benevolence."[205]

Perhaps Elizaveta desired to be similarly lauded or perhaps it was her well-known aversion to bloodshed that caused her to contemplate sending aid to Lisbon. According to Count Aleksandr Romanovitch Vorontsov, the forty-five-year-old empress "had magnanimous intentions to send timber to be used for the rebuilding of Lisbon along with iron, other materials, and a few thousand bags of flour . . . even though no formal diplomatic relationship existed [between Russia and Portugal]." The proposed convoy, consisting of a warship and several supply vessels, was to be led by a person of distinction who would personally present the tsaritsa's gift to Dom José. Also to accompany the mission was fourteen-year-old Vorontsov, whose parents saw in the undertaking a way for their son to gain some valuable diplomatic experience and see a bit of the world.[206]

Unfortunately for the teenage aristocrat, the tsaritsa changed her mind and the flotilla was never sent. Whether the notoriously mercurial Elizaveta became distracted by the two abiding passions of her life—French clothing and extravagant balls—or whether she and her advisors thought better of such a diplomatically complex undertaking is unknown. It was certainly a moment of extraordinary political flux on the continent. Over the previous year, Russia and France had engaged in secret negotiations toward a sweeping diplomatic rapprochement. To facilitate the discussions, St. Petersburg had sent a shipment of exquisite sables to Madame de Pompadour.[207] When word reached St. Petersburg of the Treaty of Westminster (January 1756), a neutrality pact between Prussia and Great Britain, the empress's counselors encouraged her to end Russia's long-standing military arrangement with the British and ally her empire with Austria and France.[208] It was the beginning of one of the most significant realignments in European history—the so-called Diplomatic Revolution of 1756—whereby the traditional alliance of Britain and Austria versus France and Prussia was transformed almost overnight into Britain and Prussia versus France, Austria, and Russia.

With such a realignment in the offing, Russia had little incentive to provide material assistance to Britain's ally Portugal—no matter how horrified the tsaritsa had been by the news. By contrast, Britain's relief efforts were not only understandable but shrewd. By aiding Portugal, Britain was providing a lifeline to a nation with which it had substantial trading interests as well as guaranteeing access to the strategic ports of Lisbon and Porto during the upcoming conflict.

As one might expect, the Portuguese took note of the British gesture. "All the kings of Europe, realizing the fatal destruction of Portugal, ordered that everything that was necessary be sent," wrote a Portuguese priest. "However, the British king, George the Second, distinguished himself above everyone." Unlike those who had promised relief, George had "acted, sending a fleet with every kind of food and thousands of cruzados." And unlike "those Catholic Kings, who ordered aid to be sent" but in the end did "nothing to address the needs of the Portuguese people," the British king, a Protestant, had come to the assistance of his fellow Christians.[209] It is odd, remarked the slightly confused cleric, "to encounter such a pious and devoted disposition in a prince and [his] vassals who follow a religion that Catholics, with good reason, consider an abomination."[210] In fact, religious affiliation appears to have played no role in the decision of states to send or not send aid, and even Portugal's notorious reputation as a bastion of the Inquisition appears not to have played into any country's calculus— evidence perhaps that the bloody sectarianism of the previous two centuries was over. In its place, a decidedly more secular world (at least, in the diplomatic sphere) had emerged.

Humanitarian concerns existed, but they were intermingled with political and economic interests. The city of Hamburg, for example, was motivated to send aid to alleviate the suffering of both the Portuguese and its own merchants as well as to secure its position as Lisbon's second most important trading partner. Spain, as has been discussed, was moved by the close familial ties between the two royal couples and, perhaps, to gain some political leverage over the Portuguese. France's offer of aid most likely reflected both the personal influence of Madame de Pompadour and a clever, albeit unsuccessful, attempt to encourage Portugal to remain neutral (i.e., not help Britain) during the imminent conflict. On the other hand, the decision of Austria to send relief (if true) was more likely evidence of Maria Theresa's kind heart than any residual Austrian allegiance to Great Britain.[211] The Great Lisbon Disaster had forced the nations of Europe to reevaluate old alliances and question the limits of their new ones.

Just as the continent began to absorb the news of the tragedy, much of central and western Europe (Germany, Switzerland, France, and Italy) was shaken by a series of powerful tremors on December 9. The apparent result of a new fault set in motion by the aftershocks of the All Saints' Day event, the earthquake shook "Languedoc, Provence, Dauphiné, Lionnois, Franche Comté, Bourgogne, and Alsace," according to the *Gazette de Cologne*—as well as "Montmedy, Caeinole, and the many cities and regions of Lorraine, Champagne, and Picardie." Thanks to "the infinite goodness" of Providence, however, "the terrible scourge" passed over the Île-de-France and its capital, Paris, as the quake on November 1 had.[212] Although no deaths or serious injuries were reported, fear and astonishment were widespread.

On the same day, Captain Augustus Hervey received word of the disaster while stationed on the island of Malta. The news made him "very uneasy" for his friends in the Portuguese capital—no doubt provoking him to wonder if any of the scores of *senhoras* and *senhorinhas* who had shared his bed had survived. "These are frightful events," Hervey confided to his journal, "[which] ought to inspire reflections that should mend the lives of individuals in order not to deserve such chastisements from Providence."[213] Whether he ever seriously contemplated mending his own ways is unknown.

MUNDUS NOVUS

In seventeen hundred fifty-five,
When vice its empire did revive,
Consuming fire, a jealous God
Call'd on New-England with his rod.

—*Lines Made after the Great Earthquake* (1755)

Over four thousand miles away on the other side of the Atlantic, *The Boston Evening-Post* on December 22 ran "a short and imperfect but surprisingly melancholy Account" of the earthquake by a Captain Collins, who had arrived in Cape Ann, Massachusetts, thirteen days before. It was, along with a similar story that day in *The Boston Gazette*, the first printed mention of the Lisbon disaster in the Western Hemisphere. "That fair, large, rich, and noble City," declared the captain, who had departed Lisbon on November 4, was "entirely shaken down by the Earthquake that did so much damage at Cádiz the same Day." According to his best estimate, "one hundred and ten thousand" people had died, "but this," the *Post*'s editors cautioned, "we have no authority to affirm."[214]

For the last two weeks, there had been indications that something unusual had occurred somewhere in the eastern Atlantic Ocean. On December 8, *The Boston Gazette* had reported the incident involving Captain Eleazer Johnson of Boston, mentioned in chapter 2.[215] But the *Gazette* could provide no explanation for this strange occurrence, and apparently the remainder of Johnson's journey across the Atlantic, which, under normal conditions, took thirty to forty days, was without incident. A week later, *The Boston Evening-Post* informed its readers that a Captain McPherson had witnessed "a surprising Ebb and Flow of the Sea" in Barbados—after which the water, "suddenly retiring to a considerable Distance . . . immediately returned again to so great a Height" that it overflowed "the Streets." No explanation was offered.[216]

When news of the Lisbon disaster finally reached British North America, many colonists were still busy discussing their own recent seismic experience: the Cape Ann Earthquake of November 18, 1755.

This "Great and Surprizing Earthquake," as one eyewitness labeled it, struck at 4:30 a.m. and measured an estimated Mw 6.0.[217] "At first," there was "a rumbling noise like low Thunder," wrote James Freeman, a Boston clergyman, "which was immediately followed with the violent shaking of the earth and buildings . . . [it] continued for about the space of 1 minute/ some say 2."[218]

Its epicenter was located about twenty-five miles off the coast of Cape Ann in the Province of Massachusetts Bay, and it was the most powerful earthquake in the history of the colony. It was felt as far north as Halifax, Nova Scotia, and as far south as the colony of South Carolina. From Maine to Connecticut, walls and chimneys buckled, broke, and collapsed. "Thousands of Bricks and Slates," recalled the Deacon John Tudor, "were scattered in the Streets."[219] In Boston alone, over 1,500 chimneys toppled over. And across the Northeast, city streets became so clogged with rubble they were rendered impassable. While no deaths or major injuries resulted, the experience caused considerable alarm.[220] "My Flesh Trembleth for fear of thee. I am afraid of thy Judgments," wrote Tudor of the God he thought responsible for the terrible event.[221]

Attempting to draw a casual connection between the earthquake in New England and the one in Iberia, *The Boston Evening-Post* noted that the Lisbon event had "happened about a Fortnight before the terrible Shock of an Earthquake felt in these parts on the 18th of November past."[222] Indeed, it seems highly likely that the dynamic stresses unleashed on the earth's tectonic plates by the Lisbon Earthquake induced not only the Cape Ann Earthquake, possibly through the activation of a new fault system, but the hundreds of aftershocks (each an earthquake in its own right) that were felt across Western Europe and North Africa over the next year.[223]

On the other hand, the much more destructive Meknes Earthquake of November 27, 1755, may have been a local seismic event not related to the Lisbon quake at all—although many confused the two at the time.[224] It nevertheless caused horrific damage to the cities of Meknes and Fez in north-central Morocco and triggered a landslide that almost completely destroyed the mountain village of Moulay Idriss Zerhoun.[225] In Fez, three thousand people purportedly died, while in Meknes "4,000 Moors were buried alive under the ruins" and eight thousand of the sixteen thousand Jews who resided in the Jewish Quarter perished, according to an exaggerated newspaper report.[226] "It

seems to me," one Christian purportedly observed, that "in delivering
the blow of Divine Justice" upon the Jews, "God wanted to express his
righteous disgust."[227]

On January 1, 1756, word of the Lisbon disaster appeared for the
first time in Benjamin Franklin's *Pennsylvania Gazette*, when a Captain
Dreson brought the "melancholy News" to Philadelphia. "By the next
Vessel," wrote the editors, "we may expect a particular Account of the
Damage, there being no Letters by Captain Dreson from any of the
Merchants relating to it."[228] Three days earlier, New Yorkers learned
of the great earthquake in *The New-York Mercury*.[229] And over the next
six weeks, the news traveled south, appearing on the second page of *The
Maryland Gazette* on January 8, 1756, and in *The South Carolina Gazette*
on February 5, 1756. But because of the outbreak of what would later
be known as the French and Indian War, a North American manifestation of the Seven Years War in Europe, *The Virginia Gazette* ceased
printing from November 1755 to August 1756 and thus ran no stories
on the disaster.[230]

In late 1755 and early 1756, the subject of war so preoccupied the
colonists of North America that the Lisbon Earthquake never came to
dominate the pages of any of the fifteen colonial newspapers, even on
the day of its first appearance. Instead, the papers focused on the movement of troops and ships, the impact of Braddock's defeat in western
Pennsylvania, and—most unsettlingly—graphic accounts of massacres
of white settlers by Native Americans that had intensified to a horrifying degree by the fall of 1755.[231] On the day *The New-York Mercury* ran
its first account of the Lisbon disaster, it published letters describing
the violence and chaos on the American frontier.

> The barbarous and bloody scene [in New Jersey] . . . is the most
> lamentable that perhaps ever appeared. . . . There may be seen
> Horror and Desolation—populous Settlements deserted—
> Villages laid in Ashes—Men, Women, and Children cruelly
> mangled and massacred—some found in the Woods, very
> nauseous for want of Internment. Some just reeking from the
> Hands of their Savage Slaughterers, and some hacked and cov-
> ered all over with wounds.[232]

With history exploding all around them and the recent experience of
their own earthquake, it is not surprising that some North American

colonists saw the Lisbon disaster as part of a larger breakdown in the natural order of things. As the editors of *The Boston Gazette* wrote on December 29,

> The Truth is the whole World is grown very corrupt, as it was in the days of Noah, and the Wickedness of Man is so great and universal in the Earth, that we need not wonder to hear of Earthquakes and Desolations abroad, or feel them, among ourselves—these Operations indeed ought to be looked upon as powerful Remonstrances against the Wickedness of Mankind, but whether we have not so long accustomed ourselves to our Sins, as to become deaf to every voice that would call off our Attention from them, is a Question that Time only can determine.[233]

God, the Divine Judge, was attempting to awaken mankind from its sinful slumber. Although many colonists were well acquainted with the scientific explanations for earthquakes, the editors shied away from such speculation and instead ran sermons and essays emphasizing how God had been the Primary Cause.[234] The seeming apocalyptic times had pushed religious explanations to the forefront of colonial minds.

In early January, a twenty-three-year-old John Dickinson, then studying law in London, wrote to his family in Pennsylvania about the earthquake in Lisbon, "a catastrophe of which I suppose some accounts as well as some signs have already reachd your world.

> To pretend to give any account of this misfortune [began the future Founding Father] would be to lessen it all I can. The curious & learned have their compassion swallowed up in fresh enquiries, when these dreadful events are the directions of Providence particularly to punish mankind, or proceed from natural causes. But great God! May not the same instructive lesson be learnt from either, that humanity is uncertainty, and *AB HOC MOMENTO PENDET AETERNITAS* [All eternity hangs on this moment]. By the very smallest computation, 20,000 lives are lost; the richest prince in Europe [José I] more wretched than a bankrupt. Accounts are just arrivd that his army are turnd dissolute & lawless & plunder the miserable remains of his subjects.[235]

Colonial newspapers (obviously responding to demand) continued their coverage of the disaster well into spring and summer. Yet no evidence has surfaced that British North America sent aid, as the mother country had, to Portugal. Embattled by marauding Indians, anxious over the territorial designs of the French, and unsure whether they had lost favor with the Deity, the American colonists (whose ancestors had crossed the Atlantic to escape the horrors of the Old World) were otherwise engaged.

On the other hand, Portugal's largest colony, Brazil, did send money. Because the sea journey between Lisbon and Portugal's South American colony took longer than to British North America, Brazilians and Portuguese colonists learned of the earthquake more than a week after their North American neighbors. Olinda, the capital of Pernambuco, received word on January 1—ten days after Boston did—in a letter from the Portuguese secretary of the navy, Diogo de Mendonça. The news was received "with a great uproar," wrote Bishop Francisco Xavier Aranha in his written reply to the secretary. "We give thanks to God for saving the life of the king, the royal family, and the Portuguese people and ask him to show mercy to the entire kingdom. We will continue praying and engaging in processions in order to placate the wrath of the Lord."[236]

Pombal, Dom José, and Secretary Mendonça all sent letters to the governors of the individual Brazilian states informing them of Lisbon's destruction. "This fatal event, which occurred not only in Lisbon but throughout the entire kingdom," wrote Mendonça to the governor of Rio de Janeiro and Minas Gerais on November 11, 1755, "was caused by an earthquake, whose purpose and range has never been seen before."[237] On December 16, Dom José ordered every Brazilian governor to take immediate steps to raise money to rebuild the imperial capital.[238] "By communicating [the details of] this sad event," he wrote to the city officials of Bahia, "I hope to rely on the fairness and honorable inclinations of my faithful vassals of this city . . . not only to deliver the praise that is due to the Divine Mercy for having suspended the punishment, when he could have annihilated us, but to do everything possible on this urgent occasion to help rebuild the capital of these kingdoms and dominions."[239]

Despite the enormous financial burden, Brazilians and Portuguese businessmen living in Brazil rallied with immediate enthusiasm and generosity to the cause. The inhabitants of Rio de Janeiro pledged the kingly sum of 3 million cruzados (£336,000) to be offered as a lump payment within the next two years, while officials in Paraíba and Recife offered 100,000 cruzados (£11,220) and 600,000 cruzados (£67,000), respectively. In Olinda, the city council pledged a hefty 900,000 cruzados (£100,000) to be taken, it was stipulated, "from the taxes of the Customs House."[240] In a letter dated July 21, 1756, São Paulo's city council informed Dom José that they had been unable to send their *donativo* (donation) because the annual fleet had already sailed, but would do so with the next fleet.[241] Whether these sums were ever paid in full is unknown. No Brazilian newspapers carried stories on the disaster because none existed. The printing press would not become a fixture in Brazil for another fifty-three years (1808), when the Portuguese royal family fled to Rio de Janeiro following Napoleon's invasion of Portugal.

CONTINUING COVERAGE

The earthquake is still on people's lips.

—*Gazette de Cologne,* JANUARY 16, 1756[242]

By the end of February 1756, most of the Western world knew of the disaster, and press coverage of it would continue well into the new year. The *Mercure de France* ran a total of 106 stories on the earthquake, while the *Courrier d'Avignon* and the *Gazette de Cologne* published more than fifty, and the *Journal de Verdun* thirty.[243] The most expansive and detailed coverage was found in Britain and Germany, with considerable interest in Spain and Russia. By the late spring of 1756, however, events related to the Seven Years War, which was formally declared on May 18, had become Europe and North America's leading news story.

Even so, the disaster continued to haunt the collective imagination. At Versailles, Cardinal de La Rochefoucauld and the Abbé Desmarets, the royal confessor, threatened Louis XV with an "earthquake" if he did not take Easter communion and forswear his mistress, Madame de Pompadour. When the king agreed, the crafty Pompadour realized she had little choice but to mimic the king's newfound piety in order to retain her influence at court. She, wrote Horace Walpole, "offered up her rouge to the daemon of earthquakes, and to sanctify her conversion and reconcile it to Court-Life, procured herself to be declared *Dame du palais* [lady-in-waiting] to the Queen."[244]

In January 1756, Spain's *Mercurio Histórico y Político* launched a special section, "From the Encampment Around the Ruins of Lisbon," which for more than a year provided readers with detailed and in-depth dispatches from a correspondent living among the city's thousands of survivors.[245] Despite its extensive coverage, the *Mercurio* never ventured to explain the causes of the quake. A recipient of monarchical protection, like the *Gaceta de Madrid* and the *Gazeta de Lisboa*, it had to tread lightly when dealing with controversial topics.[246] To suggest that the earthquake had been solely the product of natural forces might have been viewed as blasphemous, while to assert that God had been the primary instigator might have been interpreted as heretical, as Malagrida would soon discover in Portugal. Before long, debates about the causes and meaning of the disaster would explode across the continent—though most would take place not in the pages of newspapers but in letters, books, broadsheets, and printed pamphlets.

CHAPTER EIGHT

"A Chaos of Stones"

All the pomp has ended, 'twas fleeting;
No more than a sad memory
Of the famous city that someday
Only the crystals of the Tagus will enrich.

—DOMINGOS DOS REYS,
"POEM ON THE LAMENTABLE EARTHQUAKE" (1756)

DAMAGE ASSESSMENT

On February 19, 1756, more than ten weeks after the disaster, Monsignor Acciaiuoli confided to Pope Benedict XIV about the state of the Portuguese capital. "I ask Your Holiness to believe that it is much worse than what I have previously mentioned, despite the fact that there are those who would like to make it appear less."[1] Few outside the government would have disputed the nuncio's assessment, for in February 1756 central Lisbon was little more than a vast, yawning ruin. Its commercial and political core had been burned beyond recognition and much else had been shaken to the ground or damaged. The densely populated Baixa had borne the full brunt of the inferno as it had the earthquake—but other areas had suffered as well.[2] "The fire reduced to ashes a large portion of the old city and a large portion of the new," wrote Moreira de Mendonça. It "completely destroyed the neighborhoods of the Ribeira, the Rua Nova [dos Mercadores], and the Rossio, and the largest parts of the neighborhoods of the Remoulares, the Bairro Alto, the Limoeira, and the Alfama, which," he added, "are the richest and most populous seven neighborhoods of the twelve that make up the city."[3] In Father Portal's view, it destroyed "the heart of the city."[4]

While the earthquake had set the destruction in motion, it was "the fourth element [fire]," recalled one eyewitness, "that caused the most consternation, and which, without exaggeration, burned the largest and best part of Lisbon."[5] "The fire," affirmed Mr. Braddock, "may be said to have destroyed the whole city, at least everything that was grand or valuable in it."[6] In the opinion of one Portuguese priest, it was the disaster's "greatest thief."[7] Abraham Castres estimated that the "Conflagration" did "ten times more Mischief than the Earthquake itself," a reckoning that was repeated in numerous broadsheets and newspapers at the time.[8]

On the other hand, if no fires had broken out, some sections of the Baixa would have suffered only moderate damage, and many treasures would have been recovered from the rubble. On the New Street of the Merchants (Rua Nova dos Mercadores), "only a few houses initially fell," wrote Father Portal. But after the fire swept through the Baixa, it "was completely reduced to ashes."[9] It burned "those [buildings] that had fallen as well as those that still stood," wrote another priest. It was "the cruel executioner of the people of Lisbon," a "barbarous element," a "tyranny."[10]

In all, an area comprising more than one and a half square kilometers or 1,500 by 1,000 meters was destroyed by the blaze. It devoured both sides of the Rua Nova dos Mercadores, according to a priest, and all the riches possessed by those who lived there, including "the whole of the Rua do Ourives do Ouro e Prata . . . the Church of São Nicolau, the Rua dos Escudeiros, the Rua dos Odreyros, the entire area around the Rossio up to the Church of Santo Domingos, the entire Riverside Palace," and the area around the Terreiro do Paço, "the Misericordia Church" and its environs, "the Street of the Ovens, the area around the Patriarchal Square . . . the Rua Nova da Almada and passing from there to the Bairro Alto . . . to the doors of Santa Catarina and the Palace of Marialva, stopping next to the Houses of Calharis . . . then running up the Wide Street to São Roque, leaving that church undamaged, and then running downward, it devoured everything along the shoreline from the Church of São Paulo to the Cais da Pedra."[11] Within this immense half oval—"the large field where Lisbon once stood," as one person described it—the city's most prominent buildings were located and most of its population. It had become little more than "a chaos of stones," declared another survivor.[12]

What buildings did the fire destroy? According to Moreira de Mendonça, the most serious losses were the Riverside Palace (Paço da

Ribeira), the Casa da Ópera, and the extravagantly adorned Patriarchal Church.[13] For his part, Mr. Braddock marveled at the thought of all that had been destroyed.

> The damage on this occasion [cannot] be estimated, but . . . it must have been immense. . . . All the fine tapestry, paintings, plate, jewels, furniture &c[ontents]. of the King's Palace, amounting to many millions, with the rich vestments and costly ornaments of the Patriarchal church adjoining (where the service was performed with no less pomp than that of the Pope's own Chapel); all the riches of the Palace of Braganza, where the crown-jewels, and plate of inestimable value, with quantities of the finest silk tapestries, interwoven with gold and silver thread, and hangings of velvet and damask, were kept; All the rich goods and spices in the India Warehouses under the palace, those belonging to the merchants of different nations in the opposite Custom-house, as well as those in the merchants' own houses, and dispersed among the numerous shops, were utterly consumed or lost.[14]

"What is certain," wrote the philosophe and agent of the French government Ange Goudar, "is that since the reign of Pedro II [1683–1706] and the discovery of gold mines [in Brazil] there was introduced

The ruins of the Riverside Palace

into Portugal such a great luxury of things that each palace was a private treasure, as much in paintings and tapestries as other precious things, and so it is possible to estimate the general loss, including that of foreigners, at "twelve hundred million [tournois livres]."[15] If one adds "to this," wrote one *lisboeta*, "the jewels, precious stones, gilt silver of the Crown and that in private hands, the churches and the religious communities, one reaches a sum that exceeds all imagination, because the court in Lisbon was the richest in Europe in precious stones and it lost all of them, except those that the royal family had with them at the time of the disaster." Indeed, "the two streets, where the richest goldsmiths and diamond setters lived, were those that suffered the most in the earthquake and the fire."[16] In Goudar's estimation, "two hundred diamond shops were completely buried under the ruins."[17]

Also "lost were priceless suits of armor," wrote Father Portal, "especially those from the Royal Treasury belonging to his Majesty, jewels of incomparable value, diamonds, pearls, emeralds, [and] every kind of precious stone, [as well as] gold, silver, paintings, and statues."[18] Moreover, "the great cupola of the India House fell in the violence of the fire and was reduced to ashes." As one of the principal centers of commerce in Lisbon, the India House alone held "eleven or twelve million [cruzados' worth of] diamonds," reported Portal, as well as "silver, and immense quantities of gold, of which only a small quantity was ever recovered."[19] In addition, most of the precious contents of the tsunami-damaged Customs House was consumed in the blaze. In a letter to the Portuguese secretary of state for overseas affairs in May 1756, the governor of Pernambuco reports that "the merchants" of Recife lost "more than one million [cruzados] in the fire," which reduced "the Customs House . . . to ashes with all the goods that had been sent on the earlier fleet."[20]

Although much of the Torre do Tombo's contents had been saved, vast collections of public and private records, many dating back centuries, were incinerated—"registries and records, professional writings and expense accounts, books of baptism, burial, and genealogy," according to Father Figueiredo.[21] Within the area affected by the blaze, "no paper or book or similar thing was not consumed by the elements," reported another priest.[22] In the Carmelite Monastery, the fire destroyed not only "the great library," wrote Father Portal, but "the individual cells of the priests with all their book collections, papers, and furniture," as well as the archive, which was "an irreparable loss."[23]

It "burned the offices of the Ministers, those of the scholars, and the clerks, as well as the merchant houses, [and] the treaties, and lawful contracts" found within them, wrote one eyewitness.[24] And because most of the city's clerks lived in the Baixa, the fire destroyed almost all of the records and contracts in their possession.[25] On December 19, 1755, the Cabinet for Overseas Affairs began to discuss alternative measures to make up for the loss of their precious account books which had burned in the fire.[26]

The loss of the Rua Nova dos Mercadores was particularly devastating, for located here—in addition to scores of merchant houses and commercial businesses—was the Lisbon Stock Exchange, where traders and merchants from Geneva, Hamburg, Seville, Paris, London, Burgos, Amsterdam, Valladolid, and Venice came to conduct business and set prices. In this one street alone, the fire incinerated the accounting records of scores of merchants along with their private libraries and personal collections of artifacts from across the globe. One surviving notebook from the merchant house of Pedro Mendes da Costa and Matias Jorge Mendes provides rare insight into Portuguese trade during the years 1738–1750, including a description of the funeral of João V and the coronation of his son. Of the one thousand or so original accounting books that once existed from Lisbon's Royal Silk Factory for the years 1734–1750, only thirty-four survive.[27]

The amount of government records that were lost was also staggering—for the fire destroyed the principal offices of the Portuguese state, including the buildings that housed "the chief judge of the palace, the *Inquisição*, the Treasury, the War Cabinet, the board of three states, the India House, the Customs House, the War Treasury, the Cabinet of Overseas Affairs, and many others."[28] At the Customs House, the loss was particularly acute.[29] In the Seven Commodities Customs House (Alfândega das Sete Casas), which administered the import and export fees for slaves, coal, wood, fruit, meat and fish, olive oil, and wine, only a handful of records survive, while in the Grand Customs House for Sugar (Alfândega Grande de Açucar), where import-export duties were determined for Brazilian sugar, only five receipt books from the first half of the eighteenth century have come down to us. In the Treasury (Casa dos Contos do Reino), almost all the contracts, rent documents, public expense books, and financial and economic legislation—in essence, the record of the Crown's economic relationship with its subjects—were burned.[30]

According to Portugal's treasurer, Francisco da Fonseca e Sousa, "the loss of books of revenue and expenditures and documents [from the] Treasuries and [the] Royal Households" "was so damaging that it will be felt for centuries."[31] He was correct. The principal reason the economic history of early modern Portugal, which is so fundamental to our understanding of the development of the modern economy, has received less attention from scholars than it deserves is because the data from the period before the Lisbon Earthquake simply do not exist. "When we speak of archives [in Lisbon]," writes a Spanish archivist, "we should speak of the period before and after this natural disaster."[32]

But of all the property lost in the disaster, the most widely and deeply mourned by *lisboetas* were the thousands of beloved statues, sacred paintings, crosses, and reliquaries with their holy contents. In the Church of Santo Domingos, according to one heartbroken chronicler, "the fire consumed all the sacred statues *(imagens)*, including the ancient and much venerated statue of the *Crucified Lord* as well as that of the *Lady of the Rosary* and the beautiful *Lady of the Virtues*."[33] According to Father Figueiredo, "some [of these sacred objects] were broken into pieces; others were burned; others were buried below the rubble" and never found.[34] Such was the intensity of veneration for these objects that it is rather difficult to assign a meaningful modern value to their loss.

All the more cherished, therefore, were the holy objects that survived. Unlike almost everything else in the Church of São Vicente, the sacred and much venerated statue of *Maria Santissima* was spared.[35] Likewise, the beloved statue of Lisbon's patron saint, Santo António, in the church named after him, came through the catastrophe completely undamaged, reported Father João Bautista de Castro, although the church suffered terribly.[36] "One statue that deserves particular mention," wrote Father Figueiredo, was known as the *Lord with the Cross on His Back*. It had resided for centuries in the Church of Our Lady of Grace and "had been venerated by the monarchs of Portugal, the nobility, and the people . . . [and was] every year carried in Lisbon's Lenten procession." It was ordered to be recovered from the ruins by Dom João de Bragança and several members of the nobility, and was finally found after eight days of feverish digging.[37]

Money in the form of coins was also excavated from the ruins. When the main fire had largely burned itself out, "the English gentlemen began to dig for their remaining effects," wrote a British ship captain. However, "what money was saved . . . was so blackened as to cause it to be specified whether payments of any sort were to be made in black or bright money. Only iron chests [the eighteenth-century equivalent of safes] saved the ready cash of many; as to the household goods they were all consumed."³⁸ According to a German account, "many merchants dug their money chests [*Geldkisten*] out from the ruins."³⁹ Unfortunately, in many cases they proved no match for the destructive forces of the earthquake and the fire. The contents of some were "destroyed and burned to ashes." And "many collections of coins found inside them" were melted, "so that they could not be used again, and had to be melted down."⁴⁰

The fire's duration explains some of this unsparing destruction. While most survivors agree that the principal blaze (or firestorm) lasted between five and fifteen days, new evidence suggests that several fires continued to burn for more than six weeks in various parts of the city. One of the best sources on this question is the correspondence of Monsignor Acciaiuoli. Recently discovered in the Vatican Library, Acciaiuoli's letters provide a reliable and detailed record of the size and duration of the blaze.⁴¹

In his first letter, dated November 4, the monsignor informs his brother in Italy that the fire has "burnt many houses; and, moving from one to the other, has traveled throughout the whole city."⁴² A week later, he reports that the main fire, having "caused not less damage than the earthquake itself," lasted until November 7.⁴³ Yet, on November 18, he reveals that the fire is still burning, feeding on the "wood and the remaining objects of burned-out houses," as well as "straw, hay, and other combustible materials" from local "cantinas."⁴⁴ (On the very same day, Pombal reports that the government is busy "extinguishing the fires.")⁴⁵ Then, on December 16 (more than six weeks after the earthquake), Acciaiuoli writes that "the fire is still not extinguished; it continues in the basements of burned houses and . . . shops."⁴⁶

This is corroborated by Father Morganti, who, in his *Letter from One Friend to Another,* reports that "as of December 19, the fire continues to burn in many parts [of the city]."⁴⁷ Likewise, another eyewitness, an anonymous *lisboeta* writing in the margins of a copy of Moreira de Mendonça's *Universal History of Earthquakes* (1758), states unambiguously that "the fire in the city lasted more than a month."⁴⁸ While this may seem far-fetched, it should be remembered that at least one fire was still burning in the ruins of the World Trade Center in New York

City three months after its destruction on September 11, 2001. More-over, Samuel Pepys recounted in his famous diary that he could still see smoke emanating from the cellars of ruined buildings *six months* after the Great Fire of London.[49] Although we will probably never know for certain when the fires in Lisbon were ultimately extinguished, Acciaiuoli does mention the "excessive humidity caused by the substan-tial amount of rain that has fallen during the week" in a letter dated December 23, 1755.[50] Perhaps it was these winter showers which put a definitive end to the last vestiges of Lisbon's Great Firestorm.

"A SUM THAT EXCEEDS ALL ESTIMATION"

What was the total material loss in Lisbon in the disaster?* Estimates at the time varied widely. The anonymous author of the manuscript *Por-tugal: Afflicted and Disturbed* (1759) believed that a total of 400 million cruzados were lost in the earthquake, 330 million in the fire, 5 million in the tsunami, and 8 million as a result of theft—for a total loss of 743 million cruzados (or 237,000 contos de reis).[51] One survivor claimed that the loss of the Riverside Palace, the Patriarchal Church, the Cus-toms House, the Court of the Seven Houses, and the Casa da Ópera alone equaled 100 million reaes (or 4,000 contos).[52]

One modern scholar, Carlos Estorninho, put the total losses at a hefty 536,260,000 cruzados (or 215,000 contos), while the economic historian José Luis Cardoso believes that they ranged between 100,000 and 150,000 contos. As a point of reference, Portugal's annual gross domestic product in 1750 was about 150,000 contos, or 74 percent of Great Britain's GDP in the same year.[53] One judiciously systematic study in the *Journal of Economic History* (2009) by Alvaro S. Pereira reck-ons the total loss in the city of Lisbon as between 60,243 and 67,213 contos, and between 63,693 and 72,193 contos in all of Portugal—or between 32 and 48 percent of Portugal's GDP. To reach these num-bers, Pereira estimates that each dwelling in Lisbon was worth on aver-age .96 conto, a monastery 120 contos, a convent 80 contos, a smaller convent 60 contos, a hospital 100 contos, a church 80 contos, and a

---

* The basic monetary unit in eighteenth-century Portugal was the rei, although several other units were in regular use. 1 real = 40 réis. 1 conto de réis or conto (which will be used in this book to assess the damage) was equivalent to 1 million réis. 1 cruzado = 400 réis; 1 livre tornois = 160 réis; £1 (British pound sterling) = 3,600 réis; 1 peso forte = 800 réis.

palace 300 contos. Then he multiplies these by the total number of structures in each category, varying the loss somewhat depending on whether a structure was completely destroyed, damaged, or only partially damaged, to get a sum between 36,153 contos and 36,653 contos. He adds to this 4,000 contos for all the damage to those buildings in the area of the Terreiro do Paço, 1,000 to 2,000 contos for the total loss in diamonds, 10,000 to 15,000 contos for the loss of gold, silver, and furniture, 1,000 to 2,000 contos for all money (i.e., coinage) lost, 12,800 contos for all the losses by foreigners, 3,200 to 4,480 contos for all the damage to dwellings outside Lisbon, and 250 to 500 contos for the damage sustained by monasteries and convents outside of Lisbon.[54]

However granular, there is evidence from parish records that Pereira undercounts the dwellings that existed before the quake, and there is more that he undercounts.[55] It is reasonable to assume, moreover, that as many as 10,000 additional buildings sustained substantial (though not total) damage in the disaster. There is also the complicated matter of partial destruction. In a letter to Whitehall dated November 20, 1755, Abraham Castres writes that "the Houses . . . which are yet standing in this City, as well as in the Country for several Miles around it, are for the most part in such a shattered Condition, that there is hardly one in Fifty, tho' supported by props, that will hold out the winter."[56] One might therefore conclude that approximately 27,000 dwellings in Lisbon (82 percent of the total 33,000) were either completely destroyed or partially destroyed in the disaster and an even higher percentage (86 percent) of Lisbon's larger and more vulnerable buildings—churches, palaces, monasteries, convents, and government offices—suffered the same fate. The actual value of the dwellings lost in the disaster is therefore probably closer to 18,360 to 19,360 contos rather than Pereira's estimate of 15,383 to 15,883 contos.

To this, one must add the vast wealth lost inside Lisbon's churches.[57] Financed through royal and noble patronage, the opulent interiors of the capital's churches, including all the "sacred vessels, ornaments, furniture, statues, [and] paintings," according to this French source, were one of the reasons for Lisbon's status as one of the richest cities in the world.[58] One might estimate the value here at 5,000 contos.

Also generally undercounted is the wealth lost in the area of the Terreiro do Paço. The political, cultural, and financial center of both Lisbon and the empire, this section of the city suffered almost complete devastation. To quote Edward Hay, "the Part of the Town towards the Water where the Royal Palace, the public Tribunals, the Customs House, India House, and where most of the merchants dwelt for the convenience of transacting their Business, is . . . nothing but a Heap of Rubbish in many places several stories high."[59] The Royal Library and the various royal collections inside the Riverside Palace, as has been discussed, overflowed with rare tomes, one-of-a-kind manuscripts, exquisite artworks, and objects and artifacts from several centuries of Portuguese history. Their total value is difficult to calculate, as nothing of its extent has ever come up for sale. Add to this the riches found inside the Patriarchal Church, all the merchandise and the trade records of the Customs House, the India House, and the royal courts, and one could conservatively double Pereira's estimate of the losses in this area to 8,000 contos.

As to diamonds, "11 to 12 million [cruzados' worth of] diamonds" (or 1,920 contos) were lost in the India House alone, according to Father Portal, while two other authors claim that the total loss of diamonds and precious gems in the capital came to 12,800 contos and 17,920 contos, respectively.[60] To provide some perspective, the total official value of all the diamonds extracted from Brazil between 1740 and 1755 was 6,447 contos. In 1754 and 1755 alone, the value was 1,000 contos.[61] The official estimates, however, should be viewed with considerable skepticism. Since 1734, when the Portuguese Crown set up a diamond region in Brazil called the Tijuco and granted monopoly rights to certain individuals for diamond extraction there, smuggling and illegal mining were rampant. Consequently, a large percentage of all diamonds entering Portugal from Brazil were never reported. But diamonds weren't the only precious gems mined in Brazil and brought to Portugal. Emeralds and sapphires also arrived in large quantities, both legally and illegally. The total loss of all precious gems was therefore probably closer to 5,000 contos.

Particularly destructive to the early modern economy would have been the sudden and extreme loss of specie. Pereira believes that only about 1,000 to 2,000 contos of money (i.e., coins) were lost—a figure, he admits, that is much lower than that given in most contemporary accounts. His reasoning is that most of the hard currency that was "lost" was later dug up by its rightful owners and by thieves; thus, it "just changed hands."[62] But given the physical insults of the disaster, many coins were undoubtedly burned beyond recognition and then carted away with the rest of the rubble. It therefore seems reasonable to assume, even considering the heroic story of the National Mint's survival, that the total amount of money lost in the disaster approached 4,000 contos.

If one incorporates all of these newly adjusted losses—4,000 contos in money, 5,000 contos in the interiors of Lisbon's churches, 8,000 contos in the area of the Terreiro do Paço, 5,000 contos in diamonds and precious gems, and between 18,360 and 19,360 contos in dwellings—into Pereira's estimate of 60,243 to 67,213 contos, then the total material loss in the city of Lisbon climbs to between 76,220 and 82,600 contos, or 51 to 55 percent of Portugal's GDP. If one assumes that the losses outside of Lisbon were underestimated as well, and one raises Pereira's estimates of the value of all the dwellings destroyed across Portugal to 5,000 to 6,000 contos (from 3,200 to 4,480), lost monasteries and convents to 400 to 600 contos (from 250 to 500), and adds them to the total losses for Lisbon, one gets a total loss for Portugal of between 81,680 and 89,020 contos or approximately 54 to 59 percent of Portugal's GDP.[63] While it is problematic to compare economies separated by centuries, this loss would be roughly the equivalent to the United States today suffering damages of between $9.8 trillion and $10.7 trillion, or more than half the present national debt.[64] By comparison, the losses from the costliest natural disaster in American history, Hurricane Katrina, which struck the Gulf Coast of the United States in 2005, exceeded just $100 billion.[65]

MERCHANT LOSSES

Many a worthy & lately a rich Merchant have now the world to begin again.

—CHARLES DOUGLAS, EARL OF DRUMLANRIG (NOVEMBER 19, 1755)

The Portuguese were not the only people financially affected by the disaster. Also suffering substantial losses were foreign merchants and businessmen and their families. "One's blood runs cold at giving you a description of it," wrote a British merchant. "Most of the merchants are absolutely ruined; there are two [merchant] houses that have lost 50,000 [pounds] each, none of them know who are their debtors, their books of accompts having been consumed in the flames, and if they had saved them, to what purpose, the inhabitants in general becoming insolvent under this misfortune. . . . On the 31st of October," I was "in a very prosperous way, and the very next day saw myself and family overwhelmed in misery."[66] Losses would only increase when Portuguese shop owners, ruined by the disaster, walked away from their debts.[67]

Some merchants found themselves without assistance of any kind. "I alone of all my Household," wrote an elderly merchant to his colleagues in Paris, "have escap'd, and with only the Coat on my Back, from the horrible Disaster which has overwhelmed and sunk Lisbon.

> My Fortune, my Effects, all that I have in the World, are buried under the ruins of a city, which [had] become [for] me my native Country. I have lived to the age of 72, to be the Spectator of the most terrible Manifestation of the Wrath of Heaven on sinful Men. . . . This is now the fifth Day since the Overthrow of the City. I see all around me [in the fields] many Hundreds of Persons, who, like me, have nothing left but the remembrance of their former Condition. We are miserable and destitute, and shall make others so; for our Engagements were annihilated with the City where they were contracted, and from whence they derived their Consistency. In fine, Lisbon is no more.[68]

The day after the earthquake, one English merchant traveled by boat with several sailors to his house, but "could not save a Paper or Book . . . What the Seamen brought away was not worth ten Moidores [a gold coin], which, with a Night-Gown I have on, is all I have left," he lamented. "My Compting-House [Counting House], with all my Papers, Cash, Chest, & c[ontents] sunk with the first Shock. Mr. Edward Broome and Mr. James Combibrune have, by being situated near the River, saved the most valuable Part of their Effects. Mr. Stubbs has saved his Books and Cash, and so has Mr. Buller, and likewise Mr. Burn, [of] the House of Mayne, Burn, and Mayne; but the House of Bristow, Ward and Company have not saved the minutest Trifle, nor have I heard of any other that has. . . . In short, the whole country is totally ruined, and one century will not put Things to right. . . . I have no other Expectations than a total Bankruptcy and Stagnation, which will affect, and greatly too, all trading Places in Europe."[69]

Although anecdotal, such accounts provide context for what was in many ways the end of a glorious commercial era. One chronicler, for example, estimated the foreign merchant community lost a total of "48,000,000 pesos fortes," of which 32 million (or two thirds) were suffered by the English, the Irish, and the Scots; 8 million (one sixth) by the Hamburg merchants; 5 million by the Italians; 1 million by the Dutch; 1 million by the French; 500,000 by the Swedish; and 500,000 by merchants from Greater Germany.[70] Depleted capital stocks and the changing priorities and statist policies of Pombal's new regime would make it increasingly difficult for foreigners to enjoy the same level of success that they had once known. In the aftermath of the disaster, "many businessmen left for Porto, Coimbra, or their homelands, believing that Lisbon would never become Lisbon again," commented one priest. They feared "poverty because they saw that much of the city, having become like the Arabian Desert, was unfit for habitation."[71]

In a letter to Whitehall on January 14, 1756, an optimistic Edward Hay describes the state of the British factory as the new year began.

> The Loss our Trade has sustained is very great but I am far from thinking it total. The immediate Loss of Effects was those consumed in the Custom house, which were Sugars and Tobacco, Part of the Cargoes of Three Fleets that had arrived in the Summer from the Brazils, and all the English and Foreign Goods that were then in the King's Warehouses, Almost all the Goods that were in the Merchants private Warehouses, and all the Goods that were in the Hands of Shopkeepers and Algibebas or Merchant Taylors. Thus what Goods were then in Lisbon were the Bulk of the Loss the Community has sustained. Some Clothes and other Goods have been dug out of the Rubbish of the Customhouse and the Merchants upon proving their mark upon their Goods have been allowed to take them immediately.[72]

According to the *Gazeta de Lisboa*, "there was a notice that made the rounds in foreign kingdoms, that many thousands of laborers rummaging through the ruins of Lisbon have already extracted much gold, silver, and precious stones, and that the business men had a good portion of their property, and they hope to see very soon trade returning to its old level."[73] But Hay, as the advocate for British merchant interests in Lisbon, had every incentive to provide the rosiest picture he could of the state of Portugal trade; and the *Gazette* may very well have been publishing state propaganda initiated by Pombal to convince foreign powers not to curtail trade with Portugal.

Carlos Estorninho (using British estimates at the time) believed British losses in Lisbon to be £8 million out of a total of £10 million lost by foreigners, while Pereira thinks that all foreigners suffered losses of 12,800 contos (£3.5 million).[74] But one needs to calculate more than just the losses suffered by *lisboetas* and foreign merchants in Lisbon, for the disaster also did damage to the economies of those countries that traded with Portugal. "Not only in Spain, England, and France did trade suffer a great shock, but also in Germany and the northern empire," declared a German press account in 1756. "In England, many Jews suffered the greatest harm. . . . A certain Portuguese Jew in London alone suffered a loss of 100,000 [pounds]."[75] In Brazil, the merchant community of Recife, according to the governor of the *captania* of Pernambuco, lost "a million [cruzados, or £110,000] in the fire that followed the earthquake . . . and reduced the Customs House to ashes."[76]

Beyond the business community, thousands of private citizens also lost all their property and possessions in the disaster. "Some gentlemen," wrote one ship captain, "were reduced to the want of everything to keep them from the weather, for most escaped in their undress and slippers."[77] A few fortunate souls recovered a portion of their personal possessions, but many were completely ruined. A letter from a woman named Joana Tomásia Ribeiro to Dom José, dated March 26, 1756, describes the "poverty" that has overtaken her family after the "formidable fire" destroyed all of their property. She humbly petitions the king for money as well as permission to travel to Pará, Brazil, with her daughters and a female slave, to be reunited with her husband. It is not known whether her request was granted.[78]

Of course, Portugal's losses are not simply a matter of numbers, however staggering, for the disaster struck at the very heart of the empire. With the exception of Porto and a few other cities, Lisbon was an island of wealth and activity set in a sea of poverty. The undisputed national center of politics, commerce, and religion in a way that few capital cities are, it had been visited by the most extraordinary confluence of calamities. The sudden loss of so much capital, as well as tens of thousands of inhabitants, meant that Lisbon at least for the forseeable future, would cease to be a major player in European trade and politics.

Moreover, the sudden depletion of wealth controlled by the Crown, the nobility, the merchant class, and the Church rendered Portugal vulnerable to both external influences and internal entities hungry for power. Add to this the unimaginably bleak reality for the average *lisboeta* who had lost not only family members and friends but their homes and, in many cases, their livelihoods.

Much as a political revolution tears apart a society, disrupting and, in some cases, destroying institutions that had taken centuries to evolve, the dislocations caused by the Lisbon Earthquake set the stage for an audacious attempt to fundamentally transform Portugal's social, political, religious, and economic life in the second half of the eighteenth century. While some countries have recovered from natural disasters that struck at the heart of national life—Britain after the Great Fire of London in 1666, for example—Portugal was hit with a once-in-a-millennium catastrophe, which would not only disrupt the life of the nation, but exert a profound and lasting psychological effect on its inhabitants.

VÍTIMAS

The Fires, that glimm'ring still with pale'y Red,
Like Burial Tapers, nodded o'er the Dead,
Performing the last Office, as they wave,
Add Dust and Ashes to the gen'ral Grave.

—JOHN BIDDOLF, *A Poem on the Earthquake at Lisbon* (1755)

For many of Lisbon's survivors, one of the shocking realities of the disaster was the sheer randomness involved in who lived and who died. "Death went in search of many," wrote one survivor, "but with varying success."[79] "One mother," observed Moreira de Mendonça, "whose child was killed in her arms, survived, while another was slain by a falling stone, though the child at her breast suffered no injury."[80] According to an eyewitness, "as many people died in the streets as in the churches, gentlemen and knights in their chaises and servants on their beasts of burden were crushed by the walls of falling houses; all were burned together."[81] The bones of aristocrats and beggars, merchants, slaves, nuns, horses, fishermen, dogs, priests, monkeys, and mules were mixed together in the ashy heap that Lisbon had become. In lines produced just weeks after the disaster, the poet Franciso de Pina e de Mello ponders these new, unsettling realities.

> *General, Priest, Layman, Friar,*
> *Bound together by the deadly calamity;*
> *Minister, Pauper, Rich Gentleman,*
> *Merchant, Soldier, Day-Laborer,*
> *The miserable, the happy, and the annoyed,*
> *The trembling groan speaks to everyone;*
> *They have been made equal;*
> *This bitter cry of Nature brings unhappiness to all.*[82]

Parish registers reflect these sobering truths. The death register of the Church of Santa Justa lists the names of ninety-five victims along with the location where each body was found. Alongside servants and slaves, it includes Manoel Varejão e Távora, the president of the Inquisition, who perished in the palace of that institution during the earthquake. Here is a small selection:

Ana Joaquina, ruins
Manoel Dias, ruins
Manoel Gomez, ruins
Eusebia, ruins
Filippe Corrêa da Silva, ruins of his house
Simão Felix, ruins of the Royal Hospital [of All the Saints]
Bernardina, ruins of Santo Domingos
Cezilia, slave, ruins
Joam [João] Antonio Galvane, ruins
Antonio, servant, ruins
Joam [João], servant, ruins
Nicolasia, slave, ruins
Maria, slave, ruins
Padre Domingos de Oliveyra, ruins[83]

The parish register of the Church of Santa Maria Madalena records that "one hundred and thirty-seven people perished in the ruins." The list below contains some of the names of those "who died on November 1, 1755, who were parishioners of this church, and who became buried in the ruins of the earthquake."[84]

José Duarte
Elena Thereza, married to the above
Catharina Josepha, daughter of the above
Maria Rosa, servant to the above
Antonio Dinis, workman [official] to the above
Franciso da Costa and his wife Thereza de Jesus also dead, as well as four sons and a daughter
Theodorio Pereira and Joachim Manoel, workman [official] to the above
Leonardo Antonio
Andreza Maria, wife to the above
Maria, daughter
Thereza, daughter
Clemente, son of the above
Josepha Maria, wife of Manoel Lopes Dias; Ricarda, daughter of the above
Genovena Maria, assistant in the house of the above
Roza Maria Lobo and a daughter
. . .
Antonia, slave to Julião Cardoso
Joseph, apprentice to Franciso da Costa
Raymundo Paschoal, married, Spanish
A two-year-old daughter of the above Jozefa
. . .
Maria, daughter of João de Magalhães
Clemente, water seller [agoadeiro]
A day laborer
Manoel Moreira Dinis
A female servant of Antonio Alves Lage
An errand-boy [caixeiro] of Sebastião Gonçales
Clara, slave of Antonio Tavares[85]

If one looks closer, however, one sees that death was not entirely indiscriminate. Many more commoners perished as a percentage of the overall population than so-called important people. Still, the nobles

who died were not few. They include the son of the Marqueses of
Angeja and the principal of the Patriarchal Church, Dom Francisco de
Noronha; the Condessa (Countess) of Lumiares, Dona Ana Vicencia de
Noronha, and her eldest daughter; the wife of Gonçalo Xavier de Alcaçova Carneiro, Dona Ana de Moscoso, in whose house twenty-five people perished; Antonio de Mello de Castro, Roque de Sousa; the widow
of Dom Lourenço de Almeida, Dona Isabel Catharina Henriques, and
her daughter; and the Marquesa of Louriçal, Dona Maria da Graça de
Castro; and, of course, the Spanish ambassador, Count Perelada.[86]

High government officials—in most cases, aristocrats—who per-
ished include the ninety-year-old chief palace judge and high chancel-
lor, Francisco Luiz da Cunha e Ataide; the secretary of war, Pedro de
Mello Paz Ataide; Lisbon's chief inquisitor and dean of the cathedral in
Elvas, Manoel Varejão de Távora; the prelate of the Patriarchal Church,
Monsignor Gaspar Galvão Castellobranco; and the king's counselor,
Monsignor Manoel de Vasconcellos Gajo.[87]

There are several possible reasons for the small percentage of
noblemen and women among the dead. The first is that many individuals of means were spending All Saints' Day at their country estates and
quintas. "Because all of them had chapels in their country houses," Ange
Goudar explained, "they had no need to return to the city to attend
mass on feast days."[88] And for those noblemen who were in Lisbon, few
were in the churches when the earthquake began. "It is generally established in Portugal," wrote Goudar, "that people of distinction have a
chapel in their home where they hear mass. And people who live in the
vicinity collect at these houses because their owners do not deny anyone entrance. Rarely do these masses begin before 11 a.m., so everyone
was at home" when the earthquake struck.[89]

In general, research has shown that wealthier people have a greater
chance of surviving a natural disaster than those of lesser means. In
the first place, the wealthy tend to have sturdier, better-built homes.
Secondly, those with greater resources and more political and social
connections are generally better able to secure food, shelter, and proper
medical care in the aftermath of a disaster.[90] Although many noble families lost their palaces, and, as a result suffered severe financial strain,
they lived considerably better post-earthquake than the vast majority
of *lisboetas*.

Faring even worse than commoners were men and women of the
cloth. Mortality among them was particularly high. In addition to the

large numbers of secular priests and nuns who perished, those members of Lisbon's religious orders who died include 21 Observant Franciscans, "among them the esteemed theologians Father José de Apocalypte Linháres and Father José de São Gualter Lamatilde," according to Father Figueiredo, 2 Third Order Franciscans, 16 Trinitarian Fathers, 15 Shoe-Wearing Carmelites, 7 secular Monks of São João the Evangelist, 5 Hermits of Santo Agostinho (Augustine), 3 Portuguese Dominicans, 4 Hibernians, 3 Jesuits, 4 Oratorians, including Father Philip Neri, "doctor of divine and humane letters," and 1 each from Our Lady of Mercy and São Camilo (Camillus). Also killed were 10 Dominican nuns from the Convent of the Annunciation and 14 from the Convent of Salvador. Of the Franciscan nuns who died, 5 were from the Convent of Santa Ana, 22 from the Convent of the Calvary, and 63 from the Convent of Santa Clara. Eight Augustinian nuns from the Convent of Santa Mônica also perished.[91]

In Lisbon's German merchant community, a modest 8 to 10 people were lost. They include Jacob J. Ostermann, who perished in his shop; Herr Dohrmann and his wife; and two young men, Herr Schutt and twenty-year-old Johann Georg Bötefeuer, who both met their end in the house of Albert Borcher.[92] Many more Germans were injured. "Not since the destruction of Jerusalem," wrote merchants Löning, Buess, Burmester, and Krochman, "has there been such misery."[93]

As the largest foreign population in Lisbon, the British suffered the greatest number of deaths. But if one keeps in mind the overall size of that community—calculated at 2,000 by former British ambassador Lord Tyrawley—they were not shockingly high.[94] In a letter to Whitehall in December, Castres emphasized the low death toll:

Mr. Churchill a young Gentleman lately set up, and Mr. Casamajor an ancient one, are the only Men in Business I have heard of [who have died], [except] Ten or a Dozen more at furthest among the Book Keepers, Prentices, etc. Mrs. Hake's Daughter to the late Sir Charles Hardy, and Mrs. Perochon, both married to Gentlemen of the principal Houses among us, are the only English women of any note who had the misfortunes of losing their lives. Of the British and Irish Nations together, the latter were extremely numerous, particularly as to the poorer Sort, I do not hear of above Sixty missing, most of whom were so obscure as not to be known to any but the Irish Friars.[95]

One reason for the comparatively low numbers was that many British Factory members (as well as many non-British merchants) lived in the suburbs of Lisbon and not in the Baixa. Another reason, as previously mentioned, was that many Britons traveled to their country houses the night before All Saints' Day in order to avoid acts of religious bigotry directed at them.

The day after Castres penned his letter, Edward Hay mailed to Whitehall what he believed to be an accurate list of the 77 British and Irish dead (28 men and 49 women).[96] The actual numbers, however, may be substantially higher because, as Castres mentions, many poor Irish victims, who were not generally known, may not have found their way onto the list. Four Irish priests from the Church of Corpo Santo, for example—Thomas M. de Burgo, Patrick McCabe, Anthony McDonnell, and Brien Morilly—also died in the disaster.[97] Because only one person on the list is specifically identified as a child, and because one would expect relatively high fatalities among the very young, it seems reasonable to assume that some infants and small children were also not included. As a rule, Lisbon's priests did not record the names of children seven years of age and younger on their church death rolls because they had not yet received the sacraments. Perhaps British Protestants shared this custom as well. Below is Hay's list.[98]

MEN	WOMEN
Daniel Casamajor, Merch[ant]	Mariana Pershon, wife of Elias Peroshon, Merch.
John Churchill, [Merchant]	Elizabeth Hake, wife of Christ. Hake, Jun., Merch.
Giles Vincent, [Merchant]	
John Legay Jun., [Merchant]	Mary Sherman, widow of John Sherman, Merch.
Charles Holford, a young Gentleman apprentice	
Samuel Seale, [Apprentice]	Elizabeth Legay, wife of John Legay, Jun., Merch.
Henry Hutchins, [Apprentice]	
Richard Hammond, Bookkeeper	Elizabeth Legay, Jun. a child
	Mary Dohrman, English Wife of Doorman, Hamburgher Merch.
William Shea, Merchant	
Thomas Doran, [Merchant]	Mary Morrogh, wife of Andrew Morrogh, Merchant
Richard Roche, [Merchant]	
Charles McCarthy, Jun.	Mary Rochford
Anthony French	Jane Campion
Thomas Fulton	Anstice Roche

Jonathan Thomas
Joseph Sandford
Daniel Adams
Francis Lawson
John Fulton
Anthony Lawrence Morrogh
Anthony Moore
Mathias Moore
George Groves
Maurice Keating
John Morrogh
Michael Collins
Michael Grace
Edward Wall

Anne Moore
Elenor Oates
Jane Purcell
Mary Rice
Anne McGrath
Margaret Smith
Lucy Francklin
Mary Donnelan
Elenor Collins
Anne Warren
Alice Martin
Anne Fulton
Margaret Keefe
Anne Welsh
Mary Kidney
Christianna Johnson
Mary Philips
Elenor MacMahon
Elenor McCarthy
Margaret Radley
Anstice Hussey
Margaret Keating
Anne Williams
Elenor Power
Elizabeth Burgess
Catherine Rewark
Elizabeth Gibbons
Elenor Welsh
Mary Brett
Mary Clare
Catherine Ward
Mary O'Neil
Catherine Lyne
Margaret Thompson
Catherine Bates
Mary Shannon
Mary Glasson
Mary Cooke

One conspicuous feature of the list is the disproportional number of female victims (forty-nine out of a total of seventy-seven, or 75 percent more). Why should this be? According to studies, females generally suffer higher mortality rates during natural disasters than men. This is especially true in societies where the socioeconomic status of women is lower than that of men, as in the Europe of 1755. And the disparity tends to grow with the size and severity of the disaster. There are several reasons for this. In the first place, women are in general smaller, slower, and physically weaker than men and therefore have more difficulty escaping from the effects of a disaster, like running from tsunami waves or the flames of a fire or extricating themselves from under a pile of heavy stones. Likewise, women generally have thinner skulls and smaller bones than men and are thus at a greater risk of suffering fractures and other severe trauma. And in societies that do not encourage female athleticism, physical activities like climbing tend to be easier for men than women. Pregnant women are especially vulnerable.[99] Although one might expect acts of male chivalry to have mitigated some of these realities, the unequal death ratio between the sexes—as well as the anecdotal evidence that the first allegiance of many, if not most, victims was to their own survival—tells a different story.

Women would have also found themselves at an increased risk of injury, disease, and death during the period of lawlessness that followed the earthquake as well as the many months that survivors lived in the fields. On the whole, research has shown that females tend to be more sensitive to poor hygienic conditions than men. In the newly erected settlements inside and outside the capital, women faced not only a lack of hygiene and fresh food and water, but also legions of fleas, lice, bedbugs, and rats, as well as the very real risk of sexual assault.[100]

The disparity in deaths by sex holds true not just for the British but for the Portuguese population as well, as the death records of five parishes chosen at random reveal, even allowing for what may have been a slightly larger female population in Lisbon in the middle of the eighteenth century. In the parish of Santa Catarina, for example, a total of 16 male and 22 female victims are listed (38 percent more females than males), while in the parish of the Angels (Anjos), 5 male and 11 female victims are recorded (120 percent more females). In the Baixa parish of the Madalena, 48 male and 73 female victims are listed (52 percent more females), while in the parish of Santo André, 4 male and 8 female victims are recorded (100 percent more females). In the hard-hit Baixa parish of Santa Justa, 43 male and 52 female victims are recorded (20 percent more females), while in the parish of Socorro (Help), 14 male and only 10 female victims are listed (40 percent more males than females). In the parish of the Pena (Pity), 19 male and 28 female victims are listed (47 percent more females).[101]

Another reason for this disparity may be that non-noblewomen were more frequent churchgoers than non-noblemen. And Saturday, November 1 was a confession day, which normally attracted more women to church. Thus, not only were more women in attendance at the 9 a.m. mass, when the chances were greatest for being killed by collapsing church and chapel roofs, but there were more women in the equally dangerous streets making their way to the 10 a.m. mass (or, in the case of British Protestant women, walking to the Factory Church services). And because it was All Saints' Day, many non-noblewomen (housewives, female servants, and slaves) may have been in the streets running last-minute errands for the feast day. Joining them would have been hundreds of female street vendors, a common sight in Lisbon for centuries. Lacking the capital to purchase their own stores, they sold sardines, shellfish, tobacco, and bread from carts. On this festival day, they were no doubt in the streets and squares in large numbers, selling their wares to housewives and servant women, as well as pious travelers who had come to celebrate the holiday.[102]

THE DEATH TOLL

How many people perished in the Lisbon disaster? Widely divergent death tolls were reported in newspapers throughout Europe. According to one German compilation of European news reports in the years 1755 and 1756, "the [death] numbers are 30,000, 40,000, 50,000, 60,000, 100,000 and one French report of 150,000. . . . Our computation [of] . . . 100,000 . . . is the best number."[103] Another German source, which tallies deaths reported in letters from Lisbon, gives estimates of 20,000, 30,000, 40,000, and 50,000 dead, and a few of "only 8 to 10,000 souls."[104] *The Whitehall Evening Post* of November 22–25, 1755, reported that "60,000 people perished," while *The London Evening Post* for the same period, repeating accounts from France, claims that "about 100,000 people have lost their lives."[105] A few days later the number had fallen to "50,000 Souls."[106]

Two days after the earthquake, the Prussian ambassador to Lisbon, Hermann Braamcamp, informed Frederick the Great that "two thirds [of Lisbon's population] was entombed beneath the rubble" (which would have been at least 130,000 victims), while a French survivor, J. Perrot, believed the number of deaths reached 60,000.[107] In a similarly exaggerated vein, two anonymous Frenchmen thought that 45,000 and 50,000 had been killed, respectively. "The bloodiest battle never destroyed so many people," wrote one of them.[108]

The passage of years would not significantly narrow the range of death estimates. In Moreira de Mendonça's seminal *History of Earthquakes* (1758), the Torre do Tombo archivist claims that a total of 10,000 people died in Lisbon: 5,000 in the ruins and 5,000 more during the month of November.[109] In his *Latin and Portuguese Commentary on the Earthquake and Fire of Lisbon* (1756), Father Figueiredo proposes that around 15,000 perished. "Those who raised the number to seventy thousand," he wrote, "did not understand that the mortality was not equal to the proportion of buildings destroyed."[110] In his *New and Faithful Account of the Earthquake* (1756), Miguel Pedegache claims that between 20,000 and 24,000 people died, adding that "all other calculations are imaginary or exaggerated," while Ange Goudar asserts in his *Historical Account of the Earthquake in Lisbon* (1756) that "according to accounts that seem the most accurate by people who do not have an interest in increasing or decreasing the loss, the number of deaths [in Lisbon] was from twenty-five to thirty thousand."[111] In the "Lisbon" entry in the *Encyclopédie*, the official organ of the European Enlightenment, the author, Louis Jaucourt, estimates that "between 15 and 20,000 souls" perished in the ruins of the city on account of the earthquake and fire.[112]

In estimating death tolls, modern scholars have tended to be more conservative than the foreign newspapers of the time, which, in many cases, exaggerated wildly.[113] While no "official" death estimates for the Lisbon disaster were ever produced, it seems plausible—particularly with so many exaggerated numbers being printed in European newspapers and broadsheets—that the Portuguese government may have disseminated lower casualty figures in order to deter foreign invasion and discourage the loss of foreign investment. Benjamin Keene certainly thought so. "Ever since [Portugal] had recovered from its First Terrors," he informed Whitehall on December 28, 1755, "it has endeavored to show its Sufficiency, and to hide its Distresses; and more particularly, in Reducing the Number of Their Subjects who have perished in the late Calamity, as low as possible."[114] Although Keene doesn't reveal his sources, he was certainly in a position, as the current British ambassador to Spain and former ambassador to Portugal, to acquire the kind of inside information needed to make such a claim.

Intriguingly, this purported Portuguese interest in providing a lower death toll runs counter to the behavior of most modern states who regularly inflate the mortality numbers after a disaster in order to increase the amount of aid they receive. (This may be one of the principal reasons why most modern scholars have shown a bias in favor of the lower estimates.)[115] But, as has already been mentioned, the Portuguese Crown was leery of foreign aid at the time and may have wished to discourage it.

In a letter to foreign governments and Portuguese officials across the globe dated November 18, 1755, Pombal declared that "the number of deaths was much less than were believed at the beginning." Four months later, on April 14, 1756, he explained to the governor of Rio de Janeiro, Minas Gerais, and São Paulo that while "the number of deaths seemed more considerable in the first days, it was later ascertained that that number did not exceed six to eight thousand people."[116] This number is suspiciously low—certainly lower than in any contemporary source—and reflects a Pombalian agenda.

Of course, Pombal could hardly downplay the physical damage to Lisbon with any credibility. The ruins of the capital were there for all to see and would be for years to come. Yet, in another letter, he reports that "we suffered a horrible earthquake that was equal to [the earthquake] . . . that ruined the city of Lisbon in the year 1531."[117] The claim here is telling. For, while the 1531 quake was certainly destructive, it was dwarfed by the Great Earthquake of 1755—and it stretches credulity to believe that Pombal was not aware of this.[118]

No official death count ever appeared in the *Gazeta de Lisboa;* and it is plausible to assume that those Portuguese writers who published books on the disaster were unofficially encouraged to aim low in their counting. Although no direct proof of such pressure exists, death estimates in books published in Portugal are generally lower, with the exception of Pedegache's *New and Faithful Account of the Earthquake,* than those found in foreign newspapers or in unpublished sources like private letters or manuscripts. In his unpublished manuscript *The History of the Ruin of the City of Lisbon,* Father Portal estimates that 12,000 to 15,000 perished in the disaster as a whole and 1,000 of them in the fire, while the anonymous author-priest of the manuscript *Portugal: Afflicted and Disturbed* claimed that 26,800 victims perished in the entire disaster: 20,000 in the earthquake and 5,000 to 6,000 in the fire, though he admitted that the number could be "greater than ten thousand." He cites an additional 800 in the tsunami or "flood," as he called it.[119]

To be fair, higher estimates found in letters to friends and relatives may, in some cases, reflect the lure of rumor or hyperbole. Richard Goddard, for example, wrote to his brother on November 18, 1755, that "'tis generally agreed that 30,000 Persons must have perished. Though there are [a] great Variety of Opinions on that."[120] Monsignor Acciaiuoli, who believed himself privy to information available only to high officials in the Portuguese regime (Pombal, he wrote, "has orders to share everything with me"), stated in a letter to the cardinal secretary of the Vatican on December 2, 1755, that "the number of deaths, according to a generic calculus, will rise to more than forty thousand." While accepting this number, he disagrees with Secretary Mendonça's view (important because he was a rival of Pombal) that it was "exact and not exaggerated." In the end, Acciaiuoli thought "a true accounting [of the dead]" was beyond reach because of the impossibility of locating and excavating all the bodies buried "in the ruins of houses and churches."[121]

Unfortunately, parish registers in Lisbon cannot provide us with precise death totals. Many were themselves destroyed by the fire. "The number of dead persons," wrote Father Morganti, "is almost indecipherable because of the burning of many parish registers and confessional books. This would be the best way to arrive at an understanding closest to the truth, one only has recourse to an estimate with little certitude."[122] Nevertheless, data gleaned from those parish records and primitive census figures that survived can provide guidance.

In his study on the disaster, Alvaro S. Pereira argues persuasively using population figures before and after the earthquake that the death toll in Lisbon was between 20,000 and 30,000, a considerable increase over most modern estimates.[123] One reason for this, according to Pereira, is that estimates of Lisbon's pre-earthquake population fail to account for the fact that children under seven years of age are omitted from parish population records as non-communicants and thus are not found on the confession rolls (*rol de confessados*). There is reason to revise death estimates for Lisbon upward by at least 20 percent, roughly the percentage of child casualties in the disaster.[124] One recent study of excavated human remains reveals that Lisbon was a relatively young city, with a high proportion in the age range of seventeen to thirty-four.[125] Pereira also points out that both Moreira de Mendonça and Manoel Portal were not basing their figures on all the parishes of the city. Adding those parishes omitted, the death estimates rise from 10,000 and 15,000, respectively, to 20,000 and 25,000.[126]

Several factors, however, may drive the toll even higher. The first is that the population of Lisbon grew significantly on All Saints' Day. Perhaps as many as 10,000 or more people from the surrounding regions would have traveled to the capital for the holiday. And because many may have lacked a proper place to stay (Lisbon was known to have few inns), these visitors may have found themselves in three of the most dangerous places when the earthquake struck: in the churches, in the streets, or encamped along the river. Therefore, the death rate among these 10,000 pilgrims was probably much higher than among *lisboetas*; and because they were unknown to the local parishes and government authorities, they were not likely to be included in church or government tallies.

There is also little doubt that many bodies were rendered unidentifiable by the extraordinary trauma inflicted upon them. Skulls, limbs, and torsos were crushed by the collapse of ceilings and walls. And those bodies that were not immediately recovered from the ruins would have been further disfigured by the enormous pressure of the rubble that lay on top of them. After a few days of decomposition, grimy, swollen, and discolored faces would have been unrecognizable even to close family members and friends. After a few months, many corpses would have broken into pieces, become intermingled with other bodies, or been torn apart by rats.

As an example, a Mr. Vincent, who had come to Lisbon on the night of October 31 after a long absence, presumably for the holiday, "never left the house he slept in," wrote Mr. Braddock, for he was "suddenly crushed to death before he was dressed, and buried in the ruins, which is the only tomb he is ever like to have; for though his friends, after many fruitless searches, discovered, as they supposed, the remains of this body, they found them so putrid, broken, and scattered that it was impossible to remove them."[127] Likewise, the intense heat of the firestorm would have made even the counting of corpses extremely difficult, if not impossible.[128] Numerous bodies undoubtedly disintegrated altogether. According to one priest, the fire was so "violent" that "it burned the flesh off people's and animals' bodies, so that they became mere skeletons."[129]

It is instructive to point out that Lisbon's "burned parishes" (*freguesias queimadas*) suffered the greatest loss of population in the disaster.[130] Many more people died in the fires that followed the San Francisco and Kwanto Earthquakes, for example, than in the earthquakes themselves.[131] While this may not have been the case in Lisbon, many thousands were said to have been trapped beneath the ruins—and hundreds, if not thousands, more were unable to escape because of injuries or infirmities—when the fire swept through the city. One can therefore estimate that 6,000 to 7,000, and perhaps as many as 10,000, people perished in the Great Firestorm of Lisbon.

A vexing reason for inexactitude in the numbers is the enormous pressure on the authorities and religious communities to bury as many corpses as quickly as possible before they could fester and cause an epidemic or outbreak of the plague. "When they gathered up the bodies to cart them away," writes José Luis Cardoso, a Portuguese archaeologist who excavated a grave of disaster victims, "they [in their haste] also scooped up bits of whatever else was lying around"—pottery shards, clay pipes, medallions, buttons, rosaries, thimbles, and animal and fish bones. Also found with the bodies was the skeleton of a monkey that was probably a pet but was perhaps mistaken for a small child.[132]

An analysis of 214 of the disaster victims mentioned above (found under the floor of the former Monastery of Our Lady of Jesus in the Bairro Alto) reveals evidence of "heavy fire exposure, sometimes with skull opening and splitting," suggesting that the cranium had "exploded."[133] Accompanying the charred bones were pieces of charcoal and charred wood.[134] What is unknown is how many perished in the fire and how many were burned after death. Interestingly, the chemical alteration of several silver objects mixed in with the bodies suggests contact with saltwater, indicating that at least a few of the victims may have died in the tsunami.[135] Other skeletons show evidence of blunt-force trauma from falling objects or bullet wounds.[136] One skull of a three-year-old female has a sharp stone driven into it, most likely by the collapse of a building.[137] Researchers believe that altogether the site contains the remains of over 3,000 hastily interred victims. That a single burial site far from the corpse-filled Baixa could contain so many bodies, when it is well documented that many corpses were disposed of near where they lay in locations throughout the city, is further evidence of a higher overall death toll.[138] This is to say nothing of the large numbers of corpses and living people swept out to sea by the powerful receding waves of the tsunami who were never included in any of the official or unofficial death estimates. At least one ship captain (mentioned in chapter 2) reported seeing corpses floating off the coast of Lisbon several days after the disaster.[139]

For many survivors, the mental strain of the disaster must have been unbearable. "Numbers [of people] have since died of the fright and the Apprehension of further Danger," wrote one correspondent.[140] In the months that followed, many thousands undoubtedly succumbed to their injuries or to infections like gangrene, septicemia, sepsis, and tetanus, as well as respiratory illnesses caused by the inhalation of smoke, dust, and other materials thrown into the air by the collapsing buildings. Moreira de Mendonça believed that as many people died of their injuries in the month following the disaster as on the actual day of the earthquake. If so, the number of those who died in subsequent months was probably also high. "Many of the injured are going to die," wrote Monsignor Acciaiuoli bluntly on November 18. "Their injuries are not being cured because no doctors, surgeons, or hospitals have been provided. Taken to the medical stations ordered by the King, the surgeons encounter gangrene and thus are unable to help."[141]

On January 14, 1756, Acciaiuoli informed Pope Benedict that his friend the Abbot Bartolucci had just died from gangrene more than ten weeks after the disaster. His condition had arisen "from injuries [he had] sustained while escaping" from his falling house during the earthquake.[142] On December 23, 1755, the nuncio complained in the letter to the cardinal secretary of state of the Vatican that he himself was still bedridden from a "festering inflamed infection" that had developed from wounds received when the stairs in his home had collapsed in the quake.[143] Although Acciaiuoli would survive, many of the 40,000 to 50,000 who were injured in the disaster, according to Sousa, undoubtedly did not.[144]

To this number, one can add all those who died of infectious diseases like pneumonia, influenza, and measles as well as various waterborne and diarrheal afflictions like leptospirosis, hepatitis A, and hepatitis E. Although there were no reports of major outbreaks of disease immediately after the disaster (and, indeed, several studies suggest that communicable disease epidemics are less common in the aftermath of disasters than one might suppose), there was a newspaper account of a cholera epidemic that occurred in Lisbon in June 1756 which, apparently, claimed "the lives of many people" as well as an outbreak of the "plague."[145] It is therefore not unreasonable to assume that in the cramped, unsanitary conditions of the camps at least several thousand immunocompromised survivors died of illness.[146] Like many of those who later succumbed to stress or injury, one suspects that few of these victims were officially or unofficially counted as disaster deaths by either the church or the government.

To determine the overall death toll in Lisbon, one should add the estimated (by this author) 2,000 people visiting Lisbon for the feast day who died in the disaster, the 3,000 whose bodies were lost in the ruins, burned, or swept out to sea and never counted, and the 5,000 people who died from injuries and disease in the months after the event to Pereira's base estimate of 30,000 deaths. The result is 40,000 dead, the same number provided by Acciaiuoli and Edward Hay. Thus, 38,000 (or 19 percent) of Lisbon's pre-earthquake population of 200,000 perished in the disaster. Normally, such a high percentage would strain credulity, but the Lisbon disaster was exceptional in that it was actually three distinct disasters. Of the 40,000 total victims, approximately 25,000 perished in the earthquake, 7,000 in the fire, 3,000 in the tsunami, and an additional 5,000 later died of their injuries or disease. Over a hundred years after the disaster (in 1864), Lisbon's population was just 190,000, about 10,000 fewer than what it had been before the earthquake.[147]

Along Portugal's southern coast, mortality was especially grim. Cities in the Algarve—like Albufeira, Lagos, Portimão, and Alvor—were ravaged by the twin impacts of the earthquake and the tsunami, with the official death toll for the region coming in at a conservative 1,020.[148] Nearer to Lisbon, the regions of Alentejo and Ribatejo were also severely afflicted. The city of Setúbal, thirty miles south of the capital, suffered more destruction than any place in Portugal other than Lisbon, first from the earthquake and the tsunami and then from a serious fire of its own that burned out a section of the city center. If one considers its remoteness and the probability that the tsunami carried many bodies out to sea—bodies not counted by parish priests—the Algarve may have suffered closer to 1,500 deaths. If an additional 1,500 deaths throughout the rest of the kingdom (excluding Lisbon) are added, then one arrives at 43,000 Portuguese victims in total.

Outside Portugal, there were also many deaths. In Spain, the official death tally, as already mentioned, was 1,214. But again, many victims of the tsunami were likely not reported and, as in Portugal, small children were probably not included in the death records; it thus seems probable that the number of Spanish victims was actually closer to 2,000. The other country that suffered a substantial number of deaths was Morocco, which bore the full brunt of both the earthquake and the tsunami. Unfortunately, reliable death records for North Africa do not exist or have yet to be discovered. Some accounts from the region conflate the All Saints' Day earthquake with an earthquake on November 18, which was felt throughout large sections of Europe, as well as the powerful Meknes Earthquake of November 27.[149]

In any case, the death toll in Morocco on November 1 was no doubt considerable. Therefore, if one estimates that roughly 10,000 people died across Morocco and add the 50 or so people who may have died in the West Indies in the tsunami and another 100 possible deaths in places scattered across the Atlantic like the Azores and the western Mediterranean—Sardinia and other islands—and then add the 3 reported fatalities in northeastern Brazil, we obtain a grand total of 53,153 (plus or minus 3,000 to 4,000) who died worldwide in the Great Lisbon Earthquake disaster. Of those deaths, 75 percent (about 40,000) occurred in and around the Portuguese capital.

CHAPTER NINE

Uma Lisboa Nova

There can be cases where, to establish a state, it is necessary for it to be
partially destroyed, and to be destroyed by some extraordinary event.

—ANGE GOUDAR, *Discours politique* (1756)

OUT OF THE ASHES

In a moment of despondency, while gazing at the ruins of Lisbon a
few days after the disaster, Dom José announced to all within earshot
that he had decided to relocate "his residence and his city" to Maranhão in northeastern Brazil.[1] No one, of course, believed the king. For
despite its lucrative sugar and tobacco industries and its fields and forests thick with cacao, indigo, and cloves, Maranhão was remote, lacking
in infrastructure, and, because of its proximity to the equator, oppres-
sively hot.[2]

Still, the idea of transferring the Portuguese capital to the New
World was no fantasy. When Spain's Philip II seized the vacant Portuguese throne in 1580, an advisor to his principal challenger, the Prior of
Crato, recommended that the court flee into exile in Brazil. Though the
prior chose France instead, when Portugal finally broke free of Spanish
control sixty years later, counselors to the House of Bragança called for
the establishment of a new Portuguese kingdom in South America far
from the predatory reach of its European rivals.[3]

While the risk-averse Braganças decided to remain in Lisbon,
the rationale for relocation became stronger when, at the end of the
seventeenth century, gold was discovered in Minas Gerais and Brazil

became the undisputed economic driver, if not the heart, of the empire. In 1736, Portugal's ambassador to France, Luiz da Cunha, gave voice to these new realities, arguing that Portugal could escape both its economic dependence on Britain and its vulnerability to invasion by moving its capital to South America. Portugal, Cunha argued, was but an "ear of land," while Brazil was an "immense continent" where João V could assume the title of "Emperor of the West" and the Portuguese could fulfill their imperial destiny. If, on the other hand, the king chose to stay in Lisbon, Cunha warned, he would "never sleep in peace and security" again.[4]

After November 1, 1755, the idea of transferring the capital was (perhaps inevitably) revived—but with a twist. In early 1756, the Spanish Jesuit José Francisco de Isla sent an extended letter to the editor of the *Gazeta de Lisboa* in which he advised Dom José to move his capital permanently to Braga, an ancient city in northern Portugal. Though widely known for his satires, Padre Isla was, in this matter, manifestly serious. He had been deeply shaken by Lisbon's fall and had conceived of his idea after emerging from a fever that had lasted ten days.[5]

The principal strength of the plan, according to Isla, was that there would be no need to rebuild a new capital. Dom José could move into Braga's sizable and much admired archbishop's palace without fuss or delay.[6] And Braga enjoyed advantages that Lisbon did not. The region was renowned for "its fertility, its riches, and its air," according to Isla. Its wine was of the finest quality, as was its wheat, fruit, pastureland, and livestock.[7] A potential bastion of military strength on account of the region's burgeoning population, Braga could call up thousands of militiamen at a moment's notice. And while its proximity to the Spanish border might cause the Portuguese some concern, they had only to consider the rough mountain terrain to realize that a Spanish invasion would be folly. Of course, moving the entire Portuguese government would take effort—but rebuilding Lisbon on its original site, where it would take years just to clear the rubble, was, in Isla's view, nothing short of impossible.[8]

But Pombal and Dom José had no choice but to do the impossible. The king could not abandon his capital in its darkest hour. His sense of duty obligated him to be near his subjects and see them through the difficult days, weeks, months, and years ahead. "If one thing can console us in our general grief and distress," wrote one *lisboeta*, "it is that our monarch, the true father of his vassals . . . occupies his days and nights attempting to alleviate our misery. He has been advised to establish his residence temporarily in Porto or in another part of the frontier of the kingdom. But His Majesty refuses to leave us so that he can provide the relief that we need and maintain good order with his presence, which is absolutely necessary."[9]

For all Dom José and Pombal knew, warships from a foreign power were, at that very moment, readying an attack on the city. To leave abruptly would be to invite such an attack. But even if no attack came, the king could not abandon tens of thousands of his subjects to an uncertain future, possibly triggering a mass exodus from the region.

Relocating to Brazil was also unfeasible and, under the circumstances, the logistics were simply too daunting. As for relocating to Braga, it would have entailed moving backward more than a thousand years in Portuguese history. Braga (or Braccara Augusta, as it was once known) had been the capital of the Swabian kingdom in the fifth and sixth centuries AD after the nomadic Suebi invaded Galicia. But Pombal was at war with Portugal's past. He viewed the rebuilding of Lisbon as not only an opportunity to expand his powers but as a chance to transform the nation. For this he would have to be patient.

A MINISTER'S EDUCATION

Pombal had been patient before. For seven lonely years, he had lived as an outcast on his parents' rural estate, when, in 1738 (after a recommendation from the king's close advisor, Cardinal da Motta), he was abruptly and unexpectedly appointed minister plenipotentiary to Great Britain. It was his first important government post.[10] Never one to waste an opportunity, Pombal threw himself into his new responsibilities with gusto, shedding the last vestiges of his provincialism and dutifully educating himself on all the scientific and cultural advances that had been taking place over the previous two centuries.

Although Pombal never learned to speak English during his five years in London, relying exclusively on his diplomatic French, he did frequent the circles of the Royal Society and become acquainted with the work of Isaac Newton, Francis Bacon, John Locke, as well as the manifold achievements of René Descartes.[11] The impact of these five formative years (1739–1743) on Pombal was comparable in their transformative effect to the three years that Voltaire had spent in London a decade earlier. Arguably the cradle if not the epicenter of the eighteenth-century Enlightenment, Great Britain represented for both men the archetype of a modern, innovative, and forward-thinking society.[12]

Although Britain, when Pombal arrived there, had yet to embark on its Industrial Revolution, it was a country in the throes of enormous change. In the countryside, an agricultural revolution had taken hold. Crop yields had increased dramatically due to more efficient use of the land, and the resultant rise in caloric intake per capita had resulted in a population explosion that would provide legions of workers for the upcoming Industrial Age. The backdrop for all of this was the profound political realignment that had occurred at the end of the seventeenth century, the so-called Glorious Revolution of 1688, in which the new monarch, William of Orange, had entered into a power-sharing agreement with Parliament (codified in the Bill of Rights of 1689) that had provided badly needed social, political, and economic stability after two centuries of strife, discord, and civil war. Pombal was not, to be sure, interested in a similar constitutional settlement for Portugal. He loathed the Portuguese aristocracy, which he considered backward and corrupt. In Pombal's view, change would not come by giving more power to the *Cortes*, the corporate body of nobles established in the Middle Ages, but by concentrating it in the hands of the Crown—i.e., the state.

While in London, Pombal may have imbibed some of the anti-Catholicism and anticlericalism then in vogue. Though he remained a devout Catholic throughout his life, at some point he began to view the institutions of the Church as backward, unproductive, and later, in the case of the Jesuits and Oratorians, seditious. In the aristocratic circles that Pombal frequented in the early 1740s, religion was decidedly out of fashion and Catholicism was viewed with contempt and fear. Though in a few years John Wesley and his evangelical fervor would capture the imagination of the upper classes, the world of Sir Robert Walpole, prime minister from 1721 to 1742, was dominated by bankers and merchants rather than bishops and preachers.

Pombal's own concern with commerce was reflected in the substantial library (for which a catalogue exists) that he amassed while in London. There were books on mining, tobacco, sugar, wool, navigation, and the various British trading companies. If there was an organizing theme, it was the rising political and economic dominance of Great Britain. "I found on coming to this Court," Pombal wrote to his superiors in Lisbon, "that the most interesting [i.e., important] duty of the

Portuguese Minister in London is to investigate the causes which have resulted in the decadence of Portuguese commerce at a time when the commerce of England and that of other countries are in expansion."[13]

Pombal was particularly vexed by the Methuen Treaty of 1703, which gave the British the right to sell textiles in Portugal tariff-free, while Portuguese wines sold in Britain were taxed at a rate one third less than those from France. Pombal believed the benefits of the treaty greatly favored the British, whose merchants and businessmen had flooded into Lisbon and Porto while British ports harbored relatively few Portuguese.[14]

Pombal became convinced that Britain sought global dominion above all things, and would stop at nothing to achieve its goals—even if it meant turning on its oldest ally. His principal anxiety was what he perceived as Britain's covetousness for Brazil, the economic jewel in Portugal's crown. "The envy of our Brazil," he predicted, "so strong in British hearts, would eventually lead them to an attack on Portuguese America."[15] When it came to the interests of nations, Pombal was under no illusions. States, he believed, were at heart only concerned with their own interests. "All the nations of Europe," he wrote Cardinal da Motta, "are augmenting their powers by imitation of each other."[16] Pombal's error was that he saw economics as a zero-sum game. He could not conceive that trade could be beneficial to two countries engaged in economic interaction.

And so, Pombal would assert what he perceived to be Portugal's interests with a ferocity and doggedness that no Portuguese ambassador to London had ever before ventured. Believing the British had taken their ally for granted, he hounded them for not aiding the Portuguese in defending the island of Salsete from Indian attacks and berated them for harassing French and Spanish ships in neutral Portugal's waters.

When these issues appeared to reach a fever pitch, Pombal threatened Walpole with a complete break in diplomatic relations. But the prime minister correctly calculated that Portugal would never make good on its threat. Still, Pombal continued to apply pressure. Citing the abuse that British sailors frequently hurled at Portuguese authorities in the harbor at Porto, Pombal wrote to the British cabinet: "Such a scandal and such an insult are sufficiently outrageous in themselves to call for a severe punishment . . . and . . . to serve as an example . . . [to] British subjects who find in Portuguese ports . . . hospitality and help."[17]

For their part, the British were quickly losing patience with Portugal's proud and prickly ambassador. "This man has done us great harm," wrote Benjamin Keene, the British ambassador to Lisbon, to Abraham Castres, the British consul. "He has no method to make himself personally considered, and he construes all slights as national ones. It is as poor a Coimbrian pate as ever I met with: to be as stubborn, as dull, is the true asinine quality."[18]

In 1745, a combination of British pressure and the conniving of Pombal's enemies at home led to a new posting. Pombal was ordered to Vienna to broker a rapprochement between the Vatican and the Queen of Hungary and Bohemia, the future Empress Maria Theresa. He considered it a demotion (which it was), though he never formally relinquished his ambassadorship to Britain.

While in Vienna, Pombal, whose first wife, Teresa, had died in 1739, began to pursue the Countess Maria Leonor Ernestina Daun, the niece of the former head of the Austrian military and one of the heroes of the War of Austrian Succession, Marshal Heinrich Graf von Daun. In December 1745, they were married. Though not rich, the Countess Daun had a pedigree that stretched back to the twelfth century and possessed sufficient quarterings to impress even the most exacting member of Portugal's upper crust. The marriage received the blessing of Maria Theresa and, even more importantly, Portugal's Austrian-born queen, Maria Ana, who made Pombal's new wife, Leonor, one of her ladies-in-waiting upon Pombal's return to Lisbon in 1749.

The trip home had been particularly bitter. Pombal's ambassadorship to Britain had been given to someone else and, adding insult to injury, the British offered him a monetary gift that was only a fraction of what was normally bestowed upon departing ambassadors. An irate Pombal refused it altogether and, as a consequence, was forced to pawn his household silver to pay for his journey back to Portugal.

In the eyes of his countrymen, his years abroad had made Pombal an *estrangeirado*. Adapted from the word *estrangeiro* (abroad), it described Portuguese writers, scientists, and statesmen who, in the seventeenth and eighteenth centuries, traveled outside Portugal and became inspired—some would say infected— with ideas of the Scientific Revolution and Enlightenment culture. A few *estrangeirados* (like the New Christians escaping the Inquisition) fled into permanent exile, while others, like Pombal, eventually returned to Portugal.

London and Vienna proved decisive for Pombal. It was there that he gained not only confidence and experience, but a long list of friends and acquaintances (many among the *estrangeirados*) that he would consult and call upon in the future. He also began to formulate a strategy in the tradition of many *estrangeirados* about what needed to be done to reform Portuguese society. But what differentiated Pombal from most of these other potential reformers was that he was given the opportunity, with his appointment as secretary of state in 1750, to implement his blueprint.[19] When the earthquake struck, that program accelerated dramatically.

THE SEARCH FOR A PLAN

Within days of the quake, Pombal directed General Manoel da Maia to submit a plan for rebuilding the capital. A lifelong bachelor, the fleshy-faced seventy-eight-year-old was Portugal's chief architect as well as the director of the Royal Archives.[20] As a young military engineer, he had learned the techniques of fortress building and siege laying in the grand tradition of the Marquis of Vauban and had designed forts and towers in Lisbon and across the kingdom. As regent of the School of Fortification, he had once taught Dom José when he was the Prince of Brazil and heir apparent.[21]

Although nearly eighty, Maia was associated with the most visionary building project in Portuguese history: the Aqueduct of the Free Waters, for which he had served as chief engineer during the almost twenty years of its construction (1729–1748). Unlike the palace at Mafra—the other great building project in the kingdom in the first half of the eighteenth century—the aqueduct looked to the future rather than the past. While Mafra utilized the aesthetic language of the Baroque to exalt both Church and Crown, the massive aqueduct was stylistically spare, utilitarian, and, in that its sole purpose was to supply the inhabitants of Lisbon with clean water, democratic. It was also one of the engineering marvels of the age.

When the earthquake hit occurred, Maia left his house in the Baixa to the mercy of the fires and rushed to save the royal archives. "I declare," he later wrote in his will, "that the fire which followed the earthquake on November 1, 1755, burned the building in which I lived on Salema Lane in the parish of the Holy Sacrament and destroyed all that I owned along with all my memories acquired over many years in documents, architectural plans, and instruments of my principal profession."[22] For Maia, as for many, there was no turning back.

On November 29, Pombal ordered those in charge of Lisbon's dozen neighborhoods to provide "an exact description of their respective *bairros*" as well as the measurements of "each of the squares, streets, alleys, and public buildings ... in addition to [the measurements of] each private property ... front and the back ... [including] the yards, with the elevations or heights of each." Although much of the Baixa was still covered in a layer of bricks, stones, ash, and debris several stories high, this accounting needed to be completed before the rebuilding could proceed.[23]

Earlier in the month, serious consideration had been given to the idea of relocating the capital just a few miles downriver to Belém or Alcântara. "I believe that the King is thinking of building a new Lisbon *[une nouvelle Lisbonne]* in the neighborhood of Belém," wrote Miguel Pedegache in his letter to the *Journal étranger* dated November 11, 1755.[24] But only nine days later, after consulting with Pombal, Abraham Castres informed Whitehall that "it is the undoubted Resolution of this Court to rebuild the City on the very Spot it stood before it was destroyed."[25] The decision had been made.

On December 4, 1755, General Maia presented his "dissertation" on the five rebuilding options available to the Crown—along with his views on the strengths and weaknesses of each plan. Option #1 mandated that Lisbon be rebuilt exactly as it had been before. This was the strategy that had been used in the past when sections of the capital had been destroyed by fire or earthquake. Economically, it was the least disruptive. The idea was that much of the city could be rebuilt using the rubble that lay in the streets, and landlords could rent the same spaces at the same prices as they had before. A major drawback was that Lisbon would remain essentially unchanged—no steps would be taken to improve the life of the city and its inhabitants.[26]

Option #2 was similar to Option #1, except that some of the main streets would be widened, while Option #3 called for the broadening of most streets and the limiting of buildings to three stories in order to reduce the potential destruction from future earthquakes. One problem with limiting vertical construction, according to Maia, was that, while the mandate might be followed in the short term, ultimately it would be forgotten when the horrors of November 1, 1755, began to fade from memory.[27]

Option #4, the most radical, entailed "razing the entire Baixa [and] building it up with rubble" in order to prevent future inundations from the Tagus. After this, the entire city would be reconfigured with wide thoroughfares and buildings that were no higher than the width of the facing street. Option #5, which Maia and his team favored, had already been ruled out. It called for abandoning the old city and reconstructing a new capital along the river just west of rural Belém. Construction could begin almost immediately with little perceived risk, for it was widely believed at the time that buildings constructed east of Lisbon had a better chance of surviving a future quake because the intensity of the November 1 earthquake had been considerably less in this area.[28] It was also generally believed that earthquakes caused more destruction in populated (or previously populated) areas because human excreta (feces and urine) that had entered the soil intensified the forces that caused seismic tremors.[29]

The problem with constructing a new capital at or near Belém was that it would invade the royal family's recreational space. Although the king's personal views on the subject are unknown, one may assume that he and his family wished to maintain their permanent refuge from the crowded Baixa. Moreover, it was in Pombal's interest to separate the court and the capital. The farther Dom José was kept from Lisbon—with all its political, economic, and religious interests—the easier it would be for Pombal to control him.

One threat to Pombal's plan was the building boom that had spontaneously broken out all across the city as people sought to mend their damaged homes or replace their tents with more permanent *barracas*. On December 30, 1755, an edict was issued prohibiting anyone from rebuilding a damaged structure or building a new one of brick or stone in a neighborhood that had suffered fire damage until after the official accounting of all properties had been concluded and the king had issued new orders for the rebuilding of the city. Those who disregarded it would have their properties "demolished at the owner's cost" in addition to other penalties imposed at the discretion of His Majesty.[30]

Not wasting any time, Pombal ordered the Duke of Lafões on December 3 to demolish all unstable walls in the city and to clear the streets of rubble and debris.[31] On January 31, 1756, he called for an additional 150 soldiers to join those already engaged in "the public works."[32] At some point, the job of demolition was handed over to José Monterro de Carvalho, the military engineer who would come to be known as *Bota Abaixo* (the Destroyer).[33]

Soon, vast numbers of *lisboetas*—soldiers, convicts, and the poor—

were compelled to participate in this vast undertaking. In the spring, Pombal pressed the city's Gypsy population into service in public work gangs—"as there was no ship at the time that might transport them to Angola," he explained.[34] The work was difficult, dangerous, and sometimes heartbreaking. One six-mule coach was unearthed many feet below the surface with four corpses inside.[35] And because of the common belief that vapors from decomposing corpses caused disease, the anxiety level was high. By September 1756, twenty thousand workers, augmented by provincial regiments, were engaged in the enterprise.[36] Now all that was needed was a specific plan.

Initially, Maia refused to abandon his dream of a new Portuguese capital in Belém. According to a newspaper account, in the late winter several architects and engineers raised "an Abundance of Objections" to rebuilding Lisbon in the "old Spot." They had good reasons to protest. The aftershocks showed no sign of abating (thus making any near-term construction impossible); and perhaps more ominously, water had begun to seep into the ruins.[37]

At some point, Maia realized that Pombal had made up his mind. The wholesale demolition and the clearing of rubble in the Baixa signaled that the city center would be rebuilt according to a new design. In time, it would offer almost as clean a slate as the western suburbs. One problem, however, was the lack of instructive precedents for such an undertaking. The near-complete destruction of a major European city was exceedingly rare, if not unprecedented.

Maia was well aware that the great British architect Christopher Wren had, in 1666, submitted a sketch that would have completely refashioned the streets and squares of central London after the Great Fire of that year. But Wren's pioneering design was never used. The concerns of property owners convinced the British government to rebuild the capital to the same dimensions as before. Maia had also studied the expansion of Turin by the architect Filippo Juvarra in 1714 after the destructive French siege that had devastated the city eight years earlier. But that was on a much smaller scale than Lisbon. Compared to the hard work of rebuilding the Portuguese capital, Turin, wrote Maia, was merely "play."[38]

In the months that followed, the great project attracted inquiries from across Europe. French architects sent letters of introduction to the king; and one civic-minded citizen offered his thoughts on the rebuilding in *The Gentleman's Magazine*.[39]

1st. Let the new city be built upon as even ground as possible, and the seven hills, mentioned in a late description . . . left free from all kinds of buildings, and entirely open, as so many areas, instead of those squares, which the people ran to . . . because they will not only secure the fugitives from falling houses, but from the overflowing of the water upon the swell of the sea.

2dly, Let the houses be built low and broad, for it is evident, that a low and broad house will bear more shaking than a high one, and that the centre of gravity will be longer preserved within the walls.

3dly, Let the streets be three times as wide as the houses are high; that supposing the houses to be thrown down on both sides, the materials of which they are built may not meet in the middle of the street.

4thly, Let the roofs be flat, and the diminishings of the walls in the different stories all on the outside, that they may be perpendicular within from top to bottom.[40]

It was a brief but visionary treatise.

In Rome, the twenty-seven-year-old architect Robert Adam immediately interpreted the disaster as "a heavenly judgment on my behalf."[41] The self-confident Scotsman, who was then studying under the French architect Charles-Louis Clérisseau and the Italian artist Giovanni Battista Piranesi, saw the rebuilding of Lisbon as an opportunity to both make his mark in the field and improve his social station. "I should, if things succeeded [i.e., if he was appointed chief architect of the project], be made noble by the King and have money to support the dignity of it without competition or rival and after a few years spent in an honourable way in a fine climate and where reside many of our countrymen, return to England with all these honours on my head," he giddily wrote his family back in Edinburgh.[42]

To demonstrate his virtuosity, Adam produced several preliminary sketches and sent them to the Portuguese court. In them, he envisioned Lisbon as a Baroque showplace with a grand basin draining into the Tagus and an aristocratic quarter rising directly behind it.[43] It is an image strongly reminiscent of eighteenth-century Rome and in keeping with the visual style and extravagant pretensions of the now defunct reign of João V. What Adam failed to grasp was Pombal's intention of making a clean break with the past.

By the spring of 1756, Adam had become increasingly anxious and excited about his chances of appointment—he was "thinking, talking, and dreaming" of little else. There is no evidence, however, that his application ever made it to Pombal's desk. The first minister had no interest in outside advice or alternative foreign visions for Lisbon (especially from a Briton). In 1758, Adam returned to his native land, where he would become the most important architect of the second half of the eighteenth century.[44]

In order to provide Pombal with different design choices for the city, Maia organized three teams of military architects, each working furiously over the winter of 1755–1756. Their guiding principles were symmetry, uniformity, and utility. "The streets," Maia vowed in his dissertation, would be "freely drawn"—and "each street [would] conserve the same symmetry in doors, windows, and height." Wider streets would provide better ventilation, improve public health, facilitate the evacuation of the populace during a natural disaster, and increase the amount of light entering the Baixa, which would help to deter crime. To expedite the flow of traffic, streets (40 palmos or 29 feet wide) would be reserved for horses, carts, and coaches, while pedestrians and sedan cars would travel in paths (10 palmos or 7 feet wide) on either side.[45]

Another serious concern so common in early modern European cities was how to transport sewage and refuse out of the center of the city. To do this more efficiently, Maia proposed installing sewers under the principal streets, instituting a system of garbage carts that would collect the refuse thrown from windows each day, and building narrow courtyards (*alfugeres*) behind each building where residents could dump their trash and debris.[46] All would be instituted with varying degrees of success.

It was this unique opportunity to transform Lisbon into a model of health and hygiene that drew the attention of Portugal's most famous physician: Dr. António Nunes Ribeiro Sanches. Educated at Coimbra, Salamanca, Geneva, London, Paris, and Leiden, where he studied under the most celebrated doctor of his day, Hermann Boerhaave, Ribeiro Sanches was now living in exile in Paris, having fled Portugal years before when a cousin denounced him (a New Christian and later

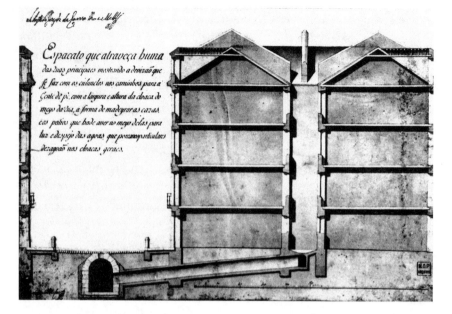

Cross section of a building showing its connection to a sewer running under
one of Lisbon's principal streets

an observant Jew) to the Inquisition. In 1731, after a recommendation
from Boerhaave, he traveled to Russia, where he became the personal
physician of Empress Anna Ivanovna and was credited with saving the
life of Princess Ekaterina Alekseyevna—the future empress Catherine
the Great—who years later would reward him with a pension.

Upon learning of Lisbon's destruction and the horrendous living
conditions experienced by its survivors, Ribeiro Sanches conceived
his *Treatise on the Preservation of the Health of the Public* (1756). It was
a visionary book that sought to safeguard the health of urban areas
everywhere—now and into the future. "Every nation," wrote Ribeiro
Sanches, "should institute laws and regulations to defend against disease
and maintain the health of its citizens." If such laws are not followed,
"the science of medicine is of little use, because it will be impossible
for doctors, [and] surgeons, however learned and experienced, to stop
an epidemic or any other disease inside a city when the air is corrupted
and the soil soaked in water."[47] The central pillar of Ribeiro Sanches's
reforms, following the prevailing medical wisdom of the day, was the
promotion of cleanliness and fresh air.

His approach—which he christened "Political Medicine"—involved the full cooperation of leaders from both the state and civil society. "Magistrates, generals, [and] captains of the sea and war could, through the strength of the new laws," be enlisted to fight disease. Such information would, he felt, be useful to "abbots, abbesses, inspectors of hospitals, and fathers of families" as well as prison wardens and architects.[48]

Regarding architecture, Ribeiro Sanches believed that too much thought went into ensuring that a city was beautiful and too little into making it healthy.[49] Of special interest to Ribeiro Sanches, who was an expert on venereal disease, was the well-being of soldiers and sailors, who were capable of carrying and transmitting diseases from the farthest corners of the empire.[50] Hearing of the book, Pombal, who relished this kind of state-sponsored reform, not only financed its publication, he mandated that copies be given to every public and religious official in the kingdom.[51]

Few, however, could have failed to notice that the much feared post-earthquake epidemic, which was supposed to have been triggered by the gases given off by decaying corpses, had not taken place. In March of 1756, Dr. José Alvares da Silva, the house physician of the powerful Távora family, published a pamphlet that attempted to explain why. Most plagues, Silva argued, appear to originate in Africa, and while dead bodies do pose some public health dangers, in this instance the fire had sanitized most of them through the process of cremation and the winter temperatures had provided refrigeration. Moreover, a brisk and constant north wind had swept many of the foul and dangerous odors away from the city. As for the survivors of the disaster, Dr. Silva recommended a healthy diet, clean clothes, ample disinfectants, and a positive mental attitude, which might be buoyed and sustained through music.[52]

On April 19, 1756, General Maia submitted six new city plans to Pombal.[53] All substantially widened Lisbon's streets and all connected the Rossio directly to the Terreiro do Paço. The city would be divided into large orthogonal blocks that would provide stability during future earthquakes and increased frontage for businesses and shops. While this grid pattern echoed the Roman Castrum and the layout of several cities built in the New World over the past century and a half—Candelaria, Argentina (1627), Mexico City (1680), Quito (1734), and Caracas (1750)—it had never been used on such a grand scale before.[54]

The sketch Pombal ultimately chose was Plan #5. It was the brain-child of architect and military engineer Captain Eugénio dos Santos, with the assistance of the Hungarian-born Carlos Mardel. After Maia, Dos Santos was the second most important architect in the kingdom. From conspicuously humble origins—both his father and grandfather had been stonemasons—he had risen through a combination of talent and his marriage into one of the architectural families of the court to become the inspector of royal buildings and works and the official architect of the Senate.[55]

Dos Santos's Plan #5 was a revelation. Instead of employing curved streets and thoroughfares that conformed to Lisbon's undulating topography, Dos Santos favored bold straight lines, as Maia and, presumably, Pombal wished him to. Between the Rossio and the Terreiro do Paço, nine streets were traversed by eight others at right angles, creating approximately forty rectangular blocks of almost equal size. Unlike the former, largely medieval, city center, there were no distinct locations that drew the eye's attention, and the number of churches was substantially reduced. Those churches that were allowed to remain were given smaller plots on the peripheries, and each was obliged to conform to the newly mandated Neoclassical style.[56]

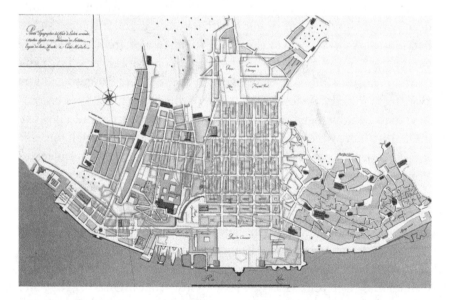

Plan #5, conceived by Eugénio dos Santos and Carlos Mardel, and chosen by Pombal

To ratify and reinforce the transformation of a city once controlled by the Church, the Crown, and the nobility into one dominated by the middle class, the names of Lisbon's principal streets were changed. Beautiful Queen Street (Rua da Bela Rainha) became Silver Street (Rua da Prata), New Princess Street (Rua da Nova Princesa) became Drapers Street (Rua dos Fanqueiros), and Immaculate Conception Street (Rua da Conceição) became Haberdashers Street (Rua dos Retrozeiros). Even more significant was Pombal's decision to build the new royal palace in Belém (and not to rebuild the old Riverside Palace). Thus were both king and court sundered from the capital.[57]

Integral to the rebuilding effort were innovations intended to help Lisbon survive the next major earthquake and fire. To this end, buildings were secured into the sandy soil with flexible pine logs treated with salt to inhibit combustion and decay.[58] And because it was believed that the earthquake tremors had moved from north to south, following the path of the two streams that flow under the Baixa, the foundations of all new structures were aligned to this axis in order to produce greater strength and stability.[59]

The most impressive innovations, however, were found in the design of the buildings themselves. Most were enclosed in a wooden frame or cage (gaiola), whose diagonal beams—set in the shape of a St. Andrew's Cross—were specifically constructed to absorb the vibrations of an earthquake. Produced after several years of experimentation (and inspired by the observation that many timber-framed structures on São Jorge's Hill had survived the disaster), the Pombaline cage (gaiola pombalina), as it was called, was required of every new building in the city and represented a revolutionary advance in architectural design.[60] Although built to withstand small to moderate earthquakes, in the event of a powerful temblor, the facade was designed to collapse into the street, thereby allowing the remainder of the building to remain intact. To limit the amount of debris that might fall on pedestrians, and to maintain stylistic uniformity throughout the Baixa, the frontages of buildings bore few decorations.

To fireproof the city, ground floors were constructed of vaulted stone, not wood, and every basement had a cistern. Firebreaks—walls extending up through the roof of a building to impede fires from moving from one structure to another—were installed, and fire pumps were positioned next to every parish church along with a generous supply of leather buckets.[61] Because it was believed that several of the initial fires

An eighteenth-century model of the *gaiola pombalina* (Pombaline cage)

that broke out on November 1, 1755, started in bakeries, all *padarias* were to be grouped together behind a high wall along the Walkway of St. Francis (Calçada de São Francisco).[62] Perhaps Maia and Pombal were also aware that the Great Fire of London had begun in a bakery in Pudding Lane.[63]

Another innovation spurred by the rebuilding effort was the pre-fabrication and standardization of building components like wall tiles, windows, doors, and wrought-iron staircase parts. To encourage the mass production and importation of these products, Pombal uncharac-teristically yielded to market forces by relaxing the import duties, taxes, and tariffs on them.[64]

One of the inevitable (and, for Pombal, desired) consequences of the rebuilding and recovery efforts was the pronounced increase in centralized power. In Portugal, laws regulating private property were

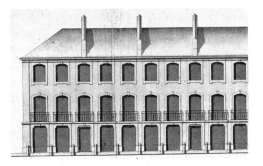

The unadorned facade of a typical Pombaline building. Firebreaks can be seen along the roof between the windows.

less stringent than in Britain, for example. As a consequence, the government could more aggressively exercise its right to eminent domain. On June 12, 1758, a decree signed by Dom José, and no doubt written by Pombal, articulated the Crown's new policy in this regard. "I wish [my subjects] to prefer, as they should . . . the public utility of regularity and beauty over and above private interests . . . in all of the

Dom José directing the rebuilding of the capital

streets whose buildings were ruined by the earthquake and burnt by the fires."[65] Royal geometry would now trump individual rights, and public aesthetics supersede private concerns.

Yet the Pombaline state did support some groups. The new building regulations decisively favored those with ready cash like merchants and businessmen, Pombal's allies, while the nobility, whose assets were largely tied up in land, were forced to rebuild their palaces outside the city center or retire on their landed estates.[66] Because landowners would, by law, lose their city plots if they did not rebuild within five years (they did, however, receive compensation), the government was able to acquire substantial property—then sell the abandoned plots to those individuals and groups it favored. In this way, Pombal and his government employed the rebuilding process to orchestrate a quiet social revolution in the capital.

One person who undoubtedly admired Pombal's statist agenda was Ange Goudar, the French writer, adventurer, and spy.[67] From 1751 to 1754, he had lived in the Portuguese capital, where as an agent of the French government he had advised Pombal and studied Portugal's economy and culture. On the whole, he was not impressed. The Portuguese, he felt, lived in a state of barbaric ignorance. Their economy and the fount of their wealth, the Brazilian gold mines, were, in his opinion, controlled entirely by the British, who, because of favorable trade agreements, supplied the Portuguese with almost all their textiles and grain, leaving Portugal vulnerable to unforeseen events, like a bad harvest in Britain.

In Goudar's view, the catastrophe of All Saints' Day offered the Portuguese a rare opportunity to reform their institutions, throw off their commercial yoke, and reclaim their country. "I believe that Portugal must take advantage of this misfortune, and I have produced this little book to prove it," Goudar wrote in the opening of his *Discours politique* of 1756.[68] He, of course, had an ulterior motive. As a Frenchman, Goudar was envious of Britain's special status in Portugal and saw it as one of the foundations of British strength. If, however, Portugal could find a way to end what Goudar believed was its servile dependence on Britain, then France might not only penetrate the Portuguese market, it might acquire a new ally; then the balance of power between France and its nemesis, Great Britain, might shift decisively.

With the Seven Years War testing alliances across Europe, the *Discours* was read throughout the continent and went through several

editions—four in 1756 alone.[69] On October 8, 1756, the Portuguese
Inquisition banned Goudar's book for what it saw as its seditious,
insulting, and incendiary attacks on the Portuguese nation—though
clandestine copies would circulate throughout Portugal, Brazil, and
Portugal's Asian possessions well into the nineteenth century. Although
Pombal largely agreed with Goudar's characterization of Portugal's
economic dependence on Britain, he could not countenance the slan-
der against his country nor support Goudar's wish to weaken Portugal's
military alliance with Britain, which he still wished to maintain. Such
was Pombal's concern that after an edition of the *Discours* was published
in Madrid in 1762, he wrote a letter to *The London Chronicle* in which
he, pretending to be an anonymous British subject, railed against that
"famous lampoon" that tried to "paint" the British "with such colours
as to make them odious and unbearable" to "the Portuguese people."[70]

There were other reasons that Pombal wished to preserve the alli-
ance with Britain. In late February 1756, the first of sixteen British
relief ships escorted by the sixty-six-gun *Hampton Court*, the twenty-gun
Greyhound, and the twenty-gun *Gibraltar* began to arrive in Lisbon.[71]
According to the *Mercurio Histórico y Político*, the British ambassador,
Abraham Castres, "had the honor of [personally] delivering the aid to
His Majesty, who received it with much satisfaction."[72] To ensure its
equitable distribution, officials were specially appointed to oversee the
process. The initial allotment was given to the poor, by order of Dom
José, and £2,000 was set aside for the British survivors, to be doled out
by Edward Hay.[73] It is "very just," said the king, "that this honorable
nation enjoys the first fruits."[74]

Priests and monks also were given substantial quantities of aid
because it was believed that they knew where the greatest need existed.
(Because of this, some *lisboetas* began masquerading as men of God in
order to be so entrusted.) So widespread was the misery in Lisbon that
Dom José mandated that some relief be specifically directed to members of the nobility. While the majority of nobles accepted the *donativo*
(gift)—it would have been ill-mannered not to, they said—the Marquês
de Valença conspicuously refused. There were many others, he said, in
greater need than himself, though "in truth," recalled one priest, "the
Marquês suffered the same poverty as the majority."[75] Even Dom José
was the recipient of some munificence. One of the last British relief
ships from Great Britain carried a personal gift from George II to the
Portuguese king: several complete sets of silver service, made to order

in London, to replace the royal plate that had melted in the ruins of the Riverside Palace.[76]

The aid from Britain came not a moment too soon. For as the winter dragged on, the morale and circumstances of the survivors would reach new lows. "Sitting on the banks of the Tagus, as the Jews in another time sat on the banks of the rivers of Babylonia, we cry here, as they cried, over the desolation of our beloved country," wrote one Portuguese. "We have no refuge or habitation other than a few badly-made tents and huts that have failed to protect us from half the rigors of this cruel season."[77] Adding to the anxiety was the fact that the earth stubbornly refused to remain still. We live "always in the misery, anguish, and fear that a much more destructive earthquake than the one we experienced [on All Saints' Day] will come to pass," admitted another *lisboeta*.[78] Soon, some would associate that more destructive force with Pombal himself.

CHAPTER TEN

Reverberations

The master I would not offend, yet wish
This gulf of fire and sulphur had outpoured
Its baleful flood amid the desert wastes.

—VOLTAIRE, "POEM ON THE LISBON DISASTER" (1756)

THE GREAT EARTHQUAKE DEBATE

Johann Wolfgang von Goethe was only six years old when the news of the Lisbon disaster arrived in his hometown of Frankfurt am Main. "The peace of mind of a little boy," recalled the author of *Faust*, "was most profoundly disturbed by an event of worldwide significance.

> The little boy, who heard everybody talking about the event, was deeply impressed. God, the creator and preserver of Heaven and Earth, God, said to be omniscient and merciful, had shown himself to be a very poor sort of father, for he had struck down equally the just and the unjust. In vain, the young mind sought to combat this idea; but it was clear that even learned theologians could not agree about the way to account for such a disaster.[1]

Fortunately, the young Goethe found reassurance in his pastor's declaration that "God was well aware that no harm could come to the immortal soul through an evil act."[2] For others, however, there was no such consolation.

Everywhere, it seemed, there was disagreement and vigorous debate. In the five years following the disaster, hundreds of books, articles, letters, treatises, poems, reviews, sermons, and scientific tracts on the subject were published across the continent. A Pandora's box of questions almost as capacious as the tectonic chasm itself had been opened up in a continent that stood, in the eyes of many, upon the precipice of a new age. Who, or what, was responsible for Lisbon's destruction? Was God solely to blame or had nature or a combination of natural forces played the leading role? And perhaps most importantly: how could a just and all-powerful God have sanctioned the deaths of so many innocent people?

The ensuing debate was arguably the most significant of the European Enlightenment. And because it engaged not only philosophers and professors, but ordinary people in church pews and front parlors from Lima to St. Petersburg, it was, in the fullest sense, a public event, involving a considerable proportion of the population of the Western world. Yet it will probably always be chiefly remembered for the spirited participation of several of the most influential thinkers of the age.

THE SORCERER AWAKENS

By the summer of 1754, Voltaire was ready for a change. Through the better part of six decades, the celebrated dramatist and popular philosopher had engaged in a relentless and highly visible pursuit of both the Truth, as he understood it, and the adulation of his many admirers. Now, in the twilight of his notorious career, all was not well. A three-year sojourn at the court of Frederick the Great had ended badly and a much anticipated letter from Louis XV contained perhaps the worst news that any Frenchman could possibly receive: exile from Paris and Versailles.[3] "Life is one vast shipwreck," he wrote a friend in his sorrow, "and it's a case of every man for himself."[4] And so, desperate and ailing, surrounded by enemies real and imagined, Europe's most famous gadfly took the fateful step that would raise his sagging spirits and—at least temporarily—transform his life. He purchased a home.

Situated on a hillside along the Rhône River in Switzerland, Les Délices, with its sumptuous gardens and miraculous views, would become the sanctuary Voltaire had always dreamed of. It had not come cheap—but the work of a prophet could be quite lucrative and it would allow the hitherto peripatetic writer to live out his days in comfort

Voltaire with his niece, Madame Denis

and safety many miles from the jailers of the Bastille. Joining him was Madame Denis—his increasingly rotund forty-three-year-old niece and lover—whom he had wooed with letters so anatomically explicit they had been written in Italian to render them indecipherable to prying servant eyes.* "I feel every day that I must devote the last days of my life to you," he gushed in one of his more tender (and modest) exchanges, "and after a springtime of folly, a stormy winter, and a languishing autumn, you alone will be able to soften the rigors of my winter."[5]

Together, both niece and lovesick uncle would refashion the estate after their own vision of an earthly paradise. "The foundations of Carthage must be laid," Voltaire proclaimed.[6] To this end, the central château and several of the outlying buildings were expanded and the garden completely redone. "[We] are building accommodations for our friends and our hens," he joked. Plants of every conceivable variety were procured, herbs for the kitchen: "lavender, thyme, rosemary, mint,

---

* Such uncle-niece relationships were not rare in eighteenth-century France. It is possible Voltaire, who believed himself to be illegitimate, considered her only a half niece.

basil, rue, strawberries . . . and hyssop to cleanse us of our sins" as well
as hundreds of apple and peach trees, turnips, gooseberries, Egyptian
onions, peas, and carrots (though no tomatoes or eggplants, as they had
yet to be introduced into Europe). There was even a greenhouse where
asparagus and artichokes could be grown year-round in emulation of
Louis XIV.[7] Before the vineyard was operational, wine was purchased
in great quantities and shipped in large wooden casks: Beaujolais for
Madame Denis and a rich, full-bodied Burgundy for Voltaire, whose
famously delicate stomach could not abide the more acidic whites.[8]

Like any Eden worthy of its name, Les Délices possessed fauna
as well as flora. To the usual menagerie of barnyard stock and the six
horses employed to pull his enormous painted coach, Voltaire would
add a pet eagle, a fox, and a much adored monkey named Luc. There
was a small army of husbandrymen and gardeners to complement the
legion of chefs, coachmen, and valets—not to mention Voltaire's sour-
tempered and long-suffering personal secretary, Cosimo Collini, who
tended to his master's and Mme Denis's every whim.[9] For Voltaire, the
former courtier and aspiring aristocrat, Les Délices had become his
own private feudal domain. *"O maison d'Aristippe! ô jardins d'Epicure!"*
wrote the new manor lord. "Receive your new possessor! May he be,
like you, solitary and peaceful."[10]

Soon, Voltaire's life—in imitation of his art—settled into an agreeable routine of work and pleasure. In the mornings and afternoons, he
toiled over his writing. In the evenings, wrapped in a luxurious ermine
and velvet coat that had cost a princely 432 livres, he would descend
from his study to dine with friends and the many visitors who flocked
to his doorstep from every corner of Europe. Although well past middle
age, he still cut a commanding, if slightly awkward, figure. A then lofty
five feet ten inches, he was slender and spindle-legged, though the years
had left him partially stooped. "Tall, dried-up, and bony" was how he
described himself as a young man.[11] It was his face, however, that was
most remarked upon by contemporaries. Large protruding eyes ("the
most intelligent I've ever seen," conceded one critic), firm, jutting chin,
a mocking mouth, and a prominent nose made all the more so by the
loss of most of his teeth, produced an effect that was at once noble and
wickedly comic.[12] Secure in his pastoral lair, he resembled a wizened
old satyr: careworn and battle-scarred, yet supremely capable of drawing up all the virile, subversive spirits of his youth.

At Les Délices in the 1750s, the *seigneur* of the house could be seen each evening presiding over the elongated and always sumptuously laid dining table. Arms at his side, head attentively cocked to catch a guest's comment or query, Voltaire radiated patriarchal pride as host and master of ceremonies. Although he consumed little food himself, he felt duty-bound to provide the very best for those who called. Indeed, meals at the château, as in most great houses of the day, were elaborate affairs, consisting of up to six courses, each of which might include several different dishes. Although a maverick in the world of ideas, he had little tolerance for innovation in the kitchen, preferring hearty, standard fare, generously supplied. "I swear my stomach cannot get used to this *nouvelle cuisine*," he wrote to a friend. "As for cooks, I cannot stand the ham essences, mushrooms, pepper, and nutmeg with which they disguise dishes that are, left by themselves, perfectly fine and healthful."[13] Occasionally, for dessert the rare and regal pineapple made an appearance, as did Voltaire's favorite, the orange, which he liked to believe had been the original "forbidden fruit."[14]

After dinner, guests would retire either to the makeshift theater, where their host would indulge himself by acting in and directing his own plays, or to the drawing room, where earlier discussions continued by candlelight. As a conversationalist—and monologist—Voltaire had few equals. Witty, charming, an inveterate gossip and wag, he could hold court for hours in the presence of any audience. Alone in his study during the day, he would, upon his escape in the evenings, explode in a torrent of pent-up observations, humorous stories, aphorisms, rants, and prophetic pronouncements. Talleyrand, recalling a meeting he'd had as a young man with his idol, wrote that words "flew from him, so rapid, so neat, yet so distinct and so clear. . . . He spoke quickly and nervously with the play of features I have never seen in any man except him. . . . His eye kindled with vivid fire, almost dazzling." Like so many who entered into the presence of Voltaire, the future diplomat was transfixed and deeply moved. "Every line in that remarkable countenance is engraved in my memory," he would write about the incident years later. "I see it now before me—the small fiery eyes staring from shrunken sockets not unlike those of a chameleon."[15]

More than just an aging luminary, Voltaire had by midcentury become the venerable symbol of a new vision of society: one that was tolerant, civilized, rational, and committed to the general advancement of man. The imperative to replace dogma and superstition with science and reason—long a central tenet of the Voltairean catechism—was now

one of the prevailing maxims of the age. No call to arms or revolution—the former courtier was essentially conservative in his politics—
his emphasis was on reform and education, preferably inspired by the
writings of men like himself. Yet, as the renowned philosopher feath-
ered his Swiss nest in the fall of 1755, there was a growing sense among
friends and enemies alike that his greatest battles were now behind him,
that soon he would be little more than a museum piece to be trundled
out whenever a visitor wished to gaze upon what had once been the
most brilliant light in this, *le siècle des Lumières*.

Then came the news from Lisbon. Early reports reaching Switzerland, as in most places, were either exaggerated or wholly inaccurate.
In one account, the earthquake had opened up gigantic underground
caverns and laid waste to all the significant cities of Portugal (except for
the narrator's hometown, which the Almighty had mercifully spared).[16]

"My dear sir," Voltaire wrote his banker in Lyon immediately upon
hearing of the tragedy,

> Nature is very cruel. One would find it hard to imagine how the
> laws of movement cause such frightful disasters in the best of all
> possible worlds. A hundred thousand ants, our fellows, crushed
> all at once in our anthill, and half of them perishing, no doubt
> in unspeakable agony, beneath the wreckage from which they
> cannot be drawn. Families ruined all over Europe, the fortunes
> of a hundred businessmen, your compatriots, swallowed up in
> the ruins of Lisbon. What a wretched gamble is the game of
> human life![17]

The news hit Voltaire like a thunderbolt. "All it lacked was a trum-
pet," he remarked bitterly.[18] From the window of his study at Les
Délices, the world had seemed so ordered, so tranquil, so full of won-
drous possibility. Now it appeared merely capricious and cruel. "I no
longer dare complain about my colic," he wrote.[19]

This was no small matter for Voltaire. For early in his youth, as
he moved effortlessly from one theatrical and romantic triumph to
the next, he had been won over by the lures of what would later be
called optimism, a belief in the ultimate perfection of God's Creation.
Through the first half of the eighteenth century, this "apologia for
the status quo" had become for many educated Europeans the closest
thing to a religious and metaphysical certainty.[20] To the "optimists," the

world was on the whole a magnificent, splendid place, its many marvels proof of a wise and benevolent Deity. Although they never denied that evil existed, they believed it was rendered insignificant when set against the flawless totality of His handiwork. In the words of the English poet Alexander Pope in his *Essay on Man* (1734):

> *All nature is but Art, unknown to thee;*
> *All Chance, Direction, which thou canst not see;*
> *All Discord, Harmony not understood;*
> *All partial Evil, universal Good:*
> *And, spite of Pride, in erring Reason's spite,*
> *One truth is clear, Whatever is, is right.*[21]

Philosophical legitimacy had been provided by the towering figure of Gottfried Wilhelm von Leibniz, who argued in his highly influential treatise *Théodicée** (1710) that an infinitely benevolent Deity had created the universe with the greatest possible excess of good over evil. "If we could sufficiently understand the order of the universe," Leibniz wrote reassuringly, "we should find it adequately exceeds all the desires of the wisest men, and that it is impossible to make it better than it is."[22] To him, the nature of existence proved incontrovertibly that this was truly "the best of all possible worlds."[23]

For many, this seemed readily apparent. The early decades of the eighteenth century held such tantalizing promise for the advancement of mankind. The wars of religion, in which millions had been killed, were now over and the great scientific and technological discoveries of the last two centuries were improving the lives of Europeans across the entire socioeconomic spectrum. Most significantly, increases in food production, made possible by recent advances in land management and new agricultural techniques, had sparked the beginning of a historic rise in population that would allow Europe to cast off its Malthusian straitjacket for good.[24] Even the climate was improving. Average temperatures had risen dramatically from their seventeenth-century lows, when rivers like the Thames regularly froze over and much of Europe had shivered through what historians would later dub the "Little Ice Age."

But in Voltaire's eyes, the horrors of Lisbon called into question

---

* The term "theodicy"—the inquiry into the existence of evil given a benevolent deity—was coined by Leibniz. He wrote his treatise in the spirit of having settled the matter.

this happy progress toward Eden. The quake was more than just a horrific event; it was an affront to the natural order of things—the embodiment of all the blind and destructive forces that plagued human history. It was also the perfect occasion (and subject) to seize the attention of the public and once again thrust himself into the spotlight. "Sixty years of fame have not reassured him sufficiently to permit a day of rest," a disciple would later write. "It is not enough for him to be the hero of the century, he wants to be the news of the day, for he knows that the news of the day often makes people forget the hero of the century."[25] And so, retreating to his writing table, his indignation overflowing in a torrent of words, Voltaire produced the first draft of his *Poème sur le désastre de Lisbonne.* "Why had Lisbon been leveled?" he asked mockingly. "Was she more vicious than London . . . [or] Paris, plunged in pleasures? Lisbon is shattered, and Paris dances."

To the woolly-headed pedants who insisted that the earthquake had been a necessary evil, he replied: "Would the entire universe have been worse without this hellish abyss, without swallowing up Lisbon? Could not [God] plunge us into this wretched world without placing flaming volcanoes beneath our feet?"

> *Come, ye philosophers, who cry, "All's well,"*
> *And contemplate the ruin of a world.*
> *Behold these shreds and cinders of your race.*
> *This child and mother heaped in a common wreck.*
> *These scattered limbs beneath marble shafts—*
> *A hundred thousand whom, the earth devours,*
> *Who, torn and bloody, palpitating yet,*
> *Entombed beneath their hospitable roofs,*
> *In racking torment end their stricken lives.*
> *To those expiring murmurs of distress,*
> *To that appalling spectacle of woe,*
> *Will ye reply: "You do but illustrate*
> *The iron laws that chain the will of God?"*
> *Say ye, o'er that yet quivering mass of flesh:*
> *"God is avenged: the wage of sin is death?"*[26]

After Lisbon, how can the so-called philosophers still assert a near-perfect and benevolent world? "Leibniz," he wrote, "does not tell me by what invisible twists an eternal disorder, a chaos of misfortunes, mingles real sorrows with our vain pleasures in the best arranged of possible universes, nor why the innocent and the guilty suffer alike this inevitable evil." The situation could not have been clearer: *"Le mal est sur la terre."*

Less an argument than a full-throated cri de coeur, Voltaire's "sermon" appeals more to the emotions than the intellect—a mode of discourse that would become more common as the Age of Reason gave way to the Age of Sentiment. In this sense, Voltaire resembles not his Enlightenment colleagues so much as Lisbon's preacher-priests, like Malagrida. Like them, he reserves a special animus for the sins of humanity. Men, he writes, "do themselves more harm on their little mole-hill than does Nature. More . . . are slaughtered in our wars than are swallowed up by earthquakes."[27]

Of course, personal disappointment and sorrow were not unknown to Voltaire, his late-life Swiss idyll notwithstanding. In the five years preceding the purchase of Les Délices, he had had his share of travails: frequent illness, a bitter falling-out with his old chum Frederick the Great, and, most painful of all, the death in 1749 of Émilie du Châtelet, his longtime mistress, intellectual companion, and confidante. Without the buffer of Madame du Châtelet, his world had suddenly become bleaker, less bearable. "How stupid and paltry this mid-eighteenth century is!" he wrote in the depths of his mourning.[28] The earthquake then had transported Voltaire back to the grim realities of his own recent past and, in many respects, a more traditional conception of the human condition.

It is also likely that Voltaire was drawing upon a tradition of philosophical pessimism that is rarely acknowledged as playing a significant role in eighteenth-century thought. Though optimism and providentialism were clearly in vogue in 1755, there were many prolific and influential thinkers—like the theologian, William Wollaston; the satirist, Jonathan Swift; the mathematician and philosopher, Pierre Maupertuis; and the philosopher, David Hume—who challenged the view that the world presented a felicitous harmony.

> Look round this universe [wrote Hume in his *Dialogues Concerning Human Understanding* (1751)]. What an immense profusion of beings, animated and organised, sensible and active! You admire this prodigious variety and fecundity. But inspect

a little more narrowly these living existences. . . . How hostile and destructive to each other! . . . How contemptible or odious to the spectator! The whole presents nothing but the idea of a blind Nature, impregnated by a great vivifying principle, and pouring forth from her lap, without discernment or parental care, her maimed and abortive children![29]

For Hume, the world reflected not order, but randomness and indifference.

But how would the public react to his *Poème*? Eighteenth-century readers (not to mention government censors) were notoriously fickle and unforgiving, and even he—the intrepid philosophe—had no interest in endangering his future ability to publish. Time and again over the years, Voltaire had made compromises to further his career: subtly altering works to ensure their widest acceptance or burying a particularly controversial piece in a large compendium. Perhaps, as he suggested to a friend, the *Poème* should be distributed privately. Why should he risk being labeled an eighteenth-century Jeremiah?[30]

But Voltaire had crossed the Rubicon, both intellectually and politically. He now saw clearly that there was nothing inevitable about human progress—that change, if it were to come at all, would be the result of bitter struggle and sacrifice. "I am ashamed to be at peace and ease at home, and on occasion to have twenty persons to dinner, when three-quarters of Europe live in misery."[31]

The earthquake, in short, had freed Voltaire to be Voltaire. For the first time since he had dedicated his life to the ideals of the Enlightenment, the silk gloves had come off. Armed with a subject that had riveted all of Europe, he sought to serve up a coup de grâce to the self-satisfaction of his age.

But the earthquake did not affect everyone in the same way. In 1755, the Swiss writer Jean-Jacques Rousseau was living in a small house in Montmorency, about ten miles north of Paris, with his domestic partner, Marie-Thérèse Levasseur. He had not yet achieved the overwhelming fame that would come to him in a few years, but his star was certainly on the rise. Five years before, his clever, counterintuitively negative reply to the question posed by the organizers of an essay contest at the Dijon Academy—"Has the restoration of the sciences and arts contributed to the purification of morals?"—won him first prize and made him known throughout France. His second attempt at social criticism, *On the Origins of Inequality* (1755), had cemented his claim to be considered one of Europe's most original minds.

It is not known how Rousseau reacted when he first heard, presumably in late November 1755, of the Lisbon disaster. But he could hardly have been more dismayed than when he received a copy of Voltaire's *Poème sur le désastre de Lisbonne* in August 1756, possibly from Voltaire himself.

He immediately put pen to paper and fashioned a reply. "Forgive me, great man, for my zealousness—it may be indiscreet, but it would not overflow so much, if I did not esteem you so highly." In truth, Rousseau had been deeply wounded by Voltaire's characterization of a world overflowing with misery and suffering. And he suspected Voltaire of disingenuousness when the author asserted at the end of the *Poème* that he still believed that God guided the destiny of man and the universe. "If the problem of the origin of evil drives you to challenge God's perfection, why not uphold His powerfulness at the cost of His goodness? If one is an error, I prefer it to be the first. You do not want us, Monsieur, to read your poem as denying Providence."[32]

Much of the unhappiness in the world, Rousseau argued in a theme that ran through most of his works, was caused by man. While natural or physical evil clearly existed, moral evil (which is caused by man) was significantly worse. According to Rousseau, most of the suffering in Lisbon on and after November 1 could be shown to be the fault of man rather than Nature. True, the earthquake was an act of Nature, "but it was hardly Nature that had assembled there twenty-thousand houses of six or seven stories. If the residents of this large city had been more evenly dispersed and less densely housed, the losses would have been fewer or perhaps none at all. Everyone would have fled at the first shock, and would have been seen two days later, twenty leagues away and as happy as if nothing had happened."[33]

But people had decided to stay in the city, Rousseau claimed, because they could not part from their personal belongings. "How many unfortunates perished in this disaster for wanting to take—one his clothing, another his papers, a third his money?"[34] In reply to Voltaire's preference that earthquakes should occur only in the middle of deserts instead of under cities, Rousseau refused to relinquish his optimism.

Can we doubt that they also happen in deserts? But no one talks about those, because they have no ill effects for city gentlemen (the only men about whom anyone cares). . . . Will we say [as Voltaire does] that the order of the world must change to suit our whims, that nature must be subject to our laws, that in order to prevent an earthquake in a certain spot, all we have to do is build a city there?[35]

Rousseau even went so far as to reject the notion that the sudden deaths of so many people at Lisbon was somehow regrettable. "A rapid death," he wrote, "is not always a true misfortune and can sometimes be considered a relative blessing. Of the many persons crushed under Lisbon's ruins, some, no doubt, escaped greater misfortunes." What Rousseau could not abide was Voltaire's seeming contempt for life itself. "Who should I imagine you consulted on this question? The rich, perhaps, satiated with imitation pleasures but not knowing the real ones; always bored of life and always afraid of losing it. Maybe you spoke with some men of letters: of all the orders of man, the most sedentary, the most unhealthy, the most thoughtful, and, as a consequence, the most unhappy. . . . If it is not always a misfortune to die, it is only very rarely one to have lived."[36]

To Rousseau, Voltaire's belief in God and his simultaneous contempt for the evils of the world were simply not logically compatible. "If God exists, He is perfect, He is wise, powerful, and just; if He is wise and powerful, all is well; if He is just and powerful, my soul is immortal, thirty years of life are nothing to me and are perhaps necessary to maintain the universe. If you grant me the first, then never can the rest be shaken; if you deny it, what is the good of arguing about the consequences?"[37] Secretly, he distrusted the old gadfly. "Voltaire believes only in the Devil," he later wrote, "for his God is a maleficent being who takes pleasure only in doing harm."[38]

After this relentless barrage, Rousseau thought a bit of a diplomatic retreat would be prudent. "I would prefer a Christian of your sort," he added in intellectual solidarity, "than one of those [pedants] from the Sorbonne." Nevertheless, his class envy could not be entirely suppressed. "I cannot prevent myself, Monsieur, from noting a strange contrast between you and me as regards the subject of this letter. Satiated with glory and disabused of vanity, you live free in the midst of affluence. Certain of your immortality, you peacefully philosophize on the nature of the soul and, if your body or heart suffer, you have Tronchin as doctor and friend. You however find only evil on earth."[39]

It was something of an intellectual tour de force. Unlike his Enlightenment peers, Rousseau separated evil into natural and moral categories, which allowed him to attack society while still maintaining a belief in God and Providence. The letter on Lisbon allowed Rousseau to engage directly and candidly with one of the principal thinkers of the age on a question of central importance to his intellectual project. As such, Rousseau's letter signals his arrival as a major figure in the history of eighteenth-century thought.

What Voltaire thought of Rousseau's letter is not known. He informed Rousseau of its receipt, but because of an illness, he said he would reply later. That letter never came—although Rousseau always believed that Voltaire's masterpiece, *Candide*, had been his rejoinder.[40]

Also electrified by Lisbon was Immanuel Kant, a thirty-one-year-old instructor of philosophy at the University of Königsberg in Prussia and an ardent admirer of Rousseau. (In fact, the only picture in Kant's unadorned home was a portrait of the Swiss writer that hung above his desk.)[41] When the Lisbon Earthquake occurred, Kant was slightly known in scholarly circles and had published only a few works, as he had just recently earned his doctorate. Sparked by the disaster at Lisbon, the young savant, who would become the most important philosopher since Aristotle by some lights, was inspired to publish three essays on the catastrophe.[42] They would mark the beginning of his transformation into a major European thinker.[43]

Like many in Prussia, Kant had closely followed the news of the disaster in the *Gazette de Cologne*. He was particularly interested in the material aspects of the earthquake and tsunami as well as their impact on other parts of the continent. This should not be surprising. To this point in his career, Kant had thought of himself as much a naturalist as a philosopher, seeing in Nature the imprint of Providence. Like many German thinkers influenced by Leibniz, Kant sought to rationalize the catastrophe at Lisbon within the context of a larger universal harmony. In Kant's view, the same subterranean fire that causes deadly tremors also gave us hot springs and baths, helped to create iron ore and encourage the growth of vegetation. If energy was not periodically released through seismic means, there would be even larger and more terrible "Holocausts" in the future.

In a section of his treatise entitled "On the Usefulness of Earth-quake," he wrote: "One will be shocked to see such a terrible punishing rod for humans being praised as having a useful side."[44] Many of the horrors of Lisbon, Kant believed, could have been averted if the Portuguese had properly prepared for such an event. The Peruvians, for example, had suffered less damage in 1746 than the Portuguese in 1755 because they lived in low-storied houses. "Man is not born," he wrote, "to build eternal huts on this stage of vanity."[45]

Over time, the earthquake would force Kant to alter his thinking. Hitherto, his works were filled with speculative reference to the Divine. After Lisbon, he embraced a more empirical approach to knowledge and the universe. Nature, he had come to believe, was enigmatic, and only when one realizes this, only when one truly and honestly confronts the vastness and inscrutability of the world, can one attain true freedom. It would become a central theme of Kant's later paradigm-shifting philosophical writings. In his essay "The Conjectural Beginning of Human History" of 1786, he would write:

> [Man] must not blame providence in any way for the troubles that harm him . . . his own destruction cannot be ascribed to an original sin committed by his primitive parents . . . but that he recognizes every single event as if it in all respects were produced by himself, and that he therefore must accept himself the full responsibility for his own hardships.[46]

Voltaire's concern that his *Poème* might elicit criticism was, apparently, justified. He was forced under pressure from his friends to change the ending several times to allow for the possibility of hope. With few exceptions—like the freethinking Marquis de Ximénès, who mocked Portuguese piety as a reason for the country's not having prevented the disaster—the religious and philosophically minded used the occasion to justify their own providential views.[47]

Some emphasized, as Kant would, the natural benefits of earthquakes. "Let us not doubt," wrote the Swiss pastor and naturalist Elie Bertrand, "that these agitations of the earth have a physical use as well as a moral one. . . . I don't know how they could be imagined not to be useful for the conservation of the Mechanism of the Earth."[48] The only remaining mystery was what physical forces had produced them.

THE BOWELS OF THE EARTH: SCIENCE RESPONDS

Embarrassing for the professors of physics
and humiliating for the theologians.

—EDMOND-JEAN BARBIER, *Chronique de la régence et du règne de Louis XV*

On January 20, 1756, Pombal ordered Portugal's bishops to distribute a questionnaire concerning the recent disaster to every parish priest in the kingdom. He had been encouraged to do this by a circle of government-friendly scientists, scholars, and writers, which included Ribeiro Sanches, Padre Luís Cardoso, Miguel Pedegache, Soares de Barros, and João Jacinto de Magalhães.[49] One assumes he was aware of the similar questionnaire sent to Spanish priests by Fernando VI on November 8. But the Portuguese "inquiry," as it was called, was different in several ways. It contained thirteen questions instead of eight; and it asked about changes "in the sea, the fountains, and the rivers" as well as whether a fire had accompanied the earthquake.[50] It had to be completed and returned within a month.

1. At what time did the earthquake of November 1 begin and how long did it last?
2. Was it possible to perceive the tremor moving from one direction to another? From the north to the south, or to the contrary, for example, did it appear that the ruins fell in one direction more than another?
3. How many houses were destroyed in each parish, were any buildings of note, and what condition were they in?
4. Who died and were some of the dead distinguished?
5. What new things were observed in the sea, in the fountains, and in the rivers?
6. Did the sea first recede or rise, and how many *palmos* did it rise more than usual, how many times was the rise and fall perceived, how much time did it take for the water to recede, and how much time to rise?
7. Did the caverns open up in the earth, and if so did they create new fountains?
8. What measures were immediately taken in each place by the Church, the military, government officials?

9. What earthquakes occurred after that of November 1, when, and what damage was done?

10. Do you remember other earthquakes, and what damage did they cause?

11. How many people live in each parish, how many are confessing Catholics, how many of each sex?

12. Was there a shortage of food?

13. If there was a fire, how long did it last, what damage did it do?[51]

Although distributed by the Church for organizational convenience, the questionnaire was a strictly scientific undertaking, whose sole aim was to collect material facts about the disaster—and as such, represented a repudiation of those who viewed the earthquake primarily as an act of God. By June 26, 1756, the Church had received 566 responses, though it is unclear what was done with the information.[52]

Outside Portugal, there was an avalanche of scholarly speculation on the disaster. Although debates about the causes of earthquakes and tsunamis had begun several years earlier in the wake of the 1746 earthquake and tsunami at Lima, which claimed thirteen thousand lives, and the London Earthquakes of 1750, they increased markedly after the destruction of Lisbon.[53] In Great Britain, the Royal Society's journal, *Philosophical Transactions*, published dozens of articles, papers, and essays on the topic over the course of several years—while in France and Germany the debate raged in the print media.[54] The French became so captivated with the subject that the *Journal des savants* began publishing précis of relevant scientific papers so no one would miss the latest theory. And in 1757, the Académie of Rouen announced an essay contest on the causes of earthquakes. Of the ten submissions that survive, no two proposed the same theory.[55]

The reasons for this are straightforward. Until the widespread acceptance of the theory of plate tectonics in the late 1950s and early 1960s, the causes of most earthquakes and tsunamis remained unknown. Although geology had made significant strides in the late seventeenth and early eighteenth centuries, it was unable to offer a convincing consensus for the origins of earthquakes as well as other related phenomena like volcanos and tsunamis. (It was not until Charles Lyell popularized James Hutton's concept of uniformitarianism in his *Principles of Geology* of 1830–1833 that a better sense of the earth's age and how its features were formed would take hold.)

And so, into this vacuum a crowd of scientists, journalists, writers, theologians, and poets poured their opinions and speculations. In "Ode on the Destruction of Lisbon," the French poet Ponce-Denis Écouchard Le Brun blends together several potential earthquake causes.

> *Sulfur, the nutrient of thunder;*
> *Its black whirlpools swirl [in the innards of the earth].*
> *Salts, niter, tar:*
> *The mixture catches fire, rumbling,*
> *Their struggles heightened by winds;*
> *And their collision, signal of tempests,*
> *Makes the heavens thunder above our heads*
> *And Hell howl beneath our feet.*[56]

Likewise, Baron d'Holbach's entry on "Earthquakes" in the *Encyclopédie* discusses many possible physical causes but provides no definitive answers.[57]

Even faraway Russia contributed to the debate. On September 6, 1757, the renowned Russian polymath Mikhail Lomonosov delivered a lecture to the Russian Academy of Sciences in St. Petersburg entitled "Discourse on the Formation of Metals from the Shaking of the Earth." He theorized, along with many in the West, that earthquakes were caused by exploding deposits of subterranean sulfur. What was potentially groundbreaking was Lomonosov's speculation—several decades before James Hutton—that the earth's surface was in a state of constant transformation and that it "now has an appearance entirely different from how it was in ancient times."[58]

Two thousand miles to the west, Catholic Spain was surprised to discover from an eighty-year-old Benedictine monk living in Oviedo that the earthquake had been caused by electricity. In 1755, Father Benito Jerónimo Feijoo y Montenegro was the most famous scholar in the kingdom. Learned, pious, and politically savvy, he began writing letters on the quake in December 1755 to calm the public's lingering anxieties.

Feijoo pointed out the unlikelihood that fires or exploding chemicals had triggered the terrible event, as tremors were felt at precisely the same time in places many hundreds of miles apart. (Clocks in both Oviedo and Cádiz, he noted, had marked the beginning of the earthquake as 9:45.) To explain this phenomenon, Feijoo latched on to a theory first put forward by two Italian naturalists: Andrea Bina and Father Giambattista Beccaria (not the more famous Beccaria from Milan). They, and now Feijoo, argued that a hitherto unknown substance called "electrical matter" (*materia eléctrica*) resided deep within the earth. Occasionally, when attempting to find its way to the surface, it exploded, causing earthquakes and volcanic eruptions sometimes hundreds of miles apart, as this electrical matter was connected by an underground system of caverns. But Feijoo's letters were not the final word on the subject. Some, like Dr. José Cevallos of Seville, were skeptical of the electrical theory as well as the belief that cities were connected by underground earthquake tracks—but most Spanish scholars were united in their conviction that the popular understanding of earthquakes as signs or punishments from God was foolishness.[59]

But there were other voices. Chief among Feijoo's critics was the bishop of Guadix, Miguel de San José, who felt that the Church had been unfairly labeled as unscientific. It was the Church, San José pointed out, that had taken the lead in teaching science in its schools and universities. In the case of the earthquake, however, San José was certain he knew its real cause: evil spirits that God had given temporary control over the earth's physical realm. In the years that followed, scores of essays, books, and treatises speculating on the causes of the earthquake were published in Spain. To assuage the censors and avoid undue criticism, most conceded at the outset that God had been the ultimate cause, before launching into their naturalistic theory.

In the first published comment on the disaster by a Spanish scientist, Juan Luis Roche of Puerto de Santa María combined a careful physical description and analysis of the event with a perfect willingness to accept many of the miraculous claims made by the people—for example, that the Virgin Mary herself had driven back the tsunami waves at Puerto de Santa María.[60] One scientist from Madrid, Antonio Nifo, felt that while most earthquakes had natural causes, the quake on All Saints' Day was caused by grave sins and atrocious behavior in church.[61]

In Portugal, Pombal backed the search for natural causes—both to calm the fears of the people and to silence what he believed to be the pernicious and destabilizing impact of the "earthquake preachers" like Malagrida who, in his opinion, had taken advantage of catastrophe to spread lies and expand their following. In the appendix to his treatise on public health, Ribeiro Sanches discusses the origins of earthquakes and underscores their physical origins. While it is possible that a few earthquakes have been sent by God to chastise mankind, he argues, the vast majority are no more mysterious than thunder and lightning.

Torre do Tombo archivist, Moreira de Mendonça concurred. In his *Universal History of Earthquakes* (1758), he describes earthquakes as physical events and nothing more. Unlike his brother, Veríssimo António, he had no patience for those who believed in fires that burned continually beneath the earth. Temblors, in his opinion, were triggered by the sudden explosion of gas and water trapped underground. His proof? Before sunrise, on the day before the earthquake, he recalled seeing in the city "a dark yellow smoke or vapor so dense" that he "could not make out any buildings in the distance."[62]

In his *New and Faithful Account of What Happened to Lisbon and All of Portugal on November 1, 1755*, Miguel Pedegache combines a detailed description of the events of All Saints' Day with a discussion of how subterranean fires, the moon, and even the heat of the sun may have caused the earthquake. He also recognized the connection between the three tsunami waves and the three tremors of the earthquake. "The bottom of the sea is a continuation of the earth," he wrote. "If the earth is agitated, it transfers this agitation to the waters."[63] Dissenting from Aristotle, Pedegache argued that tsunamis were different from wind waves, for wind only affects the water "on the surface" of the ocean. During an earthquake at sea, however, "the agitation is interior; the entire mass of the fluid is agitated."[64]

Coming tantalizingly close to an accurate description of tsunamis, Father António Pereira de Figueiredo hypothesized in his *Latin and Portuguese Commentary on the Earthquake and the Fire of Lisbon* (1756) that the "extraordinary alteration and growth of the waters might have been caused by subterranean material bursting out into the water, or because hidden underwater fires raised the waters, or because the earth communicated to the sea the same impulse that had shaken it."[65] In Spain, Father Antonio Jacobo del Barco y Gasca correctly argued that tsunamis were the result of undersea earthquakes.[66]

Immanuel Kant also displayed ingenuity in hypothesizing the true cause of both earthquakes and tsunamis. Like many at the time, Kant believed that earthquakes were the result of exploding gases ignited by underground fires. In a more original postulation, however, he proposed that tsunamis *(Wasserbewegungen)* were the result of pressure transmitted through the water by the shaking of the earth. Influenced by a French experiment, where a bullet fired into a wooden box filled with water shatters the box through water pressure, Kant theorized that the shaking earth was able to push sea water onto the shore hundreds of miles away "with the same speed" that existed at the point of origin.[67] Although fundamentally flawed (the modern theory of wave propagation had not been fully formulated), it was a perceptive application of the latest scientific theories to the observed phenomena.

More remarkable was Kant's assertion, subsequently proven correct, that seiches—standing waves in lakes, ponds, and canals—were caused by a tilt in the earth's surface produced by the largest temblors.[68] Though he remained a Christian his whole life, Kant believed that physical phenomena like tsunamis and earthquakes were not instigated by the Almighty. "We have," he wrote, "the causes under our feet." (*"Wir haben die Ursachen unter unseren Füßen."*)[69]

In 1759–1760, John Michell of Queens' College, Cambridge, correctly theorized that tsunami waves move faster in deeper water than in shallow water after he studied the arrival times of the Lisbon tsunami across the Atlantic. It was an extraordinary feat. He was mistaken, however, in believing, with many others, that earthquakes were caused by underground fires that shook the earth by igniting and expanding the gases and water in underground caverns. His explanation for the drawback phase of a tsunami, while ingenious, was also incorrect. He proposed that when the ocean floor, which had been expanded by the exploding water and gas, collapsed, water near the coast was pulled toward this sinkhole. When the vapors heated up once again, the cavity on the ocean floor expanded outward and the seawater was pushed back in the direction of the shore in the form of a tsunami wave.[70]

Many who maintained that God had been the original or first cause of both earthquakes and tsunamis conceded that the immediate or secondary cause of those events was attributable to natural phenomena. In two sermons on the earthquake that shook New England on November 18, 1755, and the Lisbon disaster, the American Congregationalist minister Charles Chauncy declared that while it is "God who maketh the earth to shake, and the pillars thereof to tremble," it is "those [subterranean gaseous] materials" that fill "the bowels of the earth . . . that are the secondary causes of that terrible phaenomenon [that] we mean by an earthquake."[71] According to the Harvard-educated minister, the origin of "Water-quakes" and "all those quick and unusual Fluxes and Refluxes of Tides; [and] those terrible Inundations from the Sea" are to be found in the "Treasury of the Winds" that emanated from the "Great Deep," a clear reference to Aristotle.[72]

Over the following years, scientific explanations abounded—in Iberia as elsewhere. In many cases, they existed side by side or intermingled with religious ones. Sometimes they were in opposition; at other times correlated. But because scientists could not agree on a definitive causality, the religious sphere could still stake a legitimate, if somewhat tenuous, claim to the truth. Scientists, for their part, were well aware of this. "Today an eclipse of the moon or the sun does not frighten us because we know its cause," wrote Ribeiro Sanches.

> [But] two centuries ago, all comets were considered omens of the death of princes, wars, and the destruction of nations. Acquainted with its true cause because of that eminent philosopher and astronomer, Isaac Newton, we view these celestial bodies today with the same serenity that we contemplate Jupiter or Saturn. If we knew the causes of earthquakes, as we know the causes of wind, thunder, and lightning, we would not see these impressive movements of Nature as punishments from Heaven, nor would we tolerate these predictions of total destruction.[73]

For more than half a century, clerics and theologians from across Europe had felt themselves besieged by Deists, natural philosophers, and scientists. They now seized on the Lisbon disaster as evidence that God was not, as the Deists said, a mere Watchmaker who had created the universe and then left it to run by its own devices, but a Deity fully engaged in the world, communicating with humanity through terrible and awesome events. If the Age of Reason had not yet superseded the Age of Faith, Lisbon did much (at least temporarily) to bolster the latter.

In Peru, Archbishop Don Antonio de Barroeta of Lima composed a pastoral letter on September 20, 1756, in which he blamed the Lisbon Earthquake on "Divine Justice." "Our crimes," he wrote, "are the true causes of earthquakes and the destruction of churches."[74] To be sure, earthquakes are more prevalent in Peru than Portugal, he added, but that was because the sins of the New World were greater than those of Iberia. The archbishop's true ire, however, was reserved for those "who, esteemed by philosophers, attribute earthquakes to subterranean volcanic eruptions and fires." For Barroeta, "the true subterranean force is the lascivious burning in men's hearts; the true volcano is concupiscence."[75] The only solution was to reconstruct the edifice of Catholic values and virtue. "If we build this structure, no earthquake, however powerful, will be able to bring it down."[76]

In the fall of 1756, John Wesley, the great Methodist leader, published his *Serious Thoughts Occasioned by the Earthquake at Lisbon*. Like the archbishop, he decried those who assigned materialist causes to earthquakes. "What then could be the Cause?" he asked. "What, indeed, but God, who arose to shake terribly the Earth." He assailed those who refused or were unable to see the Will of God in these great events. "Why should we not be convinced sooner, while that Conviction may avail, that it is not Chance that governs the World? Why should we not now, before *London* is as *Lisbon*, *Lima*, or *Catania*, acknowledge the Hand of the Almighty, arising to maintain his own Cause?"[77] Men like Wesley, Barroeta, and Malagrida used the disaster as a weapon to attack what they believed to be the disagreeable forces and sentiments of modernity. Theirs was essentially a medieval vision of the world, and it is significant that so many people at the time agreed with them.

Indeed, if there are two things that the Great Earthquake Debate reveals about the middle of the eighteenth century, it is, firstly, that the Enlightenment and its commonly shared culture was more widely distributed than many may have imagined. From the New World to the salons and academies of Russia (and most regions in between, including Iberia), scientists, philosophers, poets, and men of the cloth appeared fully conversant with the latest, wholly incorrect theories on the origins of earthquakes. The second revelation brought about by the great temblor is that religious belief was decidedly more robust among the populace and the educated classes than has generally been acknowledged. Moreover, the conflict between the religious and the scientific was, with some exceptions like the feud involving Pombal and Malagrida, not so starkly drawn. Most scientists had no trouble conceding that God was the first cause of earthquakes and other natural phenomenon, while many preachers and priests, a few of whom were scientists themselves, acknowledged that earthquakes were at least partly the result of physical forces.

In enlightened England, on Friday, February 6, 1756, the fast day was celebrated with great enthusiasm (as it was in Scotland, Wales, and Ireland) for earthquakes and the coming conflict with France. Churches were so packed that many had difficulty getting in; and although it had been organized by the Church of England, Catholics, Methodists, dissenters, and Jews eagerly joined in. In Dublin, the lord lieutenant himself along with the House of Lords were seen worshipping at Christ Church Cathedral, while in Cork, "the churches, meeting houses, and the Roman Catholic chapels were crowded from morning until night." John Wesley thought it "a glorious day, such as London has scarce seen since the Restoration." One group, the Quakers, refused to participate, opening their stores in defiance. Widely criticized for disobeying a royal proclamation, they were, in at least one instance, set upon by an angry mob. For those, like many in the press, who wished the spirit of the fast to continue into the future, there appears to have been success. In 1762, seven years after the disaster, Horace Walpole bemoaned that "We have never recovered masquerades since the earthquake at Lisbon," laying the blame on a widespread "fashion" for "enthusiasm." In addition to the British Isles, fast days were held in Massachusetts on January 8 and in Pennsylvania and New York on May 21, 1756.[78]

REIGN OF TERROR

In this prison there are nineteen cells: two are almost totally dark, and among the others there are two that have the reputation of being the worst, by their small size, and because they are close to a pipe where filth pours out.

—MARQUÊS DE ALORNA, *As Prisões da Junqueira*

It is a widely held belief that within weeks of the earthquake life in Lisbon normalized to a reasonable degree; order was restored; thieves and other criminals were apprehended; and food was liberally distributed to the survivors. Certainly, many survivors praised the vigor of the government's relief efforts. Yet, a letter from Lisbon dated July 9, 1756, and published in the *Moskovskiye Vedomosti* (*Moscow News*), provides a more sobering portrait of conditions in the capital. The anonymous author writes:

It seems to us that we have been chosen to be an example and a spectacle for other peoples at least when it comes to misfortune, for our troubles are not limited to earth tremors; riots, robberies, and murders continue to occur in our unfortunate city despite the best efforts of the First Minister [Pombal] to preserve the calm. Last week five more people were murdered and when it comes to robberies those occur daily. The robbers here are so bold that they send special tickets to rich people in which they tell them to pay up and threaten to burn down their houses if they refuse to satisfy their demands. Two such ignoble people who had crossed the river to set fire to the lower side of the city where the tents are fortunately were apprehended before they were able to realize their evil intent. Under interrogation, they confessed that there were twenty of them who agreed to start fires in different locations of the city so that they could more easily rob the tents left by the fleeing residents.[79]

Perhaps conditions deteriorated in the late spring after Pombal fell ill or perhaps they had never been tolerable for the majority of survivors.

Even the king and queen experienced hardship. When the summer of 1756 began, they were still living in tents. And on June 24, 25, and 26, they suffered through a storm so powerful, according to the *Gazette de Cologne*, that "it was only through brute force" that the king's attendants "ensured that [the wind] did not carry away the tents during the night."[80] On July 22, 1756, they finally moved into the Real Barraca (Royal Hut or Wood Palace) on the summit of Ajuda Hill. Designed by Giovanni Carlo Galli-Bibiena, who had also conceived the ill-fated Casa da Ópera, the large one-story structure was immediately filled with tapestries to add a measure of luxuriousness and keep out the cold. "Although some have advised the King to go to [the palace at] Mafra," wrote Mariana Vitória, "he is afraid to enter a building so large and so tall."[81]

As the year wore on, Pombal's powers increased—along with the list of his enemies. "He is thought to possess a greater Share than ever in his Royal Master's Esteem and Confidence," Castres wrote of Pombal in May 1756. "People begin to look upon him as Prime Minister in effect, tho' he may probably decline to be addressed under that name."[82] His main rival now after his appointment as first minister on May 4, 1756, in the wake of the death of Pedro da Mota about two weeks after the earthquake, was Diogo de Mendonça, the secretary of the navy.[83] Mendonça was gregarious and charming; the Count de Baschi considered him the pleasantest man in the kingdom, and, unfortunately, Mendonça was also headstrong and independent-minded. Once, he let it be known that he supported a Spanish husband for Dom José's eldest daughter, Maria, without consulting Pombal. Another time, during one of the lavish parties that he regularly threw on Sunday evenings at his home, which were very popular with the nobility and the diplomatic corps, he dared to criticize government policy, a breach of etiquette that Pombal soon learned about from one of his growing number of spies and informants.[84]

At some point during 1756, Mendonça decided that Pombal's tyrannical ways had become too much to bear. He joined a conspiracy to oust and replace him with a shadow cabinet directed by himself. In league with him were two Italian monks, several diplomats abroad, and a lawyer who composed the charge of speculation against the first minister. When Pombal spoke with the king about his suspicions, he learned that the conspirators had already raised their complaints with Dom José, who decided to take Pombal's side. Mendonça had permanently damaged his reputation in the eyes of the king when he had fled the capital and his duties on the day of the earthquake.

With royal support, Pombal moved swiftly against the conspirators. The traitorous lawyer was exiled to a short life in Angola. The Portuguese minister to France was immediately recalled, and the two priests were thrown in Junqueira prison, which would become a dumping ground for Pombal's enemies. At one in the morning on August 30, 1756, a company of soldiers surrounded Mendonça's house. A justice of the peace entered, handed the secretary the royal decree announcing his banishment from the capital, and informed him that he had three hours to pack his belongings and depart for a location at least forty miles from the court. Mendonça took the decree and kissed it—"and with great composure," according to Edward Hay, "gave orders to his servants to prepare for his departure." At 4 a.m., he left his keys in his office and he started off for a friend's home near Porto in the company of four dragoons, eight servants, and his confessor.[85]

To replace him, Pombal recalled his brother from Brazil. Soon afterward, Count de Baschi was recalled to Paris. Although he had been planning his departure for some time, this raised suspicions that he, too, had been involved in the plot. Incensed at the exile of his close friend, the count collected his family along with the customary parting gift of £1,100 in gold bars and left the city in a huff on September 11, 1756.[86] Not everyone was sorry to see him leave. "Pombal seems to be well pleased," wrote Abraham Castres, "with their having got rid of a Minister of his turbulent Temper, who had long ago rendered Himself disagreeable by his perpetual Disputes about Trifles, and particularly, his free and unguarded Reflexions upon the Customs and Manners of the Country, not sparing at Times the Royal Family itself."[87]

A month before, Antoinette de la Calmette, the wife of the Dutch ambassador, and her family returned to the Netherlands—presumably with their savior monkey in tow.[88] Also at some point in 1756, the Reverend Richard Goddard returned to his vicarage at Lacock with many harrowing stories, but alas, no effective cure for his deteriorating health. He died on May 2, 1758, at the age of thirty.[89]

As the year wore on, Pombal's opposition to the Jesuit order grew into a blinding hatred. Their predilection for delivering incendiary speeches blaming the earthquake on the sins of Lisbon's inhabitants reached an apogee with the publication in October of Malagrida's sermon on the subject. Immediately afterward, an edict emerged from the Inquisition, now controlled by Pombal, prohibiting people from reading impious books about the earthquake.[90] Also worrisome to the government were rumors believed to be started by the Jesuits that a second, equally destructive earthquake would strike on All Saints' Day 1756. To thwart a mass exodus, a decree was published outlawing, under penalty of prison, anyone who left the city and its environs on October 31 or November 1.[91]

For his part, Malagrida became enraged when Pombal sent him and every other religious leader in the city a copy of Ribeiro Sanches's book, which emphasized the physical causes of earthquakes. In November 1756, the controversial Jesuit was officially banished from the Portuguese capital. "What more do they want?" Malagrida raged to a Jesuit friend in a letter. "I was expelled from the royal palace. And if you knew the cause of this unpleasant situation you would be even more surprised."[92] According to Malagrida:

> Various pamphlets were distributed throughout the city of Lisbon, which attributed the earthquake to natural causes and not to providence. Because there was no one to contradict such reckless and impious assertions, I, the least of everyone, descended into the arena, buoyed by the testimony of the

Sainted Fathers, I demonstrated that the terrible earthquake tremor was a clear indication of God's anger. . . . This so upset the Prime Minster . . . that he expelled me from the city to the *colégio* of Setúbal.[93]

Before long, an opposition court began to develop around Malagrida in his house of retreat in Setúbal, thirty miles south of the capital. Ladies of the court, who idolized the saintly padre, traveled there from Belém to spend several days engaged in meditation and spiritual exercises. In Pombal's view, it was an act of defiance, and it seemed to be growing.[94]

The first minister's hostility toward the Jesuits did not begin with the earthquake. It can be traced to the New World, to a dispute in South America involving the society's rights in the region of Paraguay, where it had built an impressive power base over the course of a century and a half. Sent into the jungles to convert the indigenous peoples, these intrepid men of God had succeeded beyond their wildest dreams. Learning the Indian languages and cultures, they won their trust and, over time, coaxed the Indians to live in large settlements, where they received protection behind palisade walls. For generations, they had labored for their Jesuit masters in the fields or tended the giant herds of cattle that now numbered in the hundreds of thousands. Within the confines of their missions, which encompassed fully one quarter of the continent of South America, the Jesuits exercised enormous economic clout, selling and profiting from the fruits of their labors in the coastal ports.

In the opinion of some, the Jesuit settlements were primitive Christian Utopias, a kind of Paradise for savages, where the natives lived structured, productive lives under the vigilant but caring eyes of their Jesuit fathers. The Indians, it appeared, preferred this existence to their previous life in the jungle and so cheerfully participated in the religious processions dedicated to St. Francis de Borgia and St. Ignatius. Though these settlements (or "reductions") were actually on lands claimed by the Spanish Crown, it was the Jesuits who were in command. On the entire continent, two hundred Jesuits controlled the lives of 140,000 Indians.

Both Spanish and Portuguese colonists complained that the Jesuits controlled too much of the continent's labor force. Because independent tribes periodically attacked the reductions, and the Spanish and Portuguese regularly sent out raiding parties in search of labor, the

Jesuits felt they had little choice but to arm their Indian charges. Soon, the Jesuits were in charge of vast armies, well equipped and, in several notable engagements, devastatingly effective. Although the enslavement of Indians was forbidden, the charge was made that the Jesuit reductions were no better than slave camps.

Through his stepbrother, the governor of Grão-Pará and Maranhão, Pombal heard the cries of the large farmers and businessmen in Brazil and thereafter sought to break the power of the Jesuits.[95] A large army consisting of Portuguese and Spanish soldiers was sent to crush the Jesuit reduction in Paraguay. But Pombal's overarching strategy, which he would also employ in Portugal, was to create large government-enforced monopolies that would increase the power of certain wealthy individuals at the expense of smaller merchants and foreign businessmen—and the Jesuits. It would also substantially magnify the power of the state in economic affairs.

In 1755, the Company of Grão-Pará and Maranhão was set up to control trade in the north of Brazil. That same year, Pombal founded the General Company for the Agriculture of the Vineyards of the Upper Douro, which mandated—one hundred years before the French thought of the *appellation d'origine contrôlée*—that only certain areas along the Douro River in northern Portugal were authorized to sell their port wines to the British. One conspicuous exception was Pombal's own estate at Oeiras, which greatly added to the family's wealth.[96] "I find it absolutely necessary," Pombal wrote in 1756, "to bring all the commerce of this kingdom and its colonies into companies and then all the merchants will be obliged to enter into them, or else desist from trading, for they certainly may be assured that I know their interests better than they do themselves, and the interests of the whole kingdom."[97]

In the Douro, many large vineyard owners were overjoyed, while many smaller ones as well as the British (now buying port at higher prices because of the decreased competition) were enraged. On February 23, 1757, a crowd of five thousand laid siege to the home of the judge conservator of the Douro Company and forced him to rescind all the new restrictions on the selling of wine. It also destroyed the company's records. Although the rioters quickly dispersed, Pombal's retribution was savage.

The trial lasted seven months. Of the 478 accused, 442 were convicted, including 50 women and boys. Fourteen were hanged: 13 men and one woman. Afterward, their limbs were stuck on pikes and displayed to the public for fifteen days. Fifty-nine men and women were exiled to India and Africa. Some were whipped; others were imprisoned or delivered to the galleys. Most had their property seized by the state. To quell any future affronts to his rule, Pombal placed Porto under de facto martial law. Wearing capes, carrying weapons, holding meetings after dark, and even loitering were outlawed. Two thousand four hundred troops, led by Pombal's cousin João de Almada e Melo, descended upon the city. He would remain military governor of northern Portugal—Pombal's enforcer—for more than twenty years.[98]

Earlier that year, on May 3, 1757, Abraham Castres died suddenly in Lisbon after a protracted illness. As with all British dead, his funeral procession to the British cemetery had to take place at night for fear of inflaming the still-fierce anti-Protestant prejudices of *lisboetas*.[99] Edward Hay replaced him as envoy, and Hay was replaced as consul by Sir Harry Frankland, who, along with his wife, Agnes, returned to the city where he had once been buried alive.

Restiveness was growing in the Pombaline state, but Pombal could always turn it to his advantage. In 1758, he once again had an opportunity to exploit. On the night of September 3, at 11 p.m., the Duke of Aveiro and several accomplices fired several shots into a carriage carrying Dom José and his retainer, Pedro Teixeira. Although the coach escaped from the ambush, the coachman and the king were wounded. The details of the attack were not immediately made public, but four days later the queen was made regent while the king recovered.

The circumstances remain murky to this day, but it is likely that the assassins' target was not Dom José (it was not the royal carriage) but Teixeira, who had insulted the hotheaded duke on more than one occasion.[100] This was certainly Edward Hay's understanding.[101] But Pombal craftily decided to recast the incident as an attempted regicide and, by doing so, deal a devastating blow to his enemies in the aristocracy. To achieve his goal, he waited several months, collecting evidence and securing testimony, before officially announcing in December 1758 that there had been an assassination attempt on the king. On December 14, large-scale arrests were made. Included in the dragnet were several of the most powerful and prominent nobles in Portugal. All were interrogated and many were tortured.

After a short trial in which the defendants were denied their legal rights under the Crown's law—defense attorneys were given a mere twenty-four hours to prepare their case—the prisoners were sentenced on January 12, 1759. Some, like the Duke of Aveiro, the Marquês de Távora Velho, the Marquesa de Távora, and several other members of their family (that had once rejected Pombal many years before when he had asked for the hand of one of their daughters), were convicted of treason and rebellion against the Crown. They were executed the next day in a cruel and sadistic display on a raised platform in Belém before a crowd of more than ten thousand, over half of which, it was believed, were women.[102] While regicides were normally handled with great brutality in eighteenth-century Europe, rarely was such violence directed toward members of the aristocracy. "About half an hour after eight o'clock in the morning," recalled Edward Hay,

> The criminals were brought out one by one, each under a strong guard. The Marchioness of Tavora was the first that was brought upon the scaffold, where she was beheaded at one

The torture and execution of the Duke of Aveiro

stroke. Her body was afterwards placed upon the floor of the scaffolding, and covered with a linen cloth. Young José Maria de Tavora, the young Marquis of Tavora, the Count d'Atouguia, and three servants of the Duke of Aveiro, were strangled at a stake, and afterwards their limbs broken with an iron instrument. The Marquis of Tavora and the Duke of Aveiro had their limbs broken alive. The duke, for greater ignominy, was brought bareheaded to the place of execution. The body and limbs of each of the criminals, after they were executed, were thrown upon a wheel, and covered with a linen cloth. But when Antonio Alvares Ferreira was brought to the stake, whose sentence was to be burnt alive, the other bodies were exposed to his view. The combustible matter which had been laid under the scaffolding was set fire to; [and] the whole machine with the bodies was consumed to ashes, and then thrown into the sea.

And to further drive home the point that opposition to the regime would not be tolerated, the surname Távora was officially abolished in Portugal, and a river called Távora was renamed the "River of Death."[103]

It was the beginning of what historian Charles Boxer has called a "reign of terror." But unlike the one during the French Revolution, which lasted eleven months, this continued for eighteen years (1759–1777). The prisons and fortresses of the kingdom became filled with enemies of the regime, most of whom had never been formally charged. Some remained in their cells for years. Ordinary people feared making even private comments that might be construed as critical of Pombal. The despotism of the enlightened first minister had started to take on features of a police state.

Pombal's war with the Jesuits heated up, too. Accusing them of participating in the same conspiracy against the king as well as other crimes, he stripped them of their various positions in schools and universities and summarily rounded them up across the empire. Some were sent back to their home countries in horrendous conditions on ships; others, like Malagrida, were thrown into the Junqueira. In 1759, the Jesuit order was civilly suppressed in Portugal. But Pombal refused to relent. He directed a massive propaganda campaign against the society across Europe. Pamphlets and books listing and dissecting their crimes—which included "Machiavelianism"—were distributed throughout the continent.[104] These became required reading for government officials throughout the Portuguese empire. From Pombal's perspective, these exertions bore rich fruit. In 1764, the Jesuits were expelled from France and Spain, and in 1773—the coup de grâce—they were suppressed as an order by Pope Clement XIV.

Although a practicing Catholic, Pombal never deferred to the authority of Rome. He believed it was the state's right to remove any bishop or cleric from any office that it wished. In 1760, he even expelled the papal nuncio, Filippo Acciaiuoli, over a trivial breach of etiquette, and that same year he orchestrated a formal break between Portugal and Rome that lasted until Clement XIV gave in to all of his considerable demands ten years later.

Pombal also sought real reform across a number of fronts. In 1772, he ended the official persecution of converted Jews (New Christians) in Portugal—abolishing the legal designation forever, though he did co-opt the Inquisition into a state-run apparatus of suppression and terror against his enemies. He likewise abolished slavery in Portugal, though not for humanitarian reasons: he wanted slaves working in domestic service in Portugal to be sent to the fields and mines of Brazil, where slavery was not abolished until 1888. Yet he also got rid of the bar to miscegenation in Brazil, actively encouraging whites to marry indigenous people. "His Majesty," he wrote, "does not distinguish between his vassals by their color but by their merits."[105]

The modernization of education in Portuguese universities, particularly after the expulsion of the Jesuits, is likewise owing to Pombal, as is the founding of state schools throughout the empire. But the final judgment on Pombal's tyranny must look to the overall fortunes of the nation. Economically, Portugal suffered a notable decline in the years after the earthquake. To be sure, a steady decrease in Brazilian gold production that began at midcentury weighed heavily on the future. Nevertheless, Pombal's signature economic initiative, the creation of large national trading monopolies, which discouraged competition and foreign trade, took their toll. Add to this a marked increase in regulations, taxes, and tariffs—ostensibly to pay for the rebuilding of Lisbon—which, far from being stimulative, actually hindered growth overall. In 1750, Portugal's per capita GDP was 60 percent higher than Spain's, 28 percent higher than Sweden's, and 19 percent higher than that of German-speaking central Europe. A half century later, in 1800, Portuguese per capita GDP had declined comparatively to an astounding degree and was only 12 percent higher than Spain's, 23 percent

higher than Sweden's, and 4 percent higher than that of Germany.[106]
In the nineteenth century, Portugal's comparative economic decline
would only continue.

In short, Portugal was never the same after the earthquake. The
devastating loss of the capital it suffered would have been difficult for
any country to recover from. But coupled with Pombal's statist economic policies, conceived before Adam Smith revealed the imprudence
of such interventions, the overall effect proved stultifying.

Despite all his powers, Pombal still served at the pleasure of the
king. And so, when Dom José died on February 24, 1777, the first minister's authority evaporated.[107] Upon learning the news, jubilant priests
ran door to door announcing the end to the tyranny, and ballads deprecating Pombal filled the air. On the day after the royal funeral, the
new queen, Dom José's daughter, Maria I, commanded the prisons be
opened. At their entrances, large, emotional crowds gathered. Over
eight hundred individuals of both sexes—including priests, nobles, and
commoners—most in rags, reentered a world that some had not seen
for twenty years. They included the son of the Duke of Aveiro, who had
entered prison twenty years earlier as a seventeen-year-old. Forty-five
Jesuits of the original 124 who had been incarcerated emerged from the
Fortress of São Julião at Carcavelos. Perhaps two thousand prisoners of
the regime had died in their cells.

With public opinion turning violently against him—and the nobility and the clergy calling for his head—Pombal tendered his resigna-
tion and fled with his family into exile. On the day he left, irate mobs
surrounded his house on the Rua Formosa. However politically expedi-
ent it might have been in the short term for the queen to put the former
minister on trial, she understood that to condemn Pombal would be to
condemn her father and his reign. She also knew that every major edict
enacted had been signed by the king.

Although old and infirm, Pombal did not, as so many had hoped and
expected, die quickly. He lived six more years with his family in a one-
story house abutting the market square of the city of Pombal. When,
on May 8, 1782, at the age of eighty-two, Pombal finally breathed his
last breath after a long and excruciatingly painful illness during which
his body was covered with oozing pustules, he had become in many
ways the embodiment of the modern impulse, in both its positive and
negative aspects. In the words of the distinguished Portuguese humanist and canon lawyer António Ribeiro dos Santos:

The minister tried to follow an impossible policy; he wanted to civilize the nation and at the same time to enslave it; he wanted to spread the light of the philosophical sciences and at the same time to elevate the royal power to despotism; he greatly favored the study of the Law of Nature and of the Law of Nations, and of Universal International Law, founding chairs for these subjects in the University. But he did not realize that he was in this way enlightening the people to understand thereby that the sovereign power was solely established for the common weal of the nation and not for the benefit of the ruler, and that it had limits and boundaries in which it ought to be contained.[108]

One of the most damning indictments of Pombalism is that his signature project—the redesign and rebuilding of Lisbon—proved, ultimately, a disappointment. Despite all its innovations and its stylistic audacity, it had remarkably little influence on the history of European architecture. And many of the architects who conceived it were laid in their graves long before a substantial portion of the Baixa had been reconstituted. In the early decades of the nineteenth century, travelers to Lisbon continuously expressed their surprise and sadness at finding Lisbon in such a ruinous state. Once noteworthy structures like the Carmo monastery and church were, by design, never rebuilt and left to disintegrate. When the famous equestrian statue of Dom José was finally erected in 1775 in the Praça do Commércio—formerly the Terreiro do Paço—large sheets of cloth had to be placed over the surrounding ruins to relieve the public shame during the ceremony.

Even today, *lisboetas* regularly question the functionality and beauty of the Praça do Commércio and the Pombaline Baixa, aware that both tourists and locals prefer the older pre-earthquake architecture and layout of the Baixo Alto, the Alfama, and São Jorge's Hill. While Pombal is viewed by many in Portugal as a heroic figure who restored order and rebuilt Lisbon after the disaster, some members of the Portuguese nobility have never forgotten his crimes against their ancestors and to this day refer to him derogatorily as "Sebastião José."

For his part, Voltaire grew only more pessimistic as the epoch inaugurated by Lisbon wore on. The violence of the Seven Years War (1756–1763) had weighed heavily on him, especially the controversial trial and execution in 1757 of John Byng, the British admiral unjustly accused of neglect of duty.[109] The universe is "completely mad," Voltaire wrote. "Nothing [is] madder or more atrocious"; "happy [is] the man who can look with a tranquil eye on all the great events in this best of all possible worlds."[110] Gone was the Puckish swagger of his youth. Not even the diversions of Les Délices could rouse him from his gloom.

Yet the old sorcerer still had a few tricks up his sleeve. In the fall of 1758, he decided to purchase two adjoining estates just across the French border from his Swiss home. Nestled in the Pays de Gex and bordered by the Jura Mountains, Ferney and Tournay would allow for an easy escape if the authorities ever chose to move against him. And unlike Les Délices, the châteaus came with a village and a hundred poverty-stricken peasants, over whom Voltaire enjoyed full manorial privileges, including the right to collect dues and administer justice. The ownership of Tournay granted him the title of count. "My land is excellent," wrote Europe's newest aristocrat:

> And yet I found a hundred acres, belonging to my tenants, which remain uncultivated. The farmer has not sown half of his land. The minister has performed no marriage for seven years, and during this time no children have been produced. . . . But a far more baleful calamity is the rapacity of the [tax collectors], and the fury of their employees. Wretches who can hardly find a little black bread to eat are arrested every day, stripped of what they have. . . . One's heart is torn when one witnesses so much misery. I am buying the estate of Ferney only to do a little good.[111]

Soon, the reforming count was doing a great deal of good: draining the marshes, improving the roads, paying off the peasants' unpaid taxes, and even rebuilding the little parish church that stood near the main house at Ferney. When a young villager was nearly beaten to death by the local *curé*, Voltaire nursed the man back to health and provided him with legal assistance. In the mornings, Voltaire roamed his fields in his new farmer's clogs, personally attending to even the most minor affairs of the estate. Despite the harpings of Madame Denis that her uncle was spending 250,000 francs a year on needless improvements, Voltaire soldiered on. "Never," he wrote a friend, "has there been a more opportune moment to toil in the vineyard of the Lord."[112]

Voltaire's ambition extended far beyond the borders of his personal kingdom. In the winter of 1758, he could be found hard at work on a slender little volume that he hoped would drive the final nail in the coffin of "that cruel philosophy with a consoling name."[113] Subtitled "On Optimism," it would feature a youthful, good-natured protagonist who suffers a series of horrifying experiences—all of which, including the Lisbon Earthquake (appearing in chapter 5), are continually and systematically explained away by his tutor and Leibnizian alter ego, Dr. Pangloss. In the novella's last line, the now weary young man, having suffered a thousand indignities, finally rejects the fatalistic sunniness of his mentor and, in a remark freighted with revolutionary implications, exhorts us all to "cultivate our garden." For Candide, as for Voltaire, that garden had become the whole world.

Like Immanuel Kant, Voltaire had found freedom in the act of overcoming, or attempting to overcome, the travails of human existence. But what of optimism or providentialism? Did they both die out as a result of the publication of Voltaire's masterpiece? In Germany, support for Leibniz and optimism ran strong; and Voltaire was widely attacked. One author called *Candide* a "Mißgeburt" (or deformed child).[114] The historical record is, in fact, clear that both flourished in the second half of the eighteenth century.[115] At the time of the French Revolution, it was commonly (and perhaps unsurprisingly) accepted that even the most destructive natural phenomena were ultimately regenerative. In his *Étude de la Nature* (1793), the naturalist B. E. Manuel proposed teaching natural history to impart republican political values. "The time has come," wrote Manuel in response to the question: Will liberty triumph?, "when, in the political order of nations as in the physical order of worlds, the small masses should obey the great ones, and that these great masses, after more or less violent crises, more or less tumultuous eruptions, and more or less salutary purifications, should finally find in themselves the eternal relationships that constitute the organization of Nature. The Book of destiny is open. The march of events is outlined, and no human force can stop its course."[116]

What did slowly pass away in the wake of the Lisbon disaster was the belief, still so common in 1755, that earthquakes were acts of God sent to punish mankind. While their true physical origins would not be discovered for more than two hundred years, earthquakes would eventually be drained of their supernatural significance for the majority of people in the West. Laying the groundwork, no doubt, was the outpouring of scientific interest in the aftermath of the Lisbon disaster, though the shift may not have definitively occurred until sometime late in the nineteenth century, with the rise of positivism.

And yet, by the summer of 1756, the great earthquake had already begun to fade from memory. Though the psychic traumas of the disaster had been real, many had found a way to forget, repress, or somehow come to grips with an event that, only a few months before, appeared to threaten the survival of civilization itself. Perhaps it is not surprising then that the two great modern theorists of the idea of the sublime, Immanuel Kant and Edmund Burke, were both profoundly influenced by the catastrophe at Lisbon. The great three-pronged disaster seemed to embody perfectly their conception of the sublime as an event or object of overwhelming power and greatness that caused pleasure and awe in its beholders. Central to the idea was the ability of observers to surmount or overcome the object psychologically, and as a result gain a level of superiority over it.[117]

Perhaps, on some level, the Western world found a way to overcome the disaster in the months after November 1, 1755, or perhaps its attention simply shifted to another event of worldwide importance: the Seven Years War. This might help to explain why the Lisbon Earthquake has been mentioned so infrequently over the past two and a half centuries; and why it has never inspired a landmark work of imaginative fiction or art, other than *Candide*. In 1784, Johann Gottfried Herder, the father of German nationalism, discussed the disaster in his *Reflections on the Philosophy of the History of Mankind*; and in Mary Wollstonecraft's *Mary: A Novel* published in 1788, the ruins of Lisbon are briefly remarked upon by the protagonist. In 1811, Goethe referred to the earthquake several times in his memoir, *Poetry and Truth*; and several decades later, Charles Lyell incorporated the great temblor into his groundbreaking *Principles of Geology* (1830–1833). In 1858, Charles Dickens imagined what it must have been like to have experienced the disaster. "I saw the cloudy streets strewn with the dead and dying," he wrote, "screaming crowds, running thickly, hither and thither, like sheep when the doors of the red-slaughterhouse are closed." In October 1931, the children of the Weimar Republic learned about the disaster in a twenty-minute radio broadcast by the Marxist cultural critic and philosopher Walter Benjamin; and in 1945, those who perused Bertrand Russell's new *History of Western Philosophy* were briefly told of the earthquake's cultural impact. Over the past sixty years and most notably in the wake of the 250th anniversary of the disaster in 2005, a handful of books and articles on the earthquake have appeared, though the fact remains that the overwhelming majority of educated people in the West have never heard of it.[118]

For *lisboetas*, however, the earthquake is a constant, if not always fully articulated, presence. As Dom José stares out across the Tagus from his equestrian perch at the center of the square still commonly known as the Terreiro do Paço, Pombal gazes down over the Baixa astride a stone lion (symbolizing power) atop a triumphal column completed in 1934. Today, the population of Lisbon's urban center stands at 550,000 or a little more than twice what it was on October 31, 1755, while the metropolitan area encompasses 2.8 million people or 27 percent of Portugal's population. A much more open and inviting city than it was in 1755, Lisbon is now a modern European capital of outdoor cafés and broad thoroughfares, partly a reflection of the informality that was forced upon the populace, and amply commented upon by survivors, in the days after the disaster.[119] Gone are the gaggles of priests, monks, and nuns that once crowded the streets of pre-earthquake Lisbon as well as many other physical manifestations of the Church. Although still nominally Catholic, the city has been profoundly altered by the more than two and a half centuries of secularization that were inaugurated by the aggressive anti-clerical policies of Pombal and crowned by the dissolution of Portugal's monastic orders on May 28, 1834. Though well aware of its importance, *lisboetas* have largely made their peace with the disaster that arrived on that crisp, sunny November day in 1755.

For many who experienced it, however, the trauma could not be so easily dispelled. After returning to Hopkinton, Massachusetts, after his tenure as British consul in Lisbon, Sir Harry Frankland would, every year on the anniversary of the earthquake, retreat to a special room in his home, on whose tapestry-covered walls were hung various artifacts of his remarkable escape from beneath the ruins. There, surrounded by his damaged sword and his torn and bloody broadcloth coat, he would lock the door, close the shutters, and, in the darkness, pass the rest of the day in prayer, fasting, and personal acts of humiliation.[120]

Acknowledgments

This book is dedicated to the intellectual historians Donald H. Fleming and Stephen J. Tonsor, my graduate and undergraduate advisers at Harvard and the University of Michigan. They remain models of scholarly excellence and generosity to which I will always aspire.

To begin, I would like to express my gratitude to George Andreou, my editor at Knopf, for his patience, his commitment, and his unerring judgment in things large and small.

I owe a special debt to the following people for their help with this project: Terezia Cicelova, Brian Domitrovic, Dana Kappel, Jorge Lopez-Cortina, Peter Miskech, and Geoffrey Riklin.

I would also like to thank my present and former colleagues in the history department at Seton Hall University for their unstinting and much-appreciated support: Tracey Billado, Eliza Buhrer, George Brown, William Connell, Howard Eissenstat, Larry Greene, Sean Harvey, Williamjames Hoffer, Jane Hong, Nathaniel Knight, Brigitte Koenig, Daniel Leab, Maxine Lurie, Maxim Matusevich, Vanessa May, James McCartin, Kirsten Schultz, Dermot Quinn, Vanessa May, Murat C. Menguc, and Thomas Rzeznik.

The following people provided me with invaluable assistance: Millicent Airoldi, Nathan Alexander, Onésimo Almeida, Valerie Andrews, Miguel Telles Antunes, Adelina Axelrod, Elizabeth Bakes, Greg Bankoff, Maria Helena Barreiros, Ethan Bassoff, Frederick Booth, John Buschman, Teresa Botelho, Mariana Candido, Alberto Castro, David Chester, Missey Condie, Mark Couch, Susan Danforth, Alan Delozier, André Dourado, Philip Dray, Francis Dutra, Kathrin Enzel, Katherine Fleming, Bruce Gibson, Philippa Gibson, Ramiro Guinote, James Hankins, Lynne Harrell, John Irwin, John Klemme, Dennis Landis, Marcos León, Mary Lindemann, Uwe Luebken, Michael Mascio, Natalie Mears, Vicente Medina, John J. Miller, Jonathan Molesky, Mary Jane Molesky, Thomas Molesky, Danica Monteiro, Carlos Morais, Helga Mügge, Bernardo Nogueira de Sá, Kim Nusco, Leslie Tobias Olsen, Daniel Pace, Diego Pirillo, Andrew Presti, Allison Rich, Felicitas Ruetten, Zita Sampaio, Jordan Sand, Jennifer Seass, Thomas Shaffer, Helena Singer, Pasquale Terracciano, Maya Tolstoy, Ken Ward, and Ted Widmer.

One of my greatest debts is to the Moreira Lima-Britto family of São Luis, Maranhão (Brazil) with whom I lived for one year as an exchange student in 1985–86. It was in their home that I learned Portuguese and acquired a love and respect for the people and culture of Brazil and the Lusophone world. Their generosity to me over the years cannot be measured. Lili Moreira Lima, Zuzu Britto,

Maria Miuda Lima, Djalma Tenório Britto, Silvana Teresa Tenório Britto Ramos, Benedito Ramos, Marcelo Ramos, Fernanda Ramos, Ana Teresa Moreira Lima Tenório Britto Luna, António Luis Luna, Djalma Tenório Britto Filho, Ricardo Britto, Nathaline Britto, Luis Eugênio Britto, Andrea Britto, Luis Adriano Britto, Leila Teresa Tenório Britto Azevedo, Clarissa Azevedo, Claudia Azevedo, and Caroline Azevedo.

I would like to thank the following institutions for their generous financial support: the Earhart Foundation, the John Carter Brown Library, the National Endowment for the Humanities, the Huntington Library, and the Provost's Office and the University Research Council at Seton Hall University.

I am indebted to the following institutions and their staffs: Academia das Ciências de Lisboa e Centro de Estudos Geológicos (Lisbon), Archives des Affaires étrangères (Paris), Archivo Histórico Nacional (Madrid), Arquivo Municipal (Lisbon), the Arquivo Nacional (Rio de Janeiro), Arquivo Histórico Ultramarino (Lisbon), Arquivo Histórico do Ministério das Obras Públicas, Transportes, e Comunicações (Lisbon), Arquivo Nacional da Torre do Tombo (Lisbon), Archivio di Stato di Genova (Genoa), Archivio di Stato di Napoli (Naples), Archivum Secretum Vaticanum (Vatican City), Archivio di Stato di Venezia (Venice), Astronomical Applications Dept. U.S. Naval Observatory, Foreign Policy Archive of the Russian Empire of the Ministry of Foreign, Affairs of the Russian Federation (Moscow), Biblioteca de Ajuda, Palácio Nacional da Ajuda (Lisbon), Biblioteque de L'Arsenal, Biblioteque Nacional de France (Paris), Biblioteca Brasiliana Guita e José Mindlin (São Paulo), Biblioteca da Arte, Fundação Calouste Gulbenkian (Lisbon), Biblioteca Nacional do Brasil (Rio de Janeiro), British Library (London), Biblioteca Nacional de Portugal (Lisbon), Butler Library, Columbia University, the Centre for Kentish Studies (UK), Stiftung Hanseatisches Wirtschaftsarchiv, Commerzbibliothek (Hamburg), East Sussex Record Office (UK), Geheimes Staatsarchiv Preußischer Kulturbesitz (Berlin), Gabinete de Estudos Olisiponenses, Câmara Municipal (Lisbon), Gloucestershire Record Office (UK), the Graduate Library, University of Michigan, Ann Arbor, Houghton Library (Harvard University),the John Carter Brown Library, Brown University (Providence, RI), the Library of the British Historical Society of Portugal, Massachusetts Historical Society, the Library of Congress (Washington, D.C.), Livraria do Convento de Nossa Senhora de Jesus de Lisboa (Academia das Ciências de Lisboa), the Morgan Library (New York), the New York Public Library (Rare Books Division), Nationaal Archief (The Hague), Real Gabinete Português de Leitura (Rio de Janeiro), the Rockefeller Library (Brown University), Staatsarchiv (Hamburg), the National Archives of the UK, Public Record Office, Walsh Library (Seton Hall University), the Warwickshire Country Record Office (UK), Widener Library (Harvard University), the William L. Clements Library, University of Michigan, and the Wiltshire & Swindon Archives (UK).

A final, heartfelt thank you to my agent, Michael Carlisle, who had faith in me and the earthquake from the beginning.

Notes

PROLOGUE

The Last Victim

1. The Church and Convent of São Domingos were largely destroyed in the earthquake and fire of November 1, 1755. See M. M. de Brée, *A igreja e convento de São Domingos de Lisboa* (Lisbon: Oficinas de S. José de Lisboa, 1964), 57–64; and Manoel Portal, "Historia da ruina da cidade cauzada pello espantozo terremoto e incendio que reduzio a pó e cinza a melhor e maior parte desta infeliz cidade" (manuscript), Biblioteca da Arte, Fundação Calouste Gulbenkian, Lisbon, AP 12363, 10, 66.

2. On the execution of Malagrida (September 20–21, 1761), see *Gazeta de Lisboa*, No. 38, September 22, 1761; the *Mercurio Histórico y Político*, No. 207, November 1761, 214–271; Pe. Paul Mury, *História de Gabriel Malagrida* (São Paulo: Editora Giordano, 1992); original: Paul Mury, *Histoire de Gabriel Malagrida de la Compagnie de Jésus* (Paris: Charles Douniol, Libraire-Éditeur, 1865); P. Franciso Butiñá, *Vida del P. Malagrida de la Compania de Jesús, Quemado como Hereje por el Marqués de Pombal* (Barcelona: Franciso Rosal, 1886), 438–52; *Relation de l'Autho-da-Fé de Lisbonne; Exécution du Père Malagrida, Jésuite, Auteur du Régicide commis sur le Roi de Portugal, 3. Septembre 1758* (BNP); *Lettre de M. L'Abbé Platel, ci-devant le P. Norbert à un Évêque de France, Au sujet d l'Exécution de Gabriel Malagrida, Jésuite, par Sentences des Tribunaux de l'Inquisition & de la Supplication à Lisbonne, le 20 & 21. de Septembre 1761* (BNP); *Arrêt des Inquisiteurs, Ordinaires, et Députés de la Ste. Inquisition contre le Pére Gabriel Malagrida, Jésuite, Lû dans l'Acte public de Foi, célébré à Lisbonne le 20 de Septembre 1761* (Lisbon: Chez Antoine Rodrigues Galhardo, 1761); and *Idée Véridique du Révérend Père Gabriel de Malagrida, Jesuite Italien, Exécuté à Lisbonne, par Sentence de l'Inquisition* (Liège: Chez Syzimme, 1762).

3. Cited in Mury, 1992, 65. Although Malagrida was apparently conversant in indigenous languages, one should view the accuracy of this quote with skepticism.

4. For a discussion of Jesuit/Indian relations in Maranhão," see Dauril Alden, *The Making of an Enterprise: The Society of Jesus in Portugal, Its Empire, and Beyond, 1540–1750* (Stanford, CA: Stanford University Press, 1996), 493–501.

5. Mury, 1992, 155.

6. Ibid., 1992, 159.

7. Serafim Leite, *História da Companhia de Jesus*, Vol. 3 (of 10), (Rio de Janeiro: Instituto Nacional de Livro, 1949), 223, and Vol. 5, 159–60.

8. Mury, 1992, 159.

9. Ibid., 1992, 181.

10. The Richter scale (*M*L), or local magnitude scale, has been largely superseded by the moment magnitude scale (*M*w), which is especially helpful in determining the magnitude of large earthquakes.

11. Judite Nozes, Introduction, Translation, and Notes, *O terramoto de 1755—Testemunhos britânicos: The Lisbon Earthquake of 1755 British Accounts* (Lisbon: Lisóptima Edições, 1990), 178.

12. Ibid., 208.

13. Antonio Ribeiro, "O sismo de 1755 e o geodynâmico da Ibéria e Atlântico," *1755: O grande terramoto de Lisboa, Descrições*, 4 vols. (Lisbon: FLAD, 2005), 1: 219–36.

14. See Mark Molesky, "The Great Fire of Lisbon, 1755," in *Flammable Cities: Urban Conflagration and the Making of the Modern World*, edited by Greg Bankoff, Uwe Lubken, and Jordan Sand (Madison: University of Wisconsin Press, 2012).

15. *An Account of the Late Dreadful City of Lisbon, the Metropolis of Portugal*, 2nd ed. (Boston: Green & Russell, 1756), 23.

16. BL, Stowe #754, Correspondence of C. Lyttleton, Vol. 3, ff. 87–88, letter from John Webber (April 2, 1761); Maria Alexandra Lousada and Eduardo Brito Henriques, "Viver nos escombos: Lisboa durante a Reconstrução," in *O terremoto de 1755: Impactos históricos*, edited by Ana Cristina Araúo et al. (Lisbon: Livros Horizonte, 2007), 184–86. See also documents in the Torre do Tombo (National Archives of Portugal), #17858, which show that into the 1770s and 1780s, homes damaged in the earthquake were still being repaired by order of the government. The Italian visitor Joseph Baretti mocks the common Portuguese belief ("their fiery imaginations") in 1760 that the still devastated city will soon be rebuilt. See also Joseph Baretti, *A Journey from London to Genoa Through England, Portugal, Spain, and France* (Sussex: Centaur Press, 1970), 101–2.

17. Charles Dumouriez, *O reino de Portugal em 1766* (Casal de Cambra, Portugal: Caleidoscópio, 2007), 124. "Such a scene of horrible desolation no words are equal to. Nothing is to be seen but vast heaps of rubbish, out of which arise in numberless places the miserable remains of shattered walls and broken pillars." Baretti, 96–97 (this observation is from September 2, 1760). "The town is almost completely destroyed, which makes it very inconvenient passing from one side . . . to the other." BL, Stowe #754, ff. 48, Correspondence of C. Lyttleton, Vol. 3, letter from Thomas Pitt (March 24, 1760).

18. Baretti, 96–97 (this observation is from September 2, 1760); Dumouriez, 123.

19. William Beckford, *The Journal of William Beckford in Portugal and Spain, 1787–1788*, edited by Boyd Alexander (London: Rupert Hart-Davis, 1954), 41. Carl Ruders estimated the number of stray dogs in Lisbon at the beginning of the nineteenth century to be 80,000. Carl Israel Ruders, *Viagem em Portugal (1798–1802)* (Lisbon: Biblioteca Nacional, 1981). The Duke du Châtelet describes during a visit to Lisbon in the 1770s how soldiers accosted people in the streets for charity. Many of them lived in "subterranean caverns and cellars" amid the ruins. Bourgoing, 87.

20. BL, Stowe #754, f. 48, Correspondence of C. Lyttleton, Vol. 3, letter from Thomas Pitt (March 24, 1760).

21. Baretti, 103.

22. On autos-da-fé and *procissões* (processions), see Lilia Moritz Schwarcz, *A longa viagem da Biblioteca dos Reis: Do terremoto de Lisboa à independência do Brasil* (São Paulo: Companhia das Letras, 2002), 52–53.

23. D. João de Almeida Portugal, *As prisões da Junqueira durante o ministério do Marquês de Pombal* (Lisbon: Frenesi, 2005; original, 1857), 57–58.

24. Mury, 1992, 146.

25. Portugal, 58.

26. *Sentença contra o Pe. Malagridada Companha de Jesus* (September 24, 1761), 6. See Manuel Cadafaz de Matos, ed., *O Juizo da Verdadeira Causa do Terremoto . . . e sacrifício simbólico do Pe. Gabriel Malagrida* (Lisbon: Edições Távola Redonda, n.d.), 89–120; *The Proceedings and Sentence of the Spiritual Court of Inquisition of Portugal Against Gabriel Malagrida, Jesuit* (London: C. Marsh, 1762); and John Smith, *Memoirs of the Marquis de Pombal*, Vol. 2 (of 2), (London: Longman, Brown, Green and Longmans, 1847), 13–23. Proserpine is recast by the inquisitors as one of the "Furies of Hell."

27. Some of Malagrida's fellow prisoners believed that he had descended into madness. Portugal, 58.

28. ANTT, *Inquisição de Lisboa*, Microfilm #8086. The priest was Father Luís do Monte Carmelo.

29. ANTT, *Inquisição de Lisboa*, Microfilm #8086.

30. Mury, 1992, 225.

31. Museu da Cidade (Lisbon), 1758. See also Kenneth Maxwell, *Pombal: Paradox of the Enlightenment* (Cambridge: Cambridge University Press, 1995), 81.

32. It was a common practice in Portuguese autos-da-fé to begin the final procession at dusk in order to enhance the effect of the torchlight.

33. *Mercurio Histórico y Político*, No. 207, November 1761, 214–15; For works on Pombal and eighteenth-century Portugal, see Maxwell, 1995; José Augusto França, *Lisboa pombalina e o illuminismo* (Lisbon: Bertrand Editora, 1983); J. Lucio D'Azevedo, *O marquês de Pombal e a sua epoca* (Rio de Janeiro: Annuario do Brasil, 1922); Joaquim Veríssimo Serrão, *O marquês de Pombal: O homen, O diplomata e o estadista* (Lisbon, 1987); Marcus Cheke, *Dictator of Portugal: Marquis of Pombal* (London: Sidgwick & Jackson, 1938); and Miguel Real, *O marquês de Pombal e a cultura portuguesa* (Lisbon: QuidNovi, 2005).

34. C. R. Boxer, "Pombal's Dictatorship and the Great Lisbon Earthquake, 1755," *History Today*, November 1955, 730.

35. Cheke, 16. For information on aristocratic gangs in pre-earthquake Lisbon, see Bill M. Donovan, "Crime, Policing, and the Absolutist State in Early Modern Lisbon," *Portuguese Studies Review*, Vol. 5, No. 2, 1996–97, 63–64. Donovan argues that Pombal himself was one of the thugs.

36. Cheke, 14–15.

37. Few students at Coimbra in this period ever actually attended classes or even lived in the vicinity of the university but merely traveled to the university at the end of their term of study to collect their degrees. Ibid.

38. Ibid., 17–18.

39. Quoted in ibid., 18.

40. With Dona Teresa's fortune and the inheritance he would receive from his father and uncle, Pombal began his remarkable rise within the Portuguese state.

41. Maxwell, 1995, 1–49.

42. Boxer, 1995, 732.

43. Mury, 1992, 188.

44. See Matos; Marcus Odilon, *O livro proibido de padre Malagrida* (João Pessoa, Brazil:

UNIGRAF, 1986); and Rui Tavares, *O pequeno livro do grande terremoto ensaio sobre 1755* (Lisbon: Edições Tinta-da-China, 2005), 135–49.

45. Gabriel Malagrida, *Juizo da Verdadeira Causa do Terremoto* (Lisbon: Manoel Soares, 1756), 3–4.

46. Ibid., 5, 16.

47. Although a reformer, Pombal was no philosophe. The works of Voltaire, Rousseau, Locke, Hobbes, Diderot, and Spinoza were banned in Portugal by state censors. H. V. Livermore, *A New History of Portugal* (Cambridge: Cambridge University Press, 1966), 236–37. Note: in modern Portuguese usage, "earthquake" is spelled *terramoto*, while in Brazil the older spelling, *terremoto*, is still used.

48. Letter (November 3, 1755), in *1755 providências do marquês de Pombal* (Lisbon: FLAD e Público, 2005), 99–100.

49. Thomas D. Kendrick, *The Lisbon Earthquake* (London: Methuen, 1956), 91.

50. ANTT, #8064, no. 18, ff. 1–6.

51. Maxwell, 3.

52. Auto-da-fé means "act of faith."

53. The Rua Formosa is today called the Rua do Século.

54. For the story of Pombal and the Jesuits, see Russell R. Dynes, "The Lisbon Earthquake of 1755: The First Modern Disaster," in Theodore E. D. Braun and John B. Radner, eds., *The Lisbon Earthquake of 1755: Representations and Reactions* (Oxford: Voltaire Foundation, 2005), 34–49.

55. See Kenneth Maxwell, "The Jesuit and the Jew: The Lisbon Earthquake in Modern Perspective," in *ReVista: Harvard Review of Latin America*, "Natural Disasters: Coping with Calamity," Winter 2007, 17–18.

56. Kendrick, 72–73.

57. *Sentença contra o Pe. Malagrida da Companhia de Jesus*, 2, 4, 10.

58. Mury, 1992, 38–39. Note: Malagrida's first name is spelled "Gabriele" in Italian but "Gabriel" in Portuguese.

59. Ibid., 39.

60. Ibid., 49.

61. Contemporaries regularly compared Malagrida to John the Baptist.

62. See Lúcia Lima Rodrigues and Russell Craig, "Recovery Amid Destruction: Manoel da Maya and the Lisbon Earthquake of 1755," in *Libraries & the Cultural Record*, Vol. 43, No. 4, 2008, 397–410.

63. The Riverside Palace (Paço da Ribeira) was never rebuilt.

64. Cited in Butiñá, 444–45.

65. Ibid., 445.

66. Real, 77. *"Madelenas arrependidas."*

67. Cited in Butiñá, 446.

68. *Sentença contra o Pe. Malagrida da Companhia de Jesus*, 28.

69. See Pedro de Azevedo, ed., *O processo dos Távoras* (Lisbon: Biblioteca Nacional, 1921); Guilherme G. de Oliveira Santos, *O caso dos Távoras* (Lisbon: Livraria Portugal, 1959).

70. Butiñá, 446.

71. Cited in ibid., 447.

72. *Proceedings and Sentence of the Spiritual Court of the Inquisition of Portugal Against Gabriel Malagrida*, 50.

73. Mury, 1992, 224.

74. See *Catalogue of Prints and Drawings in the British Museum*, Division I, Political and

Personal Satires, Vol. IV, A.D. 1761–A.D. 1770, No. 3805 to No. 4838 (London: Chiswick Press, 1883), 606, footnote 1.

75. Claude-Henri Frèches, *Voltaire, Malagrida et Pombal* (Paris: Fundação Calouste Gulbenkian, 1969). Also see the sentence that Pombal had published in France to justify and explain his act: "Liste des personnes qui ont été condamnées à l'acte public de Foi, célébré dans le cloître du couvent de Dominique de Lisbonne le 20 septembre 1761" (Lisbon, 1761). In his *Philosophical Dictionary* (1764), under the category "Miracles," Voltaire wrote that he believed Malagrida was "more infatuated and mad than Nicholas Anthony" (a seventeenth-century French priest who was executed in Geneva for his embrace of Judaism). Voltaire, *The Works of Voltaire: A Philosophical Dictionary*, Vol. 7 (of 10) (New York: E. R. DuMont, 1901), 301.

76. Cited in Cheke, 157.

77. "Discurso político sobre as vantagens que o reino de Portugal pode alcançar da sua desgraça por ocasião do memorável Terramoto do 1 de novembro de 1755" (manuscript), BNP, I, 12,1, no. 14, 1–2, in Schwarcz, 96. See José Barreto, "O discurso político falsamente atribuido ao Marquês de Pombal," *Revista de História das Ideias*, Vol. 4, *O marquês de Pombal e o seu tempo*, 1982, 385–422.

78. "An Extraordinary and Surprising Agitation of the Waters . . . ," *Philosophical Transactions of the Royal Society*, Vol. 49, 1755, 351–95; *Supplement to the Gentleman's Magazine for the Year 1755*, Vol. 25, 1755, 589. See also the assessment of Harry Fielding Reid, "The Lisbon Earthquake of November 1, 1755," in *The Bulletin of the Seismological Society of America*, Vol. 4, No. 2, June 1914, 53–80; Joaquim José Moreira de Mendonça, *História universal dos terremotos, que tem havido no Mundo [. . .] com uma Narraçam Individual do Terremoto* (Lisbon: Officina de Antonio Vicente da Silva, 1758), 159.

79. *Philosophical Transactions of the Royal Society*, Vol. 49, 1755, 399–401. It is possible that the tremors felt at Derbyshire were the result of another earthquake, possibly triggered by the Lisbon quake. Francisco Luís Pereira de Sousa, *O terremoto do 1 de novembro de 1755 e um estudo demográfico*, Vol. 3 (of 4) (Lisbon: Tipografia do Comércio, 1919–32), 557.

80. *"Un altra, un altra, gran Dio, ma più forte."* Giacomo Casanova, Chevalier de Seingalt, *History of My Life*, Vol. 4 (of 12), translated by William R. Trask (Baltimore: Johns Hopkins University Press, 1997), 218–19.

81. Casanova, Vol. 4, 219.

82. Chabbar Abdelaziz, "Os efeitos do terramoto de Lisboa 1 novembro 1755," in *1755: O grande terramoto de Lisboa*, Vol. 1, 2005, 265–94.

83. A. Levret, "The Effects of the November 1, 1755, 'Lisbon' Earthquake in Morocco," *Tectonophysics*, Vol. 193, 1991, 83–94. See a letter from the governor of Pernambuco (Brazil), Luís Diogo Lobo da Silva, to the royal court on the arrival of the tsunami in the coastal villages of Itamaracá and Tamandaré in the captania of Pernambuco (February 28, 1756), AHU_ACL_CU_015_Cx. 18, D. 6689, as well as a letter from Pernambuco describing the damage at Tamandaré and Lucena in the captania of Paraíba (March 4, 1756), AHU_ACL_CU_015_Cx. 80, D. 6691.

84. Sousa, 1919–32, Vol. 3, 557–58; J. Zeilinga de Boer and D. T. Sanders. *Earthquakes in Human History: The Far-Reaching Effects of Human Disruptions* (Princeton, NJ: Princeton University Press, 2005), 94. See also Reid, 53–80; and Hans Woerle, *Der Erschutterungsbezirk des grossen Erdbebens zu Lissabon*, "Inaugural Dissertation von Hans Woerle" (Munich, 1900). See Image KZ689 in the Jan T. Kozak Col-

lection (NISEE), Pacific Earthquake Engineering Research Center, originally published in Hermann Berghaus, *Berghaus' physikalischer Atlas* (Gotha: J. Perthes, 1849–52).

85. Kendrick, 122.

86. Revelation 6:12. Authorized (King James) Version. See John Biddolf, *A Poem on the Earthquake at Lisbon* (London: W. Owen, 1756), 11. "And when on op'ning of the Sixth great Seal, With her last Earthquake this round World shall reel . . ."

87. "Haben Sie von dem Erdbeben zu Lissabon gehört? Nein, - ein Erdbeben? Ich sehe hier keine Zeitungen . . . ," Thomas Mann, *Der Zauberberg* (Berlin: S. Fischer Verlag, 1952, originally published in 1924), 325.

88. "The Cyclorama," *The Spectator*, London, December 30, 1848.

89. Ibid.

90. AHCML, FA-63, Portugal Aflito e Conturbado Pello Terremoto do Anno de 1755 (anonymous, manuscript; Manoel Portal, Historia da ruina da cidade cauzada pello espantozo terremoto e incendio que reduzio a pó e cinza a melhor e maior parte desta infeliz cidade (manuscript) Biblioteca da Arte, Fundação Calouste Gulben-kian, Lisbon, AP 12363.

91. Franciso de Pina de Mello, *Ao terremoto do primeiro de novembro de 1755, Parènesis de Francisco de Pina e de Mello* (Lisbon: Manoel Soares, 1756), in *Collecçam universal de todas as obras, que tem sahido ao publico sobre os effeitos, que cauzou o terremoto nos reinos de Portugal . . .* , Vol. 5 (Lisbon: Officina de Curiosidade, 1758).

> *Desse emporio do Mundo, onde o Tridente,*
> *Arvorava Neptuno, e todo o Oriente,*
> *A America, e as Provincias mais remotas*
> *Davão thezouros em continuas frotas*
> *Não ha mais, que huma misera lembrança.*

CHAPTER ONE

Babylonia Portugueza

The phrase *Babylonia portugueza* appears in Jospeh Moreira de Azevedo, *Desterro da iniquidade e muito necessaria consideração sobre o espantoso terremoto* (Lisbon: Manuel Soares, 1756), 5.

1. A. H. de Oliveira Marques, *História de Portugal*, Vol. 1 (of 3) (Lisbon: Editorial Presença, 1997), 220.

2. Manuel Carlos de Brito, *Opera in Portugal in the Eighteenth Century* (Cambridge: Cambridge University Press, 1989), 22. The composer was Caetano Maria Schi-assi; David Cranmer, "Opera in Portugal or Portuguese Opera," *The Musical Times*, November 1994, 692–96.

3. It would later be known as the Teatro do Tejo (Theater on the Tagus).

4. Cited in Brito, 28.

5. Brito, 27.

6. Maria Alexandra Trinidade Gago da Câmara and Vanda Anastácio, *O teatro em Lisboa no tempo do marquês de Pombal* (Lisbon: Museu Nacional do Teatro, 2005), 84; Brito, 28. See also José de Figueiredo, "Teatro Real da Ópera," in *Boletim da Academia Nacional de Belas Artes*, Vol. 3, Lisbon, 1938, 33–35; and Maria Alexandra T. Gago da Câmara, *Lisboa: Espaços teatrais setecentistas* (Lisbon: Livros Horizonte, 1996). One Englishman later wrote that the Opera House "was esteemed the rich-

est building in Europe." WRO, CR1368, Letter, John Dobson, December 15, 1755.

7. David Birmingham, *A Concise History of Portugal*, 2nd ed. (Cambridge: Cambridge University Press, 2003), 70.

8. Brito, 28–29.

9. *Gazeta de Lisboa*, No. 15, April 10, 1755, 119.

10. Brito, 28.

11. José I's father, João V, was frequently compared to Alexander the Great during his reign. Angela Delaforce, *Art and Patronage in Eighteenth-Century Portugal* (Cambridge: Cambridge University Press, 2002), 41.

12. Charles Boxer, *The Portuguese Seaborne Empire, 1415–1825* (New York: Alfred A. Knopf, 1969), 51.

13. Malagrida, 23.

14. "Everyone at the court," wrote the papal nuncio a week later, "is still talking about the opera—and nothing else." ASV Portogallo, seg. 100, fol. 132 v., April 8, 1755, in Delaforce, 2002, 284; Brito, 28.

15. *Recueil des plus belles ruines de Lisbonne causées par le tremblement et par le feu du primier novembre 1755*. Dessiné sur les lieux par M. M. Paris et Pedegache. Et gravé à Paris par Jac. Ph. Le bas premier graveur du cabinet du Roy en 1757. Avec privilège du Roy. Se vend à Paris chez Jac. Franc. Blondel. Editions also in English, Dutch, and German. José de Figueiredo, "Teatro Real da Ópera," in *Boletim da Academic Nacional de Belas-Artes*, Vol. 3, Lisbon, 1938.

16. For a detailed description of the ruins of the Opera House, see Manoel Portal, "Historia da ruina da Cidade de Lisboa cauzada pello espantozo terremoto e incendio, que reduzio a pó e cinza a melhor e major parte desta infeliz Cidade" (manuscript), BG, AP 12363, 1756?, 55–58.

17. Malcolm Jack, *Lisbon: City of the Sea—A History* (London: I. B. Tauris, 2007), 2.

18. José-Augusto França, *Lisboa história, física e Moral* (Lisbon: Livros Horizonte, 2008), 26–29. Other theories contend that Lisbon is derived from *Allis Ubo*, Phoenician for "safe harbor"—or possibly from *Lucio* or *Lisso*, from the pre-Roman names for the River Tagus. Another tradition argues that Lisbon is derived from the Phoenician *Alis Ubo* or "calm bay."

19. França, 2008, 18–26.

20. Most of these images were engravings. Jack, 4. Engravings of bulls may suggest the existence of a bull cult that was widespread in the Mediterranean at the time. Disney, Vol. 1, 8.

21. Livermore, 11; James M. Anderson and M. Sheridan Lea, *Portugal 1001 Sights: An Archaeological and Historical Guide* (Calgary: University of Calgary Press, 1994), 3–5.

22. Marques, Vol. 1, 25–28; Livermore, 11–12.

23. Disney, Vol. 1, 12–13.

24. Marques, Vol. 1, 28–30; Livermore, 12–13.

25. Birmingham, 14.

26. Disney, Vol. 1, 24.

27. Ibid., 22.

28. Livermore, 17.

29. França, 2008, 31–45; Livermore, 14–22; Disney, Vol. 1, 32–33.

30. Marques, Vol. 1, 32–40. Galician-Portuguese would also develop into the modern language of Galician. Although Portuguese, like Spanish, would absorb several

hundred words from Arabic during the Moorish occupation (as well as approximately thirty words of German origin from their Visigoth masters), the majority of the language as well as its syntax and grammatical structure is derived from its Latin source. Today Portuguese is the seventh most widely spoken language in the world.

31. Marques, Vol. 1, 53–58.
32. Ibid., 66–69; Livermore, 32–33. The majority of Arabs, who formed the elite caste, were Yemeni, while most of the immigrants were Berber. Disney, Vol. 1, 57.
33. Birmingham, 17.
34. Disney, Vol. 1, 64.
35. Marques, Vol. 1, 36–38. See also William Entwistle, "The Portuguese and the Brazilian Language," 29–47, in H. V. Livermore, *Portugal and Brazil: An Introduction* (Oxford: Oxford University Press, 1953).
36. Birmingham, 17.
37. Marques, Vol. 1, 73–103. In 732, at the Battle of Poitiers, Charlemagne's grandfather, Charles Martel, thwarted the Muslim invasion of France and perhaps saved Western Christianity.
38. When, in 1095, Pope Urban II called on Western Christians to liberate the Holy Lands of the Middle East from the Muslims (in what became known as the First Crusade), he specifically exempted the Iberians so that they could focus on freeing their own territory. Disney, Vol. 1, 80.
39. Cited in Kendrick, 85–86.
40. Kendrick, 83.
41. Livermore, 54–61.
42. See José Mattoso, *D. Afonso Henriques* (Lisbon: Temas e Debates, 2007), 239–47.
43. Disney, Vol. 1, 83.
44. See Jorge Martins, *Portugal e os Judeus: Volume I—dos primórdios da nacionalidade à legislação pombalina* (Lisbon: Nova Vega, 2006); and Meyer Kayserling, *História dos Judeus em Portugal* (São Paulo: Pioneira, 1971).
45. Disney, Vol. 1, 153; A. J. Saraiva, *Inquisição e os cristãos-novos* (Porto: Editorial Novo, 1969), 18–20, 28–31.
46. "Itinerário do Dr. Jerónimo Munzer 1492," in Paulo Henriques, Introduction, *Lisboa antes do terramoto grande vista da cidade entre 1700 & 1725* (Lisbon: Gótica, 2004), 39–40.
47. Quoted in Disney, Vol. 1, 153.
48. Jack, 23–24. See also França, 57–127.
49. Boxer, *The Portuguese Seaborne Empire*, 4.
50. Livermore, 103–4.
51. For cultural relations between Britain and Portugal, see Rose Macaulay, *They Went to Portugal* (London: Jonathan Cape, 1946) and *They Went to Portugal Too (Aspects of Portugal)* (Manchester: Carcanet, 1990).
52. Jack, 24. The plague would return to Portugal, as it would across much of Europe, every eight or nine years for the next century and a half. Disney, Vol. 1, 108.
53. Joel Serrão, ed., *Dicionário de história de Portugal*, Vol. 4 (of 9), 163–64.
54. For a list and description of earthquakes in Portugal before 1755, see Mendonça, 1–111; manuscript in BNP, Fundo Geral, Condice no. 1772, ff. 42–56. See also João José Alves Dias, "Principais sismos, em Portugal, anteriores ao de 1755," in *1755: O grande terramoto de Lisboa*, 123–42; and Antoni Roca et al., "An Outline

of Earthquake Catalogues, Databases and Studies of Historical Seismicity in the Iberian Peninsula," *Annals of Geophysics*, Vol. 47, No. 2/3, April/June 2004.

55. Mendonça, 17.

56. Ibid., 53–56. Justo and Salwa question the appearance of a tsunami, although some accounts seem to support it. J. L. Justo and C. Salwa, "The 1531 Lisbon Earthquake," *The Bulletin of the Seismological Society of America*, Vol. 88, No. 2, April 1998, 319–28. There was also a powerful earthquake in 1597. Schwarcz, 31. See also M. C. J. Henriques and M. F. F. Natividade, *O sismo de 26 de janeiro de 1531*, Lisbon, Comissão para o Catálogo Sísmico Nacional, 1988.

57. Boxer, *The Portuguese Seaborne Empire*, 18.

58. See Peter E. Russell, *Prince Henry "the Navigator": A Life* (New Haven, CT: Yale University Press, 2000), 7; and Charles Verlinden, "Prince Henry in Modern Perspective as Father of the 'Descobrimentos,'" in George Winius, ed., *Portugal the Pathfinder: Journeys from the Medieval Toward the Modern World, 1300–ca. 1600* (Madison, WI: Hispanic Seminary of Medieval Studies, 1995), 41–70.

59. In some important respects, the fruitful interaction between sailors and course-plotting mathematicians in the Portuguese court would foreshadow the empirical strides made during the Scientific Revolution in Britain. See Onésimo T. Almeida, "Science During the Portuguese Maritime Discoveries: A Telling Case of Interaction Between Experimenters and Theoreticians," in *Science in the Spanish and Portuguese Empires, 1500–1800*, eds. Daniela Bleichmar et al. (Stanford, CA: Stanford University Press, 2008); and "Portugal and the Dawn of Modern Science," in Winius, 341–61.

60. Alden, 24.

61. John Thornton, "Early Portuguese Expansion in West Africa: Its Nature and Consequences," in Winius, 121–32. Soon the Portuguese would begin the production of their famous cruzado, a coin whose high gold content made it much desired throughout Europe. Disney, Vol. 2, 148.

62. Many of these slaves had been captured in wars of conquest.

63. A. C. de C. M. Saunders, *A Social History of Black Slaves and Freedmen in Portugal, 1441–1555* (Cambridge: Cambridge University Press, 1982), 4–34, 59.

64. Although some believed the country was on the verge of finding an ocean route to Asia, others remained skeptical. When Admiral Bartolomeu Dias first rounded the Cape of Good Hope in 1488, João II's timid advisors dissuaded the king from launching a full-scale expedition to India. The Portuguese Parliament (Cortes) actually voted against the idea. It would take another decade and a new king, Manuel I, before the Portuguese would achieve their dream.

65. Bartolomeu Dias rounded the Cape of Good Hope in 1488.

66. See Carmen M. Radulet, "Vasco da Gama and His Successors" and Alfredo Pinheiro Marques, "Triumph for Da Gama and Disgrace for Columbus," in Winius, 133–44. Da Gama himself returned to Lisbon in September 1499.

67. Marques and Serrão, Vol. 5, 255; Disney, Vol. 1, 148.

68. See Francisco Bethencourt and Diogo Ramada Couto, eds. *Portuguese Oceanic Expansion, 1400–1800* (Cambridge: Cambridge University Press, 2007).

69. The Luciads were the sons of Lusus, the mythical father of Lusitania. Luís de Camões, Leonard Bacon, trans., *The Lusiads of Luís de Camões* (New York: Hispanic Society of America, 1950), 3. The author has switched the places of the words "nobler" and "valor."

70. Dom Manuel's personal animosity toward Ferdinand Magellan (Fernão de Magalhães) had driven him into the arms of the Spanish Crown, in whose name Magellan's ships would circumnavigate the globe between 1519 and 1522.

71. Bailey W. Diffie and George D. Winius, *Foundations of the Portuguese Empire, 1415–1580* (St. Paul: University of Minnesota Press, 1977), 411.

72. Boxer, *The Portuguese Seaborne Empire*, 56.

73. Ibid., 39–48.

74. Ibid., 39–64.

75. See George D. Winius, "The *Estado da India* on the Subcontinent: Portuguese as Players on a South Asia Stage," in Winius, 191–212.

76. The old royal palace on St. George's Hill was called the Paço da Alcáçova.

77. Boxer, *The Portuguese Seaborne Empire*, 48.

78. Ibid., 52, 59; A. J. R. Russell-Wood, *The Portuguese Empire, 1415–1808* (Baltimore: Johns Hopkins University Press, 1992), 126–28.

79. Russell-Wood, 1992, 123–47.

80. See Jonathan I. Israel, *European Jewry in the Age of Mercantilism, 1550–1750* (Portland, OH: Littman Library of Jewish Civilization, 1998).

81. See François Soyer, *The Persecution of the Jews and Muslims of Portugal: King Manuel I and the End of Religious Tolerance (1496–7)* (Leiden, Netherlands: Brill, 2007).

82. Disney, Vol. I, 153.

83. Ibid., 154.

84. Marques, A. H. de Oliveira and J. J. A. Dias, "A população portuguesa nos séculos XV e XVI," *Biblos*, Vol. 70, 1994, 171–96.

85. Kendrick, 51.

86. *The Scots Magazine*, Vol. 17, November 1755, 561.

87. Schwarcz, 58.

88. Damião de Góis, *Elogio da Cidade de Lisboa Urbis Olisiponis Descriptio* (Lisbon: Guimarães Editores, 2002), 171. See also França, 2008, 129–70.

89. Delaforce, 2002, 9.

90. Disney, Vol. 1, 151.

91. Delaforce, 2002, 6–7. The tapestries have been known as the *Discovery of India* or the *Conquest of India*.

92. Damião de Góis, *Elogio da Cidade de Lisboa Urbis Olisiponis Descriptio* (Lisbon: Guimarães Editores, 2002), 149.

93. Jack, 41.

94. Giovanni Botero, *The Reason of State*, "A Treatise Concerning the Causes of the Magnificency and Greatness of Cities Divided into three books by Sig. Giovanni Botero in the Italian Tongue, now done into English by Robert Peterson, 1606," Book 2, Chapter 11, "Of the residency of the prince." Special thanks to Alejandra Osorio.

95. The Battle of Alcácer-Quibir or the Battle of the Three Kings was fought on August 4, 1578.

96. The Treaty of Saragossa (or Zaragoça) of 1529 divided the Eastern Hemisphere between Spain and Portugal, giving the Moluccas to Portugal and the Philippines to Spain. On the discovery of Brazil, see Francis A. Dutra, "The Discovery of Brazil and Its Immediate Aftermath," in Winius, 145–68.

97. Boxer, *The Portuguese Seaborne Empire*, 108.

98. Russell-Wood, 1992, 23–25.

99. Ibid., 24–25. The fight for the Azores lasted from the 1530s to 1712.

100. Quoted in Schwarcz, 85.
101. See Bill M. Donovan, "The Discovery and Conquest of the Brazilian Frontier," in Winius, 229–46.
102. Charles R. Boxer, *The Golden Age of Brazil, 1695–1750* (Berkeley: University of California Press, 1962). See also Stuart B. Schwartz, "Colonial Brazil, c. 1580–c. 1750: Plantations and Peripheries," in *The Cambridge History of Latin America, Volume 2, Colonial Latin America,* ed. Leslie Bethell (Cambridge: Cambridge University Press, 1984), 423–500; as well as Schwartz's "Prata, açúcar e escravos: de como o império restaurou Portugal," *Tempo,* Vol. 12, No. 24, 2008, 201–23.
103. Cited in Boxer, 1962, 59. Bahia (or Salvador) was the capital of colonial Brazil until 1763.
104. A. J. R. Russell-Wood, "Colonial Brazil: The Gold Cycle, c. 1690–1750," 547–600, in *The Cambridge History of Latin America, Volume 2, Colonial Latin America,* ed. Leslie Bethell (Cambridge: Cambridge University Press, 1984).
105. The advisor was Dom Luís da Cunha. Kenneth Maxwell, "Eighteenth-Century Portugal: Faith and Reason, Tradition and Innovation During a Golden Age," in Jay A. Levenson, ed., *The Age of the Baroque in Portugal* (Washington, DC: National Gallery of Art, 1993), 112. See also Carl A. Hanson, "D. Luís da Cunha and Portuguese Mercantilist Thought," *Journal of the American Portuguese Society,* Vol. 15, 1981, 15–23.
106. Vitorino M. Godinho, "Portugal, as frotas do açúcar e as frotas do ouro (1870–1770)," *Revista da História,* Vol. 15, 1953.
107. Birmingham, 73–74.
108. Ibid., 4.
109. Livermore, 104.
110. For works on João V, see Maria Beatriz Nizza da Silva, *D. João V* (Lisbon: Temas e Debates, 2009); Manuel Bernardes Branco, *Portugal na época de D. João V* (Lisbon, 1885); Mário Domingues, *D. João V.: O homem e a sua época* (Lisbon: Prefácio); and Eduardo Brazão, *João V.: Subsídios para a história do seu reinado* (Porto, 1945).
111. Mário Domingues, *D. João V: O homem e a sua época* (Lisbon: Romano Torres, 1964), 5–6.
112. Once a critic of Dom João's absolutism, the British envoy, Lord Tyrawley, was eventually won over by the king's inveterate charm and charisma: "I have the utmost regard and high esteem for this person, not only for the treatment I meet with from him, but for his great qualities. For nobody ever had better parts, better sense, more wit, more quickness, and if one may use so familiar a term to so great a man, there never was one so thoroughly agreeable than the King of Portugal." Quoted in Charles R. Boxer, "Lord Tyrawley in Lisbon." *History Today,* Vol. 20, November 1970, 794. Dom João V was known to be an Anglophile.
113. P. Castrioto (painted in 1720), *Dom João V tomando chocolate que lhe servido pelo duque de Lafões,* Museu Nacional de Arte Antiga, Lisbon, Estampa No. 18, *Exposição Lisboa Joanina* (Lisbon: Câmara Municipal de Lisboa, 1950).
114. See Roy Porter, *Problems of Enlightenment in Portugal* (Minneapolis: Institute for the Study of Ideologies and Literatures, 1984); and Pedro Calafate, ed., *História do pensamento filosófico português, Volume 3: As luzes* (Lisboa: Caminho, 2001). Dom João never left Portuguese soil during his lifetime.
115. BG, AP 12363, Portal, 54; Schwarcz, 32–34, 78.
116. Schwarcz, 32.
117. Ibid., 71.

118. Ibid., 72.

119. Ibid.

120. Delaforce, 2002, 91.

121. Schwarcz, 74.

122. Delaforce, 2002, Chapter 2: "The Adornment of the Paço da Ribeira and Dom Joã's 'Precious Treasury,'" 29–66.

123. Schwarcz, 74.

124. Delaforce, 2002, 86.

125. Ibid., 87. According to the Count of Ericeira, Dom João was never happier than when in the midst of his beloved books. Delaforce, 2002, 116. Dom João once contemplated opening the library to the public, only to change his mind when he realized that the necessary renovations would disturb his beloved view of the Tagus. Delaforce, 2002, 76.

126. For a reference to João V as King Solomon, see Ignácio Barbosa Machado, *Relacam da Infermidade, Ultimas Acçoens, Morte e Sepultura do Muito Alto . . .* (Lisbon, 1750), 50.

127. Manuel Marques Resende, *Espelho da Corte ou Hum Breve Mappa de Lisboa* (Lisbon, 1720), 10, in Delaforce, 2002, 29.

128. Delaforce, 2002, 33–34.

129. Catherine of Bragança died in 1705.

130. Delaforce, 2002, 29–30.

131. Ibid., 46.

132. Ibid., 179.

133. António Manuel Hespanha and António Camões Gouveia, "A igreja," in José Mattoso, ed., *História de Portugal* (Lisbon: Editorial Estampa, 1992–93), Vol. 4 (of 8), *O Antigo Regime (1620–1807)*, 287–301.

134. Martin S. Briggs, "S. John's Chapel in the Church of S. Roque, Lisbon," *The Burlington Magazine for Connoisseurs*, Vol. 28, No. 152, November 1915; *Lisbon in the Age of Dom João V (1689–1750)* (Paris: Instituto Português de Museus, 1994), 7–11.

135. George Whitefield, *Whitefield at Lisbon: Being a Detailed Account of the Blasphemy and Idolatry of Popery as witnessed by the Late Servant of God, George Whitefield* (London: R. Greenbridge & Sons, 1851), 6.

136. Schwarcz, 51; Cheke, 4. For a catalogue of miraculous statues and images of Jesus, the Virgin Mary, and the saints located in Lisbon and throughout Portugal, see João Baptista de Castro, "Das imagens milagrosas," in *Mappa de Portugal antigo e moderno*, 2nd ed., Vol. 2 (of 3) (Lisbon: Officina Patriarcal de Francisco Luiz Ameno, 1762–63), 225–62.

137. Suzanne Chantal, *A vida quotidiana em Portugal ao tempo do terramoto* (Lisbon: Livros do Brasil, 2005), 174.

138. Ibid., 174.

139. Francisco Xavier de Oliveira, *Amusement périodique*, Vol. 1 (London, 1751), 347–57.

140. Cheke, 3; Chantal, 177.

141. Whitefield, 10 (April 3, 1754).

142. Chantal, 179.

143. Chantal, 148.

144. Piedade Braga Santos et al., *Lisboa setecentista vista por estrangeiros* (Lisbon: Livros Horizonte, 1992), 38–40; Schwarcz, 50–51; Chantal, 147–83.

145. Cheke, 7–8. The wealthiest orders were the Capuchin Franciscans, the Augustinians, the Celestines, the Bernardines, and the Carthusians.

146. See Angela Delaforce, "Lisbon, 'This New Rome': Dom João V of Portugal and Relations Between Rome and Lisbon," in Levenson, 49–79. In 1716, Dom João sent his ambassador to be received by Pope Clement XI in a procession that featured three gilded coaches of such breathtaking beauty that few could deny Lisbon's glorious rebirth. Silvana Bessone, director, *O Museu Nacional dos Coches Lisboa* (Lisbon: Instituto Português de Museus Fondation Paribas, 1993), 78–89. See also Delaforce, 2002, 117–64.

147. Delaforce, 2002, 65–66.

148. Cheke, 10.

149. Quoted in França, 1983, 46–47, from L. Moreri, *Le grand dictionnaire historique*.

150. Delaforce, 2002, 194.

151. Chantal, 147.

152. Stephen Schwartz, Lecture, Brown University, 2009.

153. See Schwarcz, 52–53; and António José Saraiva, Capítulo 6: "O que era um auto-de-fé?," in *Inquisição e Cristãos-Novos* (Lisbon: Editorial Estampa, 1969), 101–12. See also Carl A. Hanson, *Economy and Society in Baroque Portugal, 1668–1703* (Minneapolis: University of Minnesota Press, 1981), 279.

154. Chantal, 170. See also Maria Teresa Esteves Payan, *A censura literária em Portugal nos séculos XVII e XVIII* (Lisbon: Fundação Calouste Gulbenkian, 2005).

155. The University of Coimbra was founded in 1290 and was the only university in Portugal until the University of Évora opened in 1559.

156. Livermore, 208.

157. On Portugal's Enlightenment, see Manoel Cardozo, "The Internationalism of the Portuguese Enlightenment: The Role of the Estrangeirado, c. 1700–c. 1750," in A. Owen Aldridge, ed., *The Ibero-American Enlightenment* (Urbana: University of Illinois Press, 1971).

158. Schwarcz, 62, quoted in Delaforce, 2002, 166.

159. Schwarcz, 62.

160. Cheke, 10–11.

161. Quoted in Maxwell, 1995, 17.

162. Cheke, 11.

163. Ibid., 11–12.

164. Quoted in Ian Robertson, *A Traveller's History of Portugal* (New York: Interlink Books, 2002), 99.

165. Schwarcz, 60.

166. Population figures for pre-earthquake Lisbon are far from precise. While Ferro believes the population to have been 130,000, Schwarcz puts it at 250,000. João Pedro Ferro, *A População portuguesa no final do Antigo Regime (1750–1815)* (Lisbon: Editorial Presença, 1995), 50–53; Schwarzc, 31. The kingdom's second-largest city, Porto, had a population of approximately 30,000.

167. Jean-François Bourgoing, *Travels of the Duke of Châtelet in Portugal*, Vol. 1 (of 2) (London: John Stockdale, 1809), 105.

168. Quoted in Donovan, 1996–97, 60. See also Baron de Lahontan, *New Voyages to North America*, Vol. 1 (of 2) (London, 1703), 202.

169. Bourgoing, 1809, 105.

170. Ibid., 104.

171. Ibid.; Schwarcz, 47.

172. Schwarcz, 58.

173. Chantal, 110.

174. Quoted in Brito, 10.

175. Quoted in Schwarz, 51.

176. David Francis, *Portugal 1715–1808: Joanine Pombaline and Rococo Portugal as Seen by British Diplomats and Traders* (London: Tamesis, 1985).

177. António Manuel Hespanha, "A família," in José Mattoso José, ed., *História de Portugal* (Lisbon: Editorial Estampa, 1992–93), Vol. 4 (of 8), *O Antigo Regime (1620–1807)*, 277.

178. Bourgoing, 1809, 100.

179. Beckford, June 1, 1787, 54.

180. Chantal, 110.

181. Bourgoing, 1809, 101.

182. Chantal, 125, 113.

183. According to British envoy Lord Tyrawley, who was trying to solicit funds from his secretary of state: "Nobody of any rank or quality appears in Lisbon's streets with less than six horses, if it is but to the next door; six footmen behind and a gentleman servant on horseback is the least anybody goes abroad with." Quoted in Boxer, 1970, 792.

184. Schwarcz, 44.

185. Ibid., 45; Castello Branco Chaves, *O Portugal de D. João V visto por três forasteiros* (Lisbon: Biblioteca Nacional, 1989), 39.

186. Chantal, 119.

187. Schwarcz, 66; Bourgoing, 1809, 103.

188. For images of eighteenth-century Portuguese clothing, see Alberto Souza, *O trajo popular em Portugal nos seculos XVIII e XIV* (Lisbon: Sociedade Nacional de Tipografia, 1924).

189. Chantal, 101.

190. For an analysis of the political role of the Portuguese nobility in the seventeenth and eighteenth centuries, see Nuno Gonçalo Monteiro, *Elites e poder entre o Antigo Regime e o liberalismus* (Lisbon: Imprensa de Ciências Sociais, 2003).

191. Chantal, 106–9.

192. Schwarcz, 37–39; Piedade Braga Santos, Teresa Rodrigues, Margarida Sá Nogueira, eds., *Lisboa setecentista vista por estrangeiros* (Lisbon: Livros Horizonte, 1992), 70.

193. Schwarcz, 48–50; Piedade Braga Santos et al., 69–70.

194. Piedade Braga Santos et al., 69–70; Kendrick, 51.

195. Piedade Braga Santos et al., 71.

196. Kendrick, 51.

197. Cheke, 4.

198. Schwarcz, 49.

199. See Mark Kurlansky, *Cod: A Biography of the Fish That Changed the World* (New York: Walker, 1997). On Portuguese salt production, see J. Serrão and A. H. de Oliveira, eds., directors, *Nova história de Portugal*, Vol. 3, 452.

200. Piedade Braga Santos et al., 71.

201. Schwarcz, 49–50.

202. Ibid., 49; Domingos Rodrigues, *Arte de Cozinha* (Lisbon: Oficina Ferreiriana, 1732).

203. Quoted in Schwarcz, 49.

204. Schwarcz, 47; Bourgoing, 1809, 117–18.

205. Domingues, 169–75.

206. Piedade Braga Santos et al., 70–71.

207. Bourgoing, 1809, 118.

208. See David Francis, *Portugal 1715–1808*. Britain's frequent wars with France, which cut off the supply of French wines, also helped Portuguese wine growers.

209. Between 1756 and 1760, port comprised 72 percent of the wine consumed in Great Britain. Jorge Borges de Macedo, *Problemas de história da indústria portuguesa no século XVIII* (Lisbon, 1963), 48; A. B. Wallis Chapman, "The Commercial Relations of England and Portugal, 1487–1807," *TRHS*, 3rd Series, I, 1907, 177; H. E. S. Fisher, *The Portugal Trade: A Study of Anglo-Portuguese Commerce, 1700–1770* (London: Methuen, 1971), 13–40.

210. Maxwell, 1995, 43.

211. See Bill M. Donovan, "Changing Perceptions of Social Deviance: Gypsies in Early Modern Portugal and Brazil," *Journal of Social History*, Vol. 26, No. 1, Autumn 1992, 33–53.

212. Schwarcz, 45.

213. Quoted in Donovan, 1996–97, 64. Alvára (court order) dated March 31, 1742.

214. Donovan, 1996–97, 63.

215. Ibid., 62.

216. Ibid., 63.

217. Schwarcz, 40.

218. *The Scots Magazine*, Vol. 17, November 1755, 561.

219. Arthur William Costigan, *Sketches of Society and Manners in Portugal*, Vol. 2 (of 2) (London, 1787), 29.

220. Quoted in Boxer, 1955, 730.

221. See José Luís Cardoso et al., *O Tratado de Methuen (1703) diplomacia, guerra, política e economia* (Lisbon: Livros Horizonte, 2003); A. D. Francis, *The Methuens of Portugal* (Cambridge: Cambridge University Press, 1977); and José Vicente Serrão, "O Quadro Económico," in José Mattoso, ed. *História de Portugal* (Lisbon: Editorial Estampa, 1992–93), Vol. 4 (of 8), *O Antigo Regime (1620–1807)*, 71–117.

222. A. R. Walford, *The British Factory in Lisbon and Its Closing Stages Ensuing upon the Treaty of 1810* (Lisbon: Instituto Britânico em Portugal, 1940), 20.

223. See ibid.; and Richard Lodge, "The British Factory at Lisbon," *Transactions of the Royal Historical Society*, 4th Series, Vol. 16 (London, 1933), 211–47; L. M. E. Shaw, *Trade, Inquisition and the English Nation in Portugal, 1650–1690* (Manchester: Carcanet, 1989); J. B. de Macedo, *Problemas de história da indústria portuguesa no século XVIII* (Lisbon: Associação Industrial Portuguesa, 1963); J. B. de Macedo, *A situação económico no tempo de Pombal: Alguns aspectos*, 2nd ed. (Lisbon: Moraes Editores, 1982); C. R. Boxer, "Brazilian Gold and British Traders in the First Half of the Eighteenth Century," *Hispanic American Historical Review*, Vol. 49, No. 3, August 1969; Fisher, *The Portugal Trade*; S. Sideri, *Trade and Power: Informal Colonialism in Anglo-Portuguese Relations* (Rotterdam: Rotterdam University Press, 1970); J. D. Tracy, *The Political Economy of Merchant Empires: State Power and World Trade, 1350–1750* (Cambridge: Cambridge University Press, 1991); and John Delaforce, *The Factory House at Oporto*, 2nd ed. (London: Christie's Wine Publications, 1983).

224. Costigan, 29.

225. Quoted in Charles R. Boxer, "Some Contemporary Reactions to the Lisbon Earthquake of 1755," *Revista da Faculdade de Letras,* Vol. 22, No. 1, 1956, 6 (from the correspondence of Benjamin Keene, the former British envoy to Portugal).

226. Birmingham, 2. See also Virgilio Noya Pinto, *O ouro brasileiro e o comércio anglo-português* (São Paulo, 1979); and Kenneth R. Maxwell, *Conflicts and Conspiracies: Brazil and Portugal, 1750–1808* (Cambridge: Cambridge University Press, 1973).

227. Historian Olwen Hufton is skeptical of the claims of Portuguese economic historians that Portugal found itself in a compromised economic position in relation to Britain. Olwen Hufton, *Europe: Privilege and Progress, 1730–1789* (Oxford: Blackwell, 2000), 194; Cheke, 12–13.

228. Isser Wolloch, *Eighteenth-Century Europe: Tradition and Progress, 1715–1789* (New York: W. W. Norton, 1982), 273. Wolloch refers to Portugal as a "small, backward state."

229. Donovan, 1996–97, 59; Fréderic Mauro and Geoffrey Parker, "Portugal," in *An Introduction to the Sources of European Economic History, 1500–1800* (London, 1977).

230. *The Gentleman's Magazine,* Vol. 25, December 1755, 556.

231. Domingues, 376.

232. Ibid., 377; Cheke, 47–48.

233. Quoted in Cheke, 46; quoted in Boxer, 1955, 731.

234. See Nuno Gonçalo Monteiro, *D. José* (Lisbon: Temas e Debates, 2008).

235. Ibid., 82.

236. David Erskine, ed., *Augustus Hervey's Journal: The Adventures Afloat and Ashore of a Naval Casanova* (London: Chatham, 2002; first published 1953), 179.

237. Maxwell, 1993, 106; see also Godinho.

238. ASV Portugallo, seg. 100, fol. 224v., October 8, 1755, in Angela Delaforce, 2002, 285.

239. Description of the Jubilee: *Gazeta de Lisboa,* No. 44, October 30, 1755 (Mafra, October 17, 1755), 351.

240. The Battle of the Monongahela occurred on July 16, 1755.

241. *Gazeta de Lisboa,* No. 43, October 23, 1755, dispatch from London, September 12, 1755, 339–42. The total number of British soldiers who were killed or captured was around eight hundred. The majority of British casualties were probably the result of friendly fire.

CHAPTER TWO

November 1, 1755

1. *The Boston Gazette,* No. 36, December 8, 1755.

2. *Philosophical Transactions of the Royal Society,* Vol. 49, 1755, 391–94; *The Scots Magazine,* Vol. 17, November 1755, 552–53; *Supplement to the Gentleman's Magazine,* 1755, 590; *The London Evening Post,* No. 4388, December 23–25, 1755; *The London Evening Post,* No. 4376, November 25–27, 1755.

3. *The Public Advertiser,* No. 6576, November 25, 1755, 2; Pedegache, 11. See also AHCML, FA-63, *Portugal aflito e conturbado . . . ,* 438–39.

4. *The Whitehall Evening Post,* No. 1522, November 25–27, 1755; *Supplement to the Gentleman's Magazine,* 1755, 587; *The Scots Magazine,* Vol. 18, January 1756, 39; *Philosophical Transactions of the Royal Society,* Vol. 49, 1755, 643; *Supplement to The Gentleman's Magazine,* 1755, 589; *The Scots Magazine,* Vol. 17, November–December 1756, 591–92. Pedegache reports that "ship captains, who found them-

selves at sea on November 1, 1755, assured me that thirty, forty, and sixty leagues out to sea . . . their ships suddenly" felt an extremely violent movement. 11; *Gazette d'Amsterdam*, No. 97, December 5, 1755.

5. Robert Muir-Wood and Arnaud Mignan, "A Phenomenological Reconstruction of the Mw9 November 1st 1755 Earthquake Source," in Mendes Victor (2009), 141.

6. The Soviet Union's Tsar Bomba was detonated on October 30, 1961, and released the equivalent of 50 megatons of TNT.

7. The magnitude of the Lisbon Earthquake is a matter of conjecture. Comparisons to other seismic events are based on damage to natural and human structures, the extent of the area affected, and the size of the tsunami generated. Carlos Sousa Oliveira, "Descrição do terramoto de 1755, sua extensão, causos e efeitos. O sismo. O tsunami. O incêndio," *1755: O grande terramoto de Lisboa* (Lisbon, 2005), 75.

8. Susan Elizabeth Hough, *Earthshaking Science: What We Know (and Don't Know) About Earthquakes* (Princeton, NJ: Princeton University Press, 2002), 1–23.

9. Bruce A. Bolt, *Earthquakes*, 5th ed. (New York: W. H. Freeman, 2003), 53–59; Boer and Sanders, 1–15.

10. C. S. Oliveira, "Review of the 1755 Lisbon Earthquake Based on Recent Analyses of Historical Observations," in *Historical Seismology: Interdisciplinary Studies of Past and Recent Earthquakes* (London: Springer, 2008), 278.

11. E. Buforn et al., "Seismotectonics of the Ibero-Maghrebian Region," *Techtonophysics*, Vol. 1/1995, 248, 247–61; Boer and Sanders, 95–98.

12. Maria Ana Baptista et al., "Constraints on the Source of the 1755 Lisbon Tsunami Inferred from Numerical Modeling of Historical Data," *Journal of Geodynamics*, Vol. 25, No. 2, 1998, 159–74; Maria Ana Baptista et al., "New Study of the 1755 Earthquake Source Based on Multi-Channel Seismic Survey Data and Tsunami Modeling," *Natural Hazards and Earth System Sciences*, Vol. 3, 2003, 333–40; Maria Ana Baptista et al., "The 1755 Lisbon Tsunami: Evaluation of the Tsunami Parameters," *Journal of Geodynamics*, Vol. 25, 1998, 143–57; S. P. Vilanova, C. F. Nunes, and J. F. B. D. Fonseca, "Lisbon 1755: A Case of Triggered Onshore Rupture?," *Bulletin of the Seismological Society of America*, Vol. 93, 2003, 2056–68; A. A. Udias et al., "Seismotectonics of the Azores-Alboran Region," *Tectonophysics*, Vol. 31, 1976, 259–89; A. C. Johnson, "Seismic Moment Assessment of Earthquakes in Stable Continental Regions—III. New Madrid 1811–1812, Charleston 1886 and Lisbon 1755," *Geophysical Journal International*, Vol. 126, 1996, 208–21; N. Zitellini et al., "The Quest for the Africa-Eurasia Plate Boundary West of the Strait of Gibraltar," *Earth and Planetary Science Letters*, Vol. 280, 2009, 13–50; Boer and Sanders, Chapter 5; Achim Kopf, "Die geologishe Ursache des Mega-Erdbebens vom Lissabon im Jahre 1755," in Gerhard Lauer and Thorsten Unger, eds., *Das Erdbeben von Lissabon und der Katastrophendiskurs im 18. Jahrhundert* (Göttingen: Wallstein Verlag, 2008), 188–202; Oliveira, 2005, 38–43; David K. Chester and Olivia K. Chester, "The Impact of Eighteenth-Century Earthquakes on the Algarve Region, Southern Portugal," *The Geographical Journal*, Vol. 176, No. 4, December 2010, 1–22; Roy Barkan, U. S. ten Brink, and J. Lin, "Far Field Tsunami Simulation of the 1755 Lisbon Tsunami: Implications for Tsunami Hazard to the US East Coast and the Caribbean," *Geology* 164, 2009, 109–22; Marc-André Gutscher, "What Caused the Great Lisbon Earthquake?," *Science*, Vol. 305, Issue 5688, 2004, 1247–48; R. A. Hindson et al., "Sedimentary Processes Associated with the Tsunami Generated by the 1755 Lisbon Earthquake on the Algarve Coast, Portu-

gal," *Physics and Chemistry of the Earth*, Vol. 21, No. 12, 1996, 57–63; D. Banerjee et al., "Scilly Isles, UK: Optical Dating of a Possible Tsunami Deposit from the 1755 Lisbon Earthquake," *Quaternary Science Reviews*, Vol. 20, 2001, 715–18; M. A. Gutscher, "The Great Lisbon Earthquake and the Tsunami of 1755: Lessons from the Recent Sumatra Earthquakes and the Possible Link to Plato's Atlantis," *European Review*, Vol. 14, No. 2, 2006, 181–91; Luís Alberto Mendes Victor, "Os grandes terramotos," in *1755: O grande terramoto de Lisboa*, 87–122.

13. Udias et al., 1976.

14. Baptista et al., 2003; Susana Vilanova and João Fonseca, "The 1755 Lisbon Earthquake and the Onshore LTV Fault," 2003; Gutscher, 2004; Barkan et al., 109–22; Chester and Chester, 2010, 5.

15. At a "Hafen [harbor] von Suaffa," *Beschreibung des Erdbebens, welches die Hauptstadt Lissabon und viele andere Städte in Portugall und Spanien theils ganz umgeworfen, theils sehr beschädigt hat*, Vol. 2 (of 3) (Danzig, 1756), 47–48 ("On a letter from Cádiz"). The unknown author of the *Beschreibung* is skeptical of this report.

16. Robert H. Brown, *Nature's Hidden Terror: Violent Nature Imagery and Social Change in Eighteenth-Century Germany* (Columbia, SC: Camden House, 1991), 36; Johann Rudolph Anton Piderit, *Freye Betrachtungen über das neuliche Erdbeben zu Lissabon* (Marburg, 1756).

17. *Gazeta de Lisboa*, No. 11, March 18, 1756, 87; ANTT, Manuscript No. 1229; *Gazeta de Lisboa*, No. 8, February 26, 1756, 64. The newspaper did caution that because the allegation had been made by "rustics" *(pessoas rusticas)* one had to make up one's own mind as to the truth of the account.

18. Quoted in Gaston Demaree et al., "Volcano Eruptions, Earth- & Seaquakes, Dry Fogs vs. Aristotle's *Meteorologica* and the Bible in the Framework of the Eighteenth Century, *Bull. Séanc. Acad. R. Sci. Outre-Mer,* 53 (2007–3), 346.

19. *Philosophical Transactions of the Royal Society*, Vol. 49, 1755, 413–14; *The Scots Magazine*, Vol. 18, March 1756, 127.

20. The Katla volcano erupted on October 17, 1755. There were many accounts of clouds and dust in the atmosphere over the Atlantic in the weeks that followed. Demaree et al., 337–59.

21. BG, AP 12363, Portal, 19; *Mercurio Histórico y Político*, January 1756, 14.

22. Fernando López de Amezua, "Carta philosophica sobre el terremoto, que se sentió en Madrid, y en toda esta peninsula el día primero de noviembre de 1755," Madrid?, 1755?, 2; *The Maryland Gazette*, No. 561, February 5, 1756, a letter from Cork dated November 14, 1755, arriving in Philadelphia.

23. *Sankt-Peterburgskie Vedomosti*, December 15, 1755 (Julian calendar), No. 100, report from Naples dated November 12, 1755.

24. ANTT, Ministério do Reino, Maço 638, Box 743, Vila Real District, Santa Velha parish; *Philosophical Transactions of the Royal Society*, Vol. 49, 1755, 416, Letter from the Hamburg consul, Mr. Stoqueler.

25. According to two reports, the water in the river basin began to swell ominously (evidence perhaps that several small tremors, imperceptible on land, may have preceded the large quake). First Report: "Yesterday the first of November, about nine o'clock in the Morning, I was told that a vast Multitude of People, surprized at the extraordinary swelling of the Tagus, were assembled on the Banks of that River. No sooner had the Person, who brought me this frightful News, done speaking, than I felt the floor shaking under my feet." *Letter from a Portuguese Officer to a*

Friend in Paris. Giving an Account of the late dreadful Earthquake by which the City of Lisbon was Destroyed (London: M. Cooper, 1755), 3–4. Second report: "He also said that the Tagus has had a considerable rise in the water level that had preceded the earthquake." Recueil Fontanieu, 351 (quoted in Demaree et al., 352); Pedegache, 6. This source suggests that the animals also became terrified in the wake of aftershocks. AHCML, FA-63, *Portugal aflito e conturbado* . . . , 433. This source from an earthquake eyewitness claims that one of the signs of an impending earthquake is that birds become frightened and animals run terrified from their holes. It may reflect what he experienced on November 1, 1755. Scientists are unsure what causes this activity.

26. Mury, 1992, 187.
27. Kendrick, 73–74; Pedro Norberto de Aucourt e Padilha and Francisco Luís Ameno. *Carta em que se mostra falsa a profecia do terremoto do primeiro de novembro de 1755* (Lisbon: Patriarcal de Francisco Luiz Ameno, 1756), 6–7.
28. Add. 69847, Richard Goddard, letter of February 10, 1756, f. 52; Letter from Mr. Braddock to the Rev. Sandby, Chancellor of the Diocese of Norwich, England, dated November 13, 1755, in Charles Davy, *Letters Addressed Chiefly to a Young Gentleman upon Subjects of Literature* . . . , Vol. 2 (of 2) (Bury St. Edmunds, UK: J. Rackham, 1787), 13; The temperature was "14 on the Reaumur scale," while the barometer read "27 inches and seven lines." Miguel Tibério Pedegache, *Nova e Fiel Relação que Experimentou Lisboa, e Todo Portugal no 1 De Novembro de 1755* (Lisbon: Officina de Manoel Soares, 1756), 3. The Celsius scale was not used until the late eighteenth century. AHCML, FA-63, *Portugal aflito e conturbado pello terremoto do anno de 1755*, 21; AHCML, FA-63, *Portugal aflito e conturbado* . . . , 23.
29. Chantal, 16–19.
30. Johann Jakob Moritz, *The Moritz Family Chronicle, November 1, 1755 (Mortiz'schen Familienchronik)*, transcribed and excerpted in Marion Ehrhardt, "Eine unbekannter deutscher Augenzeugenbericht über das Seebeben vor Lissabons Küste 1755," in Gerhard Lauer and Thorsten Unger, eds., *Das Erdbeben von Lissabon und der Katastrophendiskurs im 18. Jahrhundert* (Göttingen: Wallstein Verlag, 2008), 48. Sunrise calculated on the website of the Astronomical Applications Department, U.S. Naval Observatory.
31. AHCML, FA-63, *portugal aflito e conturbado* . . . , 22.
32. Rui Tavares, *O pequeno livro do grande terramoto*, 73; Chantal, 20. The 11 a.m. mass was favored by the Portuguese aristocracy.
33. AHCML, FA-63, *portugal aflito e conturbado* . . . , 21.
34. Chantal, 19.
35. AHCML, FA-63, *portugal aflito e conturbado* . . . , 125–27; BA, 51_V-10-11, Book II, Folios 152–53.
36. Nozes, 136.
37. *The London Magazine*, Vol. 24, December 1755, 587. Because "insults are frequently offered to Protestant strangers, if met in the streets [on All Saints' Day], most of the gentlemen of the English factory go the night before to their country houses, and do not return till the second of November, when everything is quiet. To this unhappy bigotry, which brings many of the country inhabitants to Lisbon to see the show, the great loss of the Portuguese, and, on the other hand, the preservation of the English, is said to be owing."
38. ANTT, Maço 638, Box 743, Santarém District, Formigais parish.

39. António Pereira de Figueiredo, *Commentario Latino e Portuguez Sobre o Terremoto e o Incêndio de Lisboa de que foi testemunha ocular seu autor, Pref. de Cândido dos Santos* (Lisbon: Officina de Miguel Rodrigues, 1756), 1; Nozes, 160–62; *The Gentleman's Magazine*, Vol. 18, March 1756, 128; AHCML, FA-63, *portugal aflito e conturbado* . . . , 24; *Beschreibung des Erdbebens* . . . , Vol. 1, 32; ANTT, Maço 638, Box 743, Leiria District, Pelmá parish. Many histories of the earthquake give 9:40 a.m. as the accepted starting time of the earthquake at Lisbon. They may be consulting Francisco Luís Pereira de Sousa's seminal *O terremoto do 1 de novembro de 1755 e um estudo demográfico*. In Sousa's "General description of the earthquake," on page 516, he is not providing his own estimation of the time but merely transcribing a single, undated manuscript of unknown provenance found in the Torre do Tombo (ANTT, Manuscrito da Livraria, No. 1229). Although the times given by eyewitnesses are extremely varied, I have chosen 9:45 as it is the time given by the watch-bearing Rev. Richard Goddard, Queen Mariana of Portugal, the British merchant Thomas Chase, the priest and anonymous author of *Portugal aflito and conturbado* . . . , and British consul Edward Hay. It should be noted that Pombal gave the time as 9:40 a.m. (AHU, Lisbon, Letter to the governor of Rio de Janeiro, Minas Gerais, and São Paulo, Gomes Freire de Andrade, April 14, 1756, Caixa 50, #5036).
40. Sousa, 1919–32, Vol. 3, 530.
41. AHCML, FA-63, *portugal aflito e conturbado* . . . , 407.
42. Sousa, 1919–32, Vol. 3, 873 (from a manuscript); "When some small tremors of the earth began, everyone knew at the beginning what they were as others that had previously occurred had not caused fear or damage. However we were soon deceived . . ." Maria Teresa de Andrade e Sousa, ed. "Subsídio para o estudo do terremoto de Lisboa de 1755," 1955, 9.
43. Mendonça, 92–93; Chester and Chester, 2010.
44. *An Account of the Late Dreadful Earthquake and Fire Which Destroyed the City of Lisbon, The Metropolis of Portugal*, 2nd ed. (Boston: Green & Russell, 1756), 8–9.
45. Ibid., 9.
46. Letter from Mr. Wolfall, Surgeon to James Parsons, M.D., November 18, 1755, *Philosophical Transactions of the Royal Society*, Vol. 49, 1755, 404.
47. *The Gentleman's Magazine*, Vol. 25, December 1755, 559–60.
48. Benjamin Keene claims that Count Perelada was "indisposed in Bed" when the earthquake struck and had "hastily put on his Nightgown to go into the Street" and was killed "the Moment he put his Foot out of his" house. TNA, SP 94/149, f. 237; Figueiredo, 1756, 10–11; Richard Lodge, ed., *The Private Correspondence of Sir Benjamin Keene* (Cambridge: Cambridge University Press, 1933), 434, footnote 1; BL, 94/149, f. 237.
49. Quoted in Macaulay, 1946, 270. The English College was a seminary founded in the seventeenth century to educate English priests for the future date when their country returned to the Catholic fold.
50. Figueiredo, 1756, 2.
51. *The London Evening-Post*, No. 4390, December 27–30, 1755; *The Whitehall Evening-Post*, No. 1531, December 16–18, 1755. Williamson and his family occupied the third floor. His "Chaise-Driver" perished in the earthquake.
52. Several people thought the second tremor was more violent than the first.
53. Figueiredo, 1756, 11–12.
54. *Die denckwürdigsten Geschichte* . . . , 26.

55. The length of each tremor is a matter of conjecture. My estimates are a composite of various accounts and should not be seen as definitive; see ANTT, Manuscrito da Livraria 1229, f. 51.

56. For this reason, some seismologists have speculated that the Lisbon quake may have comprised two or more separate earthquakes. J. M. Martínez Solares and A. López Arroyo, "The Great Historical 1755 Earthquake. Effects and Damage in Spain," *Journal of Seismology*, Vol. 8, 2004, 278; Athena R. Kolbe et al., "Mortality, Crime and Access to Basic Needs Before and After the Haiti Earthquake: A Random Survey of Port-au-Prince Households," *Medicine, Conflict and Survival*, Vol. 26, No. 4, 2010.

57. Boer and Sanders, 9–10.

58. Bolt, 19–24; Solares and Arroyo, 292.

59. Bolt, 22.

60. Pedegache, 20; *The Scots Magazine*, Vol. 18, February 1756, 93. Several commas have been changed in this quote.

61. A. Vuan et al., "Suboceanic Raleigh Waves in the 1755 Lisbon Earthquake," in Mendes-Victor, 2009, 283–95.

62. Boer, 9–10; ANTT: Manuscrito da Livraria, No. 1229, f. 51; AHCML, FA-63, *Portugal aflito e conturbado . . .*, 24.

63. As told to Mr. Braddock in Davy, Vol. 2, 28.

64. *The London Evening Post*, No. 4384, December 13–16, 1755. Many houses particularly on the periphery did escape significant damage. See Cardoso, "The Opportunity of a Disaster."

65. Richard Goddard was twenty-six or twenty-seven years old on November 1, 1755.

66. BL, Add. 69847, Letter #1. Richard Goddard's Lisbon journey is told in five letters. Numbered in order of the date that they were written for purposes of this book, Letters #1, #3, #4, and #5 (dated October 22, 1755, November 18, 1755, February 10, 1756, and March 30, 1756) reside in the Manuscripts Collection of the British Library (Add. 69847), while Letter #2 (dated November 7, 1755) can be found in the Swindon and Wiltshire History Centre, National Archives (1461/2732). Letters #3 and #4 are contemporaneous copies written by Richard Goddard. The recipient of Letter #3 is unknown, while Letter #4 was probably written to John Ivory Talbot.

67. BL, Add. 69847, Letter #3.

68. Ibid.

69. Ibid.

70. Letter of November 11, 1755, to his parents in Kassel, printed in *Physikalische Betrachtungen . . .*, 211.

71. Portal's manuscript is entitled "Historia da ruina da cidade de Lisboa cauzada pello espantozo terremoto e incendio, que reduzio a pó e cinza a melhor e maior parte desta infeliz cidade," BG (Biblioteca da Arte, Fundação Calouste Gulbenkian, Lisbon), AP 12363.

72. BG, AP 12363, Portal, 18–20. Portal dedicated his account to the Oratory of Saint Philip Neri.

73. Ibid., 20–21.

74. Ibid., 21–25.

75. Quoted in Macaulay, 1946, 268–69. The manuscript is in the possession of Syon House.

76. Macaulay, 1946, 269.

77. ASV, Carte Farnesiane 18, f. 18. Letter written in Italian to a religious brother and dated November 4, 1755. Transcriptions of a number of Acciaiuoli's letters can be found in Mons. Arnaldo Pinto Cardoso, "O terramoto de Lisboa (1755), Documentos do Arquivo do Vaticano," in *Revista de História das Ideias*, Vol. 18, 1996, 448–50.

78. ASV, Segretaria di Stato Portogallo 195, f. 177, reported by Monsignor Acciaiuoli; Figueiredo, 1756, 19.

79. Elias Nason, *Sir Charles Henry Frankland, Baronet: Boston in the Colonial Times* (Albany, NY: J. Munsell, 1865), 7–8, 15–16.

80. F. Marshall Bauer, *Marblehead's Pygmalion: Finding the Real Agnes Surriage* (Charleston, SC: History Press, 2010), 71.

81. Nason, 16.

82. Ibid., 37.

83. Ibid., 7–8, 15–16.

84. Gabinete de Estudos Olisiponenses (Câmara Municipal, Lisbon), GEL_MS_Mç_265, page 31.

85. The story presented here of Frankland's escape from the ruins is based on oral interviews of relatives conducted by his nineteenth-century biographer, Elias Nason. See Nason, 63–65. An undated manuscript in the Gabinete de Estudos Olisiponenses (Câmara Municipal, Lisbon) claims that Frankland jumped out of his coach as the earthquake began and was joined under a gateway by a woman before both were buried. It also states that he dug himself out from the rubble (GEL_MS_Mç_265, pages 30–31). A letter in the Warwickshire County archives written by a John Dobson describing the condition of Lisbon to Charles Mordaunt, December 15, 1755, states: "Sir Harry Frankland and his Lady were in a Post Chaise; The very Moment they got out of it, some Stones from the Houses killed the Mules and broke the Chaise" (Warwickshire Country Record Office, UK, CR1368, Vol. 5, 16). In two German histories of the earthquake, Frankland jumps out of his carriage and runs into a house that collapses on top of him. He is dug out of the rubble two days later. *Gesammelte Nachrichten . . .* , 35; *Neunte Relation von den erschrecklichen Erdbeben zu Lissabonn, Oder: Abdruck derjenigen Briefe, Wie selbe dieses grosse Unglück von verschiedenen Orten mit mehrern Umständen berichtet haben* (Breslau, 1755). "Charles Henry Frankland Diary, 1755–1767" (manuscript), Massachusetts Historical Society, Microfilm, P-363, Reel 4.4. An account in *The Whitehall Evening Post*, No. 1531, December 16–18, 1755, gives a slightly different version: "Several have been recovered from the Ruins, among whom is Sir Harry Frankland, who has been remarkably preserved: He was in his Chariot when the Earthquake began, and on observing the Ground to undulate, opened the Door, jumped out, and ran into the first House he saw open, which he had scarce entered before it fell down and buried him in the Ruins, from which he was providentially recovered unhurt."

86. AHCML, FA-63, *Portugal aflito e conturbado . . .* , 127–28; Mendonça, 119.

87. *The Public Advertiser*, No. 6576, November 25, 1755, 2.

88. Mendonça, 119.

89. *Die denckwürdigsten Geschichte . . .* , 32–33.

90. Sousa, 1919–32, 605; BG, AP 12363.

91. AHN (Archivo Histórico Nacional, Madrid), Estado (State Papers), 2512, partially transcribed in Caetano Beirão, "Descrição inédita do terramoto de 1755 como

o viu e viveu a rainha D. Maria Vitória," *Artes & Colecções*, Vol. 1, No. 2, July 1947), 3–4.

92. The National Archives of the UK (TNA); Public Record Office, State Papers (Portugal), SP 89-50, f. 124, Letter to Sir Thomas Robinson: Lisbon (November 19, 1755).

93. Bente Scavenius, *Den Fortryllede Have* (Copenhagen: Borgen 1992), 54–55; Ulla Kjær, *En virkeliggjort drøm Oplysningstiden illustreret ved Liselund* (Nationalmuseet, 2011), 20–21.

94. ML, Literary and Historical Manuscripts (LHMS), Acc. No. MA 4543, Letter from an unknown young man to his mother, December 15, 1755.

95. Johan Paludan and Hans Jacob Paludan, *Forsøg Til En Antiqvarisk, Historisk, Statistik Og Geographisk Beskrivelse Over Møen. Udgivet Efter Forfatterens Død*, Vol. 1 (Copenhagen, 1822), 474.

96. AAE (Archives des Affaires étrangères, Paris), Correspondance Politique 87, Portugal, ff. 224–25.

97. Emil Grüneberg, "Hamburgo e o terremoto de Lisboa de 1 de novembro de 1755," in *O Instituto Revista Scientífica e Literária*, Vol. 51, No. 1, January 1904, 55, originally published in the *Zeitschrift des Vereines für Hamburgische Geschichte*, Hamburg, 1855. The following German sources erroneously state that the Swedish and Dutch consuls had died in the disaster: *Beschreibung des Erdbebens . . .*, 19–20; *Gesammelte Nachrichten von dem Erdbeben der Staat Lissabon und anderer Orte* (Leipzig and Frankfurt, 1756), 13. A printed copy of the letter from November 4, 1755, can be found in the SH, Bestandnummer 111-1 Senat, Signatur Cl. VI, No. 7, Vol. 2, Fasc. 1. Proof that the Swedish consul survived can be found in Leos Müller, *Consuls, Corsairs, and Commerce: The Swedish Consular Service and Long-Distance Shipping, 1720–1815* (Stockholm: Uppsala Universitet, 2004), 80; and Leos Müller, "Swedish-Portuguese Trade and Swedish Consular Service, 1700–1800," in *A articulação do sal português aos circuitos mundiais—The Articulation of Portuguese Salt with Worldwide Routes: antigos e novos consumos. Past and New Consumption Trends* (Porto: University of Porto, 2008). The latter article states that there are no firsthand reports of the Lisbon Earthquake in the Swedish consular records (page 100). The Dutch consul's survival is mentioned in *The Scots Magazine*, Vol. 17, November 1755, 555.

98. BAP, 3053, 209, B. S. A. F. Recueil ou Pontefeuille de M. de Paulmy, Pièces imprimées et manuscrits sur le tremblement de terre de Lisbonne, 13 (Fol. 363) (division) 1755 "Extrait d'une lettre écrite de Lisbonne, par l'ambassadeur de France, le 24. november 1755, à Madrid."

99. GSP (Geheimes Staatsarchiv Preussischer Kulturbesitz, Berlin), I. HA, Geheimer Rat, Rep. 11, Auswärtige Beziehungen, Nr. 8518 (November 3, 1755).

100. TNA, SP 89/50, f. 119 (back).

101. GRO, D2700/W/4, Letter, November 8, 1755.

102. Quoted in Macaulay, 1946, 274.

103. Letter dated December 30, 1755, in *Physikalische Betrachtungen von den Erdbeben . . .*, 214–15.

104. Jàcome Ratton, *Recordações de Jacome Ratton sobre occurrências do seu tempo em Portugal de maio de 1747 a setembro 1810* (Lisbon: Fenda Edições, 2007), 30.

105. *The Gentleman's Magazine*, Vol. 83, February 1813, 106.

106. Ibid.

107. Mr. Braddock in Davy, Vol. 2, 16; BL, Add. 69847, Letter #4.

108. ML, Acc. No. MA 4543, Letter from an unknown young man to his mother, December 15, 1755.

109. AHCML, FA-63, *Portugal aflito e conturbado* . . . , 27–28.

110. *The Gentleman's Magazine*, Vol. 25, December 1755, 558.

111. *Physikalische Betrachtungen* . . . , 212–13.

112. Quoted in Macaulay, 1946, 274.

113. *The Gentleman's Magazine*, Vol. 26, January 1756, 67.

114. Pedegache, 4.

115. BA, Ms. Av. 54-XI-16, no. 121.

116. AHCML, FA-63, *Portugal aflito e conturbado* . . . , 47.

117. Ratton, 30–31.

118. See drawing of the Cidade Baixa in Brée, 30.

119. Francisco Luís Pereira de Sousa. *Efeitos do terremoto de 1755 nas construcções de Lisboa* (Lisbon: Imprensa Nacional, 1909); M. San-Payo et al., "Contributions to the Damage Interpretation During the 1755 Lisbon Earthquake," in Luiz A. Mendes-Victor et al., eds., *The 1755 Lisbon Earthquake Revisited* (Dordrecht: Springer, 2009), 304–7.

120. BG, AP 12363, Portal, 3.

121. Boer and Sanders, 15. This was observed by the eyewitness Miguel Tibério Pedegache, who provides an explanation.

122. AHCML, FA-63, *Portugal aflito e conturbado* . . . , 212–13. The designation of "completely destroyed" is subjective. For a detailed list and discussion of individual churches and structures destroyed in the earthquake, see BG, AP 12363, Portal, Chapters 3–5; Mendonça, 131–33; and Figueiredo, 1756, 12–17.

123. Mendonça, 131–33.

124. BG, AP 12363, Portal, 11–12; see Manuel José da Cunha Brandão, *As ruínas do Carmo* (Lisbon: Typ. da Casa da Moeda e Papel Sellado, 1908); Castro, 2nd ed., Vol. 31762–63, 409; Sousa, Vol. 3, 633–41.

125. BG, AP 12363, Portal, 11.

126. Castro, 2nd edition, Vol. 3, Part 5, 395; BG, AP 12363, Portal, 30.

127. BG, AP 12363, Portal, 10.

128. Ibid., 31.

129. Mendonça, 127.

130. BL, Add. 69847, Letter #4.

131. Castro, 2nd edition, Vol. 3, Part 5, 348.

132. BL, Add. 69847, Letter #4.

133. The painting, João Glama Ströberle, *Cena de desolação junto das ruinas da desparecida Igreja de Sta. Catarina* or *Alegoria ao terramoto de 1755 na cidade de Lisboa* (c. 1760), resides in the Museu Nacional de Arte Antiga in Lisbon. See Vítor Serrão, "1755 e as imagens de Lisboa: a *Alegoria ao terramoto* de João Glama Stromberle," in Buescu and Cordeiro, 191–205. Santa Catarina Square was known as the *bairro* (neighborhood) of painters in Lisbon. Serrão, 204. For an overview of the damage the church sustained, see BG, AP 12363, Portal, 37; Castro, 2nd ed., Vol. 3, 240.

134. Letter from James O'Hara to his sister, dated November 12, 1755, in George Anne Bellamy, *An Apology for the Life of George Anne Bellamy, Late of Covent Garden Theatre*, Vol. 6 (of 6) (London: J. Bell, 1785), 59.

135. *Two Very Circumstantial Accounts of the Late Dreadful Earthquake of Lisbon*, reprint (Boston: D. Fowler, 1756), 4. Mr. Farmer is the author.

136. Mendonça, 115.

137. Nozes, 207.

138. GRO, D2700/W/4, Letter, November 8, 1755.

139. *Physikalische Betrachtungen . . .*, 215–16.

140. Macaulay, 1946, 273–74.

141. Quoted in ibid., 274.

142. *Two Very Circumstantial Accounts . . .*, 1756, 11.

143. Bellamy, 62; *Supplement to the Gentleman's Magazine*, 1755, 591.

144. Mendonça, 116.

145. Pedegache, 5.

146. Letter from Mr. Wolfall, Surgeon to James Parsons, M.D., November 18, 1755, *Philosophical Transactions of the Royal Society*, Vol. 49, 1755, 403–4.

147. *An Account of the Late Dreadful Earthquake and Fire . . .*, 1756, 13. This observation was made after the arrival of the tsunami.

148. Ibid.

149. AHCML, FA-63, *Portugal aflito e conturbado . . .*, 42–43.

150. *A Letter from a Portuguese Officer . . .*, 5; "This day that seemed so similar to that which St. John describes to us in his Apocalypse," AHCML, FA-63, *Portugal aflito e conturbado . . .*, 27.

151. *A Letter from a Portuguese Officer . . .*, 7. The provenance of this letter is unclear and may be an amalgam of several accounts.

152. *The Gentleman's Magazine*, Vol. 83, April 1813, 316–17.

153. *The Gentleman's Magazine*, Vol. 83, February 1813, 110.

154. Revelation 20:10.

155. Davy, Vol. 2, 23–24.

156. AHCML, FA-63, *Portugal aflito e conturbado . . .*, 31; Maria Teresa de Andrade e Sousa, "Subsídio para o estudo do terremoto de Lisboa de 1755 Manuscrito Coevo," Lisbon, November 1755, 11.

157. BA, Ms. Av. 54-XI-16, No. 121.

158. Mendonça, 138.

159. AHCML, FA-63, *Portugal aflito e conturbado*, 34–35.

160. MHS, Microfilm, P-363, Reel 4.4, "Charles Henry Frankland Diary, 1755–1767."

161. BL, Add. 69847, Letter #3.

162. BL, Add. 69847, Letters #3 and #4.

163. BL, Add. 69847, Letters #3 and #4.

164. BL, Add. 69847, Letter #4.

165. Ibid. See Mark Molesky, "The Vicar and the Earthquake: Conflict, Controversy, and a Christening During the Great Lisbon Disaster of 1755," *E-Journal of Portuguese History*, Vol. 10, No. 2, Winter 2012.

166. *The Gentleman's Magazine*, Vol. 83, February 1813, 106–7.

167. Ibid., 107.

168. Ibid.

169. Ibid., 107–8.

170. BG, AP 12363, Portal, 40; ANTT, Manuscritos da Livraria, No. 1229; Moreira de Mendonça, 131; Castro, 2nd edition, Vol. 3, Part 5, 266.

171. BG, AP 12363, Portal, 63; Rua Nova dos Mercadores and the Rua do Capelão, Pereira de Sousa, 679.

172. Ibid., 701.

173. Biblioteca da Ajuda (Lisbon), 51_V-10 and 11, Book No. II, Folios 152–53.

174. Sousa, 1919–32, footnote 3, 698. This quaint story is reported as hearsay.

175. *Gazeta de Lisboa*, No. 11, March 18, 1756, 85.

176. Sousa, 1919–32, 505; Dic. Geograp. (Memórias Paroquias), Tomo IX, ff. 1171. See also Olga Bettencourt, ed., et al., *Cascais em 1755 do terramoto à reconstrução* (Cascais, Portugal: Câmara Municipal, 2005); Sousa, 1919–32, 548.

177. Mendonça 149–50.

178. Ibid., 150.

179. Ibid., 150–51; *Gazeta de Lisboa*, No. 6, February 6, 1756, 47–48.

180. Mendonça, 151.

181. *Physikalische Betrachtungen von den Erdbeben . . .* , 180–81.

182. *Die denckwürdigsten Geschichte . . .* , 34; *Beschreibung des Erdbebens . . .* , 25. See *1755 terramoto no Algarve* (Faro, Portugal: Centro Ciência Viva do Algarve, 2005); and Chester and Chester, 2010.

183. *Gazeta de Lisboa*, No. 27, November 20, 1755, 375 (printed erroneously as page "535").

184. *Gazeta de Lisboa*, No. 27, November 20, 1755, 377–78; Chester and Chester, 2010, 357–58.

185. Mendonça, 154–55.

186. Ibid., 154.

187. *Gazeta de Lisboa*, No. 31, August 5, 1756, 245–46.

188. Ibid. The article states that the lecture concerned "Psalm 112," which appears to be an error.

189. *Philosophical Transactions of the Royal Society*, Vol. 49, 1755, 422.

190. *The Gentleman's Magazine*, Vol. 25, December 1755, 562–63; *Philosophical Transactions of the Royal Society*, Vol. 49, 1755, 419–20.

191. There is a variety of opinion on this matter. See Mendes-Victor et al., "Earthquake Damage Scenarios in Lisbon for Disaster Preparedness," in B. E. Tucker et al., *Issues in Urban Earthquake Risk* (Dordrecht, 1994), 265–85, 269; Rio et al., 2006; F. Tedim Pedrosa and J. Conçalves, "The 1755 Earthquake in the Algarve (South of Portugal): What Would Happen Nowdays?," *Advances in Geoscience*, Vol. 14, 2008, 62; Chester and Chester, 2010, 15; Gutscher, 2004, 1247–48; and C. S. Oliveira, "Review of the 1755 Lisbon Earthquake Based on Recent Analyses of Historical Observations," in *Historical Seismology*, Vol. 2, 2008, 297. Tsunami deposits and Roman records suggest that a powerful earthquake visited southwest Iberia in around 200 BC. Gutscher, 2006, 181.

192. United States Geological Survey (USGS) Earthquake Hazards Program website (accessed May 2011): http://earthquake.usgs.gov/learn/glossary/?termID=150.

193. See the United States Geological Survey (USGS) Earthquake Hazards Program website: http://earthquake.usgs.gov/earthquakes/world/10_largest_world .php; Hiroo Kanamori, "The Energy Release of Great Earthquakes," *Journal of Geophysical Research*, Res. 82, 1977, 2981–87; Jeffrey Park et al., "Earth's Free Oscillations Excited by the 26 December 2004 Sumatra-Andaman Earthquake," *Science*, 308, 2005, 1139–44.

194. Boer and Sanders, 23.

195. Ibid., 34–40; Ari Ben-Menahem, "Four Thousand Years of Seismicity along the Dead Sea Rift," *Journal of Geophysical Research* 96, No. B12, November 10, 1991, 20, 195–216.

196. Boer and Sanders, 45–64.

197. Ammianus Marcellinus, *The Later Roman Empire (A.D. 354–378)*, Book 26 (Mid-

dlesex: Penguin, 1986), 333. See also Edward Gibbon, *Decline and Fall of the Roman Empire*, Chapter 26; Gavin Kelly, "Ammianus and the Great Tsunami," *The Journal of Roman Studies*, 94, 2004, 141–67; and Stathis C. Stiros, "The 8.5+ Magnitude, AD 365 Earthquake in Crete: Coastal Uplift, Topography Changes, Archaeological and Historical Signature," *Quaternary International*, Vol. 216, Nos. 1–2, April 1, 2010, 54–63.

198. Stathis C. Stiros, "The AD 365 Crete Earthquake and Possible Seismic Clustering During the Fourth to Sixth Centuries AD in the Eastern Mediterranean: A Review of Historical and Archaeological Data," *Journal of Structural Geology*, Vol. 23, 2001, 549.

199. Mohamed Reda Sbeinati et al., "The Historical Earthquakes of Syria: An Analysis of Large and Moderate Earthquakes from 1365 B.C. to 1900 A.D.," *Annals of Geophysics*, Vol. 48, 2005, 347–35.

200. Jian-Jun Hou et al., "Geomorphological Observations of Active Faults in the Epicentral Region of the Huaxian Large Earthquake in 1556 in Shaanxi Province, China," *Journal of Structural Geology*, Vol. 20, No. 5, May 14, 1998, 549–57.

201. Quoted in Chabbar Abdelaziz, "Os efeitos do terramoto de Lisboa em Marracos 1 de November de 1755," in *1755: O grande terramoto de Lisboa*, Vol. 1, Descrições (Lisbon: FLAD and Público, 2005), 269, from an eight-page pamphlet originally published in Seville.

202. The figure of 750 mph was calculated by determining the time it took for the earthquake to travel from Lisbon to Madrid: 25 minutes. The distance between the two capitals: 312 miles.

203. The best account of the 1755 earthquake's impact in Spain is José Manuel Martínez Solares, *Los efectos en España del terremoto de Lisboa (1 de noviembre de 1755)* (Madrid: Instituto Geográfico Nacional, 2001).

204. *Relación Verídica, del Terremoto, y Agitación de el Mar, Acacido en la Cuidad de Ayamonte, El día primero del mes de Noviembre de este año de 1755* (Cádiz: Real de Marina, 1755–56?), 3; AHN, Estado, 3183, Mayor (Alcalde Mayor) Don Bartolomé Ramos Dávila.

205. AHN, Estado, 3183, Governor Juan de O'Brien.

206. BL, IOR: MSS EUR E313/12, "Earthquake in Lisbon," Anonymous, presumably to his uncle, dated "Cádiz 25 November 1755," 1–2.

207. *Philosophical Transactions of the Royal Society*, Vol. 49, 1755, 425; *Gazeta de Lisboa*, No. 16, November 13, 1755, 367; AHN, Estado, 3183.

208. Charles F. Walker, *Shaky Colonialism: The 1746 Earthquake-Tsunami in Lima, Peru, and Its Long Aftermath* (Durham, NC: Duke University Press, 2008), 91.

209. AHN, Estado, 3183.

210. Ibid.

211. Ibid., Report by Diego de Robles y Acuña.

212. *The London Evening Post*, No. 4383, December 16–18, 1755.

213. AHN, Estado, 3183, Royal official *(intendente)* Alberto de Suelbe; AHN, Estado, 3173, Governor Diego Adrosioriz.

214. *Completa Relación del Assombroso Terremoto, que ha padecido la Ciudad de Sevilla en el día de Todos Santos . . .* , Third Part (Seville, 1755?).

215. *The Maryland Gazette*, No. 573, April 29, 1756.

216. *Gazeta de Lisboa*, No. 46, November 13, 1755, 364–66; José Manuel Martínez Solares and Alfonso López Arroyo, "O terramoto de 1755 em Espanha," in *1755: O grande terramoto de Lisboa*, 243; Solares and Arroyo, 279.

217. *The Maryland Gazette*, No. 573, April 29, 1756.

218. Ibid.

219. Israel, 2012, 45.

220. *Gaceta de Madrid*, No. 44, November 4, 1755, 351–52; *Philosophical Transactions of the Royal Society*, Vol. 49, 1755, 423.

221. *Philosophical Transactions of the Royal Society*, Vol. 49, 1755, 423.

222. *Gaceta de Madrid*, No. 44, November 4, 1755, 351–52; *Gazeta de Lisboa*, No. 16, November 13, 1755, 361. Reference to bells in quote of the Duke of Alba from Diego Téllez Alarcia, "El Impacto del Terremoto de Lisboa en España," in Ana Cristina Araújo et al., *O terramoto de 1755: Impactos históricos* (Lisbon: Livros Horizonte, 2007), 79. *The Scots Magazine*, Vol. 17, November 1755, 554.

223. *Gaceta de Madrid*, No. 44, November 4, 1755, 352.

224. AHN, Estado 2507, 137, Letter dated November 3, 1755.

225. *Gaceta de Madrid*, No. 44, November 4, 1755, 351–52; *Philosophical Transactions of the Royal Society*, Vol. 49, 1755, 424; *The Scots Magazine*, Vol. 17, November 1755, 553–54; *Gazeta de Lisboa*, No. 16, November 13, 1755, 362.

226. Solares, 2001, 85–92.

227. AHN, Estado, 2507, Letter dated November 18, 1755.

228. These records can be found in the AHN, Estado, 2909, 3173, 3183 (Microfilm) and in the Real Academia de Historia (Madrid).

229. Solares, 2001, 73–74.

230. Ibid., 31–32.

231. Solares and Arroyo, 278; Diego Téllez Alarcia, "El impacto del terremoto de Lisboa en España," in Ana Cristina Araújo et al., *O Terramoto de 1755: Impactos históricos* (Lisbon: Livros Horizonte, 2007), 79. See also Agustín Udías and Alfonso López Arroyo, "The Lisbon Earthquake of 1755 in Spanish Contemporary Authors," in Luiz A. Mendes-Victor et al., eds., *The 1755 Lisbon Earthquake: Revisited*, 7–24.

232. *The Whitehall Evening Post*, Postscript, No. 1523, November 27–29, 1755.

233. Alexis Perrey, *Mémoire sur les tremblements de terre ressentis en France, en Belgique et en Hollande, depuis le quatrième siècle de l'ère chrétienne jusqu'à nos jours (1843 inclusiv.)* (1844), 40; *The Scots Magazine*, Vol. 17, December, 1755, 554; Reid, 58.

234. E. J. B. Rathery, *Journal and Memoirs of the Marquis d'Argenson*, Vol. 2 (of 2) (Boston: Hardy, Pratt & Co., 1901), 340.

235. For an account of the earthquake in Neuchâtel, see *Philosophical Transactions of the Royal Society*, Vol. 49, 1755, 436–37; Reid, 58; *The Scots Magazine*, Vol. 18, January 1756, 39; *The Whitehall Evening Post*, No. 1524, November 29–December 2, 1755.

236. *Die denckwürdigsten Geschichte . . .* , 80.

237. *Beschreibung des Erdbebens . . .* , Vol. 1 (of 3) (Danzig, 1756), 30.

238. *Philosophical Transactions of the Royal Society*, Vol. 49, 1755, 396–97; Hans Woerle, *Der Erschutterungsbezirk des grossen Erdbebens zu Lissabon* (Munich, 1900), 61. This source mentions shocks being felt at The Hague, *The Scots Magazine*, Vol. 17, December 1755, 553.

239. *Die denckwürdigsten Geschichte . . .* , 61–63.

240. *Philosophical Transactions of the Royal Society*, Vol. 49, 1755, 432–36. For a reference to the earthquake in Sweden and Norway, see *Supplement to the Gentleman's Magazine*, 1755, 589.

241. *The Scots Magazine*, Vol. 17, December 1755, 592–93; *Gazette de Leyde*, No. 94, November 25, 1755; *Gazette d'Amsterdam*, November 25, 1755, from a letter from

Angra, Azores, dated November 9, 1755, written by Mathias Pires, a clerk of the English merchant, Mr. Samuel Montaigu, *Journal œconomique, ou Mémoires, notes et avis sur les arts, l'agriculture, le commerce* . . . (Paris: Antoine Boudet, February 1756), 149.

242. *The Maryland Gazette*, No. 561, February 5, 1756.

243. *Philosophical Transactions of the Royal Society*, Vol. 49, 1755, 360, 365–67, 393–94, 398–402. Also for Cork, see *Supplement to the Gentleman's Magazine*, 1755, 590; and the German source "Nieder-Elbe den 5. December" in *Dritte Relation von den erschrecklichen Erdbeben zu Lissabon* (Breslau, 1755).

244. Reid, 62–65. Harry Fielding Reid had several professors examine those sources (*Boston Gazette, Connecticut Gazette, New-York Mercury, New-York Gazette, Pennsylvania Gazette*, etc.) in the early twentieth century.

245. Mendonça, 159–60. For a discussion of the European and Arabic sources, see Chabbar Abdelaziz, "Os efeitos do terramoto de Lisboa em Marracos 1 de novembro de 1755," in *1755: O grande terramoto de Lisboa*, Vol. 1, Descrições (Lisbon: FLAD and Público, 2005).

246. Quoted in Abdelaziz, 270. See also Levret, 83–94; and Giovanna Moratti et al., "The 1755 'Meknes' Earthquake (Morocco): Field Data and Geodynamic Implications," *Journal of Geodynamics*, Vol. 36, 2006, 305–22.

247. Quoted in Abdelaziz, 274.

248. *The Scots Magazine*, Vol. 18, January 1756, 41. This is undoubtedly an exaggeration.

249. Abdelaziz, 271–72. This is probably an exaggeration.

250. *The Gentleman's Magazine*, Vol. 26, January 1756, 7–8.

251. Ibid., 7.

252. Quoted in Abdelaziz, 278; *The Scots Magazine*, Vol. 18, January 1756, 41.

253. Walter C. Dudley and Min Lee, *Tsunami*, 2nd ed. (Honolulu: University of Hawai'i Press, 1998), 92–93; Solares and Arroyo, 2004, 288–90; Reid, 66.

254. Robert Muir-Wood and Arnaud Mignan, "A Phenomenological Reconstruction of the Mw9 November 1st 1755 Earthquake Source," in Mendes Victor, 2009, 129.

255. *Supplement to the Gentleman's Magazine*, 1755, 590; *The Scots Magazine*, Vol. 17, December 1755, 593.

256. *Philosophical Transactions of the Royal Society*, Vol. 49, 1755, 363.

257. Ibid., 361. Mills says this occurred "between eleven and twelve o'clock" in the morning.

258. *The Scots Magazine*, Vol. 17, December, 1755, 593–94; *Philosophical Transactions of the Royal Society*, Vol. 49, 1755, 389–91; *Philosophical Transactions of the Royal Society*, Vol. 49, 1755, 387–89.

259. *The Scots Magazine*, Vol. 17, December, 1755, 554.

260. *Die denckwürdigsten Geschichte* . . . , 80.

261. *The Scots Magazine*, Vol. 17, December, 1755, 553; *Supplement to the Gentleman's Magazine*, 1755, 589; *The Public Advertiser*, No. 6576, November 25, 1755.

262. *Philosophical Transactions of the Royal Society*, Vol. 49, 1755, 552.

263. *Die denckwürdigsten Geschichte* . . . , 62–63; *The Whitehall Evening Post*, No. 1529, December 11–13, 1755.

264. Ibid., 63–74.

265. Ibid., 74–75.

266. *The Scots Magazine*, Vol. 17, December, 1755, 553; *Supplement to the Gentleman's Magazine*, 1755, 588–89.

267. *Die denckwürdigsten Geschichte* . . . , 77–78.

268. Ibid., 76.
269. *Beschreibung des Erdbebens* . . . , Vol. 1 (of 3), 31.
270. Reid, 75.

CHAPTER THREE

An Unexpected Horror

The chapter epigraph is from Ângelo Pereira, Preface and Notes, *O terra-moto de 1755: Narrativa de uma testemunha ocular* (Lisbon: Livraria Fernin, 1953), 12. See also "II Relato" in Fernando Guedes, *O livro e a leitura em Portugal subsídios para a sua história séculos XVIII e XIX* (Lisbon: Editorial Verbo, 1987), 252–57.

1. Mendonça, 114.
2. Bellamy, 62; quote from a letter in *The London Evening Post*, No. 4384, December 13–16, 1755.
3. *Two Very Circumstantial Accounts* . . . , 4. All along the riverbank, thousands of earthquake survivors who had fled the crumbling city in the hope of securing river passage to Belém, Alcântara, and other locations throughout the country-side began to wonder whether they had in fact escaped "their Share of Danger." AHCML, FA-63, *Portugal aflito e conturbado* . . . , 53–55; BL, Add. 69847. For half an hour, ship captains had taken survivors on board and ferried them to "Belém, Alcântara . . . and their *quintas* and houses in the countryside." Goddard letter, February, 10, 1756.
4. Since the epicenter of the earthquake has not been identified, the length of the fault is not known. According to scientists, it stretched anywhere from between fifty to six hundred kilometers along the ocean floor.
5. http://wcatwc.arh.noaa.gov/characteristics.htm; Bruce Parker, *The Power of the Sea* (New York: Palgrave Macmillan, 2010), 133–38, 156–57; Bolt, 195–203; Dudley and Lee, 60–61, 90–91.
6. Parker, 136–38; Dudley and Lee, 61–62. Unlike S waves, P waves travel through water. Bruce A. Bolt, *Earthquakes*, 5th ed. (New York: W. H. Freeman, 2004), 20; Pedegache, 11.
7. National Oceanography Centre, Southampton (UK); http://www.noc.soton.ac.uk /gg/research/geohazards/lisbon_quake.php; R. Wynn, "The 1755 Lisbon Disaster: Earthquake, Tsunami and Turbidity Currents," *Ocean Zone*, Southampton Ocean-ography Centre, 2001, No. 5, 7; Douglas G. Masson et al., "Seismic Triggering of Landslides and Turbidity Currents Offshore Portugal," *Geochemistry Geophysics Geosystems*, Vol. 12, Issue 12, December 2011.
8. Dudley and Lee, 91; Parker, 138; AHCML, FA-63, *Portugal aflito e conturbado* . . . , 55. For a mention of how people are attracted to a tsunami's receding waters, see José Manuel Martínez Solares and Alfonso López Arroyo, "O terramoto de 1755 em Espanha," in *1755: O grande terramoto de Lisboa*, 244.
9. Farmer, 4; Bolt, 200–203.
10. Johann Jakob Moritz, *Mortiz'schen Familienchronik (The Moritz Family Chronicle, November 1, 1755)*, transcribed and excerpted in Ehrhardt, 47–50. One German account relates the appearance of a whirlwind *("Wirbelwind")* on the Tagus shortly before the disaster. *Beschreibung des Erdbebens* . . . , Vol. 1 (of 3) (Danzig, 1756), 16.

11. Excerpt from Moritz, *Moritz'schen Familienchronik*, in Ehrhardt, 47–50.
12. Ibid., 50–51.
13. *The London Evening Post*, No. 4384, December 13–16, 1755; Dudley and Lee, 93–97.
14. AHCML, FA-63, *portugal aflito e conturbado . . .*, 356.
15. Related by Mr. Braddock in Davy, Vol. 2, 33.
16. AHCML, FA-63, *Portugal aflito e conturbado . . .*, 361–62.
17. Quoted in Olga Bettencourt, ed., et al., *Cascais em 1755: Do terramoto à reconstrução* (Cascais, Portugal: Câmara Municipal, 2005), 18–19.
18. *The London Evening Post*, No. 4384, December 13–16, 1755.
19. AHCML, FA-63, *Portugal aflito e conturbado . . .*, 359–60.
20. The merchant, Mr. Farmer, states that "about Belem, near the Mouth of the River, the Water rose Forty Feet in an Instant; and had it not been for the great Bay, to receive and spread the great Flux, the low Part of the City must have been under Water: For as it was, it came up to the Houses, and drove the People to the Hills." *Two very Circumstantial Accounts . . .*, 4. The estimate of fifteen to twenty come from several sources, Nozes, 44, 208.
21. BL, Add. 69847, February 10, 1756.
22. Bellamy, 62, James O'Hara to his sister, November 12, 1755.
23. *The London Evening Post*, No. 4384, December 13–16, 1755.
24. BL, Add. 69847, February 10, 1756.
25. Quoted in A. Neri, "Uno scampato dal terremoto di Lisbona," in L. T. Belgrano and A. Neri, eds., *Giornale Ligustico di Archeologia, Storia, e Letteratura* (Genoa: R. Instituto Sordo-Muti, 1887), 67. The original manuscript copy of this letter could not be found in the Genoese State Archives.
26. *The Gentleman's Magazine*, Vol. 83, April 1813, 315.
27. Marginalia in a copy of Mendonça's *Historia universal dos terremotos . . .*, NYPL. See Mark Molesky, "A New Account of the Lisbon Earthquake: Marginalia in Joachim José Moreira de Mendonça's *História universal dos terremotos*," *Portuguese Studies*, Vol. 26, No. 2, September 15, 2010, 236. There are some sources which state that very few if any ships were lost in the Tagus. See British consul Edward Hay's account.
28. Pedegache, 4.
29. *The Gentleman's Magazine*, Vol. 25, December 1755, 561. The Genoese consul, Ferdinando Aniceto Vigánego, also mentions that the timber from the royal arsenal was strewn across an area of "six or seven leagues." *Relazione dal Console Viganego alla Signoria Genovese*, in Guido Battelli, "Il terremoto di Lisbona nelle memorie degli scrittori italiani contemporanei" (Coimbra: Coimbra Editora, 1929), 14.
30. ASV, Secretaria Segreta Portogallo, 231.
31. Frederic Christian Sternleuw, "1755 Breve testemunho dum sueco," Instituto Ibero-Americano, Gothenburg, Sweden (Lisbon: Casa Portuguesa, 1958), 14–15, 18–19.
32. Sternleuw, 16–19. It is possible that he is discussing the Terreiro do Paço, as another witness saw a boat deposited there and the water never reached the Rossio.
33. *The London Evening Post*, No. 4384, December 13–16, 1755.
34. Mr. Braddock in Davy, Vol. 2, 26.
35. Ibid., 26–27.
36. *Philosophical Transactions of the Royal Society*, Vol. 49, 1755, 412.
37. *An Account of the Late Dreadful Earthquake and Fire . . .*, 1756, 12.

38. AHCML, FA-63, *Portugal aflito e conturbado* . . . , 56.

39. BL, Add. 69847, Goddard letter, February 10, 1756.

40. Quoted in Baptista et al., "The 1755 Lisbon Tsunami," 1998, 143–157, from *Nueva Relacíon de lo Acoecido en la Ciudad de Lisboa* . . . (Seville: Imprenta de Joseph de Navarro, 1755).

41. AHCML, FA-63, *Portugal aflito e conturbado* . . . , 55.

42. José de Oliveira Trovão e Sousa, *Carta em que hum amigo dá noticia a outro do lamentavel successo de Lisboa* (Coimbra, 1755), 3. This early account of the earthquake disaster has been much criticized for its accuracy.

43. Pedegache, 4.

44. *Mercurio Histórico y Político*, January 1756, 15.

45. See Paulo Henriques, Introduction, *Lisboa antes do terramoto grande vista da cidade entre 1700 & 1725* (Lisbon; Gótica, 2004).

46. AHU, ACL, CU, 17, Cx. 49, D. 4937.

47. AHCML, FA-63, *Portugal aflito e conturbado* . . . , 251.

48. BNP, Fundo Geral, No. 1772, ff. 42–56.

49. AHCML, FA-63, *Portugal aflito e conturbado* . . . , 253.

50. Manuscript in Sousa, 1955, 10.

51. AHCML, FA-63, *Portugal aflito e conturbado* . . . , 250–51.

52. Mark Molesky, 2010, 240–41; *The Whitehall Evening Post*, No. 1529, December 11–13, 1755; BG, AP 12363, Portal, 7.

53. BG, AP 12363, Portal, 7.

54. Mr. Braddock in Davy, Vol. 2, 29.

55. *Supplement to the Gentleman's Magazine*, 1755, 593.

56. Nozes, 152; BNP, Fundo Geral, No. 1772; *The Scots Magazine*, Vol. 18, February 1756, 93.

57. José Acursio de Tavares, *Verdade Vindicada, ou Resposta a Huma Carta escrita de Coimbra, em que se dá noticia do lamantavel successo de Lisboa no dia de 1. de Novembro de 1755* (Lisbon: Miguel Manescal da Costa, 1756), 21–22. There is no report that Tavares and his pearl diver ever found any bodies on the sunken quay.

58. BL, Add. 69847, February 10, 1756.

59. Mr. Braddock in Davy, Vol. 2, 29.

60. Mendonça, 134.

61. Charles Lyell hypothesizes that the quay fell into a subterranean chasm in his widely read and immensely influential *Principles of Geology*, 2nd ed., Vol. 1 (of 3) (London: Charles Murray, 1832), 505–6. Presumably, this is the primary reason for the account's longevity. *1755: O grande terramoto de Lisboa*, 197–202.

62. Celeste Jorge and António Gomes Coelho, "Zonamento do potencial de liquefacção. Tentativa de aplicação a Portugal," *Geotecnia*, No. 83, July 1998, 43–45; Oliveira, 2005, 68–69; José Manuel Martínez Solares and Alfonso López Arroyo, "O terramoto de 1755 em Espanha," in *1755: O grande terramoto de Lisboa*, 253–56; J. M. Martínez Solares and A. López Arroyo, "The Great Historical 1755 Earthquake. Effects and Damage in Spain," *Journal of Seismology*, Vol. 8, 2004, 288–89.

63. Solares, 2001, 49.

64. Joachim José Moreira de Mendonça was one of the first investigators to demonstrate that the quay did not, as many believed, disappear into an underground cavern. Mendonça, 134.

65. One ship captain afloat off the Terreiro do Paço stated that "the water rose in five minutes about 16 feet, and fell in the same time for three times." Nozes, 208.

66. *The Scots Magazine*, Vol. 17, December 1755, 586.

67. Ibid., 585.

68. BG, AP 12363, Portal, 48.

69. *Philosophical Transactions of the Royal Society*, Vol. 49, 1755, 414.

70. Boer and Sanders, 12.

71. Dudley and Lee, 62.

72. Walker, 2008, 1–20; Charles F. Walker, "Lisbon and Lima: A Tale of Two Cities and Catastrophes," in Gerhard Lauer and Thorsten Unger, eds., *Das Erdbeben von Lissabon und der Katastrophendiskurs im 18. Jahrhundert* (Göttingen: Wallstein Verlag, 2008), 377–91.

73. Mendonça, 160; Figueiredo, 1756, 17.

74. AHN, Estado 3183 (Huelva); *Relación Verídica*, 4–5; *Verídica Relación, En Que Se Declara el estupendo prodigo, que a vila de innumerable Pueblo de esta Cuidad de Sanlucar de Barrameda he obrado* . . . (Seville: Joseph Padrino, 1755–56?). The majority of British observers used the words "waves" and "inundation," "flux and reflux," and even "the great Flux," while German eyewitnesses and commentators noted the "out-of-the-ordinary movement of the waters" (*ausserordentliche Wasserbewegung*), the "flood" (*Fluth*), and the assault of the "ocean waves" (*Meereswellen*). The Dutch spoke of "a frightful rising of the water" (*eene schrikkelyke Steigering van het Water*), the French, the "flux and reflux" (*flux et reflux*) and "the angry waves" (*les flots en courroux*), and the Italians, the "extraordinary growth of the water" (*straordinario accrescimento di aque*) and the "growth of the sea" (*crescimento del mare*). The Russians referred to the "cruelty of the water" (*zhestokost'iu vody*), the "cruel flood" (*zhestokim uavodneniem*), and the "walls of water." According to a report in the St. Petersburg News, "the sea performed a terrifying, sad, and shameful spectacle for those who were on it." Farmer, 4 ("the great Flux"); *Physikalische Betrachtungen* . . . , 38; *Beschreibung des Erdbebens* . . . , Vols. 1–3. (Danzig, 1756); *Die denckwürdigsten Geschichte* . . . ; *Nederlandsch Gedenkboek of Europische Mercurius*, Vol. 46 (The Hague: Frederic Henric Scheurleer, 1755) December, 301; "Il Relato," in Fernando Guedes, *O livro e a Leitura em Portugal subsídios para a sua história séculos XVIII e XIX* (Lisbon: Editorial Verbo, 1987), 252–57; BA, Ms. Av. 54-XI-15(64), 4, *Relato enviado por un italiano, em Portugal, a uma Madre, em Itália*, 1755; Battelli, 14; *Sankt-Peterburgskie Vedomosti*, December 12, 1755 (Julian calendar), No. 99; *Sankt-Peterburgskie Vedomosti*, December 19, 1755 (Julian calendar), No. 101; *Sankt-Peterburgskie Vedomosti*, December 29, 1755 (Julian calendar), Report: November 19, 1755, No. 104. Translation: Nathaniel Knight and Maxim Matusevich; *Sankt-Peterburgskie Vedomosti*, December 29, 1755 (Julian calendar), Report: November 19, 1755, No. 104.

75. *Verídica Relación* . . . ; Charles Chauncy, *Dr. Chauncy's Sermon Occasioned by the late Earthquakes the World in which there is No Curse* (Boston, 1756), 55.

76. Julyan H. E. Cartwright and Hisami Nakamura, "Tsunami: A History of the Term and of Scientific Understanding of the Phenomenon in Japanese and Western Culture," *Notes & Records of the Royal Society*, Vol. 62, No. 2, June 20, 2008, 151–66.

77. Ibid.

78. Parker, 136.

79. AHCML, FA-63, *Portugal aflito e conturbado* . . . , 60, 256–59.

80. Figueiredo, 1756, 17.

81. Baptista, Heitor, Miranda, Miranda, and Victor believe that the tsunami only penetrated about 250 meters into the city. Baptista et al., "The 1755 Lisbon Tsunami,"

1998, 143; António Correia Mineiro, "A propósito das medidas de remediação e da opção política de reedificar a cidade de Lisboa sobre os seus escombros, após o sismo de 1 de novembro de 1755: Reflexões," in *1755: O grande terramoto de Lisboa*, 206.

82. ASV, Secretaria Stato Portogallo 231.

83. BG, AP 12363, Portal, 2.

84. Pedegache, 11.

85. *Two Very Circumstantial Accounts . . .* , 4.

86. This contradicts the work of at least two scholars who claim that the tsunami arrived at low tide. See following note.

87. Dr. J. M. Saccheti states in a letter: "The water in the sea rose several times, and in a few minutes made three fluxes and refluxes, rising above the greatest spring-tides two spawns, or fifteen English feet. This phenomenon happened three days before the new moon, and the earthquake, when the high tide had run up three parts of it." *Philosophical Transactions of the Royal Society*, Vol. 49, 1755, 410–11. Saccheti's account is confirmed by comparing the tides at Lisbon on November 1, 2002, which had a similar phase of the moon to November 1, 1755. Low tide on that date occurred on 5:45 a.m. and high tide was achieved at 12:18 p.m. As Lisbon was just three days away from a new moon on November 1, 1755, the waters would have been close to spring tide and thus high tide would have been slightly more elevated than at other high tides farther from the day of a new moon. Information on phases of the moon and tides at Lisbon, Cádiz, the Algarve, and the coast of Morocco have been obtained on websites of the United States Naval Observatory, Astronomical Applications Department and/or the Instituto Hidrográfico, Marinha-Portugal. I would like to thank Dana Kappel for her help in this matter. This view contradicts at least two scholars who assert that the tide was a low tide when the tsunami arrived. António Correia Mineiro, "A propósito das medidas de remediação e da opção política de reedificar a cidade de Lisboa sobre os seus escombros, após o sismo de 1 de novembro de 1755: Reflexões," in *1755: O grande terramoto de Lisboa*, 206; C. S. Oliveira, "Review of the 1755 Lisbon Earthquake Based on Recent Analyses of Historical Observations," in *Historical Seismology: Interdisciplinary Studies of Past and Recent Earthquakes* (London: Springer, 2008), 269.

88. "Dissertação de Manuel da Maia" in França, 1983, 312. This calculation assumes that waters reached the Rua Nova. Tsunami run-ups vary widely because of the differing shore angles and depths. Maria Viana Baptista believes the water penetrated 250 meters into the city. See her map in Mineiro, "A propósito das medidas de remediação a da opção política de reedificar a cidade de Lisboa sobre os seus escombos, após o sismo de 1 de novembro de 1755: Reflexões," in *1755: O grande terramoto de Lisboa*, 206.

89. AHCML, FA-63, *Portugal aflito e conturbado . . .* , 56.

90. Pedegache, 4. A Spaniard observed that the receding sea "devoured a great number of people." ASV, Secretaria Stato Portogallo 231.

91. *The Whitehall Evening Post*, No. 1531, December 16–18, 1755.

92. Sousa, 1919–32, 847.

93. Miguel Telles Antunes, "Vítimas do terremoto de 1755 no convento de Jesus (Academia das Ciências de Lisboa)," *Revista Electrónica de Ciências da Terra Geosciences On-Line Journal*, Vol. 3, No. 1, 2006, 2, 9.

94. AHCML, FA-63, *Portugal aflito e conturbado* . . . , 253–54.

95. Baptista et al., "The 1755 Lisbon Tsunami," 1998, 143.

96. Ibid. According to Charles Walker, after the 1746 Lima Earthquake-Tsunami "bodies washed up on shore for weeks." Walker, 2008, 10.

97. Sousa, *Carta em que hum amigo* . . . , 3. This, one of the first accounts of the earthquake disaster in Portugal, has been criticized for its inaccuracies. It nevertheless provides an evocative and poetic description of the tsunami's impact.

98. BA, 49-III-55, 208.

99. See Maria Ana Baptista and Jorge Miguel Miranda, "Revision of the Portuguese Catalogue of Tsunamis," *Natural Hazards and Earth System Sciences*, Vol. 9, 2009, 25–42.

100. Mendonça, 153; Portal also discusses the damage to Setúbal. BG, AP 12363, Portal, 819.

101. BG, AP 12363, Portal, 127.

102. Quoted in Alexandre Costa, et al., *1755 Terramoto no Algarve* (Faro, Portugal: Centro Ciência Viva do Algarve), 2005, 114 (from Faria e Castro, 1786, 33). See also Chester and Chester, 2010.

103. See *Mapa do Reino do Algarve* by Laurent Sculp (Paris, 1700), in Costa et al., 29.

104. Chester and Chester, 2010, 11–13; It is difficult to determine run-up heights for many regions of the Algarve, as many authors give differing estimates; The Portuguese league (*légua*) used in the eighteenth century referred to various lengths between 4,000 and 6,000 meters. Paul-Louis Blanc argues that the tsunami run-up averaged only 2.5 meters in the Ibero-Moroccan gulf. Paul-Louis Blanc, "The Atlantic Tsunami on November 1st, 1755: World Range and Amplitude According to Primary Documentary Sources," in Nils-Axel Mörner, ed., *The Tsunami Threat—Research and Technology*, 2011. The Portuguese sources and the proximity of the earthquake epicenter suggest that the run-up was in places considerably higher. See Joel Fantina, Tedim Pedrosa, and J. Gonçalves, "The 1755 Earthquake in the Algarve (South of Portugal): What Would Happen Nowadays?," *Advances in Geosciences*, 14, 2008, 59–63.

105. Robert A. Hindson et al., "Sedimentary Processes Associated with the Tsunami Generated by the 1755 Lisbon Earthquake on the Algarve Coast, Portugal," *Physics and Chemistry of the Earth*, Vol. 21, No. 12, 1996, 62; Chester and Chester, 2010, 36062.

106. Baptista et al., "Constraints on the Source of the 1755 Lisbon Tsunami," 1998, 162.

107. These calculations (made by the author) are based on Faro, Portugal.

108. ASV, S. Cong. Conc. 635 A, 3.

109. ANTT, MPRQ/1/69, 491: *Memórias paroquiais* (May 10, 1758), Albufeira, Lagos (Portugal).

110. Quoted in Costa et al., 126.

111. Ibid. See chart on page 44. The pre-earthquake population was estimated by adding the 204 victims of the disaster with the approximately 220 children under the age of seven, who would have been left out the population counts, to the population in 1756 (2,074). Original manuscript: *Relaçam do terremoto do primeiro de Novembro do anno de 1755 com os effeitos, que particularmente cauzou neste Reino do Algarve*, 1756, Faro, Portugal, Biblioteca da Universidade de Coimbra, Manuscrito do Códice 537, ff. 159–63.

112. Pedrosa and Gonçalves, 61.
113. Quoted in Costa et al., 121.
114. *The Whitehall Evening Post*, No. 1531, December 16–18, 1755. Quoted in Costa et al., 125.
115. Costa et al., 127; ANTT/MPRQ/29/230, *Memorias paróquias* (1758), 1624.
116. ANTT, MPRQ/19/24a, *Memorias paróquias* (1758), 135.
117. Quoted in Costa et al., 118.. For information on inland penetration at Lagos and other areas in the Algarve, see Chester and Chester, 2010, 12.
118. Chester and Chester, 2010, 363.
119. Costa et al., 44.
120. *Philosophical Transactions of the Royal Society*, Vol. 49, 1755, 419, 421.
121. AHN, Estado, 3173, Mayor José de Avilés.
122. AHN, Estado, 2909, Mayor José Pérez de Cossio; AHN, Estado, 3173.
123. José Manuel Martínez Solares and Alfonso López Arroyo, "O terramoto de 1755 em Espanha," in *1755: O grande terramoto de Lisboa*, 235–64.
124. AHN, Estado, 3183.
125. Quoted in Blanc, 2011, 433.
126. Paul-Louis Blanc, 2011, 433. The number of victims in Huelva is a matter of debate. See Solares and Arroyo, 244.
127. Solares and Arroyo, 244.
128. *Relación Verídica . . .* , 4–5.
129. AHN, Estado, 3183.
130. *Verídica Relación . . .* , 2.
131. Ibid.
132. Ibid, 2–3.
133. Ibid, 3.
134. Ibid, 3–4.
135. Solares, 2001, 31–32.
136. Baptista et al., "Constraints on the Source of the 1755 Lisbon Tsunami," 1998, 162. See also Paul-Louis Blanc, 2008, 251–61; and Solares and Arroyo, 253.
137. AHN, Estado, 3173, Anonymous.
138. *The London Evening Post*, No. 4378, November 29–December 2, 1755.
139. BL, IOR: MSS EUR E313/12, "Earthquake in Lisbon," November 25, 1755.
140. Quoted in Solana, 2006, 149.
141. BL, IOR: MSS EUR E313/12, "Earthquake in Lisbon," November 25, 1755.
142. Ibid. According to the English merchant Benjamin Berwick, the waves "carried [with it] pieces of eight or ten tun [*sic*] weight forty or fifty yards from the wall, and carried away the sand and the walls, but left the houses standing. . . . There were about forty or fifty people drowned on the causey [causeway] and a great many beasts." *Philosophical Transactions of the Royal Society*, Vol. 49, 1755, 427.
143. Solares, 2001, 32.
144. AHN, Estado, 3183; Antonio de Azlor; Ana Crespo Solana, "Manifestaciones culturales y actitudes sociales y religiosas ante las catástrofes naturales en la España del Antiguo Régimen: El maremoto de 1755 en Cádiz," in *Naturalia, mirabilia & monstrosa en los imperios ibéricos (siglos XV–XIX)*, Eddy Stols, Werner Thomas, and Johan Verberckmoes, eds. (Leuven, Belgium: Leuven University Press, 2006), 145.
145. *Lettre à M. L. Racine sur le théâtre en général, et sur les tragédies de J. Racine en particulier*, Kendrick, 127.

146. AHN, Estado, 3183, Cádiz.
147. Ibid.
148. Ibid.
149. One small area of northeastern Spain did not report any tremors.
150. Solares and Arroyo, 2004, 278; Diego Téllez Alarcia, "El impacto del terremoto de Lisboa en España," in Ana Cristina Araújo et al., eds., *O terramoto de 1755: Impactos históricos* (Lisbon: Livros Horizonte, 2007), 77–85.
151. AHN, Estado, 3183, Conil. Account of Don Miguel de Aragón y Serrano.
152. Franziska Whelan and Dieter Kelletat, "Boulder Deposits on the Southern Spanish Atlantic Coast: Possible Evidence for the 1755 AD Lisbon Tsunami?," *Science of Tsunami Hazards*, Vol. 23, No. 3, 2005, 25–38.
153. *The Whitehall Evening Post*, No. 1531, December 16–18, 1755.
154. Quoted in Blanc, 2011, 434.
155. *Gesammelte Nachrichten . . .* , 34; *Die denckwürdigsten Geschichte . . .* , 80–81; *The Whitehall Evening Post*, No. 1529, December 11–13, 1755.
156. Levret, 83–94. See also Paul-Louis Blanc, "Earthquakes and Tsunami in November 1755 in Morocco: A Different Reading of the Contemporaneous Documentary Sources," *Natural Hazards and Earth System Sciences*, 9, 2009, 725–38. Blanc believes the tsunami run-ups were exaggerated in the contemporary sources.
157. The calculations were made for Safi, which had an earlier high tide than Lisbon.
158. Quoted in Abdelaziz, 273.
159. Quoted in Abdelaziz, 285.
160. *The Scots Magazine*, Vol. 18, January, 1756, 41; *Philosophical Transactions of the Royal Society*, Vol. 49, 1755, 430.
161. Fatima Kaabouben et al., "On the Moroccan Tsunami Catalogue," *Natural Hazards and Earth System Sciences*, Vol. 9, 2009, 1230.
162. Quoted in Abdelaziz, 287. The author was four years old when the earthquake occurred. He got his information from other accounts.
163. *Supplement to the Gentleman's Magazine*, 1755, 587. See also the account of Mohammad Adu'ayyef Al-ribati in Abdelaziz, 287.
164. *The London Evening Post*, No. 4385, December 16–18, 1755.
165. *The Gentleman's Magazine*, Vol. 26, January 1756, 7.
166. *The London Evening Post*, No. 4385, December 16–18, 1755.
167. Quoted in Abdelaziz, 279.
168. Quoted in Abdelaziz, 284.
169. Quoted in Blanc, 2011, 434. *Philosophical Transactions of the Royal Society*, Vol. 49, 429–30; Blanc, 2009, 732.
170. Abdelaziz, 276.
171. *Gazeta de Lisboa*, No. 18, May 1756, 142–43 (report dated January 25, 1755).
172. Quoted in Blanc, 2011, 435.
173. Blanc, 2011, 436.
174. Baptista et al., "Constraints on the Source of the 1755 Lisbon Tsumami," 1998, 162.
175. *Philosophical Transactions of the Royal Society*, Vol. 49, 1755, 433–34.
176. Ibid., 436.
177. Quote from *The London Evening Post*, No. 4390, December 27–30, 1755.
178. *The Whitehall Evening Post*, No. 1534, December 23–25, 1755; *The London Evening Post*, No. 4390, December 27–30, 1755.

179. Quoted in Blanc, 2011, 428. Blanc does not believe that this incident was caused by the tsunami because the time given, 9 a.m., was too early. He believes it was caused by the earthquake's surface waves. While there may have been a perturbation of the waters due to surface waves in the morning, it seems entirely plausible that the time given here was incorrect and that the tsunami did in fact arrive at Brest and cause the Penfeld River to overflow the cofferdam and fill up the basin in question. Brest does, after all, lie in a direct line from the earthquake's epicenter.

180. *Philosophical Transactions of the Royal Society*, Vol. 49, 1755, 372.

181. Ibid., 373–75. For arrival estimates, see Baptista et al., "The 1755 Lisbon Tsunami," 1998, 147.

182. Ibid., 379.

183. Ibid., 380.

184. Banerjee et al., 2000, 718.

185. Jean Roger et al., "The Transoceanic 1755 Lisbon Tsunami in Martinique," *Pure and Applied Geophysics*, No. 168, 2011, 1025; Karen Fay O'Loughlin and James F. Lander, *Caribbean Tsunamis: A 500-Year History from 1498–1998* (Dordrecht, Netherlands: Kluwer Academic Publishers, 2003), 37–41.

186. *The Scots Magazine*, Vol. 18, January 1756, 41. A report by a William Hillary in Barbados states that "the Sea suddenly flowed and rose more than two Feet higher than it does in the highest Spring Tides." Blanc, 2011, 437. Special thanks to Dana Kappel for her help with the tidal calculations.

187. *Philosophical Transactions of the Royal Society*, Vol. 49, 1755, 669. "An Account of the Agitation of the Sea at Antigua, Nov. 1, 1755. By Capt. Affleck of the Advice Man of War. Communicated by Charles Gray, Esq., F. R. S. in a Letter to William Watson, F. R. S."; F. Accary and Jean Roger, "Tsunami Catalog and Vulnerability of Martinique (Lesser Antilles, France)," *Science of Tsunami Hazards*, Vol. 29, No. 3, 2010, 160.

188. Roger et al., 2011, 1019.

189. Quoted in Blanc, 2011, 438. The language of the English translation has been slightly altered to better reflect English grammar.

190. At Martinique, low tide occurred at around 3:30 p.m. on November 1, 1755. Special thanks to Jena Kent of the National Oceanic and Atmospheric Administration and Dana Kappel for their help with the calculations.

191. At Guadeloupe, low tide had been reached at approximately 7:30 a.m. and high tide would be reached at approximately 7:30 p.m. Special thanks to Jena Kent of the National Oceanic and Atmospheric Administration and Dana Kappel for their help with the calculations.

192. Quoted in Blanc, 2011, 439; see also Jean Roger et al., "The 1755 Lisbon Tsunami in Guadeloupe Archipelago: Source Sensitivity and Investigation of Resonance Effects," *The Open Oceanography Journal*, Vol. 4, 2010, 58–70.

193. *Philosophical Transactions of the Royal Society*, Vol. 49, 1755, 669.

194. Mendonça, 160.

195. P. Salterain, "Ligera resena de los temblores de tierra ocurridos en la Isla de Cuba," *Boletín de la Comisión del Mapa Geológico de España*, 1883, 10, Madrid, 372–73. In Salterain, no date is given for the tsunami, just the year 1755. This article also states that "tremors" were also felt, although this seems improbable. In Desiderio Herrera, *Memoria sobre los huracanes en la isla de Cuba* (Havana: Barcina, 1847), pages 16 and 46, few specifics are given, only the line, : "1755 Noviembro 1.0 Ter-

remoto é inundacion del Mar en Cuba" as well as the assertion that the earthquake "was felt" in the Antilles (again, this seems unlikely). Stephen Taber, "The Great Fault Troughs of the Antilles," *Journal of Geology*, Vol. 30, 1922, 89–114; James F. Lander, Lowell S. Whiteside, and Patricia A. Lockridge, "A Brief History of Tsunamis in the Caribbean Sea," *Science of Tsunami Hazards*, Vol. 20, No. 2, 2002, 64; Philip M. Hamer and George C. Rogers, Jr., eds., *The Papers of Henry Laurens, Volume Two: Nov. 1, 1755–Dec. 31, 1758* (Columbia: University of South Carolina Press, 1970), 67, as well as 64, 104–5.

196. Philip Tocque, *Newfoundland: As It Was, and As It Is in 1877* (Toronto: John B. Magurn, 1877), 145; John Adams and Michael Staveley, "Historical Seismology of Newfoundland," Earth Physics Branch Open File No. 85-22, Ottawa, Canada, September 1985, 9, 37, 50; Lucinda J. Leonard et al., "Towards a National Tsunami Hazard Map for Canada: Tsunami Sources," *Proceeedings of the 9th U.S. National and 10th Canadian Conference on Earthquake Engineering*, July 25–29, 2010, Paper No. 1844. http://www.tsunamisociety.org/Symp3rlisbon.pdf; http://www.mendeley.com/research/tsunami-impact-newfoundland-canada-due-farfield-generated-tsunamis-implications-hazard-assessment/.

197. Low tide occurred at approximately 8:30 p.m. on the evening of November 1, 1755, along this stretch of the northeastern coast of Brazil. High tide would occur at approximately 3 a.m. on November 2, 1755. Special thanks to Dana Kappel for her help with the calculations.

198. AHU, ACL, CU, 015, Cx. 80, D. 6689 (letter dated February 28, 1756); AHU, ACL, CU, 015, Cx. 80, D.6691 (letter dated March 4, 1756). Admittedly, this second report by João de Melo is hearsay, but it does provide specific, detailed information. He refers to *"a Enchente do Tarramoto"* (the earthquake flood). The time he gives for the tsunami's arrival, 10 p.m. (local time), seems too late in the evening.

199. AHCML, FA-63, *Portugal aflito e conturbado . . .* , 383.

200. Captain Affleck of the man-of-war *Advice* states in a letter dated January 3, 1756, from the island of Antigua that "the sea . . . was agitated in like manner, on these islands, and at the same time, on the coast of America, and all these islands," but provides no other details. *Philosophical Transactions of the Royal Society*, Vol. 49, 1755, 669. On January 12, 1756, Henry Laurens informed an acquaintance in Barbados that while "the extrordinary [sic] flux and reflux of the Tide at your place and the adjacent Islands . . . had the like effect at Bermuda . . . none here [in South Carolina] . . . was observed." Hamer and Rogers, 64. The name of Laurens's friend was Gidney Clarke. Muir-Wood and Mignan, 134.

201. Barkan et al., 2009, 117–21. See also Roger et al., 2011, 1021–25.

202. Baptista et al., "Constraints on the Source of the 1755 Lisbon Tsunami," 1998, 172.

203. Oliveira, 2005, 75. The Sendai Tsunami produced waves from 10 to 14 meters (and perhaps larger); Oliveira, 2008, 280–83. For a general comparison of the Lisbon Earthquake of 1755 and the 2004 Indian Ocean Earthquake, see Karl Fuchs, "The Great Earthquakes of Lisbon 1755 and Aceh 2004 Shook the World. Seismologists' Societal Responsibility," in Medes-Victor, 2009, 43–64.

204. Baptista et al., 1997; Barkan et al., 2009; Chester, 2001, 363–64.

205. Chester and Chester, 2010, 364.

206. Gutscher, 2004, 1247–48. Tsunami deposits and Roman records suggest that a

powerful earthquake visited southwest Iberia in around 200 BC. Gutscher, 2006, 181.

207. This was the Storegga Slides Tsunami.
208. Maria Teresa Pareschi et al., "Lost Tsunami," *Geophysical Research Letters*, Vol. 33, 2006.
209. Simon Winchester, *Krakatoa: The Day the World Exploded: August 27, 1883* (New York: HarperCollins, 2003).
210. Thucydides, *History of the Peloponnesian War*, Rex Warner, trans. (New York: Penguin, 1972), Book 3, Section 89, 247.
211. Herodotus, *The Histories*, David Grene, trans. (Chicago: University of Chicago Press, 1987), Book 8, Section 129, 603–4.
212. Erhard Oeser, "Historical Earthquake Theories from Aristotle to Kant," in Rudolf Gutdeutsch, Gottfried Grünthal, and Roger Musson, eds., *Historical Earthquakes in Central Europe*, Vol. 1 (Vienna: Abhandlungen der Geologischen Bundesanstalt, 1992), 13; Boer and Sanders, 62–63.
213. Oeser, 13; Boer and Sanders, 62–63.
214. Oeser, 15.
215. Ibid., 14–16.
216. Aristotle, *Meteorology*, Book 2, Chapter 8; T. C. Smid, "'Tsunamis' in Greek Literature," *Greece & Rome*, 2nd Series, Vol. 17, No. 1, April 1970, 100–104; Oeser, 17.
217. Oeser, 16; Gerard J. Pendrick, *Antiphon the Sophist: The Fragments* (Cambridge: Cambridge University Press, 2002), 306.
218. Oeser, 16.
219. Ibid., 17.
220. Ibid., 22.
221. Ibid., 26.
222. William Stukely, *Philosophical Transactions of the Royal Society*, Vol. 46, 1749, 643.
223. Benjamin Franklin, "Causes of Earthquakes," in *The Works of Benjamin Franklin*, Vol. 6 (of 10), ed. Jared Sparks (Boston: Charles Tappan, 1844), 1.
224. See Alfred Owen Aldridge, "Benjamin Franklin and Jonathan Edwards on Lightning and Earthquakes," *Isis*, Vol. 41, No. 2, July 1950, 162–64.
225. Ephraim Chambers, *Cyclopaedia*, Vol. 2 (of 2) (London, 1728), 267, article: "Earthquake."
226. *The London Evening Post*, No. 4384, December 13–16, 1755.
227. BL, Add. 69847, February 10, 1756; quoted in Sousa, 1919–32, Vol. 3 (of 4), 517. Original: ANTT, Manuscript No. 1229 (ff. 51–97).
228. *The London Evening Post*, No. 4384, December 13–16, 1755.

CHAPTER FOUR

The Great Firestorm

The chapter epigraph "Um Grandissimo Incêndio" is from Figueiredo, 1756, 20.

1. Mr. Braddock in Davy, Vol. 2, 43.
2. Quoted in Sousa, 1919–32, Vol. 3, 581.
3. AHCML, FA-63, *Portugal aflito e conturbado . . .*, 457.
4. BPL, Manuscrito No. 607, Fundo Geral, *Relação historica do terremoto de Lisboa.*
5. AHCML, FA-63, *Portugal aflito e conturbado . . .*, 459–60.
6. Mendonça, 130. Father Portal refers to "manuscripts, which had been collected

with much care and diligence by [the Marquês's] illustrious ancestors." BG, AP 12363, Portal, 59–60; Rodriques and Craig, 400.

7. One eyewitness recalled "the Flame spreading themselves [*sic*] with a Rapidity which nothing could resist." *Two Very Circumstantial Accounts . . .* , 12.

8. "Bones Throw Light on 1755 Quake,"Associated Press, April 28, 2007.

9. *Pau brasil* was also used in the production of red dye.

10. "Bones Throw Light on 1755 Quake,"Associated Press, April 28, 2007.

11. ASV, Segretaria di Stato Portogallo, 231.

12. AHCML, FA-63, *Portugal aflito e conturbado . . .* , 98. Public kitchens were places where people who did not have a fireplace could come to cook their meals.

13. Davy, Vol. 2, 42.

14. *The Gentleman's Magazine*, Vol. 25, December 1755, 558.

15. Ange Goudar, *Relation historique du tremblement de terre survenu à Lisbonne le premier novembre 1755* (The Hague: Chez Philanthrope, 1756), 183. For a further description and analysis of the Lisbon firestorm, see Molesky, "The Great Fire of Lisbon, 1755," 2012, 147–69.

16. BG, AP 12363, Portal, 49–50; Anonymous, *Destruição de Lisboa e Famosa Desgraça que padeceo no dia primeiro de Novembro de 1755* (Lisbon, 1756), 10.

17. See Molesky, "The Great Fire of Lisbon, 1755," 2012.

18. Stephan Dando-Collins, *The Great Fire of Rome: The Fall of Emperor Nero and His City* (Cambridge, MA: Da Capo, 2010), 99–110.

19. For information on the elements of the firestorm, see Neil Hanson, *The Great Fire of London: In That Apocalyptic Year* (Hoboken, NJ: John Wiley & Sons, 2002), 149–60.

20. Samuel Pepys, *The Diary of Samuel Pepys M.A. F.R.S.*, Vol. 5, Henry B. Wheatley, ed. (London: George Bell & Sons, 1895), 426 (September 5–6, 1666).

21. Karen Sawislak, *Smoldering City: Chicagoans and the Great Fire, 1871–1874* (Chicago: University of Chicago Press, 1995).

22. D. A. Hanines and R. W. Sando, "Climatic Conditions Preceding Historically Great Fires in the North Central Region," 1969, United States Forest Service, Research Paper NC-34, http://www.michigan.gov/dnr/0,1607,7-153-30301_30505_30816-24038—,00.html, accessed December 17, 2012.

23. Andrea Rees Davies, "Points of Origin: The Social Impact of the 1906 San Francisco Earthquake and Fire," in Greg Bankoff et al., eds., *Flammable Cities: Urban Conflagration and the Making of the Modern World* (Madison: University of Wisconsin, 2012), 273.

24. Quoted in Joshua Hammer, *Yokohama Burning: The Deadly 1923 Earthquake and Fire That Helped Forge the Path to World War II* (New York: Free Press, 2006), 196, 243.

25. *The Whitehall Evening Post*, No. 1529, December 11–13, 1755; França, 1983, 63.

26. AHCML, FA-63, *Portugal aflito e conturbado . . .* , 97.

27. ANTT, Manuscrito 1229, Sousa, 1919–32, 517.

28. BG, AP 12363, Portal, 2.

29. Mendonça, 118.

30. AHCML, FA-63, *Portugal aflito e conturbado . . .* , 47.

31. Sousa, 1755, 3.

32. Hanson, *The Great Fire of London*, 2002, 243–44.

33. Quoted in Sousa, 1919–32, Vol. 3, 761. A letter from a Lisbon priest to his brother in Goa (1756), *Instituto Vasco da Gama*, No. 46 (October 1875), 238 and 40.

34. AHCML, FA-63, *Portugal aflito e conturbado* . . . , 101; "Relação do terramoto de 1755," BA, Ms. Av. 54-XI-16 no. 121.

35. "Multitudes still living under the Ruins [of the churches] were burnt to Death." *Two Very Circumstantial Accounts* . . . , 6.

36. BG, AP 12363, Portal, 95–96.

37. BA, Ms. Av. 54-XI-16 no. 121, "Relação do terramoto de 1755."

38. BG, AP 12363, Portal, 116–17.

39. Davy, Vol. 2, 53–54.

40. AHCML, FA-63, *Portugal aflito e conturbado* . . . , 100.

41. Ibid., 100–101.

42. Ibid., 101.

43. *An Account of the Late Dreadful Earthquake and Fire* . . . , 2nd ed., 1756, 21.

44. Sousa, 1755, 3–4.

45. ANTT, Manuscrito 1229.

46. *The Gentleman's Magazine*, Vol. 25, December 1755, 559.

47. Relato II in Guedes, 255.

48. BG, AP 12363, Portal, 63–64.

49. *Philosophical Transactions of the Royal Society*, Vol. 49, 1755, 404.

50. Bento Morganti, *Carta de hum Amigo para outro em que se dá succinta Noticia dos Effeitos de Terremoto succedido em o Primeiro de Novembro de 1755* (Lisbon: Domingos Rodrigues, 1756), 15; Relato I in Guedes, 247; *Philosophical Transactions of the Royal Society*, Vol. 49, 1755, 411.

51. *Supplement to the Gentleman's Magazine*, 1755, "Further Particulars of the Earthquake at Lisbon," 591; originally published in *The Whitehall Evening Post*.

52. At the Royal Hospital of All the Saints, "four hundred patients died in the infirmaries, many burned to death, because no one was able to come to their aid," according to one anonymous source. Sousa, 1955, 11.

53. AHU, ACL, CU, 17, Cx. 50, D. 5036.

54. Pedegache, 5.

55. *Supplement to the Gentleman's Magazine*, 1755, "Further Particulars of the Earthquake at Lisbon," 591.

56. Ibid.

57. *The Scots Magazine*, Vol. 18, February 1756, 94.

58. *Supplement to the Gentleman's Magazine*, 1755, "Further Particulars of the Earthquake at Lisbon," 592.

59. AHCML, FA-63, *Portugal aflito e conturbado* . . . , 107.

60. Quoted in Sousa, 1955, 11. Caldas is Caldas da Rainha.

61. Sousa, 1919–32, 641.

62. Figueiredo, 1756, 7.

63. AHCML, FA-63, *Portugal aflito e conturbado* . . . , 76–78.

64. Pedegache, 6.

65. Boer and Sanders, 12.

66. Figueiredo, 1756, 9.

67. Mendonça, 160.

68. BG, AP 12363, Portal, 54.

69. Rodrigues and Craig, 399; Schwarcz, 74.

70. The Library of Alexandria may have been destroyed several times: the first in 48 BC by Julius Caesar (accidentally).

71. Figueiredo, 1756, 22; Rodriques and Lima, 400.

72. Figueiredo, 1756, 22.
73. Mendonça, 130–31.
74. BG, AP 12363, Portal, 57.
75. Ibid., 58.
76. Mendonça, 126–27.
77. Ibid., 128.
78. AHCML, FA-63, *Portugal aflito e conturbado . . .* , 244.
79. Mendonça, 127.
80. Ibid., 117.
81. BG, AP 12363, Portal, 92–94.
82. Sousa, 1919–32, 628.
83. BG, AP 12363, Portal, 65.
84. Sousa, 1919–32, 575.
85. BG, AP 12363, Portal, 30.
86. Ibid, 97.
87. Ibid, 109.
88. Sousa, 1955, 9; Mendonça, 129.
89. BG, AP 12363, Portal, 60–61.
90. Sousa, 1919–32, 629.
91. Sousa, 1919–32, 568; Lúcia Lima Rodrigues and Russell Craig, "Recovery Amid Destruction: Manoel de Maya and the Lisbon Earthquake of 1755," *Libraries & the Cultural Record,* Vol. 43, No. 4, 2008, 397–410.
92. Rodrigues and Craig, 407.
93. ANTT, MR, CUL, 01, 01, 1 (Ministério do Reino, mç. 495, doc. 4); ANTT, MR, CUL, 01, 01, 2 (Ministério do Reino, mç. 495, doc. 5). The house was to be 80 palmos in length by 30 palmos in width (58 feet × 22 feet).
94. Sousa, 1919–32, 568; Rodrigues and Craig, 397–410; *Noticia da Destruição e Restauração da Torre do Tombo, Feita por Ordem do Guarda-Mor Manule da Maia,* 1763?, Obras Várias Impressas e Manuscritas, Núcleo Antigo 892, ANTT, OVNA, 892.
95. *The Gentleman's Magazine,* Vol. 83, February 1813,108–9.
96. Ibid., 109.
97. Ibid., April 315.
98. Ibid., 109.
99. Ibid., 109–10.
100. Ibid., 110.
101. Ibid.
102. Ibid.
103. Ibid.
104. BL, Add. 69847, Letter, February 10, 1756.
105. Ibid.
106. Margaret Hay was born on October 10, 1755. Arthur Collins, *The Peerage of England . . .* , Vol. 7 (of 8), 5th ed. (London: W. Strathan et al., 1779), 229.
107. BL, Add. 69847, Letter, February 10, 1756.
108. Ibid.
109. Ibid.; BL, Egerton MS 3482, ff. 147 (back), 148, Letter to his brother dated November 14, 1755.
110. Ibid.
111. BG, AP 12363, Portal, 25.
112. Ibid., 25–26.

113. Figueiredo, 1756, 19.
114. BG, AP 12363, Portal, 26.
115. "From a domestic of Lord Drumlanrig, Nov. 8," *The Scots Magazine*, Vol. 17, December 1755, 591.
116. GRO, D2700/W/4, Letter, November 8, 1755.
117. Ibid.
118. Macaulay, 1946, 274–76.
119. *Physikalische Betrachtungen . . .*, 216.
120. Ibid., 211–12.
121. *The Gentleman's Magazine*, Vol. 25, 1755, 361.
122. Quoted in Sousa, 1919–32, 648–49 (from an article published in *A Época*, February 17, 1924).
123. ASV, Secretaria Stato 195, ff. 176–79; ASV, Carte Farnesiane 18, f. 18, Letter, November 4, 1755.
124. AHCML, FA-63, *Portugal aflito e conturbado . . .*, 35; BNP, Fundo Geral, No. 1772.
125. AHCML, FA-63, *Portugal aflito e conturbado . . .*, 35.
126. BG, AP 12363, Portal, 7.
127. AHCML, FA-63, Portugal *aflito e conturbado . . .*, 88.
128. Bellamy, 61, Letter, November 12, 1755.
129. AHCML, FA-63, *Portugal aflito e conturbado . . .*, 450.
130. AHCML, FA-63, *Portugal aflito e conturbado . . .*, 85–86.
131. Mendonça, 120.
132. AHCML, FA-63, *Portugal aflito e conturbado . . .*, 87, 281.
133. *The London Evening Post*, No. 4387, December 20–23, 1755.
134. Pedegache, 5.
135. AHCML, FA-63, *Portugal aflito e conturbado . . .*, 445, 83, 451.
136. *An Account of the Late Dreadful Earthquake and Fire . . .*, 2nd ed., 1756, 17.
137. Davy, Vol. 2, 44.
138. Some at the time and subsequently were skeptical of the claims of arson. See AHCML, FA-63, *Portugal aflito e conturbado . . .*, 457; and Boxer, 1956, 9.
139. BG, AP 12363, Portal, 130.
140. *The Gentleman's Magazine*, Vol. 25, 1755, 559; Davy, Vol. 2, 45.
141. *The Gentleman's Magazine*, Vol. 25, December 1755, 559; Cardoso, 1996 (translated from the Italian), 499.
142. AHCML, FA-63, *Portugal aflito e conturbado . . .*, 47.
143. BA, Ms. Av. 54-XI-16 no. 121, "Relação do terramoto de 1755"; Anonymous, *Destruição de Lisboa* (Lisbon, 1756), 7. "All the elements wished to avenge the offences that people had shown to their Creator." AHCML, FA-63, *Portugal aflito e conturbado . . .*, 284–85.
144. BG, AP 12363, Portal, 131–32.
145. Morganti, 15.
146. *The London Evening Post*, No. 4382, December 9–11, 1755.
147. Anonymous, in *Zwölfte Relation von den erschrecklichen Erdbeben zu Lissabon* (Breslau: 1756).

> *Und was noch deren Grimm verschont,*
> *Muss hier von Feuer aus der Erden*
> *In einen Graus verwandelt warden.*

148. *The Gentleman's Magazine*, Vol. 83, April 1813, 315.

149. Davy, Vol. 2, 31.
150. Ibid., 30–31.
151. Pedegache, 5.
152. Sousa, 1755, 15–16.
153. ASV, Secretaria di Stato Portogallo 231.
154. John Pinto, *Speaking Ruins: Piranesi, Architects and Antiquity in Eighteenth-Century Rome* (Ann Arbor: University of Michigan Press, 2012).
155. AHCML, FA-63, *Portugal aflito e conturbado . . .* , 47.
156. Mendonça, 120.
157. *Letter from a Portuguese Officer . . .* , 8–9.
158. BG, AP 12363, Portal, 220; AHCML, FA-63, *Portugal aflito e conturbado . . .* , 40; Andrade e Sousa, *Subsídio . . .* , 15.
159. Davy, Vol. 2, 42–43.
160. AHCML, FA-63, *Portugal aflito e conturbado . . .* , 163.
161. Pedegache, 5.
162. AHCML, FA-63, *Portugal aflito e conturbado . . .* , 68–69.
163. *An Account of the Late Dreadful Earthquake and Fire . . .* , 2nd ed., 1756, 21–22.
164. AHCML, FA-63, *Portugal aflito e conturbado . . .* , 41.
165. Ibid., 80.
166. Ibid.
167. Figueiredo, 1756, 24.
168. *The Gentleman's Magazine*, Vol. 25, 1755, 558.
169. Davy, Vol. 2, 46–47.

CHAPTER FIVE

The Hour of Pombal

The chapter epigraph is Benjamon Keene's description of Pombal to Abraham Castres (October 1745), Lodge, 1933, 72.

1. The Rua Formosa (Beautiful Street) is today known as the Rua do Século (Century Street).
2. BBM (Biblioteca Brasiliana Guita e José Mindlin, São Paulo), B 18 b, "Historia politica economica do reinado do S. Rey D. Jozé I," f. 10; Mullin, 3.
3. AHCML, FA-63, *Portugal aflito e conturbado . . .* , 193; BBM, B 18 b, ff. 9–10; Mullin, 3; Cheke, 49.
4. Francisco José Freire, *Memorias das Principaes Providencias, que se Derão no Terremoto, que Padeceo a Corte de Lisboa no Anno de 1755, Ordenadas, e Offerecidas à Majestade Fidelissima de El Rey D. Joseph I. Nosso Senhor* (Lisbon, 1758). This book includes orders signed by the king and other state officials. All future references and quotes will be from the 2005 reprint: *1755 Providências do Marquês de Pombal, Volume 3* (Lisbon: FLAD e Público, 2005).
5. *"Senhor, enterrar os mortos e cuidar nos vivos."* Cheke, 66.
6. Monteiro, 2008, 108.
7. Early in his reign, Dom José was purportedly so unsure of his abilities that he once dropped to his knees and begged his younger brother to take the reins of government.
8. Cheke, 25–44. Officially, Pombal's ambassadorship to Great Britain lasted from 1738 to 1748.

9. Quoted in Cheke, 50–51.

10. Ibid.

11. Maxwell, 1995, 178; Marques, 1997, Vol. 1, 398; Nuno Gonçalo Monteiro, "Poder senhorial, estatuto nobilárquico e artistocracia," in José Mattoso, ed., *História de Portugal*, Vol. 5 (of 8), 333–79. Oliveira Marques argues that the Portuguese nobility in the eighteenth century was split into two camps: the old landed aristocracy and a new nobility that embraced business and trade and encouraged the elevation of new individuals to their ranks (men of letters, etc.).

12. Cheke, 61.

13. AHCML, FA-63, *Portugal aflito e conturbado . . .*, 187. See also *1755 Providências . . .*, 249–50.

14. AHCML, CMLSB, ADMG-E, 61, 2600.

15. AHCML, FA-63, *Portugal aflito e conturbado . . .*, 187–88.

16. Ibid.

17. AHCML, CMLSB, ADMG-E, 61, 2600.

18. *1755 Providências . . .*, 93. According to the French Ambassador, Count de Baschi, it was not until December 9 (1755) that the body of his friend, Count Perelada, was recovered from "the shallow ruins" of his palace. "We should have had soldiers dig it up," he wrote. AAE, Correspondance politique, Portugal, 87, f. (reverse) 384.

19. G. de Matos Sequeira, *Depois do terremoto subsídios para a história dos bairros ocidentais de Lisboa*, Vol. 1 (of 4) (Lisbon: Academia as Sciências de Lisboa, 1916), 28; John Smith, *Memoirs of the Marquis of Pombal*, Vol. 1 (of 2) (London: Longman, Brown, Green and Longmans, 1843), 92; BG, AP 12363, Portal, 149.

20. In Helena Carvalhão Buescu and Gonçalo Cordeiro, eds., *O grande terramoto de Lisboa ficar diferente* (Lisbon: Gradiva, 2005), 207. Original in the Museu da Cidade (City Museum), Lisbon. The artist is Maurício José do Carmo Sendim.

21. TNA, SP 80-59, f. 243.

22. Azevedo, 1922, 57.

23. Quoted in Sousa, 1919–32, 679 (from C. Castelo Branco, *Perfil do Marquêz de Pombal*, 1882, 119).

24. AHCML, FA-63, *Portugal aflito e conturbado . . .*, 132–34.

25. Previous to this discovery, the earliest known use of triage was during the late eighteenth and early nineteenth centuries. Christopher R. Blagg, "Triage: Napoleon to the Present Day," *Journal of Nephrology*, 17, 2004, 629–30. See also Kenneth V. Iserson and John C. Moskop, "Triage in Medicine, Part I: Concept, History, and Types," *Annals of Emergency Medicine*, Vol. 49, No. 3, March 2008, 277.

26. AHCML, FA-63, *Portugal aflito e conturbado . . .*, 132–35.

27. Ibid., 136.

28. Ibid., 135.

29. *1755 Providências . . .*, 71; AHU, ACL, CU, 17, Cx. 50, D. 5036, Letter to Gomez Freire de Andrade, governor of Rio de Janeiro, Minas Gerais, and São Paulo, April 14, 1756.

30. *The Maryland Gazette*, No. 560, January 29, 1756.

31. Quoted in James Hutton, *A Hundred Years Ago. An Historical Sketch. 1755 to 1756.* (London: Longman, Brown, Green, Longmans and Roberts, 1857), 77–78, 177.

32. Davy, Vol. 2, 41–42.

33. *Two Very Circumstantial Accounts . . .*, 6.

34. Ratton, 32.

35. Pedegache, 6.
36. Figueiredo, 1756, 23.
37. Davy, Vol. 2, 44.
38. *The Whitehall Evening Post*, Postscript, No. 1524, November 29–December 2, 1755.
39. AHCML, FA-63, *Portugal aflito e conturbado . . .* , 99–100.
40. *The Whitehall Evening Post*, No. 1529, December 11–13, 1755.
41. *Letter to Mr. Joseph Fowke, From his Brother near Lisbon, Dated November 1755 in which is given a very minute and striking Description of the late Earthquake* (Dublin: S. Powell, 1755).
42. AHN, Estado, 2512. In a letter dated November 11, 1755, the queen speaks of her fear of spending the night indoors.
43. *The Whitehall Evening Post*, No. 1533, December 20–23, 1755. By November 11, 1755, Maria had apparently recovered from her illness.
44. *The Scots Magazine*, Vol. 18, February 1756, 94. The sun rose at approximately 6:30 a.m. on November 2, 1755.
45. *The Gentleman's Magazine*, Vol. 83, March 1813, 201.
46. Ibid., 201–2.
47. Ibid., 202.
48. Ibid.
49. Ibid.
50. Ibid.
51. Ibid., 202–3.
52. Ibid, 203–4.
53. Francis, 123.
54. *The Gentleman's Magazine*, Vol. 83, March 1813, 204–5.
55. Ibid., 205.
56. AHCML, FA-63, *Portugal aflito e conturbado . . .* , 105.
57. Ibid., 102–3.
58. ASV, Carte Farnesiane 18, f. 18.
59. ASV, Segretaria di Stato Portogallo 195, f. 182.
60. ASV, Carte Farnesiane 18, f. 18.
61. Ibid.
62. Figueiredo, 1766, 7.
63. *1755 Providências . . .* , 151.
64. Ibid.
65. AHCML, FA-63, *Portugal aflito e conturbado . . .* , 188.
66. *1755 Providências . . .* , Freire, 152–53.
67. *The Maryland Gazette*, No. 573, April 29, 1756.
68. *The Gentleman's Magazine*, Vol. 83, April 1813, 315.
69. Johan Goudsblom, *Fire and Civilization* (London: Penguin, 1992), 148.
70. AHCML, CMLSB, ADMG-E, 61, 2603.
71. *1755 Providências . . .* , 93–96.
72. AHCML, CMLSB, ADMG-E, 61, 2603.
73. *1755 Providências . . .* , 98.
74. ASV, Secretaria di Stato Portogallo 231.
75. *1755 Providências . . .* , 98.
76. AHCML, CMLSB, ADMG-E, 61, 2613; *1755 Providências . . .* , 99.
77. Quoted in Sousa, 1919–32, 632.
78. Figueiredo, 1756, 4.

79. Sousa, 1955, 12.

80. Sousa, 1955, 12; Figueiredo, 1755, 4.

81. ASV, Segretaria di Stato Portogallo 231.

82. Ibid.

83. Figueiredo, 1755, 4–5.

84. Ibid., 5.

85. One shudders to think how many lives would be lost if a future mega-quake and tsunami ever strikes this popular tourist destination whose population of permanent residents now exceeds 450,000.

86. *1755 Providências . . .* , 145–46.

87. ASV, S. Cong. Conc. 635 A; José António Pinheiro e Rosa, "A Diocese de Algarve e a Universidade de Coimbra," *Revista da Universidade de Coimbra*, Vol. 37, 1992, 77–91.

88. ASV, S. Cong. Conc. 635 A, 7.

89. Rosa, 83–85.

90. "Letters from the Pope's Nuncio" intimated "that the Survivors of the late dreadful Calamity were fearful of being put to the Sword by the neighboring Barbarians [i.e., the pirates from the Barbary Coast]." *The Whitehall Evening Post*, No. 1523, November 27–29, 1755.

91. *1755 Providências . . .* , 134–35.

92. Figueiredo, 1766, 11–12. "When enough soldiers were finally gathered together," wrote one chronicler, "they were commanded to spread out and act as guards on the beaches and in all the [largely unmanned] forts and naval towers" along the Tagus. AHCML, FA-63, *Portugal aflito e conturbado . . .* , 190.

93. GSP, I. HA, Geheimer Rat, Rep. 11, Auswärtige Beziehungen, Nr. 8518 (November 3, 1755).

94. Ibid.

95. *The Gentleman's Magazine*, Vol. 83, March 1813, 205–6.

96. *Fernere Nachricht, von den entsetzlichen Erdbeben der Stadt Lissabon welche der P. Vicarii, allda, den 3 Nov. 1755 überschrieben* (1755).

97. *The Gentleman's Magazine*, Vol. 83, March 1813, 205–6.

98. *1755 Providências . . .* , 129–30,

99. AHCML, FA-63, *Portugal aflito e conturbado . . .* , 195–96; Freire, *Providencias*, 126.

100. AHCML, FA-63, *Portugal aflito e conturbado . . .* , 193–94.

101. *1755 Providências . . .* , 126–27.

102. Quoted in Sousa, 1919–32, 518.

103. *1755 Providências . . .* , 129.

104. Figueiredo, 1756, 26–27.

105. *The Gentleman's Magazine*, Vol. 25, December 1755, 559, from a letter dated November 20, 1755, from "Bellem."

106. AHCML, FA-63, *Portugal aflito e conturbado . . .* , 195. The vintém and the tostão were Portuguese coins. The prison mentioned here is the Cadeia da Galé.

107. *1755 Providências . . .* , 135.

108. Ibid., 136–37; AHCML, FA-63, *Portugal aflito e conturbado . . .* , 196–97.

109. *1755 Providências . . .* , 130–31.

110. AHCML, FA-63, *Portugal aflito e conturbado . . .* , 88.

111. Ibid., 197–98.

112. Ibid., 199.

113. *1755 Providências . . .* , 251.

114. BG, AP 12363, Portal, 197; AHCML, FA-63, *Portugal aflito e conturbado* . . . , 199.

115. BG, AP 12363, Portal, 197. It is unclear whether Portal is referring to cruzados here.

116. *1755 Providências* . . . , 250–51.

117. ANTT, Hospital São José, Maço 1, No. 28, Cx. 397.

118. AHCML, FA-63, *Portugal aflito e conturbado* . . . , 192.

119. BL, Add. 46362, ff. 83–84, Letter from Englishman E. Turnville (November 19, 1755). "For about eleven o'clock the same day fires broke out in several parts of the ruins and there being no capability of extinguishing them the streets being . . . impassable by the rubbish of the fallen houses and the general panick that . . . hindered the Portuguese from giving the assistance that they might."

120. França, 1983, 56; Schwarcz, 43–44, 47.

121. Quoted in Ferreira de Andrade, *Lisboa e seus serviços de incêndios: Vol. I, 1395–1868* (Lisbon, 1969), 9.

122. Andrade, 29.

123. Ibid., 51.

124. Ibid., 53.

125. Ibid., 63.

126. Ibid., 157–58.

127. Figueiredo, 1766, 10–11.

128. AHCML, FA-63, *Portugal aflito e conturbado* . . . , 190; *1755 Providências* . . . , 102.

129. Figueiredo, 1766, 11.

130. AHCML, CMLSB, ADMG-E, 61, 2603.

131. *The Gentleman's Magazine*, Vol. 25, 1755, 561.

132. *Gesammelte Nachrichten* . . . , 27; AHCML, FA-63, *Portugal aflito e conturbado* . . . , 191–92.

133. TNA, SP 89-50, f. 119, Letter from Marvilla, near Lisbon, November 15, 1755.

134. *The Gentleman's Magazine*, Vol. 25, 1755, 561–62; *The Whitehall Evening Post*, No. 1536, December 27–29, 1755.

135. BG, AP 12363, Portal, 154. One vintém was worth 20 réis.

136. AHCML, FA-63, *Portugal aflito e conturbado* . . . , 191.

137. *The Gentleman's Magazine*, Vol. 25, 1755, 561–62.

138. *1755 Providências* . . . , 108–9.

139. *The Gentleman's Magazine*, Vol. 25, 1755, 561–62.

140. *1755 Providências* . . . , 111–12.

141. *The Gentleman's Magazine*, Vol. 25, 1755, 562.

142. Mendonça, 145.

143. Quoted in Henry E. Bourne, "Food Control and Price-Fixing in Revolutionary France: I," *Journal of Political Economy*, Vol. 27, No. 2, February 1919, 93. See also Henry E. Bourne, "Food Control and Price-Fixing in Revolutionary France: II," *Journal of Political Economy*, Vol. 27, No. 3, March 1919.

144. Holman Jenkins, "Hug a Price Gouger: The Public Doesn't Want to Hear It, but the Public Also Doesn't Like Empty Shelves, *The Wall Street Journal*, October 30, 2012.

145. Bourne, February 1919, 93.

146. *1755 Providências* . . . , 117–18.

147. BG, AP 12363, Portal, 154. The first ship sailed for Pernambuco on January 1, 1756. Kendrick, 52–53.

148. *The Whitehall Evening Post*, No. 1612, June 19–22, 1756.

149. TNA, SP 89/50, f. 313.

150. BG, AP 12363, Portal, 228–31, 224–25.
151. See the *Mercurio Histórico y Político*, March 1756, January 1757, February 1757, and March 1757.
152. AHCML, FA-63, *Portugal aflito e conturbado . . .* , 151.
153. ANTT, Manuscrito 1229.
154. Nason, 63–65, 69; "Charles Henry Frankland Diary, 1755–1767" (manuscript), MHS, Microfilm, P-363, Reel 4.4.
155. *1755 Providências . . .* , 83.
156. Ibid., 201–2.
157. Ibid., 84.
158. *The Whitehall Evening Post*, No. 1526, December 4–6, 1755.
159. *1755 Providências . . .* , 124–25, 73.
160. Ibid., 132.
161. Ibid., 127–28.

CHAPTER SIX

City of Ashes, Huts of Wood

The chapter epigraph is found in ANTT, MPRQ, 20, 93r (*Memórias paroquiais*, 1758), 845. Father Sarmento was describing his parish and his church after the disaster.

1. *Supplement to the Gentleman's Magazine*, 1755, "Further Particulars of the Earthquake at Lisbon," 591–92.
2. Bellamy, Vol. 6, 63–64, Letter November 12, 1755.
3. *An Account of the Late Dreadful Earthquake and Fire . . .* , 2nd ed., 1756, 5.
4. Davy, Vol. 2, 56. According to another eyewitness, "the sight of the bones, which remained in the streets and inside homes, was the cause of much fear and horror." Marginalia in a copy of Joaquim José Moreira de Mendonça's *Historia Universal dos Terremotos . . .* NYPL *KF 1758, 139.
5. Davy, Vol. 2, 55–56.
6. ANTT, Manuscrito 1229.
7. Morganti, 5.
8. AHCML, FA-63, *Portugal aflito e conturbado . . .* , 164–65.
9. Ibid., 160–61.
10. ANTT, Manuscrito 1229.
11. AHCML, FA-63, *Portugal aflito e conturbado . . .* , 161.
12. Macaulay, 1946, 269, 270–71.
13. TNA, SP 89-50, f. 115.
14. Sousa, 1919–32, 649 (from a 1924 article in *A Época*).
15. AHCML, FA-63, *Portugal aflito e conturbado . . .* , 182.
16. BA, Ms. Av. 54-XI-16 no. 121, "Relação do terramoto de 1755." The main culprits, according to this author, were fleas (*"pulgas"*), lice (*"piolhos"*), and bedbugs (*"percevejos"*).
17. AHCML, FA-63, *Portugal aflito e conturbado . . .* , 182.
18. Ibid., 184–85.
19. Ibid., 171.
20. *1755 Providências . . .* , 158–59.
21. Ibid., 164–65.
22. AHCML, FA-63, *Portugal aflito e conturbado . . .* , 173.

23. AIbid., 174.
24. Ibid., 17376.
25. Dumouriez, 123.
26. BG, AP 12363, Portal, 193–94.
27. Quoted in Sousa, 1955, 15.
28. ML, LHMS, Acc. No. MA 4543. It is not certain that the author was Swiss.
29. Mendonça, 146.
30. BG, AP 12363, Portal, 153.
31. Figueiredo, 1756, 27. Lisbon's patriarch orders the construction of "decent *barracas*" throughout the city so that mass can be celebrated in them.
32. BG, AP 12363, Portal, 154.
33. *Eilfte Relation von den erschrecklichen Erdbeben zu Lissabon, Oder: Abdruck derjenigen Briefe, wie selbe dieses grosse Unglück von verschiedenen Orten mit mehrern Umständen berichtet haben* (Breslau, 1756).
34. *The Whitehall Evening Post*, No. 1533, December 20–23, 1755.
35. AHCML, FA-63, *Portugal aflito e conturbado . . .* , 137–38.
36. Ibid., 145.
37. Ibid., 146–48.
38. ANTT, Manuscrito 1229.
39. Ibid., 150.
40. *1755 Providências . . .* , 99.
41. Figueiredo, 1766, 9.
42. AHCML, FA-63, *Portugal aflito e conturbado . . .* , 115–17.
43. Ibid.
44. Ibid., 116–19.
45. Ibid.
46. BG, AP 12363, Portal, 196.
47. Mendonça, 160–61.
48. *Mercurio Histórico y Político*, Vol. 82, January 1756, 24.
49. BG, AP 12363, Portal, 144, 137. The second quote is from Portal not the patriarch. Figueiredo, 1756, 27–28.
50. *1755 Providências . . .* , 241–43.
51. Mendonça, 147; Figueiredo, 1756, 28; *1755 Providências . . .* , 242.
52. His name was José Dantas Barbosa.
53. Figueiredo, 1756, 28–29; Mendonça, 148.
54. BG, AP 12363, Portal, 143.
55. Ibid.
56. *1755 Providências . . .* , 244–48.
57. Israel, 2012, 46.

CHAPTER SEVEN

Word Spreads

The second chapter epigraph is from The Huntington Library, Elizabeth Robinson Montagu Papers, Dec. 1755, M01540.

1. *The Whitehall Evening Post*, No. 1528, December 9–11, 1755; *Gazette de France*, No. 47, November 22, 1755, 567; *The London Gazette*, No. 9532, November 25–29, 1755; *The General Evening Post* (London), No. 3419, November 25, 1755.

2. *Gaceta de Madrid*, No. 44, November 4, 1755, 351–52.

3. In the eighteenth century, there was much less of an expectation that one's letters would remain private.

4. *Gazette de Cologne*, Vol. 95, November 28, 1755; Lodge, 1933, 434.

5. *The Whitehall Evening Post*, No. 1524, November 29–December 2, 1755.

6. Lodge, 1933, 434.

7. TNA, SP 94/149, 238.

8. AHN, Estado 2507, November 18, 1755.

9. *The Whitehall Evening Post*, No. 1523, November 27–29, 1755.

10. Lodge, 1933, 434.

11. TNA, SP 89-50, f. 187. A piece of eight was worth a little less than one quarter of a British pound.

12. Diego Téllez Alarcia, "Spanish Interpretations of the Lisbon Earthquake Between 1755 and the War of 1762," in T. E. D. Braun and J. B. Radner, eds., *The Lisbon Earthquake of 1755: Representations and Reactions* (Oxford: Voltaire Foundation, 2005).

13. TNA, SP 94/149, letter, November 24, 1755.

14. Despite the queen's best efforts, Spain's generosity was, in at least one case, limited by political and economic considerations. Although the Spanish administrator of the royal rents, Don José García, "had prepared . . . a very considerable Assortment of Supplies" (largely consisting of clothing) to present to the Portuguese, he soon realized after his arrival in Lisbon that he had been sent on a "fruitless Errand," according to Abraham Castres (who made it his business to know which countries were offering Portugal aid). Treaty obligations, García learned, forbade Portugal from importing clothing from Spain—even clothing that had been given as a gift. TNA, SP 89–50, ff. 165–66.

15. *Gaceta de Madrid*, No. 45, November 11, 1755, 359. On November 25, the *Gaceta* reported that Perelada had been replaced by Don Pedro Pablo Abarca de Bolea y Jiménez de Urrea, the 10th Count of Aranda. *Gaceta de Madrid*, No. 47, November 25, 1755, 376.

16. Keene estimates the boy's age at seven years. TNA, SP 94/149, December 10, 1755.

17. *Gaceta de Madrid*, No. 45, November 11, 1755, 359; *The London Gazette*, No. 9532, November 25–29, 1755.

18. AHN, Estado 2507, Letter, November 18, 1755.

19. Lodge, 1933, 435.

20. Ibid., 434.

21. *Mercurio Histórico y Político*, Vol. 80, November 1755, 12.

22. Aguilar Piñal, "Conmoción espiritual en Sevilla por el terremoto de 1755," *Archivo hispalense*, No. 171–73 (1973), 37–53. See also Carmen Espejo Cala, "Spanish News Pamphlets on the 1755 Earthquake: Trade Strategies of the Printers of Sevilla," in Braun and Radner, 66–80.

23. The printer's name was Pedro Ferreira.

24. André Belo, "A notícia do terramoto no sistema de informação do antigo Regime," in Maria Fernanda Rollo, Ana Isabel Buescu, and Pedro Cardim, eds., *História e ciência da catástrofe: 250 aniversário do terramoto de 1755* (Lisbon: Colibri, 2007), 63–66; André Belo, "A *Gazeta de Lisboa* e o terramoto de 1755: a margem do não escrito," *Análise Social*, Vol. 34 (151–52), 1999, No. 2–3, 619, footnote 4.

25. *Gazeta de Lisboa*, No. 45, November 6, 1755, 360.
26. Ibid., No. 46, November 13, 1755, 361–70. A story about repairs to the Torre do Tombo was relegated to the final lines of the issue.
27. Belo, 1999.
28. Andrew Pettegree, *The Invention of News: How the World Came to Know About Itself* (New Haven, CT: Yale University Press, 2014), 8–9, 314.
29. Belo, 2007, 55–66.
30. Belo, 1999, 615–33; Ana Cristina Araújo, "Literacy and Social Order: Writing and Reading in Lisbon in the 18th Century" (online), 93–108; Pettegree, 118.
31. *Gazette de France*, No. 47, November 22, 1755, 566.
32. Pettegree, 54.
33. This assumes that the rider left at 9 a.m. on November 4. The sources only say he departed in the "morning."
34. One ship from Lisbon, which might otherwise have been the first to deliver the news to Britain, was delayed by the weather and had to be diverted to Guernsey. Peter Gould, "Lisbon 1755: Enlightenment, Catastrophe, and Communication," in *Geography and Enlightenment*, edited by David Livingstone and Charles W. J. Withers (Chicago: University of Chicago Press, 1999), 403.
35. AAE, Correspondance Politique, 87, Portugal, ff. 224–25.
36. ASV, Segretaria di Stato Portogallo 195, f. 182; *Staats- und gelehrte Zeitung des Hamburgischer Unparteyischer Correspondent*, No. 191, December 3, 1755.
37. E. J. B. Rathery, *Journal and Memoirs of the Marquis d'Argenson*, Vol. 2 (of 2) (Boston: Hardy, Pratt & Co., 1901), 337.
38. Christine Pevitt Algrant, *Madame de Pompadour: Mistress of France* (New York: Grove, 2002), 69. Baschi had previously served as minister plenipotentiary to the elector of Bavaria.
39. TNA, SP 89/50, ff. 167, Letter from Abraham Castes, December 27, 1755.
40. *Sankt-Peterburgskie Vedomosti*, December 19, 1755 (Julian calendar), No. 101.
41. *The Whitehall Evening Post*, No. 1529, December 11–13, 1755. Baschi was particularly distraught at having lost three state coaches worth more than 30,000 livres.
42. Quoted in Poirer, 2005, 45.
43. TNA, SP 94/149, f. 321, letter from Benjamin Keene, December 28, 1755.
44. Quoted in Poirer, 2005, 42. In 1760, Baschi became the French ambassador to Venice.
45. *Gazette de France*, No. 47, November 22, 1755, 566–68.
46. Araújo, 2006.
47. *Journal étranger*, December 1755, Vol. 2, 235.
48. Ibid.
49. Ibid., 238–39.
50. *Courrier d'Avignon*, No. 95, November 28, 1755, 381, 383.
51. Ibid., No. 96, December 2, 1755, 386.
52. ANTT, MNE-ASC, C, 2, 7.
53. *The Maryland Gazette*, No. 574, May 6, 1756. The amount was worth about £16,600 at the time. Abraham Castres gleaned from his inquiries that only "a general Offer of Services" was made by Baschi. TNA, SP 89-50, f. 165, Letter dated December 27, 1755. A pistole was worth approximately .83 British pound, http://www2.vcdh.virginia.edu/gos/currency.html.

54. TNA, SP 89-50, f. 165. Father Portal claims that the French offered "400,000 cruzados each month." BG, AP 12363, Portal, 161.

55. *The Whitehall Evening Post,* No. 1521, November 22–25.

56. Ibid., No. 1520, November 20–22.

57. See Matthias Georgi, "Das Erdbeben von Lissabon in der englischen Publizistik," in Gerhard Lauer and Thorsten Unger, eds., *Das Erdbeben von Lissabon und der Katastrophendiskurs im 18. Jahrhundert* (Göttingen: Wallstein Verlag, 2008), 96–109.

58. *The Public Advertiser,* No. 6576, November 25, 1755; *The General Evening Post* (London), No. 3419, November 25, 1755.

59. *The Whitehall Evening Post,* No. 1521, November 22–25, 1755; *The London Evening Post,* No. 4375, November 22–25, 1755; *The Whitehall Evening Post,* Postscript, No. 1524, November 29–December 2, 1755.

60. *The Whitehall Evening Post,* No. 1521, November 22–25, 1755; *The London Evening Post,* No. 4375, November 22–25, 1755; *The Whitehall Evening Post,* Postscript, No. 1524, November 29–December 2, 1755.

61. *The Whitehall Evening Post,* No. 1521, November 22–25, 1755.

62. Horace Walpole, *The Letters of Horace Walpole, 4th Earl of Oxford,* Peter Cunningham, ed., Vol. 2 (of 9) (Edinburgh: John Grant, 1906), 489. Walpole continues: "There have been lately such earthquakes and waterquakes, and rocks rent, and other strange phenomena, that one would think the world exceedingly out of repair."

63. *Correspondence of John, Fourth Duke of Bedford,* Vol. 2 (of 3) (London: Longman, Brown, Green and Longmans, 1843), 174 (letter from Mr. Rigby, November 26, 1755).

64. The author continues his list of epithets: "blushless caitiffs, common plunderers, groveling treacherous plunderers, heartless thieves, vipers, doubly malignant wretches, ribalds, growling groveling bipeds, scandal-yelping crew, varlets lavish with falsehood, rogues, drones, loggerheads, journalistic fire-eaters, superlative coxcombs, crack-brained dealers in absurdity, drivellers, oafs, cubs, jack-a-lanterns, hounds, heartless, freebooting aliens, crawling vermin, unnatural fry of barbarous insects, one is a heartless witling that chokes himself with swallowing a flight, another is a little griping understrapper with a dirt-raking mind and spurious breath." *A Satirical Review of the Manifold Falsehoods and Absurdities hitherto published concerning the Earthquake; to which is annexed an authentic Account of the late catastrophe at Lisbon, and the present state of that august Capital. By a Man of Business* (London: A. and C. Corbett, 1756).

65. J. Wilson Croker, ed., *Johnsoniana or, Supplement to Boswell: Being Anecdotes and Sayings of Dr. Johnson* (Philadelphia: Cary & Hart, 1842), 57.

66. Walpole, Horace. W. S. Lewis, ed. *The Yale Edition of Horace Walpole's Correspondence.* Vol. 20 (of 48) (New Haven, CT: Yale University Press, 1937–1983). Letter to Horace Mann, April 2, 1750, 133.

67. Kendrick, 11.

68. Walpole, Letter to Horace Mann, April 2, 1750, Lewis Walpole Library, Yale University, 137.

69. Quoted in Kendrick, 13. In the opinion of one Anglican clergyman, at least half the population of London—or more than a quarter of a million people—left the city. This was undoubtedly an exaggeration.

70. Quoted in Kendrick, 14.

71. Delany, Vol. 3, 378–79.

72. Walpole, Vol. 20 (of 48), Letter to Horace Mann, December 4, 1755, 513.

73. BL, India Office Records and Private Papers, IOR/Z/E4/1/L108, p. 345.

74. Walpole, Vol. 22 (of 48), Letter to Horace Mann, March 22, 1762, 17. "We have never recovered masquerades since the earthquake at Lisbon."

75. TNA SP 36/150/157. http://www.hrionline.ac.uk/londonliveswiki/tiki-index.php ?page=Brasel%2C+Daniel+(transported+1756)#ref_footnote1.

76. http://www.londonlives.org/browse.jsp?div=s17560225-1.

77. *The Whitehall Evening Post*, No. 1523, November 27–29, 1755.

78. Ibid., No. 1524, November 29–December 2, 1755.

79. Ibid., No. 1525, December 2–4, 1755.

80. Ibid., No. 1523, November 27–29, 1755. For the British merchant community, maintaining the lines of communication with Portugal was crucial. See the praise given to British postmaster general and fellow merchant Sir Everard Fawkner. *The Whitehall Evening Post*, No. 1524, November 29–December 2, 1755.

81. *The Whitehall Evening Post*, No. 1524, November 29–December 2, 1755.

82. Horace Walpole, *Memoires of the Last Ten Years of the Reign of George II*, Vol. 1 (of 2) (London: John Murray, 1822), 431. Walpole states erroneously that he read Benjamin Keene's letter. But that did not arrive until December 2.

83. William Cobbett et al., eds., *The Parliamentary History of England from the Earliest Period to the Year 1803*, Vol. 15, *A.D. 1753–1765* (London: T. C. Hansard, 1813), 543–44.

84. Mary Lindemann, "Fundamental Values: Political Culture in Eighteenth-Century Hamburg," in Peter Uwe Hohendahl, ed., *Patriotism, Cosmopolitanism, and National Culture: Public Culture in Hamburg* (Amsterdam and New York: Editions Rodopi C.V., 2003), 23–24.

85. Gould, 404.

86. TNA, SP 89-50, ff. 110–11.

87. See Lewis Namier, *The Structure of Politics at the Accession of George II* (New York: St. Martin's, reprint, 1968).

88. TNA, SP 89-50, f. 111. A year earlier, such assistance might not have even been possible as the supply of bullion in London banks had declined so severely (due to the payment of overseas debts) that, according to one eighteenth-century historian, "you could scarcely obtain a payment of one hundred pounds sterling in the lawful gold coin of the country, and as for silver, there was scarcely any left." However, since August 1755, most of these debts had been paid and the Bank of England was now flush with bullion. Vivant de Mezague, *A General View of England Respecting Its Policy, Trade, Commerce, Taxes, Debts, Produce of Lands, Colonies, Manners . . . From the Year 1600 to 1762* (London: J. Robson, 1766), 150–51. See also Sir John Clapham, *The Bank of England*, Vol. 1 (of 2) (Cambridge: Cambridge University Press, reprint, 1966), 236.

89. *The Whitehall Evening Post*, No. 1524, November 29–December 2, 1755; *The Whitehall Evening Post*, No. 1523, November 27–29, 1755.

90. TNA, SP 89-50, ff. 110–11.

91. Clarke, [?]. *The Georgian Era: Memoirs of the Most Eminent Persons, Who Have Flourished in Great Britain, From the Accession of George the First to the Demise of George the Fourth*, Vol. I (of 4) (London: Vizetelly, Branston and Co., 1832), 295.

92. ANTT, MNE-Asc, C, 2, 9.
93. Cobbett, 544.
94. James Hutton, *A Hundred Years Ago. An Historical Sketch. 1755 to 1756* (London: Longman, Brown, Green, Longmans and Roberts, 1857), 77–78.
95. *Horace Walpole's Correspondence*, Vol. 20, 520, Letter, December 25, 1755.
96. TNA, SP 94/149, f. 313 (reverse), Letter, December 22, 1755.
97. TNA, SP 89-50, f. 94.
98. Ibid., f. 94–95.
99. Ibid., f. 105. This quote is from Henry Fox.
100. According to Edward Hay, Castres's letter of November 6 was entrusted to a Falmouth-bound ship that set sail on November 13 or 14. TNA, SP 89-50, f. 118.
101. Ibid., f. 114–15.
102. Francis, 123.
103. TNA, SP 89-50, f. 116.
104. Ibid.
105. Ibid., f. 119.
106. Ibid., f. 118.
107. Ibid., f. 120.
108. Ibid., f. 119.
109. Ibid., f. 129–30.
110. TNA, SP 89-50, f. 134, Letter, December 10, 1755.
111. Ibid., f. 134, Letter, December 10, 1755.
112. Ibid., f. 142.
113. Ibid., f. 140.
114. Ibid., f. 149.
115. Kendrick, 148.
116. *The London Evening Post*, No. 4381, December 6–9, 1755.
117. *The Whitehall Evening Post*, No. 1533, December 20–23, 1755.
118. Ibid., No. 1522, November 25–27, 1755.
119. *The London Evening Post*, No. 4386, December 18–20, 1755.
120. *The Gentleman's Magazine*, Vol. 83, March & April 1813, 206, 314.
121. Chase died on November 20, 1788, at the age of fifty-nine.
122. *The Gentleman's Magazine*, Vol. 83, April 1813, 315.
123. *The Whitehall Evening Post*, No. 1530, December 13–16, 1755.
124. *Eilfte Relation von den erschrecklichen Erdbeben zu Lissabon, Oder: Abdruck derjenigen Briefe, wie selbe dieses grosse Unglück von verschiedenen Orten mit mehrern Umständen berichtet haben* (Breslau, 1756).
125. BL, India Office Records and Private Papers, IOR/E/1/39 ff. 215–16v.
126. Quoted in Jeroen Blaak, *Literacy in Everyday Life: Reading and Writing in Early Modern Dutch Diaries* (Leiden, Netherlands: Brill, 2009), 220.
127. Blaak, 220.
128. *Gazette de Amsterdam*, Vol. 94, November 25, 1755; *Gazette de Leyde*, No. 94, November 25, 1755.
129. Quoted in Blaak, 221.
130. *Berlinischen Nachrichten*, December 4, 1755.
131. The *Leydse Courant* reported on the *"vervaarlyke Aardbeeving"* (frightful earthquake) in Portugal; and the *Gazette de Amsterdam* provided a detailed account of "the terrible shock" that destroyed "all of Lisbon's churches and the Royal Palace." *Gazette de Amsterdam*, Vol. 95, November 28, 1755; *Leydse Courant*, No. 143,

November 28, 1755; *Gazette de Leyde*, No. 95, November 28, 1755. The news plunged the Amsterdam Stock Exchange into "a great consternation."

132. Blaak, 221.

133. NAN, 1.01.02, Staten-Generaal, 11, Bestanddeel 7027.

134. *Mercurio Histórico y Político*, Vol. 82, January 1756, 21–22. "La particular estimación, que hago de la República de las Provincias Unidas, me empeñará siempre en tener tanta parte en lo que los interesa, quanta estoy persuadido que los estados de esta República tomaren en el suceso fatal, que acaba de afligir a mi Reyno."

135. De Jong, 195–98.

136. *Gazette de Cologne*, Vol. 95, November 28, 1755.

137. Ibid., Vol. 98, December 9, 1755.

138. Gould, 404.

139. ANTT, MNE, Caixa 513.

140. *Mercurio Histórico y Político*, Vol. 132, January 1756, 11; TNA, SP 89-50, f. 147, Letter from Abraham Castres.

141. Erik Lindberg, "The Rise of Hamburg as a Global Marketplace in the Seventeenth Century: A Comparative Political Economy Perspective," *Comparative Studies in Society and History*, Vol. 50, No. 3, 2008, 656.

142. *Hamburgischer Unparteyischer Correspondent*, No. 178, November 8, 1755.

143. Ibid., No. 189, November 28, 1755.

144. TNA, SP 82, Roll 75-77, f. 147 (back), letter dated November 28, 1755.

145. *Hamburgischer Unparteyischer Correspondent*, No. 190, November 29, 1755.

146. Ibid., No. 191, December 2, 1755.

147. Ibid., No. 16, January 28, 1756.

148. Jürgen Wilke, "Daß der Jammer un das Elend mit keiner Feder zu beschreiben sey," *Relation*, Vol. 3, No. 1, 1996, 62.

149. Quoted in Ulrich Löffler, *Lissabons Fall—Europas Schrecken: die Deutung des Erdbebens von Lissabon im deutschsprachigen Protestantismus des 18. Jahrhunderts* (Berlin: Walter de Gruyter, 1999), 438.

150. On December 3, a letter from Hamburg's Hanseatic agents in Madrid was read aloud to the public. It provided eagerly awaited information on the fate of the city's merchants and their families and staffs living in Lisbon. Martin Johann Lappenberg, "Hamburg und das Erdbeben zu Lissabon am 1. November 1755," Vol. 4, in *Zeitschrift des Vereins für Hamburgische Geschichte* (Hamburg: Verl. Verein für Hamburgische Geschichte, 1858), 276, 279. Letter from the Hamburg Senate to José I: "What a lamentable and ruinous fate has befallen Lisbon[!] . . . We cannot help but let your Majesty know . . . of the barely consolable grief with which we are afflicted, [and] imploring with the most ardent prayers the best and greatest God, by whose inscrutable act this most bitter unhappiness came about, that He may bring the most effective solace to your grief . . . and that the greatest prosperity might be bestowed most abundantly upon you, most Holy Prince, as the true Father of his Country, to extreme old age.

"Would that we were able . . . in some manner to provide aid worthy for the restoration of both the celebrated royal palace and the city so dear to us. For this reason, we have ordered that ships be immediately loaded with stocks of beams and rafters for the purpose of repairing buildings; and, as soon as possible, we will make sure that they are sent to Lisbon. . . . We earnestly ask that your Majesty, with a most indulgent attitude, not refuse this humble little gift as a sign of our most eager attention." Staatsarchiv Hamburg, Germany, 111-1 Senat, Cl, VI, Nr.

7 Vol. 2, Fasc. 1. I would like to thank my colleagues Frederick Booth and Michael Mascio for help in translating this letter from the original Latin.

151. Lappenberg, 279.

152. CB, Signatur S/599, Protocoll. Commercii. Lit. CC. (March 29, 1754–November 9, 1756), ff. 147–53.

153. Ibid.

154. Ibid.; BG, AP 12363, Portal, 160

155. CB, Signatur S/599, Protocoll. Commercii. Lit. CC. (March 29, 1754–November 9, 1756), ff. 147–53; BG, AP 12363, Portal, 160.

156. Mary Lindemann, *Patriots and Paupers: Hamburg, 1712–1830* (New York: Oxford University Press, 1990), 83–89.

157. Lappenberg, 279–80.

158. SH, 111-1 Senat, Cl, VI, Nr. 7 Vol. 2, Fasc. 1, copy of the letter. I would like to thank Frederick Booth and Michael Mascio for their help in translating this letter.

159. Lappenberg, 279–80.

160. *Kjøbenhavnske Danske Post-Tidender.*

161. Robert Brown, 1991, 24.

162. *Ordinari Post Tijdender*; Shrady, 116; Schäfer, 68. Quoted in Gould, 404. Both newspapers are still in existence.

163. Mitchell's letter may have arrived in Potsdam before Braamcamp's letter because presumably it was sent from London by ship.

164. *Politische Correspondenz Friedrich's des Grossen* (Berlin: Verlag von Alexander Duncker, 1883), 425. Mitchell's letter was dated December 25.

165. Andrew Hamilton, *Rheinsberg: Memorials of Frederick the Great and Prince Henry of Prussia*, Vol. 2 (of 2) (London: John Murray, 1880), 95.

166. *Politische Correspondenz*, 426.

167. Ibid., 432, Letter dated December 16, 1755.

168. *Politische Correspondenz*, 433. The ambassador's name was Wilhlem von Klinggräffen. Conversion: http://www.pierre-marteau.com/currency/converter/fra-eng.html.

169. *Politische Correspondenz*, 437; GSP, HA Geheimer Rat, Rep 11 Auswärtige Beziehungen, Akten Nr. 8518, Draft of letter from Heinrich Graf von Podewils and Karl Wilhelm Finck von Finckenstein.

170. ANTT, MNE-ASC, C, 2, 12. The rest of the letter is as follows: "The vision of that fatal event, of the destruction of so many of your loyal subjects, and of the ruin of [such] a large and flourishing city are sufficient to paint [a picture] for us of the extreme suffering that you must have naturally felt. . . . We console ourselves that the Almighty has protected the sacred person of Your Majesty as well as the Royal Family. May God keep You and provide not only the means to repair through his blessings the immense losses, [but provide you] with all his force, happiness, and prosperity. We ask Your Majesty to be assured of the sincerity of these sentiments as well as the perfect friendship and consideration [that we have for you.]"

171. *Hamburgischer Unparteyischer Correspondent*, No. 206, December 30, 1755.

172. It was known as the Treaty of Westminster.

173. For example: *Zwölfte Relation von den erschrecklichen Erdbeben zu Lissabon, Oder: Abdruck derjenigen Briefe, wie selbe dieses grosse Unglück von verschiedenen Orten mit mehrern Umständen berichtet haben* (Breslau, 1756). Still, errors like the reported

deaths of the Swedish and Dutch consuls were widespread in German accounts of the earthquake and difficult to correct. SH, 111-1 Senat, CL, VI, Nr. 7, Vol. 2, Fasc. 1. This printed letter from Lisbon (dated November 4, 1755) may have been responsible for the false reporting of these deaths.

174. See, for example, *Physikalische Betrachtungen . . .*

175. *Gazette de Cologne*, Vol. 7, January 23, 1756. There is no independent confirmation of such a gift.

176. *Wienerisches Diarium*, No. 98, December 6, 1755.

177. ANTT, MNE-ASC, C, 2, 1, Letter, December 5, 1755.

178. *La Gazette Bolognesi*, No. 1, January 7, 1755, 4. Florins were another name for gulden. Conversion: http://www.pierre-marteau.com/currency/converter/wie-eng .html.

179. *Hamburgischer Unparteyischer Correspondent*, No. 206, December 30, 1755. Conversion: http://www.pierre-marteau.com/currency/coins/default.html.

180. *The Boston Weekly News-Letter*, April 1, 1756; *The Maryland Gazette*, No. 573, April 29, 1756.

181. Smith, Vol. 1, 97, footnote.

182. *Gazette de Cologne*, Vol. 1, January 2, 1756. The people of Bologna first learned that an earthquake had occurred outside Italy in the November 25 edition of the *Gazette Bolognesi*. "A vigorous earthquake tremor was felt [in the Netherlands] on the morning of November first," read the report from The Hague. Fortunately, the shaking did not last long or cause substantial damage, though "the waters in most of Amsterdam's canals became violently swollen." On December 2, an account from Hamburg spoke of "an extraordinary agitation of the waters" near Lübeck—"phenomena that were similar," the editors observed, to those which had "occurred [on the very same day] in Amsterdam and in almost all the states of Holland." A week later, the *bolognesi* learned that "an earthquake had caused great bloodshed" in Lisbon, that the Spanish ambassador was dead, and the Portuguese royal family was living in "tents in the countryside." From Venice came conflicting reports that 50,000 to 100,000 (or more) people had perished. *La Gazette Bolognesi*, No. 48, 2, November 25, 1755, 2. For the Italian reaction, see Sergia Adamo, "Constructing an Event, Contemplating Ruins, Theorizing Nature; the Lisbon Earthquake and Some Italian Reactions," *European Review*, Vol. 14, Issue 3, July 2006, 339–49; *La Gazette Bolognesi*, No. 49, December 2, 1755, 2; and *La Gazette Bolognesi*, No. 50, December 9, 1755, 4.

183. *Gazette de Cologne*, Vol. 5, January 16, 1756; Cardoso, 1999, 510.

184. *The Maryland Gazette*, No. 572, April 22, 1756. The report is dated December 6 (1755). On December 13, the *Diario Ordinario* of Rome reported "the ominous news of a terrible earthquake" in Lisbon, which caused "considerable damage and loss of life." Four days later, the people of Rome read that this *"terribilissimo Ter-remoto"* was followed by a large fire and "an inundation of water," which left "that vast city in ruins." *Diario Ordinario*, December 13, 1755, 12; *Diario Ordinario*, December 17, 1755, 4.

185. ANTT, BUL, 0062, 04, December 10, 1755.

186. ASV, Segretaria di Stato, Portogallo 178, ff. 273–74.

187. Ibid., f. 275.

188. Ibid., ff. 276–77.

189. Quoted in Neri, 68–69.

190. ASG, Ambasciata in Portogallo 2659. Vigánego apparently wrote letters to Genoa on November 18, 1755, February 3, 1756, May 11, 1756, and June 22, 1756. Only the latter two appear to exist in manuscript form in the Genoese State Archives.

191. ASN, Ministero degli Affari esteri, Portogallo, n. 918, Letter, November 4, 1755. Special thanks to Pasquale Terracciano for helping me with this translation.

192. Quoted in Lodge, 1933, 437.

193. ASV, Segretaria di Stato Portogallo 196, f. 54.

194. See Brito, 29–31.

195. ASVe, Ambasciata in Spagna, b. 63.

196. ASVe, Senato, Dispacci . . . , Spagna, f. 168, Letters, November 4 and 11, 1755.

197. ANTT, MNE-ASC, C, 2, 17.

198. ASV, Principi 237, f. 423.

199. ANTT, MNE-ASC, C, 2, 14. The letter is dated January 31, 1756.

200. Russia used the Julian calendar until 1918. *Sankt-Peterburgskie Vedomosti*, No. 97, December 5, 1755 (Julian calendar). The report from Paris is dated November 21, 1755; *Sankt-Peterburgskie Vedomosti*, No. 99, December 12, 1755 (Julian calendar).

201. *Sankt-Peterburgskie Vedomosti*, No. 97, December 5, 1755 (Julian calendar). The report from Paris is dated November 21, 1755.

202. *Moskovskiye Vedomosti*, No. 2, April 30, 1756 (Julian calendar).

203. AVPRI, P. Snosheniia Poccuu s Angliei, November 14/25, 1755, op. 35/1, d. 769, l. 36566. I would like to thank my colleagues Nathaniel Knight and Maxim Matusevich for their help in translating these letters.

204. One pistole was worth .83 pounds. Conversion: http://www2.vcdh.virginia.edu /gos/currency.html.

205. AVPRI, P. Snosheniia Poccuu s Angliei, November 16–27, 1755, op. 35/1, d. 769, l. 370–71.

206. Quoted in *Relações diplomáticas luso-russas: Colectânea documental conjunta* (1722–1815), Vol. 1 (Lisbon: Instituto Diplomático, 2004), 67.

207. Evgeny V. Anisimov, *Empress Elizabeth: Her Reign and Her Russia, 1741–1761* (Gulf Breeze, FL: Academic International Press, 1995), 109–12.

208. Ibid., 112–13.

209. The priest makes no mention of aid given by the king and queen of Spain. Perhaps this is because of the rising tensions between Portugal and Spain when the manuscript was completed in 1759. In 1762, Spain would join the coalition opposing Portugal and Britain.

210. AHCML, FA-63, *Portugal aflito e conturbado*, 345–46.

211. See Ana Cristina Araújo, "The Lisbon Earthquake and the Seven Years War: Public Distress and Portuguese Political Propaganda," in Gerhard Lauer and Thorsten Unger, eds., *Das Erdbeben von Lissabon und der Katastrophendiskurs im 18. Jahrhundert* (Göttingen: Wallstein Verlag, 2008).

212. *Gazette de Cologne*, Vol. 5, January 6, 1756.

213. Erskine, 121, 189.

214. *The Boston Evening-Post*, No. 1060, December 22, 1755.

215. *The Boston Gazette*, No. 36, December 8, 1755.

216. *The Boston Evening-Post*, No. 1059, December 15, 1755.

217. MHS, John Tudor Papers.

218. MHS, Ms. S-578, James Freeman notebook.

219. MHS, John Tudor Papers.

220. John E. Ebel, "The Cape Ann, Massachusetts Earthquake of 1755: A 250th Anniversary Perspective," *Seismological Research Letters*, Vol. 77, No. 1, 2006, 74–86.

221. MHS, John Tudor Papers.

222. *The Boston Evening-Post*, No. 1058, December 8, 1756. See also Marguerite Carozzi, "Reaction of British Colonies in America to the 1755 Lisbon Earthquake: A Comparison to the European Response," *Earth Sciences History: Journal of the History of the Earth Sciences Society*, Vol. 2, No. 1, 1983, 17–27.

223. Mendonça, 161.

224. G. Moratti et al., "The 1755 'Meknes' Earthquake (Morocco): Field Data and Geodynamic Implications," *Journal of Geodynamics*, Vol. 36, Issue 1–2, August–September 2003, 317–18.

225. Levret, 86; Moratti, 312.

226. Miguel das Almas Santas, *Copia de huma carta escrita pelo Padre Guardiam de Real Convento de Maquinés, e Vice-Prefeito das Santas Missoens, que nas partes da Barbaria conserva a Religiosa Provincia de São Diogo dos RR. PP. Franciscanos Descalços, ao Padre Procurador dellas* (Lisbon: Manoel Soares, 1756), 8; *Hamburgischer Unparteyischer Correspondent*, No. 7, January 13, 1756. This account confuses the November 27 earthquake with the earthquake on November 18 and 19.

227. Santas, 8.

228. *The Pennsylvania Gazette*, No. 1410, January 1, 1755.

229. *The New-York Mercury*, No. 177, December 29, 1755.

230. Carozzi, 21.

231. Peter Silver, *Our Savage Neighbors: How Indian War Transformed Early America* (New York: W. W. Norton, 2008), 93.

232. *The New-York Mercury*, No. 177, December 29, 1755.

233. *The Boston Gazette*, No. 39, December 29, 1755.

234. See Kathleen Murphy, "Prodigies and Portents: Providentialism in the Eighteenth-Century Chesapeake," *Maryland Historical Magazine*, Vol. 97, No. 4, Winter 2002; Charles Edwin Clark, "Science, Reason, and an Angry God: The Literature of an Earthquake," *New England Quarterly*, Vol. 38, No. 3, September 1965, 340–62; and Eleanor Tilton, "Lightning-Rods and the Earthquake of 1755," *The New England Quarterly*, Vol. 13, No. 1, March 1940, 85–97.

235. Quoted in H. Trevor Colbourn, "A Pennsylvania Farmer at the Court of King George: John Dickinson's London Letters, 1754–1756," *The Pennsylvania Magazine of History and Biography*, Vol. 86, No. 4, October 1962, 436. The letter is dated January 8, 1756.

236. AHU, ACL, CU, 015, Cx. 80, D. 6692.

237. AHU, ACL, CU, 17, Cx. 49, D. 4937.

238. Ibid., 4992.

239. AHU, ACL, CU, 005, Cx. 126, D. 9865.

240. BG, AP 12363, Portal, 342; AHU, ACL, CU, 014, Cx. 19, D. 1488; AHU, ACL, CU, 015, Cx. 81, D. 6701; AHU, ACL, CU, 015, Cx. 81, D. 6706. Conversion: http://www.pierre-marteau.com/currency/converter/por-eng.html.

241. AHU, CU, Cx. 21, D. 2099.

242. Quoted in Araújo, 2006.

243. Hans-Jürgen Lüsenbrink, "Le tremblement de terre de Lisbonne dans des périodiques français et allemands du XVIIe siècle," in *Gazettes et Information Politique sous l'Ancien Régime* (Saint-Étienne: Publications de l'Université de Saint-Étienne,

1999), 305. See also Theo D'Haen, "On How Not to Be Lisbon If You Want to Be Modern—Dutch Reactions to the Lisbon Earthquake," *European Review*, Vol. 14, No. 3, 2006, 351–58.

244. Horace Walpole, *Memoires of the Last Ten Years of the Reign of George II*, Vol. 1 (of 2) (London: John Murray, 1822), 23–24; Walpole, Vol. 20, 530, Letter from Horace Mann to Walpole, February 23, 1756.

245. *Mercurio Histórico y Político*, Vol. 82, January 1756.

246. Rosa Cal Martínez, "La información en Madrid del terremoto de Lisboa de 1755," *Cuadernos Dieciochistas*, No. 6, 2005, 173–86.

CHAPTER EIGHT

"A Chaos of Stones"

The chapter verse epigraph is found in ASV, Segretaria di Stato Portogallo 231.

1. ASV, Segretaria di Stato Portogallo 196, f. 47.

2. E. A. Gutkind, *Urban Development in Southern Europe: Spain and Portugal*, Vol. 3 (of 8) (New York: Free Press , 1967), 153. For a detailed description of the fire damage in Lisbon's parishes, see Sousa, 1919–32, 561–654. Also see the relevant chapters in the manuscripts: *Portugal aflito e conturbado . . .* and Portal's *Historia da Ruina . . .*

3. Mendonça, 125–26.

4. BG, AP 12363, Portal, 53.

5. BNP, Fundo Geral, Codice no. 1772, 42–56; Sousa, 1919–32, 539.

6. Davy, Vol. 2, 45.

7. AHCML, FA-63, *Portugal aflito e conturbado . . .*, 281.

8. TNA, SP 89-50, f. 114, Letter to Sir Thomas Robinson: Lisbon (Nov. 6, 1755). Printed in *The London Gazette*, "From Tuesday Dec. 9–13, 1755," No. 9536, November 6, 1755. "The last Accounts [in the newspapers] assure us," wrote the British clergyman Samuel Clark, "that much more damage has been sustained by the Fire than by the earthquake itself." Samuel Clark, *A Sermon Preached at Daventry Dec. 7, 1755 on Occasion of the Late Earthquake at Lisbon Nov. 1 1755* (London, 1755), 5, footnote, Houghton Library, Harvard University.

9. BG, AP 12363, Portal, 63.

10. AHCML, FA-63, *Portugal aflito e conturbado . . .*, 273–74. In the opinion of Father Figueiredo, "the fire destroyed and consumed everything of magnificence, nobility, and worth in the city." Figueiredo, 1756, 23.

11. AHCML, FA-63, *Portugal aflito e conturbado . . .*, 179–80; According to Father Bento Morganti, "the area that the fire occupied was between the Palace of the Count de Vila Flor to the fountain [of the king], to the Church of São Paulo; and running to the north to the Castle [of São Jorge], the doors of Santo Antão, the Rua Largo de São Roque, and the Church of Our Lady of the Chagas [or Wounds of Christ]." Morganti, 4.

12. ASV, Segretaria di Stato Portogallo 231.

13. Mendonça, 129.

14. Davy, Vol. 2, 45–46.

15. Goudar, *Relation historique . . .*, 1756, 210. Goudar's book appears to have been copied and amended in a Portuguese manuscript in the Biblioteca Nacional de Portugal. "Relação histórica do terremoto Lisboa," Sousa, 1919–32, 547 (BNL, Manuscrito No. 607, Fundo Geral). It is unclear what currency Goudar is using

here, since he makes other estimates in both "cruzades" (cruzados) and "tournois" (livres tournois). The Portuguese manuscript estimates the losses to be one hundred million reais.

16. This Portuguese manuscript in the Biblioteca Nacional de Portugal appears to amend Goudar's. "Relação histórica do terremoto Lisboa," Sousa, 1919–32, 547 (BNP, Manuscrito No. 607, Fundo Geral).

17. Goudar, *Relation historique* . . . , 1756, 197. "Relação histórica do terremoto Lisboa," Sousa, 1919–32, 547 (BNP, Manuscrito No. 607, Fundo Geral). The Portuguese manuscript estimates the losses to be one hundred million reais.

18. BG, AP 12363, Portal, 52.

19. Ibid., 53–54. One assumes that Portal means cruzados here.

20. AHU, ACL, CU, 015, Cx. 81, D. 6716. The assumption is that cruzados are being used here. There is more information in the letter on the specific nature of the losses.

21. Figueiredo, 1756, 23.

22. AHCML, FA-63, *Portugal aflito e conturbado* . . . , 295.

23. BG, AP 12363, Portal, 65–66.

24. BA, Ms. Av. 54-XI-16 No. 121, "Relação histórica do terramoto de 1755."

25. AHCML, FA-63, *Portugal aflito e conturbado* . . . , 306.

26. AHU, Conselho Ultramarino, Cx. 83, 1932.

27. Rodrigues and Craig, 400–401.

28. BG, AP 12363, Portal, 55.

29. Rodrigues and Craig, 401.

30. Ibid., 401–2.

31. Quoted in ibid., 402.

32. Rodrigues and Craig, 406–7. María Paz Martín-Pozuelo Campillos, "En torno a una tradición archivística ibérica y sus consecuencias en el uso de los archivos," 6, http://conarq.arquivonacional.gov.br/Media/publicacoes/ibericas/en_torno_a_una_tradiccin_archivstica_ibrica.pdf.

33. Sousa, 1919–32, 581.

34. Figueiredo, 1756, 6.

35. Morganti, 5.

36. Sousa, 1919–32, 593.

37. Figueiredo, 1756, 6.

38. Nozes, 210; *The London Evening Post*, No. 4384, December 13–16, 1755.

39. *Gesammelte Nachrichten von dem Erdbeben der Staat Lissabon und anderer Orte* (Leipzig and Frankfurt, 1756), 26.

40. AHCML, FA-63, *Portugal aflito e aonturbado* . . . , 295.

41. See Cardoso, 1996, 441–510.

42. ASV, Carte Farnesiane 18, f. 18.

43. ASV, Segretaria di Stato Portogallo 195, f. 180.

44. Ibid., f. 188.

45. BA, Ms. Av. 54-XIII-24 No. 88.

46. ASV, Segretaria di Stato Portogallo 196, f. 18.

47. Morganti, 4.

48. Molesky, 2010; NYPL, *KF 1758, 139.

49. Pepys, *Diary*, February 28 and March 16, 1667.

50. ASV, Segretaria di Stato Portogallo 196, f. 20.

51. AHCML, FA-63, *Portugal aflito e conturbado* . . . , 282–83. All conversions are cal-

culated using the website of the Economic History Association (EH.net) and refer to 2010. One British pound in 1755 is worth 121 British pounds in 2010. The average conversion rate between the British pound and the U.S. dollar in 2010 is 1.5468. The basic monetary unit in eighteenth-century Portugal was the rei, although several other units were in regular use. One real = 40 réis. One conto de réis or conto (which will be used to assess the damage in this book) was equivalent to 1,000,000 réis. One cruzado = 400 réis; 1 livre tornois = 160 réis; £1 (British pound sterling) = 3,600 réis; 1 peso forte = 800 réis. França, *Lisboa pombalina* . . . , 347, note #17; Pereira, "Opportunity of a Disaster," 474. One anonymous French survivor claimed that the total losses in the disaster came to around 1,592 million livres tournois (or 254,720 contos), while one anonymous Portuguese eyewitness believed them to equal 120,000 contos, and another as high as 229,000 contos. *Les Nuits Parisennes à l'imitation des Nuits Attiques d'Aulu-Gelle*, Première Partie (A Londres e se trouve à Paris: Chez Lacombe, 1769), 53–55; França, *Lisboa pombalina* . . . , 68.

52. Manuscript: "Relação histórica do terremoto Lisboa," Sousa, 1919–32, 547.
53. See http://www.ggdc.net/maddison/maddison-project/home.htm; Carlos Estorninho, "O terramoto de 1755 e a sua repercussão nas relações luso-britânicas," *Faculdade de Letras*, Lisbon, 1956, 16. Portuguese GDP estimate found in Nuno Valério, "Portuguese Economic Performance, 1250–2000," Paper, 13th International Congress of Economic History, Buenos Aires, 2002. Portugal's GDP for 1750 was 150,828 contos.
54. Alvaro S. Pereira, "Opportunity of a Disaster: The Economic Impact of the 1755 Lisbon Earthquake," *The Journal of Economic History* (2009), 473–79.
55. Pereira's study does not reflect the true extent of the destruction. In the first place, he underestimates the damage done to Lisbon's infrastructure. Data gleaned from parish records (and accepted by Pereira) indicate that before the earthquake there were more than 33,000 habitable dwellings in Lisbon and only around 20,000 habitable structures three years afterward, revealing a deficit of 13,000 buildings. However, because many of the 20,000 dwellings counted in 1758 were some of the approximately 9,000 temporary structures (*barracas*, etc.) built just after the disaster, the actual number of pre-earthquake dwellings that were destroyed was probably closer to 17,000 than 13,000. José Vicente Serrão, "O quadro humano," in José Mattoso, ed., *História de Portugal*, Vol. 4 (Lisbon: Editorial Estampa, 1992), 141–63.
56. TNA, State Papers (Portugal), SP 89-50, ff. 126–27, Letter to Sir Thomas Robinson: Lisbon, November 20, 1755.
57. One French eyewitness estimated those losses at "thirty-two million" livres tournois (5,120 contos). *Les Nuits Parisennes à l'imitation des Nuits Attiques d'Aulu-Gelle*, Première Partie (A Londres e se trouve à Paris: Chez Lacombe, 1769), 54.
58. In ibid.
59. TNA, State Papers (Portugal), SP 89-50, f. 149, Letter to Henry Fox: Lisbon, December 13, 1755.
60. BG, AP 12363, Portal, 55; França, *Lisboa pombalina* . . . , 69; in *Les Nuits Parisennes à l'imitation des Nuits Attiques d'Aulu-Gelle*, Première Partie (A Londres e se trouve à Paris: Chez Lacombe, 1769), 54.
61. Alvaro S. Pereira, 476.
62. Ibid.

63. These estimates are based on Portugal's GDP in 1750.
64. The GDP of the U.S. in 2015 is approximately $18.125 billion. The national debt in January 2015 was $18 trillion.
65. http://www.ncdc.noaa.gov/special-reports/katrina.html.
66. *The Gentleman's Magazine*, Vol. 25, 1755, 560.
67. Boxer, 1956, 15.
68. *The Whitehall Evening Post*, No. 1528, December 9–11, 1755. See also "Auszug eines Schreibens von einem zu Lissabonn wohnenden Negotianten an seinen Correspondenten zu Paris," *Dritte Relation von den erschrecklichen Erdbeben zu Lissabon* (1755).
69. *The Maryland Gazette*, No. 560, January 29, 1756, a letter dated November 3, 1755, to a gentleman in Boston, Massachusetts.
70. Sousa, 1919–32, 547 (BNP, Manuscrito No. 597, Fundo Geral, f. 43). One peso forte = 800 reis. One conto = 1,000,000 reis. One anonymous French survivor estimated the total foreign losses to be 260 million livres tournois, of which English losses were 160 million livres tournois, while an anonymous Portuguese eyewitness believed that the total foreign losses reached 38,400 contos, of which British losses were 25,600 contos. França, 1983, 68; *Les Nuits Parisennes à l'imitation des Nuits Attiques d'Aulu-Gelle*, Première Partie (A Londres e se trouve à Paris: Chez Lacombe, 1769), 55.
71. AHCML, FA-63, *Portugal aflito e conturbado . . .* , 107.
72. TNA, State Papers (Portugal), SP 89-50, f. 188, Letter to Henry Fox: Lisbon, January 14, 1756.
73. *Gazeta de Lisboa*, No. 27, July 3, 1755, 79–80.
74. Carlos Estorninho, "O terramoto de 1755 e a sua Repercussão nas relações, luso-britânicas," *Faculdade de Letras*, Lisbon, 1956, 16; Alvaro S. Pereira, 479.
75. *Beschreibung des Erdbebens . . .* , Vols. 1–3 (Danzig, 1756), 51. All conversions are calculated using the website of the Economic History Association (EH.net). One British pound in 1755 is worth 121 British pounds in 2010. The average conversion rate between the British pound and the U.S. dollar in 2010 is 1.5468.
76. AHU, ACL, CU, Cx. 81, D. 6716. The governor's name was Luis Diogo Lobo da Silva.
77. *The Gentleman's Magazine*, Vol. 25, 1755, 561.
78. AHU, ACL, CU, 013, Cx. 40, D. 3726.
79. Mendonça, 116.
80. Ibid.
81. Marginalia, see Molesky, 2010, 245.
82. Franciso de Pina e de Mello, *Ao terremoto do primeiro do novembro de 1755: Parènesis de Francisco de Pina e de Mello* (Lisbon: Manoel Soares, 1756), unpaginated.

> General, Sacerdote, Leigo, Frade,
> Cingidos da fatal calamidade;
> Ministro, Pobre, Rico Cavaleiro,
> Commerciante, Soldado, Jornaleiro,
> Miseravel, Felíz, Aborrecido,
> Com todos falla o tremulo gemido,
> A todos vos iguala, a todos peza
> Neste acerbo clamor da Natureza.

83. Sousa, 1919–32, 566–67.

84. Ibid., 597.

85. Ibid., 597–600.

86. Figueiredo, 1756, 10–2; Mendonça, 139.

87. Figueiredo, 1756, 11; Mendonça, 139.

88. Goudar, *Relation historique* . . . , 1756, 196–97 (BNP, Manuscript, Fundo Geral, No. 607).

89. Goudar, *Relation historique* . . . , 1756, 196 (BNP, Manuscript, Fundo Geral, no. 607). The majority of masses in Lisbon were 10 a.m. or later.

90. Eric Neumayer and Thomas Plümper, "The Gendered Nature of Natural Disasters: The Impact of Catastrophic Events on the Gender Gap in Life Expectancy, 1981–2002," *Annals of the Association of American Geographers*, Vol. 97, No. 3, 2007, 555.

91. Figueiredo, 1756, 7–8; Mendonça, 138–39.

92. The much longer list of survivors, first compiled by four German merchants in a widely quoted letter from Portugal on November 4, includes Ostermann's companion, Jacob Haack, who was severely injured, Ullrich Jacob Süvertrub, along with everyone residing in his house, Hödel, Till, Johannes Schubad, Johann Daniel Kleseter, Vincent von Spreckelsen, Werner Löning, Johann Brüns, Johann Bues, Rudolph Burmester and his two office boys Dannecker and Tönnies, Caspar Krochman, Thompson, J. Hingstmann, Heninrich U. Wilhelm Prale, and Albert Borchers. Injured, though safe on board ship, were Albert Meyer, "the young Brauer" (who was "very bruised," "*sehr gequetscht*"), Illius, Johann Gerhard Burmester, Johann Friedrich Otto, and Johann Friedrich Carstens. Also among the survivors were Paul Poppe, Schriever, Maas, Vogelbusch, Peterson, Winken, Hey, Renner, along with his office boys Holz and Petersen, Tönnies, "Old Thor-Laden," Bostelmann, Andreas Christian Rademin and his servants Cramer and Lenz, Straus, the Müller brothers, and Capelle. Brockelmann and George were both aboard ship, while von Cluver and his family, and Merzener were all safe and residing in Sacavém, just northeast of Lisbon. However, Herr Munder, von Diess, and von Malwo, along with his servants, were missing and presumed dead. Staatsarchiv Hamburg, Bestandnummer 111-1 Senat, Signatur Cl. VI, No. 7, Vol. 2, Fasc. 1; *Gesammelte Nachrichten von dem Erdbeben der Staat Lissabon und anderer Orte* (Leipzig and Frankfurt, 1756), 20–21; *Beschreibung des Erdbebens* . . . , Vols. 1–3 (Danzig, 1756), 22–23; Lappenberg, "Hamburg und das Erdbeben zu Lissabon am 1. November 1755," 276–78.

93. SH, Bestandnummer 111-1 Senat, Signatur Cl. VI, No. 7, Vol. 2, Fasc. 1 (letter dated November 4, 1755, Chellas, Portugal).

94. Francis, 124.

95. TNA, State Papers (Portugal), SP 89-50, ff. 166–67, Letter, December 27, 1755.

96. The British population in Lisbon in 1755 before the earthquake is unknown.

97. From a transcribed document in the possession of the British Historical Society of Portugal. It is not known whether they were British subjects.

98. TNA, State Papers (Portugal), SP 89-50, f. 176, enclosed in a letter, f. 174 (December 28, 1755).

99. Neumayer and Plümper, 553–54.

100. Ibid., 554–56.

101. Sousa, 1919–32, 666, 660, 597–601, 655–56, 578–80, 687, 682–83.

102. Hanson, *Economy and Society in Baroque Portugal, 1668–1703*, 1981, 58–59, 65.

103. *Beschreibung des Erdbebens . . .* , Vols. 1–3 (Danzig, 1756), 19.

104. *Gesammelte Nachrichten . . .* , 17–18, 28, 33; Another German compilation of death tolls provided in letters give the following estimates: 40,000, 100,000, 35,000, and 30,000, respectively. *Dritte Relation von den erschrecklichen Erdbeben zu Lissabonn, Oder: Abdruck derjenigen Briefe, wie selbe dieses grosse Unglück von verschiedenen Orten mit mehrern Umständen berichtet haben* (Breslau, 1755).

105. *The Whitehall Evening Post*, No. 1521, November 22–25, 1755, *The London Evening Post*, No. 4375, November 22–25, 1755.

106. *The London Evening Post*, No. 4377, November 27–29, 1755.

107. GSP, I. HA, Geheimer Rat, Rep. 11, Auswärtige Beziehungen, Nr. 8518 (November 3, 1755); ML, LHMS, Acc. No. MA 4500. J. Perrot, Letter #1 to his brother, November 25, 1755.

108. In *Les Nuits Parisennes à l'imitation des Nuits Attiques d'Aulu-Gelle*, Première Partie (A Londres e se trouve à Paris: Chez Lacombe, 1769), 54; In Ângelo Pereira (preface and notes), "O terramoto de 1755 narrativa de uma testemunha ocular" (Lisbon: Livraria Ferin, 1953), 22.

109. Mendonça, 138.

110. Figueiredo, 1756, 9–10.

111. Pedegache, 20; Goudar, *Relation historique . . .* , 1756, 197.

112. Louis Jaucourt, "Lisbonne," *Encyclopédie, ou dictionnaire raisonné des sciences, des arts et des métiers*, First French edition, 1751–72 (Vol. 9, 573).

113. Thomas Kendrick (*The Lisbon Earthquake*, 1956) claims that there were between 10,000 and 15,000 deaths, while Fernando Portugal and Alfredo de Matos (*Lisboa em 1758: Memórias paroquiais de Lisboa*, 1974) put the death toll at 12,000. Kenneth Maxwell (*Pombal: Paradox of the Enlightenment*, 1995) thought the numbers reached 15,000, while José-Augusto França (*Pombaline and Enlightenment Lisbon*, 1977) estimated, like Moreira de Mendonça, that there were only 10,000 in total. In *The Last Day* (2008), Nicholas Shrady hypothesizes that the death toll was probably about 25,000, though he cautions that Father Portal's estimate of 12,000 to 15,000 may have been more accurate. For his part, Edward Paice (*Wrath of God*, 2008) asserts that there were between 30,000 and 40,000 deaths, while Benigno Aguirre believes that "10,000 to 17,400" people perished. In his landmark, early-twentieth-century study of the disaster, Franciso Luiz Pereira de Sousa postulates that there were 15,000 to 20,000 total victims of the earthquake, tsunami, and fire. Kendrick, 34; Fernando Portugal and Alfredo de Matos, *Lisboa em 1758: Memórias paroquiais de Lisboa* (Lisbon, 1974); Maxwell, 1995, 24; França, 1983, 66; Shrady, 51; Edward Paice, *Wrath of God: The Great Lisbon Earthquake of 1755* (London: Quercus, 2008), 172; Benigno E. Aguirre, "Better Disaster Statistics: The Lisbon Earthquake," *The Journal of Interdisciplinary History*, Vol. 43, No. 1, Summer 2012, 41; Sousa, 1919–32.

114. TNA, SP 94/149, f. 322.

115. Benigno E. Aguirre and E. L. Quarantelli, "Phenomenology of Death Counts in Disasters: The Invisible Dead in the 9/11 WTC Attack," *International Journal of Mass Emergencies and Disasters*, Vol. 26, No. 1, March 2008, 24–25.

116. BA, 54-XIII-24, No. 88; AHU, ACL, CU, 17, Cx. 50, D. 5036.

117. AHU, ACL, CU, 17, Cx. 50, D. 5036.

118. One assumes that descriptions of the 1531 earthquake would have been readily available to Pombal.

119. BG, AP 12363, Portal, 114; AHCML, FA-63, *Portugal aflito e conturbado* . . . , 284.

120. BL, Add. 69847, Letter, November 18, 1755.

121. ASV, Segretaria di Stato Portogallo 196, f. 47, Letter to Benedict XIV, February 10, 1756; ASV, Segretaria di Stato Portogallo 196, f. 10. In a letter to the cardinal secretary on December 9, 1756, Acciaiuoli repeats his belief that the dead will reach and "maybe surpass the number forty thousand." ASV, Segretaria di Stato Portogallo 196, f. 15. The British envoy, Edward Hay, also seems to agree with the generic calculus. In a letter to George II dated December 28, 1755, in which he provides the king with the list of the British dead, he wrote that "the Number of persons that perished in the Earthquake and Fire is variously computed; but it is probable that it is not less than Forty Thousand." TNA, State Papers (Portugal), SP 89-50, f. 174 (December 28, 1755). As Hay worked to compile this list—searching through the ruins, consulting government officials, etc.—one wonders whether he was provided with unofficial state estimates on the total number of deaths. As for the merchant Thomas Chase, he writes in his letter dated December 1, 1755, that "in one of their [the Portuguese] best accounts, just published," the death toll "is calculated at about *fifteen thousand*, but Mr. Bristow, Jr. has told me, as having had it from the best authority (I think it was from the Secretary of State [i.e., Pombal]), that the number of dead found and buried was *twenty-two thousand*, odd hundreds; in which case, as there must have remained still more under the ruins, the computation would seem to be moderate at *fifty thousand* people lost by the earthquake." *The Gentleman's Magazine*, Vol. 83, March 1813, 316. While "fifty thousand" is little more than a guess, it is significant that insiders in the Portuguese government and possibly Pombal himself were, at least according to Bristow and Chase, claiming privately that 22,000 corpses had been pulled from the rubble.

122. Morganti, 4.

123. Alvaro S. Pereira, 472.

124. Ibid.

125. "Bones Throw Light on 1755 Quake," Associated Press, April 28, 2007.

126. Alvaro S. Pereira, 472.

127. Davy, Vol. 2, 52–53.

128. Neil Hanson, *The Dreadful Judgement: The True Story of the Fire of London* (London: Corgi, 2002), 323–33.

129. AHCML, FA-63, *Portugal aflito e conturbado* . . . , 100.

130. Alvaro S. Pereira, 7.

131. Sousa, 1919–32, 562. Most deaths in the Kwanto Earthquake occurred in the firestorm in Tokyo and Yokahama. See Andrea Henderson, "Points of Origin: The Social Impact of the 1906 San Francisco Earthquake and Fire" (forthcoming).

132. "Bones Throw Light on 1755 Quake," Associated Press, April 28, 2007.

133. Antunes, 2.

134. Ibid., 8.

135. Ibid., 9–10.

136. Ibid., 11–14.

137. "Bones Throw Light on 1755 Quake," Associated Press, April 28, 2007.

138. See *1755 Providências* . . . , 93–102. There are references to several nonspecific locations for burial (102) as well as a plan to place the corpses on barges and sink them past the Tagus bar in the Atlantic Ocean (98).

139. *The Whitehall Evening Post*, No. 1531, December 16–18, 1755.

140. Ibid., No. 1523, December 27–29, 1755.

141. ASV, Segretaria di Stato Portogallo 195, f. 188.
142. Ibid., 196, f. 38.
143. Ibid., f. 19.
144. Mendonça estimated that 5,000 died on November 1, 1755, and another 5,000 died during the month that followed. Mendonça, 138. Sousa death toll mentioned in Alvaro S. Pereira, "Opportunity of a Disaster."
145. *Moskovskiye Vedomosti*, No. 33, August 16, 1756 (Julian calendar). The cholera report from Lisbon was dated June 20, 1756.
146. M. J. Toole, "Communicable Diseases and Disease Control," in Eric K. Noji, ed., *The Public Health Consequences of Disasters* (Oxford: Oxford University Press, 2007), 3–20.
147. Meira do Carmo Neto Akola, "Demografia," in *Dicionário de história de Portugal*, ed. Joel Serrão, Vol. 2 (Lisbon: Iniciativas Editoriais, 1993), 284.
148. Costa et al., 44. See also Chester and Chester, 2010.
149. Moratti et al, 305–22.

CHAPTER NINE

Uma Lisboa Nova

1. *Fernere Nachricht, von den entsetzlichen Erdbeben der Stadt Lissabon welche der P. Vicarii, allda, den 3 Nov. 1755 überschrieben* (1755).
2. Walter Hawthorne, *From Africa to Brazil: Culture, Identity, and an Atlantic Slave Trade, 1600–1830* (Cambridge: Cambridge University Press, 2010), 32; Peter Bakewell, *A History of Latin America to 1825*, 3rd ed. (Chichester, UK: Wiley-Blackwell, 2010), 441.
3. Kirsten Schultz, *Tropical Versailles: Empire, Monarchy, and the Portuguese Royal Court in Rio de Janeiro, 1808–1821* (New York: Routledge, 2001), 16–17.
4. Quoted in Schultz, 19.
5. *Semanario erudito*, Vol. 16 (Madrid: Don Blas Roman, 1784); JCB, A24d, 1756, manuscript in bound volume "Situación para Lisboa . . ."
6. *Semanario erudito*, Vol. 16 (Madrid: Don Blas Roman, 1784), 269.
7. Ibid., 271–72.
8. Ibid., 273.
9. *Mercurio Histórico y Político*, February 1756, 13.
10. Cheke, 19.
11. Maxwell, 1995, 10–12.
12. See Roy Porter, *Enlightenment: Britain and the Creation of the Modern World* (London: Penguin, 2000); and Gertrude Himmelfarb, *The Roads to Modernity: The British, French, and American Enlightenments* (New York: Alfred A. Knopf, 2004).
13. Quoted in Cheke, 33.
14. Maxwell, 1995, 6–7. The single book in Pombal's library written in English was *The Privileges of an Englishman in the Kingdoms and Dominions of Portugal* (1736).
15. Quoted in Maxwell, 1995, 5–6; Schwarcz, 92.
16. Quoted in Cheke, 33.
17. Ibid.
18. Ibid., 39.
19. Maxwell, 1995, 10–17.
20. Christovam Ayres, *Manuel da Maya e os engenheiros militares portugueses no terremoto de 1755* (Lisbon: Imprensa Nacional, 1910), 53.

21. Mullin, 162.
22. Quoted in Ayres, 54.
23. *1755 Providências . . .* , 264–66.
24. *Journal étranger,* Vol. 2, December 1755.
25. TNA, SP 89-50, ff. 126.
26. França, 1983, 311–15.
27. Ibid.
28. Ibid.
29. Mascarenhas, 30.
30. *1755 Providências . . .* , 268–70.
31. Figueiredo, 1766, 20. This order was given one day before Maia formally presented his dissertation.
32. *1755 Providências . . .* , 269–70.
33. Mullin, 163.
34. *1755 Providências . . .* , 132.
35. *Mercurio Histórico y Político,* May 1756, 8.
36. Ibid., September 1756, 18.
37. *The Whitehall Evening Post,* No. 1581, April 8–10, 1756; *The Whitehall Evening Post,* February 26–28, 1756.
38. Mascarenhas, 61–62.
39. BNP, MSS 34, No. 13.
40. *The Gentleman's Magazine,* February 1756, 71.
41. Quoted in Angela Delaforce, "The Dream of a Young Architect: Robert Adam and a Project for the Rebuilding of Lisbon in 1755," in Angela Delaforce, ed., *Portugal e o Reino Unido: A aliança revistada* (Lisbon: Fundação Calouste Gulbenkian, 1995), 11.
42. Quoted in John Fleming, *Robert Fleming and His Circle, in Edinburgh and Rome* (Cambridge, MA: Harvard University Press, 1962), 204–5.
43. Delaforce, 1995, 56.
44. Quoted in ibid., 59.
45. França, 1983, 88; Mascarenhas, 31, 50. The length of a palmo (or palm) in Portugal was approximately 8.64 inches.
46. França, 1983, 322.
47. António Nunes Ribeiro Sanches, *Tratado da conservaçam da Saude dos Povos* (Lisbon: Joseph Filippe, 1757), Prologue.
48. Ibid.
49. Sanches, 94–95.
50. Sanches, Prologue.
51. Kenneth Maxwell, "The Jesuit and the Jew: The Lisbon Earthquake in Modern Perspective," *ReVista: Harvard Review of Latin America,* Winter 2007; Araújo, 2006.
52. José Alvares da Silva, *Precauções Medicas contra algumas remotas consequencias, que se podem excitar do Terremoto de 1755* (Lisbon: Joseph Costa Coimbra, 1756); Kendrick, 59–60.
53. They were formally submitted to the Duke of Lafões.
54. Mascarenhas, 61.
55. Leonor Ferrão, "Um *oficial do Génio* e a Nova Lisboa," in *Monumentos, Revista Semestral de Edifícios e Monumentos,* Vol. 21, September 2004, 66–75.

56. Walter Rossa, "Do plano de 1755–1758 para a Baixa-Chiado," in *Monumentos: Revista Semestral de Edifícios e Monumentos,* Vol. 21, 2004, 22–43.

57. Mascarenhas, 65.

58. Molesky, "The Great Fire of Lisbon, 1755," 2012, 162.

59. Mascarenhas, 35.

60. Richard Penn et al., "The Pombaline Quarter of Lisbon: An Eighteenth Century Example of Prefabrication and Dimensional Co-ordination," *Construction History,* Vol. 11, 1995, 4.

61. Firebreaks were known as *guarda-fogos.* Inês Morais Viegas, ed., *Cartulário pombalino: Colecção de 70 Prospectos (1758–1846)* (Lisbon: Archivo Municipal, 1999). See no. 1, "Prospecto das fronterias"; Mascarenhas, 52.

62. AHM, D-23-4B, D-23-3B, D-23-2B, china ink drawings, José Monteiro de Carvalho.

63. Many other precautions against fire were not taken. Charcoal and firewood could still be purchased inside the city limits; and gunpowder factories could still be found in the city center. In 1769, Lisbon's first fire chief was installed, but all the old firefighting problems persisted: lack of water (despite an attempt to increase the number of fountains) as well as the inability to transport fire pumps up and down the city's steep hills. It was not until the nineteenth century that firefighting began to win its war against fire. Ferreira de Andrade, *Lisboa e seus serviços de incêndios, Volume 1, 1395–1868* (Lisbon: Câmara Municipal de Lisboa, 1969), 66–67, 76–77, 81.

64. Penn et al., 13, 5.

65. França, 1983, 108. Quote displayed in the 2008 exhibition: "Lisboa 1758: O plano da Baixa Hoje," Câmara Municipal, Lisbon. See also the decrees on April 14 and September 13, 1758. AHCML, 187, book 11, "Consultos, decretos, e avisos do D. José I 1757–1759."

66. Mascarenhas, 65.

67. See Ana Cristina Araújo, "The Lisbon Earthquake of 1755–Public Distress and Political Propaganda," *E-Journal of Portuguese History,* Vol. 4, No. 1, Summer 2006.

68. Goudar, *Discours politique . . . ,* 1756, 5. This edition was apparently not published in Lisbon.

69. Araújo, 2006.

70. Quoted in ibid., 4; José Barreto, "O discurso político falsamente atribuído ao Marquês de Pombal," *Revista de História das Ideias,* Vol. 4, No. 1, 1982, 413–15. Pombal is referring to the Spanish edition of Goudar's work: *Profecia política, verificada en lo que está sucediendo a los Portugueses por su ciega afición a los Ingleses. Hecho luego despues del Terremoto del año de mil setecientos cinquenta y cinco* (Madrid: Imprenta de la Gaceta, 1762).

71. TNA, SP 89-50, ff. 220–22. By February 29, several ships had still not entered the Tagus.

72. *Mercurio Histórico y Político,* February 1756, 15.

73. TNA, SP 89-50, ff. 228–29, Letter from Abraham Castres, March 15, 1756.

74. *Mercurio Histórico y Político,* March 1756, 15.

75. AHCML, FA-63, *Portugal aflito e conturbado . . . ,* 344–45.

76. *Mercurio Histórico y Político,* March 1756, 15.

77. Ibid., February 1756, 12.

78. Ibid., 11.

CHAPTER TEN

Reverberations

1. Quoted in Kendrick, 149. Translation slightly modified.

2. Quoted in Brown, 1992, 481.

3. Louis XV refused Voltaire entry to Paris and Versailles because of the philosopher's treacherous decision several years earlier to abandon his post as royal historiographer in the French court for Potsdam and service to Frederick the Great.

4. Quoted in Roger Pearson, *Voltaire Almighty: A Life in the Pursuit of Freedom* (London: Bloomsbury, 2005), 232.

5. Jean Orieux, *Voltaire* (Garden City, NY: Doubleday, 1979), 297.

6. Orieux, 288.

7. Besterman, *Correspondence*, D5576, Letter, April 5, 1755.

8. Pearson, 249–50. The only true cure for Voltaire's digestive woes was donkey's milk. Pearson, 59.

9. Ibid., 248.

10. Poem: *Epître de M. de Voltaire en arrivant dans sa terre près du lac de Genève, en mars, 1755.*

11. Pearson, 40.

12. Quoted in Orieux, 452.

13. Quoted from Rebecca L. Spang, *The Invention of the Restaurant: Paris and Modern Gastronomic Culture* (Cambridge, MA: Harvard University Press, 2000), 45; Letter (September 6, 1765), *The Complete Works of Voltaire*, ed. Theodore Besterman.

14. Pearson, 249.

15. Quoted in Simon Schama, *Citizens: A Chronicle of the French Revolution* (New York: Random House, 1989), 23–24.

16. Kendrick, 89–90.

17. Quoted in Besterman, 352, Letter (November 24, 1755), D5933, Vol. 28, 157.

18. Quoted in Pearson, 244, Letter (December 1, 1755), D6608, Besterman et al., eds., *Les œuvres complètes de Voltaire. The Complete Works of Voltaire* (Genève: Institut et Musée Voltaire; Oxford: The Voltaire Foundation, 1968–).

19. Quoted in Orieux, 294.

20. Basil Willey, *The Eighteenth-Century Background: Studies on the Idea of Nature in the Thought of the Period* (Boston: Beacon, 1961); Robert Mauzi, *L'Idée du bonheur dans la littérature et la pensée françaises au XVIIIe siècle* (Paris, 1960).

21. Alexander Pope, *An Essay on Man* (1734).

22. Gottfried Wilhelm Leibniz, *The Monadology* (London: Oxford University Press, 1925), 270–71; W. H. Barber, *Leibniz in France from Arnauld to Voltaire: A Study in French Reactions to Leibnizianism, 1670–1760* (Oxford: Clarendon Press, 1955).

23. The word *optimisme* was first used in 1737 in the Jesuit journal, *Mémoires de Trevoux* to characterize Leibniz's assertion that this is the best of all possible worlds.

24. Isser Wolloch, *Eighteenth-Century Europe: Tradition and Progress, 1715–1789* (New York: W. W. Norton, 1982), 135–39.

25. Quoted in Damrosch, 295.

26. Quoted in Miller, 2011, 29.

27. Letter, December 16, 1755, Besterman, D5962, 358.

28. Quoted in Andre Morize, "The Moment of *Candide* and the Ideas of Voltaire," in *Candide* (New York: W. W. Norton, First edition 1966), 104.

29. David Hume, *Dialogues Concerning Human Understanding*, Part II, 211.

30. In 1759, the Catholic Church sentenced the *Poème* to be burned. Orieux, 294.

31. Letter to the Comte D'Argental, 1759, Orieux, 312.

32. Rousseau, "Lettre à Voltaire," August 18, 1756, trans. Rebecca Spang.

33. Ibid.

34. Ibid.

35. Ibid.

36. Ibid.

37. Ibid.

38. Quoted in Orieux, 294.

39. Rousseau, "Lettre à Voltaire."

40. Ibid.

41. It is unknown when Kant first became acquainted with Rousseau's writings. He may have read his first *Discourse* in the early 1750s.

42. Immanuel Kant, "Von den Ursachen der Erderschütterungen bei Gelegenheit des Unglücks, welches die westliche Länder von Europa gegen das Ende vorigen Jahres betroffen hat," "Geschichte und Naturbeschreibung der merkwürdigsten Vorfälle des Erdbebens, welches an dem Ende des 1755sten Jarhres einen grossen Theil der Erde erschüttert hat." "Forgesetze Betrachtung der seit einiger Zeit wahrgenommen Erderschütterungen," *Kants Werke Akademie-Textausgabe*, Vol. 1 (of 9), *Vorkritische Schriften I, 1747–56* (Berlin: Walter de Gruyter, 1968).

43. See O. Reinhardt and D. R. Oldroyd, "Kant's Theory of Earthquakes and Volcanic Action," *Annals of Science*, Vol. 40, 1983, 247–72.

44. Quoted in Alexander Regier, *Fracture and Fragmentation in British Romanticism* (Cambridge: Cambridge University Press, 2010), 92.

45. Quoted in ibid., 92.

46. Quoted in Svend Erik Larsen, "The Lisbon Earthquake and the Scientific Turn in Kant's Philosophy," *European Review*, Vol. 14, No. 3, 2006, 365.

47. Monika Gisler, "Optimism and Theodicy: Perceptions of the Lisbon Earthquake in Protestant Switzerland," in Braun and Radner, 247–64.

48. Quoted in Miller, 2011, 34.

49. Araújo, 2006. See also António Ferrão, "Ribeiro Sanches e Soares de Barros: Novos elementos para as biografias desses académicos," in *Boletim de Segunda Classe da Academia das Ciências de Lisboa*, 1936, 5–99.

50. Portugal and Matos, 5–11.

51. Quoted in António Gomes Coelho, "Do 'Inquérito do Marqués de Pombal' ao estudo de Pereira de Sousa sobre o terramoto de 1 de Novembro de 1755," in *1755: O grande terramoto de Lisboa*, 158.

52. Coelho, 159. Originals in the ANTT.

53. Israel, 2012, 40.

54. Miller, 2011, 32. See also Rómulo de Carvalho, "Portugal nas 'Philosophal Transactions' nos séculos XVII e XVIII," *Revista Filosófica*, Vol. 15–16, 1956, 3–59.

55. Miller, 2011, 32–33.

56. Quoted in ibid., 33.

57. Baron Paul-Henri-Thiry d'Holbach, "Tremblemens de Terre," *Encyclopédie, ou dictionnaire raisonné des sciences, des arts et des métiers*, first French edition, 1751–72, Vol. 16, 580–84.

58. Mikhail Vasil'evich Lomonosov, *Polnoe Sobranie Sochinenii*, Vol. 5 (Moscow: Aka-

demiia Nauk, 1950–83), 295–347. I would like to thank Nathaniel Knight for translating this source. The work in question is James Hutton's *Theory of the Earth* (1785).

59. B. J. Feijoo, *Nuevo systhema . . .* (El Puerto de Santa María: Casa Real de las Cadenas, 1756), 30.

60. Juan Luis Roche, *Relación y observaciones physicas-mathematicas y morales sobre el general terremoto y la irrupción del mar del día primero de noviembre de este año 1755 que comprendió a la ciudad, y Gran Puerto de Santa María y a toda la costa, y tierra firme del Reyno de Andalucía* (Santa María, Spain, 1756). His letter was dated November 12, 1755.

61. Francisco Mariano Nifo y Cagigal, *Explicación physica, y moral de las causas, señales, diferencias, y efectos de los terremotos, con una relación muy exacta de los más formidables, y ruinosos, que ha padecido la tierra desde el principio del mundo, hasta el que se ha experimentado en España, y Portugàl el día primero de noviembre de esta año de 1755* (Madrid, 1755).

62. Mendonça, 255.

63. Pedegache, 11–12.

64. Ibid., 12. This theory is repeated probably by reading Pedegache's book by the anonymous priest who wrote *Portugal aflito e conturbado . . .* , 438 (AHCML, FA-63).

65. Figueiredo, 1756, 17.

66. Agustín Udías and Alfonso López Arroyo, "The Lisbon Earthquake of 1755 in Spanish Contemporary Authors," in Luiz A. Mendes-Victor, Carlos Sousa Oliveira, João Azevedo, and António Ribeiro, *The Lisbon Earthquake: Revisited* (New York: Springer, 2009), 17.

67. Kant, "Von den Ursachen der Erderschütterungen bei Gelegenheit des Unglücks, welches die westliche Länder von Europa gegen das Ende vorigen Jahres betroffen hat," 1756, 424–25.

68. Kant, "Geschichte und Naturbeschreibung der merkwürdigsten Vorfälle des Erdbebens, welches an dem Ende des 1755sten Jarhres einen grossen Theil der Erde erschüttert hat," 1756, 440–41.

69. Kant, "Forgesetze Betrachtung . . . ," Vol. 1, 469.

70. John Michell, "Conjectures concerning the Cause, and Observations upon the Phaenomena of Earthquakes; Particularly of That Great Earthquake of the First of November, 1755, Which Proved So Fatal to the City of Lisbon, and Whose Effects Were Felt As Far As Africa, and More or Less throughout Almost All Europe," *Philosophical Transaction of the Royal Society*, Vol. 51, 1759–60, 611–14. See also António Gomes Coelho, "Nota introdutória": "John Michell, um filósofo da Natureza do século das Luzes," in *1755: Sobre as Causas do Terramoto*, Vol. 4, 21–30.

71. Charles Chauncy, *Dr. Chauncy's Sermon Occasion'd by the Late Terrible Earthquake. Earthquakes a Token of the Righteous Anger of God* (Boston: Edes & Gill, 1755), 6; Charles Chauncy, *The earth delivered from the curse to which it is, at present, subjected. A sermon occasioned by the later earthquakes in Spain and Portugal, as well as New-England; and preached . . .* (Boston: Edes & Gill, 1756), 10.

72. Charles Chauncy, *The earth delivered from the curse . . .* , 55.

73. Coelho, in *1755: O grande terramoto*, 163.

74. Pedro Antonio Barroeta y Angel, *Carta pastoral, que el Illmo. S.D.D. Pedro Antonio de Barroeta y Angel, arzobispo de los reyes, dirige al venerable clero, y amado pueblo de su diocessis, con ocasion de las noticias, que se han participado de España del gran terromoto*

[sic], *que el dia primero de noviembre de 1755 se experimentó con grandes estragos en la Europa* (Lima: Juan Joseph Cossio, 1756), 35.

75. Quoted in Israel, 2012, 41–42.
76. Angel, 47.
77. John Wesley, *Serious Thoughts Occasioned by the Earthquake at Lisbon to which is subjoin'd an Account of all the late Earthquakes there, and in other Places*, 6th ed. (London, 1756), 10–11.
78. "British state prayers, fasts and thanksgivings, 1540s to 1940s," https://www.dur.ac.uk/history/research/research_projects/british_state_prayers/.
79. *Moskovskiye Vedomosti*, No. 39, September 6, 1756 (Julian calendar).
80. *Gazette de Cologne*, LIII, 53, July 2, 1756.
81. AHN Estado (State Papers), 2512.
82. TNA, SP 89/50, f. 246 (and back), Letter dated May 10, 1756.
83. Monteiro, 111-112.
84. Cheke, 101.
85. Ibid., 103; TNA, SP 89/50, f. 312 (back), 313.
86. TNA, SP 89/50, f. 310.
87. Ibid.
88. *Gaceta de Madrid*, Vol. 71, October, 14.
89. Molesky, "The Vicar and the Earthquake," 2012, 89.
90. Monteiro, 336.
91. Ibid.
92. Quoted in Ilário Govoni, *Malagrida no Grão Pará* (Belém do Pará: Amazônia Indústria Gráfica e Editora, 2009), 132.
93. Quoted in Govoni, 132.
94. Cheke, 103.
95. His name was Francisco Xavier de Mendonça Furtado.
96. Maxwell, 1995, 62–63.
97. Quoted in Boxer, 1969, 184.
98. Maxwell, 1995, 71.
99. Francis, 129.
100. See Francis Dutra, "The Wounding of King José I: Accident or Assassination Attempt?," *Mediterranean Studies*, Vol. 7, 1998, 221–29.
101. Smith, Vol. 1, 210.
102. Ibid., 201–2.
103. Ibid., 198.
104. ASV, Secretaria di Stato Portogallo 231, *Erros Impios e Sediciosos que os Religiosos da Companhia de Jesus ensinarão aos Reos que forão justicados e pertendarão espalhar nos Povos destes Reynos* (Lisboa: Miquel Rodrigues, undated): 32 pages of various errors of the Jesuits. "Porque, se aquelle atrocissimo golpe de 3 Setembro do anno proximo precedente, de que hoje se trata, produzisse todo o execrando effeito, a que dirigido; fazião os dittos Religiosos passar na credulidade das gentes pias e isentas de tão negras malicias, a sciencia, que tinhão do Assassinato por elles concertado, como inspiração Divina; e fazião dar áquellas suas predicçoens o culto de profecias santas e veneraveis," 32.
105. Quoted in Boxer, 1969, 192.
106. Maddison Project Database, http://www.ggde.net/madison/madison-project/data.htm.
107. In the words of the Austrian envoy the year before: "The nation, crushed by the

weight of the despotic rule exercised by the Marquis of Pombal, the King's friend, favorite and Prime Minister, believes that only the death of the Monarch can deliver the people from a yoke which they regard as tyrannical and intolerable. The nation was never in a worse plight or in a more cruel subjection." Quoted in Boxer, 1969, 190.

108. Quoted in Boxer, 1969, 191.

109. Voltaire declared that the British were "diabolic" for executing Byng "for not having killed enough Frenchmen." Letter, December 28, 1770, Besterman, 1969, 386.

110. Quoted in Besterman, 1969, 358.

111. Ibid., 392, letter, November 18, 1758.

112. Quoted in Pearson, 264, letter, January 26, 1762, D10284.

113. Quoted in Besterman, 1969, 359, letter, February 18, 1756. See also Henry Vyverberg, *Historical Pessimism in the French Enlightenment* (Cambridge, MA: Harvard University Press, 1958).

114. Thomas E. Bourke, "Vorsehung und Katastrophe. Voltaire Poème sur le désastre de Lissabon und Kleists Erdbeben in Chili," in *Klassik und Moderne. Die Weimarer Klassik als historische Ereignis und Herausforderung im kulturegeschichtlichen Prozeß*, edited by Karl Richter and Jörg Schönert (Stuttgart: Metzler, 1983), 238–39.

115. Miller, 2011, 30; Gisler, 248.

116. Quoted in Miller, 2011, 42.

117. Alexander Regier, *Fracture and Fragmentation in British Romanticism* (Cambridge: Cambridge University Press, 2010), 75–94.

118. Charles Dickens, "Lisbon," *Household Words*, December 25, 1858, 89; Johann Gottfried Herder, *Ideen zur Philosophie der Geschichte der Menschheit*, in *Herders Sämmtliche Werke*, Vol. 13, Bernhard Suphan, ed. (Berlin: Weidermannsche Buchhandlung, 1887); Walter Benjamin, "The Lisbon Earthquake," 1931 (original: "Das Erdbeben von Lissabon") in *Selected Writings, 1927–1934*, Vol. 2 (of 2), translated by Rodney Livingstone and edited by Michael W. Jennings, Howard Eiland, and Gary Smith (Cambridge, MA: Harvard University Press, 1999).

119. ANTT, Manuscript 1229, Section 30.

120. Nason, 116.

Behold the chosen room he sought
Alone, to fast and pray,
Each year, as chill November brought
The dismal earthquake day.
There hung the rapier blade he wore,
Bent in its flattened sheath;
The coat the shrieking woman tore
Caught in her clenching teeth;—

—OLIVER WENDELL HOLMES SR., "AGNES" (SELECTIONS),
OLIVER WENDELL HOLMES, *songs in many keys*
(BOSTON: TICKNOR & FIELDS, 1862), 29.

Bibliography

I. ARCHIVAL SOURCES

For a more complete list of archives and libraries consulted, please see the acknowledgments.

AAE (Archives des Affaires Étrangères, Paris)
AHCML (Arquivo Histórico da Câmara Municipal, Lisbon)
AHM (Arquivo Histórico do Ministério das Obras Públicas, Transportes, e Comunicações, Lisbon)
AHN (Archivo Histórico Nacional, Madrid)
AHU (Arquivo Histórico Ultramarino, Lisbon)
ANTT (Arquivo Nacional da Torre do Tombo, Lisbon)
ASG (Archivio di Stato di Genova, Genoa)
ASN (Archivio di Stato di Napoli, Naples)
ASV (Archivum Secretum Vaticanum, Vatican City)
ASVe (Archivio di Stato di Venezia, Venice)
AVPRI (Foreign Policy Archive of the Russian Empire of the Ministry of Foreign Affairs of the Russian Federation, Moscow)
BA (Biblioteca de Ajuda, Palácio Nacional da Ajuda, Lisbon)
BAP (Bibliothèque de l'arsenal, Bibliothèque Nationale de France, Paris)
BBM (Biblioteca Brasiliana Guita e José Mindlin, São Paulo)
BG (Biblioteca da Arte, Fundação Calouste Gulbenkian, Lisbon)
BL (British Library, London)
BNP (Biblioteca Nacional de Portugal, Lisbon)
CB (Stiftung Hanseatisches Wirtschaftsarchiv, Commerzbibliothek, Hamburg, Germany)
ESRO (East Sussex Record Office, UK)
GEL (Gabinete de Estudos Olisiponenses, Câmara Municipal, Lisbon)
GRO (Gloucestershire Record Office, UK)
GSP (Geheimes Staetsarchiv PreuBischer Kulterbesitz, Berlin)
HL (The Huntington Library, San Marino, CA)
JCB (John Carter Brown Library, Brown University, Providence, RI)
MHS (Massachusetts Historical Society, Boston)
ML (The Morgan Library, New York)
NAN (Nationaal Archief, The Hague, Netherlands)
NYPL (New York Public Library, Rare Books Division, New York)
SH (Staatsarchiv Hamburg, Germany)
TNA (The National Archives of the UK, Public Record Office, Kew Gardens, UK)
WRO (Warwickshire Country Record Office, UK)
WSA (Wiltshire & Swindon Archives, Wiltshire, UK)

II. PRINTED PRIMARY SOURCES

Account of the Earthquake which Destroyed the City of Lisbon on the First of November, 1755; And the Appearance of the City previous to the Calamity. London: W. Glendinning, 1756?

An Account of the Late Dreadful Earthquake and Fire which destroyed the city of Lisbon, The Metropolis of Portugal. In a Letter from a Merchant Resident there, to his Friend in England. London: J. Payne, 1755.

An Account of the Late Dreadful Dreadful Earthquake and Fire which destroyed the city of Lisbon, The Metropolis of Portugal. In a Letter from a Merchant Resident there, to his Friend in England, 2nd ed. Boston: Green & Russell, 1756.

Amezua, Fernando Lopez de. *Carta philosophica sobre el terremoto, que se sintió en Madrid, y en toda esta peninsula el día primero de noviembre de 1755.* Madrid?: 1755?.

Angel, Pedro Antonio Barroeta y. *Carta pastoral, que el Illmo. S.D.D. Pedro Antonio de Barroeta y Angel, arzobispo de los reyes, dirige al venerable clero, y amado pueblo de su diocessis, con ocasion de las noticias, que se han participado de España del gran terromoto [sic], que el dia primero de noviembre de 1755 se experimentó con grandes estragos en la Europa.* Lima: Juan Joseph Cossio, 1756.

Angestellte Betrachtung über die den 1. November 1755 so ausserordentliche Erdbeben und Meeresbewegungen, wodurch die Grundfeste eines grossen Theils Europens erschüttert, und einige derer Städten verunglüket worden. Augsburg: J. M. Wagner, 1755.

Arrêt de Inquisiteurs, Ordinaire, et Députés de la Ste. Inquisition contre Le Père Gabriel Malagrida, Jésuite, Lû dans l'Acte public de Foi, célébré à Lisbonne le 20 de Septembre 1761. Lisbon: Chez Antoine Rodrigues Galhardo, 1761.

Azevedo, Joseph Moreira de. *Desterro da Iniquidade e muito Necessaria Consideração sobre o Espantoso Terremoto.* Lisbon: Manoel Soares, 1756.

Baretti, Joseph. *A Journey from London to Genoa Through England, Portugal, Spain, and France.* Sussex: Centaur Press, 1970.

Beckford, William. *The Journal of William Beckford in Portugal and Spain, 1787–1788,* edited by Boyd Alexander. London: Rupert Hart-Davis, 1954.

Beirão, Caetano. "Descrição inédita do terramoto de 1755 como o viu e viveu a rainha D. Maria Vitória." *Artes & Colecções,* No. 2, Vol. 1, July 1947, 3–4.

Bellamy, George Anne. *An Apology for the Life of George Anne Bellamy, Late of Covent Garden Theatre.* Vol. 6 (of 6). London: J. Bell, 1785.

Benjamin, Walter. "The Lisbon Earthquake." 1931. Original: "Das Erdbeben von Lissabon." In *Selected Writings, 1927–1934.* Vol. 2 (of 2), translated by Rodney Livingstone; edited by Michael W. Jennings, Howard Eiland, and Gary Smith. Cambridge, MA: Harvard University Press, 1999.

Beschreibung des Erdbebens, welches di Hauptstadt Lissabon und viele andere Städte in Portugall und Spanien theils ganz umgeworfen, theils sehr beschädigt hat. Vols. 1–3. Danzig, 1756.

Besterman, Theodore, et al., ed. *Les œuvres complètes de Voltaire. The Complete Works of Voltaire.* Genève: Institut et Musée Voltaire; Oxford, UK: Voltaire Foundation, 1968–.

———. *Correspondance/Voltaire.* Paris: Gallimard, 1977–.

Bevis, John. *The History and Philosophy of Earthquakes, from the Remotest to the Present Times: Collected from the best writers on the subject. . . . By a member of the Royal Academy of Berlin.* Gale; reprint, 2012.

Biddolf, John. *A Poem on the Earthquake at Lisbon.* London: W. Owen, 1756.

Black, Jeremy, ed. "Portugal in 1730, by John Swinton." *The British Historical Society of Portugal Thirteenth Annual Report,* 1986, Lisbon, 65–87.

———, ed. "Portugal in 1760: The Journal of a British Tourist." *The British Historical Society of Portugal Fifteenth Annual Report and Review,* 1988, Lisbon, 91–112.

Bourgoing, Jean-François, baron de. *Voyage du ci-devant Duc du Chatelet en Portugal.* Paris: Chez F. Buisson, 1798.

———. *Travels of the Duke of Châtelet in Portugal.* Vol. 1 (of 2). London: John Stockdale, 1809.

Cagigal, Francisco Mariano Nifo y. *Explicación physica, y moral de las causas, señales, diferencias, y efectos de los terremotos, con una relación muy exacta de los mas formidables, y ruinosos, que ha padecido la tierra desde el principio del mundo, hasta el que se ha experimentado en España, y Portugal el día primero de noviembre de este año de 1755.* Madrid, 1755.

Camões, Luis de. *The Lusiads of Luis de Camões,* translated by Leonard Bacon. New York: Hispanic Society of America, 1950.

Cardoso, Arnaldo Pinto. "O Terramoto de Lisboa (1755) Documentos do Arquivo do Vaticano." In *Revista de História das Ideias,* Vol. 18, 1996, 441–510.

———, ed. and trans. *O Terrível Terramoto da Cidade que Foi Lisboa: Correspondência do Núncio Filippo Acciaiuoli (Arquivo Secreto do Vaticano).* Lisbon: Alétheia, 2005.

Casanova, Giacomo Chevalier de Seingalt. *History of My Life.* Vol. 4 (of 12), translated by William R. Trask. Baltimore: Johns Hopkins University Press, 1997.

Castro, João Baptista de. *Mappa de Portugal antigo e moderno.* 2nd ed., 3 Vols. Lisbon: Officina Patriarcal de Francisco Luiz Ameno, 1762–63.

Chambers, Ephraim. *Cyclopaedia.* Vol. 1 (of 2). London, 1728.

Chauncy, Charles. *Dr. Chauncy's Sermon Occasion'd by the late terrible Earthquake.* Boston: Edes & Gill, 1755.

———. *The earth delivered from the curse to which it is, at present, subjected. A sermon occasioned by the later earthquakes in Spain and Portugal, as well as New-England; and preached . . .* Boston: Edes & Gill, 1756.

Chronica oder Sammlung alter und neuer Nachrichten von denen merkwürdigsten Erdbeben und was selbige für Ursachen zum grunde haben. Frankfurt am Main: Johann Joachim Keßler, 1756.

Clark, Samuel. *A Sermon Preached at Daventry Dec. 7, 1755 on Occasion of the Late Earthquake at Lisbon Nov. 1 1755.* London, 1755.

Colbourn, H. Trevor. "A Pennsylvania Farmer at the Court of King George: John Dickinson's London Letters, 1754–1756." *The Pennsylvania Magazine of History and Biography,* Vol. 86, No. 4, October 1962.

Collecçam Universal de Todas as Obras, Que Tem Sahido ao publico sobre os effeitos, que cauzou o Terremoto Nos Reinos de Portugal . . . Vols. 1–5. Lisbon: Officina de Curiosidade, 1758.

Completa Relacion del Assombroso Terremoto, que ha padecido la Ciudad de Sevilla en el día de Todos Santos . . . Third part. Seville, 1755?

Correspondence of John, Fourth Duke of Bedford. Vol. 2. London: Longman, Brown, Green and Longmans, 1843.

Cosme, João, and José Varandas, eds. *Memórias paroquias (1758–1759).* Vols. 1–2. Lisbon: Caleidoscópio, 2009.

Costigan, Arthur William. *Sketches of Society and Manners in Portugal.* Vol. 2 (of 2). London, 1787.

Croker, J. Wilson, ed. *Johnsoniana or, Supplement to Boswell: Being Anecdotes and Sayings of Dr. Johnson.* Philadelphia: Cary & Hart, 1842.

Davy, Charles. *Letters Addressed Chiefly to a Young Gentleman upon Subjects of Literature . . .* Vol. 2 (of 2). Bury St. Edmunds: J. Rackham, 1787.

Delany, Mary. *The Autobiography and Correspondence of Mary Granville, Mrs. Delany.* Vol. 3 (of 3). London: Richard Bentley, 1861.

Destruição de Lisboa e Famosa Desgraça que padeceo no dia primeiro de Novembro de 1755. Lisbon, 1756.

Dickins, L., and M. Stanton, eds. *An Eighteenth-Century Correspondence.* New York, 1920.

Die denckwürdigsten Geschichte der Erderschütterungen und Seltenheiten der Natur, von den letztern Monaten des abgewischenen Jarhres an. Mit nöthigen Erläuterungen aus der Geschichtskunde, der Erdbeschreibung und der Naturwissenschaft. Erfurt: J. H. Nonnens, 1756.

Discripção miudamente circunstanciada da antiga igreja de S. Nicolao de Lisboa, abatida e incendiada por occasião do terramoto no dia memoravel do 10 de Novembro de 1755 [. . .] a que se ajunta a corioza memoria da reedificação da nova igreja, e diligencias até agora empregadas para o andamento da obra. Lisbon: Tip. do Gratis, 1843.

Dritte Relation von den erschrecklichen Erdbeben zu Lissabonn, Oder: Abdruck derjenigen Briefe, Wie selbe dieses grosse Unglück von verschiedenen Orten mit mehrern Umständen berichtet haben. Breslau, 1755.

Domínguez, J. de Vega. "Des bords sanglants du Tage à la mer de Cadix. El terremoto de Lisboa y sus consecuencias en Andalucia. Nuevos testimonios." *Revista Portuguesa de História,* Vol. 32, 1997–98, 243–329.

Ehrhardt, Marion. "Eine unbekannter deutscher Augenzeugenbericht über das Seebeben vor Lissabons Küste 1755." In *Das Erdbeben von Lissabon und der Katastrophendiskurs im 18. Jahrhundert,* edited by Gerhard Lauer and Thorsten Unger. Göttingen: Wallstein Verlag, 2008.

Eilfte Relation von den erschrecklichen Erdbeben zu Lissabonn, Oder: Abdruck derjenigen Briefe, Wie selbe dieses grosse Unglück von verschiedenen Orten mit mehrern Umständen berichtet haben. Breslau, 1756.

Erskine, David, ed. *Augustus Hervey's Journal: The Adventures Afloat and Ashore of a Naval Casanova.* London: Chatham, 2002; original, 1953.

Esaguy, Augusto de. "Uma carta de doutor Jacob de Castro Sarmento a Diogo de Mendonça Côrte Real (O terremoto de 1 de novembro de 1755)." Lisbon: Imprensa Médica, 1955.

Exécution du Père Malagrida, Jésuite, Auteur du Régicide commis sur le Roi de Portugal, 3. 1761?.

Faria, Ana Maria Homem Leal de. "O terramoto de 1755: Visto por um diplomata holandês em Lisboa." In *CLIO—Revista do Centro de História da Universidade de Lisboa,* Edições Colibri, 1997, 195–99.

Fernere Nachricht, von den entsetzlichen Erdbeben der Stadt Lissabon welche der P. Vicarii, allda, den 3 Nov. 1755 überschrieben. 1755.

Figueiredo, António Pereira de. *Diario dos Sucessos de Lisboa, desde o terramoto até o extermínio dos jezuitas.* Lisbon: Francisco Borges de Sousa, 1766 [1761].

———. *Commentario latino e portuguez sobre o terremoto e o incêndio de Lisboa de que foi testemunha ocular seu autor,* Pref. de Cândido dos Santos. Lisbon: Officina de Miguel Rodrigues, 1756.

Forster, John. *Reflections, Physical and Moral, Upon the Various and Numerous Uncommon Phenomena in the Air, Water, or Earth, which Have Happened from the Earthquake at Lima, to the Present Time: In a Series of Familiar Letters from a Member of Parliament in Town to His Friend in the Country.* London: A. Millar in the Strand, 1756.

Francken, Joachim. *Versuch in physischen Betrachtungen über die Ursache und Entstehungsart des Erdbebens.* Schleswig, 1756.

Franklin, Benjamin. "Causes of Earthquakes." In *The Works of Benjamin Franklin*. Vol. 6, edited by Jared Sparks. Boston: Charles Tappan, 1844, 1–14.

Freire, Francisco José. *Memorias das Principaes Providencias, que se Derão no Terremoto, que Padeceo a Corte de Lisboa no Anno de 1755, Ordenadas, e Offerecidas à Majestade Fidelissima de El Rey D. Joseph I. Nosso Senhor*. Lisbon, 1758.

Friedrich, Dirk, ed. *Das Erdbeben von Lissabon 1755: Quellen und historische Texte*. Bonn: Minifanal, 2013.

———, ed. *Die traurige Verwandlung von Lissabon in Schutt und Asche: Das Erdbeben von 1755 in zeitgenössischen Berichten*. Bonn: Minifanal, 2013.

Gesammelte Nachrichten von dem Erdbeben der Staat Lissabon und anderer Orte. Leipzig and Frankfurt, 1756.

Goethe, Johann Wolfgang von. *Werke*. Vol. 9. Munich: C. H. Beck. 1981; reprint, 1967.

Góis, Damião de. *Elogio da Cidade de Lisboa Urbis Olisiponis Descriptio*. Lisbon: Guimarães Editores, 2002.

Gottsched, Johann Christian. *Das Neueste aus der anmutigen Gelehrsamkeit*. December 1755.

Goudar, Ange. *Discours politique sur les avantages que les Portugais pourroient retirer de leur Malheur*. Lisbon: Chez Philanthrope, 1756.

———. *Relation Historique du Tremblement de Terre survenu à Lisbonne le premier Novembre 1755*. La Haye: Chez Philanthrope, 1756.

Guedes, Fernando. "Dois relatos inéditos do terramoto de Lisboa de 1755." In *O livro e a leitura em Portugal subsídios para a sua história: séculos XVIII E XIX*. Lisbon: Editorial Verbo, 1987, 239–57.

Hamer, Philip M., and George C. Rogers, Jr., eds. *The Papers of Henry Laurens, Volume Two: Nov. 1, 1755–Dec. 31, 1758*. Columbia: University of South Carolina Press, 1970.

Herder, Johann Gottfried. *Ideen zur Philosophie der Geschichte der Menschheit*. In *Herders Sämmtliche Werke*. Vol. 13, edited by Bernhard Suphan. Berlin: Weidermannsche Buchhandlung, 1887.

Herodotus. *The Histories*, translated by David Grene. Chicago: University of Chicago Press, 1987.

Holbach, Paul-Henri-Thiry, Baron de. "Tremblemens de Terre." In *Encyclopédie, ou dictionnaire raisonné des sciences, des arts et des métiers*. First French edition, 1751–72, Vol. 16, 580–584.

Idée Véridique du Révérend Père Gabriel de Malagrida, Jesuite Italien, Exécuté à Lisbonne, par Sentence de l' Inquisition. Liège: Chez Syzimme, 1762.

Jaucourt, Louis. "Lisbonne." In *Encyclopédie, ou dictionnaire raisonné des sciences, des arts et des métiers*. First French edition, 1751–72, Vol. 9, 572–73.

Kant, Immanuel. "Von den Ursachen der Erderschütterungen," "Geschichte und Naturbeschreibung der merkwürdigsten Vorfälle des Erdbebens," and "Forgesetze Betrachtung der seit einiger Zeit wahrgenommen Erderschütterungen." In *Kants Werke*. Vol. 1, 1747–56. Berlin: Walter de Gruyter, 1968; original, 1756, 417–72.

Kühnlin, J. H. *Das glückliche und unglückliche Portugall und erschreckte Europa in den Grossen und vielfältigen Erd- und Wassers Bewegungen / welche vom 1ten November 1755. Bis zu den 20. Februar dieses Jahres zu unterschiedenen Zeiten sich ereignet un so viele Städte un Länder beschädiget haben* . . . Frankfurt and Leipzig, 1756.

Kurzverfaste Beschreibung der vortreflichen, mächtigen und reichen Haupt- und residenz-Stadt Lissabon im königreiche Portugal . . . Frankfurt, 1756.

Lahontan, Baron de. *New Voyages to North America*. Vol. 1 (of 2). London, 1703.

Leibniz, Gottfried Wilhelm. *The Monadology*. London: Oxford University Press, 1925.

Leite, Braz Joseph Rebello. *Clamor Justificado na Razão, Direito, e Motivos, para a que . . .* Lisbon: Francisco Luiz Ameno, 1758.

Les Nuits Parisennes à l'imitation des Nuits Attiques d'Aulu-Gelle. Première Partie. A Londres e se trouve à Paris: Chez Lacombe, 1769.

Letter from a Portuguese Officer to a Friend in Paris. Giving an Account of the late dreadful Earthquake by which the City of Lisbon was Destroyed. London: M. Cooper, 1755.

Letter to Mr. Joseph Fowke From his Brother near Lisbon, Date November 1755, In which is given A very minute and striking Description of the late Earthquake. Dublin: S. Powell, 1755.

Lettre de M. L'Abbé Platel, ci-devant Le P. Norbert a un Evêque de France, Au sujet de l'Exécution de Gabriel Malagrida, Jésuite, par Sentences des Tribunaux de l'Inquisition & de la Supplication à Lisbonne, le 20 & 21. de Septembre 1761.

"Lines Made After The Great Earthquake, In 1755 which shook North and South America, with great destruction in Cales, in Lisbon, and most of the adjacent kingdoms." Boston, 1755?.

Liste des personnes qui ont été condamnées à l'acte public de Foi, célèbre dans le cloître du couvent de Dominique de Lisbonne le 20 septembre 1761. Lisbon, 1761.

Lodge, Richard, ed. *The Private Correspondence of Sir Benjamin Keene.* Cambridge: Cambridge University Press, 1933.

Machado, Ignácio Barbosa. *Relacam da Infermidade, Ultimas Acçoens, Morte e Sepultura do Muito Alto . . .* Lisbon, 1750.

Malagrida, Gabriel. *Juizo da Verdadeira Causa do Terremoto.* Lisbon: Manoel Soares, 1756.

Mann, Thomas. *Der Zauberberg.* Berlin: S. Fischer Verlag, 1952.

Marcellinus, Ammianus. *The Later Roman Empire (A.D. 354–378).* Middlesex: Penguin, 1986.

Mello, Franciso de Pina e de. *Ao Terremoto do Primeiro de Novembro de 1755 Parènesis de Francisco de Pina e de Mello.* Lisbon: Manoel Soares, 1756.

Memórias das Principais Providências que se deram no Terramoto que padeceu a corte de Lisboa no ano de 1755, ordenadas e oferecidas à Majestade Fidelíssima de El-Rei D. José I, Nosso Senhor. Pref. Luís Oliveira Ramos. Lisbon: FLAD/Público, 2005 [1758].

Mendonça, Joaquim José Moreira de. *História Universal dos Terremotos, que tem havido no Mundo [. . .] com uma Narraçam Individual do Terremoto.* Lisbon, Officina de Antonio Vicente da Silva, 1758.

Miguel, das Almas Santas. *Copia de huma carta escrita pelo Padre Guardiam de Real Convento de Maquinés, e Vice-Prefeito das Santas Missoens, que nas partes da Barbaria conserva a Religiosa Provincia de São Diogo dos RR. PP.* Franciscans Desecalgos, as Padre Procurador dellas. Lisbon: Manoel Soares, 1756.

———. *Franciscanos Descalços, ao Padre Procurador dellas.* Lisbon: Manoel Soares, 1756.

Montaigu, Samuel. *Journal œconomique, ou Mémoires, notes et avis sur les arts, l'agriculture, le commerce . . .* Paris: Antoine Boudet, February 1756.

Morganti, Bento. *Carta de hum Amigo para outro em que se dá succinta Noticia dos Effeitos de Terremoto succedido em o Primeiro de Novembro de 1755.* Lisbon: Domingos Rodrigues, 1756.

Moser, Friedrich Carl von. "Lissabon, 1755." In Friedrich Carl von Moser, *Moralische und politische Scriften.* Vol. 1. Frankfurt: Gebhard, 1763, 179–88.

Münzer, Hieronymus. "Itinerário do Dr. Jerónimo Munzer 1492." In *Lisboa antes do terramoto grande vista da cidade entre 1700 & 1725.* Lisbon: Gótica, 2004.

Nederlandsch Gedenkboek of Europische Mercurius. Vol. 56. The Hague: Frederic Henric Scheurleer, 1755.

Neri, A. "Uno scampato dal terremoto di Lisbona." In *Giornale Ligustico di Archeologia, Storia, e Letteratura,* edited by L. T. Belgrano and A. Neri. Genoa: R. Instituto Sordo-Muti, 1887, 66–70.

Neunte Relation von den erschrecklichen Erdbeben zu Lissabonn, Oder: Abdruck derjenigen Briefe, Wie selbe dieses grosse Unglück von verschiedenen Orten mit mehrern Umständen berichtet haben. Breslau, 1756.

Nozes, J., Introduction, translation, and notes. *O terramoto de 1755: Testemunhas Britânicos—The Lisbon Earthquake of 1755: British Accounts.* Lisbon: Lisóptima Edições, 1990.

Nueva Relación de lo Acoecido en la Ciudad de Lisboa . . . Seville: Imprenta de Joseph de Navarro, 1755.

Oliveira, Francisco Xavier de. *Amusement périodique.* Vol. 1. London, 1751.

———. *Discurso Patético sobre as calamidades sucedidas em Portugal,* translated by Jorge P. Pires. Lisbon: Frenesi, 2004; original, 1756.

———, and Francisco Luís Ameno. *Carta Em Que Se Mostra Falsa a Profecia do Terremoto do Primeiro de Novembro de 1755.* Lisbon: Patriarcal de Francisco Luiz Ameno, 1756.

Pedegache, Miguel Tibério. *Nova e Fiel Relação que Experimentou Lisboa, e Todo Portugal no 1 De Novembro de 1755.* Lisbon: Officina de Manoel Soares, 1756.

Pendrick, Gerard J. *Antiphon the Sophist: The Fragments.* Cambridge: Cambridge University Press, 2002.

Pepys, Samuel. *The Diary of Samuel Pepys M.A. F.R.S.* Vol. 5., edited by Henry B. Wheatley. London: George Bell & Sons, 1895.

Pereira, Angelo, Preface and Notes. "O Terramoto de 1755: Narrativa de uma Testemunha Ocular." *Terra Lusa,* No. 3, 1953 Separata. Lisbon: Livraria Ferin, 1953, 1–22.

Perrey, Alexis. *Mémoire sur les tremblements de terre ressentis en France, en Belgique et en Hollande, depuis le quatrième siècle de l'ère chrétienne jusqu'a nos jours (1843 inclusiv.).* 1844.

Physikalische Betrachtungen von den Erdbeben und den daraus erfolgten auserordentlichen Bewegungen der Gewässer wie auch von den anderen Natur-Begebenheiten welche am 1ten Nov. 1755. den grösten Theil von Europa und andere Welt-Theile betroffen, besonders aber die Königl. Portugiesische Haupt-Stadt Lissabon bis auf den Grund zerstöret haben . . . Frankfurt and Leipzig: Heinrich Ludwig Brönner, 1756.

Piderit, Johann Rudolph Anton. *Freye Betrachtungen über das neuliche Erdbeben zu Lissabon.* Marburg, 1756.

Politische Correspondenz Friedrich's des Grossen. Berlin: Verlag Von Alexander Duncker, 1883.

Portal, Manoel. "Historia da ruina da cidade cauzada pello espantozo terremoto e incendio que reduzio a pó e cinza a melhor e maior parte desta infeliz cidade" (manuscript). Lisbon: Biblioteca da Arte, Fundação Calouste Gulbenkian, AP 12363, n.d.

Portugal Aflito e Conturbado Pello Terremoto do Anno de 1755 (anonymous, manuscript), AHCML, FA-63.

Portugal, Fernando, and Alfredo de Matos. *Lisboa em 1758: Memórias paroquiais de Lisboa.* Coimbra: Coimbra Editora, 1974.

Portugal, José de Almeida. *As Prisões da Junqueira durante o ministério do marquês de Pombal escritas ali mesmo pelo marquês de Alorna, uma das suas vítimas.* Lisbon: Frenesi, 2005 (originally published 1857).

The Proceedings and Sentence of the Spiritual Court of Inquisition of Portugal against Gabriel Malagrida, Jesuit. London: C. Marsh, 1762.

Rathery, E. J. B. *Journal and Memoirs of the Marquis d'Argenson.* Vol. 2 (of 2). Boston: Hardy, Pratt & Co., 1901.

Ratton, Jácome. *Recordações de Jácome Ratton sobre occurrências do seu tempo em Portugal de maio de 1747 à setembro 1810.* Lisbon: Fenda Edições, 2007.

S., L. J. dF e. *Refutaçam de Alguns Erros, que com o falso, e fantastico nome de Profecias, ou Vaticinios, Se Divulgaram, E Espalham Ao presente, aonde com toda a brevidade, e clareza se monstra sua insubsistencia, e falsidade.* Lisbon: Domingos Rodrigues, 1756.

Relación Veridica, del Terremoto, y Agitación de el Mar, Acacido en la Ciudad de Ayamonte, El día primero del mes de Noviembre de este año de 1755. Cádiz: Real de Marina, 1755–56?.

Relações diplomáticas luso-russas: Colectânea documental conjunta (1722–1815). Vol. 1. Lisbon: Instituto Diplomático, 2004.

Relation de l'Autho-da-Fé de Lisbonne. 1761?.

Resende, Manuel Marques. *Espelho da Corte ou Hum Breve Mappa de Lisboa.* Lisbon, 1720.

Reys, Domingo dos. *Sylva no Lamantavel Terremoto do Primeiro de Novembro de 1755.* Lisbon, 1756.

Roche, Juan Luis. *Relación y observaciones physicas-mathematicas y morales sobre el general terremoto y la irrupción del mar del día primero de noviembre de este año 1755 que comprendió a la ciudad, y Gran Puerto de Santa María y a toda la costa, y tierra firme del Reyno de Andalucía.* Santa María, Spain, 1756.

Rodrigues, Domingos. *Arte de Cozinha.* Lisbon: Oficina Ferreiriana, 1732.

Rodriques, Matias. *Vida do padre Gabriel Malagrida*, translated by Ilário Govoni. Belém do Pará: Centro de Cultura e Formação Cristã, 2010.

Rousseau, Jean-Jacques. *Lettre de J. J. Rousseau Citoyen de Geneve, A Monsieur de Voltaire Concernant le Poème sur le Désastre de Lisbonne, Par M. de Voltaire.* 1764.

———. "Letter to Voltaire on Providence." In *Rousseau: Religious Writings*, edited by Ronald Grimsley. Oxford: Clarendon Press, 1970.

Ruders, Carl Israel. *Viagem em Portugal (1798–1802).* Lisbon: Biblioteca Nacional, 1981.

A Satirical Review of the Manifold Falsehoods and Absurdities hitherto published concerning the Earthquake; to which is annexed an authentic Account of the late catastrophe at Lisbon, and the present state of that august Capital. By a Man of Business. London: A. and C. Corbett, 1756.

Sentença contra o Pe. Malagridada Companha de Jesus. September 24, 1761.

Silva, José Alvares da. *Precauções Medicas contra algumas remotas consequencias, que se podem excitar do Terremoto de 1755.* Lisbon: Joseph Costa Coimbra, 1756.

Sousa, José de Oliveira Trovão e. *Carta em que hum amigo dá noticia a outro do lamentavel successo de Lisboa.* Coimbra, 1755.

Sousa, Maria Teresa de Andrade e. "Subsídio para o Estudo do Terremoto de Lisboa de 1755 Manuscrito Coevo." Lisbon, November 1955.

Sternleuw, Fredric Christian. "1755 Breve Testemunho dum Sueco." Lisbon: Casa Portuguesa, 1958.

Tavares, José Acursio de. *Verdade Vindicada, ou Resposta A Huma Carta escrita de Coimbra, em que se dá noticia do lamantavel successo de Lisboa no dia de 1. de Novembro de 1755.* Lisbon: Miguel Manescal da Costa, 1756.

Thucydides. *History of the Peloponnesian War*, translated by Rex Warner. New York: Penguin, 1972.

A True and Particular Account of the late Dreadful Earthquake at Lisbon. London: Printed and Sold in Bow-Church-Yard, 1755?.

Two very Circumstantial Accounts of the late dreadful Earthquake at Lisbon. Reprint, Boston: D. Fowle, 1756.

"Une description de Lisbonne en juin de 1755 par le Chevalier des Courtils." *Bulletin des Études Portugaises,* Introduction by Jacques Aman and Notes by Albert-Alain Bourdon, L'Institut Français au Portugal, Vol. 26, 1965, 111–80.

Uz, Johann P. *Sämtliche poetische Werke von J. P. Uz,* edited by A. Sauer. 1890. Reprint; Stuttgart: Nedeln/Liechtenstein, 1968.

Verdica Relación, En Que Se Declara el estupendo prodigo, que à vista de innumerable Pueblo de esta Cuidad de Sanlucar de Barrameda ha obrado . . . Seville: Joseph Padrino, 1755–56?.

Voltaire. *The Works of Voltaire: A Philosophical Dictionary.* Vol. 7 (of 10). New York: E. R. DuMont, 1901.

Walpole, Horace. *Memoires of the Last Ten Years of the Reign of George II.* Vol. 1 (of 2). London: John Murray, 1822.

———. *The Letters of Horace Walpole, 4th Earl of Oxford.* Edited by Peter Cunningham. Vol. 2. (of 9). Edinburgh: John Grant, 1906.

Wesley, John. *Serious Thoughts Occasioned by the Earthquake at Lisbon to which is subjoin'd An Account of all the late Earthquakes there, and in other Places.* 6th ed. London, 1756.

Whitefield, George. *Whitefield at Lisbon: Being a Detailed Account of the Blasphemy and Idolatry of Popery as witnessed by the Late Servant of God, George Whitefield.* London: R. Greenbridge & Sons, 1851.

Wichmannshausen, Rudolph Friedrich von. *Betrachtungen über das außerordentliche Erdbeben zu gegenwärtigen Zeiten zur Erweckung an Gott, die Welt und an sich selbst hierbey zu gedenken, aufgesetzt.* Leipzig, 1756.

Zehente Relation von den erschrecklichen Erdbeben zu Lissabonn, Oder: Abdruck derjenigen Briefe, Wie selbe dieses grosse Unglück von verschiedenen Orten mit mehrern Umständen berichtet haben. Breslau, 1756.

Zwölfte Relation von den erschrecklichen Erdbeben zu Lissabonn, Oder: Abdruck derjenigen Briefe, Wie selbe dieses grosse Unglück von verschiedenen Orten mit mehrern Umständen berichtet haben. Breslau, 1756.

III. SECONDARY WORKS (BOOKS, ARTICLES, AND THESES)

Abdelaziz, Chabbar. "Os efeitos do terramoto de Lisboa 1 november 1755." In *1755: O grande terramoto de Lisboa.* Vol. 1, 2005, 265–94.

Abecasis, Maria Isabel Braga. *A Real Barraca A Residência na Ajuda dos Reis de Portugal Após a Terramoto (1756–1794).* Lisbon: Tribuna, 2009.

Accary, F., and Jean Roger. "Tsunami Catalog and Vulnerability of Martinique (Lesser Antilles, France)." *Science of Tsunami Hazards,* Vol. 29, No. 3, 2010.

Adamo, Sergia. "Constructing an Event, Contemplating Ruins, Theorizing Nature; the Lisbon Earthquake and Some Italian Reactions." *European Review,* Vol. 14, No. 3, July 2006, 339–49.

Adams, John, and Michael Staveley. "Historical Seismology of Newfoundland." In Earth Physics Branch Open File No. 85-22, Ottawa, Canada, September 1985.

Aguirre, Benigno E., and E. L. Quarantelli. "Phenomenology of Death Counts in Disasters: The Invisible Dead in the 9/11 WTC Attack." *International Journal of Mass Emergencies and Disasters,* Vol. 26, No. 1, March 2008, 19–39.

———. "Better Disaster Statistics: The Lisbon Earthquake." *The Journal of Interdisciplinary History,* Vol. 43, No. 1, Summer 2012.

Akola, Meira do Carmo Neto. "Demografia." In *Dicionário de história de Portugal*, Vol. 2, edited by Joel Serrão. Lisbon: Iniciativas Editoriais, 1993.

Alarcia, Diego Téllez. "Spanish Interpretations of the Lisbon Earthquake Between 1755 and the War of 1762." In *The Lisbon Earthquake of 1755: Representations and Reactions*, edited by T. E. D. Braun and J. B. Radner. Oxford: Voltaire Foundation, 2005.

———. "El impacto del terremoto de Lisboa en España." In *O terramoto de 1755: Impactos históricos*, edited by Ana Cristina Araújo et al. Lisbon: Livros Horizonte, 2007.

Alden, Dauril. *The Making of an Enterprise: The Society of Jesus in Portugal, Its Empire, and Beyond, 1540–1750*. Stanford: Stanford University Press, 1996.

Aldridge, Alfred Owen. "Benjamin Franklin and Jonathan Edwards on Lightning and Earthquakes." *Isis*, Vol. 41, No. 2, July 1950, 162–64.

Algrant, Christine Pevitt. *Madame de Pompadour: Mistress of France*. New York: Grove, 2002.

Almeida, Onésimo. "Portugal and the Dawn of Modern Science." In *Portugal the Pathfinder: Journeys from the Medieval Toward the Modern World, 1300–ca. 1600*, edited by George Winius. Madison, WI: Hispanic Seminary of Medieval Studies, 1995, 341–61.

———. "Science During the Portuguese Maritime Discoveries: A Telling Case of Interaction Between Experimenters and Theoreticians." In *Science in the Spanish and Portuguese Empires, 1500–1800*, edited by Daniela Bleichar, Paula De Vos, Kristin Huffine, and Kevin Sheehan. Stanford: Stanford University Press, 2008, 78–92.

Amador, Filomena. "O terramoto de Lisboa de 1755: Colecções de textos do século XVII." *História, Ciências, Saúde Manguinhos*, Vol. 14, No. 1, January–March 2007, 285–323.

Anderson, James M., and M. Sheridan Lea. *Portugal 1001 Sights: An Archaeological and Historical Guide*. Calgary: University of Calgary Press, 1994.

Andrade, Ferreira de. *Lisboa e seus serviços de incêndios, vol. 1, 1395–1868*. Lisbon: Câmara Municipal de Lisboa, 1969.

Anisimov, Evgeny V. *Empress Elizabeth: Her Reign and Her Russia, 1741–1761*. Gulf Breeze, FL: Academic International Press, 1995.

Antunes, Miguel Telles. "Vítimas do terremoto de 1755 no Convento de Jesus (Academia das Ciências de Lisboa)." *Revista Electrónica de Ciências da Terra Geosciences On-Line Journal*, Vol. 3, No. 1, 2006.

Araújo, Ana Cristina. "Ruína e Morte em Portugal no Século XVIII." *Revista de História Das Ideias*, Vol. 9, 1987, 327–65.

———. "O Desastre de Lisboa e o opinião pública europeia." In *Estudos de História Contemporânea, Homenagem ao Professor Victor de Sá*. Lisbon: Livros Horizonte, 1991, 93–107.

———. "L'Europe tremble à Lisbonne." In *L'esprit de l'Europe, t. I, dates et lieux*, edited by A. Compagnon and J. Seebacher. Paris: Flammarion, 1993, 125–30.

———. *O Terramoto de 1755. Lisboa e a Europa*. Lisbon: CTT, 2005.

———. "The Lisbon Earthquake of 1755—Public Distress and Political Propaganda." *E-Journal of Portuguese History*, Vol. 4, No. 1, Summer 2006.

———. *O Terramoto de 1755: Impactos históricos*. Edited by Ana Cristina Araújo, et al. Lisbon: Livros Horizonte, 2007.

———. "The Lisbon Earthquake and the Seven Years War: Public Distress and Portuguese Political Propaganda." In *Das Erdbeben von Lissabon und der Katastrophendiskurs im 18. Jahrhundert*. Edited by Gerhard Lauer and Thorsten Unger. Göttingen: Wallstein Verlag, 2008.

———. "Literacy and Social Order: Writing and Reading in Lisbon in the 18th Century." (on-line), 93–108.

Arnason, H. H. *The Sculpture of Houdon.* New York: Oxford University Press, 1975.

Ayres, Christovam. *Manuel da Maya e os engenheiros militares portugueses no Terremoto de 1755.* Lisbon: Imprensa Nacional, 1910.

Azevedo, Pedro de, ed. *O processo dos Távoras.* Lisbon: Biblioteca Nacional, 1921.

Bakewell, Peter. *A History of Latin America to 1825.* 3rd ed. Chichester: Wiley-Blackwell, 2010.

Banerjee, D., A. S. Murray, and I. D. L. Foster. "Scilly Isles, UK: Optical Dating of a Possible Tsunami Deposit from the 1755 Earthquake." *Quaternary Science Review,* Vol. 20, 2001, 715–18.

Bankoff, Greg, Uwe Lübken, and Jordan Sand, eds. *Flammable Cities: Urban Conflagration and the Making of the Modern World.* Madison: University of Wisconsin Press, 2012.

Baptista, Maria Ana, et al. "Constraints on the Source of the 1755 Lisbon Tsunami Inferred from Numerical Modeling of Historical Data on the Source of the 1755 Lisbon Tsunami." *Journal of Geodynamics,* Vol. 25, No. 2, 1998, 159–74.

———, et al. "The 1755 Lisbon Tsunami; Evaluation of the Tsunami Parameters." *Journal of Geodynamics,* Vol. 25, No. 2, 1998, 143–57.

———, et al. "New Study of the 1755 Earthquake Source Based on Multi-Channel Seismic Survey Data and Tsunami Modeling." *Natural Hazards and Earth System Sciences,* Vol. 3, 2003, 333–40.

———, et al. "Short Notes: In Search of the 31 March 1761 Earthquake and Tsunami Source." *Bulletin of the Seismological Society of America,* Vol. 96, No. 2, 2006, 713–21.

———, and J. M. Miranda. "Revision of the Portuguese Catalogue of Tsunamis." *Natural Hazards and Earth System Sciences,* Vol. 9, 2009, 25–42.

Barata, Mario. *I terremoti d'Italia.* Turin: Fratelli Bocca Editori, 1901.

Barata, M. R. Themudo, et al. *Sismicidade de Portugal. Estudo da documentação dos séculos XVII e XVIII.* 2 vols. Lisbon: Ministério do Planeamento e da Administração do Território, 1988.

Barber, William Henry. *Leibniz in France from Arnauld to Voltaire: A Study in French Reactions to Leibnizianism, 1670–1760.* Oxford: Clarendon Press, 1955.

Barkan, Roy, Uri S. ten Brink, and Jian Lin. "Far Field Tsunami Simulation of the 1755 Lisbon Tsunami: Implications for Tsunami Hazard to the US East Coast and the Caribbean." *Marine Geology,* 264, 2009, 109–22.

Barreto, José. "O Discurso Político Falsamente Atribuído ao Marquês de Pombal." *Revista de História das Ideias,* Vol. 4, No. 1, 1982, 385–422.

Battelli, Guido. *Il Terremoto di Lisbona nelle memorie degli scrittori italiani contemporanei.* Coimbra: Coimbra Editora, 1929.

Bauer, F. Marshall. *Marblehead's Pygmalion: Finding the Real Agnes Surriage.* Charleston, SC: History Press, 2010.

Belo, André. "A *Gazeta de Lisboa* e o terramoto de 1755: a margem do não escrito." *Análise Social,* Vol. 34 (151–52), 1999, No. 2–3, 615–33.

———."Between History and Periodicity: Printed and Hand-Written News in 18th-Century Portugal." *E-Journal of Portuguese History,* Vol. 2, No. 2, Winter 2004.

———."A Notícia do Terramoto no Sistema de Informação do Antigo Regime." In *História e ciência da catástrofe: 250 aniversário do terramoto de 1755,* coordinated by Maria Fernanda Rollo, Ana Isabel Buescu, and Pedro Cardim. Lisbon: Colibri, 2007, 55–66.

Ben-Menahem, Ari. "Four Thousand Years of Seismicity Along the Dead Sea Rift." *Journal of Geophysical Research* 96, No. B12, November 10, 1991, 20, 195–216.

Berghaus, Hermann. *Berghaus' Physikalischer Atlas*. Gotha: J. Perthes, 1849–52.

Bessone, Silvana, ed. *O Museu National dos Coches Lisboa*. Lisbon: Instituto Português de Museus Fondation Paribas, 1993.

Besterman, Theodore. "Voltaire et le désastre de Lisbonne: ou, La mort de l'optimisme." *Studies in Voltaire and the Eighteenth Century*, Vol. 2, 1956, 7–24.

———. *Voltaire*. New York: Harcourt, Brace & World, 1969.

Bethencourt, Francisco, and Kirti Chaudhuri, eds. *História da Expansão Portuguesa*. 5 Vols. Lisbon: Círclo de Leitores, 1999.

Bethencourt, Francisco, and Diogo Ramada Curto, eds. *Portuguese Oceanic Expansion, 1400–1800*. Cambridge: Cambridge University Press, 2007.

Bettencourt, Olga, collaborator, et al. *Cascais em 1755: Do terramoto à reconstrução*. Cascais, Portugal: Câmara Municipal, 2005.

Bicalho, Maria Fernanda. *A cidade e o império: o Rio de Janeiro no século XVIII*. Rio de Janeiro: Civilização Brasileira, 2003.

Birmingham, David. *A Concise History of Portugal*. 2nd ed. Cambridge: Cambridge University Press, 2003.

Blaak, Jeroen. *Literacy in Everyday Life: Reading and Writing in Early Modern Dutch Diaries*. Leiden: Brill, 2009.

Black, Jeremy, ed. "Anglo-Portuguese Relations in the Eighteenth Century: A Reassessment." In *The British Historical Society of Portugal Fourteenth Annual Report and Review*, Lisbon, 1987, 125–42.

Blagg, Christopher R. "Triage: Napoleon to the Present Day." *Journal of Nephrology*, Vol. 17, 2004.

Blanc, Paul-Louis. "The Tsunami in Cadiz on 1 November, 1755: A Critical Analysis of Reports by Antonio de Ulloa and by Louis Godin." *Comptes Rendus Geoscience*, Vol. 340, No. 4, 2008, 251–61.

———. "Earthquakes and Tsunami in November 1755 in Morocco: A Different Reading of the Contemporaneous Documentary Sources." *Natural Hazards and Earth System Sciences*, Vol. 9, 2009, 725–38.

———. "The Atlantic Tsunami on November 1st, 1755: World Range and Amplitude According to Primary Documentary Sources." In *The Tsunami Threat—Research and Technology*, edited by Nils-Axel Mörner. Rijeka: InTech Publishing, 2011.

Boer, J. Zeilinga de, and D. T. Sanders. *Earthquakes in Human History: The Far-Reaching Effects of Human Disruptions*. Princeton, NJ: Princeton University Press, 2005.

Bolt, Bruce A. *Earthquakes*. 5th ed. New York: W. H. Freeman, 2003.

Botero, Giovanni. *The Reason of State*, "A Treatise Concerning the Causes of the Magnificency and Greatness of Cities Divided into three books by Sig. Giovanni Botero in the Italian Tongue, now done into English by Robert Peterson, 1606," Book 2, Chapter 11, n.p. ("Of the residency of the prince"): n.d.

Bourke, Thomas E. "Vorsehung und Katastrophe. Voltaire Poème sur le désastre de Lissabon und Kleists Erdbeben in Chili." In *Klassik und Moderne. Die Weimarer Klassik als historische Ereignis und Herausforderung im kulturegeschichtlichen Prozeß*, edited by Karl Richter and Jörg Schönert. Stuttgart: Metzler, 1983.

Bourne, Henry E. "Food Control and Price-Fixing in Revolutionary France: I." *Journal of Political Economy*, Vol. 27, No. 2, February 1919.

———. "Food Control and Price-Fixing in Revolutionary France: II." *Journal of Political Economy*, Vol. 27, No. 3, March 1919.

Boxer, Charles R. "Pombal's Dictatorship and the Great Lisbon Earthquake, 1755." *History Today*, November 1955, 729–36.

———. "Some Contemporary Reactions to the Lisbon Earthquake of 1755." *Revista da Faculdade de Letras*, Vol. 23, No. 1, 1956, 113–29.

———. *The Golden Age of Brazil, 1695–1750*. Berkeley: University of California Press, 1962.

———. *The Portuguese Seaborne Empire, 1415–1825*. New York: Alfred A. Knopf, 1969.

———. "Brazilian Gold and British Traders in the First Half of the Eighteenth Century." *Hispanic American Historical Review*, Vol. 49, No. 3, August 1969.

———. "Lord Tyrawley in Lisbon." *History Today*, Vol. 20, November 1970, 791–98.

Braga, Maria Luísa. "A Polémica dos Terramotos em Portugal." *Revista da Faculdade de Letras*, 2nd Series, Vol. 5, 1986, 545–73.

Branco, Manuel Bernardes. *Portugal na época de D. João V*. Lisbon, 1885.

Brandão, Manuel José da Cunha. *As ruínas do Carmo*. Lisbon: Typ. da Casa da Moeda e Papel Sellado, 1908.

Braun, T. E. D., and J. B. Radner, eds. *The Lisbon Earthquake of 1755: Representations and Reactions*. Oxford: Voltaire Foundation, 2005.

Brazão, Eduardo. *João V: Subsídios para a história do seu reinado*. Oporto, 1945.

Brée, M. M. de. *A Igreja e Convento de São Domingos de Lisboa*. Lisbon: Oficinas de S. José de Lisboa, 1964.

Briggs, Martin S. "S. John's Chapel in the Church of S. Roque, Lisbon." *The Burlington Magazine for Connoisseurs*, Vol. 28, No. 152, 11/1915.

Brightman, Edgar S. "The Lisbon Earthquake: A Study in Religious Valuation." *American Journal of Theology*, 500–18.

Brito, Manuel Carlos de. *Opera in Portugal in the Eighteenth Century*. Cambridge: Cambridge University Press, 1989.

Brown, Bahngrell W. "The Quake That Shook Christendom—Lisbon, 1755." *Southern Quarterly*, Vol. 7, No. 4, July 1969, 425–31.

Brown, Robert H. *Nature's Hidden Terror: Violent Nature Imagery and Social Change in Eighteenth-Century Germany*. Columbia, SC: Camden House, 1991.

———. "The 'Demonic' Earthquake: Goethe's Myth of the Lisbon Earthquake and Fear of Modern Change," *German Studies Review*, Vol. 15, No. 3, October 1992, 475–91.

Bryges, Egerton. *Collins's Peerage of England*. Vol. 7 (of 9). London, 1812.

Buescu, Helena Carvalhão, and Gonçalo Cordeiro, eds. *O Grande Terramoto de Lisboa: Ficar diferente*. Lisbon: Gradiva, 2005.

———. "Sobreviver à catástrofe: sem tecto, entre ruínas." In *O Grande Terramoto de Lisboa, Ficar Diferente*, edited by Helena C. Buescu and Gonçalo Cordeiro. Lisbon: Gradiva, 2005, 19–72.

Buescu, Helena Carvalhão, Manuela Carvalho, Fernanda Gil Costa, and João Almeida Flor, eds. *1755: Catástrofe, memória e arte*. Lisboa: Edições Colibri, 2006.

Buforn, E., et al. "Seismotectonics of the Ibero-Maghrebian region." *Techtonophysics*, 248, 1995.

Butiñá, P. Franciso. *Vida del P. Malagrida de la Compania de Jesús, quemado como hereje por el Marqués de Pombal*. Barcelona: Franciso Rosal, 1886.

Cala, Carmen Espejo. "Un texto de nipho sobre el Terremoto de Lisboa. La Reacción de La prensa europea y espanola ante la catástrofe." *Cuadernos Dieciochistas*, No. 6, 2005.

———. "Spanish News Pamphlets on the 1755 Earthquake: Trade Strategies of the

Printers of Sevilla." In *The Lisbon Earthquake of 1755: Representations and Reactions,* edited by T. E. D. Braun and J. B. Radner. Oxford: Voltaire Foundation, 2005, 66–80.

Calafate, Pedro. "A polémica en torno das causas do terramoto de 1755." Chapter 4 in *História do pensamento filosófico português. Volume 3: As Luzes,* edited by Pedro Calafate. Lisbon: Caminho, 2001.

———, ed. *História do pensamento filosófico português. Volume 3: As Luzes.* Lisbon: Caminho, 2001.

Câmara, Maria Alexandra T. Gago da. *Lisboa: Espaços teatrais setecentistas.* Lisbon: Livros Horizonte, 1996.

Câmara, Maria Alexandra T. Gago da, and Vanda Anastácio. *O teatro em Lisboa no tempo do Marquês de Pombal.* Lisbon: Museu Nacional do Teatro, 2005.

Campillos, Maria Paz Martín-Pozuelo. "En torno a una tradicción archivística ibérica y sus consecuencias en el uso de los archivos." Online.

Campos, Isabela M. Barreira de. *O Grande Terremoto (1755).* Lisbon: Parceria, 1998.

Cardoso, José Luís, et al. *O Tratado de Methuen (1703) diplomacia, guerra, política e economia.* Lisbon: Livros Horizonte, 2003.

Cardozo, Manoel. "The Internationalism of the Portuguese Enlightenment: The Role of the Estrangeirado, c. 1700–c. 1750." In *The Ibero-American Enlightenment,* edited by A. Owen Aldridge. Urbana: University of Illinois Press, 1971.

Carrozi, Marguerite. "Reaction of British Colonies in America to the 1755 Lisbon Earthquake: A Comparison to the European Response." *Earth Sciences History: Journal of the History of the Earth Sciences Society,* Vol. 2, Part 1, 1983, 17–27.

Cartwright, Julyan H. E., and Hisami Nakamura. "Tsunami: A History of the Term and of Scientific Understanding of the Phenomenon in Japanese and Western Culture." *Notes & Records of the Royal Society,* Vol. 62, No. 2, June 20, 2008, 151–66.

Carvalho, Carlos Correia de, and Franciso Segurado. "O Terramoto de 1755 nas terras alentejanas de jurisdição da Casa de Bragança." *Callipole,* No. 18, 2010.

Carvalho, Joaquim de. "Correspondência Científica dirigida a João Jacinto de Magalhães." *Revista da Faculdade de Ciências,* Vol. 20, 1951, 93–283.

Carvalho, Rómulo de. "Portugal nas 'Philosophal Transactions' nos séculos XVII e XVIII." *Revista Filosófica,* Vol. 15–16, 1956, 3–59.

———. "As interpretações dadas, na época, às causas do terramoto de 1 de novembro de 1755." *Memoria de Academia de Ciências de Lisboa. Classe de Ciências.* Vol. 28, Lisbon, 1987, 179–205.

Cassirer, Ernst. *The Philosophy of the Enlightenment.* Princeton, NJ: Princeton University Press, 1968; original 1932.

Castilho, Julio. *Lisboa antiga.* 4th ed., 5 Vols. Lisbon: Soc. Tipográfica, 1981.

Castinel, G. "Le désastre de Lisbonne." *Revue du Dix-huitième Siècle,* Année 1, No. 4, 1913, 396–409, and Année 2, No. 1, 1914, 72–92.

Catalogue of Prints and Drawings in the British Museum, Division I, Political and Personal Satires, Vol. 4, *A.D. 1761–A.D. 1770,* No. 3805 to No. 4838. London: Chiswick Press, 1883.

Chantal, Suzanne. *A vida quotidiana em Portugal ao tempo do Terramoto.* Lisbon: Livros do Brasil, 2005.

Chapman, A. B. Wallis. "The Commercial Relations of England and Portugal, 1487–1807." *TRHS,* 3rd Series, Vol. 1, 1907, 177.

Chaves, Castello Branco. *O Portugal de D. João V visto por três forasteiros.* Lisbon: Biblioteca Nacional, 1989.

Cheke, Marcus. *Dictator of Portugal: Marquis of Pombal*. London: Sidgwick & Jackson, 1938.

Chester, David K. "The 1755 Lisbon Earthquake." *Progress in Physical Geography*, Vol. 25, No. 3, 2001, 363–83.

———, and Angus M. Duncan. "The Bible, Theodicy and Christian Responses to Historic and Contemporary Earthquakes and Volcanic Eruptions." *Environmental Hazards*, Vol. 8, 2009, 304–32.

Chester, David K., and Olivia K. Chester. "The Impact of Eighteenth-Century Earthquakes on the Algarve Region, Southern Portugal." *The Geographical Journal*, Vol. 176, No. 4, December 2010, 350–70.

Clapham, Sir John. *The Bank of England*. Vol. 1. Cambridge: Cambridge University Press; reprint, 1966.

Clark, Charles Edwin. "Science, Reason, and an Angry God: The Literature of an Earthquake." *New England Quarterly*, Vol. 38, No. 3, September 1965, 340–62.

Clark, J. C. D. "Providence, Predestination and Progress: Or, Did the Enlightenment Fail?" *Albion: A Quarterly Journal Concerned with British Studies*, Vol. 35, No. 4, Winter 2003, 559–89.

Clarke, [?]. *The Georgian Era: Memoirs of the Most Eminent Persons, Who Have Flourished in Great Britain, From the Accession of George the First to the Demise of George the Fourth*, Vol. 1 (of 4). London: Vizetelly, Branston and Co., 1832.

Cobbett, William, et al., eds. *The Parliamentary History of England from the Earliest Period to the Year 1803*. Vol. 15, *A.D. 1753–1765*. London: T. C. Hansard, 1813.

Coelho, António Gomes. "Do 'Inquérito do Marqués de Pombal' ao estudo de Pereira de Sousa sobre o Terramoto de 1 de novembro de 1755." In *1755: O Grande Terramoto de Lisboa*. Lisbon: FLAD e Público, 2005.

———. "Nota Introdutória," "John Michell, um filósofo da Natureza do século das Luzes." In *1755: Sobre as causes dos terramotos, Volume 4*. Lisbon: FLAD e Público, 2005.

Coen, Deborah R. *The Earthquake Observers: Disaster Science from Lisbon to Richter*. Chicago: University of Chicago Press, 2013.

Coffey, John. "'Tremble Britannia!': Fear, Providence and the Abolition of the Slave Trade, 1758–1807." *The English Historical Review*, Vol. 127, No. 527, August 2012, 844–81.

Collins, Arthur. *The Peerage of England* . . . Vol. 7 (of 8), 5th ed. London: W. Strathan et al., 1779.

Costa, Alexandre, et al. *1755 Terramoto no Algarve*. Faro, Portugal: Centro Ciência Viva do Algarve, 2005.

Costigan, Arthur William. *Sketches of Society and Manners in Portugal*. Vol. 2 (of 2). London, 1787.

Couto, Dejanirah. *História de Lisboa*. 11th ed. Lisbon: Gótica, 2008.

Cranmer, David. "Opera in Portugal or Portuguese Opera." *The Musical Times*, November 1994, 692–96.

Damrosch, Leo. *Jean-Jacques Rousseau: Restless Genius*. Boston: Houghton Mifflin, 2005.

Dando-Collins, Stephan. *The Great Fire of Rome: The Fall of Emperor Nero and His City*. Cambridge, MA: Da Capo, 2010.

Darnton, Robert. "Presidential Address: An Early Information Society: News and the Media in Eighteenth-Century Paris." *The American Historical Review*, Vol. 105, No. 1, February 2000, 1–35.

Davies, Andrea Rees. "Points of Origin: The Social Impact of the 1906 San Francisco

Earthquake and Fire." In *Flammable Cities: Urban Conflagration and the Making of the Modern World*, edited by Greg Bankoff, Uwe Lübken, and Jordan Sand. Madison: University of Wisconsin Press, 2012, 273–93.

Davison, Charles. *A History of British Earthquakes*. Cambridge: Cambridge University Press, 1924.

D'Azevedo, J. Lucio. *O marquês de Pombal e a sua época*. Rio de Janeiro: Annuario do Brasil, 1922.

De Bruhl, Marshall. *Firestorm: Allied Airpower and the Destruction of Dresden*. New York: Random House, 2006.

Delaforce, Angela. "Lisbon, 'This New Rome': Dom João V of Portugal and Relations Between Rome and Lisbon." In *The Age of the Baroque in Portugal*, edited by Jay A. Levenson. Washington, DC: National Gallery of Art, 1993.

———. "The Dream of a Young Architect: Robert Adam and a Project for the Rebuilding of Lisbon in 1755." In *Portugal e o Reino Unido: A aliança revistada*, edited by Angela Delaforce. Lisbon: Fundação Calouste Gulbenkian, 1995.

———. "Paul Crespin's Silver-Gilt Bath for the King of Portugal." *The Burlington Magazine*, Vol. 139, No. 1126, January 1997, 38–40.

———. *Art and Patronage in Eighteenth-Century Portugal*. Cambridge: Cambridge University Press, 2002.

Delaforce, John. *The Factory House at Oporto*. 2nd ed. London: Christie's Wine Publications, 1983.

Demaree, Gaston, et al. "Volcano Eruptions, Earth- & Seaquakes, Dry Fogs vs. Aristotle's *Meteorologica* and the Bible in the Framework of the Eighteenth Century Science History." *Bulletin des séances de l'Académie royale des sciences d'Outre-mer*. Vol. 53 (2007–3), 337–59.

Description of the Royal Cyclorama or Music Hall . . . With Numerous Illustrations of the Earthquake at Lisbon . . . London: J. Chisman, 1849.

Dias, João José Alves. "Principais sismos, em Portugal, anteriores ao de 1755." In *1755: O Grande Terramoto de Lisboa*. Vol. 1, 123–42.

Diffie, Bailey W., and George D. Winius. *Foundations of the Portuguese Empire, 1415–1580*. St. Paul: University of Minnesota Press, 1977.

Diogo, Maria Paula, et al. "Ciência portuguesa no iluminismo. Os estrangeirados e as comunidades europeias." In *Enteados de Galileu? A semiperiferia no Sistema mundial da ciência*, edited by João Arriscado Nunes and Maria Eduarda Gonçalves. Porto, Portugal: Afrontamento, 2001, 209–38.

Disney, A. R. *A History of Portugal and the Portuguese Empire*. Vols. 1 and 2. Cambridge: Cambridge University Press, 2009.

Domingues, Mario. D. *João V: O homem e a sua época*. Lisbon: Prefácio.

Donovan, Bill M. "Changing Perceptions of Social Deviance: Gypsies in Early Modern Portugal and Brazil." *Journal of Social History*, Vol. 26, No. 1, Autumn 1992, 33–53.

———. "The Discovery and Conquest of the Brazilian Frontier." In *Portugal the Pathfinder: Journeys from the Medieval Toward the Modern World, 1300–ca. 1600*, edited by George Winius. Madison, WI: Hispanic Seminary of Medieval Studies, 1995, 229–46.

———. "Crime, Policing, and the Absolutist State in Early Modern Lisbon." *Portuguese Studies Review*, Vol. 5, No. 2, 1996–97.

Dorado, Antonio Manuel Romero. "El terremoto y el maremoto del año 1755 en Sanlúcar de Barrameda." *Cartare Boletín del Centro de Estudios de la Costa Noroeste de Cádiz*, Vol. 2, 2012.

Drumon, M. R. Mendes. *Os estrangeiros e a Inquisição portuguesa (XVI–XVII)*. Lisbon: Hugin, 2002.

Duarte, Cidália, et al. "The Early Paleolithic Human Skeleton from the Abrigo do Lagar Velho (Portugal) and Modern Human Emergence in Iberia." *Proceedings of the National Academy of Sciences of the United States of America*, Vol. 96, No. 13, 1999, 7604–9.

Dudley Walter C., and Min Lee. *Tsunami*. 2nd ed. Honolulu: University of Hawai'i Press, 1998.

Dumouriez, Charles. *O Reino de Portugal em 1766*. Casal de Cambra, Portugal: Caleidoscópio, 2007.

Dutra, Francis A. "The Discovery of Brazil and Its Immediate Aftermath." In *Portugal the Pathfinder: Journeys from the Medieval Toward the Modern World, 1300–ca. 1600*, edited by George Winius. Madison, WI: Hispanic Seminary of Medieval Studies, 1995, 145–68.

———. "The Wounding of King José I: Accident or Assassination Attempt?" *Mediterranean Studies*, Vol. 7, 1998, 221–29.

Dynes, Russell R. "The Lisbon Earthquake in 1755: Contested Meanings in the First Modern Disaster," University of Delaware Disaster Research Center (1997).

———. "The Dialogue Between Voltaire and Rousseau on the Lisbon Earthquake: The Emergence of a Social Science View." *International Journal of Mass Emergencies and Disasters*, Vol. 18, No. 1, March 2000, 97–115.

———. "The Lisbon Earthquake in 1755: The First Modern Disaster." In *The Lisbon Earthquake of 1755: Representations and Reactions*, edited by T. E. D. Braun and J. B. Radner. Oxford: Voltaire Foundation, 2005, 34–49.

Ebel, John E. "The Cape Ann, Massachusetts, Earthquake of 1755: A 250th Anniversary Perspective." *Seismological Research Letters*, Vol. 77, No. 1, 74–86.

Eifert, Christiane. "Das Erdbeben von Lissabon 1755: Zur Historizität einer Naturkatastrophe, *Historische Zeitschrift*." Band 274, 2002, 633–64.

Entwistle, William. "The Portuguese and the Brazilian Language." In *Portugal and Brazil: An Introduction*, edited by H. V. Livermore. Oxford: Oxford University Press, 1953, 29–74.

Espejo Cala, Carmen. "Spanish News Pamphlets on the 1755 Earthquake: Trade Strategies of the Printers of Seville." In *The Lisbon Earthquake of 1755: Representations and Reactions*, edited by T. E. D. Braun and J. B. Radner. Oxford: Voltaire Foundation, 2005, 66–80.

Estorninho, Carlos. "O terramoto de 1755 e a sua repercussão nas relações luso-britânicas." *Revista da Faculdade de Letras*, Vol. 22, No. 1, 1956, 198–233.

Exposição iconográfica e bibliográfica comemorativa de reconstrução da cidade depois do Terramoto de 1755. Lisbon: Câmara Municipal de Lisboa, 1955.

Exposição Lisboa joanina: Comemorativa do segundo centenário do falecimento do rei D. João V. Lisbon: Câmara Municipal de Lisboa, 1950.

Ferrão, António. "Ribeiro Sanches e Soares de Barros. Novos elementos para as biografias desses académicos." Offprint from *Boletim de Segunda Classe da Academia das Ciências de Lisboa*, Vol. 20, 1936, 5–99.

Ferrão, Leonor. "Um *oficial do Génio* e a Nova Lisboa." In *Monumentos, Revista Semestral de Edifícios e Monumentos*, Vol. 21, September 2004.

Ferro, Carolina Chaves. *Terremoto em Lisboa, tremor em Bahia: Um protesto contra a donativo para a reconstrução de Lisboa*. Niteroi, Brazil, 2009.

Ferro, João Pedro. *A populaçã portuguesa no final do Antigo Regime (1750–1815)*. Lisbon: Editorial Presença, 1995.

Figueiredo, José de. "Teatro Real da Ópera." In *Boletim da Academic Nacional de Belas Artes*, Vol. 3. Lisbon, 1938.

Fisher, H. E. S. *The Portugal Trade: A Study of Anglo-Portuguese Commerce, 1700–1770*. London: Methuen, 1971.

Fleming, John. *Robert Fleming and His Circle, in Edinburgh and Rome*. Cambridge, MA: Harvard University Press, 1962.

Fonseca, João Duarte. *1755: O Terramoto de Lisboa*. Lisbon: Argumentum, 2004.

Foster, J. *Alumni Oxonienses: The Members of the University of Oxford, 1715–1886*. Vol. 2. Oxford: Parker & Co., 1891.

Fournier, P. F. "O tremor de terra de Lisboa em 1755, segundo a correspondência dos irmãos Darrot." *Boletim do Instituto Francês em Portugal*. Vol. 2, No. 4, October 1931, 231–45.

França, José-Augusto. *A reconstrução de Lisboa e a arquitectura*. 2nd ed. Lisbon: Instituto Cultural e Língua Portuguesa, 1981.

———. *Lisboa pombalina e o Iluminismo*. Lisbon: Bertrand Editora, 1983; original, 1965.

———. "Lisbon, the Enlightened City of the Marquês de Pombal," In *The Age of the Baroque in Portugal*, edited by Jay A. Levenson. Washington, DC: National Gallery of Art, 1993.

———. *Lisboa: Urbanismo e arquitectura*. 5th ed. Lisbon: Livros Horizonte, 2005.

———. *Lisboa: História física e moral*. Lisbon: Livros Horizonte, 2008.

Francis, A. D. *The Methuens of Portugal*. Cambridge: Cambridge University Press, 1977.

Francis, David. *Portugal 1715–1808: Joanine Pombaline and Rococo Portugal as Seen by British Diplomats and Traders*. London: Tamesis, 1985.

Frèches, Claude-Henri. *Voltaire, Malagrida et Pombal*. Paris: Fundação Calouste Gulbenkian, 1969.

———. "Pombal et la Compagnie de Jésus. La campagne de pamphlets." *Revista de História das Ideias*, Vol. 4, No. 1, 1982, 299–327.

Freitas, Jordão de. "As residencias dos Tavoras e Althouguias (Condes de S. João da Pesqueira e de Alvor, marquezes de Tavora e condes de Althouguia)." *A Época*, February 17, 1924.

Fuchs, Karl. "The Great Earthquakes of Lisbon 1755 and Aceh 2004 Shook the World. Seismologists' Societal Responsibility." In *The Lisbon Earthquake: Revisited*, edited by Luiz Medes-Victor et al. New York: Springer, 2009.

Gama, Henrique Dinis da. *Baixa pombalina: a luz obscura do Iluminismo*. Lisbon: Caminho, 2005.

Georgi, Matthias. "Das Erdbeben von Lissabon in der englischen Publizistik." In *Das Erdbeben von Lissabon und der Katastrophendiskurs im 18. Jahrhundert*, edited by Gerhard Lauer and Thorsten Unger. Göttingen: Wallstein Verlag, 2008, 96–109.

Gisler, Monika. "Optimism and Theodicy: Perceptions of the Lisbon Earthquake in Protestant Switzerland." In *The Lisbon Earthquake of 1755: Representations and Reactions*, edited by T. E. D. Braun and J. B. Radner. Oxford: Voltaire Foundation, 2005, 247–64.

Godinho, Vitorino M. "Portugal, as frotas do açucar e as frotas do ouro (1870–1770)." *Revista da História*, Vol. 15, 1953.

Goudsblom, Johan. *Fire and Civilization*. London: Penguin, 1992.

Gould, Peter. "Lisbon 1755: Enlightenment, Catastrophe, and Communication." In *Geography and Enlightenment*, edited by David Livingstone and Charles W. J. Withers. Chicago: University of Chicago Press, 1999.

Govoni, Ilário. *Malagrida no Grão Pará*. Belém do Pará: Amazônia Indústria Gráfica e Editora, 2009.

Grüneberg, Emil. "Hamburgo e o Terremoto de Lisboa de 1 de Novembro de 1755." *O Instituto Revista Scientifica e Literária*, Vol. 51, No. 1, January 1904.

Guedes, Fernando. *O livro e a leitura em Portugal subsídios para a sua história—séculos XVIII e XIX*. Lisbon: Editorial Verbo, 1987.

Gunther, Horst. "Le désastre de Lisbonne." *Revista de História das Ideias*, Vol. 12, 1990, 415–27.

Gutdeutsch, Rudolf, Gottfried Grünthal, and Roger Musson, eds. *Historical Earthquakes in Central Europe*. Vol. 1 Vienna: Abhandlungen der Geologischen Bundesanstalt, 1992.

Gutkind, E. A. *Urban Development in Southern Europe: Spain and Portugal*. 8 vols. New York: Free Press 1967.

Gutscher, Marc-André. "What Caused the Great Lisbon Earthquake?" *Science*, Vol. 14, Issue 5688, 2004, 1247–48.

———. "The Great Lisbon Earthquake and Tsunami of 1755: Lessons from the Recent Sumatra Earthquakes and Possible Link to Plato's Atlantis." *European Review*, Vol. 14, No. 2, 2006, 181–91.

Haen, Theo de. "On How Not to Be Lisbon If You Want to Be Modern—Dutch Reactions to the Lisbon Earthquake." *European Review*, Vol. 14, No. 3, 2006, 351–58.

Hamilton, Andrew. *Rheinsberg: Memorials of Frederick the Great and Prince Henry of Prussia*. Vol. 2 (of 2). London: John Murray, 1880.

Hammer, Joshua. *Yokohama Burning: The Deadly 1923 Earthquake and Fire That Helped Forge the Path to World War II*. New York: Free Press, 2006.

Hampson, Norman. *The Enlightenment*. London: Penguin, 1968.

Hanines, D. A., and R. W. Sando. "Climatic Conditions Preceding Historically Great Fires in the North Central Region." Research Paper NC-34, 1969.

Hanson, Carl A. *Economy and Society in Baroque Portugal, 1668–1703*. Minneapolis: University of Minnesota Press, 1981.

———. "D. Luís da Cunha and Portuguese Mercantilist Thought." *Journal of the American Portuguese Society*, Vol. 15, 1981, 15–23.

Hanson, Neil. *The Great Fire of London: In That Apocalyptic Year*. Hoboken, NJ: John Wiley & Sons, 2002.

———. *The Dreadful Judgement: The True Story of the Fire of London*. London: Corgi, 2002.

Hart, Charles, and Edward Biddle. *Memoirs of the Life and Works of Jean-Antoine Houdon: The Sculptor of Voltaire and of Washington*. Philadelphia, 1911.

Hauc, Jean-Claude. *Ange Goudar. Un aventurier des Lumières*. Paris: Honoré Champion, 2004.

Havens, George R. "Rousseau, and the 'Lettre sur la Providence.'" *PMLA*, Vol. 59, No. 1, March 1944, 109–30.

Hawthorne, Walter. *From Africa to Brazil: Culture, Identity, and an Atlantic Slave Trade, 1600–1830*. Cambridge: Cambridge University Press, 2010.

Haydon, C. *Anti-Catholicism in Eighteenth-Century England, c. 1714–1780: A Political and Social Study*. Manchester: Manchester University Press, 1993.

Hazard, Paul. "Le problème du mal dans la conscience européenne du XVIIIe siècle." *Romanic Review*, Vol. 31, 1941, 147–70.

————. *European Thought in the Eighteenth Century from Montesquieu to Lessing.* New York: World, 1965.

————. *The Crisis of the European Mind, 1680–1715.* New York: NYRB Classics, 2013.

Henriques, M. C. J., and M. F. F. Natividade. *O Sismo de 26 de Janeiro de 1531.* Lisbon: Comissão para o Catálogo Sísmico Nacional, 1988.

Henriques, Paulo. Introduction, *Lisboa antes do Terramoto Grande vista da cidade entre 1700 & 1725.* Lisbon: Gótica, 2004.

Herrera, Desiderio. *Memoria sobre los huracanes en la isla de Cuba.* Havana: Barcina, 1847.

Hespanha, António Manuel, and António Camões Gouveia. "A igreja." In *História de Portugal,* edited by José Mattoso. Lisbon: Editorial Estampa, 1992–93. Vol. 4 (of 8), *O Antigo Regime (1620–1807),* 287–301.

————. "A Note on Two Recent Books on the Patterns of Portuguese Politics in the 18th Century." *E-Journal of Portuguese History,* Vol. 5, No. 2, Winter 2007.

Himmelfarb, Gertrude. *The Roads to Modernity: The British, French, and American Enlightenments.* New York: Alfred A. Knopf, 2004.

Hindson, R. A., et al. "Sedimentary Processes Associated with the Tsunami Generated by the Lisbon Earthquake on the Algarve Coast." *Physics and Chemistry of the Earth,* Vol. 21, No. 12, 1996, 57–63.

Hindson, R. A., and C. Andrade. "Sedimentation and Hydrodynamic Processes Associated with the Tsunami Generated by the 1755 Lisbon Earthquake." *Quaternary Review,* Vol. 56, No. 1, May 1999, 27–38.

Holm, Isak Winkel. "Earthquake in Haiti: Kleist and the Birth of the Modern Disaster Discourse." *New German Critique,* No. 115, Winter 2012, 49–66.

Hou, Jian-Jun, et al. "Geomorphological Observations of Active Faults in the Epicentral Region of the Huaxian Large Earthquake in 1556 in Shaanxi Province, China." *Journal of Structural Geology,* Vol. 20, 1998, 549–57.

Hough, Susan Elizabeth. *Earthshaking Science: What We Know (and Don't Know) About Earthquakes.* Princeton, NJ: Princeton University Press, 2002.

Hufton, Olwen. *Europe: Privilege and Progress, 1730–1789.* Oxford: Blackwell, 2000.

Hutton, James. *A Hundred Years Ago. An Historical Sketch. 1755 to 1756.* London: Longman, Brown, Green, Longmans and Roberts, 1857.

Ingram, Robert G. "The Trembling Earth in 'God's Herald': Earthquakes, Religion and Public Life in Britain During the 1750s." In *The Lisbon Earthquake of 1755: Representations and Reactions,* edited by T. E. D. Braun and J. B. Radner. Oxford: Voltaire Foundation, 2005, 97–115.

Iserson, Kenneth V., and John C. Moskop. "Triage in Medicine, Part I: Concept, History, and Types." *Annals of Emergency Medicine,* Vol. 49, No. 3, March 2008, 275–81.

Israel, Jonathan I. *European Jewry in the Age of Mercantilism, 1550–1750.* Portland, OR: Littman Library of Jewish Civilization, 1998.

————. *Democratic Enlightenment: Philosophy, Revolution, and Human Rights, 1750–1790.* Oxford: Oxford University Press, 2012.

Jack, Malcolm. *Lisbon: City of the Sea.* New York: I. B. Tauris, 2007.

Jenkins, Holman. "Hug a Price Gouger: The Public Doesn't Want to Hear It, but the Public Also Doesn't Like Empty Shelves." *Wall Street Journal,* October 30, 2012.

Johnson, A. C. "Seismic Moment Assessment of Earthquakes in Stable Continental Regions—III. New Madrid 1811–1812, Charleston 1886 and Lisbon 1755." *Geophysical Journal International,* Vol. 126, 1996, 208–21.

Jong, M. de. "Hollandse Reacties op de Verwoesting van Lissabon in 1755." *Tijdschrift voor Geschiedenis,* Vol. 68, 1955, 193–204.

Jorge, Celeste, and António Gomes Coelho. "Zonamento do potencial de liquefacção. Tentativa de aplicação a Portugal." *Geotecnia*, No. 83, July 1998.

Justo J. L., and C. Salwa. "The 1531 Lisbon Earthquake." *The Bulletin of the Seismological Society of America*, Vol. 88, No. 2, April 1998, 319–28.

Kaabouben, F., et al. "On the Moroccan Tsunami Catalogue." *Natural Hazards and Earth System Sciences*, Vol. 9, 2009.

Kanamori, H. "The Energy Release of Great Earthquakes." *Journal of Geophysical Research*, Volume 82, 1977, 2981–87.

Kayserling, Mayer. *História dos Judeus em Portugal*. São Paulo: Pioneira, 1971.

Keller, Susanne B. "Sections and Views: Visual Representation in Eighteenth-Century Earthquake Studies." *British Journal for the History of Science*, Vol. 31, 1998, 129–59.

Kelly, Gavin. "Ammianus and the Great Tsunami." *The Journal of Roman Studies*, Vol. 94, 2004, 141–67.

Kemmerer, Arthur. "Das Erdbeben von Lissbon in seiner Beziehung zum Problem des Übels in der Welt." Diss., Johannn Wolfgang Goethe Universität, Frankfurt, Germany, 1958.

Kendrick, T. D. *The Lisbon Earthquake*. London: Methuen, 1956.

Kjær, Ulla. *En virkeliggjort drøm Oplysningstiden illustreret ved Liselund*. Nationalmuseet, Copenhagen, 2011.

Kopf, Achim. "Die geologishe Ursache des Mega-Erdbebens vom Lissabon im Jahre 1755." In *Das Erdbeben von Lissabon und der Katastrophendiskurs im 18. Jahrhundert*, edited by Gerhard Lauer and Thorsten Unger. Göttingen: Wallstein Verlag, 2008, 188–202.

Krieger, Leonard. *Kings and Philosophers, 1689–1789*. New York: W. W. Norton, 1970.

Lains, Pedro, and Álvaro Ferreira da Silva, eds. *História económica de Portugal, 1700–2000*. Lisbon: Imprensa de Ciências Socias, 2005.

Lander, James F., et al. "A Brief History of Tsunamis in the Caribbean Sea." *Science of Tsunami Hazards*, Vol. 20, No. 2, 2002.

Landsman, Ned C. *From Provincials to Colonials: American Thought and Culture 1680–1760*. Ithaca, NY: Cornell University Press, 1997.

Lappenberg, Johann Martin. "Hamburg und das Erdbeben zu Lissabon am 1. November 1755." In *Zeitschrift des Vereins für Hamburgische Geschichte*. Vol. 4. Hamburg: Verl. Verein für Hamburgische Geschichte, 1858, 274–88.

———. Portuguese Translation by Emile Grünberg. "Hamburgo e o Terremoto de Lisboa do 1 de Novembro de 1755." *O Instituto Revista Scientifica e Litteraria*, Coimbra: Imprensa da Universidade, Vol. 51, No. 1, January 1904, 53–59.

Larsen, Svend Erik. "The Lisbon Earthquake and the Scientific Turn in Kant's Philosophy." *European Review*, Vol. 14, No. 3, 2006, 359–67.

Lauer, Gerhard, and Thorsten Unger, eds. *Das Erdbeben von Lissabon und der Katastrophendiskurs im 18. Jahrhundert*. Göttingen: Wallstein Verlag, 2008.

Leigh, R. A. "From 'Inégalité' to 'Candide:' Notes on a Desultory Dialogue Between Rousseau and Voltaire (1755–1759)." In *The Age of Enlightenment*, edited by W. H. Barber et al. Edinburgh and London: Oliver & Boyd, 1967, 66–92.

Leite, Serafim. *História da Companhia de Jesus*. Vols. 3 and 5. Rio de Janeiro: Instituto Nacional de Livro, 1949.

Leonard, L. J., et al. "Towards a National Tsunami Hazard Map for Canada: Tsunami Sources." *Proceeedings of the 9th U.S. National and 10th Canadian Conference on Earthquake Engineering*, July 25–29, 2010, Paper No. 1844.

Levenson, Jay A., ed. *The Age of the Baroque in Portugal*. Washington, DC: National Gallery of Art, 1993.

Levret, A. "The Effects of the November 1, 'Lisbon' Earthquake in Morocco." *Tectonophysics*, 193, 2001, 83–94.

Lima, Durval Pires de. *O Terramoto de 1755 e a freguesia de Sta. Isabel de Lisboa: Relação abreviada*. Lisbon: Imprensa Lucas, 1930.

Lindberg, Erik. "The Rise of Hamburg as a Global Marketplace in the Seventeenth Century: A Comparative Political Economy Perspective." *Comparative Studies in Society and History*, Vol. 50, No. 3, 2008.

Lindemann, Mary. *Patriots and Paupers: Hamburg, 1712–1830*. New York: Oxford University Press, 1990.

———. "Fundamental Values: Political Culture in Eighteenth-Century Hamburg." In *Patriotism, Cosmopolitanism, and National Culture: Public Culture in Hamburg*, edited by Peter Uwe Hohendahl. Amsterdam and New York: Editions Rodopi C.V., 2003.

Livermore, H. V. *A New History of Portugal*. Cambridge: Cambridge University Press, 1966.

Lodge, Richard. "The British Factory at Lisbon." *Transactions of the Royal Historical Society*. 4th Series, Vol. 16. London, 1933, 211–47.

———, ed., *The Private Correspondence of Sir Benjamin Keene*. Cambridge: Cambridge University Press, 1933.

Löffler, Ulrich. *Lissabons Fall - Europas Schrecken: die Deutung des Erdbebens von Lissabon im deutschsprachigen Protestantismus des 18. Jahrhunderts*. Berlin: Walter de Gruyter, 1999.

———. " 'Erbauliche Trümmerstadt'? Das Erdbeben von 1755 und der Horizone seiner Deutung in Protestantismus des 18. Jahrhunderts." In *Um Himmels Willen: Religion in Katastrophen Zeiten*, edited by Manfred Jakubowski-Tiessen and Hartmut Lehmann. Göttingen: Vandenhoeck & Ruprecht, 2003.

Lousada, Maria Alexandra, and Eduardo Brito Henriques. "Viver nos escombos: Lisboa durante a reconstrução." In *O Terremoto de 1755: Impactos históricos*, edited by Ana Cristina Araújo. Lisbon: Livros Horizonte, 2007.

Lüsenbrink, Hans-Jürgen. "Le tremblement de terre de Lisbonne dans des périodiques français et allemands du XVIIe siècle." In *Gazettes et Information Politique sous l'Ancien Régime*. Saint-Étienne: Publications de l'Université de Saint-Étienne, 1999.

Lyell, Charles. *Principles of Geology*. 2nd ed., Vol. 1 (of 3). London: Charles Murray, 1832.

Macaulay, Rose. *They Went to Portugal*. London: Jonathan Cape, 1946.

———. *They Went to Portugal Too (Aspects of Portugal)*. Manchester: Carcanet, 1990.

Macedo, J. B. de. *Problemas de história da indústria portuguesa no século XVIII*. Lisbon: Associação Industrial Portuguesa, 1963.

———. *A situação económico no tempo de Pombal: Alguns aspectos*. 2nd ed. Lisbon: Moraes Editores, 1982.

Macedo, Luís de. *O Terramoto de 1755 na Freguesia da Madalena*. Lisbon: Solução, n.d.

Madureira, Nuno Luis. *Cidade: Espaço e quotidiano—Lisboa 1740–1830*. Lisbon: Livros Horizonte, 1992.

Marques, Alfredo Pinheiro. "Triumph for Da Gama and Disgrace for Columbus." In George Winius, ed., *Portugal the Pathfinder: Journeys from the Medieval Toward the Modern World, 1300–ca. 1600*. Madison, WI: Hispanic Seminary of Medieval Studies, 1995, 133–44.

Marques, A. H. de Oliveira. *História de Portugal: Desde os tempos mais antigas até ao governo do Sr. Pinheiro de Azevedo*. 6th ed., 2 Vols. Lisbon: Palas, 1976.

———. *História de Portugal*. Vol. 1. Lisbon: Editorial Presença, 1997.

———, and Joel Serrão, eds. *Nova história da expansão portuguesa*. 11 Vols. Lisbon: Estampa, 1986–98.

———, and J. J. A. Dias. "A população portuguesa nos séculos XV e XVI." *Biblos*, Vol. 70, 1994, 171–96.

Marques, José. "The Paths of Providence: Voltaire and Rousseau on the Lisbon Earthquake." *Cadernos de História e Filosofia da Ciência*, Series 3, Vol. 15, No. 1, January–June 2005, 33–57.

Martínez, Rosa Cal. "La Información en Madrid del Terremoto de Lisboa de 1755." *Cuadernos Dieciochistas*, No. 6, 2005, 173–86.

Martins, Jorge. *Portugal e os Judeus: Volume I—dos primórdios da nacionalidade à legislação pombalina*. Lisbon: Nova Vega, 2006.

Mascarenhas, Jorge Morarji Dias. "A Study of the Design and Construction of Buildings in the Pombaline Quarter of Lisbon." PhD diss., University of Glamorgan, UK, July 2006.

Masson, D. G., et al. "Seismic Triggering of Landslides and Turbidity Currents Offshore Portugal." *Geochemistry Geophysics Geosystems*, 12/2011, 12(12).

Matos, Manuel Cadafaz de, ed. *O Juizo da Verdadeira Causa do Terremoto . . . e sacrifício simbólico do Pe. Gabriel Malagrida*. Lisbon: Edições Távola Redonda, 2006?.

Mattoso, José, ed. *História de Portugal*. 8 Vols. Lisbon: Editorial Estampa, 1992–93.

———. *D. Afonso Henriques*. Lisbon: Temas e Debates, 2007.

Mauro, Frédérico, and Geoffrey Parker. "Portugal," Chapter 3. In *An Introduction to the Sources of European Economic History, 1500–1800*, edited by Charles Wilson and Geoffrey Parker. Ithaca, NY: Cornell University Press, 1977.

Mauzi, Robert. *L'idée du bonheur dans la littérature et la pensée françaises au XVIIIe siècle*. Paris: A. Colin, 1960.

Maxwell, Kenneth. "Pombal and the Nationalization of the Luso-Brazilian Economy." *The Hispanic American Historical Review*, Vol. 48, No. 4, November 1968, 608–31.

———. "Eighteenth-Century Portugal: Faith and Reason, Tradition and Innovation During a Golden Age." In *The Age of the Baroque in Portugal*, edited by Jay A. Levenson. Washington, DC: National Gallery of Art, 1993.

———. *Pombal: Paradox of the Enlightenment*. Cambridge: Cambridge University Press, 1995.

———. "The Spark: Pombal, the Amazon and the Jesuits." *Portuguese Studies*, Vol. 17, Homage to Charles Boxer, 2001, 168–83.

———. "Lisbon: The Earthquake of 1755 and Urban Recovery Under the Marquês de Pombal." In *Out of Ground Zero: Case Studies in Urban Reinvention*, edited by Joan Ockman. New York: Prestel, 2002.

———. "The Historical Context of the Treaty of Methuen." *The British Historical Society of Portugal Thirtieth Annual Report and Review*, 2003, Quinta Nova, Carcavelos, 65–76.

———. *Conflicts and Conspiracies: Brazil and Portugal, 1750–1808*. Cambridge: Cambridge University Press, 1973.

———. "The Jesuit and the Jew: The Lisbon Earthquake in Modern Perspective." *ReVista: Harvard Review of Latin America*, Natural Disasters: Coping with Calamity, Winter 2007, 17–18.

McKendrick, Neil. "The End of Optimism." *Horizon*, Vol. 16, No. 2, 1974.

Mendes-Victor, Luiz A., et al. "Earthquake Damage Scenarios in Lisbon for Disaster Preparedness." In *Issues in Urban Earthquake Risk*, edited by B. E. Tucker, Mustafa Özder Erdik, and Christina N. Hwang. Dordrecht, Netherlands, 1994, 265–85.

————, et al. *The Lisbon Earthquake: Revisited*. New York: Springer, 2009.

Mendonça, Joachim Joseph Moreira de. *História universal dos terremotos, que tem havido no mundo, de que ha noticia, desde a sua creação até o seculo presente: Com huma narração individual do terremoto do primeiro de novembro de 1755*. Lisbon: Antonio Vicente da Silva, 1758.

Mercier-Faivre, Anne-Marie, and Chantal Thomas, eds. *L'invention de la catastrophe au XVIIIe siècle: du châtiment divin au désastre naturel*. Geneva: Libraire Droz, 2008.

Mezague, Vivant de. *A General View of England Respecting its Policy, Trade, Commerce, Taxes, Debts, Produce of Lands, Colonies, Manners . . . From the Year 1600 to 1762*. London: J. Robson, 1766.

Miller, Mary Ashburn. *A Natural History of Revolution: Violence and Nature in the French Revolutionary Imagination, 1789–1794*. Ithaca, NY: Cornell University Press, 2011.

Mineiro, António Correia. "A propósito das medidas de remediação e da opção política de reedificar a cidade de Lisboa sobre os seus escombros, após o sismo de 1 de novembro de 1755: Reflexões." In *1755: O grande terramoto de Lisboa, Volume 1, Descrições*. Lisbon: FLAD e Público, 2005.

Miranda, M. A., et al. "Constraints on the Source of the 1755 Lisbon Tsunami Inferred from Numerical Modeling of Historical Data." *Journal of Geodynamics*, Vol. 25, No. 2, 1998.

Molesky, Mark. "The Lisbon Earthquake and the Enlightenment Theodicy Debate: A Reexamination." Senior honors thesis, History Department, University of Michigan, Ann Arbor, 1990.

————. "Abandoning Lisbon (Or What Was Left of It): Father José Franciso de Isla's Plan for a New Portuguese Capital." *John Carter Brown Library Online Publication*, Brown University, November 2009.

————. "A New Account of the Lisbon Earthquake: Marginalia in Joachim José Moreira de Mendonça's *História universal dos terremotos*." *Portuguese Studies*, Vol. 26, No. 2, September 15, 2010.

————. "The Great Fire of Lisbon, 1755." In *Flammable Cities: Urban Conflagration and the Making of the Modern World*, edited by Greg Bankoff, Uwe Lübken, and Jordan Sand. Madison: University of Wisconsin Press, 2012.

————. "The Vicar and the Earthquake: Conflict, Controversy, and a Christening During the Great Lisbon Disaster of 1755." *E-Journal of Portuguese History*, Vol. 10, No. 2, Winter 2012.

Molina Cortón, Juan. *Reformismo y neutralidad. José de Cavajal y la diplomacia de la España preilustrada*. Mérida: Regional de Extramadura, 2003.

Monteiro, Nuno Gonçalo. "Poder senhorial, estatuto nobilárquico e artistocracia." In *História de Portugal*, Vol. 5, edited by José Mattoso. Lisbon: Editorial Estampa, 1978–.

————. *Elites e poder entre o Antigo Regime e o liberalismus*. Lisbon: Imprensa de Ciências Sociais, 2003.

————. *D. José*. Lisbon: Temas e Debates, 2008.

Monumentos, Revista Semestral de Edifícios e Monumentos. Vol. 21, September 2004.

Moratti, G., et al. "The 1755 'Meknes' Earthquake (Morocco): Field Data and Geodynamic Implications." *Journal of Geodynamics*, Vol. 36, 2003, 305–22.

Morize, Andre. "The Moment of *Candide* and the Ideas of Voltaire." In Voltaire, *Candide*, edited by Robert M. Adams. New York: Norton, First edition, 1966.

Muir-Wood, Robert, and Arnaud Mignan. "A Phenomenological Reconstruction of the Mw9 November 1st 1755 Earthquake Source." In *The Lisbon Earthquake: Revisited*, edited by Luiz A. Mendes-Victor et al. New York: Springer, 2009, 121–46.

Müller, Leos. *Consuls, Corsairs, and Commerce: The Swedish Consular Service and Long-distance Shipping, 1720–1815*. Stockholm: Uppsala Universitet, 2004.

———. "Swedish-Portuguese Trade and Swedish Consular Service, 1700–1800." In *A articulação do sal português aos circuitos mundiais—The Articulation of Portuguese Salt with Worldwide Routes : antigos e novos consumos—Past and New Consumption Trends*. Porto, Portugal: University of Porto, 2008.

Mullin, John R. "The Reconstruction of Lisbon Following the Earthquake of 1755: A Study in Despotic Planning." *Planning Perspectives*, Vol. 7, 1992, 157–79.

Murphy, Kathleen. "Prodigies and Portents: Providentialism in the Eighteenth-Century Chesapeake." *Maryland Historical Magazine*, Vol. 97, No. 4, Winter 2002.

Mury, Paul. *História de Gabriel Malagrida*. São Paulo: Editora Giordano, 1992. Original: Paul Mury. *Histoire de Gabriel Malagrida de la Compagnie de Jésus*. Paris: Charles Douniol, Libraire-Éditeur, 1865.

Muteira, Helena. *Lisboa da Resturação à Luzes*. Lisbon: Editoria Presença, 1996.

Namier, Lewis, and J. Brooke. *The History of Parliament: The House of Commons, 1754–1790*. London: Secker & Warburg, 1964.

———. *The Structure of Politics at the Accession of George II*. New York: St. Martin's Press; reprint, 1968.

Nason, Elias. *Sir Charles Henry Frankland, Baronet: or, Boston in the Colonial Times*. Albany: J. Munsell, 1865.

Neiman, S. *Evil in Modern Thought*. Princeton, NJ: Princeton University Press, 2002.

Neumayer, Eric, and Thomas Plümper. "The Gendered Nature of Natural Disasters: The Impact of Catastrophic Events on the Gender Gap in Life Expectancy, 1981–2002." *Annals of the Association of American Geographers*, Vol. 97, No. 3, 2007, 551–66.

Nur, Amos. *Apocalypse: Earthquakes, Archaeology, and the Wrath of God*. Princeton, NJ: Princeton University Press, 2008.

Odilon, Marcus. *O livro proibido de Padre Malagrida*. João Pessoa, Brazil: UNIGRAF, 1986.

Oeser, Erhard. "Historical Earthquake Theories from Aristotle to Kant." In *Historical Earthquakes in Central Europe*, edited by Rudolf Gutdeutsch, Gottfried Grünthal, and Roger Musson. Vol. 1. Vienna: Geologische Bundesanstalt, 1992.

Oliveira, Carlos Sousa. "Descrição do terramoto de 1755, sua extensão, causos e efeitos. O Sismo. O Tsunami. O Incêndio." In *1755: O grande terramoto de Lisboa, Volume 1, Descrições*. Lisbon: FLAD e Público, 2005.

———. "Review of the 1755 Lisbon Earthquake Based on Recent Analyses of Historical Observations." *Historical Seismology: Interdisciplinary Studies of Past and Recent Earthquakes*. London: Springer, 2008.

Oliveira, Martins. *História de Portugal*. Lisbon: Guimarães Editores, 1987; first edition, 1879.

O'Loughlin, Karen Fay, and James F. Lander. *Caribbean Tsunamis: A 500-Year History from 1498–1998*. Dordrecht, Netherlands: Kluwer Academic Publishers, 2003.

Omira, R., et al. "The November, 1st 1755 Tsunami in Morocco: Can Numerical Modeling Clarify the Uncertainties of Historical Reports?" In *Tsunami—Analysis of a Hazard—From Physical Interpretation to Human Impact*, edited by Gloria I. Lopez. InTech, 2012.

Orieux, Jean. *Voltaire*. Garden City, NY: Doubleday, 1979.

Osório, Baltasar. *O terremoto de Lisboa de 1531*. Coimbra: Imprensa da Universidade, 1919.

Paice, Edward. *Wrath of God: The Great Lisbon Earthquake of 1755*. London: Quercus, 2008.

Paludan, Johan, and Hans Jacob Paludan. *Forsøg Til En Antiqvarisk, Historisk, Statistik Og Geographisk Beskrivelse Over Møen. Udgivet Efter Forfatterens Død*. Vol. 1. Copenhagen, 1822.

Pardal, Maria João Martins. *O terramoto de 1755: A urbanização da Nova Lisboa*. Lisbon: Sete Caminhos, 2005.

Pareschi, Maria Teresa, et al. "Lost Tsunami." *Geophysical Research Letters*, Vol. 33, 2006.

Park, J., et al. "Earth's Free Oscillations Excited by the 26 December 2004 Sumatra-Andaman Earthquake." *Science*, Vol. 308, 2005, 1139–44.

Parker, Bruce. *The Power of the Sea*. New York: Palgrave Macmillan, 2010.

Payan, Maria Teresa Esteves. *A censura literária em Portugal nos séculos XVII e XVIII*. Lisbon: Fundação Calouste Gulbenkian, 2005.

Pearson, Roger. *Voltaire Almighty: A Life in the Pursuit of Freedom*. London: Bloomsbury, 2005.

Pedreira, Jorge. "From Growth to Collapse: Portugal, Brazil, and the Breakdown of the Old Colonial System, 1760–1830." *Hispanic American Historical Review*, Vol. 80, No. 4, 2000, 840–64.

Pedrosa, F. Tedim, and J. Gonçalves. "The 1755 Earthquake in the Algarve (South of Portugal): What Would Happen Nowadays?" *Advanced Geoscience*, 14, 2008, 59–63.

Penn, Richard, et al. "The Pombaline Quarter of Lisbon: An Eighteenth Century Example of Prefabrication and Dimensional Co-ordination." *Construction History*, Vol. 11, 1995, 3–17.

Pereira, Alvaro S. "Opportunity of a Disaster: The Economic Impact of the 1755 Lisbon Earthquake." *The Journal of Economic History*, Vol. 69, No. 2, June 2009, 466–99.

Pereira, E. J. "The Earthquake of Lisbon." *Transactions of the Seismological Society of Japan*, Vol. 12, 1988, 5–19.

Pereira, José Fernandes, Leonor Ferrão, and Luísa d'Orey Capucho Arruda. *Lisbon in the Age of Dom João V (1689–1750)*. Paris: Instituto Português de Museus, 1994.

Perrey, Alexis. *Mémoire sur les tremblements de terre ressentis en France, en Belgique et en Hollande, depuis le quatrième siècle de l'ère chrétienne jusqu'à nos jours (1843 inclusiv)*. 1844.

Pettegree, Andrew. *The Invention of News: How the World Came to Know About Itself*. New Haven, CT: Yale University Press, 2014.

Piñal, Aguilar. "Commoción espiritual en Sevilla por el terremoto de 1755." *Archivo hispalense: Revista histórica, literaria y artística*, Vol. 56, No. 171–173, I, 1973, 37–53.

Pinheiro e Rosa, José António. "A diocese de Algarve e a universidade de Coimbra." *Revista da Universidade de Coimbra*, Vol. 37, 1992, 77–91.

Pinto, John. *Speaking Ruins: Piranesi, Architects and Antiquity in Eighteenth-Century Rome*. Ann Arbor: University of Michigan Press, 2012.

Pinto, Virgilio Noya. *O ouro brasileiro e o comércio anglo-português*. São Paulo, 1979.

Poirier, J. P. *Le tremblement de terre de Lisbonne*. Paris: Odile Jacob, 2005.

———. "The 1755 Lisbon Disaster, the Earthquake That Shook Europe." *European Review*, Vol. 14, No. 2, 2006, 169–80.

Pomeau, René. *Voltaire et son temps*. 2 Vols. Paris: Fayard & Voltaire Foundation, 1995.

Porter, Roy. *Enlightenment: Britain and the Creation of the Modern World*. London: Penguin, 2000.

———. *Problems of Enlightenment in Portugal*. Minneapolis: Institute for the Study of Ideologies and Literatures, 1984.

Quenet, G. *Les tremblements de terre aux XVII et XVIII siècles: La naissance d'un Risqué*. Seyssel, France: Champ Vallon, 2005.

Radulet, Carmen M. "Vasco da Gama and His Successors." In *Portugal the Pathfinder: Journeys from the Medieval Toward the Modern World 1300–ca. 1600*, edited by George Winius. Madison, WI: Hispanic Seminary of Medieval Studies, 1995, 133–43.

Raeff, Marc. *The Well-Ordered Police State: Social and Institutional Change Through Law in the Germanies and Russia, 1600–1800*. New Haven, CT: Yale University Press, 1983.

Ray, Gene. "Reading the Lisbon Earthquake: Adorno, Lyotard, and the Contemporary Sublime." *Yale Journal of Criticism*, Vol. 17, No. 1, Spring 2004, 1–18.

Real, Miguel. *O marquês de Pombal e a cultura portuguesa*. Lisbon: QuidNovi, 2005.

Regier, Alexander. *Fracture and Fragmentation in British Romanticism*. Cambridge: Cambridge University Press, 2010.

Reid, Harry Fielding. "The Lisbon Earthquake of November 1, 1755." *The Bulletin of The Seismological Society of America*, Vol. 4, No. 2, June 1914, 53–80.

Reinhardt, O., and D. R. Oldroyd. "Kant's Theory of Earthquakes and Volcanic Action." *Annals of Science*, Vol. 40, 1983, 247–72.

Ribeiro, A. "O sismo de 1755 e o geodynâmico da Ibéria e Atlântico." in *1755: O grande terramoto de Lisboa: Descrições*. Lisbon: FLAD, 2005.

Rio Maior, Marquês de. "No centário do terremoto grande." *Separata de Estremadura*, Série II, Nos. 33, 34, 35. Lisbon, 1955.

Robertson, Ian. *A Traveller's History of Portugal*. New York: Interlink, 2002.

Robinson, Andrew. *Earthquake: Nature and Culture*. London: Reaktion Books, 2012.

Roca, Antoni, et al. "An Outline of Earthquake Catalogues, Databases and Studies of Historical Seismicity in the Iberian Peninsula." *Annals of Geophysics*, Vol. 47, No. 2/3, April/June 2004.

Rocha, M. J. P. *Monografia de Lagos*. Reprint, 1991; original, 1909.

Roche, Daniel. *La France des Lumières*. Paris, 1993.

Rodrigues, A. Gonçalves. *O protestante lusitano. Estudo biográfico e crítico sobre o Cavaleiro de Oliveira, 1702–1783*. Coimbra: Offprint from *Biblos*, 1950.

———. "Uma obra desconhecida do Cavaleiro de Oliveira contra a Inquisição." *Biblos*, Vol. 52, 1976, 305–17.

Rodrigues, Lúcia Lima, and Russell Craig. "Recovery Amid Destruction: Manoel de Maya and the Lisbon Earthquake of 1755." *Libraries & the Cultural Record*, Vol. 43, No. 4, 2008, 397–410.

Roger, Jean, et al. "The 1755 Lisbon Tsunami in Guadeloupe Archipelago: Source Sensitivity and Investigation of Resonance Effects." *The Open Oceanography Journal*, Vol. 4, 2010, 58–70.

———. "The Transoceanic 1755 Lisbon Tsunami in Martinique." *Pure and Applied Geophysics*, No. 168, 2011.

Rohrer, B. "Das Erdbeben von Lissabon in der französischen Literatur des achtzehnten Jahrhunderts." Diss., Universität Heidelberg, Brausdruck, 1933.

Rollo, Maria Fernanda, Ana Isabel Buescu, and Pedro Cardim, coordinators. *História e ciência da catástrofe: 250 aniversário do terramoto de 1755*. Lisbon: Colibri, 2007.

Rosa, José António Pinheiro e. "A diocese de Algarve e a universidade de Coimbra." *Revista da Universidade de Coimbra*, Vol. 37, 1992, 77–91.

Rossa, Walter. *Beyond Baixa: Signs of Urban Planning in Eighteenth Century Lisbon*. Lisbon: Instituto Português do Património Arquitectónico, 1998.

———. "Do plano de 1755–1758 para a Baixa-Chiado." *Monumentos: Revista Semestral de Edifícios e Monumentos*, Vol. 21, 2004, 22–43.

Rousseau, Jean-Jacques. *Rousseau: "The Discourses" and Other Early Political Writings*, edited by Victor Gourevitch. Cambridge: Cambridge University Press, 1997.

Russell, Peter E. *Prince Henry "the Navigator": A Life*. New Haven, CT: Yale University Press, 2000.

Russell-Wood, A. J. R. "Colonial Brazil: The Gold Cycle, c. 1690–1750." In *The Cambridge History of Latin America, Volume 2, Colonial Latin America*, edited by Leslie Bethell. Cambridge: Cambridge University Press, 1984, 547–600.

———. *The Portuguese Empire, 1415–1808*. Baltimore: Johns Hopkins University Press, 1992.

———. "Portugal and the World in the Age of Dom João V." In *The Age of the Baroque in Portugal*, edited by Jay A. Levenson. Washington, DC: National Gallery of Art, 1993.

Salterain, P. "Ligera resena de los temblores de tierra ocurridos en la Isla de Cuba." *Boletín de la Comisión del Mapa Geológico de España*, 1883.

Sanches, António Nunes Ribeiro. *Tratado da conservaçam da saude dos povos*. Lisbon: Joseph Filippe, 1757.

San-Payo, M., et al. "Contributions to the Damage Interpretation During the 1755 Lisbon Earthquake." In *The 1755 Lisbon Earthquake Revisited*, edited by Luiz A. Mendes-Victor et al. Dordrecht, Netherlands: Springer, 2009.

Santos, Guilherme G. de Oliveira. *O caso dos Távoras*. Lisbon: Livraria Portugal, 1959.

Santos, Maria Helena Ribeiro dos, and Ferran Sagarra i Trias. "Trading Perspectives After the Earthquake: The Rebuilding of Eighteenth-Century Lisbon." *Planning Perspectives*, Vol. 26, No. 2, April 2011, 301–11.

Santos, Piedade Braga, et al. *Lisboa setecentista vista por estrangeiros*. Lisbon: Livros Horizonte, 1992.

Saraiva, A. J. *Inquisição e os cristãos-novos*. Porto, Portugal: Editorial Novo, 1969.

Sarti, Raffaella. *Europe at Home: Family and Material Culture, 1500–1800*. New Haven, CT: Yale University Press, 2002.

Saunders, A. C. de C. M. *A Social History of Black Slaves and Freedmen in Portugal, 1441–1555*. Cambridge: Cambridge University Press, 1982.

Sawislak, Karen. *Smoldering City: Chicagoans and the Great Fire, 1871–1874*. Chicago: University of Chicago Press, 1995.

Sbeinati, M. R., et al. "The Historical Earthquakes of Syria: an Analysis of Large and Moderate Earthquakes from 1365 B.C. to 1900 A.D." *Annals of Geophysics*, 48, 2005, 347–435.

Scavenius, Bente. *Den Fortryllede Have*. Copenhagen: Borgen, 1992.

Schäfer, Christina. *Das Erdbeben von Lissabon 1755 unter dem Aspekt der medialen Rezeption*. Bonn, Germany: Minifanal, 2013.

Schama, Simon. *Citizens: A Chronicle of the French Revolution*. New York: Random House, 1989.

Schultz, Kirsten. *Tropical Versailles: Empire, Monarchy, and the Portuguese Royal Court in Rio de Janeiro, 1808–1821*. New York: Routledge, 2001.

Schwarcz, Lilia Moritz. *A longa viagem da biblioteca dos reis: Do terremoto de Lisboa à independência do Brasil*. São Paulo: Companhia da Letras, 2005.

Schwartz, Stuart B. "Colonial Brazil, c. 1580–c. 1750: Plantations and Peripheries." In *The Cambridge History of Latin America, Volume 2, Colonial Latin America*, edited by Leslie Bethell. Cambridge: Cambridge University Press, 1984, 423–500.

———. "Prata, açúcar e escravos: de como o império restaurou Portugal." *Tempo*, Vol. 12, No. 24, 2008, 201–23.

Sequeira, Gustavo de Matos. *Depois do terremoto: Subsidios para a história dos bairros ocidentais de Lisboa.* 4 vols. Lisbon: Academia das Ciências de Lisboa, 1916–34.

Serrão, Joaquim Veríssimo. *História de Portugal.* 2nd ed., 18 Vols. Lisbon: Editorial Verbo, 1978– especially Vol. 5, *A restauração e a monarquia absoluta (1650–1750)*, and Vol. 6, *O despotismo iluminado (1750–1807).*

———. *Marquês de Pombal. O homem, o diplomata e o estadista.* Lisbon: Câmaras Municipais de Oeiras e Pombal, 1982.

Serrão, Joel, ed. *Dicionário de história de Portugal.* 9 Vols. Porto: Livrarias Figueirinhas, 1984–2000.

Serrão, José Vicente. "O Quadro Económico." In *História de Portugal,* edited by José Mattoso. Lisbon: Editorial Estampa, 1992–93. Vol. 4 (of 8). *O Antigo Regime* (1620–1807), 71–117.

Serrão, Vítor. "1755 e as imagens de Lisboa: a *Alegoria ao Terramoto* de João Glama Stromberle." In *O grande terramoto de Lisboa ficar diferente,* edited by Helena C. Buescu and Gonçalo Cordeiro. Lisbon: Gradiva, 2005, 191–205.

———. *1755: O Grande Terramoto de Lisboa, Volume 1, Descrições.* Lisbon: FLAD e Público, 2005.

———. *1755: O Grande Terramoto de Lisboa, Volume 2, A Proteção.* Lisbon: FLAD e Público, 2005.

———. *1755: Providências do Marquês de Pombal, Volume 3.* Lisbon: FLAD e Público, 2005.

———. *1755: Sobre as causes dos terramotos, Volume 4.* Lisbon: FLAD e Público, 2005.

Shaw, L. M. E. *Trade, Inquisition and the English Nation in Portugal, 1650–1690.* Manchester: Carcanet, 1989.

Sheehan, James. "Enlightenment, Religion, and the Enigma of Secularization." *The American Historical Review,* Vol. 108, 2003, 1061–80.

Shrady, Nicholas. *The Last Day: Wrath, Ruin, and Reason in the Great Lisbon Earthquake of 1755.* New York: Viking, 2008.

Sideri, S. *Trade and Power: Informal Colonialism in Anglo-Portuguese Relations.* Rotterdam: Rotterdam University Press, 1970.

Silbert, Alberto. *Do Portugal de antigo regime ao Portugal oitocentista.* Lisbon: Livros Horizonte,, 1977.

Silva, A. Vieira da. *As Muralhas da Ribeira,* 3rd ed. Lisbon: Câmara Municipal, 1987.

Silva, Maria Beatriz Nizza da. *D. João V.* Lisbon: Temas e Debates, 2009.

Silver, Peter. *Our Savage Neighbors: How Indian War Transformed Early America.* New York: W. W. Norton, 2008.

Smid, T. C. "'Tsunamis' in Greek Literature." *Greece & Rome,* 2nd Series, Vol. 17, No. 1, April, 1970, 100-104.

Smith, John. *Memoirs of the Marquis de Pombal.* 2 Vols. London: Longman, Brown, Green and Longmans, 1847.

Solana, Ana Crespo. "Manifestaciones culturales y actitudes sociales y religiosas ante las catástrofes naturales en la España del Antiguo Régimen: El Maremoto de 1755 en Cádiz." In *Naturalia, mirabilia & monstrosa en los imperios ibéricos (siglos XV–XIX),* edited by Eddy Stols, Werner Thomas, and Johan Verberckmoes. Leuven, Belgium: Leuven University Press, 2006.

Solares, José Manuel Martínez. *Los efectos en España del terremoto de Lisboa (1 de Noviembre de 1755).* Madrid: Instituto Geográfico Nacional, 2001.

———, and Julio Mezcua Rodríguez. *Catálogo sísmico de la Península Ibérica (880 a. C.– 1900).* Madrid: Dirección General del Instituto Geográfico Nacional, 2002.

———, and A. López Arroyo. "The Great Historical 1755 Earthquake. Effects and Damage in Spain." *Journal of Seismology*, Vol. 8, 2004, 275–94.

Sorkin, David. *The Religious Enlightenment: Protestants, Jews, and Catholics from London to Vienna*. Princeton, NJ: Princeton University Press, 2008.

Sousa, Francisco Luís Pereira de. *Efeitos do terremoto de 1755 nas construções de Lisboa*. Lisbon: Imprensa Nacional, 1909.

———. *O terremoto do 1 de Novembro de 1755 e um estudo demográfico*. 4 Vols. Lisbon: Tipografia do Comércio, 1919–32. Vol. 1: *Districts of Faro, Beja, and Évora*. Vol. 2: *Districts of Santarem and Portalegre*. Vol. 3: *District of Lisbon*. Vol. 4: *Districts of Leiria, Castelo Branco, Coimbra, Guarda, Aveiro, Viseu*.

Souza, Alberto. *O trajo popular em Portugal nos seculos XVIII e XIV*. Lisbon: Sociedade Nacional de Tipografia, 1924.

Soyer, François. *The Persecution of the Jews and Muslims of Portugal: King Manuel I and the End of Religious Tolerance (1496–7)*. Leiden, Netherlands: Brill, 2007.

Spang, Rebecca L. *The Invention of the Restaurant: Paris and Modern Gastronomic Culture*. Cambridge, MA: Harvard University Press, 2000.

Starobinski, Jan. *La Remède dans le mal. Critique et légitimation de l'artifice à l'âge des Lumières*. Paris: Gallimard, 1989.

Stiros, Stathis C. "The AD 365 Crete Earthquake and Possible Seismic Clustering During the Fourth to Sixth Centuries AD in the Eastern Mediterranean: A Review of Historical and Archaeological Data." *Journal of Structural Geology*, Vol. 23, 2001.

———. "The 8.5+ Magnitude, AD365 Earthquake in Crete: Coastal Uplift, Topography Changes, Archaeological and Historical Signature." *Quaternary International*, April 1, 2010, 54–63.

Stuber, Martin. "Divine Punishment or Object of Research? The Resonance of Earthquakes, Floods, Epidemics and Famine in the Correspondence Network of Albrech von Haller." *Environment and History*, Vol. 9, 2003, 173–93.

Subtil, José. *O terramoto político (1755–1759): Memória e poder*. Lisbon: UAL Universidade Autónoma: 2006.

Sutherland, L. Stuart. "The Accounts of an Eighteenth-Century Merchant: The Portuguese Ventures of William Braund." *The Economic History Review*, Vol. 3, No. 3, April 1932, 367–87.

Taber, Stephen. "The Great Fault Troughs of the Antilles." *Journal of Geology*, Vol. 30, 1922, 89–114.

Tavares, Rui. *o pequeno livro do grande terremoto ensaio sobre 1755*. Lisbon: Edições Tinta-da-China, 2005.

Téllez Alarcia, Diego. "Spanish Interpretations of the Lisbon Earthquake Between 1755 and the War of 1762." In *The Lisbon Earthquake of 1755: Representations and Reactions*, edited by T. E. D. Braun and John B. Radner. Oxford: SVEC, 2005, 50–65.

Thornton, John. "Early Portuguese Expansion in West Africa: Its Nature and Consequences." In *Portugal the Pathfinder: Journeys from the Medieval Toward the Modern World, 1300–ca. 1600*, edited by George Winius. Madison, WI: Hispanic Seminary of Medieval Studies, 1995, 121–32.

Tillman, Barrett. *Whirlwind: The Air War Against Japan, 1942–1945*. New York: Simon & Schuster, 2010.

Tilton, Eleanor. "Lightning-Rods and the Earthquake of 1755." *The New England Quarterly*, Vol. 13, No. 1, March 1940, 85–97.

Tobriner, Stephen. "Earthquake and Planning in the 17th and 18th Centuries." *Journal of Architectural Education*, Vol. 33, No. 4, 1980.

Tocque, Philip. *Newfoundland: As It Was, And As It Is in 1877*. Toronto: John B. Magurn, 1877.

Toole, M. J. "Communicable Diseases and Disease Control." In *The Public Health Consequences of Disasters*, edited by Eric K. Noji. Oxford: Oxford University Press, 2007.

Tostões, Ana, and Walter Rossa, eds. *Lisboa 1758: O plano da Baixa Hoje*. Lisboa: Câmara Municipal, 2008.

Tracy, J. D. *The Political Economy of Merchant Empires: State Power and World Trade, 1350–1750*. Cambridge: Cambridge University Press, 1991.

Tumbleson, R. *Catholicism in the English Protestant Imagination: Nationalism, Religion, and Literature, 1660–1745*. Cambridge: Cambridge University Press, 1998.

Udias, A. A., et al. "Seismotectonics of the Azores-Alboran region." *Tectonophysics*, Vol. 31, 1976, 259–89.

Udías, Agustín, and Alfonso Lópex Arroyo. "The Lisbon Earthquake of 1755 in Spanish Contemporary Authors," In *The 1755 Lisbon Earthquake: Revisited*, edited by Luiz A. Mendes-Victor et al. New York: Springer, 2009, 7–24.

Vallina, Agustín Udías. *El terremoto de Lisboa en España* (testimonios inéditos). Brenes, Spain: Muñoz Moya Editores, 2010.

Vereker, Charles. *Eighteenth-Century Optimism: Interrelations Between Moral and Social Theory*. Liverpool: Liverpool University Press, 1967.

Verlinden, Charles. "Prince Henry in Modern Perspective as Father of the 'Descobrimentos.'" In *Portugal the Pathfinder: Journeys from the Medieval Toward the Modern World, 1300–ca. 1600*, edited by George Winius. Madison, WI: Hispanic Seminary of Medieval Studies,, 1995, 41–70.

Victor, Luís Alberto Mendes. "Os grandes terramotos." In *1755: O grande terramoto de Lisboa, Volume 1, Descrições*. Lisbon: FLAD e Público, 2005, 87–122.

Viegas, Inês Morais, ed. *Cartulário pombalino colecção de 70 prospectos (1758–1846)*. Lisbon: Archivo Municipal, 1999.

Vilanova, S. P., et al. "Lisbon 1755: A Case of Triggered Onshore Rupture?" *Bulletin of the Seismological Society of America*, Vol. 93, 2003, 2056–68.

———, and João Fonseca. "The 1755 Lisbon Earthquake and the Onshore LTV Fault." 2003, online.

Villiers, John. "Singers, Sailors, Watches and Wigs: Foreign Influences in Portugal in the Reign of D. João V." *The British Historical Society of Portugal*, Fourteenth Annual Report and Review, 1987, 57–77.

Vincent, Bernard. "Les tremblements de terre en Espagne et au Portugal." *In Les catastrophes naturelles dans l'Europe médiévale et moderne*, edited by B. Bernasser. Toulouse, France: Presses Universitaires du Mirail, 1996, 77–94.

Viner, Jacob. *The Role of Providence in the Social Order*. Princeton, NJ: Princeton University Press, 1972.

Vuan, A., et al. "Suboceanic Raleigh Waves in the 1755 Lisbon Earthquake." In *The Lisbon Earthquake: Revisited*, edited by Luiz A. Mendes-Victor et al. New York: Springer, 2009, 283–95.

Vyverberg, Henry. *Historical Pessimism in the French Enlightenment*. Cambridge, MA: Harvard University Press, 1958.

Wade, Ira O. *The Intellectual Development of Voltaire*. Princeton, NJ: Princeton University Press, 1969.

Walford, A. R. *The British Factory in Lisbon and Its Closing Stages Ensuing upon the Treaty of 1810*. Lisbon: Instituto Britânico em Portugal, 1940.

———. "The British Community in Lisbon 1755: The Earthquake Census?" *The*

Historical Association Lisbon Branch Tenth Annual Report and Review, 1946–50, Lisbon, 639–52.

Walker, Charles F. *Shaky Colonialism: The 1746 Earthquake-Tsunami in Lima: Peru, and Its Long Aftermath*. Durham, NC: Duke University Press, 2008.

———. "Lisbon and Lima: A Tale of Two Cities and Catastrophes." *Das Erdbeben von Lissabon und der Katastrophendiskurs im 18. Jahrhundert*, edited by Gerhard Lauer and Thorsten Unger. Göttingen: Wallstein Verlag, 2008, 377–91.

Walker, Timothy D. "Enlightened Absolutism and the Lisbon Earthquake: Asserting State Dominance over Religious Sites and the Church in Eighteenth-Century Portugal," *Eighteenth-Century Studies*, Vol. 48, No. 3, 2015, 307–28.

Walpole, Horace. W. S. Lewis, ed. *The Yale Edition of Horace Walpole's Correspondence*. 48 vols. New Haven, CT: Yale University Press, 1937–1983.

Webster, Robert. "The Lisbon Earthquake." In *The Lisbon Earthquake of 1755: Representations and Reactions*, edited by T. E. D. Braun and John B. Radner. Oxford: SVEC, 2005, 116–26.

Weinrich, Harald. "Voltaire, Hiob und das Erdbeben von Lissabon." *Aufsätze zur portugiesischen Kulturgeschichte*, Vol. 4, 1964, 96–104.

———. "Literaturgeschichte eines Weltereignisses: Das Erdbeben von Lissabon." In *Literatur für Leser: Essays and Aufsätze zur Literaturwissenschaft*, edited by Harald Weinrich. Berlin: Verlag W. Kohlhammer, 1971, 64–76.

Whelan, Franziska, and Dieter Kelletat. "Boulder Deposits on the Southern Spanish Atlantic Coast: Possible Evidence for the 1755 AD Lisbon Tsunami?" *Science of Tsunami Hazards*, Vol. 23, No. 3, 2005.

Wilke, Jürgen. "Daß der Jammer un das Elend mit keiner Feder zu beschreiben sey," Vol. 3, No. 1, 1996, *Relation*, 59–71.

———. "Das Erdbeben von Lissabon als Medienereignis." In *Das Erdbeben von Lissabon und der Katastrophendiskurs im 18. Jahrhundert*, edited by Gerhard Lauer and Thorsten Unger. Göttingen: Wallstein Verlag, 2008.

Willey, Basil. *The Eighteenth-Century Background: Studies on the Idea of Nature in the Thought of the Period*. Boston: Beacon, 1961.

Wilson, Charles, and Geoffrey Parker, eds. *An Introduction to the Sources of European Economic History, 1500–1800*. Ithaca, NY: Cornell University Press, 1977.

Winchester, Simon. *Krakatoa: The Day the World Exploded: August 27, 1883*. New York: HarperCollins, 2003.

Winius, George, ed. *Portugal the Pathfinder: Journeys from the Medieval Toward the Modern World, 1300–ca. 1600*. Madison, WI: Hispanic Seminary of Medieval Studies, 1995.

———. "The *Estado da India* on the Subcontinent: Portuguese as Players on a South Asia Stage." In *Portugal the Pathfinder: Journeys from the Medieval Toward the Modern World, 1300–ca. 1600*, edited by George Winius. Madison, WI: Hispanic Seminary of Medieval Studies, 1995, 191–212.

Woerle, Hans. *Der Erschütterungsbezirk des grossen Erdbebens zu Lissabon*. "Inaugural Dissertation von Hans Woerle." Munich, 1900.

Wolloch, Isser. *Eighteenth-Century Europe: Tradition and Progress, 1715–1789*. New York: W. W. Norton, 1982.

Wynn, R. "The 1755 Lisbon Disaster: Earthquake, Tsunami and Turbidity Currents." *Ocean Zone, Southampton Oceanography Centre*, No. 5, 2001.

Zitellini, Nevio, et al. "The Quest for the Africa-Eurasia Plate Boundary West of the Strait of Gibraltar." *Earth and Planetary Science Letters*, Vol. 280, 2009, 13–50.

Index

Page numbers in *italics* refer to illustrations. Pages beginning with 361 refer to endnotes.

ILLUSTRATION CREDITS

page 316   Courtesy of Zita Sampaio director of the Museum of Civil Engineering of
            the University of Lisbon
page 317   Museu de Lisboa (both)
page 323   New-York Historical Society
page 350   Biblioteca Nacional de Portugal

INSERT

The Riverside Palace: Museu de Lisboa
A royal coach: Henrique Ruas, Museu Nacional dos Coches, Coche
    da embaixada ao Papa Clemente XI–dos Oceanos, estações do ano,
    alçado traseiro, Direção-Geral do Património Cultural / Arquivo de
    Documentação Fotográfica (DGPC/ADF)
Dom João: Museu de Lisboa
Dom José and Mariana Vitória: Ministry of Foreign Affairs, Lisbon
Pombal flanked by his two brothers: Museu de Lisboa
Pombal at seventy: Museu de Lisboa
Allegory of the Earthquake: Kozak Collection, NISEE-PEER, University of
    California, Berkeley
Calmette family's tribute: © Pernille Klemp
Painting of a young girl: Kozak Collection, NISEE-PEER, University of
    California, Berkeley
Public execution: Museu de Lisboa
Pombal gestures: Câmara Municipal de Oeiras
Carmelite Church today: © Tommaso Baldovino
Statue of José I: © Leandro Neumann Ciuffo
The Lisbon riverfront today: © Archive—Turismo de Lisboa

Mark Molesky is a graduate of the University of Michigan, Ann Arbor. He received his MA and PhD in history from Harvard University, where he served as a lecturer on history and literature. He is currently associate professor of history at Seton Hall University. He lives in New York City.

A NOTE ON THE TYPE

This book was set in Janson, a typeface long thought to have been made by the Dutchman Anton Janson, who was a practicing type-founder in Leipzig during the years 1668–1687. However, it has been conclusively demonstrated that these types are actually the work of Nicholas Kis (1650–1702), a Hungarian, who most probably learned his trade from the master Dutch typefounder Dirk Voskens. The type is an excellent example of the influential and sturdy Dutch types that prevailed in England up to the time William Caslon (1692–1766) developed his own incomparable designs from them.

Composed by North Market Street Graphics,
Lancaster, Pennsyvania

Printed and bound by Berryville Graphics,
Berryville, Virginia